Engage. Prepare. Educate.

Founded in 2000 by economist and Stanford professor Paul Romer, Aplia is dedicated to improving learning by increasing student effort and engagement. The most successful online product in Economics by far, Aplia has been used by over 800,000 students at over 850 institutions. For students, Aplia offers a way to stay on top of coursework with regularly scheduled homework assignments. For professors, Aplia offers high-quality, auto-graded assignments, which ensure that students put forth effort on a regular basis throughout the term.

The Baumol/Blinder Aplia product contains assignments closely aligned to the text, using the same language, level and style as the book. A digital edition of the textbook is embedded within the Aplia program, so the student's text material is always only a click away. Visit **www.aplia.com/cengage** for more details.

TOMLINSON ECONOMICS VIDEOS

Our Tomlinson Economics Videos are an inexpensive and optional set of online video segments written by—and featuring award-winning teacher, actor and playwright—Steven Tomlinson. These videos are organized to follow each section of the Baumol/Blinder text. Every segment has downloadable class notes and a quiz for extra practice. Students can use these videos for:

- Catching up in class
- Reviewing for a test
- Pre-class studying
- And more!

Visit **academic.cengage.com/economics/tomlinson** for more information!

MACROECONOMICS
Principles and Policy
Eleventh Edition

William J. Baumol

New York University and Princeton University

Alan S. Blinder

Princeton University

SOUTH-WESTERN
CENGAGE Learning

Australia • Brazil • Japan • Korea • Mexico • Singapore • Spain • United Kingdom • United States

Macroeconomics: Principles and Policy, 11e
William J. Baumol, Alan S. Blinder

VP/Editorial Director: Jack W. Calhoun

Editor-in-Chief: Alex von Rosenburg

Executive Editor: Mike Worls

Developmental Editor: Katie Yanos

Marketing Manager: John Carey

Marketing Communications Manager: Sarah Greber

Content Project Manager: Heather Mann

Manager, Editorial Media: John Barans

Technology Project Editor: Deepak Kumar

Senior Buyer—Manufacturing: Sandee Milewski

Production Service: Pre-PressPMG

Compositor: Pre-PressPMG

Senior Art Director: Michelle Kunkler

Cover Design: Lisa Albonetti

Internal Design: Lisa Albonetti

Cover Images: © Getty Images; © First Light Associated Photographers, Inc.

Senior Permissions Rights Acquisitions Account Manager—Images: Deanna Ettinger

For product information and technology assistance, contact us at
Cengage Learning Academic Resource Center, 1-800-423-0563

For permission to use material from this text or product,
submit all requests online at **www.cengage.com/permissions**
Further permissions questions can be emailed to
permissionrequest@cengage.com

ExamView® and ExamView Pro® are registered trademarks of FSCreations, Inc. Windows® is a registered trademark of the Microsoft Corporation used herein under license.

Library of Congress Control Number: 2007922480
Library of Congress Control Number: 2008926814
Student Edition ISBN-13: 978-0-324-58621-3
Student Edition ISBN-10: 0-324-58621-3
Instructor's Edition ISBN-13: 978-0-324-58631-2
Instructor's Edition ISBN-10: 0-324-58631-0

South-Western Cengage Learning
5191 Natorp Boulevard
Mason, OH 45040
USA

Cengage Learning products are represented in Canada by Nelson Education, Ltd.

For your course and learning solutions, visit **academic.cengage.com**

Purchase any of our products at your local college store or at our preferred online store **www.ichapters.com**

Printed in the United States
1 2 3 4 5 6 7 12 11 10 09 08

WILLIAM J. BAUMOL

William J. Baumol was born in New York City and received his BSS at the College of the City of New York and his Ph.D. at the University of London.

Alan Blinder and Will Baumol

He is the Harold Price Professor of Entrepreneurship and Academic Director of the Berkley Center for Entrepreneurial Studies at New York University, where he teaches a course in introductory microeconomics, and the Joseph Douglas Green, 1895, Professor of Economics Emeritus and Senior Economist at Princeton University. He is a frequent consultant to the management of major firms in a wide variety of industries in the United States and other countries as well as to a number of governmental agencies. In several fields, including the telecommunications and electric utility industries, current regulatory policy is based on his explicit recommendations. Among his many contributions to economics are research on the theory of the firm, the contestability of markets, the economics of the arts and other services—the "cost disease of the services" is often referred to as "Baumol's disease"—and economic growth, entrepreneurship, and innovation. In addition to economics, he taught a course in wood sculpture at Princeton for about 20 years and is an accomplished painter (you may view some of his paintings at http://pages.stern.nyu.edu/~wbaumol/).

Professor Baumol has been president of the American Economic Association and three other professional societies. He is an elected member of the National Academy of Sciences, created by the U.S. Congress, and of the American Philosophical Society, founded by Benjamin Franklin. He is also on the board of trustees of the National Council on Economic Education and of the Theater Development Fund. He is the recipient of 11 honorary degrees.

Baumol is the author of more than 35 books and hundreds of journal and newspaper articles. His writings have been translated into more than a dozen languages.

ALAN S. BLINDER

Alan S. Blinder was born in New York City and attended Princeton University, where one of his teachers was William Baumol. After earning a master's degree at the London School of Economics and a Ph.D. at MIT, Blinder returned to Princeton, where he has taught since 1971, including teaching introductory macroeconomics since 1977. He is currently the Gordon S. Rentschler Memorial Professor of Economics and co-director of Princeton's Center for Economic Policy Studies, which he founded.

In January 1993, Blinder went to Washington as part of President Clinton's first Council of Economic Advisers. Then, from June 1994 through January 1996, he served as vice chairman of the Federal Reserve Board. He thus played a role in formulating both the fiscal and monetary policies of the 1990s, topics discussed extensively in this book. He has also advised several presidential campaigns.

Blinder has consulted for a number of the world's largest financial institutions, testified dozens of times before congressional committees, and been involved in several entrepreneurial start-ups. For many years, he has written newspaper and magazine articles on economic policy, and he currently has a regular column in the *New York Times* Sunday Business Section. In addition, Blinder's op-ed pieces still appear periodically in other newspapers. He also appears frequently on PBS, CNN, CNBC, and Bloomberg TV.

Blinder has served as president of the Eastern Economic Association and vice president of the American Economic Association and is a member of the American Philosophical Society, the American Academy of Arts and Sciences, and the Council on Foreign Relations. He has two grown sons, two grandsons, and lives in Princeton with his wife, where he plays tennis as often as he can.

BRIEF CONTENTS

TABLE OF CONTENTS

PREFACE

As usual, when preparing a new edition, we have made many small changes to improve clarity of exposition and to update the text both for recent economics events and for relevant advances in the literature. But this time we have focused on one particular addition that will, so far as we have been able to find out, differentiate this book from all other introductory texts.

We have included in the eleventh edition a substantial discussion of the role of the entrepreneurs and of the microtheory of their activities, their pricing and their earnings, and the implications for economic growth. Several studies of the place of the entrepreneur in economics textbooks (including earlier editions of this one) have all reached the same conclusion: that entrepreneurs are either completely invisible or are virtually so. Indeed, in a substantial set of the textbooks the word *entrepreneur* does not even appear in the index.

Now, this omission should appear strange because entrepreneurs are often classified as one of the four factors of production—but the only one to which no chapter is devoted. More than that, it seems universally recognized by economists that economic growth is the prime contributor to the general welfare and that more than 80 percent of the current income of the average American was contributed by growth in the past century alone. Moreover, it is clear that, even though entrepreneurs did not produce this growth by themselves, much if not most of this historically unprecedented achievement would not have occurred without them. Yet, in the textbooks, they have been the invisible men and women.

This eleventh edition is the product of nearly 30 years of the existence and modification of this book. In the responses to a survey of faculty users, it became clear that a number of chapters were generally not covered by instructors for lack of time, although the material is of considerable interest to students and is not—or need not be—technically demanding. So we simplified several such chapters further—notably Chapter 9 on the stock and bond markets, Chapter 13 on regulation and antitrust, Chapter 17 on environmental economics, and Chapter 21 on poverty and inequality—to make it practical for an instructor to assign any or all of them to the students for reading entirely by themselves.

In the macroeconomic portions of the book, we try to make the links between the short run and the long run clearer and more explicit with each passing edition. For the eleventh edition, we have also added much new material on the problems in the subprime mortgage markets, the ensuing financial crisis and possible recession, and several economic issues in the 2008 presidential campaign—even though, at this writing, no one yet knows who the Democratic nominee will be! As is our practice, these new materials are scattered over many chapters of the text, so as to locate the discussions of current events and policy close to the places where the relevant principles are taught. This edition also adds a bit more material on China; sadly, the experience in Zimbabwe has provided a contemporary example of hyperinflation.

We ended this section of the preface to the tenth edition by singling out the critical contributions of one colleague and friend of amazingly long duration. We now repeat some of our words about the late Sue Anne Batey Blackman, who worked closely with us through 10 editions of this book; for all practical purposes, she had become a coauthor. Indeed, the chapter on environmental matters is now largely her product. Her creative mind guided our efforts; her eagle eyes caught our errors; and her stimulating and pleasant company kept us going. Perhaps most important, we loved and valued her most profoundly. Unfortunately, she has been taken from us much too young. Our children and grandchildren will understand and surely support our decision, for once, not to dedicate this edition of the book to them, but rather to our precious lost friend, Sue Anne.

NOTE TO THE STUDENT

May we offer a suggestion for success in your economics course? Unlike some of the other subjects you may be studying, economics is cumulative: Each week's lesson builds on what you have learned before. You will save yourself a lot of frustration—and a lot of work—by keeping up on a week-to-week basis.

To assist you in doing so, we provide a chapter summary, a list of important terms and concepts, a selection of questions to help you review the contents of each chapter, as well as the answers to odd-numbered Test Yourself questions. Making use of these learning aids will help you to master the material in your economics course. For additional assistance, we have prepared student supplements to help in the reinforcement of the concepts in this book and provide opportunities for practice and feedback.

The following list indicates the ancillary materials and learning tools that have been designed specifically to be helpful to you. If you believe any of these resources could benefit you in your course of study, you may want to discuss them with your instructor. Further information on these resources is available at http://academic.cengage.com/economics/baumol.

We hope our book is helpful to you in your study of economics and welcome your comments or suggestions for improving student experience with economics. Please write to us in care of Baumol and Blinder, Editor for Economics, South-Western/Cengage Learning 5191 Natorp Boulevard, Mason, Ohio, 45040, or through the book's web site at http://academic.cengage.com/economics/baumol.

EconCentral

Multiple resources for learning and reinforcing principles concepts are now available in one place! EconCentral is your one-stop shop for the learning tools and activities to help you succeed.

Access online resources like ABC News Videos, Ask the Instructor Videos, Flash Cards, Interactive Quizzing, the Graphing Workshop, News Articles, Economic debates, Links to Economic Data, and more. Visit academic.cengage.com/economics/baumol/11e/econcentral to see the study options available with this text.

Study Guide

The study guide assists you in understanding the text's main concepts. It includes learning objectives, lists of important concepts and terms for each chapter, quizzes, multiple-choice tests, lists of supplementary readings, and study questions for each chapter—all of which help you test your understanding and comprehension of the key concepts.

IN GRATITUDE

Finally, we are pleased to acknowledge our mounting indebtedness to the many who have generously helped us in our efforts through the nearly 30-year history of this book. We often have needed help in dealing with some of the many subjects that an introductory textbook must cover. Our friends and colleagues Charles Berry, *Princeton University;* Rebecca Blank, *University of Michigan;* William Branson, *Princeton University;* Gregory Chow, *Princeton University;* Avinash Dixit, *Princeton University;* Susan Feiner, *University of Southern Maine,* Claudia Goldin, *Harvard University;* Ronald Grieson, *University of California, Santa Cruz;* Daniel Hamermesh, *University of Texas;* Yuzo Honda, *Osaka University;* Peter Kenen, *Princeton University;* Melvin Krauss, *Stanford University;* Herbert Levine, *University of Pennsylvania;* Burton Malkiel, *Princeton University;* Edwin Mills, *Northwestern University;* Janusz Ordover, *New York University;* David H. Reiley Jr., *University of Arizona;*

Uwe Reinhardt, *Princeton University;* Harvey Rosen, *Princeton University;* Laura Tyson, *University of California, Berkeley;* and Martin Weitzman, *Harvard University* have all given generously of their knowledge in particular areas over the course of 10 editions. We have learned much from them and have shamelessly relied on their help.

Economists and students at colleges and universities other than ours offered numerous useful suggestions for improvements, many of which we have incorporated into this eleventh edition. We wish to thank Larry Allen, *Lamar University,* Gerald Bialka, *University of North Florida,* Kyongwook Choi, *Ohio University,* Basil G. Coley, *North Carolina A & T State University,* Carol A. Conrad, *Cerro Coso Community College,* Brendan Cushing-Daniels, *Gettysburg College,* Edward J. Deak, *Fairfield University,* Kruti Dholakia, *The University of Texas at Dallas,* Aimee Dimmerman, *George Washington University,* Mark Gius, *Quinnipiac University,* Ahmed Ispahani, *University of La Verne,* Jin Kim, *Georgetown University,* Christine B. Lloyd, *Western Illinois University,* Laura Maghoney, *Solano Community College,* Kosmas Marinakis, *North Carolina State University,* Carl B. Montano, *Lamar University,* Steve Pecsok, *Middlebury College,* J. M. Pogodzinski, *San Jose State University,* Adina Schwartz, *Lakeland College,* David Tufte, *Southern Utah University,* and Thierry Warin, *Middlebury College* for their insightful reviews.

Obviously, the book you hold in your hands was not produced by us alone. An essential role was played by Susan Walsh, who stepped into the space vacated by Sue Anne and handled the tasks superbly, with insight and reliability, and did so in a most pleasant manner. We also appreciate the contribution of the staff at South-Western Cengage Learning, including Alex von Rosenberg, Editor-in-Chief; Michael Worls, Executive Editor; John Carey, Senior Marketing Manager; Katie Yanos, Developmental Editor; Heather Mann, Senior Content Project Manager; Deepak Kumar, Media Editor; Michelle Kunkler, Senior Art Director; Deanna Ettinger, Photo Manager; and Sandee Milewski, Senior Manufacturing Coordinator. It was a pleasure to deal with them, and we appreciate their understanding of our approaches, our goals, and our idiosyncrasies. We also thank our intelligent and delightful assistants at Princeton University and New York University, Kathleen Hurley and Janeece Roderick Lewis, who struggled successfully with the myriad tasks involved in completing the manuscript.

And, finally, we must not omit our continuing debt to our wives, Hilda Baumol and Madeline Blinder. They have now suffered through 11 editions and the inescapable neglect and distraction the preparation of each new edition imposes. Their tolerance and understanding has been no minor contribution to the project.

William J. Baumol
Alan S. Blinder

To Sue Anne Batey Blackman: wise, beloved, and irreplaceable.

GETTING ACQUAINTED WITH ECONOMICS

Welcome to economics! Some of your fellow students may have warned you that "econ is boring." Don't believe them—or at least, don't believe them too much. It is true that studying economics is hardly pure fun. But a first course in economics can be an eye-opening experience. There is a vast and important world out there—the economic world—and this book is designed to help you understand it.

Have you ever wondered whether jobs will be plentiful or scarce when you graduate? Or why a college education becomes more and more expensive? Should the government be suspicious of big firms? Why can't pollution be eliminated? How did the U.S. economy manage to grow so rapidly in the 1990s while Japan's economy stagnated? If any of these questions have piqued your curiosity, read on. You may find economics to be more interesting than you had thought!

It is only in later chapters that we will begin to give you the tools you need to begin carrying out your own economic analyses. However, the four chapters of Part 1 that we list next will introduce you to both the subject matter of economics and some of the methods that economists use to study their subject.

CHAPTERS

WHAT IS ECONOMICS?

Why does public discussion of economic policy so often show the abysmal ignorance of the participants? Why do I so often want to cry at what public figures, the press, and television commentators say about economic affairs?

**ROBERT M. SOLOW, WINNER OF THE
1987 NOBEL PRIZE IN ECONOMICS**

conomics is a broad-ranging discipline, both in the questions it asks and the methods it uses to seek answers. Many of the world's most pressing problems are economic in nature. The first part of this chapter is intended to give you some idea of the sorts of issues that economic analysis helps to clarify and the kinds of solutions that economic principles suggest. The second part briefly introduces the tools that economists use—tools you are likely to find useful in your career, personal life, and role as an informed citizen, long after this course is over.

CONTENTS

IDEAS FOR BEYOND THE FINAL EXAM

Elephants may never forget, but people do. We realize that most students inevitably forget much of what they learn in a course—perhaps with a sense of relief—soon after the final exam. Nevertheless, we hope that you will remember some of the most significant economic ideas and, even more important, the ways of thinking about economic issues that, later, will help you evaluate the economic issues that arise in our economy.

To help you identify some of the most crucial concepts, we have selected seven from the many in this book. Some offer key insights into the workings of the economy. Several bear on important policy issues that appear in newspapers. Others point out common misunderstandings that occur among even the most thoughtful lay observers. Most of them indicate that it takes more than just good common sense to analyze economic issues effectively. As the opening quote of this chapter suggests, many learned judges, politicians, and university administrators who failed to understand basic economic principles could have made wiser decisions than they did.

Try this one on for size. Imagine that Mexican workers, who earn much lower wages than American workers, can both grow tomatoes and manufacture t-shirts more cheaply than their American counterparts can. (And imagine that these are the only two goods in question.) If the United States opens its border to trade with Mexico, will American workers face mass unemployment? Will our country be made worse off by trade with Mexico? It may appear that the common sense answer to both of these questions is "yes." And many people think so. But a surprising economic principle introduced on the next page (in Idea 3), and then explained more fully in Chapters 3 and 17, says that in fact the answers are probably "no." We will see why shortly.

**IDEAS FOR
BEYOND THE
FINAL EXAM**

Each of the seven *Ideas for Beyond the Final Exam*, many of which are counterintuitive, will be sketched briefly here. More important, each will be discussed in depth when it occurs in the course of the book, where it will be called to your attention by a special icon in the margin. So don't expect to master these ideas fully now. But do notice how some of the ideas arise again and again as we deal with different topics. By the end of the course you will have a better grasp of when common sense works and when it fails. And you will be able to recognize common fallacies that are all too often offered as pearls of wisdom by public figures, the press, and television commentators.

Idea 1: How Much Does It Really Cost?

Because no one has infinite riches, people are constantly forced to make choices. If you purchase a new computer, you may have to give up that trip you had planned. If a business decides to retool its factories, it may have to postpone its plans for new executive offices. If a government expands its defense program, it may be forced to reduce its outlays on school buildings.

Economists say that the true costs of such decisions are not the number of dollars spent on the computer, the new equipment, or the military, but rather *the value of what must be given up in order to acquire the item*—the vacation trip, the new executive offices, and the new schools. These are called **opportunity costs** because they represent the *opportunities* the individual, firm, or government must forgo to make the desired expenditure. Economists maintain that rational decision making must be based on opportunity costs, not just dollar costs (see Chapter 3 and elsewhere).

The **opportunity cost** of some decision is the value of the next best alternative that must be given up because of that decision (for example, working instead of going to school).

The cost of a college education provides a vivid example. How much do you think it *costs* to go to college? Most people are likely to answer by adding together their expenditures on tuition, room and board, books, and the like, and then deducting any scholarship funds they may receive. Suppose that amount comes to $15,000.

Economists keep score differently. They first want to know how much you would be earning if you were not attending college. Suppose that salary is $20,000 per year. This may seem irrelevant, but because you *give up* these earnings by attending college, they must be added to your tuition bill. You have that much less income because of your education. On the other side of the ledger, economists would not count *all* of the university's bill for room and board as part of the costs of your education. They would want to know how much *more* it costs you to live at school rather than at home. Economists would count only these *extra* costs as an educational expense because you would have incurred these costs whether or not you attend college. On balance, college is probably costing you much more than you think. And, as we will see later, taking opportunity cost into account in any personal planning you do will help you to make more rational decisions.

Idea 2: Attempts to Repeal the Laws of Supply and Demand—The Market Strikes Back

When a commodity is in short supply, its price naturally tends to rise. Sometimes disgruntled consumers badger politicians into "solving" this problem by making the high prices illegal—by imposing a ceiling on the price. Similarly, when supplies are plentiful—say, when fine weather produces extraordinarily abundant crops—prices tend to fall. Falling prices naturally dismay producers, who often succeed in getting legislators to impose price floors.

But such attempts to repeal the laws of supply and demand usually backfire and sometimes produce results virtually the opposite of those intended. Where rent controls are adopted to protect tenants, housing grows scarce because the law makes it unprofitable to build and maintain apartments. When price floors are placed under agricultural products, surpluses pile up because people buy less.

As we will see in Chapter 4 and elsewhere in this book, such consequences of interference with the price mechanism are no accident. They follow inevitably from the way in which free markets work.

Idea 3: The Surprising Principle of Comparative Advantage

China today produces many products that Americans buy in huge quantities—including toys, textiles, and electronic equipment. American manufacturers often complain about Chinese competition and demand protection from the flood of imports that, in their view, threatens American standards of living. Is this view justified?

Economists think that it is often false. They maintain that both sides normally gain from international trade. But what if the Chinese were able to produce *everything* more cheaply than we can? Wouldn't Americans be thrown out of work and our nation be impoverished?

A remarkable result, called the law of *comparative advantage*, shows that, even in this extreme case, the two nations could still benefit by trading and that each could gain as a result! We will explain this principle first in Chapter 3 and then more fully in Chapter 17. But for now a simple parable will make the reason clear.

Suppose Sally grows up on a farm and is a whiz at plowing. But she is also a successful country singer who earns $4,000 per performance. Should Sally turn down singing engagements to leave time to work the fields? Of course not. Instead, she should hire Alfie, a much less efficient farmer, to do the plowing for her. Sally may be better at plowing, but she earns so much more by singing that it makes sense for her to specialize in that and leave the farming to Alfie. Although Alfie is a less skilled farmer than Sally, he is an even worse singer.

So Alfie earns his living in the job at which he at least has a *comparative* advantage (his farming is not as inferior as his singing), and both Alfie and Sally gain. The same is true of two countries. Even if one of them is more efficient at everything, both countries can gain by producing the things they do best *comparatively*.

Idea 4: Trade Is a Win-Win Situation

One of the most fundamental ideas of economics is that both parties must expect to gain something in a voluntary exchange. Otherwise, why would they both agree to trade? This principle seems self-evident. Yet it is amazing how often it is ignored in practice.

For example, it was widely believed for centuries that in international trade one country's gain from an exchange must be the other country's loss (Chapter 17). Analogously, some people feel instinctively that if Ms. A profits handsomely from a deal with Mr. B, then Mr. B must have been exploited. Laws sometimes prohibit mutually beneficial exchanges between buyers and sellers—as when an apartment rental is banned because the rental rate is "too high" (Chapter 4), or when a willing worker is condemned to remain unemployed because the wage she is offered is "too low," or when the resale of tickets to sporting events ("ticket scalping") is outlawed even though the buyer is happy to get the ticket that he could not obtain at a lower price (Chapter 4).

In every one of these cases—and many more—well-intentioned but misguided reasoning blocks the possible mutual gains that arise from voluntary exchange and thereby interferes with one of the most basic functions of an economic system (see Chapters 3 and 4).

Idea 5: Government Policies Can Limit Economic Fluctuations—But Don't Always Succeed

One of the most persistent problems of market economies has been their tendency to go through cycles of boom and bust. The booms, as we shall see, often bring inflation. The busts always raise unemployment. Years ago, economists, businesspeople, and politicians viewed these fluctuations as inevitable: There was nothing the government could or should do about them.

That view is now considered obsolete. As we will learn in Part 2, and especially Part 3, modern governments have an arsenal of weapons that they can and do deploy to try to mitigate fluctuations in their national economies—to limit both inflation and unemployment. Some of these weapons constitute what is called *fiscal policy*: control over taxes and government spending. Others come from *monetary policy*: control over money and interest rates.

But *trying* to tame the business cycle is not the same as *succeeding*. Economic fluctuations remain with us, and one reason is that the government's fiscal and monetary policies sometimes fail—for both political and economic reasons. As we will see in Part 3, policy makers do not always make the right decisions. And even when they do, the economy does not always react as expected. Furthermore, for reasons we will explain later, it is not always clear what the "right" decision is.

Idea 6: The Short-Run Trade-Off between Inflation and Unemployment

The U.S. economy was lucky in the second half of the 1990s. A set of fortuitous events—falling energy prices, tumbling computer prices, a rising dollar, and so on—pushed inflation down even while unemployment fell to its lowest level in almost 30 years. During the 1970s and early 1980s, the United States was not so fortunate. Skyrocketing prices for food and, especially, energy sent both inflation and unemployment up to extraordinary heights. In both episodes, then, inflation and unemployment moved in the same direction.

But economists maintain that neither of these two episodes was "normal." When we are experiencing neither unusually good luck (as in the 1990s) nor exceptionally bad luck (as in the 1970s), there is a *trade-off between inflation and unemployment*—meaning that low unemployment normally makes inflation rise and high unemployment normally makes inflation fall. We will study the mechanisms underlying this trade-off in Parts 2 and 3, especially in Chapter 16. It poses one of the fundamental dilemmas of national economic policy.

Idea 7: Productivity Growth Is (Almost) Everything in the Long Run

In Geneva, Switzerland, today, workers in a watch factory turn out more than 100 times as many mechanical watches per year as their ancestors did three centuries earlier. The productivity of labor (output per hour of work) in cotton production has probably gone up more than 1,000-fold in 200 years. It is estimated that rising labor productivity has increased the standard of living of a typical American worker approximately sevenfold in the past century (see Chapter 7).

Other economic issues such as unemployment, monopoly, and inequality are important to us all and will receive much attention in this book. But in the long run, nothing has as great an effect on our material well-being and the amounts society can afford to spend on hospitals, schools, and social amenities as the rate of growth of productivity—the amount that an average worker can produce in an hour. Chapter 7 points out that what appears to be a small increase in productivity growth can have a huge effect on a country's standard of living over a long period of time because productivity compounds like the interest on savings in a bank. Similarly, a slowdown in productivity growth that persists for a substantial number of years can have a devastating effect on living standards.

Epilogue

These ideas are some of the more fundamental concepts you will find in this book—ideas that we hope you will retain beyond the final exam. There is no need to master them right now, for you will hear much more about each as you progress through the book. By the end of the course, you may be amazed to see how natural, or even obvious, they will seem.

INSIDE THE ECONOMIST'S TOOL KIT

We turn now from the kinds of issues economists deal with to some of the tools they use to grapple with them.

Economics as a Discipline

Although economics is clearly the most rigorous of the social sciences, it nevertheless looks decidedly more "social" than "scientific" when compared with, say, physics. An economist must be a jack of several trades, borrowing modes of analysis from numerous fields. Mathematical reasoning is often used in economics, but so is historical study. And neither looks quite the same as when practiced by a mathematician or a historian. Statistics play a major role in modern economic inquiry, although economists had to modify standard statistical procedures to fit their kinds of data.

The Need for Abstraction

Some students find economics unduly abstract and "unrealistic." The stylized world envisioned by economic theory seems only a distant cousin to the world they know. There is an old joke about three people—a chemist, a physicist, and an economist—stranded on an desert island with an ample supply of canned food but no tools to open the cans. The chemist thinks that lighting a fire under the cans would burst the cans. The physicist advocates building a catapult with which to smash the cans against some boulders. The economist's suggestion? "Assume a can opener."

Economic theory *does* make some unrealistic assumptions; you will encounter some of them in this book. But some abstraction from reality is necessary because of the incredible complexity of the economic world, not because economists like to sound absurd.

Compare the chemist's simple task of explaining the interactions of compounds in a chemical reaction with the economist's

SOURCE: From *The Wall Street Journal.* Permission, Cartoon Features Syndicate.

"Yes, John, we'd all like to make economics less dismal . . . "

NOTE: The nineteenth-century British writer Thomas Carlyle described economics as the "dismal science," a label that stuck.

complex task of explaining the interactions of people in an economy. Are molecules motivated by greed or altruism, by envy or ambition? Do they ever imitate other molecules? Do forecasts about them influence their behavior? People, of course, do all these things and many, many more. It is therefore vastly more difficult to predict human behavior than to predict chemical reactions. If economists tried to keep track of every feature of human behavior, they would never get anywhere. Thus:

Abstraction from unimportant details is necessary to understand the functioning of anything as complex as the economy.

Abstraction means ignoring many details so as to focus on the most important elements of a problem.

An analogy will make clear why economists **abstract** from details. Suppose you have just arrived for the first time in Los Angeles. You are now at the Los Angeles Civic Center—the point marked *A* in Maps 1 and 2, which are alternative maps of part of Los Angeles. You want to drive to the Los Angeles County Museum of Art, point *B* on each map. Which map would be more useful?

Map 1 has complete details of the Los Angeles road system. This makes it hard to read and hard to use as a way to find the art museum. For this purpose, Map 1 is far too detailed, although for some other purposes (for example, locating some small street in Hollywood) it may be far better than Map 2.

In contrast, Map 2 omits many minor roads—you might say they are *assumed away*—so that the freeways and major arteries stand out more clearly. As a result of this simplification, several routes from the Civic Center to the Los Angeles County Museum of Art emerge. For example, we can take the Hollywood Freeway west to Alvarado Boulevard, go south to Wilshire Boulevard, and then head west again. Although we *might* find a shorter route by poring over the details in Map 1, most strangers to the city would be better off with Map 2. Similarly, economists try to *abstract* from a lot of confusing details while retaining the essentials.

Map 3, however, illustrates that simplification can go too far. It shows little more than the major interstate routes that pass through the greater Los Angeles area and therefore

MAP 1

Detailed Road Map of Los Angeles

NOTE: Point A marks the Los Angeles Civic Center and Point B marks the Los Angeles County Museum of Art.

will not help a visitor find the art museum. Of course, this map was never intended to be used as a detailed tourist guide, which brings us to an important point:

> There is no such thing as one "right" degree of abstraction and simplification for all analytic purposes. The proper degree of abstraction depends on the objective of the analysis. A model that is a gross oversimplification for one purpose may be needlessly complicated for another.

Economists are constantly seeking analogies to Map 2 rather than Map 3, treading the thin line between useful generalizations about complex issues and gross distortions of the pertinent facts. For example, suppose you want to learn why some people are fabulously rich while others are abjectly poor. People differ in many ways, too many to enumerate, much less to study. The economist must ignore most of these details to focus on the important ones. The color of a person's hair or eyes is probably not important for the problem but, unfortunately, the color of his or her skin probably is because racial discrimination can depress a person's income. Height and weight may not matter, but education probably does. Proceeding in this way, we can pare Map 1 down to the manageable dimensions of Map 2. But there is a danger of going too far, stripping away some of the crucial factors, so that we wind up with Map 3.

The Role of Economic Theory

Some students find economics "too theoretical." To see why we can't avoid it, let's consider what we mean by a **theory**.

To an economist or natural scientist, the word *theory* means

MAP 2

Major Los Angeles Arteries and Freeways

Map © by Rand McNally, R.L.04-S-14. Reprinted by permission.

MAP 3

Greater Los Angeles Freeways

SOURCE: California Department of Transportation

something different from what it means in common speech. In science, a theory is *not* an untested assertion of alleged fact. The statement that aspirin provides protection against heart attacks is not a theory; it is a *hypothesis*, that is, a reasoned guess, which will prove

A **theory** is a deliberate simplification of relationships used to explain how those relationships work.

to be true or false once the right sorts of experiments have been completed. But a theory is different. It is a deliberate simplification (abstraction) of reality that attempts to explain how some relationships work. It is an *explanation* of the mechanism behind observed phenomena. Thus, gravity forms the basis of theories that describe and explain the paths of the planets. Similarly, Keynesian theory (discussed in Parts 2 and 3) seeks to describe and explain how government policies affect unemployment and prices in the national economy.

People who have never studied economics often draw a false distinction between *theory* and *practical policy.* Politicians and businesspeople, in particular, often reject abstract economic theory as something that is best ignored by "practical" people. The irony of these statements is that

> **It is precisely the concern for policy that makes economic theory so necessary and important.**

To analyze policy options, economists are forced to deal with *possibilities that have not actually occurred.* For example, to learn how to shorten periods of high unemployment, they must investigate whether a proposed new policy that has never been tried can help. Or to determine which environmental programs will be most effective, they must understand how and why a market economy produces pollution and what might happen if the government taxed industrial waste discharges and automobile emissions. Such questions require some *theorizing,* not just examination of the facts, because we need to consider possibilities that have never occurred.

The facts, moreover, can sometimes be highly misleading. Data often indicate that two variables move up and down together. But this statistical **correlation** does not prove that either variable *causes* the other. For example, when it rains, people drive their cars more slowly and there are also more traffic accidents. But no one thinks that it is the slower driving that causes more accidents when it's raining. Rather, we understand that both phenomena are caused by a common underlying factor—more rain. How do we know this? Not just by looking at the correlation between data on accidents and driving speeds. Data alone tell us little about cause and effect. We must use some simple *theory* as part of our analysis. In this case, the theory might explain that drivers are more apt to have accidents on rain-slicked roads.

Similarly, we must use theoretical analysis, and not just data alone, to understand *how,* if at all, different government policies will lead to lower unemployment or *how* a tax on emissions will reduce pollution.

> **Statistical correlation need not imply causation. Some theory is usually needed to interpret data.**

Two variables are said to be **correlated** *if they tend to go up or down together. Correlation need not imply causation.*

What Is an Economic Model?

An **economic model** *is a simplified, small-scale version of some aspect of the economy. Economic models are often expressed in equations, by graphs, or in words.*

An **economic model** is a representation of a theory or a part of a theory, often used to gain insight into cause and effect. The notion of a "model" is familiar enough to children; and economists—like other researchers—use the term in much the same way that children do.

A child's model airplane looks and operates much like the real thing, but it is much smaller and simpler, so it is easier to manipulate and understand. Engineers for Boeing also build models of planes. Although their models are far larger and much more elaborate than a child's toy, they use them for much the same purposes: to observe the workings of these aircraft "up close" and to experiment with them to see how the models behave under different circumstances. ("What happens if I do this?") From these experiments, they make educated guesses as to how the real-life version will perform.

Economists use models for similar purposes. The late A. W. Phillips, the famous engineer-turned-economist who discovered the "Phillips curve" (discussed in Chapter 16), was talented enough to construct a working model of the determination of national income in a simple economy by using colored water flowing through pipes. For years this contraption has graced the basement of the London School of Economics. Although we will explain the models with words and diagrams, Phillips's engineering background enabled him to depict the theory with tubes, valves, and pumps.

Because many of the models used in this book are depicted in diagrams, for those of you who need review, we explain the construction and use of various types of graphs in the appendix to this chapter. Don't be put off by seemingly abstract models. Think of them as useful road maps. And remember how hard it would be to find your way around Los Angeles without one.

Reasons for Disagreements: Imperfect Information and Value Judgments

"If all the earth's economists were laid end to end, they could not reach an agreement," the saying goes. Politicians and reporters are fond of pointing out that economists can be found on both sides of many public policy issues. If economics is a science, why do economists so often disagree? After all, astronomers do not debate whether the earth revolves around the sun or vice versa.

SOURCE: Science Museum/Science & Society Picture Library

A. W. Phillips built this model in the early 1950s to illustrate Keynesian theory.

This question reflects a misunderstanding of the nature of science. Disputes are normal at the frontier of any science. For example, astronomers once did argue vociferously over whether the earth revolves around the sun. Nowadays, they argue about gamma-ray bursts, dark matter, and other esoterica. These arguments go mostly unnoticed by the public because few of us understand what they are talking about. But economics is a *social* science, so its disputes are aired in public and all sorts of people feel competent to join economic debates.

Furthermore, economists actually agree on much more than is commonly supposed. Virtually all economists, regardless of their politics, agree that taxing polluters is one of the best ways to protect the environment, that rent controls can ruin a city (Chapter 4), and that free trade among nations is usually preferable to the erection of barriers through tariffs and quotas (see Chapter 17). The list could go on and on. It is probably true that the issues about which economists agree *far* exceed the subjects on which they disagree.

Finally, many disputes among economists are not scientific disputes at all. Sometimes the pertinent facts are simply unknown. For example, you will learn in Chapter 17 that the appropriate financial penalty to levy on a polluter depends on quantitative estimates of the harm done by the pollutant. But good estimates of this damage may not be available. Similarly, although there is wide scientific agreement that the earth is slowly warming, there are disagreements over how costly global warming may be. Such disputes make it difficult to agree on a concrete policy proposal.

Another important source of disagreements is that economists, like other people, come in all political stripes: conservative, middle-of-the-road, liberal, radical. Each may have different values, and so each may hold a different view of the "right" solution to a public policy problem—even if they agree on the underlying analysis. Here are two examples:

1. We suggested early in this chapter that policies that lower inflation are likely to raise unemployment. Many economists believe they can measure the amount of unemployment that must be endured to reduce inflation by a given amount. But they disagree about whether it is worth having, say, three million more people out of work for a year to cut the inflation rate by 1 percent.

2. In designing an income tax, society must decide how much of the burden to put on upper-income taxpayers. Some people believe the rich should pay a disproportionate share of the taxes. Others disagree, believing it is fairer to levy the same income tax rate on everyone.

Economists cannot answer questions like these any more than nuclear physicists could have determined whether dropping the atomic bomb on Hiroshima was a good idea. The decisions rest on moral judgments that can be made only by the citizenry through its elected officials.

Although economic science can contribute theoretical and factual knowledge on a particular issue, the final decision on policy questions often rests either on information that is not currently available or on social values and ethical opinions about which people differ, or on both.

| SUMMARY |

1. To help you get the most out of your first course in economics, we have devised a list of seven important ideas that you will want to retain beyond the final exam. Briefly, they are the following:

   a. *Opportunity cost* is the correct measure of cost.

   b. Attempts to fight market forces often backfire.

   c. Nations can gain from trade by exploiting their *comparative advantages*.

   d. Both parties can gain in a voluntary exchange.

   e. Governments have tools that can mitigate cycles of boom and bust, but these tools are imperfect.

   f. In the short run, policy makers face a trade-off between inflation and unemployment. Policies that reduce one normally increase the other.

   g. In the long run, *productivity* is almost the only thing that matters for a society's material well-being.

2. Common sense is not always a reliable guide in explaining economic issues or in making economic decisions.

3. Because of the great complexity of human behavior, economists are forced to *abstract* from many details, to make generalizations that they know are not quite true, and to organize what knowledge they have in terms of some theoretical structure called a "model."

4. Correlation need not imply causation.

5. Economists use simplified models to understand the real world and predict its behavior, much as a child uses a model railroad to learn how trains work.

6. Although these models, if skillfully constructed, can illuminate important economic problems, they rarely can answer the questions that confront policy makers. Value judgments involving such matters as ethics are needed for this purpose, and the economist is no better equipped than anyone else to make them.

| KEY TERMS |

Opportunity cost 4	Theory 9	Economic model 10
Abstraction 8	Correlation 10	

| DISCUSSION QUESTIONS |

1. Think about how you would construct a model of how your college is governed. Which officers and administrators would you include and exclude from your model if the objective were one of the following:

   a. To explain how decisions on financial aid are made

   b. To explain the quality of the faculty

   Relate this to the map example in the chapter.

2. Relate the process of abstraction to the way you take notes in a lecture. Why do you not try to transcribe every word uttered by the lecturer? Why don't you write down just the title of the lecture and stop there? How do you decide, roughly speaking, on the correct amount of detail?

3. Explain why a government policy maker cannot afford to ignore economic theory.

| APPENDIX | *Using Graphs: A Review*[1]

As noted in the chapter, economists often explain and analyze models with the help of graphs. Indeed, this book is full of them. But that is not the only reason for studying how graphs work. Most college students will deal with graphs in the future, perhaps frequently. You will see them in newspapers. If you become a doctor, you will use graphs to keep track of your patients' progress. If you join a business firm, you will use them to check profit or performance at a glance. This appendix introduces some of the techniques of graphic analysis—tools you will use throughout the book and, more important, very likely throughout your working career.

GRAPHS USED IN ECONOMIC ANALYSIS

Economic graphs are invaluable because they can display a large quantity of data quickly and because they facilitate data interpretation and analysis. They enable the eye to take in at a glance important statistical relationships that would be far less apparent from written descriptions or long lists of numbers.

TWO-VARIABLE DIAGRAMS

Much of the economic analysis found in this and other books requires that we keep track of two **variables** simultaneously.

A **variable** is something measured by a number; it is used to analyze what happens to other things when the size of that number changes (varies).

For example, in studying how markets operate, we will want to keep one eye on the *price* of a commodity and the other on the *quantity* of that commodity that is bought and sold.

For this reason, economists frequently find it useful to display real or imaginary figures in a two-variable diagram, which simultaneously represents the behavior of two economic variables. The numerical value of one variable is measured along the horizontal line at the bottom of the graph (called the *horizontal axis*), starting from the **origin** (the point labeled "0"), and the numerical value of the other variable is measured up the vertical line on the left side of the graph (called the *vertical axis*), also starting from the origin.

The "0" point in the lower-left corner of a graph where the axes meet is called the **origin**. Both variables are equal to zero at the origin.

Figures 1(a) and 1(b) are typical graphs of economic analysis. They depict an imaginary *demand curve*, represented by the brick-colored dots in Figure 1(a) and the heavy brick-colored line in Figure 1(b). The graphs show the price of natural gas on their vertical axes and the quantity of gas people want to buy at each price on the horizontal axes. The dots in Figure 1(a) are

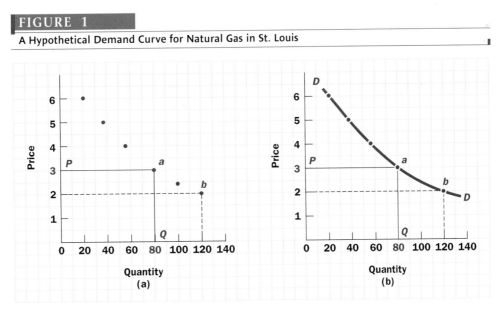

FIGURE 1

A Hypothetical Demand Curve for Natural Gas in St. Louis

NOTE: Price is in dollars per thousand cubic feet; quantity is in billions of cubic feet per year.

---

[1] Students who have some acquaintance with geometry and feel quite comfortable with graphs can safely skip this appendix.

connected by the continuous brick-colored curve labeled *DD* in Figure 1(b).

Economic diagrams are generally read just as one would read latitudes and longitudes on a map. On the demand curve in Figure 1, the point marked *a* represents a hypothetical combination of price and quantity of natural gas demanded by customers in St. Louis. By drawing a horizontal line leftward from that point to the vertical axis, we learn that at this point the average price for gas in St. Louis is $3 per thousand cubic feet. By dropping a line straight down to the horizontal axis, we find that consumers want 80 billion cubic feet per year at this price, just as the statistics in Table 1 show. The other points on the graph give similar information. For example, point *b* indicates that if natural gas in St. Louis were to cost only $2 per thousand cubic feet, quantity demanded would be higher—it would reach 120 billion cubic feet per year.

TABLE 1

Quantities of Natural Gas Demanded at Various Prices

Price (per thousand cubic feet)	$2	$3	$4	$5	$6
Quantity demanded (billions of cubic feet per year)	120	80	56	38	20

Notice that information about price and quantity is *all* we can learn from the diagram. The demand curve will not tell us what kinds of people live in St. Louis, the sizes of their homes, or the condition of their furnaces. It tells us about the quantity demanded at each possible price—no more, no less.

A diagram abstracts from many details, some of which may be quite interesting, so as to focus on the two variables of primary interest—in this case, the price of natural gas and the amount of gas that is demanded at each price. All of the diagrams used in this book share this basic feature. They cannot tell the reader the

"whole story," any more than a map's latitude and longitude figures for a particular city can make someone an authority on that city.

THE DEFINITION AND MEASUREMENT OF SLOPE

One of the most important features of economic diagrams is the rate at which the line or curve being sketched runs uphill or downhill as we move to the right. The demand curve in Figure 1 clearly slopes downhill (the price falls) as we follow it to the right (that is, as consumers demand more gas). In such instances, we say that *the curve has a negative slope, or is negatively sloped, because one variable falls as the other one rises.*

The **slope of a straight line** is the ratio of the vertical change to the corresponding horizontal change as we move to the right along the line between two points on that line, or, as it is often said, the ratio of the "rise" over the "run."

The four panels of Figure 2 show all possible types of slope for a straight-line relationship between two unnamed variables called *Y* (measured along the vertical axis) and *X* (measured along the horizontal axis). Figure 2(a) shows a *negative slope*, much like our demand curve in the previous graph. Figure 2(b) shows a *positive slope*, because variable *Y* rises (we go uphill) as variable *X* rises (as we move to the right). Figure 2(c) shows a *zero slope*, where the value of *Y* is the same irrespective of the value of *X*. Figure 2(d) shows an *infinite slope*, meaning that the value of *X* is the same irrespective of the value of *Y*.

Slope is a numerical concept, not just a qualitative one. The two panels of Figure 3 show two positively sloped straight lines with different slopes. The line in Figure 3(b) is clearly steeper. But by how much? The labels should help you compute the answer. In

FIGURE 2

Different Types of Slope of a Straight-Line Graph

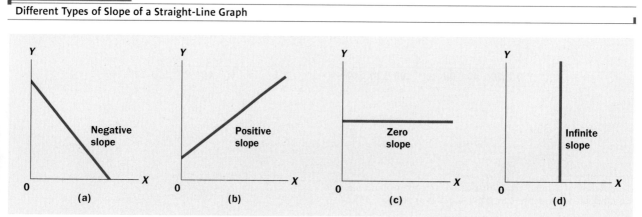

FIGURE 3
How to Measure Slope

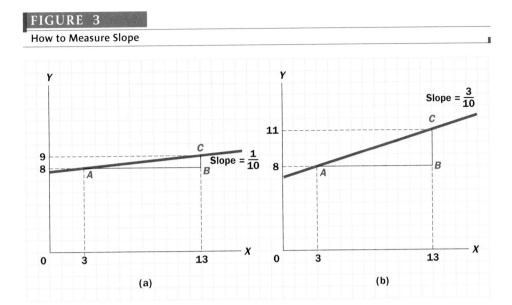

(a)   (b)

Figure 3(a) a horizontal movement, *AB*, of 10 units (13 − 3) corresponds to a vertical movement, *BC*, of 1 unit (9 − 8). So the slope is *BC*/*AB* = 1/10. In Figure 3(b), the same horizontal movement of 10 units corresponds to a vertical movement of 3 units (11 − 8). So the slope is 3/10, which is larger—the rise divided by the run is greater in Figure 3(b).

By definition, the slope of any particular straight line remains the same, no matter where on that line we choose to measure it. That is why we can pick any horizontal distance, *AB*, and the corresponding slope triangle, *ABC*, to measure slope. But this is not true for curved lines.

Curved lines also have slopes, but the numerical value of the slope differs at every point along the curve as we move from left to right.

The four panels of Figure 4 provide some examples of *slopes of curved lines*. The curve in Figure 4(a) has a negative slope everywhere, and the curve in Figure 4(b) has a positive slope everywhere. But these are not the only possibilities. In Figure 4(c) we encounter a curve that has a positive slope at first but a negative slope later on. Figure 4(d) shows the opposite case: a negative slope followed by a positive slope.

We can measure the slope of a smooth curved line numerically *at any particular point* by drawing a *straight* line that *touches*, but does not *cut*, the curve at the point in question. Such a line is called a **tangent** to the curve.

The **slope of a curved line** at a particular point is defined as the slope of the straight line that is tangent to the curve at that point.

Figure 5 shows tangents to the brick-colored curve at two points. Line *tt* is tangent at point *T*, and line *rr* is tangent at point *R*. We can measure the slope of the

FIGURE 4
Behavior of Slopes in Curved Graphs

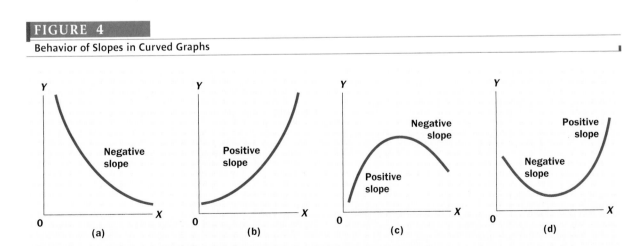

(a)   (b)   (c)   (d)

FIGURE 5

How to Measure Slope at a Point on a Curved Graph

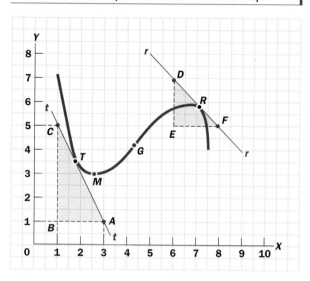

curve at these two points by applying the definition. The calculation for point T, then, is the following:

$$\text{Slope at point } T = \text{Slope of line } tt$$

$$= \frac{\text{Distance BC}}{\text{Distance BA}}$$

$$= \frac{(1 - 5)}{(3 - 1)} = \frac{-4}{2} = -2$$

A similar calculation yields the slope of the curve at point R, which, as we can see from Figure 5, must be smaller numerically. That is, the tangent line rr is less steep than line tt:

$$\text{Slope at point } R = \text{Slope of line } rr$$

$$= \frac{(5 - 7)}{(8 - 6)} = \frac{-2}{2} = -1$$

Exercise Show that the slope of the curve at point G is about 1.

What would happen if we tried to apply this graphical technique to the high point in Figure 4(c) or to the low point in Figure 4(d)? Take a ruler and try it. The tangents that you construct should be horizontal, meaning that they should have a slope exactly equal to zero. It is always true that where the slope of a *smooth* curve changes from positive to negative, or vice versa, there will be at least one point whose slope is zero.

Curves shaped like smooth hills, as in Figure 4(c), have a zero slope at their *highest* point. Curves shaped like valleys, as in Figure 4(d), have a zero slope at their *lowest* point.

RAYS THROUGH THE ORIGIN AND 45° LINES

The point at which a straight line cuts the vertical (Y) axis is called the **Y-intercept**.

> The **Y-intercept** of a line or a curve is the point at which it touches the vertical axis (the Y-axis). The X-intercept is defined similarly.

For example, the Y-intercept of the line in Figure 3(a) is a bit less than 8.

> Lines whose Y-intercept is zero have so many special uses in economics and other disciplines that they have been given a special name: a **ray through the origin**, or a **ray**.

Figure 6 shows three rays through the origin, and the slope of each is indicated in the diagram. The ray in the center (whose slope is 1) is particularly useful in many economic applications because it marks points where X and Y are equal (as long as X and Y are measured in the same units). For example, at point A we have $X = 3$ and $Y = 3$; at point B, $X = 4$ and $Y = 4$. A similar relation holds at any other point on that ray.

How do we know that this is always true for a ray whose slope is 1? If we start from the origin (where both X and Y are zero) and the slope of the ray is 1, we know from the definition of slope that

$$\text{Slope} = \frac{\text{Vertical change}}{\text{Horizontal change}} = 1$$

This implies that the vertical change and the horizontal change are always equal, so the two variables

FIGURE 6

Rays Through the Origin

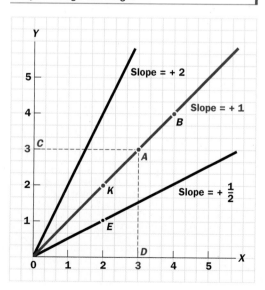

must always remain equal. Any point along that ray (for example, point A) is exactly equal in distance from the horizontal and vertical axes (length DA = length CA)—the number on the X-axis (the abscissa) will be the same as the number on the Y-axis (the ordinate).

> Rays through the origin with a slope of 1 are called 45° lines because they form an angle of 45° with the horizontal axis. A **45° line** marks off points where the variables measured on each axis have equal values.[2]

If a point representing some data is above the 45° line, we know that the value of Y exceeds the value of X. Similarly, whenever we find a point below the 45° line, we know that X is larger than Y.

SQUEEZING THREE DIMENSIONS INTO TWO: CONTOUR MAPS

Sometimes problems involve more than two variables, so two dimensions just are not enough to depict them on a graph. This is unfortunate, because the surface of a sheet of paper is only two-dimensional. When we study a business firm's decision-making process, for example, we may want to keep track simultaneously of three variables: how much labor it employs, how much raw material it imports from foreign countries, and how much output it creates.

Luckily, economists can use a well-known device for collapsing three dimensions into two—a *contour map*. Figure 7 is a contour map of the summit of the highest mountain in the world, Mt. Everest, on the border of Nepal and Tibet. On some of the irregularly shaped "rings" on this map, we find numbers (like 8500) indicating the height (in meters) above sea level at that particular spot on the mountain. Thus, unlike the more usual sort of map, which gives only latitudes and longitudes, this contour map (also called a topographical map) exhibits *three* pieces of information about each point: latitude, longitude, and altitude.

Figure 8 looks more like the contour maps encountered in economics. It shows how some third variable, called Z (think of it as a firm's output, for example), varies as we change either variable X (think of it as a firm's employment of labor) or variable Y (think of it as the use of imported raw material). Just like the map of Mt. Everest, any point on the diagram conveys three pieces of data. At point A, we can read off the values of X and Y in the conventional way (X is 30 and Y is 40), and we can also note the value of Z by finding out on which contour line point A falls. (It is on the $Z = 20$ contour.) So point A is able to tell us that 30 hours of labor and 40 yards of cloth produce 20 units of output per day. The contour line that indicates 20 units of output shows the various combinations of labor and cloth a manufacturer can use to

FIGURE 7

A Geographic Contour Map

SOURCE: Mount Everest, Alpenvereinskarte. Vienna: Kartographische Anstalt Freytag-Berndt und Artaria, 1957, 1988.

[2] The definition assumes that both variables are measured in the same units.

FIGURE 8

An Economic Contour Map

produce 20 units of output. Economists call such maps **production indifference maps.**

A **production indifference map** is a graph whose axes show the quantities of two inputs that are used to produce some output. A curve in the graph corresponds to some given quantity of that output, and the different points on that curve show the different quantities of the two inputs that are just enough to produce the given output.

Although most of the analyses presented in this book rely on the simpler two-variable diagrams, contour maps do find many applications in economics.

| SUMMARY |

1. Because graphs are used so often to portray economic models, it is important for students to acquire some understanding of their construction and use. Fortunately, the graphics used in economics are usually not very complex.

2. Most economic models are depicted in two-variable diagrams. We read data from these diagrams just as we read the latitude and longitude on a map: each point represents the values of two variables at the same time.

3. In some instances, three variables must be shown at once. In these cases, economists use contour maps, which, as the name suggests, show "latitude," "longitude," and "altitude" all at the same time.

4. Often, the most important property of a line or curve drawn on a diagram will be its slope, which is defined as the ratio of the "rise" over the "run," or the vertical change divided by the horizontal change when one moves along the curve. Curves that go uphill as we move to the right have positive slopes; curves that go downhill have negative slopes.

5. By definition, a straight line has the same slope wherever we choose to measure it. The slope of a curved line changes, but the slope at any point on the curve can be calculated by measuring the slope of a straight line tangent to the curve at that point.

| KEY TERMS |

Variable   13

Origin (of a graph)   13

Slope of a straight (or curved) line   15

Tangent to a curve   15

Y-intercept   16

Ray through the origin, or ray   16

45° line   17

Production indifference map   18

| TEST YOURSELF |

1. Portray the following hypothetical data on a two-variable diagram:

Academic Year	Total Enrollment	Enrollment in Economics Courses
1994–1995	3,000	300
1995–1996	3,100	325
1996–1997	3,200	350
1997–1998	3,300	375
1998–1999	3,400	400

Measure the slope of the resulting line, and explain what this number means.

2. From Figure 5, calculate the slope of the curve at point M.

3. Colin believes that the number of job offers he will get depends on the number of courses in which his grade is B+ or better. He concludes from observation that the following figures are typical:

Number of grades of B+ or better	0	1	2	3	4
Number of job offers		1	3	4	5	6

Put these numbers into a graph like Figure 1(a). Measure and interpret the slopes between adjacent dots.

4. In Figure 6, determine the values of X and Y at point K and at point E. What do you conclude about the slopes of the lines on which K and E are located?

5. In Figure 8, interpret the economic meaning of points A and B. What do the two points have in common? What is the difference in their economic interpretation?

THE ECONOMY: MYTH AND REALITY

E pluribus unum (Out of many, one)

MOTTO ON U.S. CURRENCY

This chapter introduces you to the U.S. economy and its role in the world. It may seem that no such introduction is necessary, for you have probably lived your entire life in the United States. Every time you work at a summer or part-time job, pay your college bills, or buy a slice of pizza, you not only participate in the American economy—you also observe something about it.

But the casual impressions we acquire in our everyday lives, though sometimes correct, are often misleading. Experience shows that most Americans—not just students—either are unaware of or harbor grave misconceptions about some of the most basic economic facts. One popular myth holds that most of the goods that Americans buy are made in China. Another is that business profits account for something like a third of the price we pay for a typical good or service. Also, "everyone knows" that federal government jobs have grown rapidly over the past few decades. In fact, none of these things is remotely close to true.

So, before we begin to develop theories of how the economy works, it is useful to get an accurate picture of what our economy is really like.

CONTENTS

THE AMERICAN ECONOMY: A THUMBNAIL SKETCH

"And may we continue to be worthy of consuming a disproportionate share of this planet's resources."

The U.S. economy is the biggest national economy on earth, for two very different reasons. First, there are a lot of us. The population of the United States is just over 300 million—making it the third most populous nation on earth after China and India. That vast total includes children, retirees, full-time students, institutionalized people, and the unemployed, none of whom produce much output. But the *working population* of the United States numbers about 150 million. As long as they are reasonably productive, that many people are bound to produce vast amounts of goods and services. And they do.

But population is not the main reason why the U.S. economy is by far the world's biggest. After all, India has nearly four times the population of the United States, but its economy is smaller than that of Texas. The second reason why the U.S. economy is so large is that we are a very rich country. Because American workers are among the most productive in the world, our economy produces more than $45,000 worth of goods and services for every living American—over $90,000 for every *working* American. If each of the 50 states was a separate country, California would be the fifth largest national economy on earth!

Inputs or **factors of production** are the labor, machinery, buildings, and natural resources used to make outputs.

Outputs are the goods and services that consumers and others want to acquire.

Why are some countries (like the United States) so rich and others (like India) so poor? That is one of the central questions facing economists. It is useful to think of an economic system as a machine that takes **inputs**, such as labor and other things we call **factors of production**, and transforms them into **outputs**, or the things people want to consume. The American economic machine performs this task with extraordinary efficiency, whereas the

U.S. Share of World GDP—It's Nice To Be Rich

The approximately 6.6 billion people of the world produced approximately $50 trillion worth of goods and services in 2007. The United States, with only about 4.5 percent of that population, turned out approximately 27 percent of total output. As the accompanying graph shows, the United States is still the leader in goods and services, with over $45,000 worth of GDP produced per person (or per capita). Just seven major industrial economies (the United States, Japan, Germany, France, Italy, the United Kingdom, and Canada—which account for just 11 percent of global population) generated 59 percent of world output. But their share has been falling as giant nations like China and India grow rapidly.

SOURCE: International Monetary Fund, *World Economic Outlook Database*, October 2007, http://www.imf.org, accessed February 2008, and Central Intelligence Agency, *The World Factbook*, 2008. Note: Foreign GDPs are converted to U.S. dollars using exchange rates.

2007 Gross Domestic Product (GDP) per Capita in 7 Industrial Countries

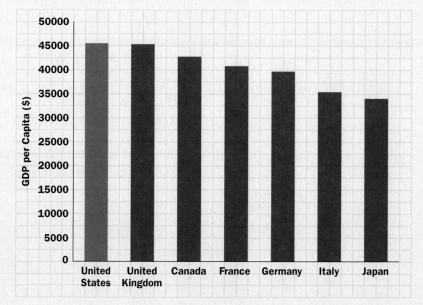

Indian machine runs quite inefficiently (though it is improving rapidly). Learning why this is so is one of the chief reasons to study economics.

Thus, what makes the American economy the center of world attention is our unique combination of prosperity and population. There are other rich countries in the world, like Switzerland, and there are other countries with huge populations, like India. But no nation combines a huge population with high per-capita income the way the United States does. Japan, with an economy well under half the size of ours, is the only nation that comes close—although China, with its immense population, is moving up rapidly.

Although the United States is a rich and populous country, the 50 states certainly were not created equal. Population density varies enormously—from a high of about 1,200 people per square mile in crowded New Jersey to a low of just one person per square mile in the wide-open spaces of Alaska. Income variations are much less pronounced. But still, the average income in West Virginia is only about half that in Connecticut.

A Private-Enterprise Economy

Part of the secret of America's economic success is that free markets and private enterprise have flourished here. These days more than ever, private enterprise and capitalism are the rule, not the exception, around the globe. But the United States has taken the idea of free markets—where individuals and businesses voluntarily buy and sell things—further than almost any other country. It remains the "land of opportunity."

Every country has a mixture of public and private ownership of property. Even in the darkest days of communism, Russians owned their own personal possessions. In our country, the post office and the electricity-producing Tennessee Valley Authority are enterprises of the federal government, and many cities and states own and operate mass transit facilities and sports stadiums. But the United States stands out among the world's nations as one of the most "privatized." Few industrial assets are publicly owned in the United States. Even many city bus companies and almost all utilities (such as electricity, gas, and telephones) are run as private companies in the United States. In Europe, they are often government enterprises, though there is substantial movement toward transfer of government firms to private ownership.

The United States also has one of the most "marketized" economies on earth. The standard measure of the total output of an economy is called **gross domestic product (GDP)**, a term that appears frequently in the news. The share of GDP that passes through markets in the United States is enormous. Although government purchases of goods and services amount to about 18 percent of GDP, much of that is purchased from private businesses. Direct government production of goods is extremely rare in our society.

> **Gross domestic product (GDP)** is a measure of the size of the economy—the total amount it produces in a year. *Real GDP* adjusts this measure for changes in the purchasing power of money, that is, it corrects for inflation.

A Relatively "Closed" Economy

All nations trade with one another, and the United States is no exception. Our annual exports exceed $1.7 trillion and our annual imports exceed $2.4 trillion. That's a lot of money, and so is the gap between them. But America's international trade often gets more attention than it deserves. The fact is that we still produce most of what we consume and consume most of what we produce, although the shares of imports and exports have been growing, as Figure 1 shows. In 1959, the average of exports and imports was only about 4 percent of GDP, a tiny fraction of the total. It has since gone up to over 14 percent. While this is no longer negligible, it still means that almost 86 percent of what Americans buy every year is made in the United States.

Among the most severe misconceptions about the U.S. economy is the myth that this country no longer manufactures anything but, rather, imports everything from, say, China. In fact, only about 17 percent of U.S. GDP is imported, with imports from China making up only about one seventh of this—or a little over 2 percent of GDP. It may surprise you to learn that we actually import more merchandise from Canada than we do from China.

Economists use the terms *open* and *closed* to indicate how important international trade is to a nation. A common measure of "openness" is the average of exports and imports,

FIGURE 1

Share of U.S. Gross Domestic Product (GDP) Exported and Imported, 1959–2007

SOURCE: *Economic Report of the President* (Washington, DC: U.S. Government Printing Office, various years).

An economy is called relatively **open** if its exports and imports constitute a large share of its GDP.

An economy is considered relatively **closed** if they constitute a small share.

expressed as a share of GDP. Thus, the Netherlands is considered an extremely **open economy** because it imports and exports about two thirds of its GDP. (See Table 1.) By this criterion, the United States stands out as among the most **closed economies** among the advanced, industrial nations. We export and import a smaller share of GDP than nearly all of the countries listed in the table.

A Growing Economy . . .

The next salient fact about the U.S. economy is its growth; it gets bigger almost every year (see Figure 2). Gross domestic product in 2007 was nearly $14 trillion; as noted earlier, that's over $45,000 per American. Measured in dollars of constant purchasing power,[1] the U.S. GDP was almost 5 times as large in 2007 as it was in 1959. Of course, there were many more people in America in 2007 than there were 48 years earlier. But even correcting for population growth, America's real GDP *per capita* was about 2.8 times higher in 2007 than in 1959. That's still not a bad performance: Living standards nearly tripled in 48 years.

Looking back further, the purchasing power of the average American increased nearly 600 percent over the entire 20th century! That's a remarkable number. To get an idea of what it means, just think how much poorer your family would become if it started out with an average U.S. income and then, suddenly, six dollars out of seven were taken away. Most Americans at the end of the 19th century could not afford vacations, the men had one good suit of clothing which they listed in their wills, and they wrote with ink that was kept in inkwells (and that froze every winter).

A **recession** is a period of time during which the total output of the economy falls.

TABLE 1

Openness of Various National Economies, 2007

	Openness
Netherlands	67%
Germany	41
China	37
Canada	36
Mexico	35
Russia	25
United Kingdom	20
United States	**14**
Japan	12

NOTE: Openness calculated as the average of imports and exports as a percentage of GDP.

SOURCE: For United States, Bureau of Economic Analysis; for all other countries, Central Intelligence Agency, *The World Factbook*, https://www.cia.gov/library/publications/the-world-factbook/index.html accessed February 2008.

But with Bumps along the Growth Path

Although the cumulative growth performance depicted in Figure 2 is impressive, America's economic growth has been quite irregular. We have experienced alternating periods of good and bad times, which are called *economic fluctuations* or sometimes just *business cycles*. In some years—five since 1959, to be exact—GDP actually declined. Such periods of *declining* economic activity are called **recessions.**

---

[1] This concept is called *real* GDP.

FIGURE 2

Real Gross Domestic Product (GDP) Since 1959

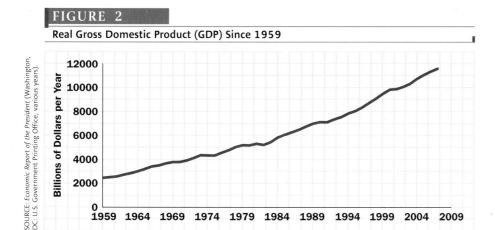

SOURCE: *Economic Report of the President* (Washington, DC: U.S. Government Printing Office, various years).

NOTE: Real (inflation-adjusted) GDP figures are in 2000 dollars.

The bumps along the American economy's historic growth path are barely visible in Figure 2. But they stand out more clearly in Figure 3, which displays the same data in a different way. Here we plot not the *level* of real GDP each year but, rather, its *growth rate*—the percentage change from one year to the next. Now the booms and busts that delight and distress people—and swing elections—stand out clearly. From 1983 to 1984, for example, real GDP grew by over 7 percent, which helped ensure Ronald Reagan's landslide reelection. But from 1990 to 1991, real GDP actually fell slightly, which helped Bill Clinton defeat (the first) George Bush.

One important consequence of these ups and downs in economic growth is that *unemployment* varies considerably from one year to the next (see Figure 4 on the next page). During the Great Depression of the 1930s, unemployment ran as high as 25 percent of the workforce. But it fell to barely over 1 percent during World War II. Just within the past few years, the national unemployment rate has been as high as 6.3 percent (in June 2003) and as low as 3.8 percent (in April 2000). In human terms, that 2.5 percentage point difference represents nearly four million jobless workers. Understanding why joblessness varies so dramatically, and what we can do about it, is another major reason for studying economics.

FIGURE 3

The Growth Rate of Real Gross Domestic Product (GDP) in the United States Since 1959

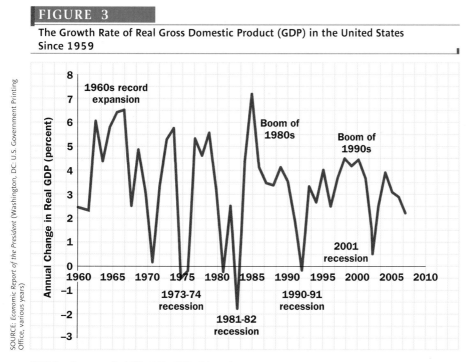

SOURCE: *Economic Report of the President* (Washington, DC: U.S. Government Printing Office, various years).

NOTE: Growth rates are for 1959–1960, 1960–1961, and so on.

FIGURE 4

The Unemployment Rate in the United States since 1929

SOURCE: *Economic Report of the President* (Washington, DC: U.S. Government Printing Office, various years); and Bureau of the Census, *Historical Statistics of the United States, Colonial Times to 1970* (Washington, DC: U.S. Government Printing Office, 1975).

THE INPUTS: LABOR AND CAPITAL

Let's now return to the analogy of an economy as a machine turning inputs into outputs. The most important input is human labor: the men and women who run the machines, work behind the desks, and serve you in stores.

Unemployment Rates in Europe

For roughly the first quarter-century after World War II, unemployment rates in the industrialized countries of Europe were significantly lower than those in the United States. Then, in the mid-1970s, rates of joblessness in Europe leaped, with double digits becoming common. And they have been higher than U.S. unemployment rates more or less ever since. Where employment is concerned, the U.S. economy has become the envy of Europe—with the exception of the United Kingdom. Put on a comparable basis by the U.S. Bureau of Labor Statistics, unemployment rates in the various countries in the fall of 2007 were:

U.S.	4.7%
Canada	5.2
Australia	4.3
Japan	3.8
France	8.6
Germany	8.6
Italy	6.0
Sweden	5.8
United Kingdom	5.4

SOURCE: U.S. Bureau of Labor Statistics.

The American Workforce: Who Is in It?

We have already mentioned that about 150 million Americans hold jobs. Almost 54 percent of these workers are men; over 46 percent are women. This ratio represents a drastic change from two generations ago, when most women worked only at home (see Figure 5). Indeed, the massive entrance of women into the paid labor force was one of the major social transformations of American life during the second half of the twentieth century. In 1950, just 29 percent of women worked in the marketplace; now almost 60 percent do. As Figure 6 shows, the share of women in the labor forces of other industrial countries has also been growing. The expanding role of women in the labor market has raised many controversial questions—whether they are discriminated against (the evidence suggests that they are), whether the government should compel employers to provide maternity leave, and so on.

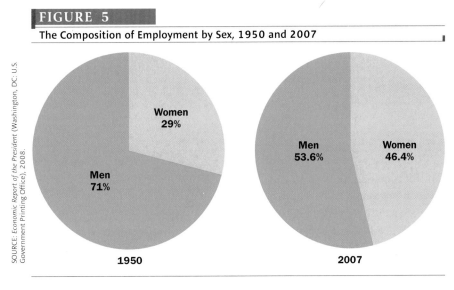

FIGURE 5

The Composition of Employment by Sex, 1950 and 2007

SOURCE: *Economic Report of the President* (Washington, DC: U.S. Government Printing Office), 2008.

Women 29%
Men 71%
1950

Men 53.6%
Women 46.4%
2007

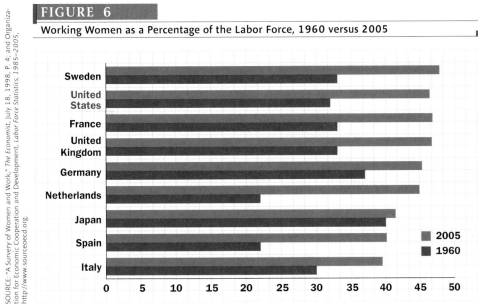

FIGURE 6

Working Women as a Percentage of the Labor Force, 1960 versus 2005

SOURCE: "A Survey of Women and Work," *The Economist,* July 18, 1998, P. 4; and Organization for Economic Cooperation and Development, *Labor Force Statistics, 1985–2005,* http://www.sourceoecd.org.

Sweden
United States
France
United Kingdom
Germany
Netherlands
Japan
Spain
Italy

■ 2005
■ 1960

0   5   10   15   20   25   30   35   40   45   50

In contrast to women, the percentage of teenagers in the workforce has dropped significantly since its peak in the mid-1970s (see Figure 7 on the next page). Young men and women aged 16 to 19 accounted for 8.6 percent of employment in 1974 but only 4.0 percent in 2007. As the baby boom gave way to the baby bust, people under 20 became scarce resources! Still,

FIGURE 7

Teenage Employment as a Percentage of Total Employment, 1950–2006

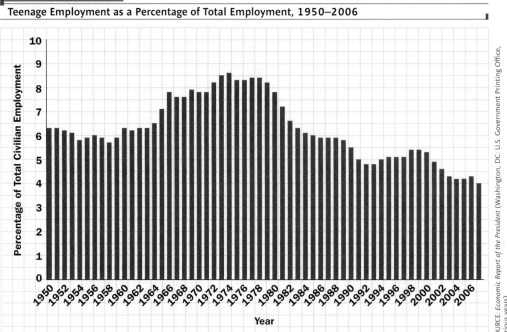

SOURCE: *Economic Report of the President* (Washington, DC: U.S. Government Printing Office, various years).

nearly 6 million teenagers hold jobs in the U.S. economy today—a number that has been pretty stable in the past few years. Most teenagers fill low-wage jobs at fast-food restaurants, amusement parks, and the like. Relatively few can be found in the nation's factories.

The American Workforce: What Does It Do?

What do these 150 million working Americans do? The only real answer is: almost anything you can imagine. In 2006, America had 101,010 architects, 396,020 computer programmers, more than 985,000 carpenters, more than 2.6 million truck drivers, 547,710 lawyers, roughly 3.9 million secretaries, 165,780 kindergarten teachers, 28,930 pediatricians, 62,860 tax preparers, 6,810 geological engineers, 283,630 fire fighters, and 12,970 economists.[2]

Figure 8 shows the breakdown by sector. It holds some surprises for most people. The majority of American workers—like workers in all developed countries—produce services, not goods. In 2007, almost 68 percent of all non-farm workers in the United States were employed by private service industries, whereas only about 16 percent produced goods. These legions of service workers included about 18.4 million in educational and health services, about 17.9 million in business and professional services, and over 15 million in retail trade. (The biggest single employer in the country is Wal-Mart.) By contrast, manufacturing companies in the United States employed only 14 million people, and almost a third of those worked in offices rather than in the factory. The Homer Simpson image of the typical American worker as a blue-collar worker is really quite misleading.

FIGURE 8

Civilian Non-Farm Payroll Employment by Sector, 2007

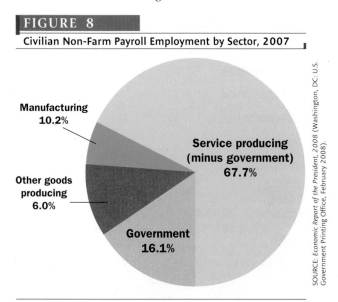

SOURCE: *Economic Report of the President, 2008* (Washington, DC: U.S. Government Printing Office, February 2008).

NOTE: Numbers may not add to 100% due to rounding.

---

[2] Source: U.S. Bureau of Labor Statistics, *Occupational Employment and Wages, May 2006,* http://www.bls.gov, accessed January 2008.

Federal, state, and local governments employed about 22 million people but, contrary to another popular misconception, few of these civil servants work for the *federal* government. Federal *civilian* employment is about 2.7 million—about 10 percent lower than it was in the 1980s. (The armed forces employ about another 1.4 million men and women in uniform.) State and local governments provide about 19.5 million jobs—or about seven times the number of federal government jobs. In addition to the jobs categorized in Figure 8, approximately 2 million Americans work on farms and over 10 million are self-employed.

As Figure 9 shows, *all* industrialized countries have become "service economies" in recent decades. To a considerable degree, this shift to services reflects the arrival of the "Information Age." Activities related to computers, to research, to the transmission of information by teaching and publication, and other information-related activities are providing many of the new jobs. This means that, in the rich economies, workers who moved out of manufacturing jobs into the service sectors have not gone predominantly into low-skill jobs such as dishwashing or housecleaning. Many found employment in service jobs in which education and experience provide a great advantage. At the same time, technological change has made it possible to produce more and more manufactured products using fewer and fewer workers. Such labor-saving innovation in manufacturing has allowed a considerable share of the labor force to move out of goods-producing jobs and into services.

FIGURE 9

The Growing Share of Service Sector Jobs, 1967 versus 2005

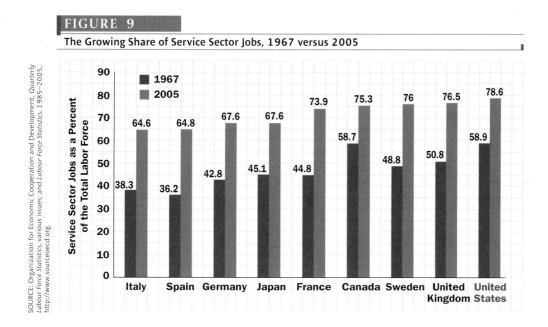

SOURCE: Organization for Economic Cooperation and Development, *Quarterly Labour Force Statistics,* various issues; and *Labour Force Statistics, 1985–2005,* http://www.sourceoecd.org.

The American Workforce: What It Earns

Altogether, these workers' wages account for over 70 percent of the income that the production process generates. That figures up to an average hourly wage of over $17—plus fringe benefits like health insurance and pensions, which can contribute an additional 30 to 40 percent for some workers. Because the average workweek is about 34 hours long, a typical weekly paycheck in the United States is about $600 before taxes (but excluding the value of benefits). That is hardly a princely sum, and most college graduates can expect to earn substantially more.[3] But it is typical of average wage rates in a rich country like the United States.

---

[3] These days, male college graduates typically earn almost 80 percent more than men with only high school diplomas, and female college grads almost 75 percent more than high-school-educated women. Source: *The State of Working America, 2006/2007,* Economic Policy Institute, http://www.epinet.org, accessed December 2006.

Wages throughout northern Europe are similar. Indeed, workers in a number of other industrial countries now receive higher compensation than American workers do—a big change from the situation a few decades ago. According to the U.S. Bureau of Labor Statistics, in 2006 workers in U.S. manufacturing industries made less than those in many European countries (see Figure 10). However, U.S. compensation levels still remain above those in Japan, Italy, and many other countries.

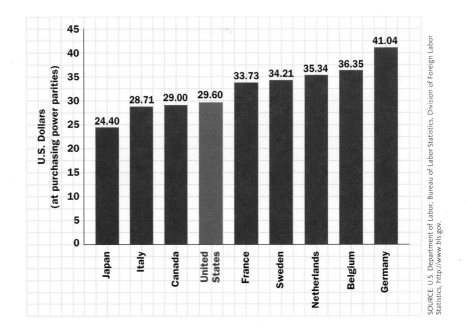

SOURCE: U.S. Department of Labor, Bureau of Labor Statistics, Division of Foreign Labor Statistics, http://www.bls.gov.

Capital and Its Earnings

The rest of national income (after deducting the small sliver of income that goes to the owners of land and natural resources) mainly accrues to the owners of *capital*—the machines and buildings that make up the nation's industrial plant.

The total market value of these business assets—a tough number to estimate—is believed to be in the neighborhood of $30 trillion. Because that capital earns an average rate of return of about 10 percent before taxes, total earnings of capital—including corporate profits, interest, and all the rest—come to about $3 trillion.

Public opinion polls routinely show that Americans have a distorted view of the level of business profits in our society. The man and woman on the street believe that corporate profits after tax account for about 30 percent of the price of a typical product (see the box "Public Opinion on Profits" on the next page). The right number is closer to 8 percent.

THE OUTPUTS: WHAT DOES AMERICA PRODUCE?

What does all this labor and capital produce? Consumer spending accounts for about 70 percent of GDP. And what an amazing variety of goods and services it buys. American households spend roughly 60 percent of their budgets on services, with housing commanding the largest share. They also spend about $140 billion annually on their telephone bills, over $35 billion on airline tickets, and $90 billion on dentists. The other 40 percent of American budgets goes for goods—ranging from about $375 billion per year on motor vehicles to almost $60 billion on shoes.

Public Opinion on Profits

Most Americans think corporate profits are much higher than they actually are. One public opinion poll years ago found that the average citizen thought that corporate profits *after taxes* amounted to 32 percent of sales for the typical manufacturing company. The actual profit rate at the time was closer to 4 percent!* Interestingly, when a previous poll asked how much profit was "reasonable," the response was 26 cents on every dollar of sales—more than six times as large as profits actually were.

* This poll was conducted in 1986. Corporate profit rates increased considerably in the 1990s and 2000s.

SOURCE: "Public Attitudes toward Corporate Profits," *Public Opinion Index* (Princeton, NJ: Opinion Research Corporation, June 1986).

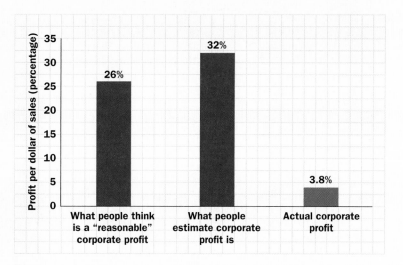

This leaves about 30 percent of GDP for all *nonconsumption* uses. That includes government services (buying such things as airplanes, guns, and the services of soldiers, teachers, and bureaucrats), business purchases of machinery and industrial structures, and consumer purchases of new houses.

THE CENTRAL ROLE OF BUSINESS FIRMS

Calvin Coolidge once said that "the business of America is business." Although this statement often has been ridiculed, he was largely right. When we peer inside the economic machine that turns inputs into outputs, we see mainly private companies. Astonishingly, the United States has more than 25 million business firms—about one for every 12 people!

The owners and managers of these businesses hire people, acquire or rent capital goods, and arrange to produce things consumers want to buy. Sound simple? It isn't. Over 80,000 businesses fail every year. A few succeed spectacularly. Some do both. Fortunately for the U.S. economy, however, the lure of riches induces hundreds of thousands of people to start new businesses every year—against the odds.

A number of the biggest firms do business all over the world, just as foreign-based *multinational corporations* do business here. Indeed, some people claim that it is now impossible to determine the true "nationality" of a multinational corporation—which may have factories in ten or more countries, sell its wares all over the world, and have stockholders in dozens of nations. (See the box "Is That an American Company?" on the next page). General Motors and Ford, for example, generate more profits abroad than they do at home, and the Toyota you drive was probably assembled in the U.S.

Firms compete with other companies in their *industry*. Most economists believe that this *competition* is the key to industrial efficiency. A sole supplier of a commodity will find it easy to make money, and may therefore fail to innovate or control costs. Its management is liable to become relaxed and sloppy. But a company besieged by dozens of competitors eager to take its business away must constantly seek ways to innovate, to cut costs, and to

Is That an American Company?

Robert Reich, who was Secretary of Labor in the Clinton administration, argued some years ago that it was already nearly impossible to define the nationality of a multinational company. Although many scholars think Reich exaggerated the point, no one doubts that he had one—nor that the nationalities of corporations have become increasingly blurred since then. He wrote in 1991:

> What's the difference between an "American" corporation that makes or buys abroad much of what it sells around the world and a "foreign" corporation that makes or buys in the United States much of what it sells? . . . The mind struggles to keep the players straight. In 1990, Canada's Northern Telecom was selling to its American customers telecommunications equipment made by Japan's NTT at NTT's factory in North Carolina.
>
> If you found that one too easy, try this: Beginning in 1991, Japan's Mazda would be producing Ford Probes at Mazda's plant in Flat Rock, Michigan. Some of these cars would be exported to Japan and sold there under Ford's trademark.
>
> A Mazda-designed compact utility vehicle would be built at a Ford plant in Louisville, Kentucky, and then sold at Mazda dealerships in the United States. Nissan, meanwhile, was designing a new light truck at its San Diego, California, design center. The trucks would be assembled at Ford's Ohio truck plant, using

panel parts fabricated by Nissan at its Tennessee factory, and then marketed by both Ford and Nissan in the United States and in Japan. Who is Ford? Nissan? Mazda?

SOURCE: © AP IMAGES/Greg Campbell

SOURCE: Robert B. Reich, *The Work of Nations* (New York: Knopf, 1991), pp. 124, 131.

build a better mousetrap. The rewards for business success can be magnificent. But the punishment for failure is severe.

WHAT'S MISSING FROM THE PICTURE? GOVERNMENT

Thus far, we have the following capsule summary of how the U.S. economy works: More than 25 million private businesses, energized by the profit motive, employ about 150 million workers and about $30 trillion of capital. These firms bring their enormously diverse wares to a bewildering variety of different markets, where they try to sell them to over 300 million consumers.

It is in *markets*—places where goods and services are bought and sold—that these millions of households and businesses meet to conduct transactions, as depicted in Figure 11. Only a few of these markets are concrete physical locations, such as fish markets or stock exchanges. Most are more abstract "places," where business may be conducted by telephone or the Internet—even if the commodity being traded is a physical object. For example, there are no centralized *physical* marketplaces for buying cars or computers. But there are highly competitive markets for these goods nonetheless.

As Figure 11 suggests, firms use their receipts from selling goods and services in the markets for *outputs* to pay wages to employees and interest and profits to the people who provide capital in the markets for *inputs*. These income flows, in turn, enable consumers to purchase the goods and services that companies produce. This circular flow of money, goods, and factors of production lies at the center of the analysis of how the national economy works. All these activities are linked by a series of interconnected markets, some of which are highly competitive and others of which are less so.

FIGURE 11

The Circular Flow of Goods and Money

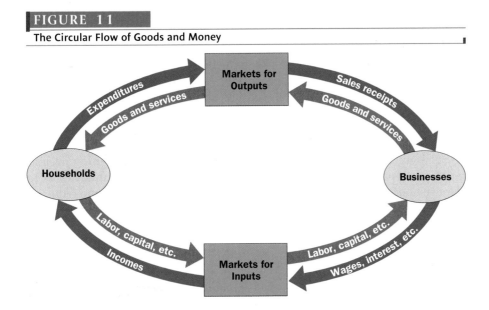

All very well and good. But the story leaves out something important: the role of *government*, which is pervasive even in our decidedly free-market economy. Just what does government do in the U.S. economy—and why?

Although an increasing number of tasks seem to get assigned to the state each year, the traditional role of government in a market economy revolves around five jobs:

- Making and enforcing the laws
- Regulating business
- Providing certain goods and services such as national defense
- Levying taxes to pay for these goods and services
- Redistributing income

Every one of these tasks is steeped in controversy and surrounded by intense political debate. We conclude this chapter with a brief look at each.

The Government as Referee

For the most part, power is diffused in our economy, and people "play by the rules." But, in the scramble for competitive advantage, disputes are bound to arise. Did Company A live up to its contract? Who owns that disputed piece of property? In addition, some unscrupulous businesses are liable to step over the line now and then—as we saw in many cases of fraud that helped bring on the debacle in sub-prime mortgages in 2007–2008.

Enter the government as rule maker, referee, and arbitrator. Congress and state and local legislatures pass the laws that define the rules of the economic game. The executive branches of all three governmental levels share the responsibility for enforcing them. And the courts interpret the laws and adjudicate disputes.

The Government as Business Regulator

Nothing is pure in this world of ours. Even in "free-market" economies, governments interfere with the workings of free markets in many ways and for myriad reasons. Some government activities seek to make markets work better. For example, America's *antitrust laws* are used to protect competition against possible encroachment by monopoly. Some regulations seek to promote social objectives that unfettered markets do not foster—environmental regulations are a particularly clear case. But, as critics like to point out, some economic regulations have no clear rationale at all.

We mentioned earlier that the American belief in free enterprise runs deep. For this reason, the regulatory role of government is more contentious here than in most other countries. After all, Thomas Jefferson said that government is best that governs least. Two hundred years later, Presidents Reagan, Bush (both of them), and Clinton all pledged to dismantle inappropriate regulations—and sometimes did. But the financial crisis of 2007–2008 has led to many calls for new and tighter regulations.

Government Expenditures

The most contentious political issues often involve taxing and spending because those are the government's most prominent roles. Democrats and Republicans, both in the White House and in Congress, have frequently battled fiercely over the federal budget. In 1995 and 1996, such disputes even led to some temporary shutdowns of the federal government. Under President Bill Clinton, the government managed to achieve a sizable surplus in its budget—meaning that tax receipts exceeded expenditures. But it didn't last long. Today the federal budget is back in the red, and prospects for getting it balanced are poor.

During fiscal year 2008, the federal government spent over $2.9 *trillion*—a sum that is literally beyond comprehension. Figure 12 shows where the money went. Over 34 percent went for *pensions and income security programs,* which include both social insurance programs (such as Social Security and unemployment compensation) and programs designed to assist the poor. About 21 percent went for *national defense.* Another 23 percent was absorbed by *health-care* expenditures, mainly on Medicare and Medicaid. Adding in *interest on the national debt,* these four functions alone accounted for over 86 percent of all federal spending. The rest went for a miscellany of other purposes including education, transportation, agriculture, housing, and foreign aid.

Government spending at the state and local levels was about $2.1 trillion. Education claimed the largest share of state and local government budgets (34 percent), with health and public welfare programs a distant second (18 percent). Despite this vast outpouring of public funds, many observers believe that serious social needs remain unmet. Critics claim that our public infrastructure (such as bridges and roads) is adequate, that our educational system is lacking, that we are not spending enough on homeland defense, and so on.

Although the scale and scope of government activity in the United States is substantial, it is quite moderate when we compare it to other leading economies, as we will see next.

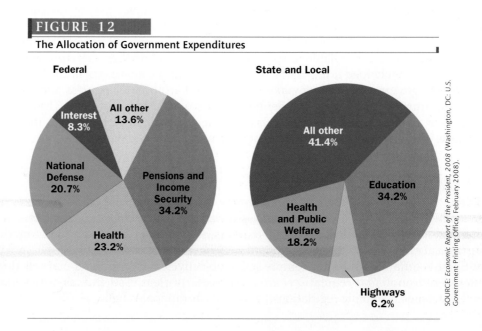

FIGURE 12

The Allocation of Government Expenditures

SOURCE: *Economic Report of the President, 2008* (Washington, DC: U.S. Government Printing Office, February 2008).

Taxes in America

Taxes finance this array of goods and services, and sometimes it seems that the tax collector is everywhere. We have income and payroll taxes withheld from our paychecks, sales taxes added to our purchases, property taxes levied on our homes; we pay gasoline taxes, liquor taxes, and telephone taxes.

Americans have always felt that taxes are both too many and too high. In the 1980s and 1990s, antitax sentiment became a dominant feature of the U.S. political scene. The old slogan "no taxation without representation" gave way to the new slogan "no new taxes." Yet, by international standards, Americans are among the most lightly taxed people in the world. Figure 13 compares the fraction of income paid in taxes in the United States with those paid by residents of other wealthy nations. The tax share in the United States fell notably during the early years of George W. Bush's presidency, but has since crept up a bit.

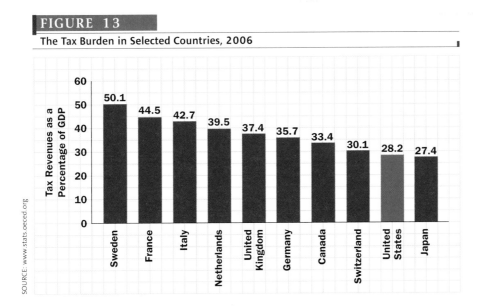

FIGURE 13

The Tax Burden in Selected Countries, 2006

SOURCE: www.stats.oecd.org

The Government as Redistributor

In a market economy, people earn incomes according to what they have to sell. Unfortunately, many people have nothing to sell but unskilled labor, which commands a paltry price. Others lack even that. Such people fare poorly in unfettered markets. In extreme cases, they are homeless, hungry, and ill. Robin Hood transferred money from the rich to the poor. Some think the government should do the same; others disagree.

If poverty amid riches offends your moral sensibilities—a personal judgment that each of us must make for ourselves—two basic remedial approaches are possible. The socialist idea is to force the distribution of income to be more equal by overriding the decisions of the market. "From each according to his ability, to each according to his needs" was Marx's ideal. In practice, things were not quite so noble under socialism, but there was little doubt that incomes in the old Soviet Union were more equally distributed than those in the United States.

The liberal idea is to let free markets determine the distribution of *before-tax* incomes, but then to use the tax system and **transfer payments** to reduce inequality—just as Robin Hood did. This is the rationale for, among other things, **progressive taxation** and antipoverty programs. Americans who support redistribution line up solidly behind the liberal approach. But which ways are the best, and how much is enough? No simple answers have emerged from many decades of debate on these highly contentious questions. Lately, as wage disparities have widened, the inequality issue has gained prominence on the national political agenda. It figured prominently in the 2008 presidential campaign, for example.

Transfer payments are sums of money that certain individuals receive as outright grants from the government rather than as payments for services rendered.

A tax is **progressive** if the ratio of taxes to income rises as income rises.

CONCLUSION: IT'S A MIXED ECONOMY

A **mixed economy** is one with some public influence over the workings of free markets. There may also be some public ownership mixed in with private property.

Ideology notwithstanding, all nations at all times blend public and private ownership of property in some proportions. All rely on markets for some purposes, but all also assign some role to government. Hence, people speak of the ubiquity of **mixed economies**. But mixing is not homogenization; different countries can and do blend the state and market sectors in different ways. Even today, the Russian economy is a far cry from the Italian economy, which is vastly different from that of Hong Kong.

Shortly after most of you were born, a stunning historical event occurred: Communism collapsed all over Europe. For years, the formerly socialist economies suffered through a painful transition from a system in which private property, free enterprise, and markets played subsidiary roles to one in which they are central. These nations have changed the mix, if you will—and dramatically so. To understand why this transformation is at once so difficult and so important, we need to explore the main theme of this book: *What does the market do well, and what does it do poorly?* This task begins in the next chapter.

| SUMMARY |

1. The U.S. economy is the biggest national economy on earth, both because Americans are rich by world standards and because we are a populous nation. Relative to most other advanced countries, our economy is also exceptionally "privatized" and **closed**.

2. The U.S. economy has grown dramatically over the years. But this growth has been interrupted by periodic **recessions**, during which unemployment rises.

3. The United States has a big, diverse workforce whose composition by age and sex has been changing substantially. Relatively few workers these days work in factories or on farms; most work in service industries.

4. Employees take home most of the nation's income. Most of the rest goes, in the forms of interest and profits, to those who provide the capital.

5. Governments at the federal, state, and local levels employ one-sixth of the American workforce (including the armed forces). These governments finance their expenditures by taxes, which account for about 28 percent of GDP. This percentage is one of the lowest in the industrialized world.

6. In addition to raising taxes and making expenditures, the government in a market economy serves as referee and enforcer of the rules, regulates business in a variety of ways, and redistributes income through taxes and **transfer payments**. For all these reasons, we say that we have a **mixed economy**, which blends private and public elements.

| KEY TERMS |

Factors of production, or Inputs 22	Open economy 24	Transfer payments 35
Outputs 22	Closed economy 24	Progressive tax 35
Gross domestic product (GDP) 23	Recession 24	Mixed economy 36

| DISCUSSION QUESTIONS |

1. Which are the two biggest national economies on earth? Why are they so much bigger than the others?

2. What is meant by a "factor of production?" Have you ever sold any on a market?

3. Why do you think per-capita income in Connecticut is nearly double that in West Virginia?

4. Roughly speaking, what fraction of U.S. labor works in factories? In service businesses? In government?

5. Most American businesses are small, but most of the output is produced by large businesses. That sounds paradoxical. How can it be true?

6. What is the role of government in a mixed economy?

The Fundamental Economic Problem:
Scarcity and Choice

Our necessities are few but our wants are endless.

INSCRIPTION ON A FORTUNE COOKIE

Understanding what the market system does well and what it does badly is this book's central task. But to address this complex issue, we must first answer a simpler one: What do economists expect the market to accomplish?

The most common answer is that the market resolves what is often called *the* fundamental economic problem: how best to manage the resources of society, doing as well as possible with them, despite their scarcity. All decisions are constrained by the scarcity of available resources. A dreamer may envision a world free of want, in which everyone, even in Africa and Central America, drives a BMW and eats caviar, but the earth lacks the resources needed to make that dream come true. Because resources are scarce, all economic decisions involve *trade-offs*. Should you use that $5 bill to buy pizza or a new writing pad for econ class? Should General Motors invest more money in improving assembly lines or in research? A well-functioning market system facilitates and guides such decisions, assigning each hour of labor and each kilowatt-hour of electricity to the task where, it is hoped, the input will best serve the public.

This chapter shows how economists analyze choices like these. The same basic principles, founded on the concept of *opportunity cost*, apply to the decisions made by business firms, governments, and society as a whole. Many of the most basic ideas of economics, such as *efficiency, division of labor, comparative advantage, exchange,* and *the role of markets* appear here for the first time.

CONTENTS

For roughly 15 years, from the early 1980s until the late 1990s, the top economic issue of the day was how to reduce the federal budget deficit. Presidents Ronald Reagan, George H. W. Bush, and Bill Clinton all battled with Congress over tax and spending *priorities*. Which programs should be cut? What taxes should be raised?

Then, thanks to a combination of strong economic growth and deficit-reducing policies, the budget deficit melted away like springtime snow and actually turned into a budget *surplus* for a few fiscal years (1998 through 2001). For a while, the need to make agonizing *choices* seemed to disappear—or so it seemed. But it was an illusion. Even during that brief era of budget surpluses, hard choices still had to be made. The U.S. government could not afford *everything*. Then, as the stock market collapsed, the economy slowed, and President George W. Bush pushed a series of tax cuts through Congress, the budget surpluses quickly turned back into deficits again—the largest deficits in our history.

The fiscal questions in the 2004 presidential campaign were the familiar ones of the 1980s and 1990s. Which spending programs should be cut and which ones should be increased? Which, if any, of the Bush tax cuts should be repealed? Even a government with an annual budget of over $2 *trillion* was forced to set priorities and make hard choices.

Even when resources are quite generous, they are never unlimited. So everyone must still make tough choices. An *optimal* decision is one that chooses the most desirable alternative *among the possibilities permitted by the available resources*, which are always scarce in this sense.

SCARCITY, CHOICE, AND OPPORTUNITY COST

Resources are the instruments provided by nature or by people that are used to create goods and services. Natural resources include minerals, soil, water, and air. Labor is a scarce resource, partly because of time limitations (the day has only 24 hours) and partly because the number of skilled workers is limited. Factories and machines are resources made by people. These three types of resources are often referred to as *land, labor,* and *capital.* They are also called *inputs* or *factors of production.*

One of the basic themes of economics is scarcity—the fact that **resources** are always limited. Even Philip II, of Spanish Armada fame and ruler of one of the greatest empires in history, had to cope with frequent rebellions in his armies when he could not meet their payrolls or even get them basic provisions. He is reported to have undergone bankruptcy an astonishing eight times during his reign. In more recent years, the U.S. government has been agonizing over difficult budget decisions even though it spends more than $2 *trillion* annually.

But the scarcity of *physical resources* is more fundamental than the scarcity of funds. Fuel supplies, for example, are not limitless, and some environmentalists claim that we should now be making some hard choices—such as keeping our homes cooler in winter and warmer in summer and saving gas by living closer to our jobs. Although energy may be the most widely discussed scarcity, the general principle applies to all of the earth's resources—iron, copper, uranium, and so on. Even goods produced by human effort are in limited supply because they require fuel, labor, and other scarce resources as inputs. We can manufacture more cars, but the increased use of labor, steel, and fuel in auto production will mean that we must cut back on something else, perhaps the production of refrigerators.

This all adds up to the following fundamental principle of economics, which we will encounter again and again in this text:

> Virtually all resources are *scarce*, meaning that people have less of them than they would like. Therefore, choices must be made among a *limited* set of possibilities, in full recognition of the inescapable fact that a decision to have more of one thing means that people will have less of something else.

In fact, one popular definition of economics is the study of how best to use *limited* means to pursue *unlimited* ends. Although this definition, like any short statement, cannot possibly cover the sweep of the entire discipline, it does convey the flavor of the economist's stock in trade.

To illustrate the true cost of an item, consider the decision to produce additional cars and therefore to produce fewer refrigerators. Although the production of a car may cost $15,000 per vehicle, or some other money amount, *its real cost to society is the refrigerators that society must forgo to get an additional car.* If the labor, steel, and energy needed to manufacture a car would be sufficient to make 30 refrigerators instead of the car, the **opportunity cost** of a car is 30 refrigerators. The principle of opportunity cost is so important that we will spend most of this chapter elaborating on it in various ways.

The **opportunity cost** of any decision is the value of the next best alternative that the decision forces the decision maker to forgo.

HOW MUCH DOES IT REALLY COST? The Principle of Opportunity Cost Economics examines the options available to households, businesses, governments, and entire societies, given the limited resources at their command. It studies the logic of how people can make optimal decisions from among competing alternatives. One overriding principle governs this logic—a principle we introduced in Chapter 1 as one of the *Ideas for Beyond the Final Exam:* With limited resources, a decision to have *more* of one thing is simultaneously a decision to have *less* of something else. Hence, the relevant *cost* of any decision is its *opportunity cost*—the value of the next best alternative that is given up. Optimal decision making must be based on opportunity-cost calculations.

Opportunity Cost and Money Cost

Because we live in a market economy where (almost) everything has its price, students often wonder about the connection or difference between an item's *opportunity cost* and its *market price.* This statement seems to divorce the two concepts: The true opportunity cost of a car is not its market price but the value to their potential purchasers of the other things (like refrigerators) that could have been made or purchased instead.

"O.K. who can put a price on love? Jim?"

But isn't the opportunity cost of a car related to its money cost? The normal answer is yes. The two costs are usually closely tied to one another because of the way in which a market economy sets prices. Steel, for example, is used to manufacture both automobiles and refrigerators. If consumers value items that can be made with steel (such as refrigerators) highly, then economists would say that the *opportunity cost* of making a car is high. But, under these circumstances, strong demand for this highly valued resource will bid up its market price. In this way, a well-functioning price system will assign a high price to steel, which will therefore make the *money cost* of manufacturing a car high as well. In summary:

> If the market functions well, goods that have high opportunity costs will also have high money costs. In turn, goods that have low opportunity costs will also have low money costs.

Yet it would be a mistake to treat opportunity costs and explicit monetary costs as identical. For one thing, sometimes the market does not function well and hence assigns prices that do not accurately reflect opportunity costs. Moreover, some valuable items may not bear explicit price tags at all. We encountered one such example in Chapter 1, where we noted that the opportunity cost of a college education may differ sharply from its explicit money cost. Why? Because one important item is typically omitted from the money-cost calculation: the *market value of your time*, that is, the wages you could earn by working instead of attending college. Because you give up these potential wages, which can amount to $15,000 per year or more, in order to acquire an education, they must be counted as a major part of the opportunity cost of going to college.

Other common examples where money costs and opportunity costs diverge are goods and services that are given away "free." For example, some early settlers of the American West destroyed natural amenities such as forests and buffalo herds, which had no market price, leaving later generations to pay the opportunity costs in terms of lost resources. Similarly, you incur no explicit monetary cost to acquire an item that is given away for free. But if you must wait in line to get the "free" commodity, you incur an opportunity cost equal to the value of the next best use of your time.

Optimal Choice: Not Just *Any* Choice

How do people and firms make decisions? There are many ways, some of them based on hunches with little forethought; some are even based on superstition or the advice of a fortune teller. Often, when the required information is scarce and the necessary research and calculations are costly and difficult, the decision maker will settle on the first possibility that he can "live with"—a choice that promises to yield results that are not too bad and that seem fairly safe. The decision maker may be willing to choose this course even though he recognizes that there might be other options that are better but are unknown to him. This way of deciding is called "satisficing."

In this book, like most books on economic theory, we will assume that decision makers seek to do better than mere satisficing. Rather, we will assume that they seek to reach decisions that are optimal—decisions that do better in achieving the decision makers' goals than any other possible choice. We will assume that the required information is available to the decision makers and study the procedures that enable them to determine which of the possible choices is optimal.

> An **optimal decision** for individual X is one that is selected *after implicit or explicit comparison of the consequences of each of the possible choices* and that is shown by analysis to be the one that most effectively promotes the goals of person X.

We will study optimal decision making by various parties—by consumers, by producers, and by sellers—in a variety of situations. The methods of analysis for determining what choice is optimal in each case will be remarkably similar. So, if you understand one of them, you will already be well on your way to understanding them all. A technique called "marginal analysis" will be used for this purpose. But one fundamental idea underlies any method used for optimal decision making: *To determine whether a possible decision is or is not optimal, its consequences must be compared with those of each of the other possible choices.*

An **optimal decision** is one that best serves the objectives of the decision maker, whatever those objectives may be. It is selected by explicit or implicit comparison with the possible alternative choices. The term *optimal* does not mean that we, the observers or analysts, approve or disapprove of the objective itself.

SCARCITY AND CHOICE FOR A SINGLE FIRM

The **outputs** of a firm or an economy are the goods and services it produces.

The **inputs** used by a firm or an economy are the labor, raw materials, electricity, and other resources it uses to produce its outputs.

The nature of opportunity cost is perhaps clearest in the case of a single business firm that produces two **outputs** from a fixed supply of **inputs**. Given current technology and the limited resources at its disposal, the more of one good the firm produces, the less of the other it will be able to make. Unless managers explicitly weigh the desirability of each product against the other, they are unlikely to make rational production decisions.

Consider the example of Jones, a farmer whose available supplies of land, machinery, labor, and fertilizer are capable of producing the various combinations of soybeans and wheat listed in Table 1. Obviously, devoting more resources to soybean production means that Jones will produce less wheat. Table 1 indicates, for example, that if Jones grows only soybeans, the harvest will be 40,000 bushels. But if he reduces his soybean production to 30,000 bushels, he can also grow 38,000 bushels of wheat. Thus, *the opportunity cost of obtaining 38,000 bushels of wheat is 10,000 fewer bushels of soybeans*. Put another way, the opportunity cost of 10,000 more bushels of soybeans is 38,000 bushels of wheat. The other numbers in Table 1 have similar interpretations.

TABLE 1

Production Possibilities Open to a Farmer

Bushels of Soybeans	Bushels of Wheat	Label in Figure 1
40,000	0	A
30,000	38,000	B
20,000	52,000	C
10,000	60,000	D
0	65,000	E

NOTE: Quantities are in thousands of bushels per year.

FIGURE 1

Production Possibilities Frontier for Production by a Single Farmer

The situation becomes a little more complicated when the objective of the farmer is to earn as large a *money profit* as possible, rather than maximizing quantity of wheat or soybeans. Suppose producing 38,000 bushels of wheat requires Jones to give up 10,000 bushels of soybeans and $4,000 is the profit he would earn if he chose the wheat output while $1,200 is the profit offered by the soybean option (that would have to be given up if wheat specialization were decided upon). Then the opportunity cost that our farmer would incur is not the 10,000 bushels of soybeans, but the $12,000 in profits that substitution of soybean production would offer.

The Production Possibilities Frontier

Figure 1 presents this same information graphically. Point *A* indicates that one of the options available to the farmer is to produce 40,000 bushels of soybeans and 0 wheat. Thus, point *A* corresponds to the first line of Table 1, point *B* to the second line, and so on. Curves similar to *AE* appear frequently in this book; they are called **production possibilities frontiers.** Any point *on or inside* the production possibilities frontier is attainable because it does not entail larger outputs than currently available resources permit. Points *outside* the frontier, representing very large quantities of output, are figments of the imagination given current circumstances because they cannot be achieved with the available resources and technology.

A **production possibilities frontier** shows the different combinations of various goods, any one of which a producer can turn out, given the available resources and existing technology.

Because resources are limited, the production possibilities frontier always slopes downward to the right. The farmer can *increase* wheat production (move to the right in Figure 1) only by devoting more land and labor to growing wheat. But this choice simultaneously *reduces* soybean production (the curve must move downward) because less land and labor remain available for growing soybeans.

Notice that, in addition to having a negative slope, our production possibilities frontier *AE* has another characteristic: It is "bowed outward." What does this curvature mean? In short, as larger and larger quantities of resources are transferred from the production of one output to the production of another, the additions to the second product decline.

Suppose farmer Jones initially produces only soybeans, using even land that is comparatively most productive in wheat cultivation (point *A*). Now he decides to switch some land from soybean production into wheat production. Which part of the land will he switch? If Jones is sensible, he will use the part that, because of its chemical content, direction in relation to sunlight, and so on, is relatively most productive in growing wheat. As he shifts to point *B*, soybean production falls from 40,000 bushels to 30,000 bushels as wheat production rises from 0 to 38,000 bushels. A sacrifice of only 10,000 bushels of soybeans "buys" 38,000 bushels of wheat.

Imagine now that our farmer wants to produce still more wheat. Figure 1 tells us that the sacrifice of an additional 10,000 bushels of soybeans (from 30,000 bushels to 20,000 bushels) will yield only 14,000 more bushels of wheat (see point *C*). Why? The main reason is that *inputs tend to be specialized.* As we noted at point *A*, the farmer was using resources for soybean production that were relatively more productive in growing wheat.

Consequently, their relative productivity in soybean production was low. When these resources are switched to wheat production, the yield is high.

But this trend cannot continue forever, of course. As more wheat is produced, the farmer must utilize land and machinery with a greater productivity advantage in growing soybeans and a smaller productivity advantage in growing wheat. This is why the first 10,000 bushels of soybeans forgone "buys" the farmer 38,000 bushels of wheat, whereas the second 10,000 bushels of soybeans "buys" only 14,000 bushels of wheat. Figure 1 and Table 1 show that these returns continue to decline as wheat production expands: The next 10,000-bushel reduction in soybean production yields only 8,000 bushels of additional wheat, and so on.

If the farmer's objective is to maximize the amount of wheat or soybean product he gets out of his land and labor then, as we can see, the *slope* of the production possibilities frontier graphically represents the concept of *opportunity cost*. Between points C and B, for example, the opportunity cost of acquiring 10,000 additional bushels of soybeans is shown on the graph to be 14,000 bushels of forgone wheat; between points B and A, the opportunity cost of 10,000 bushels of soybeans is 38,000 bushels of forgone wheat. In general, as we move upward to the left along the production possibilities frontier (toward more soybeans and less wheat), the opportunity cost of soybeans in terms of wheat increases. Looking at the same thing the other way, as we move downward to the right, the opportunity cost of acquiring wheat by giving up soybeans increases—more and more soybeans must be forgone per added bushel of wheat and successive addition to wheat output occur.

The Principle of Increasing Costs

We have just described a very general phenomenon with applications well beyond farming. The **principle of increasing costs** states that as the production of one good expands, the opportunity cost of producing another unit of this good generally increases. This principle is not a universal fact—exceptions do arise. But it does seem to be a technological regularity that applies to a wide range of economic activities. As our farming example suggests, the principle of increasing costs is based on the fact that resources tend to be at least somewhat specialized. So we lose some of their productivity when those resources are transferred from doing what they are relatively *good* at to what they are relatively *bad* at. In terms of diagrams such as Figure 1, the principle simply asserts that the production possibilities frontier is bowed outward.

Perhaps the best way to understand this idea is to contrast it with a case in which no resources are specialized so costs do not increase as output proportion changes. Figure 2 depicts a production possibilities frontier for producing black shoes and brown shoes. Because the labor and machinery used to produce black shoes are just as good at producing brown shoes, the frontier is a straight line. If the firm cuts back its production of black shoes by 10,000 pairs, it can produce 10,000 additional pairs of brown shoes, no matter how big the shift between these two outputs. It loses no productivity in the switch because resources are not specialized.

> The **principle of increasing costs** states that as the production of a good expands, the opportunity cost of producing another unit generally increases.

More typically, however, as a firm concentrates more of its productive capacity on one commodity, it is forced to employ inputs that are better suited to making another commodity. The firm is forced to vary the proportions in which it uses inputs because of the limited quantities of some of those inputs. This fact also explains the typical curvature of the firm's production possibilities frontier.

FIGURE 2

Production Possibilities Frontier with No Specialized Resources

NOTE: Quantities are in thousands of pairs per week.

SCARCITY AND CHOICE FOR THE ENTIRE SOCIETY

Like an individual firm, the entire economy is also constrained by its limited resources and technology. If the public wants more aircraft and tanks, it will have to give up some boats and automobiles. If it wants to build more factories and stores, it will have to build fewer homes and sports arenas. In general:

> The position and shape of the production possibilities frontier that constrains society's choices are determined by the economy's physical resources, its skills and technology, its willingness to work, and how much it has devoted in the past to the construction of factories, research, and innovation.

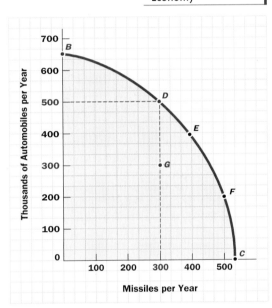

FIGURE 3

Production Possibilities Frontier for the Entire Economy

Because so many nations have long debated whether to reduce or augment military spending, let us exemplify the nature of society's choices by deciding between military might (represented by missiles) and civilian consumption (represented by automobiles). Just like a single firm, the economy as a whole faces a production possibilities frontier for missiles and autos, determined by its technology and the available resources of land, labor, capital, and raw materials. This production possibilities frontier may look like curve *BC* in Figure 3. If most workers are employed in auto plants, car production will be large, but the output of missiles will be small. If the economy transfers resources out of auto manufacturing when consumer demand declines, it can, by congressional action, alter the output mix toward more missiles (the move from *D* to *E*). However, something is likely to be lost in the process because physical resources are specialized. The fabric used to make car seats will not help much in missile production. The principle of increasing costs strongly suggests that the production possibilities frontier curves downward toward the axes.

We may even reach a point where the only resources left are not very useful outside of auto manufacturing. In that case, even a large sacrifice of automobiles will get the economy few additional missiles. That is the meaning of the steep segment, *FC*, on the frontier. At point *C*, there is little additional output of missiles as compared to point *F*, even though at *C* automobile production has been given up entirely.

> The downward slope of society's production possibilities frontier implies that hard choices must be made. Civilian consumption (automobiles) can be increased only by decreasing military expenditure, not by rhetoric or wishing. The curvature of the production possibilities frontier implies that as defense spending increases, it becomes progressively more expensive to "buy" additional military strength ("missiles") in terms of the resulting sacrifice of civilian consumption.

Scarcity and Choice Elsewhere in the Economy

We have emphasized that limited resources force hard choices on business managers and society as a whole. But the same type of choices arises elsewhere—in households, universities, and other nonprofit organizations, as well as the government.

The nature of opportunity cost is perhaps most obvious for a household that must decide how to divide its income among the goods and services that compete for the family's attention. If the Simpson family buys an expensive new car, it may be forced to cut back sharply on some other purchases. This fact does not make it unwise to buy the car. But it does make it unwise to buy the car until the family considers the full implications for its overall budget. If the Simpsons are to utilize their limited resources most effectively, they must recognize the opportunity costs of the car—the things they will forgo as a result—perhaps a vacation and an expensive new TV set. The decision to buy the car will be rational if the benefit to the family from the automobile (however measured) is greater than the opportunity cost—their benefit if they buy an equally expensive vacation or TV set instead.

Hard Choices in the Real World

Two excerpts from recent newspaper stories bring home the realities of scarcity and choice:

"As Deficit Shrinks, Battle Looms; Bush and Democrats Prepare to Face off On 2008 Budget," Washington, July 11—. . . . Yesterday, Mr. Bush seized on the latest White House budget estimates, which predict the 2007 deficit will drop to $205 billion from last year's $248 billion, to press his point that Republican tax cuts and spending policies are working. He charged that Democrat's proposals to raise taxes and expand health care and other domestic programs pose a long-term threat to the country's economic health. . . . Democrats sought to downplay the latest good news, focusing on the continued high cost of the Iraq War, the tax breaks Mr. Bush has given to the wealthy and the resulting run-up in federal debt. . . .

SOURCE: John D. McKinnon and Deborah Solomon, *Wall Street Journal*, Eastern Edition, July 12, 2007, p. A4.

"Some NYC Transit Fares Will Rise," New York (AP), December 19, 2007 —. . . . The Metropolitan Transportation Authority voted Wednesday to raise fares for monthly and weekly passes and multiple-ride MetroCards, while keeping the single-use bus and subway fare at $2. Only 14 percent of subway and bus riders pay the $2 single-use fare, but transportation officials argue they are among the poorest customers. . . . Riders' advocates and elected officials, however, said that it's tourists who will see most of the benefit, while the vast majority of New York's millions of commuters watch their costs go up by about 10 cents a ride. . . . New York City Public Advocate Betsy Gotbaum, speaking to the board before the vote, said, "New Yorkers cannot

afford the increase. They just can't afford it." Gene Russianoff of the Straphangers Campaign gave the board 4,000 anti-fare-increase petition signatures tied up with a red bow. MTA officials were unmoved, saying they need to offset $6 billion in deficits over the next four years. "Today's vote is an important step in putting the transit system on a sound financial footing," MTA chairman H. Dale Hemmerdinger said. . . . The new increases will take effect in March. The MTA had proposed increasing base fares but backed off last month after an additional $220 million was found in its updated budget forecasts. . . .

SOURCE: Karen Matthews, "Some NYC Transit Fares Will Rise," *Associated Press*, December 19, 2007

SOURCE: © AP IMAGES/Jacquelyn Martin

ISSUE REVISITED   COPING WITH THE BUDGET DEFICIT

As already noted, even a rich and powerful nation like the United States must cope with the limitations implied by scarce resources. The necessity for choice imposed on governments by the limited amount they feel they can afford to spend is similar in character to the problems faced by business firms and households. For the goods and services that it buys from others, a government must prepare a budget similar to that of a very large household. For the items it produces itself—education, police protection, libraries, and so on—it faces a production possibilities frontier much like a business firm does. Even though the U.S. government spent over $2.6 trillion in 2006, some of the most acrimonious debates between President Bush and his critics arose from disagreements about how the government's limited resources should be allocated among competing uses. Even if unstated, the concept of opportunity cost is central to these debates.

THE CONCEPT OF EFFICIENCY

So far, our discussion of scarcity and choice has assumed that either the firm or the economy always operates on its production possibilities frontier rather than *below* it. In other words, we have tacitly assumed that whatever the firm or economy decides to do, it does so **efficiently.**

Economists define efficiency as the absence of waste. An efficient economy wastes none of its available resources and produces the maximum amount of output that its technology permits.

To see why any point on the economy's production possibilities frontier in Figure 3 (in a choice between missiles or automobiles or some combination of the two) represents an efficient decision, suppose for a moment that society has decided to produce 300 missiles. The production possibilities frontier tells us that if 300 missiles are to be produced, then the maximum number of automobiles that can be made is 500,000 (point *D* in Figure 3). The economy is therefore operating efficiently only if it produces 500,000 automobiles (when it manufactures 300 missiles) rather than some smaller number of cars, such as 300,000 (as at point *G*).

Point *D* is efficient, but point *G* is not, because the economy is capable of moving from *G* to *D*, thereby producing 200,000 more automobiles without giving up any missiles (or anything else). Clearly, failure to take advantage of the option of choosing point *D* rather than point *G* constitutes a wasted opportunity—an inefficiency.

Note that the concept of efficiency does not tell us which point on the production possibilities frontier is *best*. Rather, it tells us only that any point *below* the frontier cannot be best, because any such point represents wasted resources. For example, should society ever find itself at a point such as *G*, the necessity of making hard choices would (temporarily) disappear. It would be possible to increase production of *both* missiles *and* automobiles by moving to a point such as *E*.

Why, then, would a society ever find itself at a point below its production possibilities frontier? Why are resources wasted in real life? The most important reason in today's economy is *unemployment.* When many workers are unemployed, the economy must be at a point such as *G*, below the frontier, because by putting the unemployed to work, some in each industry, the economy could produce both more missiles *and* more automobiles. The economy would then move from point *G* to the right (more missiles) and upward (more automobiles) toward a point such as *E* on the production possibilities frontier. Only when no resources are wasted is the economy operating on the frontier.

Inefficiency occurs in other ways, too. A prime example is assigning inputs to the wrong task—as when wheat is grown on land best suited to soybean cultivation. Another important type of inefficiency occurs when large firms produce goods that smaller enterprises could make better because they can pay closer attention to detail, or when small firms produce outputs best suited to large-scale production. Some other examples are the outright waste that occurs because of favoritism (for example, promotion of an incompetent brother-in-law to a job he cannot do very well) or restrictive labor practices (for example, requiring a railroad to keep a fireman on a diesel-electric locomotive where there is no longer a fire to tend).

A particularly deplorable form of waste is caused by discrimination against minority or female workers. When a job is given, for example, to a white male in preference to an African-American woman who is more qualified, society sacrifices potential output and the entire community is apt to be affected adversely. Every one of these inefficiencies means that the community obtains less output than it could have, given the available inputs.

> A set of outputs is said to be produced **efficiently** if, given current technological knowledge, there is no way one can produce larger amounts of any output without using larger input amounts or giving up some quantity of another output.

■ THE THREE COORDINATION TASKS OF ANY ECONOMY

In deciding how to **allocate its scarce resources,** every society must somehow make three sorts of decisions:

- First, as we have emphasized, it must figure out *how to utilize its resources efficiently;* that is, it must find a way to reach its production possibilities frontier.
- Second, it must decide *which of the possible combinations of goods to produce*—how many missiles, automobiles, and so on; that is, it must select one specific point on

> **Allocation of resources** refers to the society's decisions on how to divide up its scarce input resources among the different outputs produced in the economy and among the different firms or other organizations that produce those outputs.

the production possibilities frontier among all of the points (that is, all of the output combinations) on the frontier.

• Third, it must decide *how much of the total output of each good to distribute to each person*, doing so in a sensible way that does not assign meat to vegetarians and wine to teetotalers.

There are many ways in which societies can and do make each of these decisions—to which economists often refer as *how, what,* and *to whom?* For example, a central planner may tell people how to produce, what to produce, and what to consume, as the authorities used to do, at least to some extent, in the former Soviet Union. But in a market economy, no one group or individual makes all such resource allocation decisions explicitly. Rather, consumer demands and production costs allocate resources *automatically* and *anonymously* through a system of prices and markets. As the formerly socialist countries learned, markets do an impressively effective job in carrying out these tasks. For our introduction to the ways in which markets do all this, let's consider each task in turn.

TASK 1. HOW THE MARKET FOSTERS EFFICIENT RESOURCE ALLOCATION

Production efficiency is one of the economy's three basic tasks, and societies pursue it in many ways. But one source of efficiency is so fundamental that we must single it out for special attention: the tremendous productivity gains that stem from *specialization*.

The Wonders of the Division of Labor

Division of labor means breaking up a task into a number of smaller, more *specialized* tasks so that each worker can become more adept at a particular job.

Adam Smith, the founder of modern economics, first marveled at how **division of labor** raises efficiency and productivity when he visited a pin factory. In a famous passage near the beginning of his monumental book *The Wealth of Nations* (1776), he described what he saw:

> One man draws out the wire, another straightens it, a third cuts it, a fourth points it, a fifth grinds it at the top for receiving the head. To make the head requires two or three distinct operations; to put it on is a peculiar business, to whiten the pins is another; it is even a trade by itself to put them into the paper.[1]

Smith observed that by dividing the work to be done in this way, each worker became quite skilled in a particular specialty, and the productivity of the group of workers as a whole was greatly en-hanced. As Smith related it:

> I have seen a small manufactory of this kind where ten men only were employed. . . . Those ten persons . . . could make among them upwards of forty-eight thousand pins in a day. . . . But if they had all wrought separately and independently . . . they certainly could not each of them have made twenty, *perhaps not one pin in a day.*[2]

In other words, through the miracle of division of labor and specialization, 10 workers accomplished what might otherwise have required thousands. This was one of the secrets of the Industrial Revolution, which helped lift humanity out of the abject poverty that had been its lot for centuries.

Adam Smith L.L.D.

SOURCE: © Courtesy of the Library of Congress

---

[1] Adam Smith, *The Wealth of Nations* (New York: Random House, 1937), p. 4.
[2] Ibid., p. 5.

The Amazing Principle of Comparative Advantage

But specialization in production fosters efficiency in an even more profound sense. Adam Smith noticed that *how* goods are produced can make a huge difference to productivity. But so can *which* goods are produced. The reason is that people (and businesses, and nations) have different abilities. Some can repair automobiles, whereas others are wizards with numbers. Some are handy with computers, and others can cook. An economy will be most efficient if people specialize in doing what they do best and then trade with one another, so that the accountant gets her car repaired and the computer programmer gets to eat tasty and nutritious meals.

This much is obvious. What is less obvious—and is one of the great ideas of economics—is that two people (or two businesses, or two countries) can generally gain from trade *even if one of them is more efficient than the other in producing everything.* A simple example will help explain why.

Some lawyers can type better than their administrative assistants. Should such a lawyer fire her assistant and do her own typing? Not likely. Even though the lawyer may type better than the assistant, good judgment tells her to concentrate on practicing law and leave the typing to a lower-paid assistant. Why? Because the *opportunity cost* of an hour devoted to typing is the amount that she could earn from an hour less time spent with clients, which is a far more lucrative activity.

This example illustrates the principle of **comparative advantage** at work. The lawyer specializes in arguing cases despite her advantage as a typist because she has a *still greater* advantage as an attorney. She suffers some direct loss by leaving the typing to a less efficient employee, but she more than makes up for that loss by the income she earns selling her legal services to clients.

Precisely the same principle applies to nations. As we shall learn in greater detail in Chapter 34, comparative advantage underlies the economic analysis of international trade patterns. A country that is particularly adept at producing certain items—such as aircraft in the United States, coffee in Brazil, and oil in Saudi Arabia—should specialize in those activities, producing more than it wants for its own use. The country can then take the money it earns from its exports and purchase from other nations items that it does not make for itself. And this is still true if one of the trading nations is the most efficient producer of almost everything. The underlying logic is precisely the same as in our lawyer-typist example. The United States might, for example, be better than South Korea at manufacturing both computers and television sets. But if the United States is vastly more efficient at producing computers, but only slightly more efficient at making TV sets, it pays for the United States to specialize in computer manufacture, for South Korea to specialize in TV production, and for the two countries to trade.

This principle, called the *law of comparative advantage,* was discovered by David Ricardo, another giant in the history of economic analysis, almost 200 years ago. It is one of the *Ideas for Beyond the Final Exam* introduced in Chapter 1.

> One country is said to have a **comparative advantage** over another in the production of a particular good *relative to other goods* if it produces that good less inefficiently than it **produces** other goods, as compared with the other country.

THE SURPRISING PRINCIPLE OF COMPARATIVE ADVANTAGE Even if one country (or one worker) is worse than another country (or another worker) in the production of *every* good, it is said to have a *comparative advantage* in making the good at which it is *least inefficient*—compared to the other country. Ricardo discovered that two countries can gain by trading even if one country is more efficient than another in the production of *every* commodity. Precisely the same logic applies to individual workers or to businesses.

IDEAS FOR
BEYOND THE
FINAL EXAM

In determining the most efficient patterns of production and trade, it is *comparative* advantage that matters. Thus, a country can gain by importing a good from abroad even if that good can be produced more efficiently at home. Such imports make sense if they enable the country to specialize in producing those goods at which it is *even more efficient.* And the other, less efficient country should specialize in exporting the goods in whose production it is *least inefficient.*

TASK 2. MARKET EXCHANGE AND DECIDING HOW MUCH OF EACH GOOD TO PRODUCE

The gains from specialization are welcome, but they create a problem: With specialization, people no longer produce only what they want to consume themselves. The workers in Adam Smith's pin factory had no use for the thousands of pins they produced each day; they wanted to trade them for things like food, clothing, and shelter. Similarly, the administrative assistant in our law office example has no personal use for the legal briefs he types. Thus, specialization requires some mechanism by which workers producing pins can *exchange* their wares with workers producing such things as cloth and potatoes and office workers can turn their typing skills into things they want to consume.

> Without a system of exchange, the productivity miracle achieved by comparative advantage and the division of labor would do society little good, because each producer in an efficient arrangement would be left with only the commodities in whose production its comparative efficiency was greatest and would have no other goods to consume. With it, standards of living have risen enormously.

Although people can and do trade goods for other goods, a system of exchange works better when everyone agrees to use some common item (such as pieces of paper with unique markings printed on them) for buying and selling things. Enter *money.* Then workers in pin factories, for example, can be paid in money rather than in pins, and they can use this money to purchase cloth and potatoes. Textile workers and farmers can do the same.

But in a market in which trading is carried out by means of exchange between money and goods or services, the market mechanism also makes the second of our three crucial decisions: how much of each good should be produced with the resources that are available to the economy. For what happens is that if more widgets are produced than consumers want to buy at current prices, those who make widgets will be left with unsold widgets on their hands. Widget price will be driven down, and manufacturers will be forced to cut production, with some being driven out of business altogether. The opposite will happen if producers supply fewer widgets than consumers want at the prevailing prices. Then prices will be driven up by scarcity and manufacturers will be led to increase their output. In this way, the output and price of each and every commodity will be driven toward levels at which supply matches demand or comes very close to it. That is how the market automatically deals with the second critical decision: how much of each commodity will be produced by the economy given the economy's productive capacity (as shown by the production possibility frontier).

TASK 3. HOW TO DISTRIBUTE THE ECONOMY'S OUTPUTS AMONG CONSUMERS

These two phenomena—specialization and exchange (assisted by money)—working in tandem led to vast increases in the abundance that the more prosperous economies of the world were able to supply. But that leaves us with the third basic issue: What forces allow those outputs to be distributed among the population in reasonable ways? What forces establish a smoothly functioning system of exchange so that people can first exploit their comparative advantages and then acquire what they want to consume? One alternative is to have a central authority telling people what to do. Adam Smith explained and extolled yet another way of organizing and coordinating economic activity—markets and prices can coordinate those activities. Smith noted that people are adept at pursuing their own self-interests and that a **market system** harnesses this self-interest remarkably well. As he put it—with clear religious overtones—in doing what is best for themselves, people are "led by an invisible hand" to promote the economic well-being of society as a whole.

Those of us who live in a well-functioning market economy like that found in the United States tend to take the achievements of the market for granted, much like the daily rising and setting of the sun. Few bother to think about, say, the reason why Hawaiian pineapples show up daily in Vermont supermarkets in quantities desired by Vermont consumers. The

A **market system** is a form of economic organization in which resource allocation decisions are left to individual producers and consumers acting in their own best interests without central direction.

market deals with this issue through the profit motive, which guides firms' output decisions, matching quantities produced to consumer preferences. A rise in the price of wheat because of increased demand for bread, for example, will persuade farmers to produce more wheat and devote less of their land to soybeans. Such a price system also distributes goods among consumers in accord with their tastes and preferences, using voluntary exchange to determine who gets what. Consumers spend their incomes on the things they like best (among those they can afford). Vegetarians waste none of their incomes on beef, and teeto-

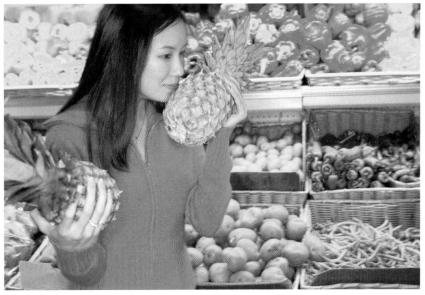

talers do not have to spend money on gin. So consumers, by their control of their spending patterns, can ensure that the bundle of goods they buy at the supermarket is compatible with their preferences. That is how the market mechanism en-sures that the products of the economy are divided among consumers in a rational manner, meaning that this distribution tends to fit in with the preferences of the different purchasers. But there is at least one problem here; the ability to buy goods is hardly divided equally. Workers with valuable skills and owners of scarce resources can sell what they have at attractive prices. With the incomes they earn, they can purchase generous amounts of goods and services. Those who are less successful in selling what they own receive lower incomes and so can afford to buy less. In extreme cases, they may suffer severe deprivation.

The past few pages explain, in broad terms, how a market economy solves the three basic problems facing any society: how to produce any given combination of goods efficiently, how to select an appropriate combination of goods to produce, and how to distribute these goods sensibly among people. As we proceed through the following chapters, you will learn much more about these issues. You will see that they constitute the central theme that permeates not only this text but the work of economists in general. As you progress through this book, keep in mind two questions:

- What does the market do well?
- What does it do poorly?

There are numerous answers to both questions, as you will learn in subsequent chapters.

Society has many important goals. Some of them, such as producing goods and services with maximum efficiency (minimum waste), can be achieved extraordinarily well by letting markets operate more or less freely.

Free markets will not, however, achieve all of society's goals. For example, they often have trouble keeping unemployment low. In fact, the unfettered operations of markets may even run counter to some goals, such as protection of the environment. Many observers also believe that markets do not necessarily distribute income in accord with ethical or moral norms. But even in cases in which markets do not perform well, there may be ways of harnessing the power of the market mechanism to remedy its own deficiencies, as you will learn in later chapters.

Economic debates often have political and ideological overtones. So we will close this chapter by emphasizing that the central theme we have just outlined is neither a *defense of* nor an *attack on* the capitalist system. Nor is it a "conservative" position. One does not have to be a conservative to recognize that the market mechanism can be an extraordinarily helpful instrument for the pursuit of economic goals. Most of the formerly socialist countries of Europe have been working hard to "marketize" their economies, and even the communist People's Republic of China has made huge strides in that direction.

The point is not to confuse ends with means in deciding how much to rely on market forces. Liberals and conservatives surely have different goals. But the means chosen to pursue these goals should, for the most part, be chosen on the basis of how effective the selected means are, not on some ideological prejudgments. Even Karl Marx emphasized that the market is remarkably efficient at producing an abundance of goods and services that had never been seen in precapitalist history. Such wealth can be used to promote conservative goals, such as reducing tax rates, or to facilitate goals favored by liberals, such as providing more generous public aid for the poor.

Certainly, the market cannot deal with every economic problem. Indeed, we have just noted that the market is the *source* of a number of significant problems. Even so, the evidence accumulated over centuries leads economists to believe that most economic problems are best handled by market techniques. The analysis in this book is intended to help you identify both the objectives that the market mechanism can reliably achieve and those that it will fail to promote, or at least not promote very effectively. We urge you to forget the slogans you have heard—whether from the left or from the right—and make up your own mind after learning the material in this book.

| SUMMARY |

1. Supplies of all **resources** are limited. Because resources are **scarce,** an **optimal decision** is one that chooses the best alternative among the options that are possible with the available resources.

2. With limited resources, a decision to obtain more of one item is also a decision to give up some of another. The value of what we give up is called the **opportunity cost** of what we get. The opportunity cost is the true cost of any decision. This is one of the *Ideas for Beyond the Final Exam.*

3. When markets function effectively, firms are led to use resources efficiently and to produce the things that consumers want most. In such cases, opportunity costs and money costs (prices) correspond closely. When the market performs poorly, or when important, socially costly items are provided without charging an appropriate price, or are given away free, opportunity costs and money costs can diverge.

4. A firm's **production possibilities frontier** shows the combinations of goods it can produce, given the current technology and the resources at its disposal. The frontier is usually bowed outward because resources tend to be specialized.

5. The **principle of increasing costs** states that as the production of one good expands, the opportunity cost of producing another unit of that good generally increases.

6. Like a firm, the economy as a whole has a production possibilities frontier whose position is determined by its technology and by the available resources of land, labor, capital, and raw materials.

7. A firm or an economy that ends up at a point below its production possibilities frontier is using its resources inefficiently or wastefully. This is what happens, for example, when there is unemployment.

8. Economists define **efficiency** as the absence of waste. It is achieved primarily by the gains in productivity brought about through **specialization** that exploits **division of labor** and **comparative advantage** and by a system of exchange.

9. Two countries (or two people) can gain by specializing in the activity in which each has a *comparative* advantage and then trading with one another. These gains from trade remain available even if one country is inferior at producing everything but specializes in producing those items at which it is least inefficient. This so-called principle of comparative advantage is one of our *Ideas for Beyond the Final Exam.*

10. If an exchange between two individuals is voluntary, both parties must benefit, even if no additional goods are produced. This is another of the *Ideas for Beyond the Final Exam.*

11. Every economic system must find a way to answer three basic questions: How can goods be produced most efficiently? How much of each good should be produced? How should goods be distributed among users?

12. The **market system** works very well in solving some of society's basic problems, but it fails to remedy others and may, indeed, create some of its own. Where and how it succeeds and fails constitute the central theme of this book and characterize the work of economists in general.

| KEY TERMS |

Resources   40

Opportunity cost   41

Optimal decision   42

Outputs   42

Inputs   42

Production possibilities frontier   43

Principle of increasing costs   44

Efficiency   47

Allocation of scarce resources   47

Division of labor   48

Comparative advantage   49

Market system   50

| TEST YOURSELF |

1. A person rents a house for which she pays the landlord $24,000 per year. The house can be purchased for $200,000, and the tenant has this much money in a bank account that pays 4 percent interest per year. Is buying the house a good deal for the tenant? Where does opportunity cost enter the picture?

2. Graphically show the production possibilities frontier for the nation of Stromboli, using the data given in the following table. Does the principle of increasing cost hold in Stromboli?

Stromboli's 2002 Production Possibilities	
Pizzas per Year	Pizza Ovens per Year
75,000,000	0
60,000,000	6,000
45,000,000	11,000
30,000,000	15,000
15,000,000	18,000
0	18,000

3. Consider two alternatives for Stromboli in 2007. In case (a), its inhabitants eat 60 million pizzas and build 6,000 pizza ovens. In case (b), the population eats 15 million pizzas but builds 18,000 ovens. Which case will lead to a more generous production possibilities frontier for Stromboli in 2007?

4. Jasmine's Snack Shop sells two brands of potato chips. She produces them by buying them from a wholesale supplier. Brand X costs Jasmine $1 per bag, and Brand Y costs her $1.40. Draw Jasmine's production possibilities frontier if she has $280 budgeted to spend on the purchase of potato chips from the wholesaler. Why is it not "bowed out"?

| DISCUSSION QUESTIONS |

1. Discuss the resource limitations that affect
   a. the poorest person on earth
   b. Bill Gates, the richest person on earth
   c. a farmer in Kansas
   d. the government of Indonesia

2. If you were president of your college, what would you change if your budget were cut by 10 percent? By 25 percent? By 50 percent?

3. If you were to leave college, what things would change in your life? What, then, is the opportunity cost of your education?

4. Raising chickens requires several types of feed, such as corn and soy meal. Consider a farm in the former Soviet Union. Try to describe how decisions on the number of chickens to be raised, and the amount of each feed to use in raising them, were made under the old communist regime. If the farm is now privately owned, how does the market guide the decisions that used to be made by the central planning agency?

5. The United States is one of the world's wealthiest countries. Think of a recent case in which the decisions of the U.S. government were severely constrained by scarcity. Describe the trade-offs that were involved. What were the opportunity costs of the decisions that were actually made?

SUPPLY AND DEMAND:
AN INITIAL LOOK

The free enterprise system is absolutely too important to be left to the voluntary action of the marketplace.

FLORIDA CONGRESSMAN RICHARD KELLY, 1979

I n this chapter, we study the economist's most basic investigative tool: the mechanism of supply and demand. Whether your econ course concentrates on macroeconomics or microeconomics, you will find that the so-called law of supply and demand is a fundamental tool of economic analysis. Economists use supply and demand analysis to study issues as diverse as inflation and unemployment, the effects of taxes on prices, government regulation of business, and environmental protection. Supply and demand curves—graphs that relate price to quantity supplied and quantity demanded, respectively—show how prices and quantities are determined in a free market.[1]

A major theme of the chapter is that governments around the world and throughout recorded history have tampered with the price mechanism. As we will see, these bouts with Adam Smith's "invisible hand" have produced undesirable side effects that often surprised and dismayed the authorities. The invisible hand fights back!

CONTENTS

[1] This chapter, like much of the rest of this book, uses many graphs like those described in the appendix to Chapter 1. If you have difficulties with these graphs, we suggest that you review that material before proceeding.

PUZZLE:	WHAT HAPPENED TO OIL PRICES?

Since 1949, the dollars of purchasing power that a buyer had to pay to buy a barrel of oil had remained remarkably steady, and gasoline had generally remained a bargain. But during two exceptional time periods—one from about 1975 through 1985 and one beginning in 2003—oil prices exploded, and filling up the automobile gas tank became painful to consumers. Clearly, supply and demand changes must have been behind these developments. But what led them to change so much and so suddenly? Later in the chapter, we will provide excerpts from a newspaper story about how dramatic and unexpected events can suddenly shift supply and will help to bring the analysis of this chapter to life.

SOURCE: © AP Images/Paul Sakuma

THE INVISIBLE HAND

Invisible hand is a phrase used by Adam Smith to describe how, by pursuing their own self-interests, people in a market system are "led by an invisible hand" to promote the well-being of the community.

Adam Smith, the father of modern economic analysis, greatly admired the price system. He marveled at its accomplishments—both as an efficient producer of goods and as a guarantor that consumers' preferences are obeyed. Although many people since Smith's time have shared his enthusiasm for the concept of the **invisible hand,** many have not. Smith's contemporaries in the American colonies, for example, were often unhappy with the prices produced by free markets and thought they could do better by legislative decree. Such attempts failed, as explained in the accompanying box "Price Controls at Valley Forge." In countless other instances, the public was outraged by the prices charged on the open market, particularly in the case of housing rents, interest rates, and insurance rates.

Attempts to control interest rates (which are the price of borrowing money) go back hundreds of years before the birth of Christ, at least to the code of laws compiled under the Babylonian king Hammurabi in about 1800 B.C. Our historical legacy also includes a rather long list of price ceilings on foods and other products imposed in the reign of Diocletian, emperor of the declining Roman Empire. More recently, Americans have been offered the "protection" of a variety of price controls. Laws have placed ceilings on some prices (such as rents) to protect buyers, whereas legislation has placed floors under other prices (such as farm products) to protect sellers. Yet, somehow, everything such regulation touches seems to end up in even greater disarray than it was before. Despite rent controls, rents in New York City have soared. Despite laws against "scalping," tickets for popular shows and sports events sell at tremendous premiums—tickets to the Super Bowl, for example, often fetch thousands of dollars on the "gray" market. To understand what goes wrong when we tamper with markets, we must first learn how they operate unfettered. This chapter takes a first step in that direction by studying the machinery of supply and demand. Then, at the end of the chapter, we return to the issue of price controls.

Every market has both buyers and sellers. We begin our analysis on the consumers' side of the market.

Price Controls at Valley Forge

George Washington, the history books tell us, was beset by many enemies during the winter of 1777–1778, including the British, their Hessian mercenaries, and the merciless winter weather. But he had another enemy that the history books ignore—an enemy that meant well but almost destroyed his army at Valley Forge. As the following excerpt explains, that enemy was the Pennsylvania legislature:

> In Pennsylvania, where the main force of Washington's army was quartered . . . the legislature . . . decided to try a period of price control limited to those commodities needed for use by the army. . . . The result might have been anticipated by those with some knowledge of the trials and tribulations of other states. The prices of uncontrolled goods, mostly imported, rose to record heights. Most farmers kept back their produce, refusing to sell at what they regarded as an unfair price. Some who had large families to take care of even secretly sold their food to the British, who paid in gold.
>
> After the disastrous winter at Valley Forge when Washington's army nearly starved to death (thanks largely to these well-intentioned but misdirected laws), the ill-fated experiment in price controls was finally ended. The Continental Congress on June 4, 1778, adopted the following resolution:
>
> "Whereas . . . it hath been found by experience that limitations upon the prices of commodities are not only ineffectual for

SOURCE: Engraving "Men Gathering Wood at Valley Forge." Metropolitan Museum of Art, bequest of Charles Allen Munn, 1924 [24.90.1828]. All Rights Reserved, The Metropolitan Museum of Art.

Valley Forge

the purposes proposed, but likewise productive of very evil consequences . . . resolved, that it be recommended to the several states to repeal or suspend all laws or resolutions within the said states respectively limiting, regulating or restraining the Price of any Article, Manufacture or Commodity."

SOURCE: Robert L. Schuettinger and Eamonn F. Butler, *Forty Centuries of Wage and Price Controls* (Washington, DC: Heritage Foundation, 1979), p. 41. Reprinted by permission.

DEMAND AND QUANTITY DEMANDED

People commonly think of consumer demands as fixed amounts. For example, when product designers propose a new computer model, management asks: "What is its market potential?" That is, just how many are likely to be sold? Similarly, government bureaus conduct studies to determine how many engineers or doctors the United States will require (demand) in subsequent years.

Economists respond that such questions are not well posed—that there is no single answer to such a question. Rather, they say, the "market potential" for computers or the number of engineers that will be "required" depends on a great number of influences, including the price charged for each.

> **The quantity demanded of any product normally depends on its price. Quantity demanded also depends on a number of other determinants, including population size, consumer incomes, tastes, and the prices of other products.**

Because prices play a central role in a market economy, we begin our study of demand by focusing on how quantity demanded depends on price. A little later, we will bring the other determinants of quantity demanded back into the picture. For now, we will consider all influences other than price to be fixed. This assumption, often expressed as "other things being equal," is used in much of economic analysis. As an example of the relationship between price and demand, let's think about the quantity of beef demanded. If the price of beef is very high, its "market potential" may be very small. People will find ways to get along with less beef, perhaps by switching to pork or fish. If the price of beef declines, people will tend to eat more beef. They may serve it more frequently or eat larger portions or switch away from fish. Thus:

> **There is no one demand figure for beef, or for computers, or for engineers. Rather, there is a different quantity demanded at each possible price, all other influences being held constant.**

The **quantity demanded** is the number of units of a good that consumers are willing and can afford to buy over a specified period of time.

The Demand Schedule

A demand schedule is a table showing how the quantity demanded of some product during a specified period of time changes as the price of that product changes, holding all other determinants of quantity demanded constant.

A demand curve is a graphical depiction of a demand schedule. It shows how the quantity demanded of some product will change as the price of that product changes during a specified period of time, holding all other determinants of quantity demanded constant.

Table 1 shows how such information for beef can be recorded in a **demand schedule.** It indicates how much beef consumers in a particular area are willing and able to buy at different possible prices during a specified period of time, other things held equal. Specifically, the table shows the quantity of beef that will be demanded in a year at each possible price ranging from $6.90 to $7.50 per pound. At a relatively low price, such as $7.00 per pound, customers wish to purchase 70 (million) pounds per year. But if the price were to rise to, say, $7.40 per pound, quantity demanded would fall to 50 million pounds.

Common sense tells us why this happens.[2] First, as prices rise, some customers will reduce the quantity of beef they consume. Second, higher prices will induce some customers to drop out of the market entirely—for example, by switching to pork or fish. On both counts, quantity demanded will decline as the price rises.

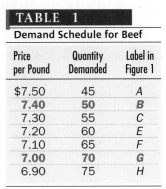

TABLE 1
Demand Schedule for Beef

Price per Pound	Quantity Demanded	Label in Figure 1
$7.50	45	A
7.40	50	B
7.30	55	C
7.20	60	E
7.10	65	F
7.00	70	G
6.90	75	H

NOTE: Quantity is in pounds per year.

> **As the price of an item rises, the quantity demanded normally falls. As the price falls, the quantity demanded normally rises, all other things held constant.**

FIGURE 1
Demand Curve for Beef

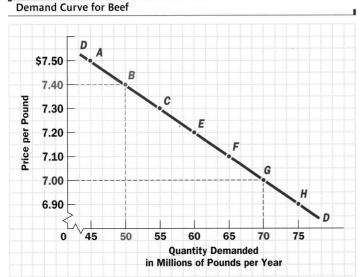

Quantity Demanded
in Millions of Pounds per Year

The Demand Curve

The information contained in Table 1 can be summarized in a graph like Figure 1, which is called a **demand curve.** Each point in the graph corresponds to a line in the table. This curve shows the relationship between price and quantity demanded. For example, it tells us that to sell 55 million pounds per year, the price must be $7.10 per pound. This relationship is shown at point G in Figure 1. If the price were $7.40, however, consumers would demand only 50 million pounds (point B). Because the quantity demanded declines as the price increases, the demand curve has a negative slope.[3]

Notice the last phrase in the definitions of the demand schedule and the demand curve: "holding all other determinants of quantity demanded constant." What are some of these "other things," and how do they affect the demand curve?

Shifts of the Demand Curve

The quantity of beef demanded is subject to a variety of influences other than the price of beef. Changes in population size and characteristics, consumer incomes and tastes, and the prices of alternative products such as pork and fish presumably change the quantity of beef demanded, even if the price of beef does not change.

Because the demand curve for beef depicts only the relationship between the quantity of beef demanded and the price of beef, holding all other factors constant, a change in beef

---

[2] This common-sense answer is examined more fully in later chapters.

[3] If you need to review the concept of slope, refer back to the appendix to Chapter 1.

price moves the market for beef from one point on the demand curve to another point on the same curve. However, a change in any of these other influences on demand causes a **shift of the entire demand curve.** More generally:

> A change in the price of a good produces a movement *along* a fixed demand curve. By contrast, a change in any other variable that influences quantity demanded produces a shift of the *entire* demand curve.

If consumers want to buy more beef at every given price than they wanted previously, the demand curve shifts to the right (or outward). If they desire less at every given price, the demand curve shifts to the left (or inward toward the origin).

Figure 2 shows this distinction graphically. If the price of beef falls from $7.30 to $7.10 per pound, and quantity demanded rises accordingly, we move along demand curve D_0D_0 from point C to point F, as shown by the blue arrow. If, on the other hand, consumers suddenly decide that they like beef better than they did formerly, or if they embrace a study that reports the health benefits of beef, the entire demand curve shifts outward from D_0D_0 to D_1D_1, as indicated by the brick arrows, meaning that at *any* given price consumers are now willing to buy more beef than before. To make this general idea more concrete, and to show some of its many applications, let us consider some specific examples of those "other things" that can shift demand curves.

A **shift in a demand curve** occurs when any relevant variable other than price changes. If consumers want to buy *more* at any and all given prices than they wanted previously, the demand curve shifts to the right (or outward). If they desire *less* at any given price, the demand curve shifts to the left (or inward).

FIGURE 2

Movements along versus Shifts of a Demand Curve

Consumer Incomes

If average incomes rise, consumers will purchase more of most goods, including beef, even if the prices of those goods remain the same. That is, increases in income normally shift demand curves outward to the right, as depicted in Figure 3(a), where the demand curve shifts outward from D_0D_0 to D_1D_1, establishing a new price and output quantity.

Quantity Demanded in Millions of Pounds per year

Population

Population growth affects quantity demanded in more or less the same way as increases in average incomes. For instance, a larger population will presumably want to consume more beef, even if the price of beef and average incomes do not change, thus shifting the entire demand curve to the right, as in Figure 3(a). The equilibrium price and quantity both rise. Increases in particular population segments can also elicit shifts in demand—for example, the United States experienced a miniature population boom between the late 1970s and mid-1990s. This group (which is dubbed Generation Y and includes most users of this book) has sparked higher demand for such items as cell phones and video games.

In Figure 3(b), we see that a decrease in population should shift the demand curve for beef to the left, from D_0D_0 to D_2D_2.

Consumer Preferences

If the beef industry mounts a successful advertising campaign extolling the benefits of eating beef, families may decide to buy more at any given price. If so, the entire demand curve for beef would shift to the right, as in Figure 3(a). Alternatively, a medical report on the dangers of high cholesterol may persuade consumers to eat less beef, thereby shifting the demand curve to the left, as in Figure 3(b). Again, these are general phenomena:

> If consumer preferences shift in favor of a particular item, its demand curve will shift outward to the right, as in Figure 3(a).

FIGURE 3
Shifts of the Demand Curve

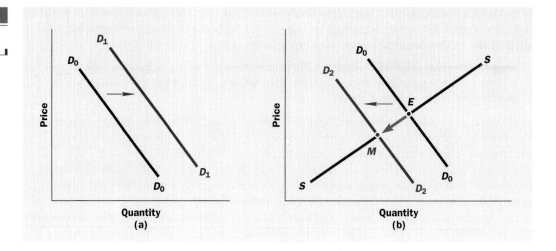

An example is the ever-shifting "rage" in children's toys—be it Yu-Gi-Oh! cards, electronic Elmo dolls, or the latest video games. These items become the object of desperate hunts as parents snap them up for their offspring, and stores are unable to keep up with the demand.

Prices and Availability of Related Goods   Because pork, fish, and chicken are popular products that compete with beef, a change in the price of any of these other items can be expected to shift the demand curve for beef. If any of these alternative

Volatility in Electricity Prices

The following newspaper story excerpts highlight the volatility of the electricity industry and its susceptibility to manipulation of the supply-demand mechanism and soaring prices. Although the industry was deregulated more than a decade ago, electricity prices have generally not fallen and, in many cases, have risen sharply. The Federal Energy Regulatory Commission contends that allowing competition among producers should guarantee the lowest possible price. Why have electricity prices not fallen, unlike other previously regulated industries?

Rising fuel costs are one major reason. . . . Another factor is the very nature of electricity, which must be produced, transmitted and consumed in an instant . . . electricity cannot be held in inventory.

Critics point to opportunities for suppliers to interfere in the market system, including the withholding of power or limiting of production during periods of high demand, leading to skyrocketing prices.

"Shutting down a power plant in July is like the mall closing on the weekend before Christmas, but in July last year, 20 percent of generating capacity was shut down in California," said Robert McCullough, an economist whose Oregon consulting business is advising some of those contending in lawsuits that prices are being manipulated.

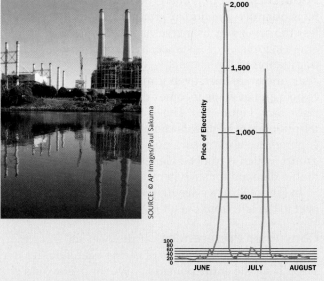

SOURCE: © AP Images/Paul Sakuma

NOTE: Quantity is in billions of quarts per year.

SOURCE: "Flaws Seen In Market for Utilities; Power Play: The Bidding Game" by David Cay Johnston, *The New York Times*, Late Edition (East Coast), November 21, 2006, p.C1.

items becomes cheaper, some consumers will switch away from beef. Thus, the demand curve for beef will shift to the left, as in Figure 3(b). Other price changes may shift the demand curve for beef in the opposite direction. For example, suppose that hamburger buns and ketchup become less expensive. This may induce some consumers to eat more beef and thus shift the demand curve for beef to the right, as in Figure 3(a). In general:

> **Increases in the prices of goods that are substitutes for the good in question (as pork, fish, and chicken are for beef) move the demand curve to the right. Increases in the prices of goods that are normally used together with the good in question (such as hamburger buns and beef) shift the demand curve to the left.**

This is just what happened when a frost wiped out almost half of Brazil's coffee bean harvest in 1995. The three largest U.S. coffee producers raised their prices by 45 percent, and, as a result, the demand curve for alternative beverages such as tea shifted to the right. Then in 1998, coffee prices dropped about 34 percent, which in turn caused the demand curve for tea to shift toward the left (or toward the origin).

Although the preceding list does not exhaust the possible influences on quantity demanded, we have said enough to suggest the principles followed by demand and shifts of demand. Let's turn now to the supply side of the market.

SUPPLY AND QUANTITY SUPPLIED

Like quantity demanded, the quantity of beef that is supplied by business firms such as farms is not a fixed number; it also depends on many things. Obviously, we expect more beef to be supplied if there are more farms or more cows per farm. Cows may provide less meat if bad weather deprives them of their feed. As before, however, let's turn our attention first to the relationship between the price and quantity of beef supplied.

Economists generally suppose that a higher price calls forth a greater **quantity supplied.** Why? Remember our analysis of the principle of increasing cost in Chapter 3 (page 44). According to that principle, as more of any farmer's (or the nation's) resources are devoted to beef production, the opportunity cost of obtaining another pound of beef increases. Farmers will therefore find it profitable to increase beef production only if they can sell the beef at a higher price—high enough to cover the additional costs incurred to expand production. In other words, it normally will take higher prices to persuade farmers to raise beef production. This idea is quite general and applies to the supply of most goods and services.[4] As long as suppliers want to make profits and the principle of increasing costs holds:

> **As the price of any commodity rises, the quantity supplied normally rises. As the price falls, the quantity supplied normally falls.**

The Supply Schedule and the Supply Curve

Table 2 shows the relationship between the price of beef and its quantity supplied. Tables such as this one are called **supply schedules;** they show how much sellers are willing to provide during a specified period at alternative possible prices. This particular supply schedule tells us that a low price like $7.00 per pound will induce suppliers to provide only 50 million pounds, whereas a higher price like $7.30 will induce them to provide much more—55 million pounds.

*The **quantity supplied** is the number of units that sellers want to sell over a specified period of time.*

*A **supply schedule** is a table showing how the quantity supplied of some product changes as the price of that product changes during a specified period of time, holding all other determinants of quantity supplied constant.*

---

[4] This analysis is carried out in much greater detail in later chapters.

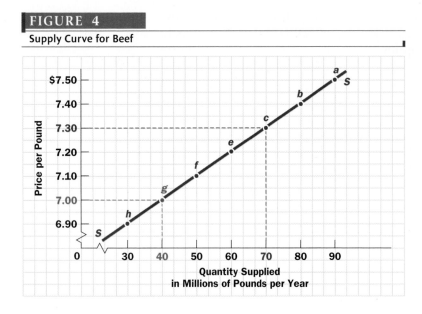

FIGURE 4

Supply Curve for Beef

TABLE 2		
Supply Schedule for Beef		
Price per Pound	Quantity Supplied	Label in Figure 4
$7.50	90	*a*
7.40	80	*b*
7.30	**70**	*c*
7.20	60	*e*
7.10	50	*f*
7.00	**40**	*g*
6.90	30	*h*

NOTE: Quantity is in pounds per year.

A **supply curve** is a graphical depiction of a supply schedule. It shows how the quantity supplied of some product will change as the price of that product changes during a specified period of time, holding all other determinants of quantity supplied constant.

As you might have guessed, when such information is plotted on a graph, it is called a **supply curve.** Figure 4 is the supply curve corresponding to the supply schedule in Table 2, showing the relationship between the price of beef and the quantity supplied. It slopes upward—it has a positive slope—because quantity supplied is higher when price is higher. Notice again the same phrase in the definition: "holding all other determinants of quantity supplied constant." What are these "other determinants"?

Shifts of the Supply Curve

Like quantity demanded, the quantity supplied in a market typically responds to many influences other than price. The weather, the cost of feed, the number and size of farms, and a variety of other factors all influence how much beef will be brought to market. Because the supply curve depicts only the relationship between the price of beef and the quantity of beef supplied, holding all other influences constant, a change in any of these other determinants of quantity supplied will cause the entire supply curve to shift. That is:

> A change in the price of the good causes a movement *along* a fixed supply curve. Price is not the only influence on quantity supplied, however. If any of these other influences change, the *entire* supply curve shifts.

Figure 5 depicts this distinction graphically. A rise in price from $7.10 to $7.30 will raise quantity supplied by moving along supply curve S_0S_0 from point *f* to point *c*. Any rise in quantity supplied attributable to an influence other than price, however, will shift the *entire* supply curve outward to the right, from S_0S_0 to S_1S_1, as shown by the brick arrows. Let us consider what some of these other influences are and how they shift the supply curve.

Size of the Industry   We begin with the most obvious influence. If more farmers enter the beef industry, the quantity supplied at any given price will increase. For example, if each farm provides 60,000 pounds of beef per year at a price of $7.10 per pound, then 100,000 farmers would provide 600 million pounds, but 130,000 farmers would provide 780,000 million. Thus, when more farms are in the industry, the quantity of beef supplied will be greater at any given price—and hence the supply curve will move farther to the right.

Figure 6(a) illustrates the effect of an expansion of the industry from 100,000 farms to 130,000 farms—a rightward shift of the supply curve from S_0S_0 to S_1S_1. Figure 6(b) illustrates the opposite case: a contraction of the industry from 100,000 farms to 62,500 farms. The supply curve shifts inward to the left, from S_0S_0 to S_2S_2. Even if no farmers enter or leave the industry, results like those depicted in Figure 6 can be produced by expansion or contraction of the *existing* farms.

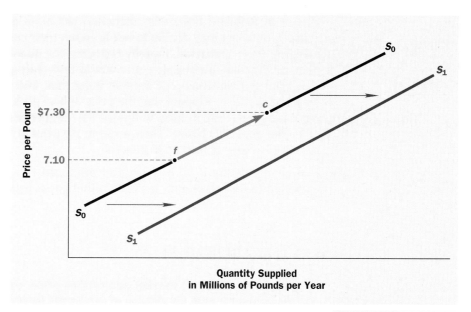

Technological Progress

Another influence that shifts supply curves is technological change. Suppose some enterprising farmer invents a new growth hormone that increases the body mass of cattle. Thereafter, at any given price, farms will be able to produce more beef; that is, the supply curve will shift outward to the right, as in Figure 6(a). This example, again, illustrates a general influence that applies to most industries:

Technological progress that reduces costs will shift the supply curve outward to the right.

Automakers, for example, have been able to reduce production costs since industrial technology invented robots that can be programmed to work on several different car models. This technological advance has shifted the supply curve outward.

Prices of Inputs

Changes in input prices also shift supply curves. Suppose a drought raises the price of animal feed. Farmers will have to pay more to keep their cows alive and healthy and consequently will no longer be able to provide the same quantity of beef at each possible price. This example illustrates that

Increases in the prices of inputs that suppliers must buy will shift the supply curve inward to the left.

FIGURE 5

Movements along versus Shifts of a Supply Curve

FIGURE 6

Shifts of the Supply Curve

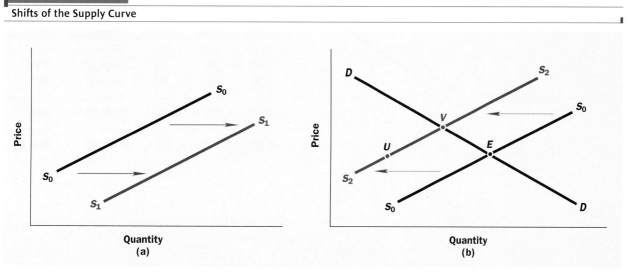

Prices of Related Outputs   Ranchers sell hides as well as meat. If leather prices rise sharply, ranchers may decide to not to fatten their cattle as much as they used to, before bringing them to market, thereby reducing the quantity of beef supplied. On a supply-demand diagram, the supply curve would then shift inward, as in Figure 6(b).

Similar phenomena occur in other industries, and sometimes the effect goes the other way. For example, suppose that the price of beef goes up, which increases the quantity of meat supplied. That, in turn, will raise the number of cowhides supplied even if the price of leather does not change. Thus, a rise in the price of beef will lead to a rightward shift in the supply curve of leather. In general:

> A change in the price of one good produced by a multiproduct industry may be expected to shift the supply curves of other goods produced by that industry.

SUPPLY AND DEMAND EQUILIBRIUM

A **supply-demand diagram** graphs the supply and demand curves together. It also determines the equilibrium price and quantity.

To analyze how the free market determines price, we must compare the desires of consumers (demand) with the desires of producers (supply) to see whether the two plans are consistent. Table 3 and Figure 7 help us do this.

Table 3 brings together the demand schedule from Table 1 and the supply schedule from Table 2. Similarly, Figure 7 puts the demand curve from Figure 1 and the supply curve from Figure 4 on a single graph. Such graphs are called **supply-demand diagrams,** and you will encounter many of them in this book. Notice that, for reasons already discussed, the demand curve has a negative slope and the supply curve has a positive slope. That is generally true of supply-demand diagrams.

In a free market, price and quantity are determined by the intersection of the supply and demand curves. At only one point in Figure 7, point E, do the supply curve and the demand curve intersect. At the price corresponding to point E, which is $7.20 per pound, the quantity supplied and the quantity demanded are both 60 million pounds per year. This means that at a price of $7.20 per pound, consumers are willing to buy exactly what producers are willing to sell.

At a lower price, such as $7.00 per pound, only 40 million pounds of beef will be supplied (point g), whereas 70 million pounds will be demanded (point G).

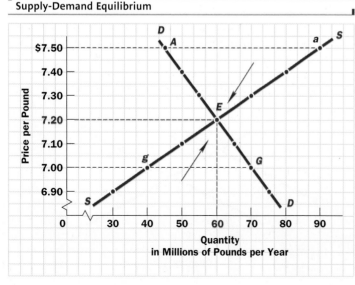

FIGURE 7

Supply-Demand Equilibrium

TABLE 3

Determination of the Equilibrium Price and Quantity of Beef

Price per Pound	Quantity Demanded	Quantity Supplied	Surplus or Shortage	Price Direction
$7.50	45	90	Surplus	Fall
7.40	50	80	Surplus	Fall
7.30	55	70	Surplus	Fall
7.20	60	60	Neither	Unchanged
7.10	65	50	Shortage	Rise
7.00	70	40	Shortage	Rise
6.90	75	30	Shortage	Rise

Thus, quantity demanded will exceed quantity supplied. There will be a **shortage** equal to 70 minus 40, or 30 million pounds. Price will thus be driven up by unsatisfied demand. Alternatively, at a higher price, such as $7.50 per pound, quantity supplied will be 90 million pounds (point *a*) and quantity demanded will be only 45 million (point *A*). Quantity supplied will exceed quantity demanded—creating a **surplus** equal to 90 minus 45, or 45 million pounds. The unsold output can then be expected to push the price down.

Because $7.20 is the only price in this graph at which quantity supplied and quantity demanded are equal, we say that $7.20 per pound is the equilibrium price (or the "market clearing" price) in this market. Similarly, 60 million pounds per year is the equilibrium quantity of beef. The term **equilibrium** merits a little explanation, because it arises so frequently in economic analysis.

An equilibrium is a situation in which there are no inherent forces that produce change. Think, for example, of a pendulum resting at its center point. If no outside force (such as a person's hand) comes to push it, the pendulum will remain exactly where it is; it is therefore in equilibrium.

If you give the pendulum a shove, however, its equilibrium will be disturbed and it will start to move. When it reaches the top of its arc, the pendulum will, for an instant, be at rest again. This point is not an equilibrium position, for the force of gravity will pull the pendulum downward. Thereafter, gravity and friction will govern its motion from side to side. Eventually, the pendulum will return to its original position. The fact that the pendulum tends to return to its original position is described by saying that this position is a *stable* equilibrium. That position is also the only equilibrium position of the pendulum. At any other point, inherent forces will cause the pendulum to move.

The concept of equilibrium in economics is similar and can be illustrated by our supply-and-demand example. Why is no price other than $7.20 an equilibrium price in Table 3 or Figure 7? What forces will change any other price?

Consider first a low price such as $7.00, at which quantity demanded (70 million pounds) exceeds quantity supplied (40 million pounds). If the price were this low, many frustrated customers would be unable to purchase the quantities they desired. In their scramble for the available supply of beef, some would offer to pay more. As customers sought to outbid one another, the market price would be forced up. Thus, a price below the equilibrium price cannot persist in a free market because a shortage sets in motion powerful economic forces that push the price upward.

Similar forces operate in the opposite direction if the market price exceeds the equilibrium price. If, for example, the price should somehow reach $7.50, Table 3 tells us that quantity supplied (90 million pounds) would far exceed the quantity demanded (45 million pounds). Producers would be unable to sell their desired quantities of beef at the prevailing price, and some would undercut their competitors by reducing price. Such competitive price cutting would continue as long as the surplus remained—that is, as long as quantity supplied exceeded quantity demanded. Thus, a price above the equilibrium price cannot persist indefinitely.

We are left with a clear conclusion. The price of $7.20 per pound and the quantity of 60 million pounds per year constitute the only price-quantity combination that does not sow the seeds of its own destruction. It is thus the only equilibrium for this market. Any lower price must rise, and any higher price must fall. It is as if natural economic forces place a magnet at point *E* that attracts the market, just as gravity attracts a pendulum.

The pendulum analogy is worth pursuing further. Most pendulums are more frequently in motion than at rest. However, unless they are repeatedly buffeted by outside forces (which, of course, is exactly what happens to economic equilibria in reality), pendulums gradually return to their resting points. The same is true of price and quantity in a free market. They are moved about by shifts in the supply and demand curves that we have already described. As a consequence, markets are not always in equilibrium. But, if nothing interferes with them, experience shows that they normally move toward equilibrium.

A **shortage** is an excess of quantity demanded over quantity supplied. When there is a shortage, buyers cannot purchase the quantities they desire at the current price.

A **surplus** is an excess of quantity supplied over quantity demanded. When there is a surplus, sellers cannot sell the quantities they desire to supply at the current price.

An **equilibrium** is a situation in which there are no inherent forces that produce change. Changes away from an equilibrium position will occur only as a result of "outside events" that disturb the status quo.

The **law of supply and demand** states that in a free market the forces of supply and demand generally push the price toward the level at which quantity supplied and quantity demanded are equal.

The Law of Supply and Demand

In a free market, the forces of supply and demand generally push the price toward its equilibrium level, the price at which quantity supplied and quantity demanded are equal. Like most economic "laws," some markets will occasionally disobey the **law of supply and demand**. Markets sometimes display shortages or surpluses for long periods of time. Prices sometimes fail to move toward equilibrium. But the "law" is a fair generalization that is right far more often than it is wrong.

EFFECTS OF DEMAND SHIFTS ON SUPPLY-DEMAND EQUILIBRIUM

Figure 3 showed how developments other than changes in price—such as increases in consumer income—can shift the demand curve. We saw that a rise in income, for example, will shift the demand curve to the right, meaning that at any given price, consumers—with their increased purchasing power—will buy more of the good than before. This, in turn, will move the equilibrium point, changing both market price and quantity sold.

This market adjustment is shown in Figure 8(a). It adds a supply curve to Figure 3(a) so that we can see what happens to the supply-demand equilibrium. In the example in the graph, the quantity demanded at the old equilibrium price of $7.20 increases from 60 million pounds per year (point E on the demand curve D_0D_0) to 75 million pounds per year (point R on the demand curve D_1D_1). We know that $7.20 is no longer the equilibrium price, because at this price quantity demanded (75 million pounds) exceeds quantity supplied (60 million pounds). To restore equilibrium, the price must rise. The new equilibrium occurs at point T, the intersection point of the supply curve and the shifted demand curve, where the price is $7.30 per pound and both quantities demanded and supplied are 70 million pounds per year. This example illustrates a general result, which is true when the supply curve slopes upward:

Any influence that makes the demand curve shift outward to the right, and does not affect an upward-sloped supply curve, will raise the equilibrium price and the equilibrium quantity.[5]

FIGURE 8

The Effects of Shifts of the Demand Curve

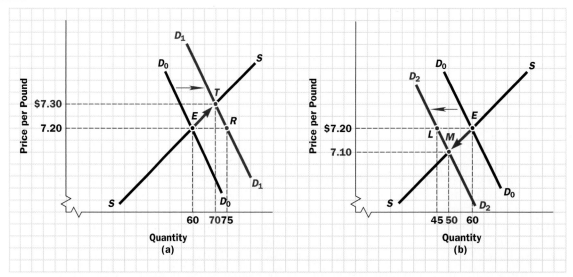

NOTE: Quantity is in millions of pounds per year.

---

[5] For example, when incomes rise rapidly, in many developing countries the demand curves for a variety of consumer goods shift rapidly outward to the right. In Japan, for example, the demand for used Levi's jeans and Nike running shoes from the United States skyrocketed in the early 1990s as status-conscious Japanese consumers searched for outlets for their then-rising incomes.

The Ups and Downs of Milk Consumption

The following excerpt from a U.S Department of Agriculture publication discusses some of the things that have affected the consumption of milk in the last century.

In 1909, Americans consumed a total of 34 gallons of fluid milk per person—27 gallons of whole milk and 7 gallons of milks lower in fat than whole milk, mostly buttermilk. . . . Fluid milk consumption shot up from 34 gallons per person in 1941 to a peak of 45 gallons per person in 1945. War production lifted Americans' incomes but curbed civilian production and the goods consumers could buy. Many food items were rationed, including meats, butter and sugar. Milk was not rationed, and consumption soared. Since 1945, however, milk consumption has fallen steadily, reaching a record low of just under 23 gallons per person in 2001 (the latest year for which data are available). Steep declines in consumption of whole milk and buttermilk far outpaced an increase in other lower fat milks. By 2001, Americans were consuming less than 8 gallons per person of whole milk, compared with nearly 41 gallons in 1945 and 25 gallons in 1970. In contrast, per capita consumption of total lower fat milks was 15 gallons in 2001, up from 4 gallons in 1945 and 6 gallons

in 1970. These changes are consistent with increased public concern about cholesterol, saturated fat, and calories. However, decline in per capita consumption of fluid milk also may be attributed to competition from other beverages, especially carbonated soft drinks and bottled water, a smaller percentage of children and adolescents in the U.S., and a more ethnically diverse population whose diet does not normally include milk.

SOURCE: Judy Putnam and Jane Allshouse, "Trends in U.S. Per Capita Consumption of Dairy Products, 1909 to 2001," *Amber Waves: The Economics of Food, Farming, Natural Resources and Rural America*, June 2003, U.S. Department of Agriculture, available at http://www.usda.gov.

Americans are switching to lower fat milks

Lower fat milks include: buttermilk (1.5 percent fat), plain and flavored reduced fat milk (2 percent fat), low-fat milk (1 percent fat), nonfat milk, and yogurt made from these milks (except frozen yogurt).

Everything works in reverse if consumer incomes fall. Figure 8(b) depicts a leftward (inward) shift of the demand curve that results from a decline in consumer incomes. For example, the quantity demanded at the previous equilibrium price ($7.20) falls from 60 million pounds (point E) to 45 million pounds (point L on the demand curve D_2D_2). The initial price is now too high and must fall. The new equilibrium will eventually be established at point M, where the price is $7.10 and both quantity demanded and quantity supplied are 50 million pounds. In general:

> Any influence that shifts the demand curve inward to the left, and that does not affect the supply curve, will lower both the equilibrium price and the equilibrium quantity.

SUPPLY SHIFTS AND SUPPLY-DEMAND EQUILIBRIUM

A story precisely analogous to that of the effects of a demand shift on equilibrium price and quantity applies to supply shifts. Figure 6 described the effects on the supply curve of beef if the number of farms increases. Figure 9(a) now adds a demand curve to the supply curves of Figure 6 so that we can see the supply-demand equilibrium. Notice that at the initial price of $7.20, the quantity supplied after the shift is 780 million pounds (point I on the supply curve S_1S_1), which is 30 percent more than the original quantity demanded of 600 million pounds (point E on the supply curve S_0S_0). We can see from the graph that the price of $7.20 is too high to be the equilibrium price; the price must fall. The new equilibrium point is J, where the price is $7.10 per pound and the quantity is 650 million pounds per year. In general:

> Any change that shifts the supply curve outward to the right, and does not affect the demand curve, will lower the equilibrium price and raise the equilibrium quantity.

This must always be true if the industry's demand curve has a negative slope, because the greater quantity supplied can be sold only if the price is decreased so as to induce customers to buy more.[6] The cellular phone industry is a case in point. As more providers

---

[6] Graphically, whenever a positively sloped curve shifts to the right, its intersection point with a negatively sloping curve must always move lower. Just try drawing it yourself.

FIGURE 9

Effects of Shifts of the Supply Curve

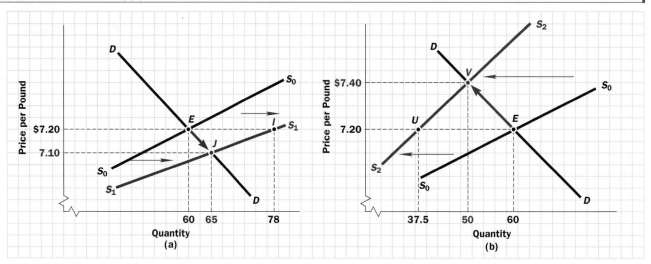

have entered the industry, the cost of cellular service has plummeted. Some cellular carriers have even given away telephones as sign-up bonuses.

Figure 9(b) illustrates the opposite case: a contraction of the industry. The supply curve shifts inward to the left and equilibrium moves from point *E* to point *V*, where the price is $7.40 and quantity is 500 million pounds per year. In general:

> **Any influence that shifts the supply curve to the left, and does not affect the demand curve, will raise the equilibrium price and reduce the equilibrium quantity.**

Many outside forces can disturb equilibrium in a market by shifting the demand curve or the supply curve, either temporarily or permanently. In 1998, for example, gasoline prices dropped because recession in Asia shifted the demand curve downward, as did a reduction in use of petroleum that resulted from a mild winter. In the summer of 1998, severely hot weather and lack of rain damaged the cotton crop in the United States, shifting the supply curve downward. Such outside influences change the equilibrium price and quantity. If you look again at Figures 8 and 9, you can see clearly that any event that causes either the demand curve or the supply curve to shift will also change the equilibrium price and quantity.

PUZZLE RESOLVED: **THOSE LEAPING OIL PRICES**

The disturbing increases in the price of gasoline, and of the oil from which it is made, is attributable to large shifts in both demand and supply conditions. Americans are, for example, driving more and are buying gas-guzzling vehicles, and the resulting upward shift in the demand curve raises price. Instability in the Middle East and Russia has undermined supply, and that also raised prices. We have seen the results at the gas pumps. The following newspaper story describes a sensational sort of change in supply conditions:

Aug. 10 (Bloomberg)—BP Plc and its partners in the Prudhoe Bay oil field in Alaska will spend about $170 million inspecting and repairing corroded pipelines that shut most of the production from the largest U.S. oil field.

Including costs to clean up and repair a line that leaked in March, the "rough estimate" rises to about $200 million, said Kemp Copeland, field manager for BP's Prudhoe Bay operations. The figures include the cost of replacing 16 miles of feeder pipeline in the field.

The worst cost to BP will probably be the hit to its reputation, said Mark Gilman, an analyst at The Benchmark Company LLC in New York, who rates the shares "sell."

"At some point this is going to prove very costly, as you're going to be competing with folks whose reputation has not been subject to the same degree of punishment," Gilman, who owns a "small" number of BP shares, said today in a phone interview.

The Prudhoe Bay shutdown is the latest blow for Chief Executive Officer John Browne, who faces a grand jury probe for an earlier Alaska spill, charges of market manipulation in the U.S. propane industry and fines from a Texas refinery blast that killed 15 workers. BP, which gets 40 percent of its sales from the U.S., last month said it will boost spending there to improve safety and maintenance.

London-based BP Plc said today it will know by the start of next week whether it can keep operating the western half of the field, which is currently producing as much as 137,000 barrels of oil a day. The entire field pumps 400,000 barrels a day, or 8 percent of U.S. output, when fully operational.

LOOKING FOR STEEL SUPPLIES

BP is asking suppliers U.S. Steel Corp. and Nippon Steel Corp. for faster delivery to a total of 51,000 feet of pipe it has already ordered for the repairs, BP Alaska President Steve Marshall said in conference call on Aug. 8. The pipe is scheduled to be delivered in October the earliest.

A supplier for another 30,000 feet of 24-inch pipe and 52,000 feet of 18-inch pipe is still needed, said Marshall.

BP, Houston-based ConocoPhillips and Exxon Mobil Corp. of Irving, Texas, are joint owners in the Prudhoe Bay field. ConocoPhillips, the third-largest U.S. oil company, earlier today declared force majeure on oil deliveries from Prudhoe Bay.

Force majeure allows companies to avoid penalties for failing to fulfill contracts because of unforeseen events. ConocoPhillips sells its Alaskan crude oil to refineries and brokers, according to spokesman Bill Tanner.

SOURCE: Ian McKinnon and Sonja Franklin, "BP Says Prudhoe Bay Repair Costs May Be $200 Million," with reporting by Jim Kennett in Houston. Editor: Jordan (rsd)

Application: Who Really Pays That Tax?

Supply-and-demand analysis offers insights that may not be readily apparent. Here is an example. Suppose your state legislature raises the gasoline tax by 10 cents per gallon. Service station operators will then have to collect 10 additional cents in taxes on every gallon they pump. They will consider this higher tax as an addition to their costs and will pass it on to you and other consumers by raising the price of gas by 10 cents per gallon. Right? No, wrong—or rather, partly wrong.

The gas station owners would certainly *like* to pass on the entire tax to buyers, but the market mechanism will allow them to shift only *part* of it—perhaps 6 cents per gallon. They will then be stuck with the remainder—4 cents in our example. Figure 10, which is just another supply-demand graph, shows why.

The demand curve is the red curve *DD*. The supply curve before the tax is the black curve $S_0 S_0$. Before the new tax, the equilibrium point is E_0 and the price is $2.54. We can interpret the supply curve as telling us at what price sellers are willing to provide any given quantity. For example, they are willing to supply quantity Q_1 = 50 million gallons per year if the price is $2.54 per gallon.

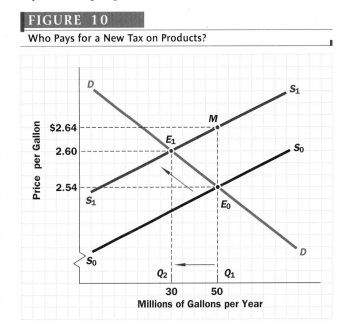

FIGURE 10

Who Pays for a New Tax on Products?

So what happens as a result of the new tax? Because they must now turn 10 cents per gallon over to the government, gas station owners will be willing to supply any given quantity only if they get 10 cents more per gallon than they did before. Therefore, to get them to supply quantity $Q_1 = 50$ million gallons, a price of \$2.54 per gallon will no longer suffice. Only a price of \$2.64 per gallon will now induce them to supply 50 million gallons. Thus, at quantity $Q_1 = 50$, the point on the supply curve will move up by 10 cents, from point E_0 to point M. Because firms will insist on the same 10-cent price increase for any other quantity they supply, the *entire* supply curve will shift up by the 10-cent tax—from the black curve S_0S_0 to the new brick supply curve S_1S_1. And, as a result, the supply-demand equilibrium point will move from E_0 to E_1 and the price will increase from \$2.54 to \$2.60.

The supply curve shift may give the impression that gas station owners have succeeded in passing the entire 10-cent increase on to consumers—the distance from E_0 to M—but look again. The *equilibrium* price has only gone up from \$2.54 to \$2.60. That is, the price has risen by only 6 cents, not by the full 10-cent amount of the tax. The gas station will have to absorb the remaining 4 cents of the tax.

Now this really *looks* as though we have pulled a fast one on you—a magician's sleight of hand. After all, the supply curve has shifted upward by the full amount of the tax, and yet the resulting price increase has covered only part of the tax rise. However, a second look reveals that, like most apparent acts of magic, this one has a simple explanation. The explanation arises from the *demand* side of the supply-demand mechanism. The negative slope of the demand curve means that when prices rise, at least some consumers will reduce the quantity of gasoline they demand. That will force sellers to give up part of the price increase. In other words, firms must absorb the part of the tax—4 cents—that consumers are unwilling to pay. But note that the equilibrium quantity Q_1 has fallen from 50 million gallons to $Q_2 = 30$ million gallons—so both consumers and suppliers lose out in some sense.

This example is not an oddball case. Indeed, the result is almost always true. The cost of any increase in a tax on any commodity will usually be paid partly by the consumer and partly by the seller. This is so no matter whether the legislature says that it is imposing the tax on the sellers or on the buyers. Whichever way it is phrased, the economics are the same: The supply-demand mechanism ensures that the tax will be shared by both of the parties.

BATTLING THE INVISIBLE HAND: THE MARKET FIGHTS BACK

IDEAS FOR BEYOND THE FINAL EXAM

As we noted in our *Ideas for Beyond the Final Exam* in Chapter 1, lawmakers and rulers have often been dissatisfied with the outcomes of free markets. From Rome to Reno, and from biblical times to the space age, they have battled the invisible hand. Sometimes, rather than trying to adjust the workings of the market, governments have tried to raise or lower the prices of specific commodities by decree. In many such cases, the authorities felt that market prices were, in some sense, immorally low or immorally high. Penalties were therefore imposed on anyone offering the commodities in question at prices above or below those established by the authorities. Such legally imposed constraints on prices are called "price ceilings" and "price floors." To see their result, we will focus on the use of price ceilings.

Restraining the Market Mechanism: Price Ceilings

The market has proven itself a formidable foe that strongly resists attempts to get around its decisions. In case after case where legal **price ceilings** are imposed, virtually the same series of consequences ensues:

A **price ceiling** is a maximum that the price charged for a commodity cannot legally exceed.

1. *A persistent shortage develops because quantity demanded exceeds quantity supplied.* Queuing (people waiting in lines), direct rationing (with everyone getting a fixed allotment), or any of a variety of other devices, usually inefficient and unpleasant, must substitute for the distribution process provided by the price mechanism. Example: Rampant shortages in Eastern Europe and the former Soviet Union helped precipitate the revolts that ended communism.

POLICY DEBATE

ECONOMIC ASPECTS OF THE WAR ON DRUGS

For years now, the U.S. government has engaged in a highly publicized "war on drugs." Billions of dollars have been spent on trying to stop illegal drugs at the country's borders. In some sense, interdiction has succeeded: Federal agents have seized literally tons of cocaine and other drugs. Yet these efforts have made barely a dent in the flow of drugs to America's city streets. Simple economic reasoning explains why.

When drug interdiction works, it shifts the supply curve of drugs to the left, thereby driving up street prices. But that, in turn, raises the rewards for potential smugglers and attracts more criminals into the "industry," which shifts the supply curve back to the right. The net result is that increased shipments of drugs to U.S. shores replace much of what the authorities confiscate. This is why many economists believe that any successful antidrug program must concentrate on reducing demand, which would lower the street price of drugs, not on reducing supply, which can only raise it.

Some people suggest that the government should go even further and legalize many drugs. Although this idea remains a highly controversial position that few are ready to endorse, the reasoning behind it is straightforward. A stunningly high fraction of all the violent crimes committed in America—especially robberies and murders—are drug-

SOURCE: © AP Images/Angela Gaul

related. One major reason is that street prices of drugs are so high that addicts must steal to get the money, and drug traffickers are all too willing to kill to protect their highly profitable "businesses."

How would things differ if drugs were legal? Because South American farmers earn pennies for drugs that sell for hundreds of dollars on the streets of Los Angeles and New York, we may safely assume that legalized drugs would be vastly cheaper. In fact, according to one estimate, a dose of cocaine would cost less than 50 cents. That, proponents point out, would reduce drug-related crimes dramatically. When, for example, was the last time you heard of a gang killing connected with the distribution of cigarettes or alcoholic beverages?

The argument against legalization of drugs is largely moral: Should the state sanction potentially lethal substances? But there is an economic aspect to this position as well: The vastly lower street prices of drugs that would surely follow legalization would increase drug use. Thus, while legalization would almost certainly reduce crime, it may also produce more addicts. The key question here is, How many more addicts? (No one has a good answer.) If you think the increase in quantity demanded would be large, you are unlikely to find legalization an attractive option.

2. *An illegal, or "black" market often arises to supply the commodity.* Usually some individuals are willing to take the risks involved in meeting unsatisfied demands illegally. Example: Although most states ban the practice, ticket "scalping" (the sale of tickets at higher than regular prices) occurs at most popular sporting events and rock concerts.

3. *The prices charged on illegal markets are almost certainly higher than those that would prevail in free markets.* After all, lawbreakers expect some compensation for the risk of being caught and punished. Example: Illegal drugs are normally quite expensive. (See the accompanying Policy Debate box "Economic Aspects of the War on Drugs.")

4. A substantial portion of the price falls into the hands of the illicit supplier instead of going to those who produce the good or perform the service. Example: A constant complaint during the public hearings that marked the history of theater-ticket price controls in New York City was that the "ice" (the illegal excess charge) fell into the hands of ticket scalpers rather than going to those who invested in, produced, or acted in the play.

5. *Investment in the industry generally dries up.* Because price ceilings reduce the monetary returns that investors can legally earn, less money will be invested in industries that are subject to price controls. Even fear of impending price controls can have this effect. Example: Price controls on farm products in Zambia have prompted peasant farmers and large agricultural conglomerates alike to cut back production rather than grow crops at a loss. The result has been thousands of lost jobs and widespread food shortages.

Case Study: Rent Controls in New York City

These points and others are best illustrated by considering a concrete example involving price ceilings. New York is the only major city in the United States that has continuously legislated rent controls in much of its rental housing, since World War II. Rent controls, of course, are intended to protect the consumer from high rents. But most economists believe that rent control does not help the cities or their residents and that, in the long run, it leaves almost everyone worse off. Elementary supply-demand analysis shows us why.

Supply-Demand Diagram for Rental Housing

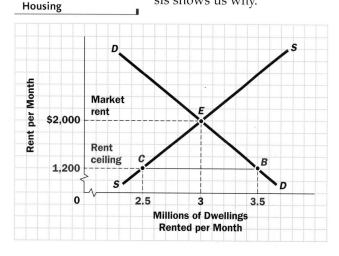

Figure 11 is a supply-demand diagram for rental units in New York. Curve *DD* is the demand curve and curve *SS* is the supply curve. Without controls, equilibrium would be at point *E*, where rents average $2,000 per month and 3 million housing units are occupied. If rent controls are effective, the ceiling price must be below the equilibrium price of $2,000. But with a low rent ceiling, such as $1,200, the quantity of housing demanded will be 3.5 million units (point *B*), whereas the quantity supplied will be only 2.5 million units (point *C*).

The diagram shows a shortage of 1 million apartments. This theoretical concept of a "shortage" manifests itself in New York City as an abnormally low vacancy rate, that is, a low share of unoccupied apartments available for rental—typically about half the national urban average. Naturally, rent controls have spawned a lively black market in New York. The black market raises the effective price of rent-controlled apartments in many ways, including bribes, so-called key money paid to move up on a waiting list, or the requirement that prospective tenants purchase worthless furniture at inflated prices.

According to Figure 11, rent controls reduce the quantity supplied from 3 million to 2.5 million apartments. How does this reduction show up in New York? First, some property owners, discouraged by the low rents, have converted apartment buildings into office space or other uses. Second, some apartments have been inadequately maintained. After all, rent controls create a shortage, which makes even dilapidated apartments easy to rent. Third, some landlords have actually abandoned their buildings rather than pay rising tax and fuel bills. These abandoned buildings rapidly become eyesores and eventually pose threats to public health and safety.

An important implication of these last observations is that rent controls—and price controls more generally—harm consumers in ways that offset part or all of the benefits to those who are fortunate enough to find and acquire at lower prices the product that the reduced prices has made scarce. Tenants must undergo long waits and undertake time-consuming searches to find an apartment, the apartment they obtain is likely to be poorly maintained or even decrepit, and normal landlord services are apt to disappear. Thus, even for the lucky beneficiaries, rent control is always far less of a bargain than the reduced monthly payments make them appear to be. The same problems generally apply with other forms of price control as well.

With all of these problems, why does rent control persist in New York City? And why do other cities sometimes move in the same direction?

Part of the explanation is that most people simply do not understand the problems that rent controls create. Another part is that landlords are unpopular politically. But a third, and very

"If you leave me, you know, you'll never see this kind of rent again."

important, part of the explanation is that not everyone is hurt by rent controls—and those who benefit from controls fight hard to preserve them. In New York, for example, many tenants pay rents that are only a fraction of what their apartments would fetch on the open market. They are, naturally enough, quite happy with this situation. This last point illustrates another very general phenomenon:

Virtually every price ceiling or floor creates a class of people that benefits from the regulations. These people use their political influence to protect their gains by preserving the status quo, which is one reason why it is so difficult to eliminate price ceilings or floors.

Restraining the Market Mechanism: Price Floors

Interferences with the market mechanism are not always designed to keep prices low. Agricultural price supports and minimum wage laws are two notable examples in which the law keeps prices *above* free-market levels. Such **price floors** are typically accompanied by a standard series of symptoms:

> A **price floor** is a legal minimum below which the price charged for a commodity is not permitted to fall.

1. *A surplus develops as sellers cannot find enough buyers.* Example: Surpluses of various agricultural products have been a persistent—and costly—problem for the U.S. government. The problem is even worse in the European Union (EU), where the common agricultural policy holds prices even higher. One source estimates that this policy accounts for half of all EU spending.[7]

2. *Where goods, rather than services, are involved, the surplus creates a problem of disposal.* Something must be done about the excess of quantity supplied over quantity demanded. Example: The U.S. government has often been forced to purchase, store, and then dispose of large amounts of surplus agricultural commodities.

3. *To get around the regulations, sellers may offer discounts in disguised—and often unwanted—forms.* Example: Back when airline fares were regulated by the government, airlines offered more and better food and more stylishly uniformed flight attendants instead of lowering fares. Today, the food is worse, but tickets cost much less.

4. *Regulations that keep prices artificially high encourage overinvestment in the industry.* Even inefficient businesses whose high operating costs would doom them in an unrestricted market can survive beneath the shelter of a generous price floor. Example: This is why the airline and trucking industries both went through painful "shakeouts" of the weaker companies in the 1980s, after they were deregulated and allowed to charge market-determined prices.

Once again, a specific example is useful for understanding how price floors work.

Case Study: Farm Price Supports and the Case of Sugar Prices

America's extensive program of farm price supports began in 1933 as a "temporary method of dealing with an emergency"—in the years of the Great Depression, farmers were going broke in droves. These price supports are still with us today, even though farmers account for less than 2 percent of the U.S. workforce.[8]

One of the consequences of these price supports has been the creation of unsellable surpluses—more output of crops such as grains than consumers were willing to buy at the inflated prices yielded by the supports. Warehouses were filled to overflowing. New storage facilities had to be built, and the government was forced to set up programs in

---

[7] *The Economist*, February 20, 1999.

[8] Under major legislation passed in 1996, many agricultural price supports were supposed to be phased out over a seven-year period. In reality, many support programs, especially that for sugar, have changed little.

which grain from the unmanageable surpluses was shipped to poor foreign countries to combat malnutrition and starvation in those nations. Realistically, if price supports are to be effective in keeping prices above the equilibrium level, then *someone* must be prepared to purchase the surpluses that invariably result. Otherwise, those surpluses will somehow find their way into the market and drive down prices, undermining the price support program. In the United States (and elsewhere), the buyer of the surpluses has usually turned out to be the government, which makes its purchases at the expense of taxpayers who are forced to pay twice—once through taxes to finance the government purchases and a second time in the form of higher prices for the farm products bought by the American public.

One of the more controversial farm price supports involves the U.S. sugar industry. Sugar producers receive low-interest loans from the federal government and a guarantee that the price of sugar will not fall below a certain level.

In a market economy such as that found in the United States, Congress cannot simply set prices by decree; rather, it must take some action to enforce the price floor. In the case of sugar, that "something" is limiting both domestic production and foreign imports, thereby shifting the supply curve inward to the left. Figure 12 shows the mechanics involved in this price floor. Government policies shift the supply curve inward from S_0S_0 to S_1S_1 and drive the U.S. price up from 25¢ to 50¢ per pound. The more the supply curve shifts inward, the higher the price.

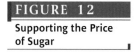

FIGURE 12

Supporting the Price of Sugar

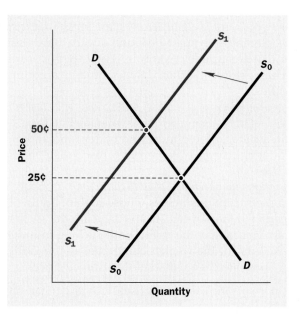

The sugar industry obviously benefits from the price-control program. But consumers pay for it in the form of higher prices for sugar and sugar-filled products such as soft drinks, candy bars, and cookies. Although estimates vary, the federal sugar price support program appears to cost consumers approximately $1.5 billion per year.

If all of this sounds a bit abstract to you, take a look at the ingredients in a U.S.-made soft drink. Instead of sugar, you will likely find "high-fructose corn syrup" listed as a sweetener. Foreign producers generally use sugar, but sugar is simply too expensive to be used for this purpose in the United States.

A Can of Worms

Our two case studies—rent controls and sugar price supports—illustrate some of the major side effects of price floors and ceilings but barely hint at others. Difficulties arise that we have not even mentioned, for the market mechanism is a tough bird that imposes suitable retribution on those who seek to evade it by government decree. Here is a partial list of other problems that may arise when prices are controlled.

Favoritism and Corruption   When price ceilings or floors create shortages or surpluses, someone must decide who gets to buy or sell the limited quantity that is available. This decision-making process can lead to discrimination along racial or religious lines, political favoritism, or corruption in government. For example, many prices were held at artificially low levels in the former Soviet Union, making queuing for certain goods quite common. Even so, Communist Party officials and other favored groups were somehow able to purchase the scarce commodities that others could not get.

Unenforceability   Attempts to limit prices are almost certain to fail in industries with numerous suppliers, simply because the regulating agency must monitor the behavior of so many sellers. People will usually find ways to evade or violate the law, and something like the free-market price will generally reappear. But there is an important difference: Because the evasion process, whatever its form, will have some operating costs, those costs must be borne by someone. Normally, that someone is the consumer, who must pay higher prices to the suppliers for taking the risk of breaking the law.

Auxiliary Restrictions   Fears that a system of price controls will break down invariably lead to regulations designed to shore up the shaky edifice. Consumers may be told when and from whom they are permitted to buy. The powers of the police and the courts may be used to prevent the entry of new suppliers. Occasionally, an intricate system of market subdivision is imposed, giving each class of firms a protected sphere in which others are not permitted to operate. For example, in New York City, there are laws banning conversion of rent-controlled apartments to condominiums.

Limitation of Volume of Transactions   To the extent that controls succeed in affecting prices, they can be expected to reduce the volume of transactions. Curiously, this is true regardless of whether the regulated price is above or below the free-market equilibrium price. If it is set above the equilibrium price, the quantity demanded will be below the equilibrium quantity. On the other hand, if the imposed price is set below the free-market level, the quantity supplied will be reduced. Because sales volume cannot exceed either the quantity supplied or the quantity demanded, a reduction in the volume of transactions is the result.[9]

Misallocation of Resources   Departures from free-market prices are likely to result in misuse of the economy's resources because the connection between production costs and prices is broken. For example, Russian farmers used to feed their farm animals bread instead of unprocessed grains because price ceilings kept the price of bread ludicrously low. In addition, just as more complex locks lead to more sophisticated burglary tools, more complex regulations lead to the use of yet more resources for their avoidance.

Economists put it this way: Free markets are capable of dealing efficiently with the three basic coordination tasks outlined in Chapter 3: deciding what to produce, how to produce it, and to whom the goods should be distributed. Price controls throw a monkey wrench into the market mechanism. Although the market is surely not flawless, and government interferences often have praiseworthy goals, good intentions are not enough. Any government that sets out to repair what it sees as a defect in the market mechanism runs the risk of causing even more serious damage elsewhere. As a prominent economist

---

[9] See Discussion Question 4 at the end of this chapter.

once quipped, societies that are too willing to interfere with the operation of free markets soon find that the invisible hand is nowhere to be seen.

A SIMPLE BUT POWERFUL LESSON

Astonishing as it may seem, many people in authority do not understand the law of supply and demand, or they act as if it does not exist. For example, a few years ago the *New York Times* carried a dramatic front-page picture of the president of Kenya setting fire to a large pile of elephant tusks that had been confiscated from poachers. The accompanying story explained that the burning was intended as a symbolic act to persuade the world to halt the ivory trade.[10] One may certainly doubt whether the burning really touched the hearts of criminal poachers, but one economic effect was clear: By reducing the supply of ivory on the world market, the burning of tusks forced up the price of ivory, which raised the illicit rewards reaped by those who slaughter elephants. That could only encourage more poaching—precisely the opposite of what the Kenyan government sought to accomplish.

| SUMMARY |

1. An attempt to use government regulations to force prices above or below their equilibrium levels is likely to lead to **shortages** or **surpluses,** to black markets in which goods are sold at illegal prices, and to a variety of other problems. The market always strikes back at attempts to repeal the law of supply and demand.

2. The quantity of a product that is demanded is not a fixed number. Rather, **quantity demanded** depends on such influences as the price of the product, consumer incomes, and the prices of other products.

3. The relationship between quantity demanded and price, holding all other things constant, can be displayed graphically on a **demand curve.**

4. For most products, the higher the price, the lower the quantity demanded. As a result, the demand curve usually has a negative slope.

5. The quantity of a product that is supplied depends on its price and many other influences. A **supply curve** is a graphical representation of the relationship between **quantity supplied** and price, holding all other influences constant.

6. For most products, supply curves have positive slopes, meaning that higher prices lead to supply of greater quantities.

7. A change in quantity demanded that is caused by a change in the price of the good is represented by a movement *along* a fixed demand curve. A change in quantity demanded that is caused by a change in any other determinant of quantity demanded is represented by a **shift of the demand curve.**

8. This same distinction applies to the supply curve: Changes in price lead to movements along a fixed supply curve; changes in other determinants of quantity supplied lead to shifts of the entire supply curve.

9. A market is said to be in **equilibrium** when quantity supplied is equal to quantity demanded. The equilibrium price and quantity are shown by the point on the supply-demand graph where the supply and demand curves intersect. The **law of supply and demand** states that price and quantity tend to gravitate to this point in a free market.

10. Changes in consumer incomes, tastes, technology, prices of competing products, and many other influences lead to shifts in either the demand curve or the supply curve and produce changes in price and quantity that can be determined from **supply-demand diagrams.**

11. A tax on a good generally leads to a rise in the price at which the taxed product is sold. The rise in price is generally less than the tax, so consumers usually pay less than the entire tax.

12. Consumers generally pay only part of a tax because the resulting rise in price leads them to buy less and the cut in the quantity they demand helps to force price down.

---

[10] *The New York Times,* July 19, 1989.

| KEY TERMS |

Invisible hand   56

Quantity demanded   57

Demand schedule   58

Demand curve   58

Shift in a demand curve   59

Quantity supplied   61

Supply schedule   61

Supply curve   62

Supply-demand diagram   64

Shortage   65

Surplus   65

Equilibrium   65

Law of supply and demand   66

Price ceiling   70

Price floor   73

| TEST YOURSELF |

1. What shapes would you expect for demand curves for the following:

   a. A medicine that means life or death for a patient

   b. French fries in a food court with kiosks offering many types of food

2. The following are the assumed supply and demand schedules for hamburgers in Collegetown:

Demand Schedule		Supply Schedule	
Price	Quantity Demanded per Year (thousands)	Price	Quantity Supplied per Year (thousands)
$2.75	14	$2.75	32
2.50	18	2.50	30
2.25	22	2.25	28
2.00	26	2.00	26
1.75	30	1.75	24
1.50	34	1.50	22

   a. Plot the supply and demand curves and indicate the equilibrium price and quantity.

   b. What effect would a decrease in the price of beef (a hamburger input) have on the equilibrium price and quantity of hamburgers, assuming all other things remained constant? Explain your answer with the help of a diagram.

   c. What effect would an increase in the price of pizza (a substitute commodity) have on the equilibrium price and quantity of hamburgers, assuming again that all other things remain constant? Use a diagram in your answer.

3. Suppose the supply and demand schedules for bicycles are as they appear below.

   a. Graph these curves and show the equilibrium price and quantity.

Price	Quantity Demanded per Year (millions)	Quantity Supplied per Year (millions)
$170	43	27
210	39	31
250	35	35
300	31	39
330	27	43
370	23	47

   b. Now suppose that it becomes unfashionable to ride a bicycle, so that the quantity demanded at each price falls by 9 million bikes per year. What is the new equilibrium price and quantity? Show this solution graphically. Explain why the quantity falls by less than 9 million bikes per year.

   c. Suppose instead that several major bicycle producers go out of business, thereby reducing the quantity supplied by 9 million bikes at every price. Find the new equilibrium price and quantity, and show it graphically. Explain again why quantity falls by less than 9 million.

   d. What are the equilibrium price and quantity if the shifts described in Test Yourself Questions 3(b) and 3(c) happen at the same time?

4. The following table summarizes information about the market for principles of economics textbooks:

Price	Quantity Demanded per Year	Quantity Supplied per Year
$45	4,300	300
55	2,300	700
65	1,300	1,300
75	800	2,100
85	650	3,100

   a. What is the market equilibrium price and quantity of textbooks?

b. To quell outrage over tuition increases, the college places a $55 limit on the price of textbooks. How many textbooks will be sold now?

c. While the price limit is still in effect, automated publishing increases the efficiency of textbook production. Show graphically the likely effect of this innovation on the market price and quantity.

5. How are the following demand curves likely to shift in response to the indicated changes?

a. The effect of a drought on the demand curve for umbrellas

b. The effect of higher popcorn prices on the demand curve for movie tickets

c. The effect on the demand curve for coffee of a decline in the price of Coca-Cola

6. The two accompanying diagrams show supply and demand curves for two substitute commodities: tapes and compact discs (CDs).

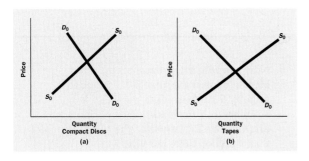

a. On the right-hand diagram, show what happens when rising raw material prices make it costlier to produce tapes.

b. On the left-hand diagram, show what happens to the market for CDs.

7. Consider the market for beef discussed in this chapter (Tables 1 through 4 and Figures 1 and 8). Suppose that the government decides to fight cholesterol by levying a tax of 50 cents per pound on sales of beef. Follow these steps to analyze the effects of the tax:

a. Construct the new supply schedule (to replace Table 2) that relates quantity supplied to the price that consumers pay.

b. Graph the new supply curve constructed in Test Yourself Question 7(a) on the supply-demand diagram depicted in Figure 7. What are the new equilibrium price and quantity?

c. Does the tax succeed in its goal of reducing the consumption of beef?

d. How much does the equilibrium price increase? Is the price rise greater than, equal to, or less than the 50 cent tax?

e. Who actually pays the tax, consumers or producers? (This may be a good question to discuss in class.)

8. **(More difficult)** The demand and supply curves for T-shirts in Touristtown, U.S.A., are given by the following equations:

$$Q = 24,000 - 500P \qquad Q = 6,000 + 1,000P$$

where P is measured in dollars and Q is the number of T-shirts sold per year.

a. Find the equilibrium price and quantity algebraically.

b. If tourists decide they do not really like T-shirts that much, which of the following might be the new demand curve?

$$Q = 21,000 - 500P \qquad Q = 27,000 - 500P$$

Find the equilibrium price and quantity after the shift of the demand curve.

c. If, instead, two new stores that sell T-shirts open up in town, which of the following might be the new supply curve?

$$Q = 4,000 + 1,000P \qquad Q = 9,000 + 1,000P$$

Find the equilibrium price and quantity after the shift of the supply curve.

| DISCUSSION QUESTIONS |

1. How often do you rent videos? Would you do so more often if a rental cost half as much? Distinguish between your demand curve for home videos and your "quantity demanded" at the current price.

2. Discuss the likely effects of the following:

a. Rent ceilings on the market for apartments

b. Floors under wheat prices on the market for wheat

Use supply-demand diagrams to show what may happen in each case.

3. U.S. government price supports for milk led to an unceasing surplus of milk. In an effort to reduce the surplus about a decade ago, Congress offered to pay dairy farmers to slaughter cows. Use two diagrams, one for the milk market and one for the meat market, to illustrate how this policy should have affected the price of meat. (Assume that meat is sold in an unregulated market.)

4. It is claimed in this chapter that either price floors or price ceilings reduce the actual quantity exchanged in a market. Use a diagram or diagrams to test this conclusion, and explain the common sense behind it.

5. The same rightward shift of the demand curve may produce a very small or a very large increase in quantity, depending on the slope of the supply curve. Explain this conclusion with diagrams.

6. In 1981, when regulations were holding the price of natural gas below its free-market level, then-Congressman Jack Kemp of New York said the following in an interview with the *New York Times*: "We need to decontrol natural gas, and get production of natural gas up to a higher level so we can bring down the price."[11] Evaluate the congressman's statement.

7. From 1990 to 1997 in the United States, the number of working men grew by 6.7 percent; the number of working women grew by 11 percent. During this time, average wages for men grew by 20 percent, while average wages for women grew by 25 percent. Which of the following two explanations seems more consistent with the data?

a. Women decided to work more, raising their relative supply (relative to men).

b. Discrimination against women declined, raising the relative (to men) demand for female workers.

[11] *The New York Times,* December 24, 1981.

THE MACROECONOMY:
AGGREGATE SUPPLY AND DEMAND

Macroeconomics is the headline-grabbing part of economics. When economic news appears on the front page of your daily newspaper or is reported on the nightly television news, you are most likely reading or hearing about some macroeconomic development in the national or world economy. The Federal Reserve has just cut interest rates. Inflation remains low. Jobs are scarce—or plentiful. The federal government's budget is in deficit. The euro is rising in value. These developments are all macroeconomic news. But what do they mean?

Part 2 begins your study of macroeconomics. It will first acquaint you with some of the major concepts of macroeconomics—things that you hear about every day, such as gross domestic product (GDP), inflation, unemployment, and economic growth (Chapters 5 and 6). Then it will introduce the basic theory that we use to interpret and understand macroeconomic events (Chapters 7 through 10). By the time you finish Chapter 10—which is only six chapters away—those newspaper articles will make a lot more sense.

CHAPTERS

AN INTRODUCTION TO MACROECONOMICS

Where the telescope ends, the microscope begins. Which of the two has the grander view?

VICTOR HUGO

By time-honored tradition, economics is divided into two fields: *microeconomics* and *macroeconomics*. These inelegant words are derived from the Greek, where *micro* means something small and *macro* means something large. Chapters 3 and 4 introduced you to microeconomics. This chapter does the same for macroeconomics.

How do the two branches of the discipline differ? It is *not* a matter of using different tools. As we shall see in this chapter, supply and demand provide the basic organizing framework for constructing macroeconomic models, just as they do for microeconomic models. Rather, the distinction is based on the issues addressed. For an example of a macroeconomic question, turn the page.

CONTENTS

The U.S. economy grew strongly from early 2003 to early 2006, at a compound annual growth rate of 3.5 percent. Then, starting in the second quarter of 2006, growth slowed down and averaged only 2.2 percent per annum over the ensuing seven quarters. Why was that?

There is, of course, no simple answer to this question. But beginning in this chapter and continuing throughout Parts 2 and 3, we will learn a great deal about the factors that make economic growth fluctuate from one year to the next. Among those factors, as we will see, are a number of government policies.

DRAWING A LINE BETWEEN MACROECONOMICS AND MICROECONOMICS

In microeconomics, the spotlight is on *how individual decision-making units behave.* For example, the dairy farmers of Chapter 4 are individual decision makers; so are the consumers who purchase the milk. How do they decide which actions are in their own best interests? How are these millions of decisions coordinated by the market mechanism, and with what consequences? Questions such as these lie at the heart of microeconomics.

Although Plato and Aristotle might wince at the abuse of their language, microeconomics applies to the decisions of some astonishingly large units. The annual sales of General Electric and General Motors, for example, exceed the total production of many nations. Yet someone who studies GE's pricing policies is a microeconomist, whereas someone who studies inflation in a small country like Monaco is a macroeconomist. The micro-macro distinction in economics is certainly not based solely on size.

What, then, is the basis for this long-standing distinction? The answer is that, whereas microeconomics focuses on the *decisions of individual units,* no matter how large, macroeconomics concentrates on *the behavior of entire economies,* no matter how small. Microeconomists might look at a single company's pricing and output decisions. Macroeconomists study the overall price level, unemployment rate, and other things that we call *economic aggregates.*

Aggregation and Macroeconomics

An "economic aggregate" is simply an *abstraction* that people use to describe some salient feature of economic life. For example, although we observe the prices of gasoline, telephone calls, and movie tickets every day, we never actually see "the price level." Yet many people—not just economists—find it meaningful to speak of "the cost of living." In fact, the government's attempts to measure it are widely publicized by the news media each month.

Among the most important of these abstract notions is the concept of *domestic product,* which represents the total production of a nation's economy. The process by which real objects such as software, baseballs, and theater tickets are combined into an abstraction called total domestic product is **aggregation,** and it is one of the foundations of macroeconomics. We can illustrate it by a simple example.

Aggregation means combining many individual markets into one overall market.

An imaginary nation called Agraria produces nothing but foodstuffs to sell to consumers. Rather than deal separately with the many markets for pizzas, candy bars, hamburgers, and so on, macroeconomists group them all into a single abstract "market for output." Thus, when macroeconomists announce that output in Agraria grew 10 percent last year, are they referring to more potatoes or hot dogs, more soybeans or green peppers? The answer is: They do not care. In the aggregate measures of macroeconomics, output is output, no matter what form it takes.

The Foundations of Aggregation

Amalgamating many markets into one means ignoring distinctions among different products. Can we really believe that no one cares whether the national output of Agraria consists of $800,000 worth of pickles and $200,000 worth of ravioli rather than $500,000 each of lettuce and tomatoes? Surely this is too much to swallow.

Macroeconomists certainly do not believe that no one cares; instead, they rest the case for aggregation on two foundations:

1. Although the *composition* of demand and supply in the various markets may be terribly important for *some* purposes (such as how income is distributed and the diets people enjoy), it may be of little consequence for the economy-wide issues of growth, inflation, and unemployment—the issues that concern macroeconomists.

2. During economic fluctuations, markets tend to move up or down together. When demand in the economy rises, there is more demand for potatoes *and* tomatoes, more demand for artichokes *and* pickles, more demand for ravioli *and* hot dogs.

Although there are exceptions to these two principles, both are serviceable enough as approximations. In fact, if they were not, there would be no discipline called macroeconomics, and a full-year course in economics could be reduced to a half-year. Lest this cause you a twinge of regret, bear in mind that many people believe that unemployment and inflation would be far more difficult to control without macroeconomics—which would be a lot worse.

The Line of Demarcation Revisited

These two principles—that the composition of demand and supply may not matter for some purposes, and that markets normally move together—enable us to draw a different kind of dividing line between microeconomics and macroeconomics.

In macroeconomics, we typically assume that most details of resource allocation and income distribution are relatively unimportant to the study of the overall rates of inflation and unemployment. In microeconomics, we generally ignore inflation, unemployment, and growth, focusing instead on how individual markets allocate resources and distribute income.

To use a well-worn metaphor, a macroeconomist analyzes the size of the proverbial economic "pie," paying scant attention to what is inside it or to how it gets divided among the dinner guests. A microeconomist, by contrast, assumes that the pie is of the right size and shape, and frets over its ingredients and who gets to eat it. If you have ever baked or eaten a pie, you will realize that either approach alone is a trifle myopic.

Economics is divided into macroeconomics and microeconomics largely for the sake of pedagogical clarity: We can't teach you everything at once. But in reality, the crucial interconnection between macroeconomics and microeconomics is with us all the time. There is, after all, only one economy.

SUPPLY AND DEMAND IN MACROECONOMICS

Whether you are taking a course that concentrates on macroeconomics or one that focuses on microeconomics, the discussion of supply and demand in Chapter 4 served as an invaluable introduction. Supply and demand analysis is just as fundamental to macroeconomics as it is to microeconomics.

A Quick Review

Figure 1 shows two diagrams that should look familiar from Chapter 4. In Figure 1(a), we find a downward-sloping demand curve, labeled *DD*, and an upward-sloping supply curve, labeled *SS*. Because the figure is a multipurpose diagram, the "Price" and "Quantity" axes do not specify any particular commodity. To start on familiar terrain, first imagine that this graph depicts the market for milk, so the vertical axis measures the price of milk and the horizontal axis measures the quantity of milk demanded and supplied. As we know, if nothing interferes with the operation of a free market, equilibrium will be at point *E* with a price P_0 and a quantity of output Q_0.

Next, suppose something happens to shift the demand curve outward. For example, we learned in Chapter 4 that an increase in consumer incomes might do that. Figure 1(b) shows this shift as a rightward movement of the demand curve from D_0D_0 to D_1D_1. Equilibrium shifts from point *E* to point *A*, so both price and output rise.

Moving to Macroeconomic Aggregates

The **aggregate demand curve** shows the quantity of domestic product that is demanded at each possible value of the price level.

The **aggregate supply curve** shows the quantity of domestic product that is supplied at each possible value of the price level.

Now let's switch from microeconomics to macroeconomics. To do so, we reinterpret Figure 1 as representing the market for an abstract object called "domestic product"—one of those economic aggregates that we described earlier. No one has ever seen, touched, or eaten a unit of domestic product, but these are the kinds of abstractions we use in macroeconomic analysis.

Consistent with this reinterpretation, think of the price measured on the vertical axis as being another abstraction—the overall price index, or "cost of living."[1] Then the curve DD in Figure 1(a) is called an **aggregate demand curve**, and the curve SS is called an **aggregate supply curve**. We will develop an economic theory to derive these curves explicitly in Chapters 7 through 10. As we will see there, the curves have rather different origins from the microeconomic counterparts we encountered in Chapter 4.

FIGURE 1

Two Interpretations of a Shift in the Demand Curve

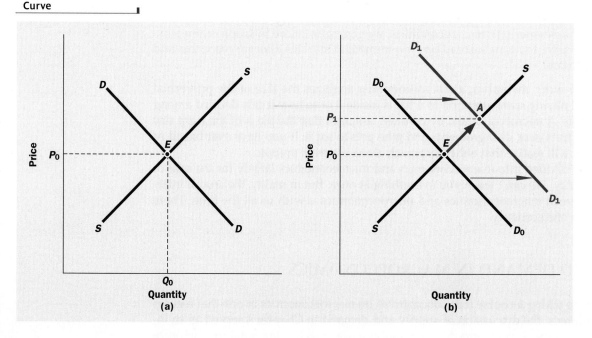

---

[1] The appendix to Chapter 6 explains how such price indexes are calculated.

Inflation

With this macroeconomic reinterpretation, Figure 1(b) depicts the problem of **inflation.** We see from the figure that the outward shift of the aggregate demand curve, whatever its cause, pushes the price level up. If aggregate demand keeps shifting out month after month, the economy will suffer from inflation—meaning a sustained increase in the general price level.

Inflation refers to a sustained increase in the general price level.

Recession and Unemployment

The second principal issue of macroeconomics, recession and unemployment, also can be illustrated on a supply-demand diagram, this time by shifting the demand curve in the opposite direction. Figure 2 repeats the supply and demand curves of Figure 1(a) and in addition depicts a leftward shift of the aggregate demand curve from $D_0 D_0$ to $D_2 D_2$. Equilibrium now moves from point E to point B so that domestic product (total output) declines. This is what we normally mean by a **recession**—a period of time during which production falls and people lose jobs.

A **recession** is a period of time during which the total output of the economy declines.

Economic Growth

Figure 3 illustrates macroeconomists' third area of concern: the process of economic growth. Here the original aggregate demand and supply curves are, once again, $D_0 D_0$ and $S_0 S_0$, which intersect at point E. But now we consider the possibility that both curves shift to the right over time, moving to $D_1 D_1$ and $S_1 S_1$, respectively. The new intersection point is C, and the brick-colored arrow running from point E to point C shows the economy's growth path. Over this period of time, domestic product grows from Q_0 to Q_1.

FIGURE 2

An Economy Slipping into a Recession

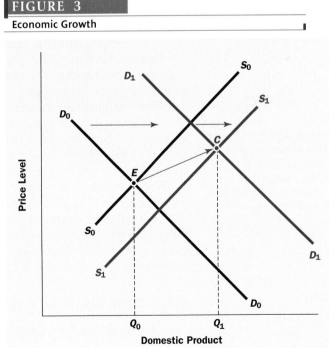

FIGURE 3

Economic Growth

GROSS DOMESTIC PRODUCT

Up to now, we have been somewhat cavalier in using the phrase "domestic product." Let's now get more specific. Of the various ways to measure an economy's total output,

Gross domestic product (GDP) is the sum of the money values of all final goods and services produced in the domestic economy and sold on organized markets during a specified period of time, usually a year.

the most popular choice by far is the **gross domestic product,** or **GDP** for short—a term you have probably encountered in the news media. GDP is the most comprehensive measure of the output of all the factories, offices, and shops in the United States. Specifically, it is the sum of the *money values* of all *final* goods and services *produced* in the *domestic* economy within the year.

Several features of this definition need to be underscored.[2] First, you will notice that

We add up the money values of things.

Money as the Measuring Rod: Real versus Nominal GDP

The GDP consists of a bewildering variety of goods and services: computer chips and potato chips, tanks and textbooks, ballet performances and rock concerts. How can we combine all of these into a single number? To an economist, there is a natural way to do so: First, convert every good and service into *money* terms, and then add all the money up. Thus, contrary to the cliché, we *can* add apples and oranges. To add 10 apples and 20 oranges, first ask: How much *money* does each cost? If apples cost 20 cents and oranges cost 25 cents, then the apples count for $2 and the oranges for $5, so the sum is $7 worth of "output." The market *price* of each good or service is used as an indicator of its *value* to society for a simple reason: *Someone* is willing to pay that much money for it.

Nominal GDP is calculated by valuing all outputs at current prices.

This decision raises the question of what prices to use in valuing different outputs. The official data offer two choices. Most obviously, we can value each good and service at the price at which it was actually sold. If we take this approach, the resulting measure is called **nominal GDP,** or *GDP in current dollars.* This seems like a perfectly sensible choice, but it has one serious drawback as a measure of output: Nominal GDP rises when prices rise, even if there is no increase in actual production. For example, if hamburgers cost $2.00 this year but cost only $1.50 last year, then 100 hamburgers will contribute $200 to this year's nominal GDP, whereas they contributed only $150 to last year's nominal GDP. But 100 hamburgers are still 100 hamburgers—output has not grown.

Real GDP is calculated by valuing outputs of different years at common prices. Therefore, real GDP is a far better measure than nominal GDP of changes in total production.

For this reason, government statisticians have devised alternative measures that correct for inflation by valuing goods and services produced in *different* years at the *same* set of prices. For example, if the hamburgers were valued at $1.50 each in both years, $150 worth of hamburger output would be included in GDP *in each year.* In practice, such calculations can be quite complicated, but the details need not worry us in an introductory course. Suffice it to say that, when the calculations are done, we obtain **real GDP** or *GDP in constant dollars.* The news media often refer to this measure as "GDP corrected for inflation." Throughout most of this book, and certainly whenever we are discussing the nation's output, we will be concerned with *real* GDP.

The distinction between nominal and real GDP leads us to a working definition of a *recession* as a period in which *real* GDP declines. For example, between the fourth quarter of 2000 and the third quarter of 2001, America's last recession, nominal GDP *rose* from $9,954 billion to $10,135 billion, but real GDP *fell* from $9,888 billion to $9,871 billion. In fact, it has become conventional to say that a recession occurs when real GDP declines for two or more consecutive quarters.

What Gets Counted in GDP?

The next important aspect of the definition of GDP is that

The GDP for a particular year includes only goods and services produced within the year. Sales of items produced in previous years are explicitly excluded.

---

[2] Certain exceptions to the definition are dealt with in the appendix to Chapter 8. Some instructors may prefer to take up that material here.

For example, suppose you buy a perfectly beautiful 1985 Thunderbird from a friend next week and are overjoyed by your purchase. The national income statistician will not share your glee. She counted that car in the GDP of 1985, when it was first produced and sold, and will never count it again. The same is true of houses. The resale values of houses do not count in GDP because they were counted in the years they were built.

Next, you will note from the definition of gross domestic product that

Only final goods and services count in the GDP.

The adjective *final* is the key word here. For example, when Dell buys computer chips from Intel, the transaction is not included in the GDP because Dell does not want the chips for itself. It buys them only to manufacture computers, which it sells to consumers. Only the computers are considered a final product. When Dell buys chips from Intel, economists consider the chips to be **intermediate goods.** The GDP excludes sales of intermediate goods and services because, if they were included, we would wind up counting the same outputs several times.[3] For example, if chips sold to computer manufacturers were included in GDP, we would count the same chip when it was sold to the computer maker and then again as a component of the computer when it was sold to a consumer.

Next, note that

The adjective *domestic* in the definition of GDP denotes production within the geographic boundaries of the United States.

Some Americans work abroad, and many American companies have offices or factories in foreign countries. For example, roughly half of IBM's employees work outside the United States. While all of these foreign employees of American firms produce valuable outputs, none of it counts in the GDP of the United States. (It counts, instead, in the GDPs of the other countries.) On the other hand, quite a few foreign companies produce goods and services in the United States. For example, if your family owns a Toyota or a Honda, it was most likely assembled in a factory here. All that activity of foreign firms on our soil does count in our GDP.[4]

Finally, the definition of GDP notes that

For the most part, only goods and services that pass through organized markets count in the GDP.

This restriction, of course, excludes many economic activities. For example, illegal activities are not included in the GDP. Thus, gambling services in Atlantic City are part of GDP, but gambling services in Chicago are not. Garage sales, although sometimes lucrative, are not included either. The definition reflects the statisticians' inability to measure the value of many of the economy's most important activities, such as housework, do-it-yourself repairs, and leisure time. These activities certainly result in currently produced goods or services, but they all lack that important measuring rod—a market price.

This omission results in certain oddities. For example, suppose that each of two neighboring families hires the other to clean house, generously paying $1,000 per week for the services. Each family can easily afford such generosity because it collects an identical salary from its neighbor. Nothing real has changed, but GDP goes up by $104,000 per year. If this example seems trivial, you may be interested to know that,

Final goods and services are those that are purchased by their ultimate users.

An **intermediate good** is a good purchased for resale or for use in producing another good.

SOURCE: From *The Wall Street Journal*— Permission, Cartoon Features Syndicate.

"More and more, I ask myself what's the point of pursuing the meaning of the universe if you can't have a rising GNP."

---

[3] Actually, there is another way to add up the GDP by counting a portion of each intermediate transaction. This is explained in the appendix to Chapter 8.

[4] There is another concept, called gross *national* product, which counts the goods and services produced by all Americans, regardless of where they work. For consistency, the outputs produced by foreigners working in the United States are not included in GNP. In practice, the two measures—GDP and GNP—are very close.

according to one estimate made some years ago, America's GDP might be a stunning 44 percent higher if unpaid housework were valued at market prices and counted in GDP.[5]

Limitations of the GDP: What GDP Is Not

Now that we have seen in some detail what the GDP *is*, let's examine what it *is not*. In particular:

Gross domestic product is not a measure of the nation's economic well-being.

The GDP is not intended to measure economic well-being and does not do so for several reasons.

Only Market Activity Is Included in GDP

As we have just seen, a great deal of work done in the home contributes to the nation's well-being but is not counted in GDP because it has no price tag. One important implication of this exclusion arises when we try to compare the GDPs of developed and less developed countries. Americans are always amazed to hear that the per-capita GDPs of the poorest African countries are less than $250 per year. Surely, no one could survive in America on $5 per week. How can Africans do it? Part of the answer, of course, is that these people are terribly poor. But another part of the answer is that

International GDP comparisons are vastly misleading when the two countries differ greatly in the fraction of economic activity that each conducts in organized markets.

This fraction is relatively large in the United States and relatively small in the poorest countries. So when we compare their respective measured GDPs, we are not comparing the same economic activities. Many things that get counted in the U.S. GDP are not counted in the GDPs of very poor nations because they do not pass through markets. It is ludicrous to think that these people, impoverished as they are, survive on what an American thinks of as $5 per week.

A second implication is that GDP statistics take no account of the so-called underground economy—a term that includes not just criminal activities, but also a great deal of legitimate business that is conducted in cash or by barter to escape the tax collector. Naturally, we have no good data on the size of the underground economy. Some observers, however, think that it may amount to 10 percent or more of U.S. GDP—and much more in some foreign countries.

GDP Places No Value on Leisure

As a country gets richer, its citizens normally take more and more leisure time. If that is true, a better measure of national well-being that includes the value of leisure would display faster growth than conventionally measured GDP. For example, the length of the typical workweek in the United States fell steadily for many decades, which meant that growth in GDP systematically *underestimated* the growth in national well-being. But then this trend stopped and may even have reversed. (See "Are Americans Working More?" on the next page.)

"Bads" as Well as "Goods" Get Counted in GDP

There are also reasons why the GDP *overstates* how well-off we are. Here is a tragic example. Disaster struck the United States on September 11, 2001. No one doubts that this made the nation worse off. Thousands of people were killed. Buildings and businesses were destroyed. Yet the disaster almost certainly raised GDP. The government spent more for disaster relief and cleanup, and later for reconstruction. Businesses spent more to rebuild and repair damaged buildings and replace lost items. Even consumers spent more on cleanup and replacing lost possessions. No one imagines that America was better off after 9/11, despite all this additional GDP.

---

[5] Ann Chadeau, "What Is Households' Non-Market Production Worth?" *OECD Economic Studies*, 18 (1992), pp. 85–103.

Are Americans Working More?

According to conventional wisdom, the workweek in the United States is steadily shrinking, leaving Americans with more and more leisure time to enjoy. But a 1991 book by economist Juliet Schor pointed out that this view was wrong: Americans were really working longer and longer hours. Her findings were both provocative and controversial at the time. But since then, the gap between the typical American and European workweeks has widened.

> In the last twenty years the amount of time Americans have spent at their jobs has risen steadily. . . . Americans report that they have only sixteen and a half hours of leisure a week, after the obligations of job and household are taken care of. . . . If present trends continue, by the end of the century Americans will be spending as much time at their jobs as they did back in the nineteen twenties.
>
> The rise in worktime was unexpected. For nearly a hundred years, hours had been declining. . . . Equally surprising, but also hardly recognized, has been the deviation from Western Europe. After progressing in tandem for nearly a century, the United States veered off into a trajectory of declining leisure, while in Europe work has been disappearing. . . . U.S. manufacturing employees currently work 320 more hours [per year]—the equivalent of over two months—than their counterparts in West Germany or France. . . . We have paid a price for prosperity. . . .

We are eating more, but we are burning up those calories at work. We have color televisions and compact disc players, but we need them to unwind after a stressful day at the office. We take vacations, but we work so hard throughout the year that they become indispensable to our sanity.

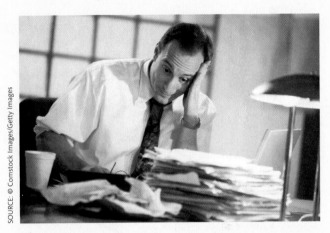

SOURCE: © Comstock Images/Getty Images

SOURCE: Juliet B. Schor, *The Overworked American* (New York: Basic Books; 1991), pp. 1–2, 10–11.

Wars represent an extreme example. Mobilization for a war fought on some other nation's soil normally causes a country's GDP to rise rapidly. But men and women serving in the military could be producing civilian output instead. Factories assigned to produce armaments could instead be making cars, washing machines, and televisions. A country at war is surely worse off than a country at peace, but this fact will not be reflected in its GDP.

Ecological Costs Are Not Netted Out of the GDP   Many productive activities of a modern industrial economy have undesirable side effects on the environment. Automobiles provide an essential means of transportation, but they also despoil the atmosphere. Factories pollute rivers and lakes while manufacturing valuable commodities. Almost everything seems to produce garbage, which creates serious disposal problems. None of these ecological costs are deducted from the GDP in an effort to give us a truer measure of the *net* increase in economic welfare that our economy produces. Is this omission foolish? Not if we remember that national income statisticians are trying to measure economic activity conducted through organized markets, not national welfare.

Now that we have defined several of the basic concepts of macroeconomics, let us breathe some life into them by perusing the economic history of the United States.

THE ECONOMY ON A ROLLER COASTER

Growth, but with Fluctuations

The most salient fact about the U.S. economy has been its seemingly limitless *growth;* it gets bigger almost every year. Nominal gross domestic product in 2007 was around $13.8 trillion, more than 27 times as much as in 1959. The black curve in Figure 4 shows

Nominal GDP, Real GDP, and Real GDP per Capita Since 1959

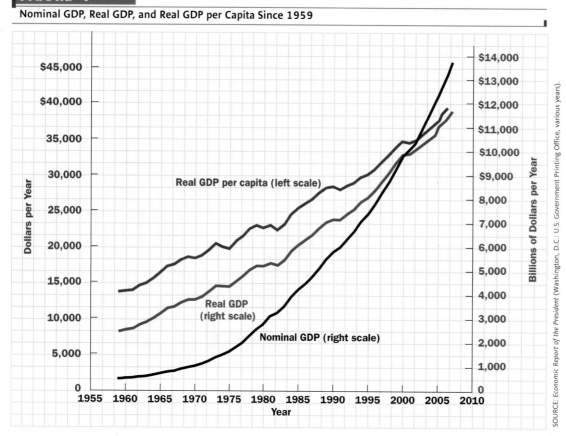

SOURCE: *Economic Report of the President* (Washington, D.C.: U.S. Government Printing Office, various years).

NOTE: Real GDP figures are in 2000 dollars.

that extraordinary upward march. But, as the discussion of nominal versus real GDP suggests, a large part of this apparent growth was simply inflation. Because of higher prices, the *purchasing power* of each 2007 dollar was less than one-fifth of each 1959 dollar. Corrected for inflation, we see that *real GDP* (the blue curve in the figure) was only about 4¾ times greater in 2007 than in 1959.

Another reason for the growth of GDP is population growth. A nation becomes richer only if its GDP grows *faster* than its population. To see how much richer the United States has actually become since 1959, we must divide real GDP by the size of the population to obtain **real GDP per capita**—which is the brick-colored line in Figure 4. It turns out that real output per person in 2007 was roughly 2.8 times as much as in 1959. That is still not a bad performance.

Real GDP per capita is the ratio of real GDP divided by population.

If aggregate supply and demand grew smoothly from one year to the next, as was depicted in Figure 3, the economy would expand at some steady rate. But U.S. economic history displays a far less regular pattern—one of alternating periods of rapid and slow growth that are called *macroeconomic fluctuations,* or sometimes just *business cycles.* In some years—five since 1959, to be exact—real GDP actually declined.[6] Such *recessions,* and their attendant problem of rising unemployment, have been a persistent feature of American economic performance—one to which we will pay much attention in the coming chapters.

The bumps encountered along the American economy's historic growth path stand out more clearly in Figure 5, which displays the same data in a different way and extends the time period back to 1870. Here we plot not the *level* of real GDP each year, but, rather, its *growth rate*—the percentage change from one year to the next. Now the booms and busts that delight and distress people—and swing elections—stand out clearly. For example, the

---

[6] The 2001 recession was so mild that real GDP for the full year 2001 was actually higher than in 2000.

FIGURE 5

The Growth Rate of U.S. Real Gross Domestic Product since 1870

SOURCE: Constructed by the authors from Commerce Department data since 1929. Data for 1869–1928 are based on research by Professor Christina Romer.

fact that real GDP grew by over 7 percent from 1983 to 1984 helped ensure Ronald Reagan's landslide reelection. Then, from 1990 to 1991, real GDP actually fell by 1 percent, which helped Bill Clinton defeat George H. W. Bush. On the other hand, weak economic growth from 2000 to 2004 did not prevent George W. Bush's reelection.

Inflation and Deflation

The history of the inflation rate depicted in Figure 6 also shows more positive numbers than negative ones—more inflation than **deflation.** Although the price level has risen roughly 16-fold since 1869, the upward trend is of rather recent vintage. Prior to World

Deflation refers to a sustained decrease in the general price level.

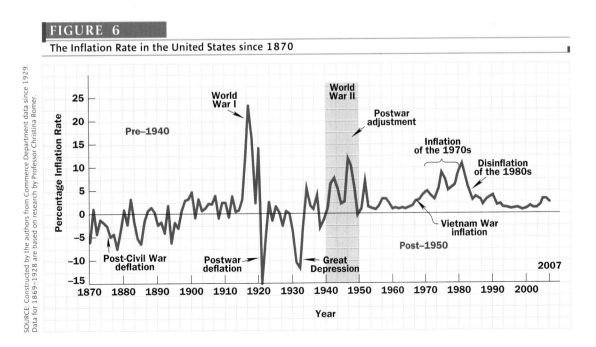

FIGURE 6

The Inflation Rate in the United States since 1870

SOURCE: Constructed by the authors from Commerce Department data since 1929. Data for 1869–1928 are based on research by Professor Christina Romer.

War II, Figure 6 shows periods of inflation and deflation, with little or no tendency for one to be more common than the other. Indeed, prices in 1940 were barely higher than those at the close of the Civil War. However, the figure does show some large gyrations in the inflation rate, including sharp bursts of inflation during and immediately after the two world wars and dramatic deflations in the 1870s, the 1880s, 1921–1922, and 1929–1933. Recently, as you can see, inflation has been both low and stable.

In sum, although both real GDP, which measures the economy's output, and the price level have grown a great deal over the past 138 years, neither has grown smoothly. The ups and downs of both real growth and inflation are important economic events that need to be explained. The remainder of Part 2, which develops a model of aggregate supply and demand, and Part 3, which explains the tools the government uses to try to manage aggregate demand, will build a macroeconomic theory designed to do precisely that.

The Great Depression

As you look at these graphs, the Great Depression of the 1930s is bound to catch your eye. The decline in economic activity from 1929 to 1933 indicated in Figure 5 was the most severe in our nation's history, and the rapid deflation in Figure 6 was extremely unusual. The Depression is but a dim memory now, but those who lived through it—including some of your grandparents—will never forget it.

Human Consequences   Statistics often conceal the human consequences and drama of economic events. But in the case of the Great Depression, they stand as bitter testimony to its severity. The production of goods and services dropped an astonishing 30 percent, business investment almost dried up entirely, and the unemployment rate rose ominously from about 3 percent in 1929 to 25 percent in 1933—one person in four was jobless! From the data alone, you can conjure up pictures of soup lines, beggars on street corners, closed factories, and homeless families. (See "Life in 'Hooverville.'")

Life in "Hooverville"

During the worst years of the Great Depression, unemployed workers congregated in shantytowns on the outskirts of many major cities. With a heavy dose of irony, these communities were known as "Hoovervilles," in honor of the then-president of the United States, Herbert Hoover. A contemporary observer described a Hooverville in New York City as follows:

> It was a fairly popular "development" made up of a hundred or so dwellings, each the size of a dog house or chickencoop, often constructed with much ingenuity out of wooden boxes, metal cans, strips of cardboard or old tar paper. Here human beings lived on the margin of civilization by foraging for garbage, junk, and waste lumber. I found some . . . picking through heaps of rubbish they had gathered before their doorways or cooking over open fires or battered oilstoves. Still others spent their days improving their rent-free homes . . . Most of them, according to the police, lived by begging or trading in junk; when all else failed they ate at the soup kitchens or public canteens. . . . They lived in fear of being forcibly removed by the authorities, though the neighborhood people in many cases helped them and the police tolerated them for the time being.

SOURCE: © American Stock/Hulton Archive/Getty Images

SOURCE: Mathew Josephson, *Infidel in the Temple* (New York: Knopf, 1967), pp. 82–83.

The Great Depression was a worldwide event; no country was spared its ravages. It literally changed the histories of many nations. In Germany, it facilitated the ascendancy of Nazism. In the United States, it enabled Franklin Roosevelt to engineer one of the most dramatic political realignments in our history and to push through a host of political and economic reforms.

A Revolution in Economic Thought   The worldwide depression also caused a much-needed revolution in economic thinking. Until the 1930s, the prevailing economic theory held that a capitalist economy occasionally misbehaved but had a natural tendency to cure recessions or inflations by itself. The roller coaster bounced around but did not run off the tracks. But the stubbornness of the Great Depression shook almost everyone's faith in the ability of the economy to correct itself. In England, this questioning attitude led John Maynard Keynes, one of the world's most renowned economists, to write *The General Theory of Employment, Interest, and Money* (1936). Probably the most important economics book of the twentieth century, it carried a message that was considered revolutionary at the time. Keynes rejected the idea that the economy naturally gravitated toward smooth growth and high levels of employment, asserting instead that if pessimism led businesses and consumers to curtail their spending, the economy might be condemned to years of stagnation.

In terms of our simple aggregate demand–aggregate supply framework, Keynes was suggesting that there were times when the aggregate demand curve shifted inward—as depicted in Figure 2 on page 87. As that figure showed, the consequence would be declining output and deflation. This doleful prognosis sounded all too realistic at the time. But Keynes closed his book on a hopeful note by showing how certain government actions—the things we now call monetary and fiscal policy—might prod the economy out of a depressed state. The lessons he taught the world then are among the lessons we will be learning in the rest of Part 2 and in Part 3—along with many qualifications that economists have learned since 1936. These lessons show how governments can manage their economies so that recessions will not turn into depressions and depressions will not last as long as the Great Depression, but they also show why this is not an easy task.

While Keynes was working on *The General Theory*, he wrote his friend George Bernard Shaw that "I believe myself to be writing a book on economic theory which will largely revolutionize . . . the way the world thinks about economic problems." In many ways, he was right.

SOURCE: © Pictorial Press Ltd/Alamy

John Maynard Keynes

From World War II to 1973

The Great Depression finally ended when the United States mobilized for war in the early 1940s. As government spending rose to extraordinarily high levels, it gave aggregate demand a big boost. Thus, **fiscal policy** was (accidentally) being used in a big way. The economy boomed, and the unemployment rate fell as low as 1.2 percent during the war.

Figure 1(b) on page 86 suggested that spending spurts such as this one should lead to inflation. But much of the potential inflation during World War II was contained by price controls. With prices held below the levels at which quantity supplied equaled quantity demanded, shortages of consumer goods were common. Sugar, butter, gasoline, cloth, and a host of other goods were strictly rationed. When controls were lifted after the war, prices shot up.

A period of strong growth marred by several recessions after the war then gave way to the fabulous 1960s, a period of unprecedented—and noninflationary—growth that was credited to the success of the economic policies that Keynes had prescribed in the 1930s. For a while, it looked as if we could avoid both unemployment and inflation, as aggregate demand and aggregate supply expanded in approximate balance. But the optimistic verdicts proved premature on both counts.

The government's **fiscal policy** is its plan for spending and taxation. It can be used to steer aggregate demand in the desired direction.

Inflation came first, beginning about 1966. Its major cause, as it had been so many times in the past, was high levels of wartime spending. The Vietnam War pushed aggregate demand up too fast. Later, unemployment also rose when the economy ground to a halt in 1969. Despite a short and mild recession, inflation continued at 5 to 6 percent per year. Faced with persistent inflation, President Richard Nixon stunned the nation by instituting wage and price controls in 1971, the first time this tactic had ever been employed in peacetime. The controls program held inflation in check for a while. But inflation worsened dramatically in 1973, mainly because of an explosion in food prices caused by poor harvests around the world.

The Great Stagflation, 1973–1980

In 1973 things began to get much worse, not only for the United States but for all oil-importing nations. A war between Israel and the Arab nations precipitated a quadrupling of oil prices by the Organization of Petroleum Exporting Countries (OPEC). At the same time, continued poor harvests in many parts of the globe pushed world food prices higher. Prices of other raw materials also skyrocketed. By unhappy coincidence, these events came just as the Nixon administration was lifting wage and price controls. Just as had happened after World War II, the elimination of controls led to a temporary acceleration of inflation as prices that had been held artificially low were allowed to rise. For all these reasons, the inflation rate in the United States soared above 12 percent during 1974.

Meanwhile, the U.S. economy was slipping into what was, up to then, its longest and most severe recession since the 1930s. Real GDP fell between late 1973 and early 1975, and the unemployment rate rose to nearly 9 percent. With both inflation and unemployment unusually virulent in 1974 and 1975, the press coined a new term—**stagflation**—to refer to the simultaneous occurrence of economic *stag*nation and rapid in*flation*. Conceptually, what was happening in this episode is that the economy's aggregate *supply* curve, which normally moves outward from one year to the next, shifted *inward* instead. When this happens, the economy moves from a point like *E* to a point like *A* in Figure 7. Real GDP declines as the price level rises.

Thanks to a combination of government actions and natural economic forces, the economy recovered. Unfortunately, stagflation came roaring back in 1979 when the price of oil soared again. This time, inflation hit the astonishing rate of 16 percent in the first half of 1980, and the economy sagged.

Stagflation is inflation that occurs while the economy is growing slowly ("stagnating") or in a recession.

The Effects of an Adverse Supply Shift

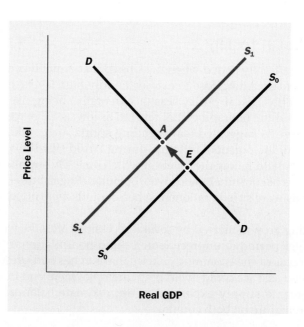

Reaganomics and Its Aftermath

Recovery was under way when President Ronald Reagan assumed office in January 1981, but high inflation seemed deeply ingrained. The new president promised to change things with a package of policies—mainly large tax cuts—that, he claimed, would both boost growth and reduce inflation.

However, the Federal Reserve under Paul Volcker was already deploying **monetary policy** to fight inflation—which meant using excruciatingly high interest rates to deter spending. So while inflation did fall, the economy also slumped—into its worst recession since the Great Depression. When the 1981–1982 recession hit bottom, the unemployment rate was approaching 11 percent, the financial markets were in disarray, and the word *depression* had reentered the American vocabulary. The U.S. government also acquired chronically large budget deficits, far larger than anyone had dreamed possible only a few years before. This problem remained with us for about 15 years.

> **Monetary policy** refers to actions taken by the Federal Reserve to influence aggregate demand by changing interest rates.

The recovery that began in the winter of 1982–1983 proved to be vigorous and long lasting. Unemployment fell more or less steadily for about six years, eventually dropping below 5.5 percent. Meanwhile, inflation remained tame. These developments provided an ideal economic platform on which George H. W. Bush ran to succeed Reagan—and to continue his policies.

But, unfortunately for the first President Bush, the good times did not keep rolling. Shortly after he took office, inflation began to accelerate a bit, and Congress enacted a deficit-reduction package (including a tax increase) not entirely to the president's liking. Then, in mid-1990, the U.S. economy slumped into another recession—precipitated by yet another spike in oil prices before the Persian Gulf War. When the recovery from the 1990–1991 recession proved to be sluggish, candidate Bill Clinton hammered away at the lackluster economic performance of the Bush years. His message apparently resonated with American voters.

Clintonomics: Deficit Reduction and the "New Economy"[7]

Although candidate Clinton ran on a platform that concentrated on spurring economic growth, the yawning budget deficit forced President Clinton to concentrate on deficit reduction instead. A politically contentious package of tax increases and spending cuts barely squeaked through Congress in August 1993, and a second deficit-reduction package passed in 1997. Transforming the huge federal budget deficit into a large surplus turned out to be the crowning achievement of Clinton's economic policy.

Whether by cause or coincidence, the national economy boomed during President Clinton's eight years in office. Business spending perked up, the stock market soared, unemployment fell rapidly, and even inflation drifted lower. Why did all these wonderful things happen at once? Some optimists heralded the arrival of an exciting "New Economy"—a product of globalization and computerization—that naturally performs better than the economy of the past.

The new economy was certainly an alluring vision. But was it real? Most mainstream economists would answer: yes and no. On the one hand, advances in computer and information technology did seem to lead to faster growth in the second half of the 1990s. In that respect, we did get a "New Economy." But something more mundane also happened: A variety of transitory factors pushed the economy's aggregate supply curve outward at an unusually rapid pace between 1996 and 1998. When this happens, the expected result is faster economic growth and lower inflation, as Figure 8 shows.

---

[7] One of the authors of this book was a member of President Clinton's original Council of Economic Advisers.

FIGURE 8

The Effects of a
Favorable Supply Shift

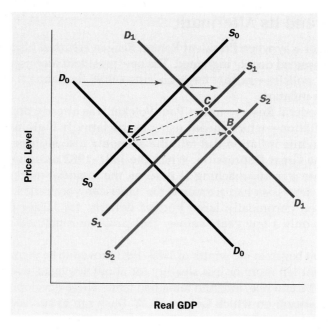

Figure 8 takes the graphical analysis of economic growth from Figure 3 and adds a new aggregate supply curve, S_2S_2, which lies to the right of S_1S_1. With supply curve S_2S_2 instead of S_1S_1, the economy moves from point E not just to point C, as in the earlier figure, but all the way to point B. Comparing B to C, we see that the economy winds up both farther to the right (that is, it grows faster) and lower (that is, it experiences less inflation). That, in a nutshell, is how our simple aggregate demand–aggregate supply framework explains this episode of recent U.S. economic history.

Tax Cuts and the Bush Economy

The Clinton boom ended around the middle of 2000—just before the election of President George W. Bush. Real GDP grew very slowly in the second half of 2000 and then actually *declined* in two quarters of 2001, marking the first recession in the United States in 10 years.

The tax cut of 2001 turned out to be remarkably well timed, however, and the war on terrorism led to a burst of government spending. Both of these components of fiscal policy helped shift the aggregate demand curve outward, thereby mitigating the recession. (Refer back to Figure 1(b) on page 86.) The Federal Reserve also lowered interest rates to encourage more spending. The recession ended late in 2001. But the recovery was extremely weak until the spring of 2003, when growth finally picked up—remaining strong through 2006 before slowing a bit late in 2007 and into 2008. The tax cuts of 2001–2003, while giving the economy a boost, also brought back large budget deficits.

ISSUE REVISITED: WHY DID THE ECONOMY SLOW DOWN?

At the start of this chapter, we asked why U.S. economic growth weakened after early 2006. The analysis in the chapter suggests that we should look for a slowdown in aggregate demand to find the answer. And, indeed, there was one—some (but not all) of it made in Washington. Why did policy makers do this? Worried about inflation, the Federal Reserve started raising interest rates in the middle of 2005. Tax cutting, which had helped propel the economy in the years 2002–2004 also petered out, partly because policy makers became worried about large budget deficits. In addition, the nation's spending on housing began to sag as the so-called housing bubble burst. Each of these factors restrained the growth of aggregate demand, as compared to 2003–2005, and therefore the growth of real GDP.

THE PROBLEM OF MACROECONOMIC STABILIZATION: A SNEAK PREVIEW

This brief look at the historical record shows that our economy has not generally produced steady growth without inflation. Rather, it has been buffeted by periodic bouts of unemployment or inflation, and sometimes it has been plagued by both. We have also hinted that government policies may have had something to do with this performance. Let us now expand upon and systematize this hint.

To provide a preliminary analysis of **stabilization policy,** the name given to government programs designed to shorten recessions and to counteract inflation, we can once again use the basic tools of aggregate supply and demand analysis. To facilitate this discussion, we have reproduced as Figures 9 and 10 two diagrams found earlier in this chapter, but we now give them slightly different interpretations.

> **Stabilization policy** is the name given to government programs designed to prevent or shorten recessions and to counteract inflation (that is, to *stabilize* prices).

Combating Unemployment

Figure 9 offers a simplified view of government policy to fight unemployment. Suppose that in the absence of government intervention, the economy would reach an equilibrium at point E, where the aggregate demand curve D_0D_0 crosses the aggregate supply curve SS. Now if the output corresponding to point E is too low, leaving many workers unemployed, *the government can reduce unemployment by increasing aggregate demand*. Subsequent chapters will consider in detail how this is done. But our brief historical review has already mentioned three methods: Congress can spend more or reduce taxes ("fiscal

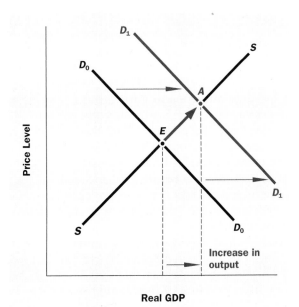

FIGURE 9

Stabilization Policy to Fight Unemployment

policy"), as it recently did with the 2008 "stimulus" bill; or the Federal Reserve can lower interest rates ("monetary policy"), as it also did in late 2007 and early 2008. In the diagram, any of these actions would shift the demand curve outward to D_1D_1, causing equilibrium to move to point A. In general:

> **Recessions and unemployment are often caused by insufficient aggregate demand. When such situations occur, fiscal or monetary policies that successfully augment demand can be effective ways to increase output and reduce unemployment. But they also normally raise prices.**

Combating Inflation

The opposite type of demand management is called for when inflation is the main macroeconomic problem. Figure 10 illustrates this case. Here again, point E, the intersection of aggregate demand curve D_0D_0 and aggregate supply curve SS, is the equilibrium the economy would reach in the absence of government policy. But now suppose the price level corresponding to point E is considered "too high," meaning that the price level would be rising too rapidly if the economy were to move to point E. Government policies that reduce demand from D_0D_0 to D_2D_2 can keep prices down and thereby reduce inflation. Some examples are reducing government spending or raising taxes, as done by the Clinton administration in the 1990s, or raising interest rates, which the Federal Reserve did in 2005–2006. Thus:

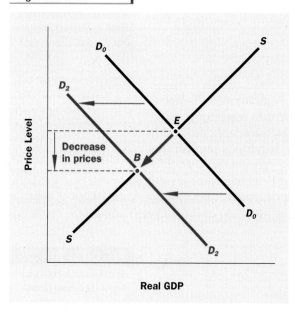

FIGURE 10

Stabilization Policy to Fight Inflation

> **Inflation is frequently caused by aggregate demand racing ahead too fast. When this is the case, fiscal or monetary policies that reduce aggregate demand can be effective anti-inflationary devices. But such policies also decrease real GDP and raise unemployment.**

This, in brief, summarizes the *intent* of stabilization policy. When aggregate demand fluctuations are the source of economic instability, the government can limit both recessions and inflations by pushing aggregate demand ahead when it would otherwise lag and restraining it when it would otherwise grow too quickly.

Does It Really Work?

Can the government actually stabilize the economy, as these simple diagrams suggest? That is a matter of some debate—a debate that is important enough to constitute one of our *Ideas for Beyond the Final Exam.*

We will deal with the pros and cons in Part 3. But a look back at Figures 5 and 6 (page 93) may be instructive right now. First, cover the portions of the two figures that deal with the period after 1940, the portions from the shaded area rightward in each figure. The picture that emerges for the 1870–1940 period is that of an economy with frequent and sometimes quite pronounced fluctuations.

Now do the reverse. Cover the data before 1950 and look only at the postwar period. There is indeed a difference. Instances of negative real GDP growth are less common and business fluctuations look less severe. Although government policies have not achieved perfection, things do look much better.

When we turn to inflation, however, matters look rather worse. Gone are the periods of deflation and price stability that occurred before World War II. Prices now seem only to rise. This quick tour through the data suggests that something *has* changed. The U.S. economy behaved differently from 1950 to 2007 than it did from 1870 to 1940.

Although controversy over this point continues, many economists attribute this shift in the economy's behavior to lessons the government has learned about managing the economy—lessons you will be learning in the next Part of this book. When you look at the prewar data, you see the fluctuations of an unmanaged economy that went through booms and recessions for "natural" economic reasons. The government did little about either. When you examine the postwar data, on the other hand, you see an economy that has been increasingly managed by government policy—sometimes successfully and sometimes unsuccessfully. Although the recessions are less severe, this improvement has come at a cost: The economy appears to be more inflation-prone than it was in the more distant past. These two changes in our economy may be connected. But to understand why, we will have to provide some relevant economic theory.

IDEAS FOR
BEYOND THE
FINAL EXAM

We have, in a sense, spent much of this chapter running before we have learned to walk—that is, we have been using aggregate demand and aggregate supply curves extensively before developing the theory that underlies them. That is the task before us in the rest of Part 2.

| SUMMARY |

1. Microeconomics studies the decisions of individuals and firms, the ways in which these decisions interact, and their influence on the allocation of a nation's resources and the distribution of income. Macroeconomics looks at how entire economies behave and studies the pressing social problems of economic growth, inflation, and unemployment.

2. Although they focus on different subjects, microeconomics and macroeconomics rely on virtually identical tools. Both use the supply-and-demand analysis introduced in Chapter 4.

3. Macroeconomic models use abstract concepts like "the price level" and "gross domestic product" that are derived by combining many different markets into one. This process is known as **aggregation;** it should not be taken literally but rather viewed as a useful approximation.

4. The best specific measure of the nation's economic output is **gross domestic product (GDP),** which is obtained by adding up the money values of all **final goods and services** produced in a given year. These outputs can be evaluated at current market prices (to get **nominal GDP**) or at some fixed set of prices (to get **real GDP**). Neither **intermediate goods** nor transactions that take place outside organized markets are included in GDP.

5. GDP measures an economy's production, not the increase in its well-being. For example, the GDP places no value on housework, other do-it-yourself activities, or leisure time. On the other hand, even commodities that might be considered as "bads" rather than "goods" are counted in the GDP (for example, activities that harm the environment).

6. America's economic history shows steady growth punctuated by periodic **recessions**—that is, periods in which real GDP declined. Although the distant past included some periods of falling prices **(deflation),** more recent history shows only rising prices **(inflation).**

7. The Great Depression of the 1930s was the worst in U.S. history. It profoundly affected both our nation and countries throughout the world. It also led to a revolution in economic thinking, thanks largely to the work of John Maynard Keynes.

8. From World War II to the early 1970s, the American economy exhibited steadier growth than in the past. Many observers attributed this more stable performance to the implementation of the **monetary and fiscal policies** (collectively called **stabilization policy**) that Keynes had suggested. At the same time, however, the price level seems only to rise—never to fall—in the modern economy. The economy seems to have become more "inflation-prone."

9. Between 1973 and 1991, the U.S. economy suffered through several serious recessions. In the first part of that period, inflation was also unusually virulent. This unhappy combination of economic stagnation with rapid inflation was nicknamed **"stagflation."** Since 1982, however, inflation has been low.

10. The United States enjoyed a boom in the 1990s, and unemployment fell to its lowest level in 30 years. Yet inflation also fell. One explanation for this happy combination of rapid growth and low inflation is that the **aggregate supply curve** shifted out unusually rapidly.

11. One major cause of inflation is that aggregate demand may grow more quickly than does aggregate supply. In such a case, a government policy that reduces aggregate demand may be able to stem the inflation.

12. Recessions often occur because aggregate demand grows too slowly. In this case, a government policy that stimulates demand may be an effective way to fight the recession.

| KEY TERMS |

Aggregation   84

Aggregate demand curve   86

Aggregate supply curve   86

Inflation   87

Recession   87

Gross domestic product (GDP)   88

Nominal GDP   88

Real GDP   88

Final goods and services   89

Intermediate good   89

Real GDP per capita   92

Deflation   93

Fiscal policy   95

Stagflation   96

Monetary policy   97

Stabilization policy   99

| TEST YOURSELF |

1. Which of the following problems are likely to be studied by a microeconomist and which by a macroeconomist?

   a. The rapid growth of Google

   b. Why unemployment in the United States fell from 2003 to 2006

   c. Why Japan's economy grew faster than the U.S. economy in the 1980s, but slower in the 2000s

   d. Why college tuition costs have risen so rapidly in recent years

2. Use an aggregate supply-and-demand diagram to study what would happen to an economy in which the aggregate supply curve never moved while the aggregate demand curve shifted outward year after year.

3. Which of the following transactions are included in gross domestic product, and by how much does each raise GDP?

   a. Smith pays a carpenter $50,000 to build a garage.

   b. Smith purchases $10,000 worth of materials and builds himself a garage, which is worth $50,000.

   c. Smith goes to the woods, cuts down a tree, and uses the wood to build himself a garage that is worth $50,000.

   d. The Jones family sells its old house to the Reynolds family for $400,000. The Joneses then buy a newly constructed house from a builder for $500,000.

   e. You purchase a used computer from a friend for $200.

   f. Your university purchases a new mainframe computer from IBM, paying $25,000.

   g. You win $100 in an Atlantic City casino.

   h. You make $100 in the stock market.

   i. You sell a used economics textbook to your college bookstore for $60.

   j. You buy a new economics textbook from your college bookstore for $100.

| DISCUSSION QUESTIONS |

1. You probably use "aggregates" frequently in everyday discussions. Try to think of some examples. (Here is one: Have you ever said, "The students at this college generally think . . ."? What, precisely, did you mean?)

2. Try asking a friend who has not studied economics in which year he or she thinks prices were higher: 1870 or 1900? 1920 or 1940? (In both cases, prices were higher in the earlier year.) Most young people think that prices have always risen. Why do you think they have this opinion?

3. Give some reasons why gross domestic product is not a suitable measure of the well-being of the nation. (Have you noticed newspaper accounts in which journalists seem to use GDP for this purpose?)

THE GOALS OF MACROECONOMIC POLICY

When men are employed, they are best contented.

BENJAMIN FRANKLIN

Inflation is repudiation.

CALVIN COOLIDGE

Someone once quipped that you could turn a parrot into an economist by teaching him just two words: supply and demand. And now that you have been through Chapter 4 and Chapter 5, you see what he meant. Sure enough, economists think of the process of economic growth as having two essential ingredients:

- The first ingredient is *aggregate supply*. Given the available supplies of **inputs** like labor and capital, and the technology at its disposal, an economy is able to produce a certain volume of **outputs,** measured by GDP. This capacity to produce normally increases from one year to the next as the supplies of inputs grow and the technology improves. The theory of aggregate supply will be our focus in Chapters 7 and 10.

- The second ingredient is *aggregate demand*. How much of the capacity to produce is actually utilized depends on how many of these goods and services people and businesses want to buy. We begin building a theory of aggregate demand in Chapters 8 and 9.

Inputs are the labor, machinery, buildings, and other resources used to produce outputs.

Outputs are the goods and services that the economy produces.

CONTENTS

Corresponding to these two ingredients, economists visualize a dual task for those who make macroeconomic policy. First, *policy should create an environment in which the economy can expand its productive capacity rapidly,* because that is the ultimate source of higher living standards. This first task is the realm of **growth policy,** and it is taken up in the next chapter. Second, *policy makers should manage aggregate demand so that it grows in line with the economy's capacity to produce,* avoiding as much as possible the cycles of boom and bust that we saw in the last chapter. This is the realm of *stabilization policy.* As we noted in the last chapter, inadequate growth of aggregate demand can lead to high *unemployment,* while excessive growth of aggregate demand can lead to high *inflation.* Both are to be avoided.

> **Growth policy** refers to government policies intended to make the economy grow faster in the long run.

Thus, the goals of macroeconomic policy can be summarized succinctly as *achieving rapid but relatively smooth economic growth with low unemployment and low inflation.* Unfortunately, that turns out to be a tall order. In chapters to come, we will explain why these goals cannot be attained with machine-like precision and why improvement on one front often spells deterioration on another. Along the way, we will pay a great deal of attention to both the *causes* of and *cures* for sluggish growth, high unemployment, and high inflation.

But before getting involved in such weighty issues of theory and policy, we pause in this chapter to take a close look at the three goals themselves. How fast can—or should—the economy grow? Why does a rise in unemployment cause such social distress? Why is inflation so loudly deplored? The answers to some of these questions may seem obvious at first. But, as you will see, there is more to them than meets the eye.

The chapter is divided into three main parts, corresponding to the three goals. An appendix explains how inflation is measured.

PART 1: THE GOAL OF ECONOMIC GROWTH

To residents of a prosperous society like ours, economic growth—the notion that standards of living rise from one year to the next—seems like part of the natural order of things. But it is not. Historians tell us that living standards barely changed from the Roman Empire to the dawn of the Industrial Revolution—a period of some 16 centuries! Closer in time, per-capita incomes have tragically declined, on net, in most of the former Soviet Union and some of the poorest countries of Africa in recent decades. Economic growth is *not* automatic.

Growth is also a very slow, and therefore barely noticeable, process. The typical American probably will consume about 1 to 2 percent more goods and services in 2008 than he or she did in 2007. Can you perceive a difference that small? Perhaps not, but such tiny changes, when compounded for decades or even centuries, transform societies. During the twentieth century, for example, living standards in the United States increased by a factor of almost 7—which means that your ancestors in the year 1900 consumed roughly one-seventh as much food, clothing, shelter, and other amenities as you do today. Try to imagine how your family would fare on one-eighth of its current income.

PRODUCTIVITY GROWTH: FROM LITTLE ACORNS . . .

Small differences in growth rates make an enormous difference—*eventually.* To illustrate this point, think about the relative positions of three major nations—the United States, the United Kingdom, and Japan—at two points in history: 1870 and 1979. In 1870, the United States was a young, upstart nation. Although already among the most prosperous countries on earth, the United States was in no sense yet a major power. The United Kingdom, by contrast, was the preeminent economic and military power of the world. The Victorian era was at its height, and the sun never set on the British Empire. Meanwhile, somewhere across the Pacific was an inconsequential island nation called Japan. In 1870, Japan had only recently opened up to the West and was economically backward.

The Wonders of Compound Interest

Growth rates, like interest rates, *compound* so that, for example, 10 years of growth at 3 percent per year leaves the economy *more than* 30 percent larger. How much more? The answer is 34.4 percent. To see how we get this figure, start with the fact that $100 left in a bank account for one year at 3 percent interest grows to $103, which is 1.03 × $100. If left for a second year, that $103 will grow another 3 percent—to 1.03 × $103 = $106.09, which is already more than $106. Compounding has begun.

Notice that 1.03 × $103 is $(1.03)^2$ × $100. Similarly, after three years the original $100 will grow to $(1.03)^3$ × $100 = $109.27. As you can see, each additional year adds another 1.03 growth factor to the multiplication. Now returning to answer our original question, after 10 years of compounding, the depositor will have $(1.03)^{10}$ × $100 = $134.39 in the bank. Thus the balance will have grown by 34.4 percent. By identical logic, an economy growing at 3 percent per year for 10 years will expand 34.4 percent in total.

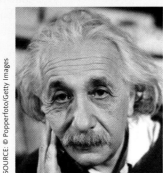

SOURCE: © Popperfoto/Getty Images

You may not be impressed by the difference between 30 percent and 34.4 percent. If so, follow the logic for longer periods. After 20 years of 3 percent growth, the economy will be 80.6 percent bigger (because $(1.03)^{20} = 1.806$), not just 60 percent bigger. After 50 years, cumulative growth will be 338 percent, not 150 percent. And after a century, it will be 1,822 percent, not just 300 percent. Now we are talking about large discrepancies! No wonder Einstein once said, presumably in jest, that compounding was the most powerful force in the universe.

The arithmetic of growth leads to a convenient "doubling rule" that you can do in your head. If something (the money in a bank account, the GDP of a country, and so on) grows at an annual rate of *g* percent, how long will it take to double? The approximate answer is $70/g$, so the rule is often called "the Rule of 70." For example, at a 2 percent growth rate, something doubles in about $70/2 = 35$ years. At a 3 percent growth rate, doubling takes roughly $70/3 = 23.33$ years. Yes, small differences in growth rates can make a large difference.

Now fast-forward more than a century. By 1979, the United States had become the world's preeminent economic power, Japan had emerged as the clear number two, and the United Kingdom had retreated into the second rank of nations. Obviously, the Japanese economy grew faster than the U.S. economy during this century, while the British economy grew more slowly, or else this stunning transformation of relative positions would not have occurred. But the magnitudes of the differences in growth rates may astound you.

Over the 109-year period, GDP per capita in the United States grew at a 2.3 percent compound annual rate while the United Kingdom's growth rate was 1.8 percent—a difference of merely 0.5 percent per annum, but compounded for more than a century. And what of Japan? What growth rate propelled it from obscurity into the front rank of nations? The answer is just 3.0 percent, a mere 0.7 percent per year faster than the United States. These numbers show vividly what a huge difference a 0.5 or 0.7 percentage point change in the growth rate makes, *if sustained for a long time*.

Economists define the *productivity* of a country's labor force (or **"labor productivity"**) as the amount of output a typical worker turns out in an hour of work. For example, if output is measured by GDP, productivity would be measured by GDP divided by the total number of hours of work. It is the growth rate of productivity that determines whether living standards will rise rapidly or slowly.

PRODUCTIVITY GROWTH IS (ALMOST) EVERYTHING IN THE LONG RUN As we pointed out in our list of *Ideas for Beyond the Final Exam*, only rising productivity can raise standards of living in the long run. Over long periods of time, small differences in rates of productivity growth compound like interest in a bank account and can make an enormous difference to a society's prosperity. Nothing contributes more to material wellbeing, to the reduction of poverty, to increases in leisure time, and to a country's ability to finance education, public health, environmental improvement, and the arts than its productivity growth rate.

Labor productivity is the amount of output a worker turns out in an hour (or a week, or a year) of labor. If output is measured by GDP, it is GDP per hour of work.

IDEAS FOR BEYOND THE FINAL EXAM

ISSUE: Is FASTER GROWTH ALWAYS BETTER?

How fast should the U.S. economy, or any economy, grow? At first, the question may seem silly. Isn't it obvious that we should grow as fast as possible? After all, that will make us all richer. In a broad sense, economists agree; faster growth is generally preferred to slower growth. But as we shall see in a few pages, further thought suggests that the apparently naive question is not quite as silly as it sounds. Growth comes at a cost. So more may not always be better.

THE CAPACITY TO PRODUCE: POTENTIAL GDP AND THE PRODUCTION FUNCTION

Potential GDP is the real GDP that the economy would produce if its labor and other resources were fully employed.

The **labor force** is the number of people holding or seeking jobs.

The economy's **production function** shows the volume of output that can be produced from given inputs (such as labor and capital), given the available technology.

Questions like how fast our economy can or should grow require quantitative answers. Economists have invented the concept of **potential GDP** to measure the economy's normal capacity to produce goods and services. Specifically, potential GDP is the real gross domestic product (GDP) an economy *could* produce if its **labor force** was fully employed.

Note the use of the word *normal* in describing capacity. Just as it is possible to push a factory beyond its normal operating rate (by, for example, adding a night shift), it is possible to push an economy beyond its normal full-employment level by working it very hard. For example, we observed in the last chapter that the unemployment rate dropped as low as 1.2 percent under abnormal conditions during World War II. So when we talk about employing the labor force fully, we do not mean a measured unemployment rate of zero.

Conceptually, we estimate potential GDP in two steps. First, we count up the available supplies of labor, capital, and other productive resources. Then we estimate how much *output* these *inputs* could produce if they were all fully utilized. This second step—the transformation of inputs into outputs—involves an assessment of the economy's *technology*. The more technologically advanced an economy, the more output it will be able to produce from any given bundle of inputs—as we emphasized in Chapter 3's discussion of the production possibilities frontier.

To help us understand how technology affects the relationship between inputs and outputs, it is useful to introduce a tool called the **production function**—which is simply a mathematical or graphical depiction of the relationship between inputs and outputs. We will use a graph in our discussion.

For a given level of technology, Figure 1 shows how output (measured by real GDP on the vertical axis) depends on labor input (measured by hours of work on the horizontal

---

FIGURE 1

The Economy's Production Function

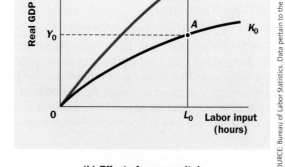

(a) Effect of better technology   (b) Effect of more capital

SOURCE: Bureau of Labor Statistics. Data pertain to the nonfarm business sector.

axis). To read these graphs, and to relate them to the concept of potential GDP, begin with the black curve OK in Figure 1(a), which shows how GDP depends on labor input, *holding both capital and technology constant.* Naturally, output rises as labor inputs increase as we move outward along the curve OK, just as you would expect. If the country's labor force can supply L_0 hours of work when it is fully employed, then *potential GDP is Y_0* (see point A). If the technology improves, the production function will shift upward—say, to the brick-colored curve labeled OM—meaning that the *same* amount of labor input will now produce *more* output. The graph shows that potential GDP increases to Y_1.

Now what about capital? Figure 1(b) shows two production functions. The black curve OK_0 applies when the economy has some lower capital stock, K_0. The higher, brick-colored curve OK_1 applies when the capital stock is some higher number, K_1. Thus, the production function tells us that potential GDP will be Y_0 if the capital stock is K_0 (see point A) but Y_1 if the capital stock is K_1 instead (see point B). Once again, this relationship is just what you would expect: The economy can produce *more* output with the *same* amount of labor if workers have more capital to work with.

You can hardly avoid noticing the similarities between the two panels of Figure 1: Better technology, as in Figure 1(a), or more capital, as in Figure 1(b), affect the production function in more or less the same way. In general:

> **Either more capital or better technology will shift the production function upward and therefore raise potential GDP.**

THE GROWTH RATE OF POTENTIAL GDP

With this new tool, it is but a short jump to potential growth rates. If the *size* of potential GDP depends on the size of the economy's labor force, the amount of capital and other resources it has, and its technology, it follows that the *growth rate* of potential GDP must depend on

- The growth rate of the labor force
- The growth rate of the nation's capital stock
- The rate of technical progress

To sharpen the point, observe that real GDP is, by definition, the product of the total hours of work in the economy times the amount of output produced per hour—what we have just called *labor productivity:*

GDP = Hours of work × Output per hour = Hours of work × Labor productivity.

For example, in the United States today, in round numbers, GDP is about $14 trillion and total hours of work per year are about 250 billion. Thus labor productivity is roughly $14 trillion/250 billion hours = $56 per hour.

How fast can the economy increase its productive capacity? By transforming the preceding equation into growth rates, we have our answer: The growth rate of potential GDP is the *sum* of the growth rates of labor input (hours of work) and labor productivity:[1]

Growth rate of potential GDP = Growth rate of labor input + Growth rate of labor productivity

In the United States in recent years, labor input has been increasing at a rate of about 1 percent per year. But labor productivity growth, which was very slow until the mid-1990s, has leaped upward since then—averaging about 2.6 percent per annum from 1995 to 2007. Together, these two figures imply an estimated growth rate of potential GDP in the 3.6 percent range over the past dozen years.

---

[1] You may be wondering about what happened to capital. The answer, as we have just seen in our discussion of the production function, is that one of the main determinants of potential GDP, and thus of labor productivity, is the amount of capital that each worker has to work with. Accordingly, the role of capital is incorporated into the productivity number, that is, the growth rate of labor productivity depends on the growth rate of capital.

TABLE 1	
Recent Growth Rates of Real GDP in the United States	
Years	Growth Rate per Year
1995–1997	4.1%
1997–1999	4.3
1999–2001	2.2
2001–2003	2.1
2003–2005	3.4
2005–2007	2.5
1995–2007	**3.1**

SOURCE: U.S. Department of Commerce.

Do the growth rates of potential GDP and actual GDP match up? The answer is an important one to which we will return often in this book:

Over long periods of time, the growth rates of actual and potential GDP are normally quite similar. But the two often diverge sharply over short periods owing to cyclical fluctuations.

Table 1 illustrates this point with some recent U.S. data. Since 1994, GDP growth rates over two-year periods have ranged from as low as 2.1 percent per annum to as high as 4.3 percent. Over the entire 12-year period, GDP growth averaged 3.1 percent, which is probably just a bit above current estimates of the growth rate of potential GDP.

The next chapter is devoted to studying the *determinants* of economic growth and some *policies* that might speed it up. But we already know from the production function that there are two basic ways to boost a nation's growth rate—other than faster population growth and simply working harder. One is accumulating more capital. Other things being equal, a nation that builds more capital for its future will grow faster. The other way is by improving technology. When technological breakthroughs are coming at a fast and furious pace, an economy will grow more rapidly. We will discuss both of these factors in detail in the next chapter. First, however, we need to address the more basic question posed earlier in this chapter.

ISSUE REVISITED: IS FASTER GROWTH ALWAYS BETTER?

It might seem that the answer to this question is obviously yes. After all, faster growth of either labor productivity or GDP per person is the route to higher living standards. But exceptions have been noted.

For openers, some social critics have questioned the desirability of faster economic growth as an end in itself, at least in the rich countries. Faster growth brings more wealth, and to most people the desirability of wealth is beyond question. "I've been rich and I've been poor. Believe me, honey, rich is better," singer Sophie Tucker once told an interviewer. And most people seem to share her sentiment. To those who hold this belief, a healthy economy is one that produces vast quantities of jeans, pizzas, cars, and computers.

Yet the desirability of further economic growth for a society that is already quite wealthy has been questioned on several grounds. Environmentalists worry that the sheer increase in the volume of goods imposes enormous costs on society in the form of crowding, pollution, global climate change, and proliferation of wastes that need disposal. It has, they argue, dotted our roadsides with junkyards, filled our air with pollution, and poisoned our food with dangerous chemicals.

Some psychologists and social critics argue that the never-ending drive for more and better goods has failed to make people happier. Instead, industrial progress has transformed the satisfying and creative tasks of the artisan into the mechanical and dehumanizing routine of the assembly-line worker. In the United States, it even seems to be driving people to work longer and longer hours. The question is whether the vast outpouring of material goods is worth all the stress and environmental damage. In fact, surveys of self-reported happiness show that residents of richer countries are no happier, on average, than residents of poorer countries.

But despite this, most economists continue to believe that more growth is better than less. For one thing, slower growth would make it extremely difficult to finance programs that improve the quality of life—including efforts to protect the environment. Such programs are costly, and the evidence suggests that people are willing to pay for them only after their incomes reach a certain level. Second, it would be difficult to prevent further economic growth even if we were so inclined. Mandatory controls are abhorrent to most Americans; we cannot order people to stop being inventive and hardworking. Third, slower economic growth would seriously hamper efforts to eliminate poverty—both within our own country and throughout the world. Much of the earth's population still lives in a state of extreme want. These unfortunate people are far less interested in clean air and fulfillment in the workplace than they are in more food, better clothing, and sturdier shelters.

All that said, economists concede that faster growth is not always better. One important reason will occupy our attention later in Parts 2 and 3: An economy that grows too fast may generate inflation. Why? You were introduced to the answer at the end of the last chapter: Inflation rises when aggregate demand races ahead of aggregate supply. In plain English, an economy will become inflationary when people's demands for goods and services expand faster than its capacity to produce them. So we probably do not want to grow faster than the growth rate of potential GDP, at least not for long.

Should society then seek the maximum possible growth rate of *potential* GDP? Maybe, but maybe not. After all, more rapid growth does not come for free. We have noted that building more capital is one good way to speed the growth of potential GDP. But the resources used to manufacture jet engines and computer servers could be used to make home air conditioners and video games instead. Building more capital imposes an obvious cost on a society: The citizens must consume less today. Saying this does not argue against investing for the future. Indeed, most economists believe we need to do more of that. But we must realize that faster growth through capital formation comes at a cost—an *opportunity cost*. Here, as elsewhere, you don't get something for nothing.

▨ PART 2: THE GOAL OF LOW UNEMPLOYMENT

We noted earlier that actual GDP growth can differ sharply from potential GDP growth over periods as long as several years. These *macroeconomic fluctuations* have major implications for employment and unemployment. In particular:

> **When the economy grows more *slowly* than its potential, it fails to generate enough new jobs for its ever-growing labor force. Hence, *the unemployment rate* rises. Conversely, GDP growth *faster* than the economy's potential leads to a *falling unemployment rate*.**

The **unemployment rate** is the number of unemployed people, expressed as a percentage of the labor force.

High unemployment is socially wasteful. When the economy does not create enough jobs to employ everyone who is willing to work, a valuable resource is lost. Potential goods and services that might have been produced and enjoyed by consumers are lost forever. This lost output is the central economic cost of high unemployment, and we can measure it by comparing actual and potential GDP.

That cost is considerable. Table 2 summarizes the idleness of workers and machines, and the resulting loss of national output, for some of the years of lowest economic activity in recent decades. The second column lists the civilian unemployment rate and thus measures unused labor resources. The third lists the percentage of industrial capacity that U.S. manufacturers were actually using, which indicates the extent to which plant and equipment went unused. The fourth column estimates the shortfall between potential and actual real GDP. We see that unemployment has cost the people of the United States as much as an 8.1 percent reduction in their real incomes.

Although Table 2 shows extreme examples, our inability to utilize all of the nation's available resources was a persistent economic problem for decades. The blue line in Figure 2 shows actual real GDP in the United States from 1954 to 2007, while the black line shows potential GDP. The graph makes it clear that actual GDP has fallen short of potential GDP more often than it has exceeded it, especially during the 1973–1993 period. In fact:

> **A conservative estimate of the cumulative gap between actual and potential GDP over the years 1974 to 1993 (all evaluated in 2000**

TABLE 2

The Economic Costs of High Unemployment

Year	Civilian Unemployment Rate	Capacity Utilization Rate	Real GDP Lost Due to Idle Resources
1958	6.8%	75.0%	4.8%
1961	6.7	77.3	4.1
1975	8.5	73.4	5.4
1982	9.7	71.3	8.1
1992	7.5	79.4	2.6
2003	6.0	73.4	2.2

SOURCES: Bureau of Labor Statistics, Federal Reserve System, and Congressional Budget Office.

FIGURE 2

Actual and Potential GDP in the United States since 1954

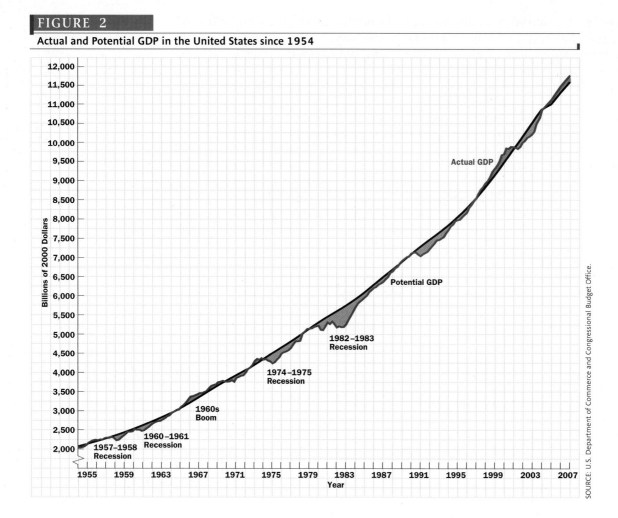

SOURCE: U.S. Department of Commerce and Congressional Budget Office.

prices) is roughly $1,750 billion. At 2007 levels, this loss in output as a result of unemployment would be over one-and-a-half months worth of production. And there is no way to redeem those losses. The labor wasted in 1992 cannot be utilized in 2007.

THE HUMAN COSTS OF HIGH UNEMPLOYMENT

If these numbers seem a bit dry and abstract, think about the human costs of being unemployed. Years ago, job loss meant not only enforced idleness and a catastrophic drop in income, it often led to hunger, cold, ill health, even death. Here is how one unemployed worker during the Great Depression described his family's plight in a mournful letter to the governor of Pennsylvania:

> I have been out of work for over a year and a half. Am back almost thirteen months and the landlord says if I don't pay up before the 1 of 1932 out I must go, and where am I to go in the cold winter with my children? If you can help me please for God's sake and the children's sakes and like please do what you can and send me some help, will you, I cannot find any work. . . . Thanksgiving dinner was black coffee and bread and was very glad to get it. My wife is in the hospital now. We have no shoes to were [sic]; no clothes hardly. Oh what will I do I sure will thank you.[2]

---

[2] From *Brother, Can You Spare a Dime? The Great Depression 1929–1933,* by Milton Meltzer, p. 103. Copyright 1969 by Milton Meltzer. Reprinted by permission of Alfred A. Knopf, Inc.

Nowadays, unemployment does not hold quite such terrors for most families, although its consequences remain dire enough. Our system of unemployment insurance (discussed later in this chapter) has taken part of the sting out of unemployment, as have other social welfare programs that support the incomes of the poor. Yet most families still suffer painful losses of income and, often, severe noneconomic consequences when a bread-winner becomes unemployed.

Even families that are well protected by unemployment compensation suffer when joblessness strikes. Ours is a work-oriented society. A man's place has always been in the office or shop, and lately this has become true for women as well. A worker forced into idleness by a recession endures a psychological cost that is no less real for our inability to measure it. Martin Luther King, Jr. put it graphically: "In our society, it is murder, psychologically, to deprive a man of a job. . . . You are in substance saying to that man that he has no right to exist."[3] High unemployment has been linked to psychological and physical disorders, divorces, suicides, and crime.

It is important to realize that these costs, whether large or small in total, are distributed most unevenly across the population. In 2007, for example, the unemployment rate among all workers averaged just 4.6 percent. But, as Figure 3 shows, 8.3 percent of black workers were unemployed. For teenagers, the situation was much worse, with unemployment at 15.7 percent, and that of black male teenagers a shocking 33.8 percent. Married men had the lowest rate—just 2.5 percent. Overall unemployment varies from year to year, but these relationships are typical:

> In good times and bad, married men suffer the least unemployment and teenagers suffer the most; nonwhites are unemployed much more often than whites; blue-collar workers have above-average rates of unemployment; well-educated people have below-average unemployment rates.[4]

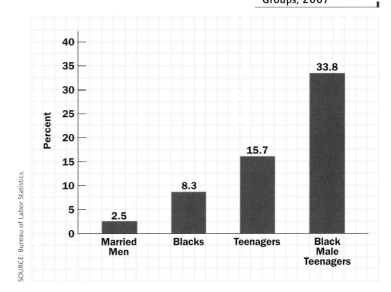

FIGURE 3

Unemployment Rates for Selected Groups, 2007

SOURCE: Bureau of Labor Statistics.

It is worth noting that unemployment in the United States has been much lower than in most other industrialized countries in recent years. For example, during 2006, when the U.S. unemployment rate averaged 4.6 percent, the comparable figures were 5.5 percent in Canada, 9.5 percent in France, 6.9 percent in Italy, and 10.4 percent in Germany.[5]

COUNTING THE UNEMPLOYED: THE OFFICIAL STATISTICS

We have been using unemployment figures without considering where they come from or how accurate they are. The basic data come from a monthly survey of about 60,000 households conducted for the U.S. Bureau of Labor Statistics. The census taker asks several questions about the employment status of each member of the household and, on the basis of the answers, classifies each person as *employed, unemployed,* or *not in the labor force.*

---

[3] Quoted in Coretta Scott King (ed.), *The Words of Martin Luther King* (New York: Newmarket Press; 1983), p. 45.

[4] Unemployment rates for men and women are about equal.

[5] The numbers for foreign countries are based (approximately) on U.S. unemployment concepts.

The Employed   The first category is the simplest to define. It includes everyone currently at work, including part-time workers. Although some part-timers work less than a full week by choice, others do so only because they cannot find suitable full-time jobs. Nevertheless, these workers are counted as employed, even though many would consider them "underemployed."

The Unemployed   The second category is a bit trickier. For persons not currently working, the survey first determines whether they are temporarily laid off from a job to which they expect to return. If so, they are counted as unemployed. The remaining workers are asked whether they actively sought work during the previous four weeks. If they did, they are also counted as unemployed.

Out of the Labor Force   But if they failed to look for a job, they are classified as *out of the labor force* rather than unemployed. This seems a reasonable way to draw the distinction—after all, not *everyone* wants to work. Yet there is a problem: Research shows that many unemployed workers give up looking for jobs after a while. These so-called **discouraged workers** are victims of poor job prospects, just like the officially unemployed. But when they give up hope, the measured unemployment rate—which is the ratio of the number of unemployed people to the total labor force—actually declines.

A **discouraged worker** is an unemployed person who gives up looking for work and is therefore no longer counted as part of the labor force.

Involuntary part-time work, loss of overtime or shortened work hours, and discouraged workers are all examples of "hidden" or "disguised" unemployment. People concerned about such phenomena argue that we should include them in the official unemployment rate because, if we do not, the magnitude of the problem will be underestimated. Others, however, argue that measured unemployment overestimates the problem because, to count as unemployed, potential workers need only *claim* to be looking for jobs, even if they are not really interested in finding them.

TYPES OF UNEMPLOYMENT

Frictional unemployment is unemployment that is due to normal turnover in the labor market. It includes people who are temporarily between jobs because they are moving or changing occupations, or are unemployed for similar reasons.

Structural unemployment refers to workers who have lost their jobs because they have been displaced by automation, because their skills are no longer in demand, or because of similar reasons.

Cyclical unemployment is the portion of unemployment that is attributable to a decline in the economy's total production. Cyclical unemployment rises during recessions and falls as prosperity is restored.

Providing jobs for those willing to work is one principal goal of macroeconomic policy. How are we to define this goal?

We have already noted that a zero measured unemployment rate would clearly be an *incorrect* answer. Ours is a dynamic, highly mobile economy. Households move from one state to another. Individuals quit jobs to seek better positions or retool for more attractive occupations. These and other decisions produce some minimal amount of unemployment—people who are literally between jobs. Economists call this **frictional unemployment,** and it is unavoidable in our market economy. The critical distinguishing feature of frictional unemployment is that it is short-lived. A frictionally unemployed person has every reason to expect to find a new job soon.

A second type of unemployment can be difficult to distinguish from frictional unemployment but has very different implications. **Structural unemployment** arises when jobs are eliminated by changes in the economy, such as automation or permanent changes in demand. The crucial difference between frictional and structural unemployment is that, unlike frictionally unemployed workers, structurally unemployed workers cannot realistically be considered "between jobs." Instead, their skills and experience may be unmarketable in the changing economy in which they live. They are thus faced with either prolonged periods of unemployment or the necessity of making major changes in their skills or occupations.

The remaining type of unemployment, **cyclical unemployment,** will occupy most of our attention. Cyclical unemployment rises when the level of economic activity declines, as it does in a recession. Thus, when macroeconomists speak of maintaining "full employment," they mean limiting unemployment to its frictional and structural components—which means, roughly, producing at potential GDP. A key question, therefore, is: How much measured unemployment constitutes full employment?

DOES THE MINIMUM WAGE CAUSE UNEMPLOYMENT?

Elementary economic reasoning—summarized in the simple supply-demand diagram to the right—suggests that setting a minimum wage (*W* in the graph) above the free-market wage (*w* in the graph) must cause unemployment. In the graph, unemployment is the horizontal gap between the quantity of labor supplied (point *B*) and the quantity demanded (point *A*) at the minimum wage. Indeed, the conclusion seems so elementary that generations of economists took it for granted. The argument seems compelling. Indeed, earlier editions of this book, for example, confidently told students that a higher minimum wage must lead to higher unemployment.

But some surprising economic research published in the 1990s cast serious doubt on this conventional wisdom.* For example, economists David Card and Alan Krueger compared employment changes at fast-food restaurants in New Jersey and nearby Pennsylvania after New Jersey, but not Pennsylvania, raised its minimum wage in 1992. To their surprise, the New Jersey stores did *more* net hiring than their Pennsylvania counterparts. Similar results were found for fast-food stores in Texas after the federal minimum wage was raised

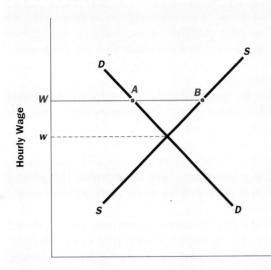

Number of Workers

in 1991, and in California after the statewide minimum wage was increased in 1988. In none of these cases did a higher minimum wage seem to reduce employment—in contrast to the implications of simple economic theory.

The research of Card and Krueger, and of others who reached similar conclusions, was controversial from the start, and remains so. Thus, a policy question that had been deemed closed now seems to be open: Does the minimum wage really cause unemployment?

Resolution of this debate is of more than academic interest. In 1996, President Clinton recommended and Congress passed an increase in the federal minimum wage—justifying its action, in part, by the new research suggesting that unemployment would not rise as a result. The same research was cited in 2007, when Congress debated and then enacted a three-stage increase in the minimum wage that will bring it up to $7.25 by the summer of 2009. Economic research can have consequences.

*See David Card and Alan Krueger, *Myth and Measurement: The New Economics of the Minimum Wage* (Princeton, N.J.: Princeton University Press; 1995).

HOW MUCH EMPLOYMENT IS "FULL EMPLOYMENT"?

John F. Kennedy was the first president to commit the federal government to a specific numerical goal for unemployment. He picked a 4 percent target, which was rejected as being unrealistically ambitious in the 1970s. But when the government abandoned the 4 percent unemployment target, no new number was put in its place. Instead, we have experienced a long-running national debate over exactly how much measured unemployment corresponds to **full employment**—a debate that continues to this day.

In the early 1990s, many economists believed that full employment came at a measured unemployment rate as high as 6 percent. Others disputed that estimate as unduly pessimistic. Then real-world events decisively rejected the 6 percent estimate. The boom of the late 1990s pushed the unemployment rate below 5 percent by the summer of 1997, and it remained there every month until September 2001—even falling as low as 3.9 percent in 2000. All this left economists guessing where full employment might be. Official government reports issued in early 2008 estimated the full-employment unemployment rate to be around 5 percent. But no one was totally confident in such estimates.

Full employment is a situation in which everyone who is willing and able to work can find a job. At full employment, the measured unemployment rate is still positive.

UNEMPLOYMENT INSURANCE: THE INVALUABLE CUSHION

One major reason why America's unemployed workers no longer experience the complete loss of income that devastated so many during the 1930s is our system of

Unemployment insurance is a government program that replaces some of the wages lost by eligible workers who lose their jobs.

unemployment insurance—one of the most valuable institutional innovations to emerge from the trauma of the Great Depression.

Each of the 50 states administers an unemployment insurance program under federal guidelines. Although the precise amounts vary, the average weekly benefit check in 2007 was $288, which amounted to just under half of average weekly earnings. While a 50 percent drop in earnings poses very serious problems, the importance of this 50 percent income cushion can scarcely be exaggerated, especially because it may be supplemented by funds from other welfare programs. Families that are covered by unemployment insurance rarely go hungry or are dispossessed from their homes when they lose their jobs.

Eligibility for benefits varies by state, but some criteria apply quite generally. Only experienced workers qualify, so persons just joining the labor force (such as recent college graduates) or reentering after prolonged absences (such as women returning to the job market after years of child rearing) cannot collect benefits. Neither can those who quit their jobs, except under unusual circumstances. Also, benefits end after a stipulated period of time, normally six months. For all of these reasons, only 37 percent of the 7.1 million people who were unemployed in an average week in 2007 actually received benefits.

The importance of unemployment insurance to the unemployed is obvious. But significant benefits also accrue to citizens who never become unemployed. During recessions, billions of dollars are paid out in unemployment benefits. And because recipients probably spend most of their benefits, unemployment insurance limits the severity of recessions by providing additional purchasing power when and where it is most needed.

The unemployment insurance system is one of several cushions built into our economy since 1933 to prevent another Great Depression. By giving money to those who become unemployed, the system helps prop up aggregate demand during recessions.

Although the U.S. economy is now probably "depression-proof," this should not be a cause for too much rejoicing, for the many recessions we have had since the 1950s—most recently in 2001 (plus concern about another in 2008)—amply demonstrate that we are far from "recession-proof."

The fact that unemployment insurance and other social welfare programs replace a significant fraction of lost income has led some skeptics to claim that unemployment is no longer a serious problem. But the fact is that unemployment insurance is just what the name says—an *insurance* program. And insurance can never prevent a catastrophe from occurring; it simply spreads the costs among many people instead of letting all of the costs fall on the shoulders of a few unfortunate souls. As we noted earlier, unemployment robs the economy of output it could have produced, and no insurance policy can insure society against such losses.

Our system of payroll taxes and unemployment benefits spreads the costs of unemployment over the entire population. But it does not eliminate the basic economic cost.

In that case, you might ask, why not cushion the blow even more by making unemployment insurance much more generous, as many European countries have done? The answer is that there is also a downside to unemployment insurance. When unemployment benefits are very generous, people who lose their jobs may be less than eager to look for new jobs. The right level of unemployment insurance strikes an appropriate balance between the benefits of supporting the incomes of unemployed people and the costs of raising the unemployment rate a bit.

PART 3: THE GOAL OF LOW INFLATION

Both the human and economic costs of inflation are less obvious than the costs of unemployment. But this does not make them any less real, for if one thing is crystal clear about inflation, it is that people do not like it.

When inflation is low, it barely registers as a problem in national public opinion polls. But when inflation is high, it often heads the list—generally even ahead of unemployment. Surveys also show that inflation, like unemployment, makes people unhappy. Finally, studies of elections suggest that voters penalize the party that occupies the White House when inflation is high. The fact is beyond dispute: People dislike inflation. The question is, why?

The **purchasing power** of a given sum of money is the volume of goods and services that it will buy.

INFLATION: THE MYTH AND THE REALITY

At first, the question may seem ridiculous. During inflationary times, people pay higher prices for the same quantities of goods and services they had before. So more and more income is needed just to maintain the same standard of living. Is it not obvious that this erosion of **purchasing power**—that is, the decline in what money will buy—makes everyone worse off?

Inflation and Real Wages

This would indeed be the case were it not for one very significant fact. The wages that people earn are also prices—prices for labor services. During a period of inflation, wages also rise. In fact, the average wage typically rises more or less in step with prices. Thus, contrary to popular myth, workers as a group are not usually victimized by inflation.

The purchasing power of wages—what is called the real wage rate—is not systematically eroded by inflation. Sometimes wages rise faster than prices, and sometimes prices rise faster than wages. In the long run, wages tend to outstrip prices as new capital equipment and innovation increase output per worker.

Figure 4 illustrates this simple fact. The brick-colored line shows the rate of increase of prices in the United States for each year since 1948, and the black line shows the rate of increase of wages. The difference between the two, shaded in blue in the diagram, indicates the rate of growth of *real* wages. Generally, wages rise faster than prices, reflecting the

SOURCE: *The Wall Street Journal*—Permission, Cartoon Features Syndicate.

"Sure, you're raising my allowance. But am I actually gaining any purchasing power?"

The **real wage rate** is the wage rate adjusted for inflation. Specifically, it is the nominal wage divided by the price index. The real wage thus indicates the volume of goods and services that the nominal wages will buy.

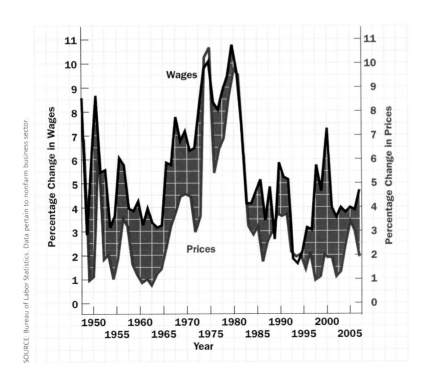

SOURCE: Bureau of Labor Statistics. Data pertain to nonfarm business sector.

FIGURE 4

Rates of Change of Wages and Prices in the United States since 1948

Calculating the Real Wage: A Real Example

The *real* wage shows not how many dollars a worker is paid for an hour of work (that is called the *nominal* wage), but rather the *purchasing power* of that money. It indicates what an hour's worth of work can buy. As noted in the definition of the real wage in the margin on the previous page, we calculate the real wage by *dividing* the nominal wage by the price level. The rule is

$$\text{Real wage} = \frac{\text{Nominal wage}}{\text{Price level}}$$

Here's a concrete example. Between 1998 and 2007, the average hourly wage in the United States rose from $13.01 to $17.41, an increase of 34 percent over nine years. Sounds pretty good for

American workers. But over those same nine years, the Consumer Price Index (CPI), the most commonly used index of the price level, rose by 27 percent, from 163.0 to 207.3. This means that the real wages in the two years were

$$\text{Real wage in 1998} = \frac{\$13.01}{163} = .0798$$

$$\text{Real wage in 2007} = \frac{\$17.41}{207.3} = .0840$$

for an increase of just 5.2 percent over the nine years, which is a small fraction of 34 percent.[6]

steady advance of labor productivity; therefore, real wages rise. But this is not always the case; the graph shows several instances in which inflation outstripped wage increases.

The feature of Figure 4 that virtually jumps off the page is the way the two lines dance together. Wages normally rise rapidly when prices rise rapidly, and they rise slowly when prices rise slowly. But you should not draw any hasty conclusions from this association. It does not, for example, imply that rising prices *cause* rising wages or that rising wages *cause* rising prices. Remember the warnings given in Chapter 1 about trying to infer causation just by looking at data. But analyzing cause and effect is not our purpose right now. We merely want to dispel the myth that inflation inevitably erodes real wages.

Why is this myth so widespread? Imagine a world without inflation in which wages are rising 2 percent per year because of the increasing productivity of labor. Now imagine that, all of a sudden, inflation sets in and prices start rising 3 percent per year but nothing else changes. Figure 4 suggests that, with perhaps a small delay, wage increases will accelerate to 2 + 3 = 5 percent per year.

Will workers view this change with equanimity? Probably not. To each worker, the 5 percent wage increase will be seen as something he earned by the sweat of his brow. In his view, he *deserves* every penny of his 5 percent raise. In a sense, he is right because "the sweat of his brow" earned him a 2 percent increment in real wages that, when the inflation rate is 3 percent, can be achieved only by increasing his money wages by 5 percent. An economist would divide the wage increase in the following way:

Reason for Wages to Increase	Amount
Higher productivity	2%
Compensation for higher prices	3%
Total	5%

But the worker will probably keep score differently. Feeling that he earned the entire 5 percent raise by his own merits, he will view inflation as having "robbed" him of three-fifths of his just deserts. The higher the rate of inflation, the more of his raise the worker will feel has been stolen from him.

Of course, nothing could be farther from the truth. Basically, the economic system rewards the worker with *the same 2 percent real wage increment for higher productivity, regardless of the rate of inflation.* The "evils of inflation" are often exaggerated because people fail to understand this point.

---

[6] As explained in the appendix, it is conventional to multiply index numbers by 100, which would make the two real wage numbers 7.98 and 8.40, respectively. That does not alter the percentage change.

The Importance of Relative Prices

A related misperception results from failure to distinguish between a *rise in the general price level* and a change in **relative prices,** which is a rise in one price relative to another. To see the distinction most clearly, imagine first a *pure inflation* in which every price rises by 10 percent during the year, so that relative prices do not change. Table 3 gives an example in which the price of movie tickets increases from $6.00 to $6.60, the price of candy bars from 50 cents to 55 cents, and the price of automobiles from $9,000 to $9,900. After the inflation, just as before, it will still take 12 candy bars to buy a movie ticket, 1,500 movie tickets to buy a car, and so on. A person who manufactures candy bars in order to purchase movie tickets is neither helped nor harmed by the inflation. Neither is a car dealer with a sweet tooth.

An item's **relative price** is its price in terms of some other item rather than in terms of dollars.

TABLE 3
Pure Inflation

Item	Last Year's Price	This Year's Price	Increase
Candy bar	$0.50	$0.55	10%
Movie ticket	6.00	6.60	10
Automobile	9,000	9,900	10

But real inflations are not like this. When there is 10 percent general inflation—meaning that the "average price" rises by 10 percent—some prices may jump 20 percent or more while others actually fall.[7] Suppose that, instead of the price increases shown in Table 3, prices rise as shown in Table 4. Movie prices go up by 25 percent, but candy prices do not change. Surely, candy manufacturers who love movies will be disgruntled because it now costs 15 candy bars instead of 12 to get into the theater. They will blame inflation for raising the price of movie tickets, even though their real problem stems from the *increase in the price of movies relative to candy.* (They would have been hurt as much if movie tickets had remained at $6 while the price of candy fell to 40 cents.) Because car prices have risen by only 5 percent, theater owners in need of new cars will be delighted by the fact that an auto now costs only 1,260 movie admissions—just as they would have cheered if car prices had fallen to $7,560 while movie tickets remained at $6. However, they are unlikely to attribute their good fortune to inflation. Indeed, they should not. What has actually happened is that *cars became cheaper relative to movies.*

TABLE 4
Real-World Inflation

Item	Last Year's Price	This Year's Price	Increase
Candy bar	$0.50	$0.50	0%
Movie ticket	6.00	7.50	25
Automobile	9,000	9,450	5

Because real-world inflations proceed at uneven rates, relative prices are always changing. There are gainers and losers, just as some would gain and others lose if relative prices were to change without any general inflation. Inflation, however, gets a bad name because losers often blame inflation for their misfortune, whereas gainers rarely credit inflation for their good luck.

Inflation is not usually to blame when some goods become more expensive *relative to others.*

---

[7] How statisticians figure out "average" price increases is discussed in the appendix to this chapter.

These two kinds of misconceptions help explain why respondents to public opinion polls often cite inflation as a major national issue, why higher inflation rates depress consumers, and why voters express their ire at the polls when inflation is high. But not all of the costs of inflation are mythical. Let us now turn to some of the real costs.

INFLATION AS A REDISTRIBUTOR OF INCOME AND WEALTH

We have just seen that the *average* person is neither helped nor harmed by inflation. But almost no one is exactly average! Some people gain from inflation and others lose. For example, senior citizens trying to scrape by on pensions or other fixed incomes suffer badly from inflation. Because they earn no wages, it is little solace to them that wages keep pace with prices. Their pension incomes do not.[8]

This example illustrates a general problem. Think of pensioners as people who "lend" money to an organization (the pension fund) when they are young, expecting to be paid back with interest when they are old. Because of the rise in the price level during the intervening years, the unfortunate pensioners get back dollars that are worth less in purchasing power than those they originally loaned. In general:

Those who lend money are often victimized by inflation.

Although lenders may lose heavily, borrowers may do quite well. For example, homeowners who borrowed money from banks in the form of mortgages back in the 1950s, when interest rates were 3 or 4 percent, gained enormously from the surprisingly virulent inflation of the 1970s. They paid back dollars of much lower purchasing power than those that they borrowed. The same is true of other borrowers.

Borrowers often gain from inflation.

Because the redistribution caused by inflation generally benefits borrowers at the expense of lenders, and because both lenders and borrowers can be found at every income level, we conclude that

Inflation does not systematically steal from the rich to aid the poor, nor does it always do the reverse.

Why, then, is the redistribution caused by inflation so widely condemned? Because its victims are selected capriciously. No one legislates the redistribution. No one enters into it voluntarily. The gainers do not earn their spoils, and the losers do not deserve their fate. Moreover, inflation robs particular classes of people of purchasing power year after year—people living on private pensions, families who save money and "lend" it to banks, and workers whose wages and salaries do not adjust to higher prices. Even if the average person suffers no damage from inflation, that fact offers little consolation to those who are its victims. This is one fundamental indictment of inflation.

Inflation redistributes income in an arbitrary way. Society's income distribution should reflect the interplay of the operation of free markets and the purposeful efforts of government to alter that distribution. Inflation interferes with and distorts this process.

REAL VERSUS NOMINAL INTEREST RATES

But wait. Must inflation always rob lenders to bestow gifts upon borrowers? If both parties see inflation coming, won't lenders demand that borrowers pay a higher interest rate as compensation for the coming inflation? Indeed they will. For this reason, economists draw a sharp distinction between *expected* inflation and *unexpected* inflation.

---

[8] The same is not true of Social Security benefits, which are automatically increased to compensate recipients for changes in the price level.

What happens when inflation is fully expected by both parties? Suppose Diamond Jim wants to borrow $1,000 from Scrooge for one year, and both agree that, in the absence of inflation, a fair rate of interest would be 3 percent. This means that Diamond Jim would pay back $1,030 at the end of the year for the privilege of having $1,000 now.

If both men expect prices to increase by 6 percent, Scrooge may reason as follows: "If Diamond Jim pays me back $1,030 one year from today, that money will buy less than what $1,000 buys today. Thus, I'll really be *paying him* to borrow from me! I'm no philanthropist. Why don't I charge him 9 percent instead? Then he'll pay back $1,090 at the end of the year. With prices 6 percent higher, this will buy roughly what $1,030 is worth today. So I'll get the same 3 percent increase in purchasing power that we would have agreed on in the absence of inflation and won't be any worse off. That's the least I'll accept."

Diamond Jim may follow a similar chain of logic. "With no inflation, I was willing to pay $1,030 one year from now for the privilege of having $1,000 today, and Scrooge was willing to lend it. He'd be crazy to do the same with 6 percent inflation. He'll want to charge me more. How much should I pay? If I offer him $1,090 one year from now, that will have roughly the same purchasing power as $1,030 today, so I won't be any worse off. That's the most I'll pay."

This kind of thinking may lead Scrooge and Diamond Jim to write a contract with a 9 percent interest rate—3 percent as the increase in purchasing power that Diamond Jim pays to Scrooge and 6 percent as compensation for expected inflation. Then, if the expected 6 percent inflation actually materializes, neither party will be made better or worse off by inflation.

This example illustrates a general principle. The 3 percent increase in purchasing power that Diamond Jim agrees to turn over to Scrooge is called the **real rate of interest.** The 9 percent contractual interest charge that Diamond Jim and Scrooge write into the loan agreement is called the **nominal rate of interest.** The nominal rate of interest is calculated by adding the *expected rate of inflation* to the real rate of interest. The general relationship is

> **Nominal interest rate = Real interest rate + Expected inflation rate**

Expected inflation is added to compensate the lender for the loss of purchasing power that the lender expects to suffer as a result of inflation. Because of this,

> **Inflation that is accurately predicted need not redistribute income between borrowers and lenders. If the *expected* rate of inflation that is embodied in the nominal interest rate matches the *actual* rate of inflation, no one gains and no one loses. However, to the extent that expectations prove incorrect, inflation will still redistribute income.[9]**

It need hardly be pointed out that errors in predicting the rate of inflation are the norm, not the exception. Published forecasts bear witness to the fact that economists have great difficulty in predicting the rate of inflation. The task is no easier for businesses, consumers, and banks. This is another reason why inflation is so widely condemned as unfair and undesirable. It sets up a guessing game that no one likes.

> The **real rate of interest** is the percentage increase in purchasing power that the borrower pays to the lender for the privilege of borrowing. It indicates the increased ability to purchase goods and services that the lender earns.

> The **nominal rate of interest** is the percentage by which the money the borrower pays back exceeds the money that was borrowed, making no adjustment for any decline in the purchasing power of this money that results from inflation.

INFLATION DISTORTS MEASUREMENTS

So inflation imposes costs on society because it is difficult to predict. But other costs arise even when inflation is predicted accurately. Many such costs stem from the fact that people are simply unaccustomed to thinking in inflation-adjusted terms and so make errors in thinking and calculation. Many laws and regulations that were designed for an inflation-free economy malfunction when inflation is high. Here are some important examples.

---

[9] *Exercise:* Who gains and who loses if the inflation turns out to be only 4 percent instead of the 6 percent that Scrooge and Diamond Jim expected? What if the inflation rate is 8 percent?

Confusing Real and Nominal Interest Rates

People frequently confuse *real* and *nominal* interest rates. For example, most Americans viewed the 12 percent mortgage interest rates that banks charged in 1980 as scandalously high but saw the 6½ percent mortgage rates of 2006 as great bargains. In truth, with inflation around 2½ percent in 2006 and 10 percent in 1980, the real interest rate in 2004 (about 4 percent) was well above the bargain-basement real rates in 1980 (about 2 percent).

The Malfunctioning Tax System

The tax system is probably the most important example of inflation illusion at work. The law does not recognize the distinction between nominal and real interest rates; it simply taxes *nominal* interest regardless of how much real interest it represents. Similarly, **capital gains**—the difference between the price at which an investor sells an asset and the price paid for it—are taxed in nominal, not real, terms. As a result, our tax system can do strange things when inflation is high. An example will show why.

Between 1984 and 2007, the price level roughly doubled. Consider some stock that was purchased for $20,000 in 1984 and sold for $35,000 in 2007. The investor actually *lost* purchasing power while holding the stock because $20,000 of 1984 money could buy roughly what $40,000 could buy in 2007. Yet because the law levies taxes on nominal capital gains, with no correction for inflation, the investor would have been taxed on the $15,000 *nominal* capital gain—even though suffering a *real* capital loss of $5,000.

Many economists have proposed that this (presumably unintended) feature of the law be changed by taxing only real capital gains, that is, capital gains in excess of inflation. To date, Congress has not agreed. This little example illustrates a pervasive and serious problem:

> **Because it fails to recognize the distinction between nominal and real capital gains, or between nominal and real interest rates, our tax system levies high, and presumably unintended, tax rates on capital income when there is high inflation. Thus the laws that govern our financial system can become counterproductive in an inflationary environment, causing problems that were never intended by legislators. Some economists feel that the high tax rates caused by inflation discourage saving, lending, and investing—and therefore retard economic growth.**

Thus, failure to understand that high *nominal* interest rates can still be low *real* interest rates has been known to make the tax code misfire, to impoverish savers, and to inhibit borrowing and lending. And it is important to note that *these costs of inflation are not purely redistributive.* Society as a whole loses when mutually beneficial transactions are prohibited by dysfunctional legislation.

Why, then, do such harmful laws stay on the books? The main reason appears to be a lack of understanding of the difference between real and nominal interest rates. People fail to understand that it is normally the *real* rate of interest that matters in an economic transaction because only that rate reveals how much borrowers pay and lenders receive *in terms of the goods and services that money can buy.* They focus on the high *nominal* interest rates caused by inflation, even when these rates correspond to low real interest rates.

> **The difference between real and nominal interest rates, and the fact that the real rate matters economically whereas the nominal rate is often politically significant, are matters that are of the utmost importance and yet are understood by very few people—including many who make public policy decisions.**

A **capital gain** is the difference between the price at which an asset is sold and the price at which it was bought.

OTHER COSTS OF INFLATION

Another cost of inflation is that rapidly changing prices make it risky to enter into long-term contracts. In an extremely severe inflation, the "long term" may be only a few days from now. But even moderate inflations can have remarkable effects on long-term loans. Suppose a corporation wants to borrow $1 million to finance the purchase of some new equipment and needs the loan for 20 years. If inflation averages 2 percent over this period, the $1 million it repays at the end of 20 years will be worth $672,971 in today's purchasing power. But if inflation averages 5 percent instead, it will be worth only $376,889.

Lending or borrowing for this long a period is obviously a big gamble. With the stakes so high, the outcome may be that neither lenders nor borrowers want to get involved in long-term contracts. But without long-term loans, business investment may become impossible. The economy may stagnate.

Inflation also makes life difficult for the shopper. You probably have a group of stores that you habitually patronize because they carry the items you want to buy at (roughly) the prices you want to pay. This knowledge saves you a great deal of time and energy. But when prices are changing rapidly, your list quickly becomes obsolete. You return to your favorite clothing store to find that the price of jeans has risen drastically. Should you buy? Should you shop around at other stores? Will they have also raised their prices? Business firms have precisely the same problem with their suppliers. Rising prices force them to shop around more, which imposes costs on the firms and, more generally, reduces the efficiency of the entire economy.

THE COSTS OF LOW VERSUS HIGH INFLATION

The preceding litany of the costs of inflation alerts us to one very important fact: *Predictable inflation is far less burdensome than unpredictable inflation.* When is inflation most predictable? When it proceeds year after year at a modest and more or less steady rate. Thus, the *variability of the inflation rate* is a crucial factor. Inflation of 3 percent per year for three consecutive years will exact lower social costs than inflation that is 2 percent in the first year, zero in the second year, and 7 percent in the third year. In general:

Steady inflation is more predictable than variable inflation and therefore has smaller social and economic costs.

But the *average level of inflation* also matters. Partly because of the inflation illusions mentioned earlier and partly because of the more rapid breakdown in normal customer relationships that we have just mentioned, steady inflation of 6 percent per year is more damaging than steady inflation of 3 percent per year.

Economists distinguish between *low inflation,* which is a modest economic problem, and *high inflation,* which can be a devastating one, partly on the basis of the average level of inflation and partly on its variability. If inflation remains steady and low, prices may rise for a long time, but at a moderate and fairly constant pace, allowing people to adapt. For example, inflation in the United States, as measured by the Consumer Price Index, has been remarkably steady since 1991, never dropping below 1.6 percent nor rising above 4.1 percent.

Very high inflations typically last for short periods of time and are often marked by highly variable inflation rates from month to month or year to year. In recent decades, for example, countries ranging from Argentina to Russia to Zimbabwe have experienced bouts of inflation exceeding 100 percent or even 1,000 percent per year. (See "How to Make Hyperinflation Even Worse" on the next page.) Each of these episodes severely disrupted the affected country's economy.

The German hyperinflation after World War I is perhaps the most famous episode of runaway inflation. Between December 1922 and November 1923, when a hard-nosed reform program finally broke the spiral, wholesale prices in Germany increased by almost 100 million percent! But even this experience was dwarfed by the great Hungarian inflation of 1945–1946, the greatest inflation of them all. For a period of one year, the *monthly* rate of inflation averaged about 20,000 percent. In the final month, the price level skyrocketed 42 quadrillion percent!

If you review the costs of inflation that have been discussed in this chapter, you will see why the distinction between low and high inflation is so fundamental. Many economists think we can live rather nicely in an environment of steady, low inflation. No one believes we can survive very well under extremely high inflation. When inflation is steady and low, the rate at which prices rise is relatively easy to predict. It can therefore be taken into account in setting interest rates. Under high inflation, especially if prices are rising at ever-increasing or highly variable rates, this is extremely difficult, and perhaps impossible, to do. The potential redistributions become monumental, and lending and borrowing may cease entirely.

Any inflation makes it difficult to write long-term contracts. Under low, creeping inflation, the "long term" may be 20 years, or 10 years, or 5 years. By contrast, under high, galloping inflation, the "long term" may be measured in days or weeks. Restaurant prices may change daily. Airfares may go up while you are in flight. When it is impossible to enter into contracts of any duration longer than a few days, economic activity becomes paralyzed. We conclude that

The horrors of hyperinflation are very real. But they are either absent in low, steady inflations or present in such muted forms that they can scarcely be considered horrors.

How to Make Hyperinflation Even Worse

For some years now, the world's highest inflation rate has been in the impoverished African country of Zimbabwe. And recently, it has escalated into the first episode of virulent hyperinflation in decades.

After averaging around 20 percent per year in the mid 1990s, Zimbabwean inflation began to accelerate at the end of the 1990s and really took off starting in 2002. According to the International Monetary Fund (IMF), consumer prices in Zimbabwe rose 132 percent in 2002, 350 percent in 2004, and a stunning 1,017 percent in 2006. Then things really got out of control, with inflation rising month after month. At this writing, the IMF estimates that inflation in Zimbabwe reached the astonishing rate of 16,000 percent for 2007 as a whole, and press reports state that it topped 66,000 percent at an annual rate in December! The root cause, of course, was what it always is in hyperinflations: the Zimbabwean government was printing colossal amounts of money to pay its bills.

While printing too much money was bad enough, Zimbabwe's dictator, Robert Mugabe, decided to compound the sin by instituting price controls in July 2007. After all, if inflation is running too high, he apparently reasoned, why not just decree that it stop? Well, even an absolute dictator must contend with the laws of economics—especially if he keeps running the printing presses at full tilt. (In the summer of 2007, Zimbabwe's central bank was forced to introduce a 200,000 Zimbabwean dollar (Z$) bill so that people could conduct business.) The result was predictable: commodities, including basic foodstuffs, quickly disappeared from the shelves. Long queues and even riots developed as Zimbabwe's starved citizens scrambled to purchase what little there was to buy. Neighboring South Africa reported Zimbabweans pouring over the border—some to flee the chaos, but some just to shop.

A newspaper story in July 2007 reported that "buying meat in Zimbabwe these days is like buying an illegal substance."* While the government price ceiling for beef was Z$87,000 per kilogram, the article reported one of the few shopkeepers with meat to sell asking Z$300,000 per kilo for the precious substance—while carefully watching the door for government inspectors. The local newspaper in one of Zimbabwe's cities reported that trying to find beef for sale was "like looking for a snowflake in the Sahara desert." Why? Because the government's only licensed meat processor was slaughtering only 100 cattle per day—to feed a population of 12 million people!

And meat was by no means a special case. Within weeks after price controls were instituted, such basics as bread, cornmeal, sugar, salt, flour, and even matches were difficult to find, thousands of shopkeepers had been arrested, and many stores were opening only at night to avoid the inspectors. Zimbabwe was barreling full-speed-ahead toward economic chaos.

SOURCE: "Zimbabwe's Shopping Nightmare," *The Scotsman,* July 26, 2007.

LOW INFLATION DOES NOT NECESSARILY LEAD TO HIGH INFLATION

We noted earlier that inflation is surrounded by a mythology that bears precious little relation to reality. It seems appropriate to conclude this chapter by disposing of one particularly persistent myth: that low inflation is a slippery slope that invariably leads to high inflation.

There is neither statistical evidence nor theoretical support for the belief that low inflation inevitably leads to high inflation. To be sure, inflations sometimes speed up. At other times, however, they slow down.

Although creeping inflations have many causes, runaway inflations have occurred only when the government has printed incredible amounts of money, usually to finance wartime expenditures. In the German inflation of 1923, the government finally found that its printing presses could not produce enough paper money to keep pace with the exploding prices. Not that it did not try—by the end of the inflation, the *daily* output of currency exceeded 400 quadrillion marks! The Hungarian authorities in 1945–1946 tried even harder: The average growth rate of the money supply was more than 12,000 percent *per month.* Needless to say, these are not the kind of inflation problems that are likely to face industrialized countries in the foreseeable future.

But that does not mean there is nothing wrong with low inflation. We have spent several pages analyzing the very real costs of even modest inflation. A case against moderate inflation can indeed be built, but it does not help this case to shout slogans like "Creeping inflation always leads to galloping inflation." Fortunately, it is simply not true.

These children in Germany during the hyperinflation of the 1920s are building a pyramid with cash, worth no more than the sand or sticks used by children elsewhere.

SOURCE: © Camera Press/Globe Photos, Inc.

| SUMMARY |

1. Macroeconomic policy strives to achieve rapid and reasonably stable growth while keeping both unemployment and inflation low.

2. Only rising productivity can raise standards of living in the long run. And seemingly small differences in productivity growth rates can compound to enormous differences in living standards. This is one of our *Ideas for Beyond the Final Exam.*

3. The **production function** tells us how much output the economy can produce from the available supplies of labor and capital, given the state of technology.

4. The growth rate of **potential GDP** is the sum of the growth rate of the **labor force** plus the growth rate of **labor productivity.** The latter depends on, among other things, technological change and investment in new capital.

5. Over long periods of time, the growth rates of actual and potential GDP match up quite well. But, owing to macroeconomic fluctuations, the two can diverge sharply over short periods.

6. Although some psychologists, environmentalists, and social critics question the merits of faster economic growth, economists generally assume that faster growth of potential GDP is socially beneficial.

7. When GDP is below its potential, unemployment is above **"full employment."** High unemployment exacts heavy financial and psychological costs from those who are its victims, costs that are borne quite unevenly by different groups in the population.

8. **Frictional unemployment** arises when people are between jobs for normal reasons. Thus, most frictional unemployment is desirable.

9. **Structural unemployment** is due to shifts in the pattern of demand or to technological change that makes certain skills obsolete.

10. **Cyclical unemployment** is the portion of unemployment that rises when real GDP grows more slowly than potential GDP and falls when the opposite is true.

11. Today, after years of extremely low unemployment, economists are unsure where full employment lies.

Many think it may be at a measured unemployment rate around 5 percent.

12. **Unemployment insurance** replaces about half of the lost income of unemployed persons who are insured. But barely over one-third of the unemployed actually collect benefits, and no insurance program can bring back the lost output that could have been produced had these people been working.

13. People have many misconceptions about inflation. For example, many believe that inflation systematically erodes **real wages** and blame inflation for any unfavorable changes in relative prices. Both of these ideas are myths.

14. Other costs of inflation are real, however. For example, inflation often redistributes income from lenders to borrowers.

15. This redistribution is ameliorated by adding the expected rate of inflation to the interest rate. But such expectations often prove to be inaccurate.

16. The **real rate of interest** is the **nominal rate of interest** minus the **expected rate of inflation.**

17. Because the real rate of interest indicates the command over real resources that the borrower surrenders to the lender, it is of primary economic importance. But public attention often is riveted on nominal rates of interest, and this confusion can lead to costly policy mistakes.

18. Because nominal—not real—**capital gains** and interest are taxed, our tax system levies heavy taxes on income from capital when inflation is high.

19. Low inflation that proceeds at moderate and fairly predictable rates year after year carries far lower social costs than does high or variable inflation. But even low, steady inflations entail costs.

20. The notion that low inflation inevitably accelerates into high inflation is a myth with no foundation in economic theory and no basis in historical fact.

| KEY TERMS |

Inputs 105	Unemployment rate 111	Real wage rate 117
Outputs 105	Discouraged workers 114	Relative prices 119
Growth policy 106	Frictional unemployment 114	Redistribution by inflation 120
Economic growth 106	Structural unemployment 114	Real rate of interest 121
Labor productivity 107	Cyclical unemployment 114	Nominal rate of interest 121
Potential GDP 108	Full employment 115	Expected rate of inflation 121
Labor force 108	Unemployment insurance 116	Capital gain 122
Production function 108	Purchasing power 117	

| TEST YOURSELF |

1. Two countries start with equal GDPs. The economy of Country A grows at an annual rate of 3 percent while the economy of Country B grows at an annual rate of 4 percent. After 25 years, how much larger is Country B's economy than Country A's economy? Why is the answer *not* 25 percent?

2. If output rises by 35 percent while hours of work increase by 40 percent, has productivity increased or decreased? By how much?

3. Most economists believe that from 2000 to 2003, actual GDP in the United States grew slower than potential GDP. What, then, should have happened to the unemployment rate over those three years? Then, from 2003 to 2006, actual GDP likely grew faster than potential GDP. What should have happened to the unemployment rate over those three years? (Check the data on the inside back cover of this book to see what actually happened.)

4. Country A and Country B have identical population growth rates of 1 percent per annum, and everyone in each country always works 40 hours per week. Labor productivity grows at a rate of 2 percent in Country A and a rate of 2.5 percent in Country B. What are the growth rates of potential GDP in the two countries?

5. What is the *real interest rate* paid on a credit card loan bearing 18 percent nominal interest per year, if the rate of inflation is

   a. zero?

   b. 4 percent?

   c. 8 percent?

   d. 15 percent?

   e. 20 percent?

6. Suppose you agree to lend money to your friend on the day you both enter college at what you both expect to be a zero *real* rate of interest. Payment is to be made at graduation, with interest at a fixed *nominal* rate. If inflation proves to be *lower* during your college years than what you both had expected, who will gain and who will lose?

| DISCUSSION QUESTIONS |

1. If an earthquake destroys some of the factories in Poorland, what happens to Poorland's potential GDP? What happens to Poorland's potential GDP if it acquires some new advanced technology from Richland and starts using it?

2. Why is it not as terrible to become unemployed nowadays as it was during the Great Depression?

3. "Unemployment is no longer a social problem because unemployed workers receive unemployment benefits and other benefits that make up for most of their lost wages." Comment.

4. Why is it so difficult to define *full employment?* What unemployment rate should the government be shooting for today?

5. Show why each of the following complaints is based on a misunderstanding about inflation:

    a. "Inflation must be stopped because it robs workers of their purchasing power."

    b. "Inflation makes it impossible for working people to afford many of the things they were hoping to buy."

    c. "Inflation must be stopped today, for if we do not stop it, it will surely accelerate to ruinously high rates and lead to disaster."

| APPENDIX | *How Statisticians Measure Inflation*

INDEX NUMBERS FOR INFLATION

Inflation is generally measured by the change in some index of the general price level. For example, between 1977 and 2007 the Consumer Price Index (CPI), the most widely used measure of the price level, rose from 60.6 to 207.3—an increase of 242 percent. The meaning of the *change* is clear enough. But what are the meanings of the 60.6 figure for the price level of 1977 and the 207.3 figure for 2007? Both are **index numbers.**

> A **price index** expresses the cost of a market basket of goods relative to its cost in some "base" period, which is simply the year used as a basis of comparison.

Because the CPI currently uses 1982–1984 as its base period, the CPI of 207.3 for 2007 means that it cost $207.30 in 2007 to purchase the same basket of several hundred goods and services that cost $100 in 1982–1984.

Now in fact, the particular list of consumer goods and services under scrutiny did not actually cost $100 in 1982–1984. When constructing index numbers, by convention the index is set at 100 in the base period. This conventional figure is then used to obtain index numbers for other years in a very simple way. Suppose that the budget needed to buy the hundreds of items included in the CPI was $2,000 per month in 1982–1984 and $4146 per month in 2007 Then the index is defined by the following rule:

$$\frac{\text{CPI in 2007}}{\text{CPI in 1982–1984}}$$

$$= \frac{\text{Cost of market basket in 2007}}{\text{Cost of market basket in 1982–1984}}$$

Because the CPI in 1982–1984 is set at 100:

$$\frac{\text{CPI in 2007}}{100} = \frac{\$4,146}{\$2,000} = 2.073$$

or

$$\text{CPI in 2007} = 207.3$$

Exactly the same sort of equation enables us to calculate the CPI in any other year. We have the following rule:

$$\text{CPI in given year} = \frac{\text{Cost of market basket in given year}}{\text{Cost of market basket in base year}} \times 100$$

Of course, not every combination of consumer goods that cost $2,000 in 1982–1984 rose to $4,146 by 2007. For example, a color TV set that cost $400 in 1983 might still have cost $400 in 2007, but a $400 hospital bill in 1983 might have ballooned to $3,000. The index number problem refers to the fact that there is no perfect cost-of-living index because no two families buy precisely the same bundle of goods and services, and hence no two families suffer precisely the same increase in prices. Economists call this the **index number problem:**

> When relative prices are changing, there is no such thing as a "perfect price index" that is correct for every consumer. Any statistical index will understate the increase in the cost of living for some families and overstate it for others. At best, the index can represent the situation of an "average" family.

THE CONSUMER PRICE INDEX

The **Consumer Price Index (CPI),** which is calculated and announced each month by the Bureau of Labor Statistics (BLS), is surely the most closely watched price index. When you read in the newspaper or see on television that the "cost of living rose by 0.2 percent last month," chances are the reporter is referring to the CPI.

> The **Consumer Price Index (CPI)** is measured by pricing the items on a list representative of a typical urban household budget.

To know which items to include and in what amounts, the BLS conducts an extensive survey of spending habits roughly once every decade. As a consequence, the *same* bundle of goods and services is used as a standard for 10 years or more, whether or not spending habits change.[10] Of course, spending habits do change, and this variation introduces a small error into the CPI's measurement of inflation.

A simple example will help us understand how the CPI is constructed. Imagine that college students purchase only three items—hamburgers, jeans, and movie tickets—and that we want to devise a cost-of-living index (call it SPI, or "Student Price Index") for them. First, we would conduct a survey of spending habits in the base year. (Suppose it is 1983.) Table 5 represents the hypothetical results. You will note that the frugal students of that day spent only $100 per month: $56 on hamburgers, $24 on jeans, and $20 on movies.

TABLE 5

Results of Student Expenditure Survey, 1983

Item	Average Price	Average Quantity Purchased per Month	Average Expenditure per Month
Hamburger	$ 0.80	70	$56
Jeans	24.00	1	24
Movie ticket	5.00	4	20
Total			$100

Table 6 presents hypothetical prices of these same three items in 2007. Each price has risen by a different amount, ranging from 25 percent for jeans up to 50 percent for hamburgers. By how much has the SPI risen?

TABLE 6

Prices in 2007

Item	Price	Increase over 1983
Hamburger	$1.20	50%
Jeans	30.00	25
Movie ticket	7.00	40

Pricing the 1983 student budget at 2007 prices, we find that what once cost $100 now costs $142, as the calculation in Table 7 shows. Thus, the SPI, based on 1983 = 100, is

$$\text{SPI} = \frac{\text{Cost of budget in 2007}}{\text{Cost of budget in 1983}} \times 100$$

$$= \frac{\$142}{\$100} \times 100 = 142$$

TABLE 7

Cost of 1983 Student Budget in 2007 Prices

70 Hamburgers at $1.20	$84
1 pair of jeans at $30	30
4 movie tickets at $7	28
Total	$142

So, the SPI in 2007 stands at 142, meaning that students' cost of living has increased 42 percent over the 24 years.

USING A PRICE INDEX TO "DEFLATE" MONETARY FIGURES

One of the most common uses of price indexes is in the comparison of monetary figures relating to two different points in time. The problem is that if there has been inflation, the dollar is not a good measuring rod because it can buy less now than it did in the past.

Here is a simple example. Suppose the average student spent $100 per month in 1983 but $140 per month in 2007. If there was an outcry that students had become spendthrifts, how would you answer the charge?

The obvious answer is that a dollar in 2007 does not buy what it did in 1983. Specifically, our SPI shows us that it takes $1.42 in 2007 to purchase what $1 would purchase in 1983. To compare the spending habits of students in the two years, we must divide the 2007 spending figure by 1.42. Specifically, *real* spending per student in 2007 (where "real" is defined by 1983 dollars) is:

$$\frac{\text{Real spending}}{\text{in 2007}} = \frac{\text{Nominal spending in 2007}}{\text{Price index of 2007}} \times 100$$

---

[10] Economists call this a *base-period weight index* because the relative importance it attaches to the price of each item depends on how much money consumers actually chose to spend on the item during the base period.

Thus:

$$\text{Real spending in 2007} = \frac{\$140}{142} \times 100 = \$98.59$$

This calculation shows that, despite appearances to the contrary, the change in nominal spending from $100 to $140 actually represented a small *decrease* in real spending.

This procedure of dividing by the price index is called **deflating,** and it serves to translate noncomparable monetary figures into more directly comparable real figures.

Deflating is the process of finding the real value of some monetary magnitude by dividing by some appropriate price index.

A good practical illustration is the real wage, a concept we have discussed in this chapter. As we saw in the boxed insert on page 118, we obtain the real wage by dividing the nominal wage by the price level.

USING A PRICE INDEX TO MEASURE INFLATION

In addition to deflating nominal magnitudes, price indexes are commonly used to measure *inflation,* that is, the *rate of increase* of the price level. The procedure is straightforward. The data on the inside back cover (Column 13) show that the CPI was 49.3 in 1974 and 44.4 in 1973. The ratio of these two numbers, 49.3/44.4, is 1.11, which means that the 1974 price level was 11 percent greater than the 1973 price level. Thus, the *inflation rate* between 1973 and 1974 was 11 percent. The same procedure holds for any two adjacent years. Most recently, the CPI rose from 201.6 in 2006 to 207.3 in 2007. The ratio of these two numbers is 207.3/201.6 = 1.028, meaning that the inflation rate from 2006 to 2007 was 2.8 percent.

THE GDP DEFLATOR

In macroeconomics, one of the most important of the monetary magnitudes that we have to deflate is the nominal gross domestic product (GDP).

The price index used to deflate nominal GDP is called the GDP deflator. It is a broad measure of economy-wide inflation that includes the prices of all goods and services in the economy.

Our general principle for deflating a nominal magnitude tells us how to go from nominal GDP to real GDP:

$$\text{Real GDP} = \frac{\text{Nominal GDP}}{\text{GDP deflator}} \times 100$$

As with the CPI, the 100 simply serves to establish the base of the index as 100, rather than 1.00.

Some economists consider the GDP deflator to be a better measure of overall inflation than the Consumer Price Index. The main reason is that the GDP deflator is based on a broader market basket. As mentioned earlier, the CPI is based on the budget of a typical urban family. By contrast, the GDP deflator is constructed from a market basket that includes *every* item in the GDP—that is, every final good and service produced by the economy. Thus, in addition to prices of consumer goods, the GDP deflator includes the prices of airplanes, lathes, and other goods purchased by businesses—especially computers, which fall in price every year. It also includes government services. For this reason, the two indexes rarely give the same measure of inflation. Usually the discrepancy is minor. But sometimes it can be noticeable, as in 2000 when the CPI recorded a 3.4 percent inflation rate over 1999 while the GDP deflator recorded an inflation rate of only 2.2 percent.

| SUMMARY |

1. Inflation is measured by the percentage increase in an **index number** of prices, which shows how the cost of some basket of goods has changed over a period of time.

2. Because relative prices are always changing, and because different families purchase different items, no price index can represent precisely the experience of every family.

3. The **Consumer Price Index (CPI)** tries to measure the cost of living for an average urban household by pricing a typical market basket every month.

4. Price indexes such as the CPI can be used to **deflate** nominal figures to make them more comparable. Deflation amounts to dividing the nominal magnitude by the appropriate price index.

5. The inflation rate between two adjacent years is computed as the percentage change in the price index between the first year and the second year.

6. The **GDP deflator** is a broader measure of economy-wide inflation than the CPI because it includes the prices of all goods and services in the economy.

| KEY TERMS |

Price index   127

Index number problem   127

Consumer Price Index (CPI)   128

Deflating   129

GDP deflator   129

| TEST YOURSELF |

1. Below you will find the yearly average values of the Dow Jones Industrial Average, the most popular index of stock market prices, for four different years. The Consumer Price Index for each year (on a base of 1982–1984 = 100) can be found on the inside back cover of this book. Use these numbers to deflate all five stock market values. Do real stock prices always rise every decade?

Year	Dow Jones Industrial Average
1970	753
1980	891
1990	2,679
2000	10,735

2. Below you will find nominal GDP and the GDP deflator (based on 2000 = 100) for the years 1987, 1997, and 2007.

   a. Compute real GDP for each year.

   b. Compute the percentage change in nominal and real GDP from 1987 to 1997, and from 1997 to 2007.

   c. Compute the percentage change in the GDP deflator over these two periods.

GDP Statistics	1987	1997	2007
Nominal GDP (Billions of dollars)	4,740	8,304	13,843
GDP deflator	73.2	95.4	119.7

3. Fill in the blanks in the following table of GDP statistics:

	2005	2006	2007
Nominal GDP	12,434		13,843
Real GDP	11,003	11,319	
GDP deflator		116.6	119.7

4. Use the following data to compute the College Price Index for 2007 using the base 1982 = 100.

Item	Price in 1982	Quantity per Month in 1982	Price in 2007
Button-down shirts	$10	1	$25
Loafers	25	1	55
Sneakers	10	3	35
Textbooks	12	12	40
Jeans	12	3	30
Restaurant meals	5	11	14

5. Average hourly earnings in the U.S. economy during several past years were as follows:

1970	1980	1990	2000
$3.23	$6.66	$10.01	$13.75

Use the CPI numbers provided on the inside back cover of this book to calculate the real wage (in 1982–1984 dollars) for each of these years. Which decade had the fastest growth of money wages? Which had the fastest growth of real wages?

6. The example in the appendix showed that the Student Price Index (SPI) rose by 42 percent from 1983 to 2007. You can understand the meaning of this better if you do the following:

a. Use Table 5 to compute the fraction of total spending accounted for by each of the three items in 1983. Call these values the "expenditure weights."

b. Compute the weighted average of the percentage increases of the three prices shown in Table 6, using the expenditure weights you just computed.

You should get 42 percent as your answer. This shows that inflation, as measured by the SPI, is a weighted average of the percentage price increases of all the items that are included in the index.

ECONOMIC GROWTH: THEORY AND POLICY

Once one starts to think about . . . [differences in growth rates among countries],
it is hard to think about anything else.

ROBERT E. LUCAS, JR.,
1995 NOBEL PRIZE WINNER IN ECONOMICS

Why do some economies grow rapidly while others grow slowly—or not at all? As the opening quotation suggests, there is probably no more important question in all of economics. From 1990 to 2005, according to the World Bank, the American economy grew at a 3.2 percent annual rate, while China's grew 10.3 percent per year and Russia's *declined* (on average) by 1.2 percent per year. Those are very large differences. What factors account for such disparities?

The discussion in Chapter 6 of the goal of economic growth focused our attention on two crucial but distinct tasks for macroeconomic policy makers, both of which are quite difficult to achieve:

- *Growth policy:* Ensuring that the economy sustains a high long-run growth rate of potential GDP (although not necessarily the *highest possible* growth rate)
- *Stabilization policy:* Keeping actual GDP reasonably close to potential GDP in the short run, so that society is plagued by neither high unemployment nor high inflation

This chapter is devoted to the theory of economic growth and to the policies that this theory suggests.

Corresponding to the two tasks listed just above, there are two ways to think about what is to come in this and subsequent chapters. In discussing *growth policy* in this chapter, we study the factors that determine an economy's *long-run* growth rate of *potential GDP*, and we consider how policy makers can try to speed it up. When we turn to *stabilization policy*, starting in the next chapter, we will investigate how and why *actual GDP* deviates from potential GDP in the *short run* and how policy makers can try to minimize these deviations. Thus the two views of the macroeconomy complement one another.

CONTENTS

PUZZLE: WHY DOES COLLEGE EDUCATION KEEP GETTING MORE EXPENSIVE?

Have you ever wondered why the cost of a college education rises more rapidly than most other prices year after year? If you have not, your parents surely have! And it's not a myth. Between 1978 and 2007, the component of the Consumer Price Index (CPI) that measures college tuition costs rose by about 800 percent—compared to about 218 percent for the overall CPI. That is, the relative price of college tuition increased massively.

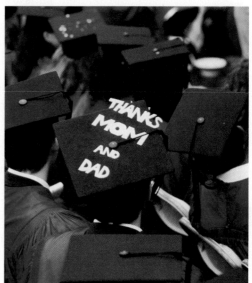

Economists understand at least part of the reason, and it has little, if anything, to do with the efficiency (or lack thereof) with which colleges are run. Rather, it is a natural companion to the economy's long-run growth rate. Furthermore, there is good reason to expect the relative price of college tuition to keep rising, and to rise more rapidly in faster-growing societies. Economists believe that the same explanation for the unusually rapid growth in the cost of attending college applies to services as diverse as visits to the doctor, theatrical performances, and restaurant meals—all of which also have become relatively more expensive over time. Later in this chapter, we shall see precisely what this explanation is.

THE THREE PILLARS OF PRODUCTIVITY GROWTH

As we learned in the previous chapter, the growth rate of potential GDP is the *sum* of the growth rates of *hours of work* and *labor productivity*. It is hardly mysterious that an economy will grow if its people keep working harder and harder, year after year. And a few societies have followed that recipe successfully for relatively brief periods of time. But there is a limit to how much people can work or, more important, to how much they want to work. In fact, people typically want more leisure time, not longer hours of work, as they get richer. In consequence, the natural focus of growth policy is on enhancing productivity—on working *smarter* rather than working *harder*.

The last chapter introduced a tool called the *production function,* which tells us how much *output* the economy can produce from specified *inputs* of labor and capital, given the state of *technology.* The discussion there focused on two of the three main determinants of productivity growth:[1]

- The rate at which the economy builds up its stock of *capital*
- The rate at which *technology* improves

Before introducing the third determinant, let us review how these first two pillars work.

---

[1] If you need review, see pages 108–110 of Chapter 6.

Capital

Figure 1 resembles Figure 1 of the last chapter (see page 108). The lower curve $0K_1$ is the production function when the capital stock is some low number K_1. Its upward slope indicates, naturally enough, that more labor input produces more output. (Remember, technology is held constant in this graph.) The middle curve $0K_2$ is the production function corresponding to some larger capital stock K_2, and the upper curve $0K_3$ pertains to an even larger capital stock K_3.

To keep things simple at first, suppose hours of work do not grow over time, but rather remain fixed at L_1. However, the nation's businesses invest in new plant and equipment, so the capital stock grows from K_1 in the first year to K_2 in the second year and K_3 in the third year. Then the economy's capacity to produce will move up from point *a* in year 1 to point *b* in year 2 and point *c* in year 3. Potential GDP will therefore rise from Y_a to Y_b to Y_c. Because hours of work do not change in this example (by assumption), every bit of this growth comes from rising *productivity*, which is in turn due to the accumulation of more capital.[2] In general:

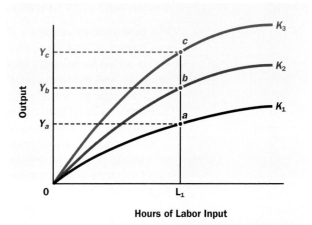

FIGURE 1

Production Functions Corresponding to Three Different Capital Stocks

> For a given technology and a given labor force, labor productivity will be higher when the capital stock is larger.

This conclusion is hardly surprising. Employees who work with more capital can obviously produce more goods and services. Just imagine manufacturing a desk, first with only hand tools, then with power tools, and finally with all the equipment available in a modern furniture factory. Or think about selling books from a sidewalk stand, in a bookstore, or over the Internet. Your productivity would rise in each case. Furthermore, workers with *more* capital are almost certainly blessed with *newer*—and, hence, *better*—capital as well. This advantage, too, makes them more productive. Again, compare one of Henry Ford's assembly-line workers of a century ago to an autoworker in a Ford plant today.

Technology

In Chapter 6, we saw that a graph like Figure 1 can also be used to depict the effects of *improvements in technology*. So now imagine that curves $0K_1$, $0K_2$, and $0K_3$ all correspond to the same capital stock, but to *different* levels of technology. Specifically, the economy's technology improves as we move up from $0K_1$ to $0K_2$ to $0K_3$. The graphical (and common-sense) conclusion is exactly the same: Labor becomes more productive from year 1 to year 2 to year 3, so improving technology leads directly to growth. In general:

> For given inputs of labor and capital, labor productivity will be higher when the technology is better.

Once again, this conclusion hardly comes as a surprise—indeed, it is barely more than the definition of technical progress. When we say that a nation's technology improves, we mean, more or less, that firms in the country can produce *more output* from the *same inputs*. And of course, superior technology is a major factor behind the vastly higher productivity of workers in rich countries versus poor ones. Textile plants in North Carolina, for example, use technologies that are far superior to those employed in Africa.

---

[2] Because productivity is the ratio Y/L, it is shown on the graph by the *slope* of the straight line connecting the origin to point *a*, or point *b*, or point *c*. Clearly, that slope is rising over time.

Labor Quality: Education and Training

It is now time to introduce the third pillar of productivity growth, the one not mentioned in Chapter 6: *workforce quality*. It is generally assumed—and supported by reams of evidence—that better-educated workers can produce more goods and services in an hour than can less well-educated workers. And the same lesson applies to training that takes place outside the schools, such as on the job: Better-trained workers are more productive. The amount of education and training embodied in a nation's labor force is often referred to as its stock of **human capital**.

Conceptually, an increase in human capital has the same effect on productivity as an increase in physical capital or an improvement in technology, that is, the same *quantity* of labor input becomes capable of producing more output. So we can use the ever-adaptable Figure 1 for yet a third purpose—to represent increasing *workforce quality* as we move up from $0K_1$ to $0K_2$ to $0K_3$. Once again, the general conclusion is obvious:

> **For a given capital stock, labor force, and technology, labor productivity will be higher when the workforce has more education and training.**

This third pillar is another obvious source of large disparities between rich nations, which tend to have well-educated populations, and poor nations, which do not. So we can add a third item to complete our list of the three principal determinants of a nation's productivity growth rate:

- The rate at which the economy builds up its stock of *capital*
- The rate at which *technology* improves
- The rate at which *workforce quality* (or "human capital") is improving

In the contemporary United States, average educational attainment is high and workforce quality changes little from year to year. But in some rapidly developing countries, improvements in education can be an important engine of growth. For example, average years of schooling in South Korea soared from less than five in 1970 to more than nine in 1990, which contributed mightily to South Korea's remarkably rapid economic development.

Although there is no unique formula for growth, the most successful growth strategies of the post–World War II era, beginning with the Japanese "economic miracle," made ample use of all three pillars. Starting from a base of extreme deprivation after World War II, Japan showed the world how a combination of high rates of investment, a well-educated workforce, and the adoption of state-of-the-art technology could catapult a poor nation into the leading ranks within a few decades. The lessons were not lost on the so-called Asian Tigers—including Taiwan, South Korea, Singapore, and Hong Kong—which developed rapidly using their own versions of the Japanese model. Today, a number of other countries, most notably China, are applying variants of this growth formula once again. It works.

Human capital is the amount of skill embodied in the workforce. It is most commonly measured by the amount of education and training.

LEVELS, GROWTH RATES, AND THE CONVERGENCE HYPOTHESIS

Notice that, where productivity *growth rates* are concerned, it is the *rates of increase* of capital, technology, and workforce quality that matter, rather than their current *levels*. This distinction may sound boring, but it is important.

Productivity *levels* are vastly higher in the rich countries—that is why they are called rich. The wealthy nations have more bountiful supplies of capital, more highly skilled workers, and superior technologies. Naturally, they can produce more output per hour of work. Table 1 shows, for example, that an hour of labor in France in 2005 produced 99 percent as much output as an hour of labor in the United States, when evaluated in U.S. dollars, whereas the corresponding figure for Brazil was only 23 percent.

But the *growth rates* of capital, workforce skills, and technology are not necessarily higher in the rich countries. For example, Country A might have abundant capital, but the amount might be increasing at a snail's pace, whereas in Country B capital might be scarce but growing rapidly. When it comes to determining the long-run growth rate, it is the *growth rates* rather than the current *levels* of these three pillars that matter.

In fact, GDP per hour of work actually grew faster over the 25 years covered in Table 1 in several countries that have lower average incomes than the United States. For example, productivity in South Korea, Ireland, France, and the United Kingdom all grew faster than in the United States. Why? While a typical Irish worker in 1980 had far less physical and human capital than a typical American worker, and used substantially less-advanced technology, the capital stock, average educational attainment, and level of technology all *increased* faster in Ireland than in the United States.

The level of productivity in a nation depends on its supplies of human and physical capital and the state of its technology. But the growth rate of productivity depends on the rates of increase of these three factors.

TABLE 1

Productivity Levels and Productivity Growth Rates in Selected Countries

Country	GDP per Hour of Work 1980 (as percentage of U.S.)	GDP per Hour of Work 2005 (as percentage of U.S.)	Growth Rate
United States	**100**	**100**	**1.7**
France	86	99	2.3
United Kingdom	71	85	2.4
Spain	62	62	1.7
Ireland	57	96	3.9
Argentina	51	37	0.4
Mexico	44	25	− 0.5
Brazil	33	23	0.2
South Korea	20	48	5.4

NOTE: All productivity data are measured *in U.S. dollars*. So countries whose currencies rise relative to the U.S. dollar gain on the United States, whereas countries whose currencies fall relative to the U.S. dollar lose ground.

SOURCE: International Labour Organization, *Key Indicators of the Labour Market* (Geneva: 2007), Table 18A (at http://www.ilo.org/kilm).

The distinction between productivity levels and productivity growth rates may strike you as a piece of pedantic arithmetic, but it has many important practical applications. Here is a particularly striking one. If the productivity growth rate is higher in poorer countries than in richer ones, then poor countries will close the gap on rich ones. The so-called **convergence hypothesis** suggests that this is what normally happens.

The Convergence Hypothesis: The productivity growth rates of poorer countries tend to be higher than those of richer countries.

The idea behind the convergence hypothesis, as illustrated in Figure 2, is that productivity growth will typically be faster where the initial level of productivity is lower. In this hypothetical example, the poorer country starts out with a per-capita GDP of $2,000, just one-fifth that of the richer country. But the poor country's real GDP per capita grows faster, so it gradually narrows the relative income gap.

Why might we expect such convergence to be the norm? In some poor countries, the supply of capital may be growing very rapidly. In others, educational attainment may be rising quickly, albeit from a low base. But the main reason to expect convergence in the long run is that *low-productivity countries should be able to learn from high-productivity countries* as scientific and managerial know-how spreads around the world.

A country that is operating at the technological frontier can improve its technology only by *innovating.* It must constantly figure out ways to do things better. But a less advanced country can boost its productivity simply by *imitating,* by adopting technologies that are already in common use in the advanced countries. Not surprisingly, it is much easier to "look it up" than to "think it up."

Modern communications assist the convergence process by speeding the flow of information around the globe. The Internet was invented mainly in the United States and the United Kingdom, but it quickly spread to almost every corner of the world. Likewise, advances in human genomics and stem-cell research are now originating in some of the most advanced countries, but they are communicated rapidly to scientists all over the world. A poor country that is skilled at importing scientific and engineering advances from the rich

The **convergence hypothesis** holds that nations with low levels of productivity tend to have high productivity growth rates, so that international productivity differences shrink over time.

FIGURE 2

The Convergence Hypothesis

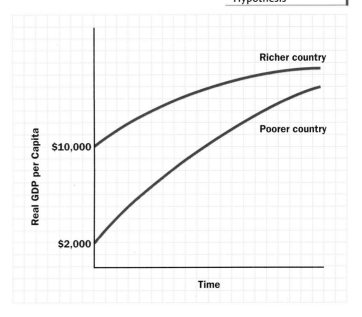

TABLE 2

Levels and Growth Rates of GDP per Capita in Selected Poor Countries

Country	GDP per Capita, 2005*	GDP Per Capita Growth Rate, 1990–2005
Belarus	$1,868	2.0%
Russia	2,445	−0.4
Ukraine	960	−2.4
Peru	2,337	2.3
Haiti	434	−2.4
Burundi	105	−2.5
Sierra Leone	218	−0.9

* In constant 2000 U.S. dollars.

SOURCE: World Bank, World Development Indicators, 2007.

countries can achieve very rapid productivity growth. Indeed, when Japan was a poor nation, successful imitation was one of its secrets to getting rich. India and China are trying that now—with considerable success.

Unfortunately, many poor countries seem unable to participate in the convergence process. For a variety of reasons (some of which will be mentioned later in this chapter), a number of developing countries seem incapable of adopting and adapting advanced technologies. In fact, Table 1 shows that per-capita incomes in some of these nations actually grew more slowly than in the rich countries over the quarter-century covered by the table. Labor productivity in Argentina and Brazil both grew much slower than that of the United States, for example, while Mexico's productivity (when measured in U.S. dollars) actually declined. Sadly, this kind of decline is not all that unusual. Real incomes have stagnated or even fallen in some of the poorest countries of the world, especially in Africa and many of the formerly communist countries (see Table 2). Convergence certainly cannot be taken for granted.

Technological laggards can, and sometimes do, close the gap with technological leaders by imitating and adapting existing technologies. Within this "convergence club," productivity *growth rates* are higher where productivity *levels* are lower. Unfortunately, some of the world's poorest nations have been unable to join the club.

GROWTH POLICY: ENCOURAGING CAPITAL FORMATION

A nation's **capital** is its available supply of plant, equipment, and software. It is the result of past decisions to make *investments* in these items.

Investment is the *flow* of resources into the production of new capital. It is the labor, steel, and other inputs devoted to the *construction* of factories, warehouses, railroads, and other pieces of capital during some period of time.

Capital formation is synonymous with investment. It refers to the process of building up the capital stock.

Let us now see how the government might spur growth by working on these three pillars, beginning with capital.

First, we need to clarify some terminology. We have spoken of the supply of **capital,** by which we mean the volume of plant (factories, office buildings, and so on), equipment (drill presses, computers, and so on), and software currently available. Businesses *add* to the existing supply of capital whenever they make **investment** expenditures—purchases of new plant, equipment, and software. In this way, the *growth* of the capital stock depends on how much businesses spend on investment. That process is called **capital formation**—literally, forming new capital.

But you don't get something for nothing. Devoting more of society's resources to producing investment goods generally means devoting fewer resources to producing consumer goods. A *production possibilities frontier* like those introduced in Chapter 3 can be used to depict the nature of this trade-off—and the choices open to a nation. Given its technology and existing resources of labor, capital, and so on, the country can in principle select any point on the production possibilities frontier *AICD* in Figure 3. If it picks a point like *C*, its citizens will enjoy many consumer goods, but it will not be investing much for the future. *So it will grow slowly.* If, on the other hand, it selects a point like *I*, its citizens will consume less today, but the nation's higher level of investment means *it will grow more quickly.* Thus, at least within limits, the amount of capital formation and growth can be chosen.

Now suppose the government wants the capital stock to grow faster, that is, it wants to move from a point like *C* toward a point like *I* in Figure 3. In a capitalist, market economy such as ours, private businesses make almost all investment decisions—how many factories to build, how many computers to purchase, and so on. To speed up the process of capital formation, the government must somehow persuade private businesses to invest more. But how?

Real Interest Rates The most obvious way to increase investment by private businesses is to lower real interest rates. When real interest rates fall, investment normally rises. Why? Because businesses often borrow to finance their investments, and the real interest rate indicates how much firms must pay for that privilege. An investment project that looks unattractive at an interest rate of 10 percent may look highly profitable if the firm has to pay only 6 percent.

> **The amount that businesses invest depends on the real interest rate they pay to borrow funds. The lower the real rate of interest, the more investment there will be.**

In subsequent chapters, we will learn how government policy, especially monetary policy, influences interest rates—which gives policy makers some leverage over private investment decisions. That relationship, in fact, is why monetary policy will play such a crucial role in subsequent chapters. But we might as well come clean right away: For reasons to be examined later, the government's ability to control real interest rates is imperfect. Furthermore, the rate of interest is only one of several determinants of investment spending. So policy makers have only a limited ability to affect the level of investment by manipulating interest rates.

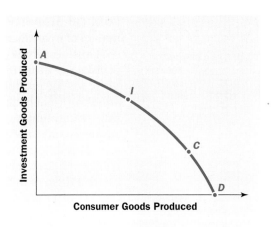

FIGURE 3

Choosing between Investment and Consumption

Tax Provisions   The government also can influence investment spending by altering various provisions of the tax code. For example, President George W. Bush and Congress reduced the tax rate on capital gains—the profit earned by selling an asset for more than you paid for it—in 2003. The major argument for lowering capital gains taxes was the claim, much disputed by the critics, that it would lead to greater investment spending. In addition, the United States imposes a tax on corporate profits and can reduce that tax to spur investment as well. There are other, more complicated tax provisions relating to investment, too.[3] To summarize:

> **The tax law gives the government several ways to influence business spending on investment goods. But influence is far from total control.**

Technical Change   Technology, which we have listed as a separate pillar of growth, also drives investment. New business opportunities suddenly appear when a new product such as the mobile telephone is invented or when a technological breakthrough makes an existing product much cheaper or better, as is happening with flat-panel TVs right now. In a capitalist system, entrepreneurs pounce on such opportunities—building new factories, stores, and offices, and buying new equipment. Thus, if the government can figure out how to spur technological progress (a subject discussed later in this chapter), those same policies will probably boost investment.

The Growth of Demand   Rapid growth itself can induce businesses to invest more. When demand presses against capacity, executives are likely to believe that new factories and machinery can be employed profitably—which creates strong incentives to build new capital. Thus it was no coincidence that investment soared in the United States during the boom years of the 1990s, collapsed when the economy slowed precipitously in 2000–2001, and then revived again starting in 2003. By contrast, if machinery and factories stand idle, businesses may find new investments unattractive. In summary:

> **High levels of sales and expectations of rapid economic growth create an atmosphere conducive to investment.**

This situation creates a kind of virtuous cycle in which high rates of investment boost economic growth, and rapid growth boosts investment. Of course, the same process can also operate in reverse—as a vicious cycle: When the economy stagnates, firms do not want to invest much, which damages prospects for further growth.

---

[3] But any kind of a tax cut will reduce government revenue. Unless that revenue is made up by a spending cut or by some other tax, the government's budget deficit will rise—which will also affect investment. We will study that channel in Chapter 15.

Political Stability and Property Rights   There is one other absolutely critical determinant of investment spending that Americans simply take for granted.

Property rights are laws and/or conventions that assign owners the rights to use their property as they see fit (within the law)—for example, to sell the property and to reap the benefits (such as rents or dividends) while they own it.

A business thinking about committing funds to, say, build a factory faces any number of risks. Construction costs might run higher than estimates. Interest rates might rise. Demand for the product might prove weaker than expected. The list goes on and on. These are the normal hazards of entrepreneurship, an activity that is not for the faint of heart. But, at a minimum, business executives contemplating a long-term investment want assurances that their property will not be taken from them for capricious or political reasons. Republican businesspeople in the United States do not worry that their property will be seized if the Democrats win the next election. Nor do they worry that court rulings will deprive them of their **property rights** without due process.

By contrast, in many less-well-organized societies, the rule of law is regularly threatened by combinations of arbitrary government actions, political instability, anticapitalist ideology, rampant corruption, or runaway crime. Such problems have posed serious impediments to long-term investment in many poor countries throughout history. They are among the chief reasons these countries have remained poor. And the litany of problems that threaten property rights is not just a matter of history—these issues remain relevant in countries as different as Russia, much of Africa, and parts of Latin America today. Where businesses fear that their property may be expropriated, a drop in interest rates of a few percentage points will not encourage much investment.

Needless to say, the strength of property rights, adherence to the rule of law, the level of corruption, and the like are not easy things to measure. Anyone who attempts to rank countries on such criteria must make many subjective judgments. Nevertheless, due to its recent interest in the subject, the World Bank currently ranks 175 countries on various aspects of their business climate, including their degree of investor protection. Some of their data are displayed in Table 3. The ranking of the various countries is roughly what you might expect.

TABLE 3	
Selected Countries Ranked by Level of Investor Protection	
Country	Rating (0–10 scale)
Singapore	9.3
United States	**8.3**
Canada	8.3
United Kingdom	8.0
Japan	7.0
Mexico	6.0
India	6.0
Sweden	5.7
Brazil	5.3
Italy	5.0
China	5.0
Swaziland	2.3

SOURCE: World Bank web site, www.doingbusiness.org, accessed August 2007. The index is constructed by rating countries on transparency of transactions, liability for self-dealing, and shareholders' ability to sue for misconduct.

GROWTH POLICY: IMPROVING EDUCATION AND TRAINING

Numerous studies in many countries confirm the fact that more-educated and better-trained workers earn higher wages. Economists naturally assume that the people who earn more are also more productive. Thus, more education and training presumably

To Grow Fast, Get the Institutions Right

A few years ago, the World Bank surveyed the ways the governments of around 100 countries either encourage or discourage market activity. Its conclusion, as summarized in *The Economist*, was that "when poor people are allowed access to the institutions richer people enjoy, they can thrive and help themselves. A great deal of poverty, in other words, may be easily avoidable."

The World Bank study highlighted the importance of making simple institutions accessible to the poor—such as protection of property rights (especially over land), access to the judicial system, and a free and open flow of information—as key ingredients in successful economic development. *The Economist* put it graphically:

If it is too expensive and time-consuming, for example, to open a bank account, the poor will stuff their savings under the mattress. When it takes 19 steps, five months and more than an average person's annual income to register a new business in Mozambique, it is no wonder that aspiring, cash-strapped entrepreneurs do not bother.

The Bank's conclusion reminded many people of the central message of a best-selling 2000 book by Peruvian economist and businessman Hernando de Soto—who found to his dismay that, in his own country, it took 700 bureaucratic steps to obtain legal title to a house!

SOURCES: "Now, Think Small," *The Economist*, September 15, 2001, pp. 40–42. Hernando de Soto, *The Mystery of Capital: Why Capitalism Triumphs in the West and Fails Everywhere Else* (New York: Basic Books), 2000.

contribute to higher productivity. Although private institutions play a role in the educational process, in most societies the state bears the primary responsibility for educating the population. So *education policy* is an obvious and critical component of growth policy.

A modern industrial society is built more on brains than on brawn. Even ordinary blue-collar jobs often require a high school education. For this reason, policies that raise rates of high school attendance and completion and, perhaps as importantly, improve the *quality* of secondary education can make genuine contributions to growth. Unfortunately, such policies have proven difficult to devise and implement. So the debate over how to improve our public schools goes on and on, with no resolution in sight. President Bush's No Child Left Behind program is only the latest in a long list of educational reforms.

Finally, if knowledge is power in the information age, then sending more young people to college and graduate school may be crucial to economic success. It is well documented that the earnings gap between high school and college graduates in the United States has risen dramatically since the late 1970s. One graphical depiction of this rising disparity is shown in Figure 4. It shows clearly that the job market was rewarding the skills acquired in college ever more generously from about 1978 until about 2000. To the extent that high wages reflect high productivity, low-cost tuition (such as that paid at many state colleges and universities), student loans to low-income families, and other policies to encourage college attendance may yield society rich dividends.

Devoting more resources to education should, therefore, raise an economy's growth rate. By suitable reinterpretation, Figure 3 (on page 139) can again be used to illustrate the trade-off between present and future. Because expenditures on education are naturally thought of as *investments* in *human* capital, just interpret the vertical axis as now representing educational investments. If a society spends more on them and less on consumer goods (thus moving from point C toward point I), it should grow faster. China, to cite the most prominent example, is doing that with great enthusiasm right now.

But education is not a panacea for all of an economy's ills. Education in the former Soviet Union was outstanding in some respects. But it proved insufficient to prevent the Soviet economy from falling ever further behind the capitalist economies in terms of economic growth.

On-the-job training may be just as important as formal education in raising productivity, but it is less amenable to influence by the government. For the most part, private

On-the-job training refers to skills that workers acquire while at work, rather than in school or in formal vocational training programs.

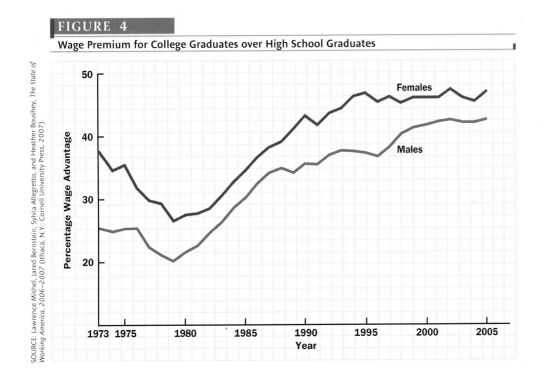

FIGURE 4

Wage Premium for College Graduates over High School Graduates

SOURCE: Lawrence Mishel, Jared Bernstein, Sylvia Allegretto, and Heather Boushey, *The State of Working America, 2006–2007* (Ithaca, N.Y.: Cornell University Press, 2007).

Percentage Wage Advantage (y-axis): 20, 30, 40, 50

Year (x-axis): 1973 1975, 1980, 1985, 1990, 1995, 2000, 2005

Females

Males

businesses decide how much, and in what ways, to train their workers. Various public policy initiatives—ranging from government-run training programs, to subsidies for private-sector training, to mandated minimum training expenditures by firms—have been tried in various countries with mixed results. In the United States, mandates on companies have always been viewed as improper interferences with private business decisions, and they have been avoided. The government runs some training programs, though the biggest (by far) is the armed forces.

GROWTH POLICY: SPURRING TECHNOLOGICAL CHANGE

Our third pillar of growth is *technology,* or getting more output from given supplies of inputs. Some of the most promising policies for speeding up the pace of technical progress have already been mentioned:

More Education   Although some inventions and innovations are the product of dumb luck, most result from the sustained application of knowledge, resources, and brainpower to scientific, engineering, and managerial problems. We have just noted that more-educated workers appear to be more productive *per se*. In addition, a society is likely to be more innovative if it has a greater supply of scientists, engineers, and skilled business managers who are constantly on the prowl for new opportunities. Modern growth theory emphasizes the pivotal role in the growth process of committing more human, physical, and financial resources to the acquisition of knowledge.

> **High levels of education, especially scientific, engineering, and managerial education, contribute to the advancement of technology.**

There is little doubt that the United States leads the world in the quality of its graduate programs in business and in many of the scientific and engineering disciplines. As evidence of this superiority, one need only look at the tens of thousands of foreign students who flock to our shores to attend graduate school—many of whom remain in America. It seems reasonable to suppose that America's unquestioned leadership in scientific and business education contributes to our leadership in productivity. On this basis, many economists and politicians endorse policies designed to induce more bright young people to pursue scientific and engineering careers—such as scholarships, fellowships, and research grants—and worry that too few young Americans are choosing these career paths.

More Capital Formation   We are all familiar with the fact that the latest versions of cell phones, PCs, personal digital assistants (PDAs), and even televisions embody new features that were unavailable a year or even six months ago. The same is true of industrial capital. Indeed, new investment is the principal way in which the latest technological breakthroughs get hard-wired into the nation's capital stock. As we mentioned in our earlier discussion of capital formation, newer capital is normally better capital. In this way,

> **High rates of investment contribute to rapid technical progress.**

So all of the policies we discussed earlier as ways to bolster capital formation can also be thought of as ways to speed up technical progress.

Research and Development   But there is a more direct way to spur **invention** and **innovation**: devote more of society's resources to **research and development (R&D)**.

Driven by the profit motive, American businesses have long invested heavily in industrial R&D. According to the old saying, "Build a better mousetrap, and the world will beat a path to your door." And innovative companies in the United States and elsewhere have been engaged in research on "better mousetraps" for decades. Polaroid invented instant photography, Xerox developed photocopying, and Apple pioneered the desktop computer. Boeing improved jet aircraft several times. U.S.-based pharmaceutical companies

Invention is the act of discovering new products or new ways of making products.

Innovation is the act of putting new ideas into effect by, for example, bringing new products to market, changing product designs, and improving the way in which things are done.

Research and development (R&D) refers to activities aimed at inventing new products or processes, or improving existing ones.

have discovered many new, life-enhancing drugs. Intel has developed generation after generation of ever-faster microprocessors. The list goes on and on.

All these companies and others have spent untold billions of dollars on R&D to discover new products, to improve old ones, and to make their industrial processes more efficient. Although many research dollars are inevitably "wasted" on false starts and experiments that don't pan out, numerous studies have shown that the average dollar invested in R&D has yielded high returns to society. Heavy spending on R&D is, indeed, one of the keys to high productivity growth.

The U.S. government supports and encourages R&D in several ways. First, it subsidizes private R&D spending through the tax code. Specifically, the Research and Experimentation Tax Credit reduces the taxes of companies that spend more money on R&D.

Second, the government sometimes joins with private companies in collaborative research efforts. The Human Genome Project may be the best-known example of such a public–private partnership (some called it a race!). But there also have been cooperative ventures in new automotive technology, alternative energy sources, and elsewhere.

Last, and certainly not least, the federal government has over the years spent a great deal of taxpayer money directly on R&D. Much of this spending has been funneled through the Department of Defense. But the National Aeronautics and Space Administration (NASA), the National Science Foundation (NSF), the National Institutes of Health (NIH), and many other agencies have also played important roles. Inventions as diverse as atomic energy, advanced ceramic materials, and the Internet were originally developed in federal laboratories. Federal government R&D spending in fiscal year 2006 amounted to roughly $134 billion, more than half of which went through the Pentagon.

Our multipurpose Figure 3 (page 139) again illustrates the choice facing society. Now interpret the vertical axis as measuring investments in R&D. Devoting more resources to R&D—that is, choosing point *I* rather than point *C*—leads to less current consumption but more growth.

THE PRODUCTIVITY SLOWDOWN AND SPEED-UP IN THE UNITED STATES

Around 1973, productivity growth in the United States suddenly and mysteriously slowed down—from the rate of about 2.8 percent per year that had characterized the 1948–1973 period to about 1.4 percent thereafter (see Figure 5). Hardly anyone anticipated this productivity slowdown. Then, starting around 1995, productivity growth suddenly speeded up again—from about 1.4 percent per year during the 1973–1995 period back to about 2.5 percent since then (see Figure 5 again). Once again, the abrupt change in the growth rate caught most people by surprise.

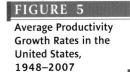

FIGURE 5

Average Productivity Growth Rates in the United States, 1948–2007

Recall from the discussion of compounding in Chapter 6 that a change in the growth rate of around 1 percentage point, if sustained for decades, makes an enormous difference in living standards. So understanding these two major events is of critical importance. Yet even now, some 35 years later, economists remain puzzled about the 1973 productivity slowdown, and the reasons behind the 1995 productivity speed-up are only partly understood. Let us see what economists know about these two episodes.

The Productivity Slowdown, 1973–1995

The productivity slowdown after 1973 was a disconcerting development, and economists have

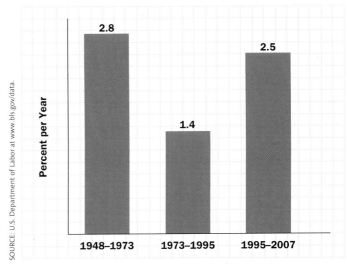

SOURCE: U.S. Department of Labor at www.bls.gov/data.

NOTE: Data pertain to the nonfarm business sector.

been struggling to explain it ever since. Among the leading explanations that have been offered are the following.

Lagging Investment   During the 1980s and early 1990s, many people suggested that inadequate investment was behind America's productivity problem. Countries such as Germany and Japan, these critics observed, saved and invested far more than Americans did, thereby equipping their workers with more modern equipment that boosted labor productivity. United States tax policy, they argued, should create stronger incentives for business to invest and for households to save.

Although the argument was logical, the facts never did support it. For example, the share of U.S. GDP accounted for by business investment did not decline during the period of slow productivity growth. Nor did the contribution of capital formation to growth fall. (See the box on growth accounting on the next page.)

High Energy Prices   A second explanation begins with a tantalizing fact: The productivity slowdown started around 1973, just when the Organization of Petroleum Exporting Countries (OPEC) jacked up the price of oil. As a matter of logic, higher oil prices should reduce business use of energy, which should make labor less productive. Furthermore, productivity growth fell just at the time that energy prices rose, not just in the United States but all over the world—which is quite a striking coincidence. This circumstantial evidence points the finger at oil. The argument sounds persuasive until you remember another important fact: When energy prices dropped sharply in the mid-1980s, productivity growth did not revive. So the energy explanation of the productivity slowdown has many skeptics.

Inadequate Workforce Skills   Could it be that the skills of the U.S. labor force failed to keep pace with the demands of new technology after 1973? Although workforce skills are notoriously difficult to measure, there was and is a widespread feeling that the quality of education in the United States has declined. For example, SAT scores peaked in the late 1960s and then declined for about 20 years.[4] Yet standard measures such as school attendance rates, graduation rates, and average levels of educational attainment all continued to register gains in the 1970s and 1980s. Clearly, the proposition that the quality of the U.S. workforce declined is at least debatable.

A Technological Slowdown?   Could the pace of innovation have slowed in the 1973–1995 period? Most people instinctively answer "no." After all, the microchip and the personal computer were invented in the 1970s, opening the door to what can only be called a revolution in computing and information technology (IT). Workplaces were transformed beyond recognition. Entirely new industries (such as those related to PCs) were spawned. Didn't these technological marvels raise productivity by enormous amounts?

The paradox of seemingly rapid technological advance coupled with sluggish productivity performance puzzled economists for years. How could the contribution of technology to growth have *fallen*? A satisfactory answer was never given. And then, all of a sudden, the facts changed.

The Productivity Speed-up, 1995–?

Figure 5 shows that productivity growth speeded up remarkably after 1995, rising from about 1.4 percent per annum before that year to about 2.5 percent from 1995 to 2007. This time, the causes are better understood—and most of them relate to the IT revolution.

Surging Investment   Bountiful new business opportunities in the IT sector and elsewhere, coupled with a strong national economy, led to a surge in business investment

---

[4] The SAT was rescaled about a decade ago to reflect this decline in average scores.

Growth Accounting in the United States

In this chapter, we have learned that labor productivity (output per hour of work) rises because more capital is accumulated, because technology improves, and because workforce quality rises. The last of these three pillars is quantitatively unimportant in the modern United States because average educational attainment has been high for a long time and has not changed much recently. But the other two pillars are very important.

The table breaks down the growth rate of labor productivity into its two main components over three different periods of time. We see that the productivity slowdown after 1973 was entirely accounted for by slower technological improvement; the contribution of capital formation did not decline at all.* Similarly, the productivity speed-up after 1995 was entirely accounted for by faster technical progress, not by higher rates of investment.

	1948–1973	1973–1995	1995–2006
Growth rate of Labor Productivity	2.8%	1.4%	2.7%
Contribution of capital formation	0.9	1.0	1.0
Contribution of technology	1.9	0.4	1.7

SOURCE: Bureau of Labor Statistics at www.bls.gov/data.

* Changes in workforce quality are included in the technology component.

spending in the 1990s. Business investment as a percentage of real GDP rose from 9.1 percent in 1991 to 14.6 percent in 2000, and most of that increase was concentrated in computers, software, and telecommunications equipment. We have observed several times in this chapter that the productivity growth rate should rise when the capital stock grows faster—and it did in the late 1990s. But then investment fell when the stock market crashed, beginning in 2000. So, over the entire 1995–2006 period, the table in the box above shows the same contribution of capital formation to productivity growth in 1995–2006 as in 1973–1995. So investment cannot be the answer.

Falling Energy Prices?   For part of this period, especially the years 1996–1998, energy prices were falling. By the same logic used earlier, falling energy prices should have enhanced productivity growth. But, as we noted earlier, this argument did not seem to work so well when energy prices fell in the 1980s. Why, then, should we believe it for the 1990s? In addition, productivity continued to surge in the early years of this decade, after energy prices had started to rise.

Advances in Information Technology   We seem to be on safer ground when we look to technological progress, especially in computers and semiconductors, to explain the speed-up in productivity growth. First, innovation seemed to have exploded in the 1990s. Computers became faster and much, much cheaper—as did telecommunications equipment and services. Corporate intranets became commonplace. The Internet grew from a scientific curiosity into a commercial reality, and so on. We truly entered the Information Age.

Second, it probably took American businesses some time to learn how to use the computer and telecommunications technologies that were invented and adopted between, say, 1980 and the early 1990s. It was only in the late 1990s, some observers argue, that U.S. industry was positioned to reap the benefits of these advances in the form of higher productivity. Such long delays are not unprecedented. Research has shown, for example, that it took a long time for the availability of electric power at the end of the nineteenth century to contribute much to productivity growth. Like electric power, computers were a novel input to production, and it may have taken years for prospective users to find the most productive ways to employ them.

In summary:

The biggest pillar of productivity growth—technological change—seems to do a credible job of explaining why productivity accelerated in the United States after 1995.

PUZZLE RESOLVED: WHY THE RELATIVE PRICE OF COLLEGE TUITION KEEPS RISING

Earlier in this chapter, we observed that the relative prices of services such as college tuition, medical care, and theater tickets seem to rise year after year. And we suggested that one main reason for this perpetual increase is tied to the economy's long-run growth rate. We are now in a position to understand precisely how that mechanism works. Rising productivity is the key. The argument is based on three simple ideas.

IDEA 1 It stands to reason, and is verified by historical experience, that *real wages tend to rise at the same rate as labor productivity.* This relationship makes sense: Labor normally gets paid more when it produces more. Thus real wages will rise most rapidly in those economies with the fastest productivity growth.

IDEA 2 Although average labor productivity in the economy increases from year to year, *there are a number of personally provided services for which productivity (output per hour) cannot or does not grow.* We have already mentioned several of them. Your college or university can increase the "productivity" of its faculty by increasing class size, but most students and parents would view that as a decrease in educational quality. Similarly, a modern doctor takes roughly as long to give a patient a physical as his counterparts did 25 or 50 years ago. It also takes *exactly* the same time for an orchestra to play one of Beethoven's symphonies today as it did in Beethoven's time.

There is a common ingredient in each of these diverse examples: The major sources of higher labor productivity that we have studied in this chapter—more capital and better technology—are completely or nearly irrelevant. It still takes one lecturer to teach a class, one doctor to examine a patient, and four musicians to play a string quartet—just as it did 100 years ago. Saving on labor by using more and better equipment is more or less out of the question.[5] These so-called *personal services* stand in stark contrast to, say, working on an automobile assembly line or in a semiconductor plant, or even to working in service industries such as telecommunications—all instances in which both capital formation and technical progress regularly raise labor productivity.

IDEA 3 *Real wages in different occupations must rise at similar rates in the long run.* This point may sound wrong at first: Haven't the wages of computer programmers risen faster than those of schoolteachers in recent years? Yes they have, and that is the market's way of attracting more young people into computer programming. But in the long run, these growth rates must (more or less) equilibrate, or else virtually no one would want to be a schoolteacher any more.

Now let's bring the three ideas together. College teachers are no more productive than they used to be, but autoworkers are (Idea 2). But in the long run, the real wages of college teachers and autoworkers must grow at roughly the same rate (Idea 3), which is the economy-wide productivity growth rate (Idea 1). As a result, wages of college teachers and doctors will rise *faster* than their productivity does, and so their services must grow ever more expensive compared to, say, computers and phone calls.

That is, indeed, the way things seem to have worked out. Compared to the world in which your parents grew up, computers and telephone calls are now very cheap while college tuition and doctors' bills are very expensive. The same logic applies to the services of police officers (two per squad car), baseball players (nine per team), chefs, and many other occupations where productivity improvements are either impossible or undesirable. All of these services have grown much more expensive over the years. This phenomenon has been called the **cost disease of the personal services.**

According to the **cost disease of the personal services,** service activities that require direct personal contact tend to rise in price relative to other goods and services.

---

[5] However, some people foresee a world in which some aspects of education and medical care will be delivered long distance over the Internet. We'll see!

Ironically, the villain of the piece is actually the economy's strong productivity growth. If manufacturing and telecommunications workers had *not* become more productive over time, their real wages would not have risen. In that case, the real wages of teachers and doctors would not have had to keep pace, so their services would not have grown ever more expensive. Paradoxically, the enormous productivity gains that have blessed our economy and raised our standard of living also account for the problem of rising tuition costs. In the most literal sense, we are the victims of our own success.

GROWTH IN THE DEVELOPING COUNTRIES[6]

Ernest Hemingway once answered a query of F. Scott Fitzgerald's by agreeing that, yes, the rich *are* different—they have more money! Similarly, whereas the main determinants of economic growth—increases in capital, improving technology, and rising workforce skills—are the same in both rich and poor countries, they look quite different in what is often called the Third World. This chapter has focused on growth in the industrialized countries so far. So let us now review the three pillars of productivity growth from the standpoint of the developing nations, using China as the most outstanding recent example of success.

The Three Pillars Revisited

Capital   We noted earlier that many poor countries are poorly endowed with capital. Given their low incomes, they simply have been unable to accumulate the volumes of business capital (factories, equipment, and the like) and public capital (roads, bridges, airports, and so on) that we take for granted in the industrialized world. In a super-rich country like the United States, $150,000 or more worth of capital stands behind a typical worker, while in a poor African country the corresponding figure may be less than $500. No wonder the American worker is vastly more productive than his African counterpart.

But accumulating more capital can be exceptionally difficult in the developing world. We noted earlier that rich countries have a *choice* about how much of their resources to devote to current consumption versus investment for the future. But building capital for the future is a far more difficult task in poor countries, where much of the population may be living on the edge of survival and have little if anything to save for the future. For this reason, it has long been believed that **development assistance**, sometimes called *foreign aid*, is a crucial ingredient for growth in the developing world. Indeed, the *World Bank* was established in 1944 precisely to make low-interest development loans to poor countries.

Development assistance has always been controversial. Critics of foreign aid argue that the money is often not well spent. Without honest and well-functioning governments, well-defined property rights, and so on, they argue, the developing countries cannot and will not make good use of the assistance they receive. Supporters of foreign aid counter that the donor countries have been far too stingy. The United States, for example, donates only about 0.1 percent of its GDP each year. Can grants that amount to $60 per person—which is a fairly typical figure for the recipient countries—really be expected to make much difference?

While foreign aid can be critical in certain instances, it has certainly *not* been the secret to China's success. Instead, the Chinese have shown a remarkable willingness and ability to save and invest—nearly half of GDP in recent years—despite their relatively low incomes. In addition, China has welcomed **foreign direct investment**, often by **multinational corporations**, which it has received in great volume.

Development assistance ("foreign aid") refers to outright grants and low-interest loans to poor countries from both rich countries and multinational institutions like the World Bank. The purpose is to spur economic development.

Foreign direct investment is the purchase or construction of real business assets—such as factories, offices, and machinery—in a foreign country.

Multinational corporations are corporations, generally large ones, that do business in many countries. Most, but not all, of these corporations have their headquarters in developed countries.

---

[6] This section can be skipped in shorter courses.

Technology   You need only visit a poor country to see that the level of technology is generally far below what we in the West are accustomed to. In principle, this handicap should be easy to overcome. As noted in our discussion of the convergence hypothesis, people in poor countries don't have to invent anything; they can just adopt technologies that have already been invented in the rich countries. And indeed, a number of formerly poor countries have followed this strategy with great success. South Korea, which was destitute in the mid-1950s, is a prime example. China is doing this today. Indeed, much of the foreign direct investment flowing into China brings Western technology along with it.

But as we observed earlier, many of the developing nations, especially the poorest ones, seem unable to join this "convergence club." They may lack the necessary scientific and engineering know-how. They may be short on educated workers. They may be woefully undersupplied with the necessary infrastructure, such as transportation and communications systems. Or they may simply be plagued by incompetent or corrupt governments. Whatever the reasons, they have been unable emulate the technological advances of the West.

There are no easy solutions to this problem. One common suggestion is to encourage foreign direct investment by multinational corporations. Industrial giants like Toyota (Japan), IBM (United States), Siemens (Germany), and others bring their advanced technologies with them when they open a factory or office in a developing nation. They can train local workers and improve local transportation and communications networks. But, of course, these companies are *foreign*, and they come to make a *profit*—both of which may cause resentment in the local population.

For this and other reasons, many developing countries have not always welcomed foreign investment. China, as mentioned above, is a big exception: It has welcomed foreign investment with enthusiasm, especially for the technology it brings, and it has learned avidly and openly from the West. However, multinational companies are rarely tempted to open factories in the poorest developing countries, such as those in sub-Saharan Africa, where skilled labor is in short supply, transportation systems may be inadequate, and governments are often unstable and unreliable.

TABLE 4	
Average Educational Attainment in Selected Countries, 2000*	
United States	**12.3**
Canada	11.4
South Korea	10.5
Japan	9.7
United Kingdom	9.4
Italy	7.0
Mexico	6.7
India	4.8
Brazil	4.6
Sudan	1.9

* For people older than 25 years of age

SOURCE: Web site accompanying R. Barro and J.-W. Lee, "International Data on Educational Attainment: Updates and Implications," CID Working paper No. 42, Harvard University, 2000, http://www.cid.harvard.edu/ciddata/ciddata.html.

Education and Training   Huge discrepancies exist between the average levels of educational attainment in the rich and poor countries. Table 4 shows some data on average years of schooling in selected countries, both developed and developing. The differences are dramatic—ranging from a high of 12.3 years in the United States to less than 5 years in India and less than 2 years in the Sudan. In most industrialized countries, universal primary education and high rates of high school completion are already realities. But in many poor countries, even completing grade school may be the exception, leaving rudimentary skills such as reading, writing, and basic arithmetic in short supply. In such cases, expanding and improving primary education—including keeping children in school until they reach the age of 12—may be among the most cost-effective growth policies available. The problem is particularly acute in many traditional societies, where women are second-class citizens—or worse. In such countries, the education of girls may be considered unimportant or even inappropriate.

China, again, offers a stunning contrast. It is raising the educational attainment of its population rapidly. It is sending legions of students abroad to study science, engineering, business, and economics (among other things). And it is seeking to develop world-class universities of its own.

Some Special Problems of the Developing Countries

Accumulating capital, improving technology, and enhancing workforce skills are common ingredients of growth in rich and poor countries alike. But many Third World countries also must contend with some special handicaps to growth that are mostly absent in the West.

Geography   Americans often forget how blessed we are geographically. We live in a temperate climate zone, on a land mass that has literally millions of acres of flat, fertile land that is ideal for agriculture. The fact that our nation literally stretches "from sea to shining sea" also means we have many fine seaports. Contrast this splendid set of geographical conditions with the situation of the world's poorest region: sub-Saharan Africa. Many African nations are landlocked, have extremely hot climates, and/or are terribly short on arable land.

Health   People in the rich countries rarely think about such debilitating tropical diseases as malaria. But they are rampant in many developing nations, especially in Africa. The AIDS epidemic, of course, is ravaging the continent. Although improvements in public health are important in all countries, they are literally matters of life and death in the poorest nations. And there is a truly vicious cycle here: Poor health is a serious impediment to economic growth, and poverty makes it hard to improve health standards.

Governance   Complaining about low-quality or dishonest government is a popular pastime in many Western democracies. Americans do it every day. But most governments in industrialized nations are paragons of virtue and efficiency compared to the governments of some (though certainly not all) developing nations. As we have noted in this chapter, political stability, the rule of law, and respect for property rights are all crucial requirements for economic growth. By the same token, corruption and overregulation of business are obvious deterrents to investment. Lawlessness, tyrannical rule, and war are even more serious impediments. Unfortunately, too many poor nations have been victimized by a succession of corrupt dictators and tragic wars. It need hardly be said that those conditions are not exactly conducive to economic growth.

FROM THE LONG RUN TO THE SHORT RUN

Most of this chapter has been devoted to explaining and evaluating the factors underpinning the growth rate of *potential* GDP. Over long periods of time, the growth rates of actual and potential GDP match up pretty well. But, just like people, economies do not always live up to their potential. As we observed in the previous chapter, GDP in the United States often diverges from potential GDP as a result of macroeconomic fluctuations. Sometimes it is higher; sometimes it is lower. Indeed, whereas this chapter has studied the factors that determine the rate at which the GDP of a particular country can *grow* from one year to the next, we know that GDP occasionally *shrinks*—during periods we call *recessions*. To study these fluctuations, we must supplement the long-run theory of *aggregate supply*, which we have just described, with a short-run theory of *aggregate demand*—a task that begins in the next chapter.

| SUMMARY |

1. More **capital,** improved workforce quality (which is normally measured by the amount of education and training), and better technology all raise labor productivity and therefore shift the production function upward. They constitute the three main pillars of growth.

2. The growth rate of labor productivity depends on the rate of capital formation, the rate of improvement of workforce quality, and the rate of technical progress. So growth policy concentrates on speeding up these processes.

3. **Capital formation** can be encouraged by low real interest rates, favorable tax treatment, rapid technical change, rapid growth of demand, and a climate of political stability that respects **property rights.** Each of these factors is at least influenced by policy.

4. Policies that increase education and training—the second pillar of growth—can be expected to make a country's workforce more productive. They range from universal primary education to postgraduate fellowships in science and engineering.

5. Technological advances can be encouraged by more education, by higher rates of **investment,** and also by direct expenditures—both public and private—on **research and development (R&D).**

6. The **convergence hypothesis** holds that countries with lower productivity levels tend to have higher productivity growth rates, so that poor countries gradually close the gap on rich ones.

7. One major reason to expect convergence is that technological know-how can be transferred quickly from the leading nations to the laggards. Unfortunately, not all countries seem able to benefit from this information transfer.

8. Productivity growth slowed precipitously in the United States around 1973, and economists are still not sure why.

9. Productivity growth in the United States has speeded up again since 1995, largely as a result of the information technology (IT) revolution.

10. Because many personal services—such as education, medical care, and police protection—are essentially handicraft activities that are not amenable to labor-saving innovations, they suffer from a **cost disease** that makes them grow ever more expensive over time.

11. The same three pillars of economic growth—capital, technology, and education—apply in the developing countries. But on all three fronts, conditions are much more difficult there—and improvements are harder to obtain.

12. The rich countries try to help with all three pillars by providing **development assistance,** and **multinational corporations** sometimes provide capital and better technology via **foreign direct investment.** But both of these mechanisms are surrounded by controversy.

13. Growth in many of the poor countries is also held back by adverse geographical conditions and/or corrupt governments.

| KEY TERMS |

Human capital   136

Convergence hypothesis   137

Capital   138

Investment   138

Capital formation   138

Property rights   140

On-the-job training   141

Invention   142

Innovation   142

Research and development (R&D)   142

Cost disease of the personal services   146

Development assistance   147

Foreign direct investment   147

Multinational corporations   147

| TEST YOURSELF |

1. The following table shows real GDP per hour of work in four imaginary countries in the years 1997 and 2007. By what percentage did labor productivity grow in each country? Is it true that productivity *growth* was highest where the initial *level* of productivity was the lowest? For which countries?

	Output per Hour	
	1997	2007
Country A	$40	$48
Country B	$25	$35
Country C	$ 2	$ 3
Country D	$ 0.50	$ 0.60

2. Imagine that new inventions in the computer industry affect the growth rate of productivity as follows:

Year of Invention	Following Year	5 Years Later	10 Years Later	20 Years Later
0%	−1%	0%	+2%	+4%

Would such a pattern help explain U.S. productivity performance since the mid-1970s? Why?

3. Which of the following prices would you expect to rise rapidly? Why?

   a. Cable television rates

   b. Football tickets

   c. Internet access

   d. Household cleaning services

   e. Driving lessons

4. Two countries have the production possibilities frontier (PPF) shown in Figure 3 on page 139. But Consumia chooses point C, whereas Investia chooses point I. Which country will have the higher PPF the following year? Why?

5. Show on a graph how capital formation shifts the production function. Use this graph to show that capital formation increases labor productivity. Explain in words why labor is more productive when the capital stock is larger.

| DISCUSSION QUESTIONS |

1. Explain the different objectives of (long-run) growth policy versus (short-run) stabilization policy.

2. Explain why economic growth might be higher in a country with well-established property rights and a stable political system compared with a country where property rights are uncertain and the government is unstable.

3. Chapter 6 pointed out that, because faster capital formation comes at a cost (reduced current consumption), it is possible for a country to invest too much. Suppose the government of some country decides that its businesses are investing too much. What steps might it take to slow the pace of capital formation?

4. Explain why the best educational policies to promote faster growth might be different in the following countries.
   a. Mozambique
   b. Brazil
   c. France

5. Comment on the following: "Sharp changes in the volume of investment in the United States help explain both the productivity slowdown in 1973 and the productivity speed-up in 1995."

6. Discuss some of the pros and cons of increasing development assistance, both from the point of view of the donor country and the point of view of the recipient country.

AGGREGATE DEMAND AND THE POWERFUL CONSUMER

Men are disposed, as a rule and on the average, to increase their consumption as their income increases, but not by as much as the increase in their income.

JOHN MAYNARD KEYNES

The last chapter focused on the determinants of *potential GDP*—the economy's capacity to produce. We turn our attention now to the factors determining *actual GDP*—how much of that potential is actually utilized. Will the economy be pressing against its capacity, and therefore perhaps also having trouble with inflation? Or will there be a great deal of unused capacity, and therefore high unemployment?

The theory that economists use to answer such questions is based on the two concepts we first introduced in Chapter 5: aggregate demand and supply. The last chapter examined the long-run determinants of *aggregate supply*, a topic to which we will return in Chapter 10. In this chapter and the next, we will construct a simplified model of *aggregate demand* and learn the origins of the aggregate demand curve.

While aggregate supply rules the roost in the long run, Chapter 5's whirlwind tour of U.S. economic history suggested that the strength of aggregate demand holds the key to the economy's condition in the short run. When aggregate demand grows briskly, the economy booms. When aggregate demand is weak, the economy stagnates.

The model we develop to understand aggregate demand in this chapter and the next will teach us much about this process. But it is too simple to deal with policy issues effectively, because the government and the financial system are largely ignored. We remedy these omissions in Part 3, where we give government spending, taxation, and interest rates appropriately prominent roles. The influence of the exchange rate between the U.S. dollar and foreign currencies is then considered in Part 4.

CONTENTS

ISSUE:	DEMAND MANAGEMENT AND THE ORNERY CONSUMER

In Chapter 5, we suggested that the government sometimes wants to shift the aggregate demand curve. It can do so a number of ways. One direct approach is to alter its own spending, spending freely when private demand is weak and tightening the budget when private demand is strong. Alternatively, the government can take a more indirect route by using taxes and other policy tools to influence *private* spending decisions. Because consumer expenditures constitute more than two-thirds of gross domestic product, the consumer presents the most tempting target.

A case in point arose after the 2000 election, when the long boom of the 1990s ended abruptly and economic growth in the United States slowed to a crawl. President George W. Bush decided that consumer spending needed a boost, and Congress passed a multiyear tax cut in 2001. One provision of the tax cut gave taxpayers an advance *rebate* on their 2001 taxes. Checks ranging as high as $600 went out starting in July 2001. There should be no mystery about how changes in personal taxes are expected to affect consumer spending. Any reduction in personal taxes leaves consumers with more after-tax income to spend; any tax increase leaves them with less. The linkage from taxes to spendable income to consumer spending seems direct and unmistakable, and, in a certain sense, it is.

Yet the congressional debate over the tax bill sent legislators and journalists scurrying to the scholarly evidence on a similar episode 26 years earlier. In the spring of 1975, as the U.S. economy hit a recessionary bottom, Congress enacted a tax rebate to spur consumer spending. But that time consumers did not follow the wishes of the president and Congress. They saved a substantial share of their tax cuts, rather than spending them. As a result, the economy did not receive the expected boost.

Perhaps the legislators should have taken the 1975 episode to heart. Early estimates of the effects of the 2001 rebates suggested that consumers spent relatively little of the money they received. Thus, in a sense, history repeated itself. But why? Why did these two temporary tax cuts seem to have so little effect? This chapter attempts to provide some answers. But before getting involved in such complicated issues, we must build some vocabulary and learn some basic concepts.

AGGREGATE DEMAND, DOMESTIC PRODUCT, AND NATIONAL INCOME

First, some vocabulary. We have already introduced the concept of gross domestic product as the standard measure of the economy's total output.[1]

For the most part, firms in a market economy produce goods only if they think they can sell them. **Aggregate demand** is the total amount that all consumers, business firms, government agencies, and foreigners spend on U.S. final goods and services. The downward-sloping aggregate demand curve of Chapter 5 alerted us to the fact that *aggregate demand is a schedule, not a fixed number*—the actual numerical value of aggregate demand depends on the price level. Several reasons for this dependence will emerge in coming chapters.

But the level of aggregate demand also depends on a variety of other factors—such as consumer incomes, various government policies, and events in foreign countries. To understand the nature of aggregate demand, it is best to break it up into its major components, as we do now.

Consumer expenditure (*consumption* for short) is simply the total value of all consumer goods and services demanded. Because consumer spending constitutes more than

Aggregate demand is the total amount that all consumers, business firms, government agencies, and foreigners spend on final goods and services.

Consumer expenditure (C) is the total amount spent by consumers on newly produced goods and services (excluding purchases of new homes, which are considered investment goods).

---

two-thirds of total spending, it is the main focus of this chapter. We represent it by the letter *C*.

Investment spending, represented by the letter *I*, was discussed extensively in the last chapter. It is the amount that firms spend on factories, machinery, software, and the like, plus the amount that families spend on new houses. Notice that this usage of the word *investment* differs from common parlance. Most people speak of *investing* in the stock market or in a bank account. But that kind of investment merely swaps one form of financial asset (such as money) for another form (such as a share of stock). When economists speak of *investment,* they mean instead the purchase of some *new physical asset,* such as a drill press, a computer, or a house. The distinction is important here because only investments by the economists' definition constitute direct additions to the demand for newly produced goods.

The third major component of aggregate demand, **government purchases** of goods and services, includes items such as paper, computers, airplanes, ships, and labor bought by all levels of government. We use the symbol *G* for this variable.

The final component of aggregate demand, **net exports,** is simply defined as U.S. exports *minus* U.S. imports. The reasoning here is simple. Part of the demand for American goods and services originates beyond our borders—as when foreigners buy our wheat, software, and banking services. So to obtain total demand for U.S. products, these goods and services must be *added* to U.S. domestic demand. Similarly, some items included in *C* and *I* are made abroad. Think, for example, of beer from Germany, cars from Japan, and shirts from Malaysia. These must be *subtracted* from the total amount demanded by U.S. consumers if we want to measure total spending *on U.S. products.* The addition of exports, *X*, and the subtraction of imports, *IM*, leads to the following shorthand definition of aggregate demand:

Aggregate demand is the sum of C + I + G + (X − IM).

The last concept we need for our vocabulary is a way to measure the total *income* of all individuals in the economy. It comes in two versions: one for before-tax incomes, called **national income,** and one for after-tax incomes, called **disposable income.**[2] The term *disposable income,* which we will abbreviate *DI*, is meant to be descriptive—it tells us how much consumers actually have available to spend or to save. For that reason, it will play a prominent role in this chapter and in subsequent discussions.

Investment spending (I) is the sum of the expenditures of business firms on new plant and equipment and households on new homes. Financial "investments" are not included, nor are resales of existing physical assets.

Government purchases (G) refer to the goods (such as airplanes and paper clips) and services (such as school teaching and police protection) purchased by all levels of government.

Net exports, or X − IM, is the difference between exports (X) and imports (IM). It indicates the difference between what we sell to foreigners and what we buy from them.

SOURCE: From *The Wall Street Journal.* Permission, Cartoon Features Syndicate

"When I refer to it as disposable income, don't get the wrong idea."

THE CIRCULAR FLOW OF SPENDING, PRODUCTION, AND INCOME

Enough definitions. How do these three concepts—domestic product, total expenditure, and national income—interact in a market economy? We can answer this best with a rather elaborate diagram (Figure 1 on the next page). For obvious reasons, Figure 1 is called a **circular flow diagram**. It depicts a large tube in which an imaginary fluid circulates in the clockwise direction. At several points along the way, some of the fluid leaks out or additional fluid is injected into the tube.

To examine this system, start on the far left. At point 1 on the circle, we find consumers. Disposable income (*DI*) flows into their pockets, and two things flow out: consumption (*C*), which stays in the circular flow, and saving (*S*), which "leaks out." This outflow depicts the fact that consumers normally spend less than they earn and save the balance. The "leakage" to saving, of course, does not disappear; it flows into the financial system via banks, mutual funds, and so on. We defer consideration of what happens inside the financial system to Chapters 12 and 13.

National income is the sum of the incomes that all individuals in the economy earn in the forms of wages, interest, rents, and profits. It excludes government transfer payments and is calculated before any deductions are taken for income taxes.

Disposable income (DI) is the sum of the incomes of all individuals in the economy after all taxes have been deducted and all transfer payments have been added.

---

[2] More detailed information on these and other concepts is provided in the appendix to this chapter.

FIGURE 1

The Circular Flow of
Expenditures and
Income

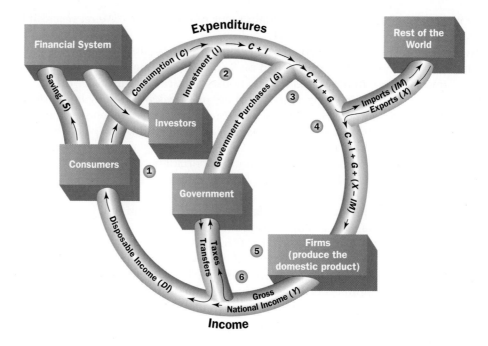

The upper loop of the circular flow represents expenditures, and as we move clockwise to point 2, we encounter the first "injection" into the flow: investment spending (*I*). The diagram shows this injection as coming from "investors"—a group that includes both business firms and home buyers.[3] As the circular flow moves past point 2, it is bigger than it was before: Total spending has increased from *C* to *C* + *I*.

At point 3, there is yet another injection. The government adds its demand for goods and services (*G*) to those of consumers and investors (*C* + *I*). Now aggregate demand has grown to *C* + *I* + *G*.

The next leakage and injection come at point 4. Here we see export spending entering the circular flow from abroad and import spending leaking out. The net effect of these two forces may increase or decrease the circular flow, depending on whether net exports are positive or negative. (In the United States today, they are strongly negative.) In either case, by the time we pass point 4, we have accumulated the full amount of aggregate demand, *C* + *I* + *G* + (*X* − *IM*).

The circular flow diagram shows this aggregate demand for goods and services arriving at the business firms, which are located at point 5. Responding to this demand, firms produce the domestic product. As the circular flow emerges from the firms, however, we rename it *gross national income*. Why? The reason is that, except for some complications explained in the appendix,

National income and domestic product must be equal.

Why is this so? When a firm produces and sells $100 worth of output, it pays most of the proceeds to its workers, to people who have lent it money, and to the landlord who owns the property on which the plant is located. All of these payments represent *income* to some individuals. But what about the rest? Suppose, for example, that the firm pays wages, interest, and rent totaling $90 million and sells its output for $100 million. What happens to the remaining $10 million? The firm's owners receive it as *profits*. Because these owners are citizens of the country, their incomes also count in national income.[4]

---

[3] You are reminded that expenditure on housing is part of *I*, not part of *C*.

[4] Some of the income paid out by American companies goes to noncitizens. Similarly, some Americans earn income from foreign firms. This complication is discussed in the appendix to this chapter.

Thus, when we add up all the wages, interest, rents, *and profits* in the economy to obtain the *national income,* we must arrive at the *value of output.*

The lower loop of the circular flow diagram shows national income leaving firms and heading for consumers. But some of the flow takes a detour along the way. At point 6, the government siphons off a portion of the national income in the form of *taxes.* But it also adds back government **transfer payments,** such as unemployment compensation and Social Security benefits, which government agencies give to certain individuals as outright *grants* rather than as payments for goods or services rendered.

By subtracting taxes from gross domestic product (GDP) and adding transfer payments, we obtain disposable income:[5]

$$DI = GDP - \text{Taxes} + \text{Transfer payments}$$
$$= GDP - (\text{Taxes} - \text{Transfers})$$
$$= Y - T$$

where Y represents GDP and T represents taxes *net of transfers* or simply *net taxes.* Disposable income flows unimpeded to consumers at point 1, and the cycle repeats.

Figure 1 raises several complicated questions, which we pose now but will not try to answer until subsequent chapters:

- Does the flow of spending and income grow larger or smaller as we move clockwise around the circle? Why?
- Is the output that firms produce at point 5 (the GDP) equal to aggregate demand? If so, what makes these two quantities equal? If not, what happens?

The next chapter provides the answers to these two questions.

- Do the government's accounts balance, so that what flows in at point 6 (net taxes) is equal to what flows out at point 3 (government purchases)? What happens if they do not balance?

This important question is first addressed in Chapter 11 and then recurs many times, especially in Chapter 15, which discusses budget deficits and surpluses in detail.

- Is our international trade balanced, so that exports equal imports at point 4? More generally, what factors determine net exports, and what consequences arise from trade deficits or surpluses?

We take up these questions in the next two chapters but deal with them more fully in Part 4.

However, we cannot dig very deeply into any of these issues until we first understand what goes on at point 1, where consumers make decisions. So we turn next to the determinants of consumer spending.

> **Transfer payments** are sums of money that the government gives certain individuals as outright grants rather than as payments for services rendered to employers. Some common examples are Social Security and unemployment benefits.

CONSUMER SPENDING AND INCOME: THE IMPORTANT RELATIONSHIP

Recall that we started the chapter with a puzzle: Why did consumers respond so weakly to tax rebates in 2001 and 1975? An economist interested in predicting how consumer spending will respond to a change in income taxes must first ask how consumption (C) relates to disposable income (DI), because a tax increase decreases after-tax income and a tax reduction increases it. So this section examines what we know about how consumer spending is influenced by changes in disposable income.

Figure 2 on the next page depicts the historical paths of *C* and *DI* for the United States since 1929. The association is extremely close, suggesting that consumption will rise whenever disposable income rises and fall whenever income falls. The vertical distance between the two lines represents personal saving: disposable income minus consumption.

---

[5] This definition omits a few minor details, which are explained in the appendix.

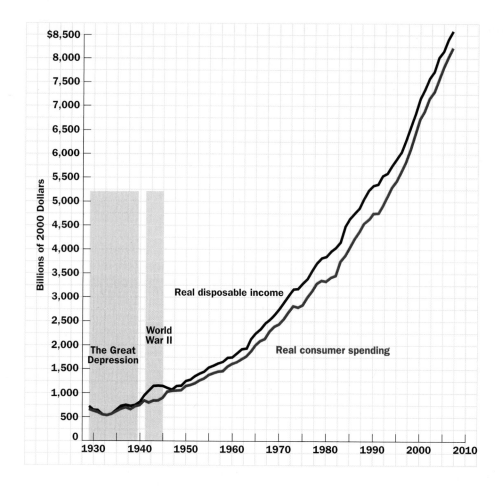

Notice how little saving consumers did during the Great Depression of the 1930s (when the two lines run very close together); how much they did during World War II, when many consumer goods were either unavailable or rationed; and how little saving consumers have done lately.

Of course, knowing that *C* will move in the same direction as *DI* is not enough for policy planners. They need to know *how much* one variable will go up when the other rises a given amount. Figure 3 presents the same data as in Figure 2, but in a way designed to help answer the "how much" question.

A **scatter diagram** is a graph showing the relationship between two variables (such as consumer spending and disposable income). Each year is represented by a point in the diagram, and the coordinates of each year's point show the values of the two variables in that year.

Economists call such pictures **scatter diagrams,** and they are very useful in predicting how one variable (in this case, consumer spending) will change in response to a change in another variable (in this case, disposable income). Each dot in the diagram represents the data on *C* and *DI* corresponding to a particular year. For example, the point labeled "1996" shows that real consumer expenditures in 1996 were $5,619 billion (which we read off the vertical axis), while real disposable incomes amounted to $6,081 billion (which we read off the horizontal axis). Similarly, each year from 1929 to 2007 is represented by its own dot in Figure 3.

To see how such a diagram can assist fiscal policy planners, imagine that you were a member of Congress way back in 1964, contemplating a tax cut. (In fact, Congress did cut taxes that year.) Legislators want to know how much additional consumer spending may be stimulated by tax cuts of various sizes. To assist your imagination, the scatter diagram in Figure 4 on page 160 removes the points for 1964 through 2007 that appear in Figure 3; after all, these data were unknown in 1964. Years prior to 1947 have also been removed because, as Figure 2 showed, both the Great Depression and wartime rationing disturbed the normal relationship between *DI* and *C*. With no more training in economics than you have right now, what would you suggest?

FIGURE 3

Scatter Diagram of Consumer Spending and Disposable Income

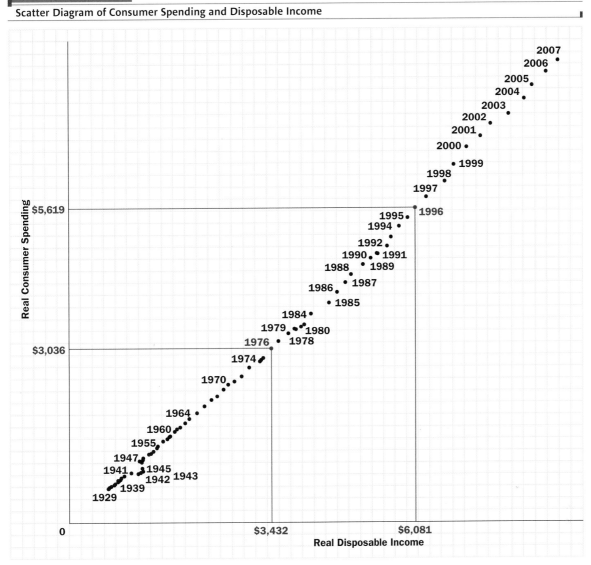

NOTE: Figures are in billions of 2000 dollars.

One rough-and-ready approach is to get a ruler, set it down on Figure 4, and sketch a straight line that comes as close as possible to hitting all the points. That has been done for you in the figure, and you can see that the resulting line comes remarkably close to touching all the points. The line summarizes, in a very rough way, the normal relationship between income and consumption. The two variables certainly appear to be closely related.

The *slope* of the straight line in Figure 4 is very important.[6] Specifically, we note that it is

$$\text{Slope} = \frac{\text{Vertical change}}{\text{Horizontal change}} = \frac{\$180 \text{ billion}}{\$200 \text{ billion}} = 0.90$$

Because the horizontal change involved in the move from *A* to *B* represents a rise in disposable income of $200 billion (from $1,300 billion to $1,500 billion), and the corresponding vertical change represents the associated $180 billion rise in consumer spending

---

[6] To review the concept of *slope*, see the appendix to Chapter 1, pages 14–16.

FIGURE 4

Scatter Diagram of
Consumer Spending
and Disposable
Income, 1947–1963

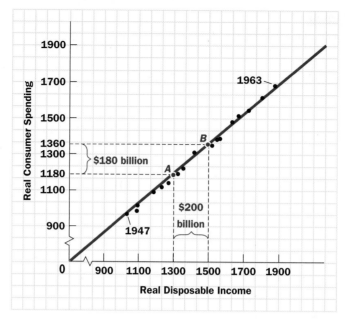

NOTE: Figures are in billions of 2000 dollars.

(from $1,180 billion to $1,360 billion), the slope of the line indicates how consumer spending responds to changes in disposable income. In this case, we see that each additional $1 of income leads to 90 cents of additional spending.

Now let us return to tax policy. First, recall that each dollar of tax cut increases disposable income by exactly $1. Next, apply the finding from Figure 4 that each additional dollar of disposable income increases consumer spending by about 90 cents. The conclusion is that a tax cut of, say, $9 billion—which is about what happened in 1964—would be expected to increase consumer spending by about $9 × 0.9 = $8.1 billion.

THE CONSUMPTION FUNCTION AND THE MARGINAL PROPENSITY TO CONSUME

The **consumption function** shows the relationship between total consumer expenditures and total disposable income in the economy, holding all other determinants of consumer spending constant.

The **marginal propensity to consume (MPC)** is the ratio of the change in consumption relative to the change in disposable income that produces the change in consumption. On a graph, it appears as the slope of the consumption function.

It has been said that economics is just systematized common sense. So let us now organize and generalize what has been a completely intuitive discussion up to now. One thing we have discovered is the apparently close relationship between consumer spending, C, and disposable income, DI. Economists call this relationship the **consumption function**.

A second fact we have gleaned from these figures is that the *slope* of the consumption function is quite constant. We infer this constancy from the fact that the straight line drawn in Figure 4 comes so close to touching every point. If the slope of the consumption function had varied widely, we could not have done so well with a single straight line.[7] Because of its importance in applications such as the tax cut, economists have given this slope a special name—the **marginal propensity to consume,** or **MPC** for short. The MPC tells us how much more consumers will spend if disposable income rises by $1.

$$\text{MPC} = \frac{\text{Change in } C}{\text{Change in } DI \text{ that produces the change in } C}$$

The MPC is best illustrated by an example, and for this purpose we turn away from U.S. data for a moment and look at consumption and income in a hypothetical country whose data come in nice round numbers—which facilitates computation.

[7] Figure 4 is limited to 17 years of data, so try fitting a single straight line to all of the data in Figure 3. You will find that you can do rather well.

Columns (1) and (2) of Table 1 below show annual consumer expenditure and disposable income, respectively, from 2002 to 2007. These two columns constitute the consumption function, and they are plotted in Figure 5. Column (3) in the table shows the marginal propensity to consume (MPC), which is the slope of the line in Figure 5; it is derived from the first two columns. We can see that between 2004 and 2005, *DI* rose by $400 billion (from $4,000 billion to $4,400 billion) while *C* rose by $300 billion (from $3,300 billion to $3,600 billion). Thus, the MPC was

$$\text{MPC} = \frac{\text{Change in } C}{\text{Change in } DI} = \frac{\$300}{\$400} = 0.75$$

As you can easily verify, the MPC between any other pair of years in Table 1 is also 0.75. This relationship explains why the slope of the line in Figure 4 was so crucial in estimating the effect of a tax cut. This slope, which we found there to be 0.90, is simply the MPC for the United States. The MPC tells us how much *additional* spending will be induced by each dollar *change* in disposable income. For each $1 of tax cut, economists expect consumption to rise by $1 times the marginal propensity to consume.

To estimate the *initial* effect of a tax cut on consumer spending, economists must first estimate the MPC and then multiply the amount of the tax cut by the estimated MPC.[8] Because they never know the true MPC with certainty, their prediction is always subject to some margin of error.

FIGURE 5

A Consumption Function

TABLE 1

Consumption and Income in a Hypothetical Economy

Year	(1) Consumption, *C*	(2) Disposable Income, *DI*	(3) Marginal Propensity to Consume, MPC
2002	$2,700	$3,200	
2003	3,000	3,600	0.75
2004	3,300	4,000	0.75
2005	3,600	4,400	0.75
2006	3,900	4,800	0.75
2007	4,200	5,200	0.75

NOTE: Amounts are in billions of dollars.

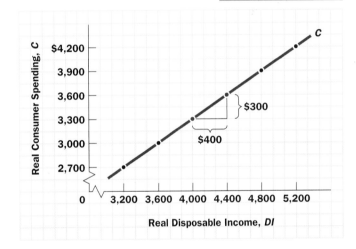

FACTORS THAT SHIFT THE CONSUMPTION FUNCTION

Unfortunately for policy planners, the consumption function does not always stand still. Recall from Chapter 4 the important distinction between a movement along a demand curve and a shift of the curve. A demand curve depicts the relationship between quantity demanded and one of its many determinants—price. Thus a change in price causes a movement along the demand curve. But a change in any other factor that influences quantity demanded causes a shift of the entire demand curve.

Because factors other than disposable income influence consumer spending, a similar distinction is vital to understanding real-world consumption functions. Look back at the definition of the consumption function in the margin of page 160. A change in disposable income leads to a *movement along the consumption function* precisely because the consumption function depicts the relationship between *C* and *DI*. Such movements, which are what we have been considering so far, are indicated by the brick-colored arrows in Figure 6.

[8] The word *initial* in this sentence is an important one. The next chapter will explain why the effects discussed in this chapter are only the beginning of the story.

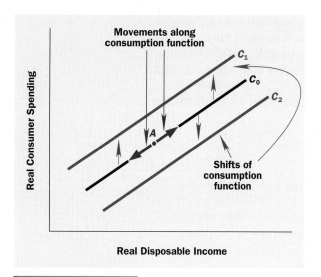

Movements along consumption function

Real Consumer Spending

Real Disposable Income

C_1
C_0
C_2

A

Shifts of consumption function

FIGURE 6

Shifts of the Consumption Function

But consumption also has other determinants, and a change in any of them will *shift the entire consumption function*—as indicated by the blue arrows in Figure 6. Such shifts account for many of the errors in forecasting consumption. To summarize:

Any change in disposable income moves us *along a given consumption function*. A change in any of the other determinants of consumption *shifts the entire consumption schedule* (see Figure 6).

Because disposable income is far and away the main determinant of consumer spending, the real-world data in Figure 3 come *close* to lying along a straight line. But if you use a ruler to draw such a line, you will find that it misses a number of points badly. These deviations reflect the influence of the "other determinants" just mentioned. Let us see what some of them are.

Wealth   One factor affecting spending is consumers' *wealth*, which is a source of purchasing power in addition to income. Wealth and income are different things. For example, a wealthy retiree with a huge bank balance may earn little current *income* when interest rates are low. But a high-flying investment banker who spends every penny of the high income she earns will not accumulate much *wealth*.

To appreciate the importance of the distinction, think about two recent college graduates, each of whom earns $40,000 per year. If one of them has $100,000 in the bank and the other has no assets at all, who do you think will spend more? Presumably the one with the big bank account. The general point is that current income is not the only source of spendable funds; households can also finance spending by cashing in some of the wealth they have previously accumulated.

One important implication of this analysis is that the stock market can exert a major influence on consumer spending. A stock market boom adds to wealth and thus raises the consumption function, as depicted by the shift from C_0 to C_1 in Figure 6. That is what happened in the late 1990s, when the stock market soared and American consumers went on a spending spree. Correspondingly, a collapse of stock prices, like the one that occurred in 2000–2002, should shift the consumption function down (see the shift from C_0 to C_2). Using the same logic, as this book went to press, many economists were worrying that falling house prices, which were making consumers less wealthy, would therefore make them less willing to spend.

The Price Level   Stocks are hardly the only form of wealth. People hold a great deal of wealth in forms that are fixed in money terms. Bank accounts are the most obvious example, but government and corporate bonds also have fixed face values in money terms. The purchasing power of such **money-fixed assets** obviously declines whenever the price level rises, which means that the asset can buy less. For example, if the price level rises by 10 percent, a $1,000 government bond will buy about 10 percent less than it could when prices were lower. This is no trivial matter. Consumers in the United States hold money-fixed assets worth well over $8 *trillion,* so that each 1 percent rise in the price level reduces the purchasing power of consumer wealth by more than $80 billion, a tidy sum. This process, of course, operates equally well in reverse, because a decline in the price level increases the purchasing power of money-fixed assets.

A **money-fixed asset** is an asset whose value is a fixed number of dollars.

The Real Interest Rate   A higher real rate of interest raises the rewards for saving. For this reason, many people believe it is "obvious" that higher real interest rates encourage saving and therefore discourage spending. Surprisingly, however, statistical studies of this relationship suggest otherwise. With very few exceptions, they show that interest rates have negligible effects on consumption decisions in the United States and other

POLICY DEBATE

USING THE TAX CODE TO SPUR SAVING

Compared to the citizens of virtually every other industrial nation, Americans save very little. Many policy makers consider this lack of saving to be a serious problem, so they have proposed numerous changes in the tax laws to increase incentives to save. In 2001, for example, Congress expanded Individual Retirement Accounts (IRAs), which allow taxpayers to save tax-free. In 2003, the taxation of dividends was reduced. Further tax incentives for saving seem to be proposed every year.

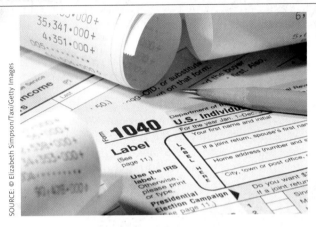

SOURCE: © Elizabeth Simpson/Taxi/Getty Images

All of these tax changes are designed to increase the after-tax return on saving. For example, if you put away money in a bank at a 5 percent rate of interest and your income is taxed at a 30 percent rate, your after-tax rate of return on saving is just 3.5 percent (70 percent of 5 percent). But if the interest is earned tax-free, as in an IRA, you

get to keep the full 5 percent. Over long periods of time, this seemingly small interest differential compounds to make an enormous difference in returns. For example, $100 invested for 20 years at 3.5 percent interest grows to $199. But at 5 percent, it grows to $265. Members of Congress who advocate tax incentives for saving argue that lower tax rates will therefore induce Americans to save more.

This idea seems reasonable and has many supporters. Unfortunately, the evidence runs squarely against it. Economists have conducted many studies of the effect of higher rates of return on saving. With very few exceptions, they detect little or no impact. Although the evidence fails to support the "common-sense" solution to the undersaving problem, the debate goes on. Many people, it seems, refuse to believe the evidence.

countries. Hence, in developing our model of the economy, we will assume that changes in real interest rates do not shift the consumption function. (See the box "Using the Tax Code to Spur Saving.")

Future Income Expectations   It is hardly earth-shattering to suggest that consumers' expectations about their *future* incomes should affect how much they spend today. This final determinant of consumer spending holds the key to resolving the puzzle posed at the beginning of the chapter: Why did tax policy designed to boost consumer spending apparently fail in 1975 and succeed only modestly in 2001?

ISSUE REVISITED: WHY THE TAX REBATES FAILED IN 1975 AND 2001

To understand how expectations of future incomes affect current consumer expenditures, consider the abbreviated life histories of three consumers given in Table 2. (The reason for giving our three imaginary individuals such odd names will be apparent shortly.) The consumer named "Constant" earned $100 in each of the years considered in the table. The consumer named "Temporary" earned $100 in three of the four years but had a good year in 1975. The consumer named "Permanent" enjoyed a permanent increase in income in 1975 and was therefore clearly the richest.

Now let us use our common sense to figure out how much each of these consumers might have spent in 1975. Temporary and Permanent had the same income that year. Do you think they spent the same amount? Not if they had some ability to foresee their future incomes, because Permanent was richer in the long run.

TABLE 2

Incomes of Three Consumers

Consumer	Incomes in Each Year				Total Income
	1974	1975	1976	1977	
Constant	$100	$100	$100	$100	**$400**
Temporary	100	120	100	100	**420**
Permanent	100	120	120	120	**460**

Now compare Constant and Temporary. Temporary had 20 percent higher income in 1975 ($120 versus $100), but only 5 percent more over the entire four-year period ($420 versus $400). Do you think his spending in 1975 was closer to 20 percent above Constant's or closer to 5 percent above it? Most people guess the latter.

The point of this example is that consumers very reasonably decide on their current consumption spending by looking at their long-run income prospects. This should come as no surprise to a college student. You are probably spending more than you earn this year, but that does not make you a foolish spendthrift. On the contrary, you know that your college education will likely give you a much higher income in the future, and you are spending with that in mind.

To relate this example to the failure of the 1975 income tax cut, now imagine that the three rows in Table 2 represent the entire economy under three different government policies. Recall that 1975 was the year of the temporary tax cut. The first row (Constant) shows the unchanged path of disposable income in the absence of a tax cut. The second (Temporary) shows an increase in disposable income attributable to a tax cut for one year only. The bottom row (Permanent) shows a policy that increases *DI* in every future year by cutting taxes permanently in 1975. Which of the two lower rows do you imagine would have generated more consumer spending in 1975? The bottom row (Permanent), of course. What we have concluded, then, is this:

Permanent cuts in income taxes cause greater increases in consumer spending than do temporary cuts of equal magnitude.

The application of this analysis to the 1975 and 2001 tax rebates is immediate. The 1975 tax cut was advertised as a one-time increase in after-tax income, like that experienced by Temporary in Table 2. No future income was affected, so consumers did not increase their spending as much as government officials had hoped. Ironically, the 2001 tax rebate checks actually represented the first installment of a projected permanent tax reduction. But they were so widely advertised as a one-time event that most people receiving the checks probably thought they were temporary.

We have, then, what appears to be a general principle, backed up by both historical evidence and common sense. Permanent changes in income taxes have more significant effects on consumer spending than do temporary ones. This conclusion may seem obvious, but it is not a lesson you would have learned from an introductory textbook prior to 1975. It is one we learned the hard way, through bitter experience.

THE EXTREME VARIABILITY OF INVESTMENT

Next, we turn to the most *volatile* component of aggregate demand: investment spending.[9] While Figure 2 showed that consumer spending follows movements in disposable income quite closely, investment spending swings from high to low levels with astonishing speed. For example, when real GDP in the United States slowed abruptly from a 3.7 percent growth rate in 2000 to a sluggish 0.8 percent rate in 2001, a drop of about 3 percentage points, the growth rate of real investment spending dropped from 5.7 percent to *minus* 7.9 percent, a swing of over 13 percentage points. What accounts for such dramatic changes in investment spending?

Several factors that influence how much businesses want to invest were discussed in the previous chapter, including interest rates, tax provisions, technical change, and the

---

[9] We repeat the warning given earlier about the meaning of the word *investment*. It *includes* spending by businesses and individuals on newly produced factories, machinery, and houses. But it *excludes* sales of used industrial plants, equipment, and homes as well as purely financial transactions, such as the purchases of stocks and bonds.

strength of the economy. Sometimes these determinants change abruptly, leading to dramatic variations in investment. But perhaps the most important factor accounting for the volatility of investment spending was not discussed much in Chapter 7: the *state of business confidence*, which in turn depends on *expectations about the future*.

Although confidence is tricky to measure, it does seem obvious that businesses will build more factories and purchase more new machines when they are optimistic. Correspondingly, their investment plans will be very cautious if the economic outlook appears bleak. Keynes pointed out that psychological perceptions such as these are subject to abrupt shifts, so that fluctuations in investment can be a major cause of instability in aggregate demand.

Unfortunately, neither economists nor, for that matter, psychologists have many good ideas about how to *measure*—much less *control*—business confidence. So economists usually focus on several more objective determinants of investment that are easier to quantify and even influence—factors such as interest rates and tax provisions.

THE DETERMINANTS OF NET EXPORTS

Another highly variable source of demand for U.S. products is foreign purchases of U.S. goods—our *exports*. As we observed earlier in this chapter, we obtain the *net* contribution of foreigners to U.S. aggregate demand by subtracting *imports*, which is the portion of domestic demand that is satisfied by foreign producers, from our exports to get *net exports*. What determines net exports?

National Incomes

Although both exports and imports depend on many factors, the predominant one is income *levels in different countries*. When American consumers and firms spend more on consumption and investment, some of this new spending goes toward the purchase of foreign goods. Therefore:

Our imports rise when our GDP rises and fall when our GDP falls.

Similarly, because our *exports* are the *imports* of other countries, our exports depend on *their* GDPs, not on our own. Thus:

Our exports are relatively insensitive to our own GDP, but are quite sensitive to the GDPs of other countries.

Putting these two ideas together leads to a clear implication: When our economy grows faster than the economies of our trading partners, our net exports tend to shrink. Conversely, when foreign economies grow faster than ours, our net exports tend to rise. Events since the 1990s illustrate this point dramatically. When the U.S. economy stagnated between 1990 and 1992, our net exports rose from −$55 billion to −$16 billion. (Remember, −16 is a *larger* number than −55!) Since then, growth in the United States has generally outstripped growth abroad, and U.S. net exports have plummeted from −$16 billion in 1992 to −$560 billion in 2007.

Relative Prices and Exchange Rates

Although GDP levels here and abroad are important influences on a country's net exports, they are not the only relevant factors. International prices matter, too.

To make things concrete, let's focus on trade between the United States and Japan. Suppose American prices rise while Japanese prices fall, making U.S. goods more expensive *relative to Japanese goods.* If American consumers react to these new relative prices by buying more Japanese goods, U.S. *imports rise.* If Japanese consumers react to the same relative price changes by buying fewer American products, U.S. *exports fall.* Both reactions reduce America's *net* exports.

Naturally, a decline in American prices (or a rise in Japanese prices) does precisely the opposite. Thus:

A rise in the prices of a country's goods will lead to a reduction in that country's net exports. Analogously, a decline in the prices of a country's goods will raise that country's net exports. Similarly, price increases abroad raise the home country's net exports, whereas price decreases abroad have the opposite effect.

This simple idea holds the key to understanding how exchange rates among the world's currencies influence exports and imports—an important topic that we will consider in depth in Chapters 18 and 19. The reason is that exchange rates translate foreign prices into terms that are familiar to home country customers—their own currencies.

Consider, for example, Americans interested in buying Japanese cars that cost ¥3,000,000. If it takes ¥100 to buy a dollar, these cars cost American buyers $30,000. But if the dollar is worth ¥150, those same cars cost Americans just $20,000, and consumers in the United States are likely to buy more of them. These sorts of responses help explain why American automakers lost market share to Japanese imports when the dollar rose against the yen in the late 1990s. They also explain why, today, so many U.S. manufacturers want to see the value of the Chinese yuan rise.

HOW PREDICTABLE IS AGGREGATE DEMAND?

We have now learned enough to see why economists often have difficulty predicting aggregate demand. Consider the four main components, starting with consumer spending.

Because wealth affects consumption, forecasts of spending can be thrown off by unexpected movements of the stock market or by poor forecasts of future prices. It may also be difficult to anticipate how taxpayers will view changes in the income tax law. If the government says that a tax cut is permanent (as for example, in 1964), will consumers take the government at its word and increase their spending accordingly? Perhaps not, if the government has a history of raising taxes after promising to keep them low. Similarly, when (as in 1975) the government explicitly announces that a tax cut is temporary, will consumers always believe the announcement? Or might they greet it with a hefty dose of skepticism? Such a reaction is quite possible if there is a history of "temporary" tax changes that stayed on the books indefinitely.

Swings in investment spending are even more difficult to predict, partly because they are tied so closely to business confidence and expectations. Developments abroad also often lead to surprises in the net export account. Even the final component of aggregate demand, government purchases (G), is subject to the vagaries of politics and to sudden military and national security events such as 9/11 and the Iraq war.

We could say much more about the determinants of aggregate demand, but it is best to leave the rest to more advanced courses. For we are now ready to apply our knowledge of aggregate demand to the construction of the first model of the economy. Although it is true that income determines consumption, the consumption function in turn helps to determine the level of income. If that sounds like circular reasoning, read the next chapter!

| SUMMARY |

1. **Aggregate demand** is the total volume of goods and services purchased by consumers, businesses, government units, and foreigners. It can be expressed as the sum $C + I + G + (X - IM)$, where C is consumer spending, I is investment spending, G is **government purchases,** and $X - IM$ is **net exports.**

2. Aggregate demand is a schedule: The aggregate quantity demanded depends on (among other things) the price level. But, for any given price level, aggregate demand is a number.

3. Economists reserve the term **investment** to refer to purchases of newly produced factories, machinery, software, and houses.

4. Gross domestic product is the total volume of final goods and services produced in the country.

5. **National income** is the sum of the before-tax wages, interest, rents, and profits earned by all individuals in the economy. By necessity, it must be approximately equal to domestic product.

6. **Disposable income** is the sum of the incomes of all individuals in the economy after taxes and transfers. It is the chief determinant of **consumer expenditures.**

7. All of these concepts, and others, can be depicted in a **circular flow diagram** that shows expenditures on all four sources flowing into business firms and national income flowing out.

8. The close relationship between consumer spending (C) and disposable income (*DI*) is called the **consumption function.** Its slope, which is used to predict the change in consumption that will be caused by a change in income taxes, is called the **marginal propensity to consume (MPC).**

9. Changes in disposable income move us along a given consumption function. Changes in any of the other variables that affect *C* shift the entire consumption function. Among the most important of these other variables are total consumer wealth, the price level, and expected future incomes.

10. Because consumers hold so many **money-fixed assets,** they lose purchasing power when prices rise, which leads them to reduce their spending.

11. The government often tries to manipulate aggregate demand by influencing private consumption decisions, usually through changes in the personal income tax. But this policy did not work well in 1975 or 2001.

12. Future income prospects help explain why. The 1975 tax cut was temporary and therefore left future incomes unaffected. The 2001 tax cut was also advertised as a one-time event.

13. Investment is the most volatile component of aggregate demand, largely because it is closely tied to confidence and expectations.

14. Policy makers cannot influence confidence in any reliable way, so policies designed to spur investment focus on more objective, although possibly less important, determinants of investment—such as interest rates and taxes.

15. Net exports depend on GDPs and relative prices both domestically and abroad.

| KEY TERMS |

Aggregate demand   154

Consumer expenditure (C)   154

Investment spending (I)   155

Government purchases (G)   155

Net exports (X − IM)   155

C + I + G + (X − IM)   155

National income   155

Disposable income (DI)   155

Circular flow diagram   155

Transfer payments   157

Scatter diagram   158

Consumption function   160

Marginal propensity to consume (MPC)   160

Movements along versus shifts of the consumption function   161–162

Money-fixed assets   162

Temporary versus permanent tax changes   164

| TEST YOURSELF |

1. What are the four main components of aggregate demand? Which is the largest? Which is the smallest?

2. Which of the following acts constitute *investment* according to the economist's definition of that term?

   a. Pfizer builds a new factory in the United States to manufacture pharmaceuticals.

   b. You buy 100 shares of Pfizer stock.

   c. A small drugmaker goes bankrupt, and Pfizer purchases its factory and equipment.

   d. Your family buys a newly constructed home from a developer.

   e. Your family buys an older home from another family. (*Hint:* Are any *new* products demanded by this action?)

3. On a piece of graph paper, construct a consumption function from the data given here and determine the MPC.

Year	Consumer Spending	Disposable Income
2003	$1,200	$1,500
2004	1,440	1,800
2005	1,680	2,100
2006	1,920	2,400
2007	2,160	2,700

4. In which direction will the consumption function shift if the price level rises? Show this on your graph from the previous question.

| DISCUSSION QUESTIONS |

1. Explain the difference between *investment* as the term is used by most people and *investment* as defined by an economist.

2. What would the circular flow diagram (Figure 1) look like in an economy with no government? Draw one for yourself.

3. The marginal propensity to consume (MPC) for the United States as a whole is roughly 0.90. Explain in words what this means. What is your personal MPC at this stage in your life? How might that change by the time you are your parents' age?

4. Look at the scatter diagram in Figure 3. What does it tell you about what was going on in this country in the years 1942 to 1945?

5. What is a consumption function, and why is it a useful device for government economists planning a tax cut?

6. Explain why permanent tax cuts are likely to lead to bigger increases in consumer spending than temporary tax cuts do.

7. In 2001 and again in 2003, Congress enacted changes in the tax law designed to promote saving. If such saving incentives had been successful, how would the consumption function have shifted?

8. **(More difficult)** Between 1990 and 1991, real disposable income (in 2000 dollars) barely increased at all, owing to a recession. (It rose from $5,324 billion to $5,352 billion.) Use the data on real consumption expenditures given on the inside back cover of this book to compare the change in C to this $28 billion change in DI. Explain why dividing the two does *not* give a good estimate of the marginal propensity to consume.

| APPENDIX | *National Income Accounting*

The type of macroeconomic analysis presented in this book dates from the publication of John Maynard Keynes's *The General Theory of Employment, Interest, and Money* in 1936. But at that time, there was really no way to test Keynes's theories because the necessary data did not exist. It took some years for the theoretical notions used by Keynes to find concrete expression in real-world data.

> The system of measurement devised for collecting and expressing macroeconomic data is called **national income accounting.**

The development of this system of accounts ranks as a great achievement in applied economics, perhaps as important in its own right as was Keynes's theoretical work. Without it, the practical value of Keynesian analysis would be severely limited. Economists spent long hours wrestling with the many difficult conceptual questions that arose as they translated the theory into numbers. Along the way, some more-or-less arbitrary decisions and conventions had to be made. You may not agree with all of them, but the accounting framework that was devised, though imperfect, is eminently serviceable.

DEFINING GDP: EXCEPTIONS TO THE RULES

We first encountered the concept of **gross domestic product (GDP)** in Chapter 5.

> **Gross domestic product (GDP)** is the sum of the money values of all final goods and services produced during a specified period of time, usually one year.

However, the definition of GDP has certain exceptions that we have not yet noted.

First, the treatment of government output involves a minor departure from the principle of using market prices. Unlike private products, the "outputs" of government offices are not sold; indeed, it is sometimes even difficult to define what those outputs are. Lacking prices for outputs, national income accountants fall back on the only prices they have: prices for the inputs from which the outputs are produced. Thus:

> **Government outputs are valued at the cost of the inputs needed to produce them.**

This means, for example, that if a clerk at the Department of Motor Vehicles who earns $20 per hour spends one-half hour torturing you with explanations of why you cannot get a driver's license, that particular government "service" increases GDP by $10.

Second, some goods that are produced but not sold during the year are nonetheless counted in that year's GDP. Specifically, goods that firms add to their *inventories* count in the GDP even though they do not pass through markets.

> **National income statisticians treat inventories as if they were "bought" by the firms that produced them, even though these "purchases" do not actually take place.**

Finally, the treatment of investment goods can be thought of as running slightly counter to the rule that GDP includes only final goods. In a broad sense, factories, generators, machine tools, and the like might be considered intermediate goods. After all, their owners want them only for use in producing other goods, not for any innate value that they possess. But this classification would present a real problem. Because factories and machines normally are never sold to consumers, when would we count them in GDP? National income statisticians avoid this problem by defining investment goods as final products demanded by the *firms* that buy them.

Now that we have a more complete definition of what the GDP is, let us turn to the problem of actually measuring it. National income accountants have devised three ways to perform this task, and we consider each in turn.

GDP AS THE SUM OF FINAL GOODS AND SERVICES

The first way to measure GDP is the most natural, because it follows so directly from the circular flow diagram (Figure 1). It also turns out to be the most useful definition for macroeconomic analysis. We simply add up the final demands of all consumers, business firms, government, and foreigners. Using the symbols Y, C, I, G, and (X − IM) as we did in the chapter, we have:

$$Y = C + I + G + (X - IM)$$

The *I* that appears in the actual U.S. national accounts is called **gross private domestic investment.** We will explain the word *gross* presently. *Private* indicates that government investment is considered part of *G*, and *domestic* means that, say, machinery sold by American firms to foreign companies is included in exports rather than in *I* (investment).

> **Gross private domestic investment (I)** includes business investment in plant, equipment, and software; residential construction; and inventory investment.

We repeat again that *only* these three things are *investment* in national income accounting terminology.

> As defined in the national income accounts, *investment* includes only newly produced capital goods, such as machinery, factories, and new homes. It does not include exchanges of existing assets.

The symbol *G*, for government purchases, represents the volume of *current goods and services purchased by all levels of government.* Thus, all government payments to its employees are counted in *G*, as are all of its purchases of goods. Few citizens realize, however, that *the federal government spends most of its money, not for purchases of goods and services, but rather on transfer payments*—literally, giving away money—either to individuals or to other levels of government.

The importance of this conceptual distinction lies in the fact that *G* represents the part of the national product that government uses up for its own purposes—to pay for armies, bureaucrats, paper, and ink—whereas transfer payments merely shuffle purchasing power from one group of citizens to another. Except for the administrators needed to run these programs, real economic resources are not used up in this process.

In adding up the nation's total output as the sum of *C* + *I* + *G* + (*X* − *IM*), we sum the shares of GDP that are used up by consumers, investors, government, and foreigners, respectively. Because transfer payments merely give someone the capability to spend on *C*, it is logical to exclude transfers from our definition of *G*, including in *C* only the portion of these transfer payments that consumers spend. If we included transfers in *G*, the same spending would get counted twice: once in *G* and then again in *C*.

The final component of GDP is net exports, which are simply exports of goods and services minus imports of goods and services. Table 3 shows GDP for 2007, in both nominal and real terms, computed as the sum of *C* + *I* + *G* + (*X* − *IM*). Note that the numbers for net exports in the table are actually negative. We will say much more about America's trade deficit in Part 4.

TABLE 3

Gross Domestic Product in 2007 as the Sum of Final Demands

Item	Nominal Amount*	Real Amount†
Personal consumption expenditures (C)	$9,734	$8,278
Gross private domestic investment (I)	2,125	1,826
Government purchases of goods and services (G)	2,690	2,022
Net exports (X − IM)	−708	−556
Exports (X)	1,643	1,410
Imports (IM)	2,351	1,965
Gross domestic product (Y)	**13,841**	**11,567**

*In billions of current dollars.
†In billions of 2000 dollars.
SOURCE: U.S. Department of Commerce. Totals do not add up precisely due to rounding and method of deflating.

GDP AS THE SUM OF ALL FACTOR PAYMENTS

We can count up the GDP another way: by *adding up all incomes in the economy.* Let's see how this method handles some typical transactions. Suppose General Electric builds a generator and sells it to General Motors for $1 million. The first method of calculating GDP simply counts the $1 million as part of *I*. The second method asks: What incomes resulted from producing this generator? The answer might be something like this:

Wages of GE employees	$400,000
Interest to bondholders	50,000
Rentals of buildings	50,000
Profits of GE stockholders	100,000

The total is $600,000. The remaining $400,000 is accounted for by inputs that GE purchased from other companies: steel, circuitry, tubing, rubber, and so on. But if we traced this $400,000 back even further, we would find that it is accounted for by the wages, interest, and rentals paid by these other companies, *plus* their profits, *plus* their purchases from other firms. In fact, for *every* firm in the economy, there is an accounting identity that says:

$$\text{Revenue from sales} = \left\{ \begin{array}{l} \text{Wages paid} + \\ \text{Interest paid} + \\ \text{Rentals paid} + \\ \text{Profits earned} + \\ \text{Purchases from} \\ \text{other firms} \end{array} \right.$$

Why must this always be true? Because profits are the balancing item; they are what is *left over* after the firm has made all other payments. In fact, this accounting identity really reflects the definition of profits: sales revenue less all costs.

Now apply this accounting identity to *all firms in the economy.* Total purchases from other firms are precisely what we call *intermediate goods.* What, then, do we get if we subtract these intermediate transactions from both sides of the equation?

$$\begin{array}{l} \text{Revenue from sales } minus \\ \text{purchases from other firms} \end{array} = \left\{ \begin{array}{l} \text{Wages paid} + \\ \text{Interest paid} + \\ \text{Rentals paid} + \\ \text{Profits earned} \end{array} \right.$$

On the right-hand side, we have the sum of all factor incomes: payments to labor, land, and capital. On the left-hand side, we have total sales minus sales of intermediate goods. This means that we have sales of *final goods,* which is precisely our definition of GDP. Thus, the accounting identity for the entire economy can be rewritten as follows:

GDP = Wages + Interest + Rents + Profits

This definition gives national income accountants another way to measure the GDP.

Table 4 shows how to obtain GDP from the sum of all incomes. Once again, we have omitted a few details in our discussion. By adding up wages, interest, rents, and profits, we obtain only $11,180 billion, whereas GDP in 2007 was $13,841 billion. When sales taxes, excise taxes, and the like are added to the sum of wages,

TABLE 4

Gross Domestic Product in 2007 as the Sum of Incomes

Item	Amount
Compensation of employees (wages)	**$7,874**
plus	
Net interest	**603**
plus	
Rental income	**65**
plus	
Profits	**2,638**
Corporate profits	1,595
Proprietors' income	1,043
plus	
Indirect business taxes and misc. items	**1,041**
equals	
National income	**12,221**
plus	
Statistical discrepancy	**29**
equals	
Net national product	**12,250**
plus	
Depreciation	1,687
equals	
Gross national product	**13,937**
minus	
Income received from other countries	**818**
plus	
Income paid to other countries	**722**
equals	
Gross domestic product	**13,841**

NOTE: Amounts are in billions of current dollars.

SOURCE: U.S. Department of Commerce. Totals do not add up precisely due to rounding.

interest, rents, and profits, we obtain what is called **national income**—the sum of all factor payments, including indirect business taxes.

> **National income** is the sum of the incomes that all individuals in the country earn in the forms of wages, interest, rents, and profits. It includes indirect business taxes but excludes transfer payments and makes no deduction for income taxes.

Notice that national income is a measure of the factor incomes of all Americans, regardless of whether they work in this country or somewhere else. Likewise, incomes earned by foreigners in the United States are excluded from (our) national income. We will return to this distinction shortly.

But, reading down Table 4, we next encounter a new concept: **net national product (NNP),** a measure of *production.* For reasons explained in the chapter, NNP is conceptually identical to national income. However, in practice, national income accountants estimate *income* and *production* independently; and so the two measures are never precisely equal. The difference in 2007 was $29 billion, or just 0.2 percent of NNP; it is called the statistical discrepancy.

Moving further down the table, the only difference between NNP and **gross national product (GNP)** is **depreciation** of the nation's capital stock. Thus the adjective "net" means excluding depreciation, and "gross" means including it. GNP is thus a measure of *all* final production, making no adjustment for the fact that some capital is used up each year and thus needs to be replaced. NNP deducts the required replacements to arrive at a net production figure.

> **Depreciation** is the value of the portion of the nation's capital equipment that is used up within the year. It tells us how much output is needed just to maintain the economy's capital stock.

From a conceptual point of view, most economists feel that NNP is a more meaningful indicator of the economy's output than is GNP. After all, the depreciation component of GNP represents the output that is needed just to repair and replace worn-out factories and machines; it is not available for anybody to consume.[10] Therefore, NNP seems to be a better measure of production than GNP.

Alas, GNP is much easier to measure because depreciation is a particularly tricky item. What fraction of his tractor did Farmer Jones "use up" last year? How much did the Empire State Building depreciate during 2007? If you ask yourself difficult questions like these, you will understand why most economists believe that we can measure GNP more accurately than NNP. For this reason, most economic models are based on GNP.

The final two adjustments that bring us to *GDP* return to a fact mentioned earlier. Some American citizens earn their incomes abroad, and some of the payments made by American companies are paid to foreign citizens. Thus, to obtain a measure of total production in the U.S. *domestic* economy (which is GDP) rather than a measure of the total production by U.S. *nationals* (which is GNP), we must *subtract* the income that Americans receive for factors supplied abroad and *add* the income that foreigners receive for factors supplied here. The net of these two adjustments is a very small number, as Table 4 shows. Thus, GDP and GNP are almost equal.

In Table 4, you can hardly help noticing the preponderant share of employee compensation in total factor payments—about 70 percent. Labor is by far the most important factor of production. The return on land is well under 1 percent of factor payments, and interest accounts for about 5 percent. Profits account for the remaining 24 percent, although the size of corporate profits (just 12 percent of GDP in 2007) is much less than the public thinks. If, by some magic stroke, we could convert all corporate profits into wages without

upsetting the economy's performance, the average worker would get a raise of about 20 percent!

GDP AS THE SUM OF VALUES ADDED

It may strike you as strange that national income accountants include only *final* goods and services in GDP. Aren't *intermediate* goods part of the nation's product? Of course they are. The problem is that, if all intermediate goods were included in GDP, we would wind up double- and triple-counting certain goods and services and therefore get an exaggerated impression of the actual level of economic activity.

To explain why, and to show how national income accountants cope with this difficulty, we must introduce a new concept, called *value added*.

> The **value added** by a firm is its revenue from selling a product minus the amount paid for goods and services purchased from other firms.

The intuitive sense of this concept is clear: If a firm buys some inputs from other firms, does something to them, and sells the resulting product for a price higher than it paid for the inputs, we say that the firm has "added value" to the product. If we sum up the values added by all firms in the economy, we must get the total value of all final products. Thus:

> GDP can be measured as the sum of the values added by all firms.

To verify this fact, look back at the accounting identity in the left column bottom of page 170. The left-hand side of this equation, sales revenue minus purchases from other firms, is precisely the firm's value added. Thus:

> Value added = Wages + Interest + Rents + Profits

Because the second method we gave for measuring GDP is to add up wages, interest, rents, and profits, we see that the value-added approach must yield the same answer.

The value-added concept is useful in avoiding double-counting. Often, however, intermediate goods are difficult to distinguish from final goods. Paint bought by a painter, for example, is an intermediate good. But paint bought by a do-it-yourselfer is a final good. What happens, then, if the professional painter buys some paint to refurbish his own garage? The intermediate good becomes a final good. You can see that the line between intermediate goods and final goods is a fuzzy one in practice.

If we measure GDP by the sum of values added, however, we need not make such subtle distinctions. In this method, every purchase of a new good or service counts, but we do not count the entire selling price, only the portion that represents value added.

---

[10] If the capital stock is used for consumption, it will decline, and the nation will wind up poorer than it was before.

To illustrate this idea, consider the data in Table 5 and how they would affect GDP as the sum of final products. Our example begins when a farmer who grows soybeans sells them to a mill for $3 per bushel. This transaction does *not* count in the GDP because the miller does not purchase the soybeans for her own use. The miller then grinds up the soybeans and sells the resulting bag of soy meal to a factory that produces soy sauce. The miller receives $4, but GDP still has not increased because the ground beans are also an intermediate product. Next, the factory turns the beans into soy sauce, which it sells to your favorite Chinese restaurant for $8. Still no effect on GDP.

TABLE 5

An Illustration of Final and Intermediate Goods

Item	Seller	Buyer	Price
Bushel of soybeans	Farmer	Miller	$3
Bag of soy meal	Miller	Factory	4
Gallon of soy sauce	Factory	Restaurant	8
Gallon of soy sauce used as seasoning	Restaurant	Consumers	10
		Total: $25	
Addendum: Contribution to GDP			**$10**

But then the big moment arrives: The restaurant sells the sauce to you and other customers as a part of your meals, and you eat it. At this point, the $10 worth of soy sauce becomes part of a final product and *does* count in the GDP. Notice that if we had also counted the three intermediate transactions (farmer to miller, miller to factory, factory to restaurant), we would have come up with $25—2½ times too much.

Why is it too much? The reason is straightforward. Neither the miller, the factory owner, nor the restaurateur values the product we have been considering *for its own sake.* Only the customers who eat the final product (the soy sauce) have increased their material well-being, so only this last transaction counts in the GDP. However, as we shall now see, value-added

calculations enable us to come up with the right answer ($10) by counting only *part* of each transaction. The basic idea is to count at each step only the contribution to the value of the ultimate final product that is made at that step, excluding the values of items produced at other steps.

Ignoring the minor items (such as fertilizer) that the farmer purchases from others, the entire $3 selling price of the bushel of soybeans is new output produced by the farmer; that is, the whole $3 is value added. The miller then grinds the beans and sells them for $4. She has added $4 minus $3, or $1 to the value of the beans. When the factory turns this soy meal into soy sauce and sells it for $8, it has added $8 minus $4, or $4 more in value. Finally, when the restaurant sells it to hungry customers for $10, a further $2 of value is added.

The last column of Table 6 shows this chain of creation of value added. We see that the total value added by all four firms is $10, exactly the same as the restaurant's selling price. This is as it must be, for only the restaurant sells the soybeans as a final product.

TABLE 6

An Illustration of Value Added

Item	Seller	Buyer	Price	Value Added
Bushel of soybeans	Farmer	Miller	$3	$3
Bag of soy meal	Miller	Factory	4	1
Gallon of soy sauce	Factory	Restaurant	8	4
Gallon of soy sauce used as seasoning	Restaurant	Consumers	10	2
		Total:	$25	$10
Addendum: Contribution to GDP				
Final Products			$10	
Sum of values added			$10	

| SUMMARY |

1. **Gross domestic product (GDP)** is the sum of the money values of all final goods and services produced during a year and sold on organized markets. There are, however, certain exceptions to this definition.

2. One way to measure the GDP is to add up the final demands of consumers, investors, government, and foreigners: GDP = $C + I + G + (X - IM)$.

3. A second way to measure the GDP is to start with all factor payments—wages, interest, rents, and profits—that

constitute the **national income** and then add indirect business taxes and **depreciation.**

4. A third way to measure the GDP is to sum up the **values added** by every firm in the economy (and then once again add indirect business taxes and depreciation).

5. Except for possible bookkeeping and statistical errors, all three methods must give the same answer.

| KEY TERMS |

National income accounting 168

Gross domestic product
(GDP) 168

Gross private domestic
investment (I) 169

National income 170

Net national product
(NNP) 170

Gross national product
(GNP) 171

Depreciation 171

Value added 171

| TEST YOURSELF |

1. Which of the following transactions are included in the gross domestic product, and by how much does each raise GDP?

   a. You buy a new Toyota, made in the United States, paying $25,000.

   b. You buy a new Toyota, imported from Japan, paying $25,000.

   c. You buy a used Cadillac, paying $12,000.

   d. Google spends $500 million to increase its Internet capacity.

   e. Your grandmother receives a Social Security check for $1,500.

   f. Chrysler manufactures 1,000 automobiles at a cost of $15,000 each. Unable to sell them, the company holds the cars as inventories.

   g. Mr. Black and Mr. Blue, each out for a Sunday drive, have a collision in which their cars are destroyed. Black and Blue each hire a lawyer to sue the other, paying the lawyers $5,000 each for services rendered. The judge throws the case out of court.

   h. You sell a used computer to your friend for $100.

2. The following outline provides a complete description of all economic activity in Trivialand for 2007. Draw up versions of Tables 3 and 4 for Trivialand showing GDP computed in two different ways.[11]

   i. There are thousands of farmers but only two big business firms in Trivialand: Specific Motors (an auto company) and Super Duper (a chain of food markets). There is no government and no depreciation.

   ii. Specific Motors produced 1,000 small cars, which it sold at $6,000 each, and 100 trucks, which it sold at $8,000 each. Consumers bought 800 of the cars, and the remaining 200 cars were exported to the United States. Super Duper bought all the trucks.

   iii. Sales at Super Duper markets amounted to $14 million, all of it sold to consumers.

   iv. All farmers in Trivialand are self-employed and sell all of their wares to Super Duper.

   v. The costs incurred by all of Trivialand's businesses were as follows:

	Specific Motors	Super Duper	Farmers
Wages	$3,800,000	$4,500,000	$ 0
Interest	100,000	200,000	700,000
Rent	200,000	1,000,000	2,000,000
Purchases of food	0	7,000,000	0

3. **(More difficult)** Now complicate Trivialand in the following ways and answer the same questions. In addition, calculate national income and disposable income.[12]

   a. The government bought 50 cars, leaving only 150 cars for export. In addition, the government spent $800,000 on wages and made $1,200,000 in transfer payments.

   b. Depreciation for the year amounted to $600,000 for Specific Motors and $200,000 for Super Duper. (The farmers had no depreciation.)

   c. The government levied sales taxes amounting to $500,000 on Specific Motors and $200,000 on Super Duper (but none on farmers). In addition, the government levied a 10 percent income tax on all wages, interest, and rental income.

   d. In addition to the food and cars mentioned in Test Yourself Question 2, consumers in Trivialand imported 500 computers from the United States at $2,000 each.

---

[11] In Trivialand, net national product and net domestic product are the same. So there are no entries corresponding to "income received from other countries" or "income paid to other countries," as in Table 4.

[12] In this context, disposable income is *national income* plus transfer payments minus taxes.

| DISCUSSION QUESTIONS |

1. Explain the difference between final goods and intermediate goods. Why is it sometimes difficult to apply this distinction in practice? In this regard, why is the concept of value added useful?

2. Explain the difference between government spending and government purchases of goods and services (*G*). Which is larger?

3. Explain why national income and gross domestic product would be essentially equal if there were no depreciation.

DEMAND-SIDE EQUILIBRIUM: UNEMPLOYMENT OR INFLATION?

A definite ratio, to be called the Multiplier, can be established between income and investment.

JOHN MAYNARD KEYNES

Let's briefly review where we have just been. In Chapter 5, we learned that the interaction of aggregate demand and aggregate supply determines whether the economy will stagnate or prosper, whether our labor and capital resources will be fully employed or unemployed. In Chapter 8, we learned that aggregate demand has four components: consumer expenditure (C), investment (I), government purchases (G), and net exports ($X - IM$). It is now time to start building a theory that puts the pieces together so we can see where the aggregate demand and aggregate supply curves come from.

Because it is best to walk before you try to run, our approach is sequential. We begin in this chapter by assuming that taxes, the price level, the rate of interest, and the international value of the dollar are all constant. None of these assumptions is true, of course, and we will dispense with all of them in subsequent chapters. But we reap two important benefits from making these unrealistic assumptions now. First, they enable us to construct a simple but useful model of how the strength of aggregate demand influences the level of gross domestic product (GDP)—a model we will use to derive specific numerical solutions. Second, this simple model enables us to obtain an initial answer to a question of great importance to policy makers: Can we expect the economy to achieve full employment if the government does not intervene?

CONTENTS

Economists are fond of pointing out, with some awe, the amazing achievements of free markets. Without central direction, they somehow get businesses to produce just the goods and services that consumers want—and to do so cheaply and efficiently. If consumers want less meat and more fish, markets respond. If people subsequently change their minds, markets respond again. Free markets seem able to coordinate literally millions of decisions effortlessly and seamlessly.

Yet for hundreds of years and all over the globe, market economies have stumbled over one particular coordination problem: the periodic bouts of mass unemployment that we call *recessions* and *depressions*. Widespread unemployment represents a failure to coordinate economic activity in the following sense. If the unemployed were hired, they would be able to buy the goods and services that businesses cannot sell. The revenues from those sales would, in turn, allow firms to pay the workers. So a seemingly straightforward "deal" offers jobs for the unemployed and sales for the firms. But somehow this deal is not made. Workers remain unemployed and firms get stuck with unsold output.

Thus, free markets, which somehow manage to get rough diamonds dug out of the ground in South Africa and turned into beautiful rings that grooms buy for brides in Los Angeles, cannot seem to solve the coordination problem posed by unemployment. Why not? For centuries, economists puzzled over this question. By the end of the chapter, we will be well on the way toward providing an answer.

THE MEANING OF EQUILIBRIUM GDP

First, let's put the four components of aggregate demand together to see how they interact, using as our organizing framework the circular flow diagram from the last chapter. In doing so, we initially ignore a possibility raised in earlier chapters: that the government might use monetary and fiscal policy to steer the economy in some desired direction. Aside from pedagogical simplicity, there is an important reason for doing so. One of the crucial questions surrounding stabilization policy is whether the economy would *automatically* gravitate toward full employment if the government simply left it alone. Contradicting the teachings of generations of economists before him, Keynes claimed it would not. But Keynes's views are controversial to this day. We can study the issue best by imagining an economy in which the government never tries to manipulate aggregate demand, which is just what we do in this chapter.

To begin to construct such a model, we must first understand what we mean by *equilibrium GDP*. Figure 1, which repeats Figure 1 from the last chapter, is a circular flow diagram that will help us do this. As explained in the last chapter, total *production* and total *income* must be equal. But the same need not be true of total *spending*. Imagine that, for some reason, the total expenditures made after point 4 in the figure, $C + I + G + (X - IM)$, exceed the output produced by the business firms at point 5. What happens then?

Because consumers, businesses, government, and foreigners together are buying more than firms are producing, businesses will start pulling goods out of their warehouses to meet demand. Thus, inventory stocks will fall—which signals retailers that they need to increase their orders and manufacturers that they need to step up production. Consequently, output is likely to rise.

At some later date, if evidence indicates that the high level of spending is not just a temporary aberration, manufacturers and retailers may also respond to buoyant sales performances by raising their prices. Economists therefore say that neither output nor the price level is in **equilibrium** when total spending exceeds current production.

Equilibrium refers to a situation in which neither consumers nor firms have any incentive to change their behavior. They are content to continue with things as they are.

The definition of *equilibrium* in the margin tells us that the economy cannot be in equilibrium when total spending exceeds production, because falling inventories demonstrate to firms that their production and pricing decisions were not quite right.[1] Thus, because we normally use GDP to measure output:

> The equilibrium level of GDP on the demand side cannot be one at which total spending exceeds output because firms will notice that they are depleting their inventory stocks. Firms may first decide to increase production sufficiently to meet the higher demand. Later they may decide to raise prices.

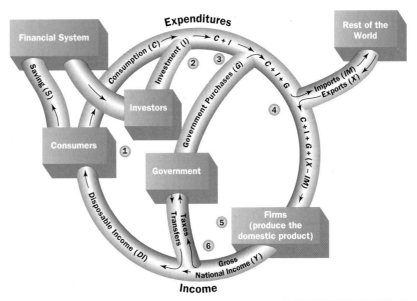

FIGURE 1

The Circular Flow Diagram

Now imagine the other case, in which the flow of spending reaching firms falls short of current production. Unsold output winds up as additional inventories. The inventory pile-up signals firms that either their pricing or output decisions were wrong. Once again, they will probably react first by cutting back on production, causing GDP to fall (at point 5 in Figure 1). If the imbalance persists, they may also lower prices to stimulate sales. But they certainly will not be happy with things as they are. Thus:

> The equilibrium level of GDP on the demand side cannot be one at which total spending is less than output, because firms will not allow inventories to pile up. They may decide to decrease production, or they may decide to cut prices in order to stimulate demand.

We have now determined, by process of elimination, the only level of output that is consistent with people's desires to spend. We have reasoned that GDP will *rise* whenever it is less than total spending, $C + I + G + (X - IM)$, and that GDP will fall whenever it exceeds $C + I + G + (X - IM)$. Equilibrium can occur, then, only when there is just enough spending to absorb the current level of production. Under such circumstances, producers conclude that their price and output decisions are correct and have no incentive to change. We conclude that

> The equilibrium level of GDP on the demand side is the level at which total spending equals production. In such a situation, firms find their inventories remaining at desired levels, so they have no incentive to change output or prices.

Thus, the circular flow diagram has helped us to understand the concept of equilibrium GDP and has shown us how the economy is driven toward this equilibrium. It leaves unanswered, however, three important questions:

* How large is the equilibrium level of GDP?
* Will the economy suffer from unemployment, inflation, or both?
* Is the equilibrium level of GDP on the demand side also consistent with firms' desires to produce? That is, is it also an equilibrium on the supply side?

The first two questions will occupy our attention in this chapter; the third is reserved to the next.

---

[1] All the models in this book assume, strictly for simplicity, that firms seek constant inventories. Deliberate inventory changes are treated in more advanced courses.

THE MECHANICS OF INCOME DETERMINATION

Our first objective is to determine precisely the equilibrium level of GDP on the demand side. To make the analysis more concrete, we turn to a numerical example. Specifically, we examine the relationship between total spending and GDP in the hypothetical economy we introduced in the last chapter.

TABLE 1

The Total Expenditure Schedule

(1)	(2)	(3)	(4)	(5)	(6)
GDP (Y)	Consumption (C)	Investment (I)	Government Purchases (G)	Net Exports (X − IM)	Total Expenditure
4,800	3,000	900	1,300	−100	5,100
5,200	3,300	900	1,300	−100	5,400
5,600	3,600	900	1,300	−100	5,700
6,000	3,900	900	1,300	−100	6,000
6,400	4,200	900	1,300	−100	6,300
6,800	4,500	900	1,300	−100	6,600
7,200	4,800	900	1,300	−100	6,900

Columns 1 and 2 of Table 1 repeat the relationship between consumption and GDP that we first encountered in the preceding chapter. They show how consumer spending, C, depends on GDP, which we symbolize by the letter Y. Columns 3 through 5 provide the other three components of total spending—I, G, and X − IM—through the simplifying assumptions that each is just a fixed number regardless of the level of GDP. Specifically, we assume that investment spending is $900 billion, government purchases are $1,300 billion, and net exports are −$100 billion—meaning that in this hypothetical economy, as in the United States at present, imports exceed exports.

By adding columns 2 through 5, we calculate C + I + G + (X − IM), or total expenditure, which appears in column 6 of Table 1. Columns 1 and 6 are highlighted in blue to show how total expenditure depends on income. We call this relationship the **expenditure schedule.**

Figure 2 shows the construction of the expenditure schedule graphically. The black line labeled C is the consumption function; it plots on a graph the numbers given in columns 1 and 2 of Table 1.

The blue line, labeled C + I, displays our assumption that investment is fixed at $900 billion. It lies a fixed distance (corresponding to $900 billion) above the C line. If investment were not always $900 billion, the two lines would either move closer together or grow farther apart. For example, our analysis of the determinants of investment spending suggested that I might be larger when GDP is higher. Such added investment as GDP rises—which is called **induced investment**—would give the resulting C + I line a steeper slope than the C line. But we ignore that possibility here for simplicity.

The green line, labeled C + I + G, adds government purchases. Because they are assumed to be $1,300 billion regardless of the size of GDP, the green line is parallel to the blue line and $1,300 billion higher.

FIGURE 2

Construction of the Expenditure Schedule

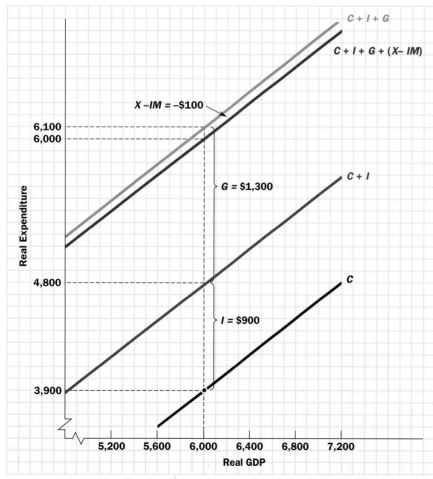

NOTE: Figures are in billions of dollars per year.

Finally, the brick-colored line labeled $C + I + G + (X - IM)$ adds in net exports. It is parallel to the green line and $100 billion lower, reflecting our assumption that net exports are always $-$$100 billion. Once again, if imports depended on GDP, as the previous chapter suggested, the $C + I + G$ and $C + I + G + (X - IM)$ lines would not be parallel. We deal with this more complicated case in Appendix B to this chapter.

We are now ready to determine demand-side equilibrium in our hypothetical economy. Table 2 presents the logic of the circular flow argument in tabular form. The first two columns reproduce the expenditure schedule that we have just constructed. The other columns explain the process by which the economy approaches equilibrium. Let us see why a GDP of $6,000 billion must be the equilibrium level.

Consider first any output level below $6,000 billion. For example, at output level $Y = $5,200 billion, total expenditure is $5,400 billion, as shown in column 2. This is $200 billion more than production. With spending greater than output, as noted in column 3, inventories will fall (see column 4). As the table suggests in column 5, this will signal producers to raise their output. Clearly, then, no output level below $Y = $6,000 billion can be an equilibrium, because output is too low.

> **An expenditure schedule** shows the relationship between national income (GDP) and total spending.
>
> **Induced investment** is the part of investment spending that rises when GDP rises and falls when GDP falls.

TABLE 2

The Determination of Equilibrium Output

(1) Output (Y)	(2) Total Spending [C + I + G + (X − IM)]	(3) Balance of Spending and Output	(4) Inventory Status	(5) Producer Response
4,800	5,100	Spending exceeds output	Falling	Produce more
5,200	5,400	Spending exceeds output	Falling	Produce more
5,600	5,700	Spending exceeds output	Falling	Produce more
6,000	**6,000**	**Spending = output**	**Constant**	**No change**
6,400	6,300	Output exceeds spending	Rising	Produce less
6,800	6,600	Output exceeds spending	Rising	Produce less
7,200	6,900	Output exceeds spending	Rising	Produce less

NOTE: Amounts are in billions of dollars.

A similar line of reasoning eliminates any output level above $6,000 billion. Consider, for example, $Y = $6,800 billion. The table shows that total spending would be $6,600 billion if output were $6,800 billion, so $200 billion would go unsold. This would raise producers' inventory stocks and signal them that their rate of production was too high.

Just as we concluded from our circular flow diagram, equilibrium will be achieved only when total spending, $C + I + G + (X - IM)$, exactly equals GDP, Y. In symbols, our condition for equilibrium GDP is

$$Y = C + I + G + (X - IM)$$

Table 2 shows that this equation holds only at a GDP of $6,000 billion, which must therefore be the equilibrium level of GDP.

Figure 3 depicts the same conclusion graphically, by adding a 45° line to Figure 2. Why a 45° line? Recall from the appendix to Chapter 1 that a 45° line marks all points on a graph at which the value of the variable measured on the horizontal axis (in this case, GDP) equals the value of the variable measured on the vertical axis (in this case, total expenditure).[2] Thus, the 45° line in Figure 3 shows all the points at which output and spending are equal—that is, where $Y = C + I + G + (X - IM)$. *The 45° line therefore displays all the points at which the economy can possibly be in demand-side equilibrium,* for firms will be content with current output levels only if total spending equals production.

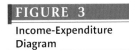

FIGURE 3

Income-Expenditure Diagram

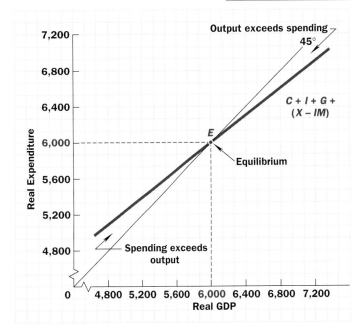

NOTE: Figures are in billions of dollars per year.

Now we must compare these *potential* equilibrium points with the *actual* combinations of spending and output that are consistent with the current behavior of consumers and investors. That behavior is described by the $C + I + G + (X - IM)$ line in Figure 3, which shows how total expenditure varies as income changes. *The economy will always be on the expenditure line* because only points on the $C + I + G + (X - IM)$ line describe the spending plans of consumers and investors. Similarly, *if* the economy is in equilibrium, it *must* be on the 45° line. As Figure 3 shows, these two requirements imply that the only viable equilibrium is at point *E*, where the $C + I + G + (X - IM)$ line intersects the 45° line. Only this point is consistent with both equilibrium and people's actual desires to consume and invest.

Notice that to the left of the equilibrium point, *E*, the expenditure line lies *above* the 45° line. This means that total spending exceeds total output, as we have already noted. Hence, inventories will be falling and firms will conclude that they should increase production. Thus, production will rise toward the equilibrium point, *E*. The opposite is true to the right of point *E*. Here spending falls short of output, inventories rise, and firms will cut back production—thereby moving closer to *E*.

In other words, whenever production is *above* the equilibrium level, market forces will drive output *down*. And whenever production is *below* equilibrium, market forces will drive output *up*. In either case, deviations from demand-side equilibrium will gradually be eliminated.

Diagrams such as Figure 3 will recur so frequently in this and the next several chapters that it will be convenient to have a name for them. We call them **income-expenditure diagrams,** because they show how expenditures vary with income, or simply **45° line diagrams.**

> An **income-expenditure diagram,** or **45° line diagram,** plots total real expenditure (on the vertical axis) against real income (on the horizontal axis). The 45° line marks off points where income and expenditure are equal.

THE AGGREGATE DEMAND CURVE

Chapter 5 introduced aggregate demand and aggregate supply curves relating aggregate quantities demanded and supplied to the price level. The expenditure schedule graphed in Figure 3 is certainly *not* the aggregate demand curve, for we have yet to bring the price level into our discussion. It is now time to remedy this omission and derive the aggregate demand curve.

To do so, we need only recall something we learned in the last chapter. As we noted on page 162, households own a great deal of *money-fixed assets* whose real value declines when the price level rises. The money in your bank account is a prime example. If prices rise, it will buy less. Because of that fact, consumers' *real* wealth declines whenever the price level rises—and that affects their spending. Specifically:

> **Higher prices decrease the demand for goods and services because they erode the purchasing power of consumer wealth. Conversely, lower prices increase the demand for goods and services by enhancing the purchasing power of consumer wealth.**

For these reasons, a change in the price level will shift the entire consumption function. To represent this shift graphically, Figure 4 (which looks just like Figure 6 from the previous chapter) shows that

> **A higher price level leads to lower real wealth and therefore to less spending *at any given level of real income.* Thus, a higher price level leads to a lower consumption function (such as C_1 in Figure 4), and a lower price level leads to a higher consumption function (such as C_2 in Figure 4).**

Because students are sometimes confused by this point, it is worth repeating that the depressing effect of the price level on consumer spending works through real *wealth*, not through real *income*. The consumption function is a relationship between *real consumer income* and *real consumer spending*. Thus, any decline in real income, regardless of its cause, moves the economy leftward *along a fixed consumption function*; it does not shift the consumption function. By contrast, a decline in *real wealth* will *shift the entire consumption function downward*, meaning that people spend less at any given level of real income.

In terms of the 45° line diagram, a rise in the price level will therefore pull down the consumption function depicted in Figure 2 and hence will pull down the total expenditure schedule as well. Conversely, a fall in the price level will raise both the C and $C + I + G + (X - IM)$ schedules in the diagram. The two panels of Figure 5 illustrate both of these shifts.

How, then, do changes in the price level affect the equilibrium level of real GDP on the demand side? Common sense says that, with lower spending, equilibrium GDP should fall; and Figure 5 shows that this conclusion is correct. Figure 5(a) shows that a rise in the price level, by shifting the expenditure schedule downward, leads to a reduction in the equilibrium quantity of real GDP demanded from Y_0 to Y_1. Conversely, Figure 5(b) shows that a fall in the price level, by shifting the expenditure schedule upward, leads to a rise in the equilibrium quantity of real GDP demanded from Y_0 to Y_2. In summary:

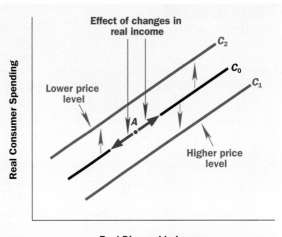

FIGURE 4

How the Price Level Shifts the Consumption Function

A rise in the price level leads to a lower equilibrium level of real aggregate quantity demanded. This relationship between the price level and real GDP (depicted in Figure 6 on the next page) is precisely what we called the aggregate demand curve in earlier chapters. It comes directly from the 45° line diagrams in Figure 5. Thus, points E_0, E_1, and E_2 in Figure 6 correspond precisely to the points bearing the same labels in Figure 5.

The effect of higher prices on consumer wealth is just one of several reasons why the aggregate demand curve slopes downward. A second reason comes from international trade. In Chapter 8's discussion of the determinants of net exports (see pages

FIGURE 5

The Effect of the Price Level on Equilibrium Aggregate Quantity Demanded

(a) Rise in Price Level

(b) Fall in Price Level

FIGURE 6

The Aggregate Demand Curve

165–166), we pointed out that higher U.S. prices (holding foreign prices constant) will depress exports (X) and stimulate imports (IM). That means that, other things equal, a higher U.S. price level will reduce the ($X - IM$) component of total expenditure, thereby shifting the $C + I + G + (X - IM)$ line downward and lowering real GDP, as depicted in Figure 5(a).

Later in this book, after we have studied interest rates and exchange rates, we will encounter still more reasons for a downward-sloping aggregate demand curve. All of them imply that

> An income-expenditure diagram like Figure 3 can be drawn only for a *specific* price level. At different price levels, the $C + I + G + (X - IM)$ schedule will be different and, hence, the equilibrium quantity of GDP demanded will also be different.

As we will now see, this seemingly technical point about graphs is critical to understanding the genesis of unemployment and inflation.

DEMAND-SIDE EQUILIBRIUM AND FULL EMPLOYMENT

We now turn to the second major question posed on page 177: Will the economy achieve an equilibrium at full employment without inflation, or will we see unemployment, inflation, or both? This question is a crucial one for stabilization policy, for if the economy always gravitates toward full employment *automatically*, then the government should simply leave it alone.

In the income-expenditure diagrams used so far, the equilibrium level of GDP demanded appears as the intersection of the expenditure schedule and the 45° line, regardless of the GDP level that corresponds to full employment. However, as we will see now, when equilibrium GDP falls above potential GDP, the economy probably will be plagued by inflation, and when equilibrium falls below potential GDP, unemployment and recession will result.

FIGURE 7

A Recessionary Gap

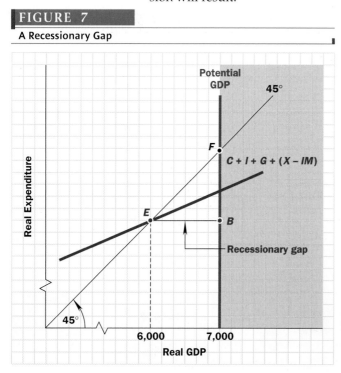

This notable fact was one of the principal messages of Keynes's *General Theory of Employment, Interest, and Money*. Writing during the Great Depression, it was natural for Keynes to focus on the case in which equilibrium falls short of full employment, leaving some resources unemployed. Figure 7 illustrates this possibility. A vertical line has been drawn at the level of *potential GDP*, a number that depends on the kinds of *aggregate supply* considerations discussed at length in Chapter 7—and to which we will return in the next chapter. Here, potential GDP is assumed to be $7,000 billion. We see that the $C + I + G + (X - IM)$ curve cuts the 45° line at point E, which corresponds to a GDP($Y = $6,000$ billion) *below* potential GDP. In this case, the expenditure curve is too low to lead to full employment. Such a situation arose in the U.S. in 2008, after the economy, hampered by a slump in housing and a variety of financial problems, slowed down abruptly late in 2007.

An equilibrium below potential GDP can arise when consumers or investors are unwilling to spend at normal rates, when government spending is low, when foreign demand is weak, or when the price level is "too high." Any of these events would depress

NOTE: Figures are in billions of dollars per year.

the $C + I + G + (X - IM)$ curve. Unemployment must then occur because not enough output is demanded to keep the entire labor force at work.

The distance between the *equilibrium* level of output demanded and the *full-employment* level of output (that is, potential GDP) is called the **recessionary gap**; it is shown by the horizontal distance from point E to point B in Figure 7. Although the figure is entirely hypothetical, real-world gaps of precisely this sort were shown shaded in blue in Figure 2 of Chapter 6 (page 112). They have been a regular feature of U.S. economic history.

The **recessionary gap** is the amount by which the equilibrium level of real GDP falls short of potential GDP.

Figure 7 clearly shows that full employment can be reached by raising the total expenditure schedule to eliminate the recessionary gap. Specifically, the $C + I + G + (X - IM)$ line must move upward until it cuts the 45° line at point F. Can this happen without government intervention? We know that a sufficiently large drop in the price level can do the job. But is that a realistic prospect? We will return to this question in the next chapter, after we bring the supply side into the picture, for we cannot discuss price determination without bringing in *both* supply *and* demand. First, however, let us briefly consider the other case—when equilibrium GDP exceeds full employment.

FIGURE 8
An Inflationary Gap

Figure 8 illustrates this possibility, which many people believe characterized the U.S. economy in 2006 and into 2007, when the unemployment rate dipped below 5 percent. Now the expenditure schedule intersects the 45° line at point E, where GDP is $8,000 billion. But this exceeds the full-employment level, $Y = \$7,000$ billion. A case such as this can arise when consumer or investment spending is unusually buoyant, when foreign demand is particularly strong, when the government spends too much, or when a "low" price level pushes the $C + I + G + (X - IM)$ curve upward.

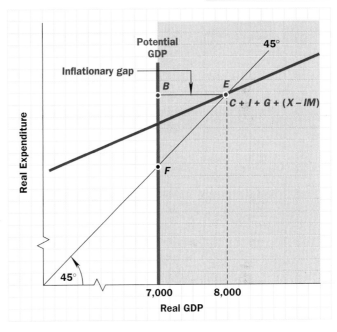

NOTE: Figures are in billions of dollars per year.

To reach an equilibrium at full employment, the price level would have to rise enough to drive the expenditure schedule *down* until it passed through point F. The horizontal distance BE—which indicates the amount by which the quantity of GDP demanded exceeds potential GDP—is now called the **inflationary gap**. If there is an inflationary gap, a higher price level or some other means of reducing total expenditure is necessary to reach an equilibrium at full employment. Rising prices will eventually pull the $C + I + G + (X - IM)$ line down until it passes through point F. Real-world inflationary gaps were shown shaded in pink-color in Figure 2 of Chapter 6 (page 112). In sum:

The **inflationary gap** is the amount by which equilibrium real GDP exceeds the full-employment level of GDP.

Only if the price level and spending plans are "just right" will the expenditure curve intersect the 45° line precisely at full employment, so that neither a recessionary gap nor an inflationary gap occurs.

Are there reasons to expect this outcome? Does the economy have a self-correcting mechanism that automatically eliminates recessionary or inflationary gaps and propels it toward full employment? And why do inflation and unemployment sometimes rise or fall together? We are not ready to answer these questions yet because we have not yet brought *aggregate supply* into the picture. However, it is not too early to get an idea about why things can go wrong during a recession.

THE COORDINATION OF SAVING AND INVESTMENT

To do so, it is useful to pose the following question: Must the full-employment level of GDP be a demand-side equilibrium? Decades ago, economists thought the answer was "yes." Since Keynes, most economists believe the answer is "not necessarily."

FIGURE 9
A Simplified Circular Flow

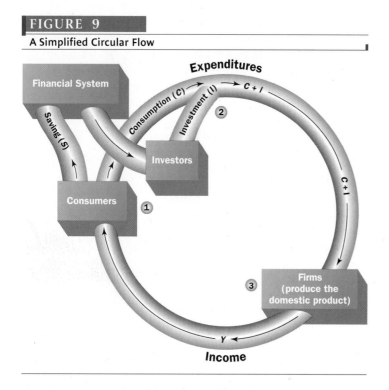

To help us see why, Figure 9 offers a simplified circular flow diagram that ignores exports, imports, and the government. In this version, income can "leak out" of the circular flow only at point 1, where consumers save some of their income. Similarly, lost spending can be replaced only at point 2, where investment enters the circular flow.

What happens if firms produce exactly the full-employment level of GDP at point 3 in the diagram? Will this income level be maintained as we move around the circle, or will it shrink or grow? The answer is that full-employment income will be maintained *only* if the spending by investors at point 2 exactly balances the saving done by consumers at point 1. In other words:

The economy will reach an equilibrium at full employment on the demand side only if the amount that consumers wish to save out of their full-employment incomes happens to equal the amount that investors want to invest. If these two magnitudes are unequal, full employment will not be an equilibrium.

Thus, the basic answer to the puzzle we posed at the start of this chapter is

The market will permit unemployment when total spending is too low to employ the entire labor force.

Now, how can that occur? The circular flow diagram shows that if saving exceeds investment at full employment, the total demand received by firms at point 3 will fall short of total output because the added investment spending will not be enough to replace the leakage to saving. With demand inadequate to support production at full employment, GDP must fall below potential. There will be a recessionary gap. Conversely, if investment exceeds saving when the economy is at full employment, then total demand will exceed potential GDP and production will rise above the full-employment level. There will be an inflationary gap.

Now, this discussion does nothing but restate what we already know in different words.[3] But these words provide the key to understanding why the economy sometimes finds itself stuck above or below full employment, for *the people who invest are not the same as the people who save.* In a modern capitalist economy, investing is done by one group of individuals (primarily corporate executives and home buyers), whereas saving is done by another group.[4] It is easy to imagine that their plans may not be well coordinated. If they are not, we have just seen how either unemployment or inflation can occur.

Neither of these problems would arise if the acts of saving and investing were perfectly coordinated. While perfection is never attainable, the analysis in the accompanying box, "Unemployment and Inflation as Coordination Failures," raises a tantalizing possibility. If both high unemployment and high inflation arise from **coordination failures,** might the government be able to do something about this problem? Keynes suggested that it could, by using its powers over monetary and fiscal policy. His ideas, which constitute one of our *Ideas for Beyond the Final Exam,* will be examined in detail in later chapters. But even the simple football analogy described in the box reminds us that a central authority may not find it easy to solve a coordination problem.

A **coordination failure** occurs when party A would like to change his behavior if party B would change hers, and vice versa, and yet the two changes do not take place because the decisions of A and B are not coordinated.

IDEAS FOR BEYOND THE FINAL EXAM

---

[3] In symbols, our equilibrium condition without government or foreign trade is $Y = C + I$. If we note that Y is also the sum of consumption plus saving, $Y = C + S$, then it follows that $C + S = C + I$, or $S = I$, is a restatement of the equilibrium condition.

[4] In a modern economy, not only do households save but businesses also save in the form of retained earnings. Nonetheless, households are the ultimate source of the saving needed to finance investment.

Unemployment and Inflation as Coordination Failures

The idea that unemployment stems from a *lack of coordination* between the decisions of savers and investors may seem abstract. But we encounter coordination failures in the real world quite frequently. The following familiar example may bring the idea down to earth.

Picture a crowd watching a football game. Now something exciting happens and the fans rise from their seats. People in the front rows begin standing first, and those seated behind them are forced to stand if they want to see the game. Soon everyone in the stadium is on their feet.

But with everyone standing, no one can see any better than when everyone was sitting. And the fans are enduring the further discomfort of being on their feet. (Never mind that stadium seats are uncomfortable!) Everyone in the stadium would be better off if everyone sat down, which sometimes happens. But the crowd rises to its feet again on every exciting play. There is simply no way to coordinate the individual decisions of tens of thousands of football fans.

Unemployment poses a similar coordination problem. During a deep recession, workers are unemployed and businesses cannot sell their wares. Figuratively speaking, everyone is "standing" and unhappy about it. If only the firms could agree to hire more workers, those newly employed people could afford to buy more of the goods and services the firms want to produce. But, as at the football stadium, there is no central authority to coordinate these millions of decisions.

SOURCE: © Thinkstock Images/Jupiterimages

The coordination failure idea also helps to explain why it is so difficult to stop inflation. Virtually everyone prefers stable prices to rising prices. But now think of yourself as the seller of a product. If all other participants in the economy would hold their prices steady, you would happily hold yours steady, too. But, if you believe that others will continue to raise their prices at a rate of, say, 5 percent per year, you may find it dangerous not to increase your prices apace. Hence, society may get stuck with 5 percent inflation even though everyone agrees that zero inflation is better.

CHANGES ON THE DEMAND SIDE: MULTIPLIER ANALYSIS

We have just learned how demand-side equilibrium depends on the consumption function and on the amounts spent on investment, government purchases, and net exports. But none of these is a constant of nature; they all change from time to time. How does equilibrium GDP change when the consumption function shifts or when I, G, or $(X - IM)$ changes? As we will see now, the answer is simple: *by more!* A remarkable result called the **multiplier** says that a change in spending will bring about an *even larger* change in equilibrium GDP on the demand side. Let us see why.

The **multiplier** is the ratio of the change in equilibrium GDP (Y) divided by the original change in spending that causes the change in GDP.

The Magic of the Multiplier

Because it is subject to abrupt swings, investment spending often causes business fluctuations in the United States and elsewhere. So let us ask what would happen if firms suddenly decided to spend more on investment goods. As we will see next, such a decision would have a *multiplied* effect on GDP, that is, each $1 of additional investment spending would add *more* than $1 to GDP.

To see why, refer first to Table 3, which looks very much like Table 1. The only difference is that we now assume that firms want to invest $200 billion more than previously—for a total of $1,100 billion. As indicated by the blue numbers, only income level $Y = \$6,800$ billion is

TABLE 3

Total Expenditure after a $200 Billion Increase in Investment Spending

(1)	(2)	(3)	(4)	(5)	(6)
Income (Y)	Consumption (C)	Investment (I)	Government Purchases (G)	Net Exports (X − IM)	Total Expenditure
4,800	3,000	1,100	1,300	−100	5,300
5,200	3,300	1,100	1,300	−100	5,600
5,600	3,600	1,100	1,300	−100	5,900
6,000	3,900	1,100	1,300	−100	6,200
6,400	4,200	1,100	1,300	−100	6,500
6,800	**4,500**	**1,100**	**1,300**	**−100**	**6,800**
7,200	4,800	1,100	1,300	−100	7,100

NOTE: Figures are in billions of dollars per year.

an equilibrium on the demand side of the economy now, because only at this level is total spending, $C + I + G + (X - IM)$, equal to production (Y).

The *multiplier* principle says that GDP will rise by *more than* the $200 billion increase in investment. Specifically, the multiplier is defined as the ratio of the change in equilibrium GDP (Y) to the original change in spending that caused GDP to change. In shorthand, when we deal with the multiplier for investment (I), the formula is

$$\text{Multiplier} = \frac{\text{Change in } Y}{\text{Change in } I}$$

Let us verify that the multiplier is, indeed, greater than 1. Table 3 shows how the new expenditure schedule is constructed by adding up C, I, G, and $(X - IM)$ at each level of Y, just as we did earlier—only now I is $1,100 billion rather than $900 billion. If you compare the last columns of Table 1 (page 178) and Table 3 (page 185), you will see that the new expenditure schedule lies uniformly above the old one by $200 billion.

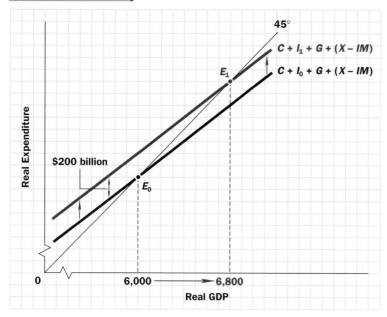

NOTE: Figures are in billions of dollars per year.

Figure 10 depicts this change graphically. The curve marked $C + I_0 + G + (X - IM)$ is derived from the last column of Table 1, while the higher curve marked $C + I_1 + G + (X - IM)$ is derived from the last column of Table 3. The two expenditure lines are parallel and $200 billion apart.

So far things look just as you might expect. But one more step will bring the multiplier rabbit out of the hat. Let us see what the upward shift of the expenditure line does to equilibrium income. In Figure 10, equilibrium moves outward from point E_0 to point E_1, or from $6,000 billion to $6,800 billion. The difference is an increase of $800 billion in GDP. All this from a $200 billion stimulus to investment? That is the magic of the multiplier.

Because the change in I is $200 billion and the change in equilibrium Y is $800 billion, by applying our definition, the multiplier is

$$\text{Multiplier} = \frac{\text{Change in } Y}{\text{Change in } I} = \frac{\$800}{\$200} = 4$$

This tells us that, in our example, each additional $1 of investment demand will add $4 to equilibrium GDP!

This result does, indeed, seem mysterious. Can something be created from nothing? Let's first check that the graph has not deceived us. The first and last columns of Table 3 show in numbers what Figure 10 shows graphically. Notice that equilibrium now comes at $Y = \$6,800$ billion, because only at that point is total expenditure equal to production (Y). This equilibrium level of GDP is $800 billion higher than the $6,000 billion level found when investment was $200 billion lower. Thus, a $200 billion rise in investment does indeed lead to an $800 billion rise in equilibrium GDP. The multiplier really is 4.

Demystifying the Multiplier: How It Works

The multiplier result seems strange at first, but it loses its mystery once we recall the circular flow of income and expenditure and the simple fact that one person's spending is another person's income. To illustrate the logic of the multiplier and see why it is exactly 4 in our example, think about what happens when businesses decide to spend $1 million on investment goods.

Suppose that Microhard—a major corporation in our hypothetical country—decides to spend $1 million on a new office building. Its $1 million expenditure goes to construction workers and owners of construction companies as wages and profits. That is, the $1 million becomes their *income.*

But the construction firm's owners and workers will not keep all of their $1 million in the bank; instead, they will spend most of it. If they are "typical" consumers, their spending will be $1 million times the marginal propensity to consume (MPC). In our example, the MPC is 0.75, so assume they spend $750,000 and save the rest. *This $750,000 expenditure is a net addition to the nation's demand for goods and services*, just as Microhard's original $1 million expenditure was. So, at this stage, the $1 million investment has already pushed GDP up by some $1.75 million. But the process is by no means over.

Shopkeepers receive the $750,000 spent by construction workers, and they in turn also spend 75 percent of their new income. This activity accounts for $562,500 (75 percent of $750,000) in additional consumer spending in the "third round." Next follows a fourth round in which the recipients of the $562,500 spend 75 percent of this amount, or $421,875, and so on. At each stage in the spending chain, people spend 75 percent of the additional income they receive, and the process continues—with consumption growing in every round.

Where does it all end? Does it all end? The answer is that, yes, it does eventually end—with GDP a total of $4 million higher than it was before Microhard built the original $1 million office building. The multiplier is indeed 4.

Table 4 displays the basis for this conclusion. In the table, "Round 1" represents Microhard's initial investment, which creates $1 million in income for construction workers. "Round 2" represents the construction workers' spending, which creates $750,000 in income for shopkeepers. The rest of the table proceeds accordingly; each entry in column 2 is 75 percent of the previous entry. Column 3 tabulates the running sum of column 2.

We see that after 10 rounds of spending, the initial $1 million investment has mushroomed to $3.77 million—and the sum is still growing. After 20 rounds, the total increase in GDP is over $3.98 million—near its eventual value of $4 million. Although it takes quite a few rounds of spending before the multiplier chain nears 4, we see from the table that it hits 3 rather quickly. If each income recipient in the chain waits, say, two months before spending his new income, the multiplier will reach 3 in only about ten months.

Figure 11 provides a graphical presentation of the numbers in the last column of Table 4. Notice how the multiplier builds up rapidly at first and then tapers off to approach its ultimate value (4 in this example) gradually.

And, of course, all this operates exactly the same—but in the opposite direction—when spending falls. For example, when the boom in housing in America ended in 2005 and 2006, spending on new houses began to decline. As this process progressed, the slowdown in housing created a negative multiplier effect on everything from appliances and furniture to carpeting and insulation. Indeed, the big macroeconomic concern in 2007 and 2008 was whether housing would "pull" the whole economy into a recession.

Algebraic Statement of the Multiplier

Figure 11 and Table 4 probably make a persuasive case that the multiplier eventually reaches 4. But for the

TABLE 4
The Multiplier Spending Chain

(1) Round Number	(2) Spending in This Round	(3) Cumulative Total
1	$1,000,000	$1,000,000
2	750,000	1,750,000
3	562,500	2,312,500
4	421,875	2,734,375
5	316,406	3,050,781
6	237,305	3,288,086
7	177,979	3,466,065
8	133,484	3,599,549
9	100,113	3,699,662
10	75,085	3,774,747
⋮	⋮	⋮
20	4,228	3,987,317
⋮	⋮	⋮
"Infinity"	0	4,000,000

FIGURE 11
How the Multiplier Builds

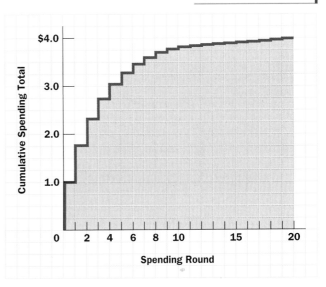

NOTE: Amounts are in millions of dollars.

remaining skeptics, we offer a simple algebraic proof.[5] Most of you learned about something called an *infinite geometric progression* in high school. This term refers to an infinite series of numbers, each one of which is a fixed fraction of the previous one. The fraction is called the *common ratio*. A geometric progression beginning with 1 and having a common ratio of 0.75 looks like this:

$$1 + 0.75 + (0.75)^2 + (0.75)^3 + \ldots$$

More generally, a geometric progression beginning with 1 and having a common ratio R would be

$$1 + R + R^2 + R^3 + \ldots$$

A simple formula enables us to sum such a progression as long as R is less than 1.[6] The formula is[7]

$$\text{Sum of infinite geometric progression} = \frac{1}{1 - R}$$

We now recognize that the multiplier chain in Table 4 is just an infinite geometric progression with 0.75 as its common ratio. That is, each \$1 that Microhard spends leads to a $(0.75) \times \$1$ expenditure by construction workers, which in turn leads to a $(0.75) \times (0.75 \times \$1) = (0.75)^2 \times \$1$ expenditure by the shopkeepers, and so on. Thus, for each initial dollar of investment spending, the progression is

$$1 + 0.75 + (0.75)^2 + (0.75)^3 + (0.75)^4 + \ldots$$

Applying the formula for the sum of such a series, we find that

$$\text{Multiplier} = \frac{1}{1 - 0.75} = \frac{1}{0.25} = 4$$

Notice how this result can be generalized. If we did not have a specific number for the marginal propensity to consume, but simply called it MPC, the geometric progression in Table 4 would have been

$$1 + \text{MPC} + (\text{MPC})^2 + (\text{MPC})^3 + \ldots$$

This progression uses the MPC as its common ratio. Applying the same formula for summing a geometric progression to this more general case gives us the following general result:

Oversimplified Multiplier Formula

$$\text{Multiplier} = \frac{1}{1 - \text{MPC}}$$

We call this formula "oversimplified" because it ignores many factors that are important in the real world. You can begin to appreciate just how unrealistic the oversimplified formula is by considering some real numbers for the U.S. economy. The MPC is over 0.95. From our oversimplified formula, then, it would seem that the multiplier should be at least

$$\text{Multiplier} = \frac{1}{1 - 0.95} = \frac{1}{0.05} = 20$$

In fact, the actual multiplier for the U.S. economy is less than 2. That is quite a discrepancy!

---

[5] Students who blanch at the sight of algebra should not be put off. Anyone who can balance a checkbook (even many who cannot!) will be able to follow the argument.

[6] If R exceeds 1, no one can possibly sum it—not even with the aid of a modern computer—because the sum is not a finite number.

[7] The proof of the formula is simple. Let the symbol S stand for the (unknown) sum of the series:
$S = 1 + R + R^2 + R^3 + \ldots$
Then, multiplying by R,
$RS = R + R^2 + R^3 + R^4 + \ldots$
By subtracting RS from S, we obtain
$S - RS = 1$ or $S = \dfrac{1}{1 - R}$

But this discrepancy does not mean that anything we have said about the multiplier so far is incorrect. Our story is simply incomplete. As we progress through this and subsequent chapters, you will learn why the multiplier in the United States is less than 2 even though the country's MPC is over 0.95. One such reason relates to *international trade*—in particular, the fact that a country's imports depend on its GDP. We deal with this complication in Appendix B to this chapter. A second factor is *inflation*, a complication we will address in the next chapter. A third factor is *income taxation*, a point we will elaborate in Chapter 11. The last important reason arises from the *financial system* and, after we discuss money and banking in Chapters 12 and 13, we will explain in Chapter 14 how the financial system influences the multiplier. As you will see, each of these factors *reduces* the size of the multiplier. So:

> **Although the multiplier is larger than 1 in the real world, it cannot be calculated accurately with the oversimplified multiplier formula. The actual multiplier is much lower than the formula suggests.**

THE MULTIPLIER IS A GENERAL CONCEPT

Although we have used business investment to illustrate the workings of the multiplier, it should be clear from the logic that *any* increase in spending can kick off a multiplier chain. To see how the multiplier works when the process is initiated by an upsurge in consumer spending, we must distinguish between two types of change in consumer spending.

To do so, look back at Figure 4 on page 181. When C rises because income rises—that is, when consumers move outward *along a fixed consumption function*—we call the increase in C an **induced increase in consumption**. (See the brick-colored arrows in the figure.) When C rises because the entire consumption function *shifts upward* (such as from C_0 to C_2 in the figure), we call it an **autonomous increase in consumption**. The name indicates that consumption changes *independently* of income. The discussion of the consumption function in Chapter 8 pointed out that a number of events, such as a change in the value of the stock market, can initiate such a shift.

If consumer spending were to rise autonomously by $200 billion, we would revise our table of aggregate demand to look like Table 5. Comparing this new table to Table 3, we note that each entry in column 2 is $200 billion *higher* than the corresponding entry in Table 3 (because consumption is higher), and each entry in column 3 is $200 billion *lower* (because in this case investment is only $900 billion).

Column 6, the expenditure schedule, is identical in both tables, so the equilibrium level of income is clearly Y = $6,800 billion once again. The initial rise of $200 billion in *consumer* spending leads to an eventual rise of $800 billion in GDP, just as it did in the case of higher *investment* spending. In fact, Figure 10 (page 186) applies directly to this case once we note that the upward shift is now caused by an autonomous change in C rather than in I. The multiplier for autonomous changes in consumer spending, then, is also 4 (= $800/$200).

The reason is straightforward. It does not matter who injects an additional dollar of spending into the economy—business investors or consumers. Whatever the source of the extra dollar, 75 percent of it will be respent if the MPC is 0.75, and the recipients of this second round of spending will, in turn, spend 75 percent of their additional income, and so on. That continued spending constitutes the multiplier process. Thus a $200 billion increase in government purchases (G) or in net exports (X − IM) would have the same multiplier effect as depicted in Figure 10. The multipliers are identical because the logic behind them is identical.

An **induced increase in consumption** is an increase in consumer spending that stems from an increase in consumer incomes. It is represented on a graph as a movement along a fixed consumption function.

An **autonomous increase in consumption** is an increase in consumer spending without any increase in consumer incomes. It is represented on a graph as a shift of the entire consumption function.

TABLE 5

Total Expenditure after Consumers Decide to Spend $200 Billion More

(1)	(2)	(3)	(4)	(5)	(6)
			Government		
Income (Y)	Consumption (C)	Investment (I)	Purchases (G)	Net Exports (X − IM)	Total Expenditure
4,800	3,200	900	1,300	−100	5,300
5,200	3,500	900	1,300	−100	5,600
5,600	3,800	900	1,300	−100	5,900
6,000	4,100	900	1,300	−100	6,200
6,400	4,400	900	1,300	−100	6,500
6,800	**4,700**	**900**	**1,300**	**−100**	**6,800**
7,200	5,000	900	1,300	−100	7,100

NOTE: Figures are in billions of dollars per year.

The idea that changes in G have multiplier effects on GDP will play a central role in the discussion of government stabilization policy that begins in Chapter 11. So it is worth noting here that

Changes in the volume of government purchases of goods and services will change the equilibrium level of GDP on the demand side in the same direction, but by a multiplied amount.

To cite a recent example, heavy federal government spending on the war in Iraq since 2003 has boosted the *G* component of $C + I + G + (X - IM)$, which had a multiplier effect on GDP.

Applying the same multiplier idea to exports and imports teaches us another important lesson: *Booms and recessions tend to be transmitted across national borders*. Why is that? Suppose a boom abroad raises GDPs in foreign countries. With rising incomes, foreigners will buy more American goods—which means that U.S. exports will increase. But an increase in our exports will, via the multiplier, raise GDP in the United States. By this mechanism, rapid economic growth abroad contributes to rapid economic growth here. And, of course, the same mechanism also operates in reverse. Thus:

The GDPs of the major economies are linked by trade. A boom in one country tends to raise its imports and hence push up exports and GDP in other countries. Similarly, a recession in one country tends to pull down GDP in other countries.

THE MULTIPLIER AND THE AGGREGATE DEMAND CURVE

One last mechanical point about the multiplier: Recall that income-expenditure diagrams such as Figure 3 (page 179) can be drawn only for a given price level. Different price levels lead to different total expenditure curves. This means that our oversimplified multiplier formula indicates *the increase in real GDP demanded that would occur if the price level were fixed*. Graphically, this means that it measures the *horizontal shift* of the economy's aggregate demand curve.

Figure 12 illustrates this conclusion by supposing that the price level that underlies Figure 3 is $P = 100$. The top panel simply repeats Figure 10 (page 186) and shows how an increase in investment spending from $900 to $1,100 billion leads to an increase in GDP from $6,000 to $6,800 billion.

The bottom panel shows two downward-sloping aggregate demand curves. The first, labeled D_0D_0, depicts

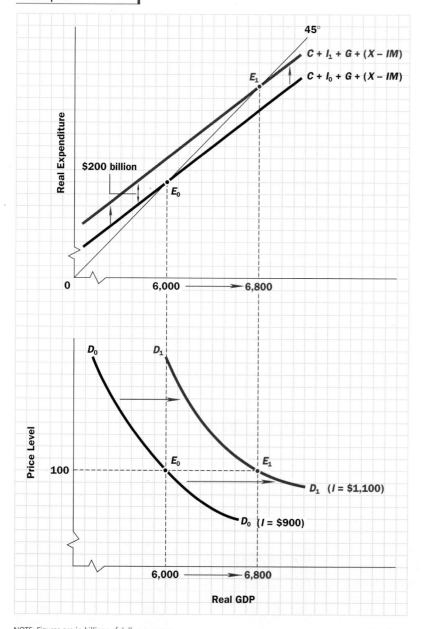

FIGURE 12

Two View of the Multiplier

NOTE: Figures are in billions of dollars per year.

the situation when investment is $900 billion. Point E_0 on this curve corresponds exactly to point E_0 in the top panel. It indicates that, at the given price level ($P = 100$), the equilibrium quantity of GDP demanded is $6,000 billion. The second aggregate demand curve, D_1D_1, depicts the situation after investment has risen to $1,100 billion. Point E_1 on this curve indicates that the equilibrium quantity of GDP demanded when $P = 100$ has risen to $6,800 billion, which corresponds exactly to point E_1 in the top panel.

As Figure 12 shows, the horizontal distance between the two aggregate demand curves is exactly equal to the increase in real GDP shown in the income-expenditure diagram—in this case, $800 billion. Thus:

> **An autonomous increase in spending leads to a horizontal shift of the aggregate demand curve by an amount given by the oversimplified multiplier formula.**

So everything we have just learned about the multiplier applies to *shifts of the economy's aggregate demand curve*. If businesses decide to increase their investment spending, if the consumption function shifts upward, or if the government or foreigners decide to buy more goods, then the aggregate demand curve moves horizontally to the right—as indicated in Figure 12. If any of these variables moves downward instead, the aggregate demand curve moves horizontally to the left.

Thus, the economy's aggregate demand curve cannot be expected to stand still for long. Autonomous changes in one or another of the four components of total spending will cause it to move around. But to understand the *consequences* of such shifts of aggregate demand, we must bring the *aggregate supply* curve back into the picture. That is the task for the next chapter.

| SUMMARY |

1. The **equilibrium level of GDP on the demand side** is the level at which total spending just equals production. Because total spending is the sum of consumption, investment, government purchases, and net exports, the condition for equilibrium is $Y = C + I + G + (X - IM)$.

2. Output levels below **equilibrium** are bound to rise because when spending exceeds output, firms will see their inventory stocks being depleted and will react by stepping up production.

3. Output levels above equilibrium are bound to fall because when total spending is insufficient to absorb total output, inventories will pile up and firms will react by curtailing production.

4. The determination of the equilibrium level of GDP on the demand side can be portrayed on a convenient **income-expenditure diagram** as the point at which the **expenditure schedule**—defined as the sum of $C + I + G + (X - IM)$—crosses the 45° line. The 45° line is significant because it marks off points at which spending and output are equal—that is, at which $Y = C + I + G + (X - IM)$, which is the basic condition for equilibrium.

5. An income-expenditure diagram can be drawn only for a specific price level. Thus, the equilibrium GDP so determined depends on the price level.

6. Because higher prices reduce the purchasing power of consumers' wealth, they reduce total expenditures on the 45° line diagram. Equilibrium real GDP demanded is therefore lower when prices are higher. This downward-sloping relationship is known as the **aggregate demand curve.**

7. Equilibrium GDP can be above or below **potential GDP,** which is defined as the GDP that would be produced if the labor force were fully employed.

8. If equilibrium GDP exceeds potential GDP, the difference is called an **inflationary gap.** If equilibrium GDP falls short of potential GDP, the resulting difference is called a **recessionary gap.**

9. Such gaps can occur because of the problem of **coordination failure:** The saving that consumers want to do at full-employment income levels may differ from the investing that investors want to do.

10. Any **autonomous increase in expenditure** has a multiplier effect on GDP; that is, it increases GDP by more than the original increase in spending.

11. The **multiplier** effect occurs because one person's additional expenditure constitutes a new source of income for another person, and this additional income leads to still more spending, and so on.

12. The multiplier is the same for an autonomous increase in consumption, investment, government purchases, or net exports.

13. A simple formula for the multiplier says that its numerical value is $1/(1 - MPC)$. This formula is too simple to give accurate results, however.

14. Rapid (or sluggish) economic growth in one country contributes to rapid (or sluggish) growth in other countries because one country's imports are other countries' exports.

| KEY TERMS |

Equilibrium   176

Expenditure schedule   179

Induced investment   179

$Y = C + I + G + (X - IM)$ 179

Income-expenditure (or 45° line)
diagram   180

Aggregate demand curve   180

Full-employment level of GDP
(or potential GDP)   182

Recessionary gap   183

Inflationary gap   183

Coordination of saving and
investment   183-184

Coordination failure   184

Multiplier   185

Induced increase in
consumption   189

Autonomous increase in
consumption   189

| TEST YOURSELF |

1. From the following data, construct an expenditure schedule on a piece of graph paper. Then use the income-expenditure (45° line) diagram to determine the equilibrium level of GDP.

Income	Consumption	Investment	Government Purchases	Net Exports
$3,600	$3,220	$240	$120	$40
3,700	3,310	240	120	40
3,800	3,400	240	120	40
3,900	3,490	240	120	40
4,000	3,580	240	120	40

Now suppose investment spending rises to $260, and the price level is fixed. By how much will equilibrium GDP increase? Derive the answer both numerically and graphically.

2. From the following data, construct an expenditure schedule on a piece of graph paper. Then use the income-expenditure (45° line) diagram to determine the equilibrium level of GDP. Compare your answer with your answer to the previous question.

Income	Consumption	Investment	Government Purchases	Net Exports
$3,600	$3,280	$180	$120	$40
3,700	3,340	210	120	40
3,800	3,400	240	120	40
3,900	3,460	270	120	40
4,000	3,520	300	120	40

3. Suppose that investment spending is always $250, government purchases are $100, net exports are always $50, and consumer spending depends on the price level in the following way:

Price Level	Consumer Spending
90	$740
95	720
100	700
105	680
110	660

On a piece of graph paper, use these data to construct an aggregate demand curve. Why do you think this example supposes that consumption declines as the price level rises?

4. **(More difficult)**[8] Consider an economy in which the consumption function takes the following simple algebraic form:

$$C = 300 + 0.75DI$$

and in which investment (I) is always $900 and net exports are always −$100. Government purchases are fixed at $1,300 and taxes are fixed at $1,200. Find the equilibrium level of GDP, and then compare your answer to Table 1 and Figure 2. (*Hint:* Remember that disposable income is GDP minus taxes: $DI = Y - T = Y - 1,200$.)

5. **(More difficult)** Keep everything the same as in Test Yourself Question 4 *except* change investment to $I = $1,100. Use the equilibrium condition $Y = C + I + G + (X - IM)$ to find the equilibrium level of GDP on the demand side. (In working out the answer, assume the price level is fixed.) Compare your answer to Table 3 and Figure 10. Now compare your answer to the answer to Test Yourself Question 4. What do you learn about the multiplier?

6. **(More difficult)** An economy has the following consumption function:

$$C = 200 + 0.8DI$$

The government budget is balanced, with government purchases and taxes both fixed at $1,000. Net exports are $100. Investment is $600. Find equilibrium GDP.

What is the multiplier for this economy? If G rises by $100, what happens to Y? What happens to Y if both G and T rise by $100 at the same time?

---

[8] The answer to this question is provided in Appendix A to this chapter.

7. Use both numerical and graphical methods to find the multiplier effect of the following shift in the consumption function in an economy in which investment is always $220, government purchases are always $100, and net exports are always −$40. (*Hint:* What is the marginal propensity to consume?)

Income	Consumption before Shift	Consumption after Shift
$1,080	$ 880	$ 920
1,140	920	960
1,200	960	1,000
1,260	1,000	1,040
1,320	1,040	1,080
1,380	1,080	1,120
1,440	1,120	1,160
1,500	1,160	1,200
1,560	1,200	1,240

| DISCUSSION QUESTIONS |

1. For over 25 years now, imports have consistently exceeded exports in the U.S. economy. Many people consider this imbalance to be a major problem. Does this chapter give you any hints about why? (You may want to discuss this issue with your instructor. You will learn more about it in later chapters.)

2. Look back at the income-expenditure diagram in Figure 3 (page 179) and explain why some level of real GDP other than $6,000 (say, $5,000 or $7,000) is *not* an equilibrium on the demand side of the economy. Do not give a mechanical answer to this question. Explain the economic mechanism involved.

3. Does the economy this year seem to have an inflationary gap or a recessionary gap? (If you do not know the answer from reading the newspaper, ask your instructor.)

4. Try to remember where you last spent a dollar. Explain how this dollar will lead to a multiplier chain of increased income and spending. (Who received the dollar? What will he or she do with it?)

| APPENDIX A | *The Simple Algebra of Income Determination and the Multiplier*

The model of demand-side equilibrium that the chapter presented graphically and in tabular form can also be handled with some simple algebra. Written as an equation, the consumption function in our example is

$$C = 300 + 0.75DI$$
$$= 300 + 0.75(Y - T)$$

because, by definition, $DI = Y - T$. This is simply the equation of a straight line with a slope of 0.75 and an intercept of $300 - 0.75T$. Because $T = 1,200$ in our example, the intercept is −600 and the equation can be written more simply as follows:

$$C = -600 + 0.75Y$$

Investment in the example was assumed to be 900, regardless of the level of income, government purchases were 1,300, and net exports were −100. So the sum $C + I + G + (X - IM)$ is

$$C + I + G + (X - IM) = -600 + 0.75Y + 900$$
$$+ 1,300 - 100$$
$$= 1,500 + 0.75Y$$

This equation describes the expenditure curve in Figure 3. Because the equilibrium quantity of GDP demanded is defined by

$$Y = C + I + G + (X - IM)$$

we can solve for the equilibrium value of Y by substituting $1,500 + 0.75Y$ for $C + I + G + (X - IM)$ to get

$$Y = 1,500 + 0.75Y$$

To solve this equation for Y, first subtract $0.75Y$ from both sides to get

$$0.25Y = 1,500$$

Then divide both sides by 0.25 to obtain the answer:

$$Y = 6,000$$

This, of course, is precisely the solution we found by graphical and tabular methods in the chapter.

We can easily generalize this algebraic approach to deal with any set of numbers in our equations. Suppose that the consumption function is as follows:

$$C = a + bDI = a + b(Y - T)$$

(In the example, $a = 300$, $T = 1,200$, and $b = 0.75$.) Then the equilibrium condition that $Y = C + I + G + (X - IM)$ implies that

$$Y = a + bDI + I + G + (X - IM)$$
$$= a - bT + bY + I + G + (X - IM)$$

Subtracting bY from both sides leads to

$$(1 - b)Y = a - bT + I + G + (X - IM)$$

and dividing through by $1 - b$ gives

$$Y = \frac{a - bT + I + G + (X - IM)}{1 - b}$$

This formula is valid for any numerical values of a, b, T, G, I, and $(X - IM)$ (so long as b is between 0 and 1).

From this formula, it is easy to derive the oversimplified multiplier formula algebraically and to show that it applies equally well to a change in investment, autonomous consumer spending, government purchases, or net exports. To do so, suppose that *any of* the symbols in the numerator of the multiplier formula increases by one unit. Then GDP would rise from the previous formula to

$$Y = \frac{a - bT + I + G + (X - IM) + 1}{1 - b}$$

By comparing this expression with the previous expression for Y, we see that a one-unit change in any component of spending changes equilibrium GDP by

$$\text{Change in } Y = \frac{a - bT + I + G + (X - IM) + 1}{1 - b} \\ - \frac{a - bT + I + G + (X - IM)}{1 - b}$$

or

$$\text{Change in } Y = \frac{1}{1 - b}$$

Recalling that b is the marginal propensity to consume, we see that this is precisely the oversimplified multiplier formula.

| TEST YOURSELF |

1. Find the equilibrium level of GDP demanded in an economy in which investment is always $300, net exports are always −$50, the government budget is balanced with purchases and taxes both equal to $400, and the consumption function is described by the following algebraic equation:

$$C = 150 + 0.75DI$$

   (*Hint:* Do not forget that $DI = Y − T$.)

2. Referring to Test Yourself Question 1, do the same for an economy in which investment is $250, net exports are 0, government purchases and taxes are both $400, and the consumption function is as follows:

$$C = 250 + 0.5DI$$

3. In each of these cases, how much saving is there in equilibrium? (*Hint:* Income not consumed must be saved.) Is saving equal to investment?

4. Imagine an economy in which consumer expenditure is represented by the following equation:

$$C = 50 + 0.75DI$$

Imagine also that investors want to spend $500 at every level of income ($I = \$500$), net exports are 0 ($X − IM = 0$), government purchases are $300, and taxes are $200.

   a. What is the equilibrium level of GDP?

   b. If potential GDP is $3,000, is there a recessionary or inflationary gap? If so, how much?

   c. What will happen to the equilibrium level of GDP if investors become optimistic about the country's future and raise their investment to $600?

   d. After investment has increased to $600, is there a recessionary or inflationary gap? How much?

5. Fredonia has the following consumption function:

$$C = 100 + 0.8DI$$

Firms in Fredonia always invest $700 and net exports are 0, initially. The government budget is balanced with spending and taxes both equal to $500.

   a. Find the equilibrium level of GDP.

   b. How much is saved? Is saving equal to investment?

   c. Now suppose that an export-promotion drive succeeds in raising net exports to $100. Answer (a) and (b) under these new circumstances.

| DISCUSSION QUESTIONS |

1. Explain the basic logic behind the multiplier in words. Why does it require b, the marginal propensity to consume, to be between 0 and 1?

2. **(More difficult)** What would happen to the multiplier analysis if $b = 0$? If $b = 1$?

| APPENDIX B | *The Multiplier with Variable Imports*

In the chapter, we assumed that net exports were a fixed number, −100 in the example. In fact, a nation's imports vary along with its GDP for a simple reason:

Higher GDP leads to higher incomes, some of which is spent on foreign goods. Thus:

Our imports rise as our GDP rises and fall as our GDP falls.

Similarly, our *exports* are the *imports* of other countries, so it is to be expected that our exports depend on *their* GDPs, not on our own. Thus:

Our exports are relatively insensitive to our own GDP, but are quite sensitive to the GDPs of other countries.

This appendix derives the implications of these rather elementary observations. In particular, it shows

that once we recognize the dependence of a nation's imports on its GDP,

International trade lowers the value of the multiplier.

To see why, we begin with Table 6, which adapts the example of our hypothetical economy to allow imports to depend on GDP. Columns 1 through 4 are the same as in Table 1; they show C, I, and G at alternative levels of GDP. Columns 5 and 6 record revised assumptions about the behavior of exports and imports.

TABLE 6

Equilibrium Income with Variable Imports

(1)	(2)	(3)	(4)	(5)	(6)	(7)	(8)
Gross Domestic Product (Y)	Consumer Expenditures (C)	Investment (I)	Government Purchases (G)	Exports (X)	Imports (IM)	Net Exports (X − IM)	Total Expenditure (C + I + G + [X − IM])
4,800	3,000	900	1,300	650	570	+80	5,280
5,200	3,300	900	1,300	650	630	+20	5,520
5,600	3,600	900	1,300	650	690	−40	5,760
6,000	**3,900**	**900**	**1,300**	**650**	**750**	**−100**	**6,000**
6,400	4,200	900	1,300	650	810	−160	6,240
6,800	4,500	900	1,300	650	870	−220	6,480
7,200	4,800	900	1,300	650	930	−280	6,720

NOTE: Figures are in billions of dollars per year.

FIGURE 13

The Dependence of Net Exports on GDP

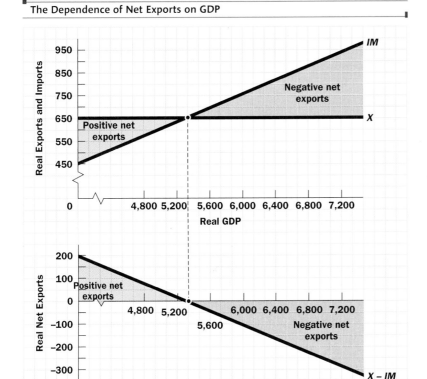

NOTE: Figures are in billions of dollars per year.

Exports are fixed at $650 billion regardless of GDP. But imports are assumed to rise by $60 billion for every $400 billion rise in GDP, which is a simple numerical example of the idea that imports depend on GDP. Column 7 subtracts imports from exports to get net exports, (X − IM), and column 8 adds up the four components of total expenditure, C + I + G + (X − IM). The equilibrium, you can see, occurs at Y = $6,000 billion, just as it did in the chapter.

Figures 13 and 14 display the same conclusion graphically. The upper panel of Figure 13 shows that exports are fixed at $650 billion regardless of GDP, whereas imports increase as GDP rises, just as in Table 6. The difference between exports and imports, or net exports, is positive until GDP approaches $5,300 billion, and negative once GDP surpasses that amount. The bottom panel of Figure 13 shows the subtraction explicitly by displaying *net exports*. It shows clearly that

Net exports decline as GDP rises.

Figure 14 carries this analysis over to the 45° line diagram. We begin with the familiar C + I + G + (X − IM) line in

FIGURE 14

Equilibrium GDP with Variable Imports

FIGURE 15

The Multiplier with Variable Imports

TABLE 7

Equilibrium Income after a $160 Billion Increase in Exports

(1)	(2)	(3)	(4)	(5)	(6)	(7)	(8)
Gross Domestic Product (Y)	Consumer Expenditures (C)	Investment (I)	Government Purchases (G)	Exports (X)	Imports (IM)	Net Exports ($X - IM$)	Total Expenditure ($C + I + G + [X - IM]$)
4,800	3,000	900	1,300	810	570	+240	5,440
5,200	3,300	900	1,300	810	630	+180	5,680
5,600	3,600	900	1,300	810	690	+120	5,920
6,000	3,900	900	1,300	810	750	+60	6,160
6,400	**4,200**	**900**	**1,300**	**810**	**810**	**0**	**6,400**
6,800	4,500	900	1,300	810	870	−60	6,640
7,200	4,800	900	1,300	180	930	−120	6,800

NOTE: Figures are in billions of dollars per year.

black. Previously, we simply assumed that net exports were fixed at −$100 billion regardless of GDP. Now that we have amended our model to note that net exports decline as GDP rises, the sum $C + I + G + (X - IM)$ rises more slowly than we previously assumed. This change is shown by the brick-colored line. Note that it is less steep than the black line.

Let us now consider what happens if exports rise by $160 billion while imports remain as in Table 6. Table 7 shows that equilibrium now occurs at a GDP of $Y = \$6,400$ billion. Naturally, higher exports have raised domestic GDP. But consider the magnitude. A $160 billion increase in exports (from $650 billion to $810 billion) leads to an increase of $400 billion in GDP (from $6,000 billion to $6,400 billion). So the multiplier is 2.5 (= $400/$160).[9]

This same conclusion is shown graphically in Figure 15, where the line $C + I + G + (X_0 - IM)$ represents the original expenditure schedule and the line $C + I + G + (X_1 - IM)$ represents the expenditure schedule after the $160 billion increase in exports. Equilibrium shifts from point E to point A, and GDP rises by $400 billion.

Notice that the multiplier in this example is 2.5, whereas in the chapter, with net exports taken to be a fixed number, it was 4. This simple example illustrates a general result: *International trade lowers the numerical value of the multiplier.* Why is this so? Because, in an open economy, any autonomous increase in spending is partly dissipated in purchases of foreign goods, which creates additional income for *foreigners* rather than for domestic citizens.

Thus, international trade gives us the first of what will eventually be several reasons why the oversimplified multiplier formula overstates the true value of the multiplier.

---

[9] *Exercise:* Construct a version of Table 6 to show what would happen if imports rose by $160 billion at every level of GDP while exports remained at $650 billion. You should be able to show that the new equilibrium would be $Y = \$5,600$.

| SUMMARY |

1. Because imports rise as GDP rises, while exports are insensitive to (domestic) GDP, net exports decline as GDP rises.

2. If imports depend on GDP, international trade reduces the value of the multiplier.

| TEST YOURSELF |

1. Suppose exports and imports of a country are given by the following:

GDP	Exports	Imports
$2,500	$400	$250
3,000	400	300
3,500	400	350
4,000	400	400
4,500	400	450
5,000	400	500

Calculate net exports at each level of GDP.

2. If domestic expenditure (the sum of $C + I + G$ in the economy described in Test Yourself Question 1) is as shown in the following table, construct a 45° line diagram and locate the equilibrium level of GDP.

GDP	Domestic Expenditures
$2,500	$3,100
3,000	3,400
3,500	3,700
4,000	4,000
4,500	4,300
5,000	4,600

3. Now raise exports to $650 and find the equilibrium again. How large is the multiplier?

| DISCUSSION QUESTION |

1. Explain the logic behind the finding that variable imports reduce the numerical value of the multiplier.

BRINGING IN THE SUPPLY SIDE: UNEMPLOYMENT *AND* INFLATION?

We might as well reasonably dispute whether it is the upper or the under blade of a pair of scissors that cuts a piece of paper, as whether value is governed by [demand] or [supply].

ALFRED MARSHALL

The previous chapter taught us that the position of the economy's total expenditure $(C + I + G + (X - IM))$ schedule governs whether the economy will experience a recessionary or an inflationary gap. Too little spending leads to a *recessionary gap.* Too much leads to an *inflationary gap.* Which sort of gap actually occurs is of considerable practical importance, because a recessionary gap translates into *unemployment* whereas an inflationary gap leads to *inflation.*

But the tools provided in Chapter 9 cannot tell us which sort of gap will arise because, as we learned, the position of the expenditure schedule depends on the price level—and the price level is determined by *both* aggregate demand *and* aggregate supply. So this chapter has a clear task: to bring the supply side of the economy back into the picture.

Doing so will put us in a position to deal with the crucial question raised in earlier chapters: Does the economy have an efficient self-correcting mechanism? We shall see that the answer is "yes, but": Yes, but it works slowly. The chapter will also enable us to explain the vexing problem of *stagflation*—the simultaneous occurrence of high unemployment *and* high inflation—which plagued the economy in the 1980s and which some people worry may stage a comeback.

CONTENTS

PUZZLE: WHAT CAUSES STAGFLATION?

The financial press in 2007 and 2008 was full of stories about the possible return of the dreaded disease of stagflation, which plagued the U.S. economy in the 1970s and early 1980s. Many economists, however, found this talk unduly alarming.

On the surface, the very existence of stagflation—the combination of economic *stag*nation and in*flation*—seems to contradict one of our *Ideas for Beyond the Final Exam* from Chapter 1: that there is a *trade-off* between inflation and unemployment. Low unemployment is supposed to make the inflation rate rise, and high unemployment is supposed to make inflation fall. (This trade-off will be discussed in more detail in Chapter 16.) Yet things do not always work out this way. For example, both unemployment and inflation rose together in the early 1980s and then fell together in the late 1990s. Why is that? What determines whether inflation and unemployment move in opposite directions (as in the trade-off view) or in the same direction (as during a stagflation). This chapter will provide some answers.

THE AGGREGATE SUPPLY CURVE

The **aggregate supply curve** shows, for each possible price level, the quantity of goods and services that all the nation's businesses are willing to produce during a specified period of time, holding all other determinants of aggregate quantity supplied constant.

In earlier chapters, we noted that aggregate demand is a schedule, not a fixed number. The quantity of real gross domestic product (GDP) that will be demanded depends on the price level, as summarized in the economy's *aggregate demand curve*. The same point applies to *aggregate supply:* The concept of aggregate supply does not refer to a fixed number, but rather to a schedule (an *aggregate supply curve*).

The volume of goods and services that profit-seeking enterprises will provide depends on the prices they obtain for their outputs, on wages and other production costs, on the capital stock, on the state of technology, and on other things. The relationship between the price level and the quantity of real GDP supplied, *holding all other determinants of quantity supplied constant,* is called the economy's **aggregate supply curve.**

Figure 1 shows a typical aggregate supply curve. It slopes upward, meaning that as prices rise, more output is produced, *other things held constant.* Let's see why.

Why the Aggregate Supply Curve Slopes Upward

Producers are motivated mainly by profit. The profit made by producing an additional unit of output is simply the difference between the price at which it is sold and the unit cost of production:

Unit profit = Price − Unit cost

The response of output to a rising price level—which is what the slope of the aggregate supply curve shows—depends on the response of costs. So the question is: Do costs rise along with selling prices, or not?

The answer is: Some do, and some do not. Many of the prices that firms pay for labor and other inputs remain fixed for periods of time—although certainly not forever. For example, workers and firms often enter into long-term labor contracts that set nominal wages a year or more in advance. Even where no explicit contracts exist, wage rates typically adjust only annually. Similarly, a variety of material inputs are delivered to firms under long-term contracts at prearranged prices.

This fact is significant because firms decide how much to produce by comparing their selling prices with their costs of production. If the selling prices of the firm's products rise

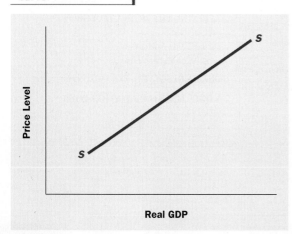

FIGURE 1

An Aggregate Supply Curve

Price Level (vertical axis)

Real GDP (horizontal axis)

while its nominal wages and other factor costs are fixed, production becomes more profitable, and firms will presumably produce more.

A simple example will illustrate the idea. Suppose that, given the scale of its operations, a particular firm needs one hour of labor to manufacture one additional gadget. If the gadget sells for $9, workers earn $8 per hour, and the firm has no other costs, its profit on this unit will be

$$\text{Unit profit} = \text{Price} - \text{Unit cost}$$

$$= \$9 - \$8 = \$1$$

If the price of the gadget then rises to $10, but wage rates remain constant, the firm's profit on the unit becomes

$$\text{Unit profit} = \text{Price} - \text{Unit cost}$$

$$= \$10 - \$8 = \$2$$

With production more profitable, the firm presumably will supply more gadgets.

The same process operates in reverse. If selling prices fall while input costs remain relatively fixed, profit margins will be squeezed and production cut back. This behavior is summarized by the upward slope of the aggregate supply curve: Production rises when the price level (henceforth, P) rises, and falls when P falls. In other words,

> **The aggregate supply curve slopes upward because firms normally can purchase labor and other inputs at prices that are fixed for some period of time. Thus, higher selling prices for output make production more attractive.**[1]

The phrase "for some period of time" alerts us to the important fact that the aggregate supply curve may not stand still for long. If wages or prices of other inputs change, as they surely will during inflationary times, then the aggregate supply curve will shift.

Shifts of the Aggregate Supply Curve

So let's consider what happens when input prices change.

The Nominal Wage Rate   The most obvious determinant of the position of the aggregate supply curve is the *nominal wage rate* (sometimes called the "money wage rate"). Wages are the major element of cost in the economy, accounting for more than 70 percent of all inputs. Because higher wage rates mean higher costs, they spell lower profits at any given selling prices. That relationship explains why companies have sometimes been known to dig in their heels when workers demand increases in wages and benefits. For example, negotiations between General Motors and the United Auto Workers led to a brief strike in September 2007 because GM felt it had to reduce its labor costs in order to survive.

Returning to our example, consider what would happen to a gadget producer if the nominal wage rate rose to $8.75 per hour while the gadget's price remained $9. Unit profit would decline from $1 to

$$\$9.00 - \$8.75 = \$0.25$$

With profits thus squeezed, the firm would probably cut back on production.

Thus, a wage increase leads to a decrease in aggregate quantity supplied at current prices. Graphically, the aggregate supply curve *shifts to the left* (or inward) when nominal wages rise, as shown in Figure 2 on the next page. In this diagram, firms are willing to supply $6,000 billion in goods and services at a price level of 100 when wages are low (point *A*). But after wages increase, the same firms are willing to supply only $5,500 billion at this

---

[1] There are both differences and similarities between the *aggregate* supply curve and the *microeconomic* supply curves studied in Chapter 4. Both are based on the idea that quantity supplied depends on how output prices move relative to input prices. But the aggregate supply curve pertains to the behavior of *the overall price level,* whereas a microeconomic supply curve pertains to the *price of some particular commodity.*

FIGURE 2

A Shift of the Aggregate Supply Curve

NOTE: Amounts are in billions of dollars per year.

price level (point *B*). By similar reasoning, the aggregate supply curve will shift to the right (or outward) if wages fall.

> **An increase in the nominal wage shifts the aggregate supply curve *inward*, meaning that the quantity supplied at any price level *declines*. A decrease in the nominal wage shifts the aggregate supply curve *outward*, meaning that the quantity supplied at any price level *increases*.**

The logic behind these shifts is straightforward. Consider a wage increase, as indicated by the brick-colored line in Figure 2. With selling prices fixed at 100 in the illustration, an increase in the nominal wage means that wages rise *relative to prices*. In other words, the *real wage rate* rises. It is this increase in the firms' real production costs that induces a contraction of quantity supplied—from *A* to *B* in the diagram.

Prices of Other Inputs   In this regard, wages are not unique. An increase in the price of *any* input that firms buy will shift the aggregate supply curve in the same way. That is,

> **The aggregate supply curve is shifted to the left (or inward) by an increase in the price of any input to the production process, and it is shifted to the right (or outward) by any decrease.**

The logic is exactly the same.

Although producers use many inputs other than labor, the one that has attracted the most attention in recent decades is energy. Increases in the prices of imported energy, such as those that took place over most of the period from 2002 until this book went to press, push the aggregate supply curve inward—as shown in Figure 2. By the same token, decreases in the price of imported oil, such as the ones we enjoyed briefly in the second half of 2006, shift the aggregate supply curve in the opposite direction—outward.

Productivity is the amount of output produced by a unit of input.

Technology and Productivity   Another factor that can shift the aggregate supply curve is the state of technology. The idea that technological progress increases the **productivity** of labor is familiar from earlier chapters. Holding wages constant, any increase of productivity will *decrease* business costs, improve profitability, and encourage more production.

Once again, our gadget example will help us understand how this process works. Suppose the price of a gadget stays at $9 and the hourly wage rate stays at $8, but gadget workers become more productive. Specifically, suppose the labor input required to manufacture a gadget *decreases* from one hour (which costs $8) to three-quarters of an hour (which costs just $6). Then unit profit rises from $1 to

$$\$9 - (\tfrac{3}{4})\,\$8 = \$9 - \$6 = \$3$$

The lure of higher profits should induce gadget manufacturers to increase output—which is, of course, why companies constantly strive to raise their productivity. In brief, we have concluded that

> **Improvements in productivity shift the aggregate supply curve outward.**

We can therefore interpret Figure 2 as illustrating the effect of a *decline* in productivity. As we mentioned in Chapter 7, a slowdown in productivity growth was a persistent problem for the United States for more than two decades starting in 1973.

Available Supplies of Labor and Capital   The last determinants of the position of the aggregate supply curve are the ones we studied in Chapter 7: The bigger the economy—as measured by its available supplies of labor and capital—the more it is capable of producing. Thus:

> **As the labor force grows or improves in quality, and as investment increases the capital stock, the aggregate supply curve shifts *outward* to the right, meaning that more output can be produced at any given price level.**

So, for example, the great investment boom of the late 1990s, by boosting the supply of capital, left the U.S. economy with a greater capacity to produce goods and services—that is, it shifted the aggregate supply curve outward.

These factors, then, are the major "other things" that we hold constant when drawing an aggregate supply curve: nominal wage rates, prices of other inputs (such as energy), technology, labor force, and capital stock. A change in the price level moves the economy *along a given supply curve,* but a change in any of these determinants of aggregate quantity supplied *shifts the entire supply schedule.*

EQUILIBRIUM OF AGGREGATE DEMAND AND SUPPLY

Chapter 9 taught us that the price level is a crucial determinant of whether equilibrium GDP falls below full employment (a "recessionary gap"), precisely at full employment, or above full employment (an "inflationary gap"). We can now analyze which type of gap, if any, will occur in any particular case by combining the aggregate supply analysis we just completed with the aggregate demand analysis from the last chapter.

Figure 3 displays the simple mechanics. In the figure, the aggregate demand curve *DD* and the aggregate supply curve *SS* intersect at point *E*, where real GDP (*Y*) is $6,000 billion and the price level (*P*) is 100. As can be seen in the graph, at any higher price level, such as 120, aggregate quantity supplied would exceed aggregate quantity demanded. In such a case, there would be a glut of goods on the market as firms found themselves unable to sell all their output. As inventories piled up, firms would compete more vigorously for the available customers, thereby forcing prices down. Both the price level and production would fall.

At any price level lower than 100, such as 80, quantity demanded would exceed quantity supplied. There would be a shortage of goods on the market. With inventories disappearing and customers knocking on their doors, firms would be encouraged to raise prices. The price level would rise, and so would output. Only when the price level is 100 are the quantities of real GDP demanded and supplied equal. Therefore, only the combination of *P* = 100 and *Y* = $6,000 is an equilibrium.

Table 1 illustrates this conclusion by using a tabular analysis similar to the one in the previous chapter. Columns (1) and (2) constitute an aggregate demand schedule corresponding to curve *DD* in Figure 3. Columns (1) and (3) constitute an aggregate supply schedule corresponding to aggregate supply curve *SS*.

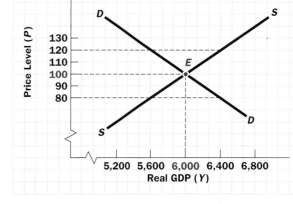

NOTE: Amounts are in billions of dollars per year.

FIGURE 3

Equilibrium of Real GDP and the Price Level

TABLE 1

Determination of the Equilibrium Price Level

(1) Price Level	(2) Aggregate Quantity Demanded	(3) Aggregate Quantity Supplied	(4) Balance of Supply and Demand	(5) Prices will be:
80	$6,400	$5,600	Demand exceeds supply	Rising
90	6,200	5,800	Demand exceeds supply	Rising
100	**6,000**	**6,000**	**Demand equals supply**	**Unchanged**
110	5,800	6,200	Supply exceeds demand	Falling
120	5,600	6,400	Supply exceeds demand	Falling

NOTE: Quantities are in billions of dollars.

The table clearly shows that equilibrium occurs only at $P = 100$. At any other price level, aggregate quantities supplied and demanded would be unequal, with consequent upward or downward pressure on prices. For example, at a price level of 90, customers demand $6,200 billion worth of goods and services, but firms wish to provide only $5,800 billion. In this case, the price level is too low and will be forced upward. Conversely, at a price level of 110, quantity supplied ($6,200 billion) exceeds quantity demanded ($5,800 billion), implying that the price level must fall.

INFLATION AND THE MULTIPLIER

To illustrate the importance of the slope of the aggregate supply curve, we return to a question we posed in the last chapter: What happens to equilibrium GDP if the aggregate demand curve shifts outward? We saw in Chapter 9 that such changes have a *multiplier* effect, and we noted that the actual numerical value of the multiplier is considerably smaller than suggested by the oversimplified multiplier formula. One of the reasons, variable imports, emerged in an appendix to that chapter. We are now in a position to understand a second reason:

Inflation reduces the size of the multiplier.

The basic idea is simple. In Chapter 9, we described a multiplier process in which one person's spending becomes another person's income, which leads to further spending by the second person, and so on. But this story was confined to the *demand* side of the economy; it ignored what is likely to be happening on the *supply* side. The question is: As the multiplier process unfolds, will firms meet the additional demand without raising prices?

If the aggregate supply curve slopes upward, the answer is no. More goods will be provided only at *higher* prices. Thus, as the multiplier chain progresses, pulling income and employment up, prices will rise, too. This development, as we know from earlier chapters, will reduce net exports and dampen consumer spending because rising prices erode the purchasing power of consumers' wealth. As a consequence, the multiplier chain will not proceed as far as it would have in the absence of inflation.

How much inflation results from a given rise in aggregate demand? How much is the multiplier chain muted by inflation? The answers to these questions depend on the slope of the economy's aggregate supply curve.

For a concrete example, let us return to the $200 billion increase in investment spending used in Chapter 9. There we found (see especially Figure 10 on page 186) that $200 billion in additional investment spending would eventually lead to $800 billion in additional spending *if the price level did not rise*—that is, *it tacitly assumed that the aggregate supply curve was horizontal.* But that is not so. The slope of the aggregate supply curve tells us how any expansion of aggregate demand gets apportioned between higher output and higher prices.

In our example, Figure 4 shows the $800-billion rightward shift of the aggregate demand curve, from D_0D_0 to D_1D_1, that we derived from the oversimplified multiplier formula in Chapter 9. We see that, as the economy's equilibrium moves from point E_0 to point E_1, real GDP does not rise by $800 billion. Instead, prices rise, cancelling out part of the increase in quantity demanded. As a result, output rises from $6,000 billion to $6,400 billion—an increase of only $400 billion. Thus, in the example, inflation reduces the multiplier from $800/$200 = 4 to $400/$200 = 2. In general:

As long as the aggregate supply curve slopes upward, any increase in aggregate demand will push up the price level. Higher prices, in turn, will drain off some of the higher real demand by eroding the purchasing power of consumer wealth and by reducing net exports. Thus, inflation reduces the value of the multiplier below what is suggested by the oversimplified formula.

Notice also that the price level in this example has been pushed up (from 100 to 120, or by 20 percent) by the rise in investment demand. This, too, is a general result:

> **As long as the aggregate supply curve slopes upward, any outward shift of the aggregate demand curve will increase the price level.**

The economic behavior behind these results is certainly not surprising. Firms faced with large increases in quantity demanded at their original prices respond to these changed circumstances in two natural ways: They raise production (so that real GDP rises), and they raise prices (so the price level rises). But this rise in the price level, in turn, reduces the purchasing power of the bank accounts and bonds held by consumers, and they, too, react in the natural way: They reduce their spending. Such a reaction amounts to a movement *along* aggregate demand curve $D_1 D_1$ in Figure 4 from point *A* to point E_1.

Figure 4 also shows us exactly where the oversimplified multiplier formula goes wrong. By ignoring the effects of the higher price level, the oversimplified formula erroneously pretends that the economy moves horizontally from point E_0 to point *A*—which it will not do unless the aggregate supply curve is horizontal. As the diagram clearly shows, output actually rises by less, which is one reason why the oversimplified formula exaggerates the size of the multiplier.

FIGURE 4

Inflation and the Multiplier

NOTE: Amounts are in billions of dollars per year.

RECESSIONARY AND INFLATIONARY GAPS REVISITED

With this understood, let us now reconsider the question we have been deferring: Will equilibrium occur at, below, or beyond potential GDP?

We could not answer this question in the previous chapter because we had no way to determine the equilibrium price level, and therefore no way to tell which type of gap, if any, would arise. The aggregate supply-and-demand analysis presented in this chapter now gives us what we need. But we find that our answer is still the same: Anything can happen.

The reason is that Figure 3 tells us nothing about where *potential* GDP falls. The factors determining the economy's capacity to produce were discussed extensively in Chapter 7. But that analysis could leave potential GDP above the $6,000 billion equilibrium level or below it. Depending on the locations of the aggregate demand and aggregate supply curves, then, we can reach equilibrium *beyond* potential GDP (an inflationary gap), *at* potential GDP, or *below* potential GDP (a recessionary gap). All three possibilities are illustrated in Figure 5 on the next page.

The three upper panels duplicate diagrams that we encountered in Chapter 9.[2] Start with the upper-middle panel, in which the expenditure schedule $C + I_1 + G + (X - IM)$ crosses the 45° line exactly at potential GDP—which we take to be $7,000 billion in the example. Equilibrium is at point *E*, with neither a recessionary nor an inflationary gap. Now suppose that total expenditures either *fall* to $C + I_0 + G + (X - IM)$ (producing the upper-left diagram) or *rise* to $C + I_2 + G + (X - IM)$ (producing the upper-right diagram). As we read across the page from left to right, we see equilibrium occurring with a recessionary gap, exactly at full employment, or with an inflationary gap—depending on the position

---

[2] Recall that each income-expenditure diagram considers *only* the demand side of the economy by treating the price level as fixed.

FIGURE 5

Recessionary and Inflationary Gaps Revisited

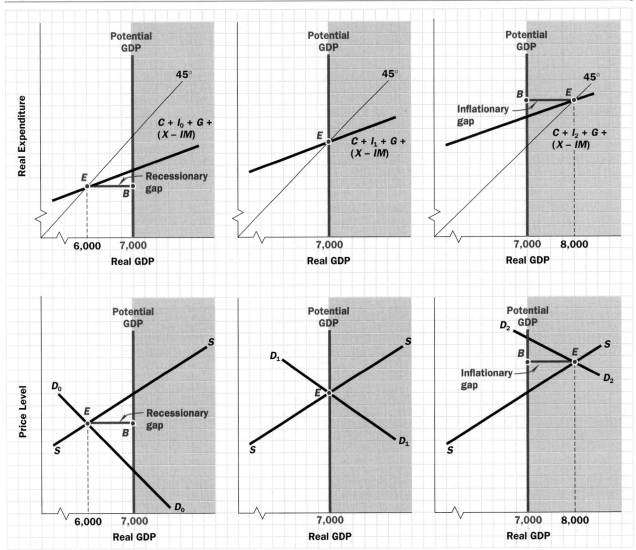

NOTE: Real GDP is in billions of dollars per year.

of the $C + I + G + (X - IM)$ line. In Chapter 9, we learned of several variables that might shift the expenditure schedule up and down in this way. One of them was the price level.

The three lower panels portray the same three cases differently—in a way that can tell us what the price level will be. These diagrams consider *both* aggregate demand *and* aggregate supply, and therefore determine *both* the equilibrium price level *and* the equilibrium GDP at point *E*—the intersection of the aggregate supply curve *SS* and the aggregate demand curve *DD*. But there are still three possibilities.

In the lower-left panel, aggregate demand is too low to provide jobs for the entire labor force, so we have a recessionary gap equal to distance *EB*, or $1,000 billion. This situation corresponds precisely to the one depicted on the income-expenditure diagram immediately above it.

In the lower-right panel, aggregate demand is so high that the economy reaches an equilibrium beyond potential GDP. An inflationary gap equal to *BE*, or $1,000 billion, arises, just as in the diagram immediately above it.

In the lower-middle panel, the aggregate demand curve D_1D_1 is at just the right level to produce an equilibrium at potential GDP. Neither an inflationary gap nor a recessionary gap occurs, as in the diagram just above it.

It may seem, therefore, that we have simply restated our previous conclusions. But, in fact, we have done much more. For now that we have studied the determination of the equilibrium price level, we are able to examine how the economy adjusts to either a recessionary gap or an inflationary gap. Specifically, because wages are fixed in the short run, any one of the three cases depicted in Figure 5 can occur. But, in the long run, wages will adjust to labor market conditions, which will shift the aggregate supply curve. It is to that adjustment that we now turn.

ADJUSTING TO A RECESSIONARY GAP: DEFLATION OR UNEMPLOYMENT?

Suppose the economy starts with a recessionary gap—that is, an equilibrium *below* potential GDP—as depicted in the lower-left panel of Figure 5. Such a situation might be caused, for example, by inadequate consumer spending or by anemic investment spending. After the financial crisis (which was centered on the home mortgage market) hit in 2007, many observers began to fear that the United States was headed in that direction for the first time in years. And these fears mounted in early 2008. But in Japan, recessionary gaps have been the norm since the early 1990s. What happens when an economy experiences such a recessionary gap?

With equilibrium GDP below potential (point *E* in Figure 6), jobs will be difficult to find. The ranks of the unemployed will exceed the number of people who are jobless because of moving, changing occupations, and so on. In the terminology of Chapter 6, the economy will experience a considerable amount of *cyclical unemployment*. Businesses, by contrast, will have little trouble finding workers, and their current employees will be eager to hang on to their jobs.

Such an environment makes it difficult for workers to win wage increases. Indeed, in extreme situations, wages may even fall—thereby shifting the aggregate supply curve *outward*. (Remember: An aggregate supply curve is drawn for a *given* nominal wage.) But as the aggregate supply curve shifts to the right—eventually moving from S_0S_0 to S_1S_1 in Figure 6—prices decline and the recessionary gap shrinks. By this process, deflation gradually erodes the recessionary gap—leading eventually to an equilibrium at potential GDP (point *F* in Figure 6).

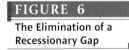

FIGURE 6

The Elimination of a Recessionary Gap

But there is an important catch. In our modern economy, this adjustment process proceeds slowly—painfully slowly. Our brief review of the historical record in Chapter 5 showed that the history of the United States includes several examples of *deflation* before World War II but none since then. Not even severe recessions have forced average prices and wages down—although they have certainly slowed their rates of increase to a crawl. The only protracted episode of deflation in an advanced economy since the 1930s is the experience of Japan over roughly the last decade, and even there the rate of deflation has been quite mild.

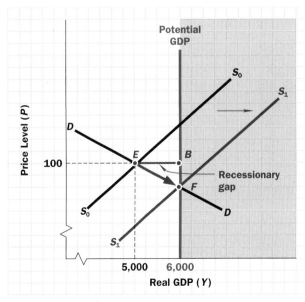

Why Nominal Wages and Prices Won't Fall (Easily)

Exactly why wages and prices rarely fall in a modern economy is still a subject of intense debate among economists. Some economists emphasize institutional factors such as minimum wage laws, union contracts, and a variety of

NOTE: Amounts are in billions of dollars per year.

government regulations that place legal floors under particular wages and prices. Because most of these institutions are of recent vintage, this theory successfully explains why wages and prices fall less frequently now than they did before World War II. But only a small minority of the U.S. economy is subject to legal restraints on wage and price cutting. So it seems doubtful that legal restrictions take us very far in explaining sluggish wage-price adjustments in the United States. In Europe, however, these institutional factors may be more important.

Other observers suggest that workers have a profound psychological resistance to accepting a wage reduction. This theory has roots in psychological research that finds people to be far more aggrieved when they suffer an absolute loss (e.g., a nominal wage reduction) than when they receive only a small gain. So, for example, business may find it relatively easy to cut the rate of wage increase from 3 percent to 1 percent, but excruciatingly hard to cut it from 1 percent to *minus* 1 percent. This psychological theory has the ring of truth. Think how you might react if your boss announced he was cutting your hourly wage rate. You might quit, or you might devote less care to your job. If the boss suspects you will react this way, he may be reluctant to cut your wage. Nowadays, genuine wage reductions are rare enough to be newsworthy. But although no one doubts that wage cuts can damage morale, the psychological theory still must explain why the resistance to wage cuts apparently started only after World War II.

A third explanation is based on a fact we emphasized in Chapter 5—that business cycles have been less severe in the postwar period than they were in the prewar period. As workers and firms came to realize that recessions would not turn into depressions, the argument goes, they decided to wait out the bad times rather than accept wage or price reductions that they would later regret.

Yet another theory is based on the old adage, "You get what you pay for." The idea is that workers differ in productivity but that the productivities of individual employees are difficult to identify. Firms therefore worry that they will lose their best employees if they reduce wages—because these workers have the best opportunities elsewhere in the economy. Rather than take this chance, the argument goes, firms prefer to maintain high wages even in recessions.

Other theories also have been proposed, none of which commands a clear majority of professional opinion. But regardless of the cause, we may as well accept it as a well-established fact that wages fall only sluggishly, if at all, when demand is weak.

The implications of this rigidity are quite serious, for a recessionary gap cannot cure itself without some deflation. And if wages and prices will not fall, recessionary gaps like *EB* in Figure 6 will linger for a long time. That is,

When aggregate demand is low, the economy may get stuck with a recessionary gap for a long time. If wages and prices fall very slowly, the economy will endure a prolonged period of production below potential GDP.

Does the Economy Have a Self-Correcting Mechanism?

Now a situation like that described earlier would, presumably, not last forever. As the recession lengthened and perhaps deepened, more and more workers would be unable to find jobs at the prevailing "high" wages. Eventually, their need to be employed would overwhelm their resistance to wage cuts. Firms, too, would become increasingly willing to cut prices as the period of weak demand persisted and managers became convinced that the slump was not merely a temporary aberration. Prices and wages did, in fact, fall in many countries during the Great Depression of the 1930s, and they have fallen in Japan for about a decade, albeit very slowly.

Thus, starting from any recessionary gap, the economy will *eventually* return to potential GDP—following a path something like the brick-colored arrow from *E* to *F* in Figure 6 on the previous page. For this reason, some economists think of the vertical line at potential GDP as representing the economy's long-run aggregate supply curve. But this "long run" might be long indeed.

Nowadays, political leaders of both parties—and in virtually all countries—believe that it is folly to wait for falling wages and prices to eliminate a recessionary gap. They agree that government action is both necessary and appropriate under recessionary conditions. Nevertheless, vocal—and highly partisan—debate continues over how much and what kind of intervention is warranted. One reason for the disagreement is that the **self-correcting mechanism** does operate—if only weakly—to cure recessionary gaps.

An Example from Recent History: Deflation in Japan

Fortunately for us, recent U.S. history offers no examples of long-lasting recessionary gaps. But the world's second-largest economy does. The Japanese economy has been weak for most of the period since the early 1990s—including several recessions. As a result, Japan has experienced persistent recessionary gaps for 15 years or so. Unsurprisingly, Japan's modest inflation rate of the early 1990s evaporated and, from 1999 through 2005, turned into a small *deflation* rate. Qualitatively, this is just the sort of behavior the theoretical model of the self-correcting mechanism predicts. But it took a long time! Hence, the practical policy question is: How long can a country afford to wait?

> The economy's **self-correcting mechanism** refers to the way money wages react to either a recessionary gap or an inflationary gap. Wage changes shift the aggregate supply curve and therefore change equilibrium GDP and the equilibrium price level.

ADJUSTING TO AN INFLATIONARY GAP: INFLATION

Let us now turn to what happens when the economy finds itself *beyond* full employment—that is, with an *inflationary* gap like that shown in Figure 7. When the aggregate supply curve is S_0S_0 and the aggregate demand curve is DD, the economy will initially reach equilibrium (point E) with an inflationary gap, shown by the segment BE.

According to some economists, a situation like this arose in the United States in 2006 and 2007 when the unemployment rate dipped below 5 percent. What should happen under such circumstances? As we shall see now, the tight labor market should produce an inflation that eventually eliminates the inflationary gap, although perhaps in a slow and painful way. Let us see how.

When equilibrium GDP exceeds potential GDP, jobs are plentiful and labor is in great demand. Firms are likely to have trouble recruiting new workers or even holding onto their old ones as other firms try to lure workers away with higher wages.

Rising nominal wages add to business costs, which shift the aggregate supply curve to the left. As the aggregate supply curve moves from S_0S_0 to S_1S_1 in Figure 7, the inflationary gap shrinks. In other words, inflation eventually erodes the inflationary gap and brings the economy to an equilibrium at potential GDP (point F).

There is a straightforward way of looking at the economics underlying this process. Inflation arises because buyers are demanding more output than the economy can produce at normal operating rates. To paraphrase an old cliché, there is too much demand chasing too little supply. Such an environment encourages price hikes.

Ultimately, rising prices eat away at the purchasing power of consumers' wealth, forcing them to cut back on consumption, as explained in Chapter 8. In addition, exports fall and imports rise, as we learned in Chapter 9. Eventually, aggregate quantity demanded is scaled back to the economy's capacity to produce—graphically, the economy moves back along curve DD from point E to point F. At this point the self-correcting process stops. In brief:

If aggregate demand is exceptionally high, the economy may reach a short-run equilibrium above full employment

FIGURE 7

The Elimination of an Inflationary Gap

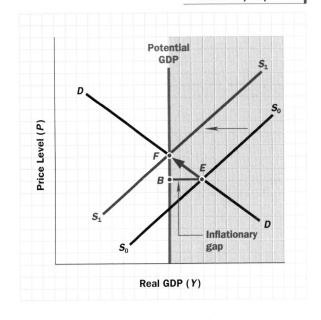

(an *inflationary gap*). When this occurs, the tight situation in the labor market soon forces nominal wages to rise. Because rising wages increase business costs, prices increase; there is inflation. As higher prices cut into consumer purchasing power and net exports, the inflationary gap begins to close.

As the inflationary gap closes, output falls and prices continue to rise. When the gap is finally eliminated, a long-run equilibrium is established with a higher price level and with GDP equal to potential GDP.

This scenario is precisely what some economists believe happened in 2006 and 2007. Because they believed that the U.S. economy had a small inflationary gap in 2006 and 2007, they expected inflation to rise slightly—which it did, before receding again. But remember once again that *the self-correcting mechanism takes time* because wages and prices do not adjust quickly. Thus, while an inflationary gap sows the seeds of its own destruction, the seeds germinate slowly. So, once again, policy makers may want to speed up the process.

Demand Inflation and Stagflation

Simple as it is, this model of how the economy adjusts to an inflationary gap teaches us a number of important lessons about inflation in the real world. First, Figure 7 reminds us that the real culprit is an *excess of aggregate demand* relative to potential GDP. The aggregate demand curve is initially so high that it intersects the aggregate supply curve beyond full employment. The resulting intense demand for goods and labor pushes prices and wages higher. Although aggregate demand in excess of potential GDP is not the only possible cause of inflation, it certainly is the cause in our example.

Nonetheless, business managers and journalists may blame inflation on rising wages. In a superficial sense, of course, they are right, because higher wages do indeed lead firms to raise product prices. But in a deeper sense they are wrong. Both rising wages and rising prices are symptoms of the same underlying malady: too much aggregate demand. Blaming labor for inflation in such a case is a bit like blaming high doctor bills for making you ill.

Second, notice that output *falls* while prices *rise* as the economy adjusts from point *E* to point *F* in Figure 7. This is our first (but not our last) explanation of the phenomenon of **stagflation**—the conjunction of in*flation* and economic *stag*nation. Specifically:

> **Stagflation** is inflation that occurs while the economy is growing slowly or having a recession.

A period of stagflation is part of the normal aftermath of a period of excessive aggregate demand.

It is easy to understand why. When aggregate demand is excessive, the economy will temporarily produce beyond its normal capacity. Labor markets tighten and wages rise. Machinery and raw materials may also become scarce and so start rising in price. Faced with higher costs, business firms quite naturally react by producing less and charging higher prices. That is stagflation.

A U.S. Example

The stagflation that follows a period of excessive aggregate demand is, you will note, a rather benign form of the dreaded disease. After all, while output is falling, it nonetheless remains above potential GDP, and unemployment is low. The U.S. economy last experienced such an episode at the end of the 1980s.

The long economic expansion of the 1980s brought the unemployment rate down to a 15-year low of 5 percent by March 1989. Almost all economists believed at the time that 5 percent was below the full-employment unemployment rate, that is, that the U.S. economy had an *inflationary gap*. As the theory suggests, inflation began to accelerate—from 4.4 percent in 1988 to 4.6 percent in 1989 and then to 6.1 percent in 1990.

In the meantime, the economy was stagnating. Real GDP growth fell from 3.5 percent during 1989 to 1.8 percent in 1990 and down to −0.5 percent in 1991. Inflation was eating away at the inflationary gap, which had virtually disappeared by mid-1990, when the

A Tale of Two Graduating Classes: 2003 Versus 2007

Timing matters in life. The college graduates of 2007 were pretty fortunate. The unemployment rate was a low 4.5 percent in May and June of that year—close to its lowest level in a generation. With employers on the prowl for new hires, starting salaries rose and many graduating seniors had numerous job offers.

Things were not nearly that good for the Class of 2003 when it hit the job market four years earlier. The U.S. economy had been sluggish for a while, and job offers were relatively scarce. The unemployment rate in May–June 2003 averaged 6.2 percent. Many companies were less than eager to hire more workers, salary increases were modest, and "perks" were being trimmed.

This accident of birth meant that the college grads of 2003 started their working careers in a less advantageous position than their more fortunate brothers and sisters four years later. What's more, recent research suggests that the initial job market advantage of the Class of 2007, compared to the Class of 2003, is likely to be maintained for many years.

SOURCE: © Creatas Images/Jupiterimages

recession started. Yet inflation remained high through the early months of the recession. The U.S. economy was in a *stagflation* phase.

Our overall conclusion about the economy's ability to right itself seems to run something like this:

The economy does, indeed, have a self-correcting mechanism that tends to eliminate either unemployment or inflation. But this mechanism works slowly and unevenly. In addition, its beneficial effects on either inflation or unemployment are sometimes swamped by strong forces pushing in the opposite direction (such as rapid increases or decreases in aggregate demand). Thus, the self-correcting mechanism is not always reliable.

STAGFLATION FROM A SUPPLY SHOCK

We have just discussed the type of stagflation that follows in the wake of an inflationary boom. However, that is not what happened when unemployment and inflation both soared in the 1970s and early 1980s. What caused this more virulent strain of stagflation? Several things, though the principal culprit was rising energy prices.

In 1973, the Organization of Petroleum Exporting Countries (OPEC) quadrupled the price of crude oil. American consumers soon found the prices of gasoline and home heating fuels increasing sharply, and U.S. businesses saw an important cost of doing business—energy prices—rising drastically. OPEC struck again in the period 1979–1980, this time doubling the price of oil. Then the same thing happened again, albeit on a smaller scale, when Iraq invaded Kuwait in 1990. Most recently, oil prices have been on an irregular upward climb since 2002 because of the Iraq war, other political issues in the Middle East and elsewhere, problems with refining capacity, and surging energy demand from China.

Higher energy prices, we observed earlier, shift the economy's aggregate supply curve *inward* in the manner shown in Figure 8 on the next page. If the aggregate supply curve shifts inward, as it surely did following each of these "oil shocks," production will decline. To reduce demand to the available supply, prices will have to rise. The result is the worst of both worlds: falling production and rising prices.

This conclusion is displayed graphically in Figure 8, which shows an aggregate demand curve, *DD,* and two aggregate supply curves. When the supply curve shifts inward, the economy's equilibrium shifts from point *E* to point *A*. Thus, output falls while prices

FIGURE 8

Stagflation from an Adverse Shift in Aggregate Supply

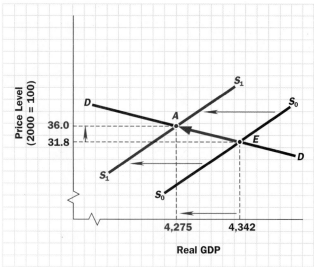

NOTE: Amounts are in billions of dollars per year.

rise, which is precisely our definition of stagflation. In sum:

> **Stagflation is the typical result of adverse shifts of the aggregate supply curve.**

The numbers used in Figure 8 are meant to indicate what the big energy shock in late 1973 might have done to the U.S. economy. Between 1973 (represented by supply curve S_0S_0 and point E) and 1975 (represented by supply curve S_1S_1 and point A), it shows real GDP falling by about 1.5 percent, while the price level rises more than 13 percent over the two years. The general lesson to be learned from the U.S. experience with supply shocks is both clear and important:

> **The typical results of an adverse supply shock are lower output and higher inflation. This is one reason why the world economy was plagued by stagflation in the mid-1970s and early 1980s. And it can happen again if another series of supply-reducing events takes place.**

APPLYING THE MODEL TO A GROWING ECONOMY

You may have noticed that ever since Chapter 5 we have been using the simple aggregate supply and aggregate demand model to determine the equilibrium *price level* and the equilibrium *level of real GDP*, as depicted in several graphs in this chapter. But in the real world, neither the price level nor real GDP remains constant for long. Instead, both normally rise from one year to the next.

The growth process is illustrated in Figure 9, which is a scatter diagram of the U.S. price level and the level of real GDP for every year from 1972 to 2007. The labeled points show the clear upward march of the economy through time—toward higher prices and higher levels of output.

Why Was There No Stagflation in 2006–2008?

As noted earlier, oil prices have climbed steeply, if irregularly, since early 2002. Yet this succession of "oil shocks" seems not to have caused much, if any, stagflation in the United States or in other industrial economies. This recent experience stands in sharp contrast to the 1970s and early 1980s. What has been different this time around?

In truth, economists do not have a complete answer to this question, and research on it continues. But we do understand a few things. Most straightforwardly, the world has learned to live with less energy (relative to GDP). In the United States and many other countries, for example, the energy content of $1 worth of GDP is now only about half of what it was in the 1970s. That alone cuts the impact of an oil shock in half.

In addition, for reasons that are not entirely understood, the United States and other economies seem to have become less volatile since the mid-1980s. Sound macroeconomic policies have probably contributed to the reduction in volatility, and so have a variety of structural changes that have made these economies more flexible. But in the view of most researchers who have studied the

question, part of the story is plain old good luck. Naturally, we cannot expect good luck to continue forever.

Finally, it can be argued that we *did* have a little bit of stagflation. In late 2007 and early 2008, growth slowed sharply and inflation rose.

SOURCE: © Creatas Images/Jupiterimages

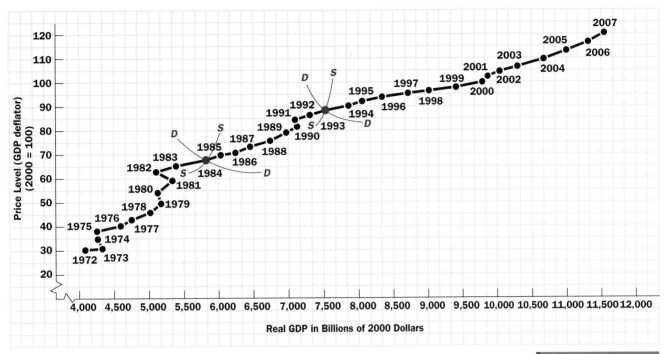

SOURCE: U.S. Department of Commerce, Bureau of Economic Analysis.

FIGURE 9

The Price Level and
Real GDP Output in
the United States,
1972–2007

This upward trend is hardly mysterious, for both the aggregate demand curve and the aggregate supply curve normally shift to the right each year. Aggregate supply grows because more workers join the workforce each year and because investment and technology improve productivity (Chapter 7). Aggregate demand grows because a growing population generates more demand for both consumer and investment goods and because the government increases its purchases (Chapters 8 and 9). We can think of each point in Figure 9 as the intersection of an aggregate supply curve and an aggregate demand curve for that particular year. To help you visualize this idea, the curves for 1984 and 1993 are sketched in the diagram.

Figure 10 is a more realistic version of the aggregate supply-and-demand diagram that illustrates how our theoretical model applies to a growing economy. We have chosen the numbers so that the black curves $D_0 D_0$ and $S_0 S_0$ roughly represent the year 2005, and the brick-colored curves $D_1 D_1$ and $S_1 S_1$ roughly represent 2006—except that we use nice round numbers to facilitate computations. Thus, the equilibrium in 2005 was at point A, with a real GDP of $11,000 billion (in 2000 dollars) and a price level of 113. A year later, the equilibrium was at point B, with real GDP at $11,330 billion and the price level at 116.5. The blue arrow in the diagram shows how equilibrium moved from 2005 to 2006. It points upward and to the right, meaning that both prices and output increased. In this case, the economy grew by 3 percent and prices also rose about 3 percent, which is close to what actually happened in the United States over that year.

FIGURE 10

Aggregate Supply and
Demand Analysis of a
Growing Economy

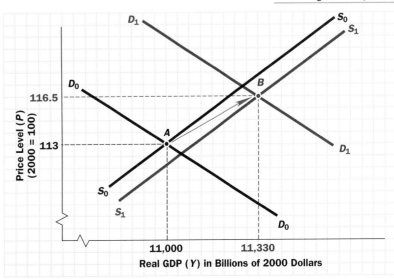

Demand-Side Fluctuations

Let us now use our theoretical model to rewrite history. Suppose that aggregate

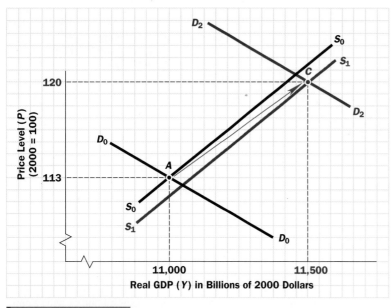

FIGURE 11

The Effects of Faster Growth of Aggregate Demand

demand grew *faster* than it actually did between 2005 and 2006. What difference would this have made to the performance of the U.S. economy? Figure 11 provides answers. Here the black demand curve D_0D_0 is exactly the same as in the previous diagram, as are the two supply curves, indicating a given rate of aggregate supply growth. But the brick-colored demand curve D_2D_2 lies farther to the right than the demand curve D_1D_1 in Figure 10. Equilibrium is at point *A* in 2005 and point *C* in 2006. Comparing point *C* in Figure 11 with point *B* in Figure 10, you can see that *both output and* prices would have increased more over the year—that is, the economy would have experienced faster *growth* and more *inflation*. This is generally what happens when the growth rate of aggregate demand speeds up.

For any given growth rate of aggregate supply, a faster growth rate of aggregate demand will lead to more inflation and faster growth of real output.

Figure 12 illustrates the opposite case. Here we imagine that the aggregate demand curve shifted out *less* than in Figure 10. That is, the brick-colored demand curve D_3D_3 in Figure 12 lies to the left of the demand curve D_1D_1 in Figure 10. The consequence, we see, is that the shift of the economy's equilibrium from 2005 to 2006 (from point *A* to point *E*) would have entailed *less inflation* and *slower growth* of real output than actually took place. Again, that is generally the case when aggregate demand grows more slowly.

For any given growth rate of aggregate supply, a slower growth rate of aggregate demand will lead to less inflation and slower growth of real output.

Putting these two findings together gives us a clear prediction:

If fluctuations in the economy's real growth rate from year to year arise primarily from variations in the rate at which *aggregate demand* increases, then the data should show the most rapid inflation occurring when output grows most rapidly and the slowest inflation occurring when output grows most slowly.

FIGURE 12

The Effects of Slower Growth of Aggregate Demand

Is it true? For the most part, yes. Our brief review of U.S. economic history back in Chapter 5 found that most episodes of high inflation came with rapid growth. But not all. Some surges of inflation resulted from the kinds of supply shocks we have considered in this chapter.

Supply-Side Fluctuations

As an historical example, let's return to the events of 1973 to 1975 that were depicted in Figure 8 (page 212). But now let's add in something we ignored there: While the aggregate supply curve was shifting *inward* because of the oil shock, the aggregate demand was

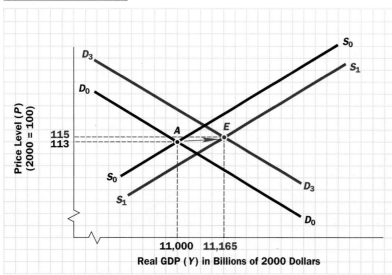

shifting *outward*. In Figure 13, the black aggregate demand curve D_0D_0 and aggregate supply curve S_0S_0 represent the economic situation in 1973. Equilibrium was at point E, with a price level of 31.8 (based on 2000 = 100) and real output of $4,342 billion. By 1975, the aggregate demand curve had shifted out to the position indicated by the brick-colored curve D_1D_1, but the aggregate supply curve had shifted *inward* from S_0S_0 to the brick-colored curve S_1S_1. The equilibrium for 1975 (point B in the figure) therefore wound up to the left of the equilibrium point for 1973 (point E in the figure). Real output declined slightly (although less than in Figure 8) and prices—led by energy costs—rose rapidly (more than in Figure 8).

FIGURE 13

Stagflation from an Adverse Supply Shock

What about the opposite case? Suppose the economy experiences a *favorable* supply shock, as it did in the late 1990s, so that the aggregate supply curve shifts *outward* at an unusually rapid rate.

Figure 14 depicts the consequences. The aggregate demand curve shifts out from D_0D_0 to D_1D_1 as usual, but the aggregate supply curve shifts all the way out to S_1S_1. (The dotted line indicates what would happen in a "normal" year.) So the economy's equilibrium winds up at point B rather than at point C. Compared to C, point B represents *faster economic growth* (B is to the right of C) and *lower inflation* (B is lower than C). In brief, the economy wins on both fronts: Inflation falls while GDP grows rapidly, as happened in the late 1990s.

Combining these two cases, we conclude that

If fluctuations in economic activity emanate mainly from the supply side, higher rates of inflation will be associated with *lower* rates of economic growth.

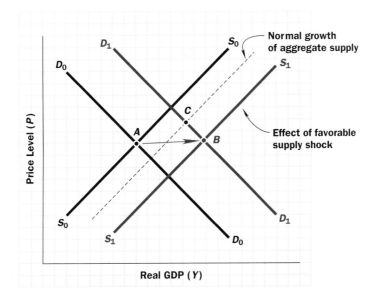

FIGURE 14

The Effects of a Favorable Supply Shock

PUZZLE RESOLVED: EXPLAINING STAGFLATION

What we have learned in this chapter helps us to understand why the U.S. economy performed so poorly in the 1970s and early 1980s, when both unemployment and inflation rose together. The OPEC cartel first flexed its muscles in 1973–1974, when it quadrupled the price of oil, thereby precipitating the first bout of serious stagflation in the United States and other oil-importing nations. Then OPEC struck again in 1979–1980, this time doubling the price of oil, and stagflation returned. Unlucky? Yes. But mysterious? No. What was happening was that the economy's aggregate supply curve was shifted *inward* by the rising price of energy, rather than moving *outward* from one year to the next, as it normally does.

Unfavorable supply shocks tend to push unemployment and inflation up at the same time. It was mainly unfavorable supply shocks that accounted for the stunningly poor economic performance of the 1970s ands early 1980s.[3]

A ROLE FOR STABILIZATION POLICY

Chapter 8 emphasized the volatility of investment spending, and Chapter 9 noted that changes in investment have multiplier effects on aggregate demand. This chapter took the next step by showing how shifts in the aggregate demand curve cause fluctuations in *both* real GDP *and* prices—fluctuations that are widely decried as undesirable. It also suggested that the economy's self-correcting mechanism works, but slowly, thereby leaving room for government stabilization policy to improve the workings of the free market. Can the government really accomplish this goal? If so, how? These are some of the important questions for Part 3.

| SUMMARY |

1. The economy's **aggregate supply curve** relates the quantity of goods and services that will be supplied to the price level. It normally slopes upward to the right because the costs of labor and other inputs remain relatively fixed in the short run, meaning that higher selling prices make input costs relatively cheaper and therefore encourage greater production.

2. The position of the aggregate supply curve can be shifted by changes in money wage rates, prices of other inputs, technology, or quantities or qualities of labor and capital.

3. The **equilibrium price level** and the **equilibrium level of real GDP** are jointly determined by the intersection of the economy's aggregate supply and aggregate demand schedules.

4. Among the reasons why the oversimplified multiplier formula is wrong is the fact that it ignores the inflation that is caused by an increase in aggregate demand. Such

inflation decreases the multiplier by reducing both consumer spending and net exports.

5. The equilibrium of aggregate supply and demand can come at full employment, below full employment (a **recessionary gap**), or above full employment (an **inflationary gap**).

6. The economy has a **self-correcting mechanism** that erodes a recessionary gap. Specifically, a weak labor market reduces wage increases and, in extreme cases, may even drive wages down. Lower wages shift the aggregate supply curve outward. But it happens very slowly.

7. If an inflationary gap occurs, the economy has a similar mechanism that erodes the gap through a process of inflation. Unusually strong job prospects push wages up, which shifts the aggregate supply curve to the left and reduces the inflationary gap.

---

[3] As we mentioned in the box on page 212, questions have been raised, and only partially answered, about why stagflation did not return in the 2003–2007 period.

8. One consequence of this self-correcting mechanism is that, if a surge in aggregate demand opens up an inflationary gap, the economy's subsequent natural adjustment will lead to a period of **stagflation**—that is, a period in which prices are rising while output is falling.

9. An inward shift of the aggregate supply curve will cause output to fall while prices rise—that is, it will produce stagflation. Among the events that have caused such a shift are abrupt increases in the price of foreign oil.

10. Adverse supply shifts like this plagued the U.S. economy when oil prices skyrocketed in 1973–1974, in 1979–1980, and again in 1990, leading to stagflation each time.

11. But things reversed in 1997–1998, when falling oil prices and rising productivity shifted the aggregate supply curve out more rapidly than usual, thereby boosting real growth and reducing inflation simultaneously.

12. Inflation can be caused either by rapid growth of aggregate demand or by sluggish growth of aggregate supply. When fluctuations in economic activity emanate from the demand side, prices will rise rapidly when real output grows rapidly. But when fluctuations in economic activity emanate from the supply side, output will grow slowly when prices rise rapidly.

| KEY TERMS |

Aggregate supply curve   200

Productivity   202

Equilibrium of real GDP and the price level   203

Inflation and the multiplier   204

Recessionary gap   205

Inflationary gap   205

Self-correcting mechanism   209

Stagflation   210

| TEST YOURSELF |

1. In an economy with the following aggregate demand and aggregate supply schedules, find the equilibrium levels of real output and the price level. Graph your solution. If full employment comes at $2,800 billion, is there an inflationary or a recessionary gap?

Aggregate Quantity Demanded	Price Level	Aggregate Quantity Supplied
$3,200	90	$2,750
3,100	95	2,900
3,000	100	3,000
2,900	105	3,050
2,800	110	3,075

NOTE: Amounts are in billions of dollars.

2. Suppose a worker receives a wage of $20 per hour. Compute the real wage (money wage deflated by the price index) corresponding to each of the following possible price levels: 85, 95, 100, 110, 120. What do you notice about the relationship between the real wage and the price level? Relate your finding to the slope of the aggregate supply curve.

3. Add the following aggregate supply and demand schedules to the example in Test Yourself Question 2 of Chapter 9 (page 192) to see how inflation affects the multiplier:

(1)	(2)	(3)	(4)
Price Level	Aggregate Demand When Investment Is $240	Aggregate Demand When Investment Is $260	Aggregate Supply
90	$3,860	$4,060	$3,660
95	3,830	4,030	3,730
100	3,800	4,000	3,800
105	3,770	3,970	3,870
110	3,740	3,940	3,940
115	3,710	3,910	4,010

Draw these schedules on a piece of graph paper.

a. Notice that the difference between columns (2) and (3), which show the aggregate demand schedule at two different levels of investment, is always $200. Discuss how this constant gap of $200 relates to your answer in the previous chapter.

b. Find the equilibrium GDP and the equilibrium price level both before and after the increase in investment. What is the value of the multiplier? Compare that to the multiplier you found in Test Yourself Question 2 of Chapter 9.

4. Use an aggregate supply-and-demand diagram to show that multiplier effects are smaller when the aggregate supply curve is steeper. Which case gives rise to more inflation—the steep aggregate supply curve or the flat one? What happens to the multiplier if the aggregate supply curve is vertical?

| DISCUSSION QUESTIONS |

1. Explain why a decrease in the price of foreign oil shifts the aggregate supply curve outward to the right. What are the consequences of such a shift?

2. Comment on the following statement: "Inflationary and recessionary gaps are nothing to worry about because the economy has a built-in mechanism that cures either type of gap automatically."

3. Give two different explanations of how the economy can suffer from stagflation.

4. Why do you think wages tend to be rigid in the downward direction?

5. Explain in words why rising prices reduce the multiplier effect of an autonomous increase in aggregate demand.

FISCAL AND MONETARY POLICY

I n Part 2, we constructed a framework for understanding the macroeconomy. The basic theory came in three parts. We started with the determinants of the long-run growth rate of *potential* GDP in Chapter 7, added some analysis of short-run fluctuations in *aggregate demand* in Chapters 8 and 9, and finally considered short-run fluctuations in *aggregate supply* in Chapter 10. Part 3 uses that framework to consider a variety of public policy issues—the sorts of things that make headlines in the newspapers and on television.

At several points in earlier chapters, beginning with our list of *Ideas for Beyond the Final Exam* in Chapter 1, we suggested that the government may be able to manage aggregate demand by using its *fiscal and monetary policies*. Chapters 11–13 pick up and build on that suggestion. You will learn how the government tries to promote rapid growth and low unemployment while simultaneously limiting inflation—and why its efforts do not always succeed. Then, in Chapters 14–16, we turn explicitly to a number of important controversies related to the government's *stabilization policy*. How should the Federal Reserve do its job? Why is it considered so important to reduce the budget deficit? Is there a trade-off between inflation and unemployment?

By the end of Part 3, you will be in an excellent position to understand some of the most important debates over national economic policy—not only today but also in the years to come.

CHAPTERS

Managing Aggregate Demand: Fiscal Policy

> *Next, let us turn to the problems of our fiscal policy. Here the myths are legion and the truth hard to find.*

JOHN F. KENNEDY

I n the model of the economy we constructed in Part 2, the government played a rather passive role. It did some spending and collected taxes, but that was about it. We concluded that such an economy has only a weak tendency to move toward an equilibrium with high employment and low inflation. Furthermore, we hinted that well-designed government policies might enhance that tendency and improve the economy's performance. It is now time to expand on that hint—and to learn about some of the difficulties that must be overcome if stabilization policy is to succeed.

We begin in this chapter with **fiscal policy.** The next three chapters take up the government's other main tool for managing aggregate demand, *monetary policy.*

The government's **fiscal policy** is its plan for spending and taxation. It is designed to steer aggregate demand in some desired direction.

CONTENTS

ISSUE: AGGREGATE DEMAND, AGGREGATE SUPPLY, AND THE CAMPAIGN OF 2008

As this book went to press, the 2008 campaign for the White House was in full swing although the name of the Democratic candidate (either Barack Obama or Hillary Clinton) had not yet been determined. One of the main economic issues between either Democrat and the Republican John McCain was what to do about the tax cuts that President Bush and the Republican Congress had enacted during Mr. Bush's first term—and which are scheduled to expire in 2010. Both Mr. Obama and Ms. Clinton advocated repeal of many of the tax cuts, especially those that benefited mainly upper-income people. But Mr. McCain opposed this change in fiscal policy, arguing that doing so would damage economic growth in two ways: by reducing consumer spending (and, thus, aggregate demand), and by impairing incentives to earn more income (thus reducing aggregate supply).

The two Democrats rejected both claims. With regard to aggregate supply, they argued that the alleged incentive effects of lower tax rates were minuscule. With regard to aggregate demand, they made two arguments: First, that wealthy taxpayers do not spend much of the money they receive from their tax cuts anyway, and second, that eliminating the tax cuts for the rich would enable the government to spend more on more important priorities, such as universal health care. On balance, they maintained (without using the term), aggregate demand would rise, not fall.

The debate over whether to repeal or extend the Bush tax cuts thus revolved around three concepts that we will study in this chapter:

* The multiplier effects of tax cuts versus higher government spending
* The multiplier effects of different types of tax cuts (e.g., those for the poor versus those for the rich)
* The incentive effects of tax cuts

By the end of the chapter, you will be in a much better position to form your own opinion on this important public policy issue.

INCOME TAXES AND THE CONSUMPTION SCHEDULE

To understand how taxes affect equilibrium gross domestic product (GDP), we begin by recalling that taxes (*T*) are *subtracted* from gross domestic product (*Y*) to obtain disposable income (*DI*):

$$DI = Y - T$$

and that disposable income, not GDP, is the amount actually available to consumers and is therefore the principal determinant of consumer spending (*C*). Thus, *at any given level of*

GDP, if taxes rise, disposable income falls—and hence so does consumption. What we have just described in words is summarized graphically in Figure 1:

Any increase in taxes shifts the consumption schedule downward, and any tax reduction shifts the consumption schedule upward.

Of course, if the C schedule moves up or down, so does the $C + I + G + (X - IM)$ schedule. And we know from Chapter 9 that such a shift will have a multiplier effect on aggregate demand. So it follows that

An increase or decrease in taxes will have a mutiplier effect on equilibrium GDP on the demand side. Tax reductions increase equilibrium GDP, and tax increases reduce it.

So far, this analysis just echoes our previous analysis of the multiplier effects of government spending. But there is one important difference. Government purchases of goods and services add to total spending *directly*—through the G component of $C + I + G + (X - IM)$. But taxes reduce total spending only *indirectly*—by lowering disposable income and thus reducing the C component of $C + I + G + (X - IM)$. As we will now see, that little detail turns out to be quite important.

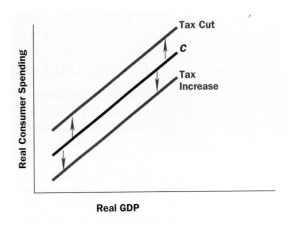

FIGURE 1

How Tax Policy Shifts the Consumption Schedule

THE MULTIPLIER REVISITED

To understand why, let us return to the example used in Chapter 9, in which we learned that the multiplier works through a chain of spending and respending, as one person's expenditure becomes another's income. In the example, the spending chain was initiated by Microhard's decision to spend an additional $1 million on investment. With a marginal propensity to consume (MPC) of 0.75, the complete multiplier chain was

$$\$1,000,000 + \$750,000 + \$562,500 + \$421,875 + \ldots .$$
$$= \$1,000,000 (1 + 0.75 + (0.75)^2 + (0.75)^3 + \ldots)$$
$$= \$1,000,000 \times 4 = \$4,000,000.$$

Thus, each dollar originally spent by Microhard eventually produced $4 in additional spending.

The Tax Multiplier

Now suppose the initiating event was a $1 million tax cut instead. As we just noted, a tax cut affects spending only indirectly. By adding $1 million to disposable income, it increases consumer spending by $750,000 (assuming that the MPC is 0.75). Thereafter, the chain of spending and respending proceeds exactly as before, to yield:

$$\$750,000 + \$562,500 + \$421,875 + \ldots .$$
$$= \$750,000 (1 + 0.75 + (0.75)2 + \ldots)$$
$$= \$750,000 \times 4 = \$3,000,000.$$

Notice that the mutiplier effect of each dollar of tax cut is 3, not 4. The reason is straightforward. Each new dollar of additional autonomous spending—regardless of whether it is C or I or G—has a multiplier of 4. But each dollar of tax cut creates only 75 cents of new consumer spending. Applying the basic expenditure multiplier of 4 to the 75 cents of first-round spending leads to a multiplier of 3 for each dollar of tax cut. This numerical example illustrates a general result:[1]

---

[1] You may notice that the tax multiplier of 3 is the spending multiplier of 4 times the marginal propensity to consume, which is 0.75. See Appendix B for an algebraic explanation.

The multiplier for changes in taxes is smaller than the multiplier for changes in government purchases because not every dollar of tax cut is spent.

Income Taxes and the Multiplier

But this is not the only way in which taxes force us to modify the multiplier analysis of Chapter 9. If the volume of taxes collected depends on GDP—which, of course, it does in reality—there is another.

To understand this new wrinkle, return again to our Microhard example, but now assume that the government levies a 20 percent *income tax*—meaning that individuals pay 20 cents in taxes for each $1 of income they receive. Now when Microhard spends $1 million on salaries, its workers receive only $800,000 in *after-tax* (that is, disposable) income. The rest goes to the government in taxes. If workers spend 75 percent of the $800,000 (because the MPC is 0.75), spending in the next round will be only $600,000. Notice that this is only *60 percent* of the original expenditure, not *75 percent*—as was the case before.

Thus, the multiplier chain for each original dollar of spending *shrinks* from

$$1 + 0.75 + (0.75)^2 + (0.75)^3 + \ldots = \frac{1}{1 - 0.75} = \frac{1}{0.25} = 4$$

in Chapter 9's example to

$$1 + 0.6 + (0.6)^2 + (0.6)^3 + \ldots = \frac{1}{1 - 0.6} = \frac{1}{0.4} = 2.5$$

now. This is clearly a large reduction in the multiplier. Although this is just a numerical example, the two appendixes to this chapter show that the basic finding is quite general:

The multiplier is reduced by an income tax because an income tax reduces the fraction of each dollar of GDP that consumers actually receive and spend.

We thus have a third reason why the oversimplified multiplier formula of Chapter 9 exaggerates the size of the multiplier: It ignores income taxes.

REASONS WHY THE OVERSIMPLIFIED FORMULA OVERSTATES THE MULTIPLIER

1. It ignores variable imports, which reduce the size of the multiplier.
2. It ignores price-level changes, which reduce the multiplier.
3. It ignores income taxes, which also reduce the size of the multiplier.

The last of these three reasons is the most important one in practice.

This conclusion about the multiplier is shown graphically in Figure 2, which can usefully be compared to Figure 10 of Chapter 9 (page 186). Here we draw our $C + I + G + (X - IM)$ schedules with a slope of 0.6, reflecting an MPC of 0.75 and a tax rate of 20 percent, rather than the 0.75 slope we used in Chapter 9. Figure 2 then illustrates the effect of a $400 billion increase in government purchases of goods and services, which shifts the total expenditure schedule from $C + I + G_0 + (X - IM)$ to $C + I + G_1 + (X - IM)$. Equilibrium moves from point E_0 to point E_1—a GDP increase from $Y = \$6,000$ billion to $Y = \$7,000$ billion.

Thus, if we ignore for the moment any increases in the price level (which would further reduce the multiplier), a $400 billion

---

FIGURE 2

The Multiplier in the Presence of an Income Tax

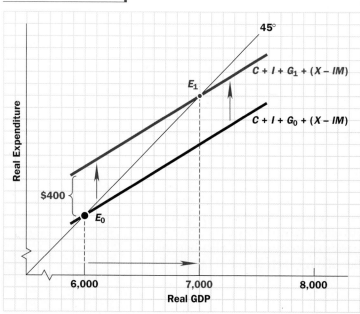

NOTE: Figures are in billions of dollars per year.

increment in government spending leads to a $1,000 billion increment in GDP. So, when a 20 percent income tax is included in our model, the multiplier is only $1,000/$400 = 2.5, as we concluded above.

So we now have noted two different ways in which taxes modify the multiplier analysis:

- Tax changes have a smaller multiplier effect than spending changes by government or others.
- An income tax reduces the multipliers for *both* tax changes *and* changes in spending.

Automatic Stabilizers

The size of the multiplier may seem to be a rather abstract notion with little practical importance. But that is not so. Fluctuations in one or another of the components of total spending—C, I, G, or X − IM—occur all the time. Some come unexpectedly; some are even difficult to explain after the fact. We know from Chapter 9 that any such fluctuation will move GDP up or down by a multiplied amount. Thus, if the multiplier is smaller, GDP will be less sensitive to such shocks—that is, the economy will be less volatile.

Features of the economy that reduce its sensitivity to shocks are called **automatic stabilizers.** The most obvious example is the one we have just been discussing: the personal income tax. The income tax acts as a shock absorber because it makes disposable income, and thus consumer spending, less sensitive to fluctuations in GDP. As we have just seen, when GDP rises, disposable income (*DI*) rises *less* because part of the increase in GDP is siphoned off by the U.S. Treasury. This leakage helps limit any increase in consumption spending. When GDP falls, *DI* falls less sharply because part of the loss is absorbed by the Treasury rather than by consumers. So consumption does not drop as much as it otherwise might. Thus, the much-maligned personal income tax is one of the main features of our modern economy that helps ensure against a repeat performance of the Great Depression.

But our economy has other automatic stabilizers as well. For example, Chapter 6 discussed the U.S. system of unemployment insurance. This program also serves as an automatic stabilizer. When GDP drops and people lose their jobs, unemployment benefits prevent disposable incomes from falling as dramatically as earnings do. As a result, unemployed workers can maintain their spending better, and consumption fluctuates less than employment does.

The list could continue, but the basic principle remains the same: Each automatic stabilizer serves, in one way or another, as a shock absorber, thereby lowering the multiplier. And each does so quickly, without the need for any decision maker to take action. In a word, they work *automatically.*

A case in point arose when the U.S. economy sagged in fiscal year 2008. The budget deficit naturally rose as tax receipts came in lower than had been expected. While there was much hand-wringing over the rising deficit, most economists viewed it as a good thing in the short run: The automatic stabilizers were propping up spending, as they should.

> An **automatic stabilizer** is a feature of the economy that reduces its sensitivity to shocks, such as sharp increases or decreases in spending.

Government Transfer Payments

To complete our discussion of multipliers for fiscal policy, let us now turn to the last major fiscal tool: *government transfer payments.* Transfers, as you will remember, are payments to individuals that are not compensation for any direct contribution to production. How are transfers treated in our models of income determination—like purchases of goods and services (*G*) or like taxes (*T*)?

The answer to this question follows readily from the circular flow diagram on page 156 or the accounting identity on page 157. The important thing to understand about transfer payments is that they intervene between gross domestic product (*Y*) and disposable income (*DI*) in precisely the *opposite* way from income taxes. They add to earned income rather than subtract from it.

Specifically, starting with the wages, interest, rents, and profits that constitute national income, we *subtract* income taxes to calculate disposable income. We do so because these taxes represent the portion of incomes that consumers *earn* but never *receive.* But then we must *add* transfer payments because they represent sources of income that are *received* although they were not *earned* in the process of production. Thus:

Transfer payments function basically as negative taxes.

As you may recall from Chapter 8, we use the symbol T to denote taxes *minus* transfers. Thus, giving consumers $1 in the form of transfer payments is treated in the 45° line diagram in the same way as a $1 decrease in taxes.

ISSUE REVISITED: THE 2008 DEBATE OVER TAXES AND SPENDING

What we have learned already has some bearing on the debate between the Republicans and Democratic in 2008. Remember that the Democrats wanted to rescind some of the Bush tax cuts for wealthy taxpayers and spend the funds on items such as government health insurance programs. We have just learned that the multiplier for T is smaller than the multiplier for G. That means that an increase in government spending balanced by an equal increase in taxes—which comes close to what the Democrats proposed—should raise total spending.

Next, consider the claim that the portions of the Bush tax cuts that went to wealthy individuals would not stimulate much spending. This assertion presumes that the rich have very low marginal propensities to consume, as many people naturally assume. Remember, a lower MPC leads to a lower multiplier. But the data actually suggest that the rich are spendthrifts, just like the rest of us. That said, poor families probably do have extremely high MPCs, so tax cuts for the poor would probably give rise to somewhat larger multipliers than tax cuts for the rich.

PLANNING EXPANSIONARY FISCAL POLICY

We will have more to say about the campaign debate later. But first imagine that you were a member of the U.S. Congress trying to decide whether to use fiscal policy to stimulate the economy back in 2001—and, if so, by how much. Suppose the economy would have had a GDP of $6,000 billion if the government simply reenacted the previous year's budget. Suppose further that your goal was to achieve a fully-employed labor force and that staff economists told you that a GDP of approximately $7,000 billion was needed to reach this target. Finally, just to keep the calculations simple, imagine that the price level was fixed. What sort of budget would you have voted for?

This chapter has taught us that the government has three ways to raise GDP by $1,000 billion. Congress can close the recessionary gap between actual and potential GDP by

- raising government purchases
- reducing taxes
- increasing transfer payments

Figure 3 illustrates the problem, and its cure through higher government spending, on our 45° line diagram. Figure 3(a) shows the equilibrium of the economy if no changes are made in the budget. With an expenditure multiplier of 2.5, you can figure out that an additional $400 billion of government spending would be needed to push GDP up by $1,000 billion and eliminate the gap ($400 × 2.5 = $1,000).

So you might vote to raise G by $400 billion, hoping to move the $C + I + G + (X - IM)$ line in Figure 3(a) up to the position indicated in Figure 3(b), thereby achieving full employment. Or you might prefer to achieve this fiscal stimulus by lowering taxes. Or you might opt for more generous transfer payments. The point is that a variety of budgets are capable of increasing GDP by $1,000 billion. Figure 3 applies equally well to any of them. President George W. Bush favored tax cuts, which is the tool the U.S government relied on in 2001. Especially after the September 11 terrorist attacks, encouraging consumers to spend their tax cuts became a national priority. (See the cartoon to the left.)

WE'RE LOOKING FOR A FEW BIG SPENDERS

JOIN THE U.S. CIVILIAN CONSUMPTION CORPS

MALL

TAX CUT

FIGHT TERRORISM AND **SAVE** OUR ECONOMY!

Source: © R. J. Matson, Roll Call

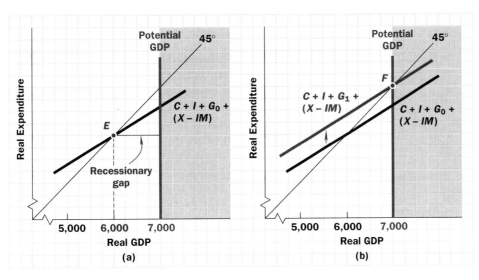

FIGURE 3

Fiscal Policy to
Eliminate a
Recessionary Gap

NOTE: Figures are in billions of dollars per year.

PLANNING CONTRACTIONARY FISCAL POLICY

The preceding example assumed that the basic problem of fiscal policy is to close a recessionary gap, as was surely the case in 2001 and then again in 2008. But only two years earlier, in 1999, most economists believed that the major macroeconomic problem in the United States was just the opposite: Real GDP exceeded potential GDP, producing an inflationary gap. And some people believed that an inflationary gap emerged once again in 2006 and 2007 when the unemployment rate dropped to around 4.5 percent. In such a case, government would wish to adopt more restrictive fiscal policies to reduce aggregate demand.

It does not take much imagination to run our previous analysis in reverse. If an inflationary gap would arise from a continuation of current budget policies, contractionary fiscal policy tools can eliminate it. By cutting spending, raising taxes, or by some combination of the two, the government can pull the $C + G + I + (X - IM)$ schedule down to a noninflationary position and achieve an equilibrium at full employment.

Notice the difference between this way of eliminating an inflationary gap and the natural self-correcting mechanism that we discussed in the last chapter. There we observed that, if the economy were left to its own devices, a cumulative but self-limiting process of inflation would eventually eliminate the inflationary gap and return the economy to full employment. Here we see that we need not put the economy through the inflationary wringer. Instead, a restrictive fiscal policy can avoid inflation by limiting aggregate demand to the level that the economy can produce at full employment.

THE CHOICE BETWEEN SPENDING POLICY AND TAX POLICY

In principle, fiscal policy can nudge the economy in the desired direction equally well by changing government spending or by changing taxes. For example, if the government wants to expand the economy, it can raise G or lower T. Either policy would shift the total expenditure schedule upward, as depicted in Figure 3(b), thereby raising equilibrium GDP on the demand side.

In terms of our aggregate demand-and-supply diagram, either policy shifts the aggregate demand curve outward, as illustrated in the shift from D_0D_0 to D_1D_1 in Figure 4 on the next page. As a result, the economy's equilibrium moves from point E to point A. Both real GDP and the price level rise. As this diagram points out,

FIGURE 4

Expansionary Fiscal Policy

Any combination of higher spending and lower taxes that produces the same aggregate demand curve leads to the same increases in real GDP and prices.

"Free gifts to every kid in the world? Are you a Keynesian or something?"

How, then, do policy makers decide whether to raise spending or to cut taxes? The answer depends mainly on how large a public sector they want to create—a major issue in the long-running debate in the United States over the proper size of government.

The small-government point of view, typically advocated by conservatives, says that we are foolish to rely on the public sector to do what private individuals and businesses can do better. Conservatives believe that the growth of government interferes too much in our everyday lives, thereby curtailing our freedom. Those who hold this view can argue for *tax cuts* when macroeconomic considerations call for expansionary fiscal policy, as President Bush did, and for *lower public spending* when contractionary policy is required.

An opposing opinion, expressed more often by liberals, holds that something is amiss when a country as wealthy as the United States has such an impoverished public sector. In this view, America's most pressing needs are not for more fast food and video games but, rather, for better schools, better transportation infrastructure, and health insurance for all of our citizens. People on this side of the debate believe that we should *increase* spending when the economy needs stimulus and pay for these improved public services by *increasing taxes* when it is necessary to rein in the economy.

It is important not to confuse the fiscal stabilization issue with the "big-government" issue. In fact,

> Individuals favoring a smaller public sector can advocate an active fiscal policy just as well as those who favor a larger public sector. Advocates of bigger government should seek to expand demand (when appropriate) through higher government spending and to contract demand (when appropriate) through tax increases. But advocates of smaller government should seek to expand demand by cutting taxes and to reduce demand by cutting expenditures.

Indeed, our two most conservative recent presidents, Ronald Reagan and George W. Bush, each pursued activist fiscal policies based on tax cuts.

ISSUE REDUX: DEMOCRATS VERSUS REPUBLICANS

While both parties favored fiscal stimulus, the choice between extending the Bush tax cuts or replacing them with spending played a central role in the economic debate during the 2008 presidential campaign. John McCain staunchly defended President Bush's tax cuts, partly on the grounds that "small government" is better than "big government." He even advocated further tax cuts. But both Barack Obama and Hillary Clinton argued, for example, that providing health insurance coverage to more Americans was a higher priority than providing tax cuts for the well-to-do. Democrats also favored other spending on such things as environmental protection and infrastructure.

SOME HARSH REALITIES

The mechanics outlined so far in this chapter make the fiscal policy planner's job look deceptively simple. The elementary diagrams make it appear that policy makers can drive GDP to any level they please simply by manipulating spending and tax programs. It seems they should be able to hit the full-employment bull's-eye every time. In fact, a better analogy is to a poor rifleman shooting through dense fog at an erratically moving target with an inaccurate gun and slow-moving bullets.

The target is moving because, in the real world, the investment, net exports, and consumption schedules constantly shift about as expectations, technology, events abroad, and other factors change. For all of these reasons and others, the policies decided on today, which will take effect at some future date, may no longer be appropriate by the time that future date rolls around.

The second misleading feature of our diagrams (the "inaccurate gun") is that we do not know multipliers as precisely as in our numerical examples. Although our best guess may be that a $20 billion increase in government purchases will raise GDP by $30 billion (a multiplier of 1.5), the actual outcome may be as little as $20 billion or as much as $40 billion. It is therefore impossible to "fine-tune" every little wobble out of the economy's growth path. Economic science is simply not that precise.

A third complication is that our target—full-employment GDP—may be only dimly visible, as if through a fog. For example, with the unemployment rate hovering around 4.5 percent for parts of 2006 and 2007, there was a vigorous debate over whether the U.S. economy was above or below full employment.

A fourth complication is that the fiscal policy "bullets" travel slowly: Tax and spending policies affect aggregate demand only after some time elapses. Consumer spending, for example, may take months to react to an income-tax cut. Because of these time lags, fiscal policy decisions must be based on *forecasts* of the future state of the economy. And forecasts are not always accurate. The combination of long lags and poor forecasts may occasionally leave the government fighting the last recession just as the new inflation gets under way.

And, finally, the people aiming the fiscal "rifle" are politicians, not economic technicians. Sometimes political considerations lead to policies that deviate markedly from what textbook economics would suggest. And even when they do not, the wheels of Congress grind slowly.

In addition to all of these operational problems, legislators trying to decide whether to push the unemployment rate lower would like to know the answers to two further questions. First, since either higher spending or lower taxes will increase the government's budget deficit, what are the long-run costs of running large budget deficits? This is a question we will take up in depth in Chapter 15. Second, how large is the inflationary cost likely to be? As we know, an expansionary fiscal policy that reduces a recessionary gap by increasing aggregate demand will lower unemployment. But, as Figure 4 reminds us, it also tends to be inflationary. This undesirable side effect may make the government hesitant to use fiscal policy to combat recessions.

Is there a way out of this dilemma? Can we pursue the battle against unemployment without aggravating inflation? For about 30 years now, a small but influential minority of economists, journalists, and politicians have argued that we can. They call their approach "supply-side economics." The idea helped sweep Ronald Reagan to smashing electoral victories in 1980 and 1984 and was revived under President George W. Bush. Just what is supply-side economics?

THE IDEA BEHIND SUPPLY-SIDE TAX CUTS

The central idea of supply-side economics is that certain types of tax cuts increase aggregate supply. For example, taxes can be cut in ways that raise the rewards for working, saving, and investing. Then, *if people actually respond to these incentives,* such tax cuts will increase the total supplies of labor and capital in the economy, thereby increasing aggregate supply.

Figure 5, on the next page, illustrates the idea on an aggregate supply-and-demand diagram. If policy measures can shift the economy's aggregate supply to position S_1S_1, then prices will be lower and output higher than if the aggregate supply curve remained at S_0S_0. Policy makers will have reduced inflation and raised real output at the same time—as shown by point *B* in the figure. The trade-off between inflation and unemployment will have been defeated, which is the goal of supply-side economics.

What sorts of policies do supply-siders advocate? Here is a sample of their long list of recommended tax cuts:

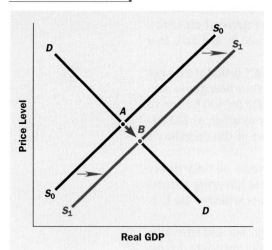

FIGURE 5

The Goal of Supply-Side Tax Cuts

Lower Personal Income-Tax Rates

Sharp cuts in personal taxes were the cornerstone of the economic strategy of George W. Bush, just as they had been for Ronald Reagan 20 years earlier. Since 2001, tax rates on individuals have been reduced in stages, and in several ways. The four upper tax bracket rates, which were 39.6 percent, 36 percent, 31 percent, and 28 percent when President Bush assumed office, have been reduced to 35 percent, 33 percent, 28 percent, and 25 percent, respectively. In addition, some very low income taxpayers have seen their tax rate fall from 15 percent to 10 percent. Lower tax rates, supply-siders argue, augment the supplies of both labor and capital.

Reduce Taxes on Income from Savings

One extreme form of this proposal would simply exempt from taxation all income from interest and dividends. Because income must be either consumed or saved, doing this would, in effect, change our present personal income tax into a tax on consumer spending. Several such proposals for radical tax reform have been considered in Washington over the years, but never adopted. However, Congress did reduce the tax rate on dividends to just 15 percent in 2003. And since then, both President Bush and a number of Democrats have proposed additional tax preferences for saving.

Reduce Taxes on Capital Gains

When an investor sells an asset for a profit, that profit is called a *capital gain*. Supply-siders argue that the government can encourage more investment by taxing capital gains at lower rates than ordinary income. This proposal was acted upon in 2003, when the top rate on capital gains was cut to 15 percent.

Reduce the Corporate Income Tax

By reducing the tax burden on corporations, proponents argue, the government can provide both greater investment incentives (by raising the profitability of investment) and more investable funds (by letting companies keep more of their earnings).

Let us suppose, for the moment, that a successful supply-side tax cut is enacted. Because *both* aggregate demand *and* aggregate supply increase simultaneously, the economy may be able to avoid the inflationary consequences of an expansionary fiscal policy shown in Figure 4 (page 228).

FIGURE 6

A Successful Supply-Side Tax Reduction

Figure 6 illustrates this conclusion. The two aggregate demand curves and the initial aggregate supply curve S_0S_0 carry over directly from Figure 4. But now we have introduced an additional supply curve, S_1S_1, to reflect the successful supply-side tax cut depicted in Figure 5. The equilibrium point for the economy moves from E to C, whereas with a conventional demand-side tax cut it would have moved from E to A. As compared with point A, which reflects only the demand-side effects of a tax cut, output is higher and prices are lower at point C.

A good deal, you say. And indeed it is. The supply-side argument is extremely attractive *in principle*. The question is: Does it work *in practice*? Can we actually do what is depicted in Figure 6? Let us consider some of the difficulties.

Some Flies in the Ointment

Critics of supply-side economics rarely question its goals or the basic idea that lower taxes improve incentives. They argue, instead, that supply-siders exaggerate the beneficial effects of tax cuts and ignore some undesirable side effects. Here is a brief rundown of some of their main objections.

Small Magnitude of Supply-Side Effects

The first objection is that supply-siders are simply too optimistic: No one really knows how to do what Figure 5 shows. Although it is easy, for example, to design tax incentives that make saving more *attractive* financially, people may not actually respond to these incentives. In fact, most of the statistical evidence suggests that we should not expect much from tax incentives for saving. As the economist Charles Schultze once quipped: "There's nothing wrong with supply-side economics that division by 10 couldn't cure."

Demand-Side Effects

The second objection is that supply-siders ignore the effects of tax cuts on aggregate demand. If you cut personal taxes, for example, individuals *may possibly* work more. But they *will certainly* spend more.

FIGURE 7

A More Pessimistic View of Supply-Side Tax Cuts

The joint implications of these two objections appear in Figure 7. This figure depicts a *small* outward shift of the aggregate supply curve (which reflects the first objection) and a *large* outward shift of the aggregate demand curve (which reflects the second objection). The result is that the economy's equilibrium moves from point E (the intersection of S_0S_0 and D_0D_0) to point C (the intersection of S_1S_1 and D_1D_1). Prices rise as output expands. The outcome differs only a little from the straight "demand-side" fiscal stimulus depicted in Figure 4.

Problems with Timing

Investment incentives are the most promising type of supply-side tax cuts. But the benefits from greater investment do not arrive by overnight mail. In particular, the *expenditures* on investment goods almost certainly come before any *expansion of capacity*. Thus, supply-side tax cuts have their primary short-run effects on aggregate demand. Effects on aggregate supply come later.

Effects on Income Distribution

The preceding objections all pertain to the likely effects of supply-side policies on aggregate supply and demand. But a different problem bears mentioning: Most supply-side initiatives increase income inequality. Indeed, some tilt toward the rich is an almost inescapable corollary of supply-side logic. The basic aim of supply-side economics is to increase the incentives for working and investing—that is, to increase the gap between the rewards of those who succeed in the economic game (by working hard, investing well, or just plain being lucky) and those who fail. It can hardly be surprising, therefore, that supply-side policies tend to increase economic inequality.

Losses of Tax Revenue

You can hardly help noticing that most of the policies suggested by supply-siders involve cutting one tax or another. Thus supply-side tax cuts are bound to raise the government budget deficit. This problem proved to be the Achilles' heel of supply-side economics in the United States in the 1980s. The Reagan tax cuts left in their wake a legacy of budget deficits that took 15 years to overcome. Opponents argue that President George W. Bush's tax cuts put us in a similar position: The tax cuts used up the budget surplus and turned it into a large deficit.

ISSUE: THE PARTISAN DEBATE ONCE MORE

Several of the items on the preceding list played prominent roles in the 2008 presidential campaign. Democrats argued that the Bush tax cuts had very small supply-side incentive effects, were unfair because they went mainly to the well-to-do, and were the primary cause of the large budgets deficits that emerged in 2002. Republicans countered that the tax cuts substantially improved the economy's growth, that it was fair to give the largest tax cuts to those who pay the highest taxes, and that the Bush tax cuts were not the major cause of the budget deficit—which they blamed on the 2001 recession and the spending required after September 11, 2001.

Supply-Side Economics and Presidential Elections

As we have mentioned, Ronald Reagan won landslide victories in 1980 and 1984 by running on a supply-side platform. But in 1992, candidate Bill Clinton attacked supply-side economics as "trickle-down economics," arguing that it had failed. He emphasized two of the drawbacks of such a fiscal policy: the effects on income inequality and on the budget deficit. The voters apparently agreed with him.

The hallmark of Clintonomics was, first, reducing the budget deficit that Clinton had inherited from the first President George Bush, and second, building up a large surplus. This policy succeeded—for a while. The huge budget deficit turned into a large surplus, the economy boomed, and Clinton, like Reagan before him, was re-elected easily.

Then, in the 2000 presidential election, the voters once again switched their allegiance. During that campaign, Democratic candidate Al Gore promised to continue the "fiscal responsibility" of the Clinton years, while Republican candidate George W. Bush echoed Reagan by offering large tax cuts. Bush won in what was virtually a dead heat. Then, in 2004, John Kerry ran against the incumbent George Bush on what amounted to a promise to roll back some of the Bush tax cuts and return to Clintonomics. Bush won again.

In 2008, the very same issue was on the agenda again. The Democrats wanted to repeal most of the Bush tax cuts because, they argued, the government needs the tax revenue. But John McCain wanted to make the tax cuts permanent features of the code.

So which approach do American voters prefer? They appear to be fickle! But one thing is clear: The debate over fiscal policy played a major role in each of the last eight presidential elections.

SOURCE: (a) © AP Images; (b) © AP Images/Greg Wahl-Stevens; (c) © Wally McNamee/CORBIS; (d) © AP Images / J. Scott Applewhite

Toward an Assessment of Supply-Side Economics

On balance, most economists have reached the following conclusions about supply-side tax initiatives:

1. **The likely effectiveness of supply-side tax cuts depends on what kinds of taxes are cut. Tax reductions aimed at stimulating business investment are likely to pack more punch than tax reductions aimed at getting people to work longer hours or to save more.**

2. **Such tax cuts probably will increase aggregate supply much more slowly than they increase aggregate demand. Thus, supply-side policies should not be regarded as a substitute for short-run stabilization policy, but, rather, as a way to promote (slightly) faster economic growth in the long run.**

3. **Demand-side effects of supply-side tax cuts are likely to overwhelm supply-side effects in the short run.**

4. **Supply-side tax cuts are likely to widen income inequalities.**

5. **Supply-side tax cuts are almost certain to lead to larger budget deficits.**

Some people will look over this list and decide in favor of supply-side tax cuts; others, perusing the same facts, will reach the opposite conclusion. We cannot say that either group is wrong because, like almost every economic policy, supply-side economics has its pros and cons and involves value judgments that color people's conclusions.

Why, then, did so many economists and politicians react so negatively to supply-side economics as preached and practiced in the early 1980s? The main reason seems to be that the claims made by the most ardent supply-siders were clearly excessive. Naturally, these claims proved wrong. But showing that wild claims are wild does not eliminate the kernel of truth in supply-side economics: Reductions in marginal tax rates *do* improve economic incentives. Any specific supply-side tax cut must be judged on its individual merits.

| SUMMARY |

1. The government's **fiscal policy** is its plan for managing aggregate demand through its spending and taxing programs. This policy is made jointly by the president and Congress.

2. Because consumer spending (*C*) depends on disposable income (*DI*), and *DI* is GDP minus taxes, any change in taxes will shift the consumption schedule on a 45° line diagram. Such shifts in the consumption schedule have multiplier effects on GDP.

3. The multiplier for changes in taxes is smaller than the multiplier for changes in government purchases because each $1 of tax cuts leads to less than $1 of increased consumer spending.

4. An income tax reduces the size of the multiplier.

5. Because an income tax reduces the multiplier, it reduces the economy's sensitivity to shocks. It is therefore considered an **automatic stabilizer**.

6. Government transfer payments are like negative taxes, rather than like government purchases of goods and services, because they influence total spending only indirectly through their effect on consumption.

7. If the multipliers were known precisely, it would be possible to plan a variety of fiscal policies to eliminate either a recessionary gap or an inflationary gap. Recessionary gaps can be cured by raising *G* or cutting *T*. Inflationary gaps can be cured by cutting *G* or raising *T*.

8. Active stabilization policy can be carried out either by means that tend to expand the size of government (by raising either *G* or *T* when appropriate) or by means that reduce the size of government (by reducing either *G* or *T* when appropriate).

9. Expansionary fiscal policy can mitigate recessions, but it also raises the budget deficit.

10. Expansionary fiscal policy also normally exacts a cost in terms of higher inflation. This last dilemma has led to a great deal of interest in "supply-side" tax cuts designed to stimulate aggregate supply.

11. **Supply-side tax cuts** aim to push the economy's aggregate supply curve outward to the right. When successful, they can expand the economy and reduce inflation at the same time—a highly desirable outcome.

12. But critics point out at least five serious problems with supply-side tax cuts: They also stimulate aggregate demand; the beneficial effects on aggregate supply may be small; the demand-side effects occur before the supply-side effects; they make the income distribution more unequal; and large tax cuts lead to large budget deficits.

| KEY TERMS |

Fiscal policy   221

Effect of income taxes on the multiplier   224

Automatic stabilizer   225

Supply-side tax cuts   229

| TEST YOURSELF |

1. Consider an economy in which tax collections are always $400 and in which the four components of aggregate demand are as follows:

GDP	Taxes	DI	C	I	G	(X − IM)
$1,360	$400	$960	$720	$200	$500	$30
1,480	400	1,080	810	200	500	30
1,600	400	1,200	900	200	500	30
1,720	400	1,320	990	200	500	30
1,840	400	1,440	1,080	200	500	30

Find the equilibrium of this economy graphically. What is the marginal propensity to consume? What is the multiplier? What would happen to equilibrium GDP if government purchases were reduced by $60 and the price level remained unchanged?

2. Consider an economy similar to that in the preceding question in which investment is also $200, government purchases are also $500, net exports are also $30, and the price level is also fixed. But taxes now vary with income and, as a result, the consumption schedule looks like the following:

GDP	Taxes	DI	C
$1,360	$320	$1,040	$810
1,480	360	1,120	870
1,600	400	1,200	930
1,720	440	1,280	990
1,840	480	1,360	1,050

Find the equilibrium graphically. What is the marginal propensity to consume? What is the tax rate? Use your diagram to show the effect of a decrease of $60 in government purchases. What is the multiplier? Compare this answer to your answer to Test Yourself Question 1 above. What do you conclude?

3. Return to the hypothetical economy in Test Yourself Question 1, and now suppose that *both* taxes and government purchases are increased by $120. Find the new equilibrium under the assumption that consumer spending continues to be exactly three-quarters of disposable income (as it is in Test Yourself Question 1).

4. Suppose you are put in charge of fiscal policy for the economy described in Test Yourself Question 1. There is an inflationary gap, and you want to reduce income by $120. What specific actions can you take to achieve this goal?

5. Now put yourself in charge of the economy in Test Yourself Question 2, and suppose that full employment comes at a GDP of $1,840. How can you push income up to that level?

| DISCUSSION QUESTIONS |

1. The federal budget for national defense has increased substantially to pay for the Iraq war. How would GDP in the United States have been affected if this higher defense spending led to

   a. larger budget deficits?

   b. less spending elsewhere in the budget, so that total government purchases remained the same?

2. Explain why *G* has the same multiplier as *I*, but taxes have a different multiplier.

3. If the government decides that aggregate demand is excessive and is causing inflation, what options are open to it? What if the government decides that aggregate demand is too weak instead?

4. Which of the proposed supply-side tax cuts appeals to you most? Draw up a list of arguments for and against enacting such a cut right now.

5. **(More difficult)** Advocates of lower taxes on capital gains argue that this type of tax cut will raise aggregate supply by spurring business investment. Compare the effects on investment, aggregate supply, and tax revenues of three different ways to cut the capital gains tax:

   a. Reduce capital gains taxes on *all* investments, including those that were made before tax rates were cut.

   b. Reduce capital gains taxes only on investments made after tax rates are cut.

   c. Reduce capital gains taxes only on certain types of investments, such as corporate stocks and bonds.

   Which of the three options seems most desirable to you? Why?

| APPENDIX A | *Graphical Treatment of Taxes and Fiscal Policy*

Most of the taxes collected by the U.S. government—indeed, by all national governments—rise and fall with GDP. In some cases, the reason is obvious: *Personal* and *corporate income-tax* collections, for example, depend on how much income there is to be taxed. *Sales tax* receipts depend on GDP because consumer spending is higher when GDP is higher. However, other types of tax receipts—such as property taxes—do not vary with GDP. We call the first kind of tax **variable taxes** and the second kind **fixed taxes.**

This distinction is important because it governs *how* the consumption schedule shifts in response to a tax change. If a *fixed tax* is increased, disposable income falls by the *same* amount regardless of the level of GDP. Hence, the decline in consumer spending is the same at every income level. In other words, the *C* schedule shifts downward in a parallel manner, as was depicted in Figure 1 in the chapter (page 223).

But many tax policies actually change disposable income by larger amounts when incomes are higher. That is true, for example, whenever Congress alters the tax rates imposed by the personal income tax, as it did in 2001 and 2003. Because higher tax rates decrease disposable income *more* when GDP is *higher*, the *C* schedule shifts down more sharply at higher income levels than at lower ones, as depicted in Figure 8. The same relationships apply for tax decreases, as the upward shift in the figure shows.

FIGURE 8

How Variable Taxes Shift the Consumption Schedule

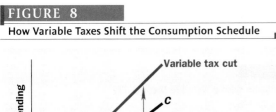

Figure 9 illustrates the second reason why the distinction between fixed and variable taxes is important. This diagram shows two different consumption lines. C_1 is the consumption schedule used in previous chapters; it reflects the assumption that tax collections are the same regardless of GDP. C_2 depicts a more realistic

FIGURE 9

The Consumption Schedule with Fixed versus Variable Taxes

case in which the government collects taxes equal to 20 percent of GDP. Notice that C_2 is flatter than C_1. This is no accident. In fact, as pointed out in the chapter:

> Variable taxes such as the income tax flatten the consumption schedule in a 45° line diagram.

We can easily understand why. Column (1) of Table 1 shows alternative values of GDP ranging from $4.5 trillion to $7.5 trillion. Column (2) then indicates that taxes are always one-fifth of this amount. Column (3) subtracts column (2) from column (1) to arrive at disposable income (*DI*). Column (4) then gives the amount of consumer spending corresponding to each level of *DI*. The schedule relating *C* to *Y*, which we need for our 45° line diagram, is therefore found in columns (1) and (4).

TABLE 1

The Effects of an Income Tax on the Consumption Schedule

(1) Gross Domestic Product	(2) Taxes	(3) Disposable Income (GDP minus Taxes)	(4) Consumption
$4,500	$ 900	$3,600	$3,000
5,000	1,000	4,000	3,300
5,500	1,100	4,400	3,600
6,000	1,200	4,800	3,900
6,500	1,300	5,200	4,200
7,000	1,400	5,600	4,500
7,500	1,500	6,000	4,800

NOTE: Figures are in billions of dollars per year.

Notice that each $500 billion increase in GDP in Table 1 leads to a $300 billion rise in consumer spending. Thus, the slope of line C_2 in Figure 9 is $300/$500, or 0.60, as we observed in the chapter. But in our earlier example in Chapter 9, consumption rose by $300 billion each time GDP increased $400 billion—making the slope $300/$400, or 0.75. (See the steeper line C_1 in Figure 9.) Table 2 compares the two cases explicitly. In the Chapter 9 example, taxes were fixed at $1,200 billion and each $400 billion rise in Y led to a $300 billion rise in C—as in the left-hand panel of Table 2. But now, with taxes variable (equal to 20 percent of GDP), each $500 billion increment to Y gives rise to a $300 billion increase in C—as in the right-hand panel of Table 2.

TABLE 2
The Relationship between Consumption and GDP

With Fixed Taxes ($T = \$1,200$) (from Table 1, Chapter 9)		With a 20 Percent Income Tax (from Table 1)	
Y	C	Y	C
$4,800	$3,000	$4,500	$3,000
5,200	3,300	5,000	3,300
5,600	3,600	5,500	3,600
6,000	3,900	6,000	3,900
6,400	4,200	6,500	4,200
6,800	4,500	7,000	4,500
7,200	4,800	7,500	4,800
Line C_1 in Figure 9		**Line C_2 in Figure 9**	

These differences sound terribly mechanical, but the economic reasoning behind them is vital to understanding tax policies. When taxes are fixed, as in line C_1, each additional dollar of GDP raises disposable income (DI) by $1. Consumer spending then rises by $1 times the marginal propensity to consume (MPC), which is 0.75 in our example. Hence, each additional dollar of GDP leads to 75 cents more spending. But when taxes vary with income, each additional dollar of GDP raises DI by less than $1 because the government takes a share in taxes. In our example, taxes are 20 percent of GDP, so each additional $1 of GDP generates just 80 cents more DI. With an MPC of 0.75, then, spending rises by only 60 cents (75 percent of 80 cents) each time GDP rises by $1. Thus, the slope of line C_2 in Figure 9 is only 0.60, instead of 0.75.

Table 3 and Figure 10 take the next step by replacing the old consumption schedule with this new one in both the tabular presentation of income determination and the 45° line diagram. We see immediately that the equilibrium level of GDP is at point E. Here gross domestic product is $6,000 billion, consumption is $3,900 billion, investment is $900 billion, net exports are −$100 billion, and government purchases are $1,300 billion. As we know from

TABLE 3
Total Expenditure Schedule with a 20 Percent Income Tax

(1)	(2)	(3)	(4)	(5)	(6)
Gross Domestic Product Y	Consumption C	Investment I	Government Purchases G	Net Exports $(X - IM)$	Total Expenditures $C + I + G + (X - IM)$
$4,500	$3,000	$900	$1,300	−$100	$5,100
5,000	3,300	900	1,300	−100	5,400
5,500	3,600	900	1,300	−100	5,700
6,000	**3,900**	**900**	**1,300**	**−100**	**6,000**
6,500	4,200	900	1,300	−100	6,300
7,000	4,500	900	1,300	−100	6,600
7,500	4,800	900	1,300	−100	6,900

previous chapters, full employment may occur above or below $Y = \$6,000$ billion. If it is below this level, an inflationary gap arises. Prices will probably start to rise, pulling the expenditure schedule down and reducing equilibrium GDP. If it is above this level, a recessionary gap results, and history suggests that prices will fall only slowly. In the interim, the economy will suffer a period of high unemployment.

In short, once we adjust the expenditure schedule for variable taxes, the determination of national income proceeds exactly as before. The effects of government spending and taxation, therefore, are fairly straightforward and can be summarized as follows:

Government purchases of goods and services add to total spending *directly* through the G component of $C + I + G + (X - IM)$. Higher taxes reduce total spending *indirectly* by lowering disposable income and thus reducing the C component of $C + I + G + (X - IM)$. On balance, then, the government's actions may raise or

FIGURE 10
Income Determination with a Variable Income Tax

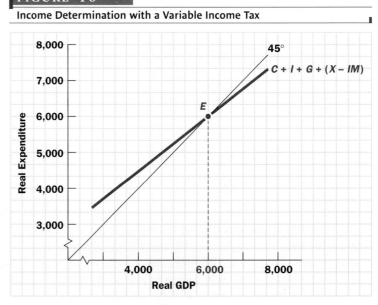

NOTE: Figures are in billions of dollars per year.

lower the equilibrium level of GDP, depending on how much spending and taxing it does.

MULTIPLIERS FOR TAX POLICY

Now let us turn our attention, as in the chapter, to multipliers for tax changes. They are more complicated than multipliers for spending because they work indirectly via consumption. For this reason, we restrict ourselves to the multiplier for fixed taxes, leaving the more complicated case of variable taxes to more advanced courses. Tax multipliers must be worked out in two steps:

1. Figure out how much any proposed or actual changes in the tax law will affect consumer spending.
2. Enter this vertical shift of the consumption schedule in the 45° line diagram and see how it affects output.

To create a simple and familiar numerical example, suppose income taxes fall by a fixed amount at each level of GDP—say, by $400 billion. Step 1 instructs us to multiply the $400 billion tax cut by the marginal propensity to consume (MPC), which is 0.75, to get $300 billion as the increase in consumer spending—that is, as the vertical shift of the consumption schedule.

Next, Step 2 instructs us to multiply this $300 billion increase in consumption by the multiplier—which is 2.5 in our example—giving $750 billion as the rise in GDP. Figure 11 verifies that this result is correct by depicting a $300 billion upward shift of the consumption function in the 45° line diagram and

noting that GDP does indeed rise by $750 billion as a consequence—from $6,000 billion to $6,750 billion.

Notice that the $400 billion tax cut raises GDP by $750 billion, whereas the multiplier effect of the $400 billion increase in government purchases depicted in the chapter in Figure 2 (page 224) raised GDP by $1,000 billion. This is a specific numerical example of something we learned in the chapter. Because some of the change in disposable income affects *saving* rather than *spending*, a dollar of tax cut does not pack as much punch as a dollar of G. That is why we multiplied the $400 billion change in taxes by 0.75 to get the $300 billion shift of the C schedule shown in Figure 11.

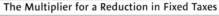

FIGURE 11

The Multiplier for a Reduction in Fixed Taxes

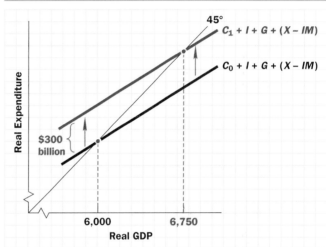

| SUMMARY |

1. Precisely *how* a tax change affects the consumption schedule depends on whether **fixed taxes** or **variable taxes** are changed.

2. Shifts of the consumption function caused by tax policy are subject to the same multiplier as autonomous shifts in G, I, or X − IM.

3. Because tax changes affect C only indirectly, the multiplier for a change in T is smaller than the multiplier for a change in G.

4. The government's net effect on aggregate demand—and hence on equilibrium output and prices—depends on whether the expansionary effects of its spending are greater or smaller than the contractionary effects of its taxes.

| KEY TERMS |

Variable taxes   235   Fixed taxes   235

| TEST YOURSELF |

1. Which of the following is considered a fixed tax and which a variable tax?

   a. The gasoline tax

   b. The corporate income tax

   c. The estate tax

   d. The payroll tax

2. In a certain economy, the multiplier for government purchases is 2 and the multiplier for changes in fixed taxes is 1.5. The government then proposes to raise both spending and taxes by $100 billion. What should happen to equilibrium GDP on the demand side?

3. (**More difficult**) Suppose real GDP is $10,000 billion and the basic expenditure multiplier is 2. If two tax changes are made at the same time:

   a. fixed taxes are raised by $100 billion,

   b. the income-tax *rate* is reduced from 20 percent to 18 percent,

   will equilibrium GDP on the demand side rise or fall?

| DISCUSSION QUESTIONS |

1. When the income-tax rate declines, as it did in the United States early in this decade, does the multiplier go up or down? Explain why.

2. Discuss the pros and cons of having a higher or lower multiplier.

| APPENDIX B | *Algebraic Treatment of Taxes and Fiscal Policy*

In this appendix, we explain the simple algebra behind the fiscal policy multipliers discussed in the chapter. In so doing, we deal only with a simplified case in which prices do not change. Although it is possible to work out the corresponding algebra for the more realistic aggregate demand-and-supply analysis with variable prices, the analysis is rather complicated and is best left to more advanced courses.

 We start with the example used both in the chapter and in Appendix A. The government spends $1,300 billion on goods and services ($G = 1,300$) and levies an income tax equal to 20 percent of GDP. So, if the symbol T denotes tax receipts,

$$T = 0.20Y$$

Because the consumption function we have been working with is

$$C = 300 + 0.75DI$$

where DI is disposable income, and because disposable income and GDP are related by the accounting identity

$$DI = Y - T$$

it follows that the C schedule used in the 45° line diagram is described by the following algebraic equation:

$$\begin{aligned} C &= 300 + 0.75(Y - T) \\ &= 300 + 0.75(Y - 0.20Y) \\ &= 300 + 0.75(0.80Y) \\ &= 300 + 0.60Y \end{aligned}$$

We can now apply the equilibrium condition:

$$Y = C + I + G + (X - IM)$$

Because investment in this example is $I = 900$ and net exports are -100, substituting for $C, I, G,$ and $(X - IM)$ into this equation gives:

$$\begin{aligned} Y &= 300 + 0.60Y + 900 + 1{,}300 - 100 \\ 0.40Y &= 2{,}400 \\ Y &= 6{,}000 \end{aligned}$$

This is all there is to finding equilibrium GDP in an economy with a government.

 To find the multiplier for government spending, increase G by 1 and solve the problem again:

$$\begin{aligned} Y &= C + I + G + (X - IM) \\ Y &= 300 + 0.60Y + 900 + 1{,}301 - 100 \\ 0.40Y &= 2{,}401 \\ Y &= 6{,}002.5 \end{aligned}$$

Thus, the multiplier is $6{,}002.5 - 6{,}000 = 2.5$, as stated in the text.

 To find the multiplier for an increase in fixed taxes, change the tax schedule as follows:

$$T = 0.20Y + 1$$

Disposable income is then

$$DI = Y - T = Y - (0.20Y + 1) = 0.80Y - 1$$

so the consumption function is

$$C = 300 + 0.75DI$$
$$= 300 + 0.75(0.80Y - 1)$$
$$= 299.25 + 0.60Y$$

Solving for equilibrium GDP as usual gives:

$$Y = C + I + G + (X - IM)$$
$$Y = 299.25 + 0.60Y + 900 + 1,300 - 100$$
$$0.40Y = 2,399.25$$
$$Y = 5,998.125$$

So a $1 increase in fixed taxes lowers Y by $1.875. The tax multiplier is −1.875, which is 75 percent of −2.5.

Now let us proceed to a more general solution, using symbols rather than specific numbers. The equations of the model are as follows:

$$Y = C + I + G + (X - IM) \tag{1}$$

is the usual equilibrium condition.

$$C = a + bDI \tag{2}$$

is the same consumption function we used in Appendix A of Chapter 9.

$$DI = Y - T \tag{3}$$

is the accounting identity relating disposable income to GDP.

$$T = T_0 + tY \tag{4}$$

is the tax function, where T_0 represents fixed taxes (which are zero in our numerical example) and t represents the tax rate (which is 0.20 in the example). Finally, I, G, and $(X - IM)$ are just fixed numbers.

We begin the solution by substituting Equations (3) and (4) into Equation (2) to derive the consumption schedule relating C to Y:

$$C = a + bDI$$
$$C = a + b(Y - T)$$
$$C = a + b(Y - T_0 - tY)$$
$$C = a - bT_0 + b(1 - t)Y \tag{5}$$

Notice that a change in fixed taxes (T_0) shifts the *intercept* of the C schedule, whereas a change in the tax rate (t) changes its *slope*, as explained in Appendix A (pages 235–237).

Next, substitute Equation (5) into Equation (1) to find equilibrium GDP:

$$Y = C + I + G + (X - IM)$$
$$Y = a - bT_0 + b(1 - t)Y$$
$$+ I + G + (X - IM)$$
$$[1 - b(1 - t)]Y = a - bT_0 + I + G + (X - IM)$$

or

$$Y = \frac{a - bT_0 + I + G + (X - IM)}{1 - b(1 - t)} \tag{6}$$

Equation (6) shows us that the multiplier for G, I, a, or $(X - IM)$ is

$$\text{Multiplier} = \frac{1}{1 - b(1 - t)}.$$

To see that this is in fact the multiplier, raise any of G, I, a, or $(X - IM)$ by one unit. In each case, Equation (6) would be changed to read:

$$Y = \frac{a - bT_0 + I + G + (X - IM) + 1}{1 - b(1 - t)}$$

Subtracting Equation (6) from this expression gives the change in Y stemming from a one-unit change in G, I, or a:

$$\text{Change in } Y = \frac{1}{1 - b(1 - t)}$$

In Chapter 9 (page 188, we noted that if there were no income tax ($t = 0$), a realistic value for b (the marginal propensity to consume) would yield a multiplier of 20, which is much bigger than the true multiplier. Now that we have added taxes to the model, our multiplier formula produces much more realistic numbers. Approximate values for these parameters for the U.S. economy are $b = 0.95$ and $t = \frac{1}{3}$. The multiplier formula then gives

$$\text{Multiplier} = \frac{1}{1 - 0.95(1 - \frac{1}{3})}$$
$$= \frac{1}{1 - 0.633} = \frac{1}{0.367} = 2.72$$

which is much closer to its actual estimated value—between 1.5 and 2.

Finally, we can see from Equation (6) that the multiplier for a change in fixed taxes (T_0) is

$$\text{Tax Multiplier} = \frac{-b}{1 - b(1 - t)}$$

For the example considered in the text and earlier in this appendix, $b = 0.75$ and $t = 0.20$, so the formula gives

$$\frac{-0.75}{1 - 0.75(1 - 0.20)} = \frac{-0.75}{1 - 0.75(0.80)}$$
$$= \frac{-0.75}{1 - 0.60} = \frac{-0.75}{0.40} = -1.875$$

According to these figures, each $1 *increase* in T_0 *reduces* Y by $1.875.

| TEST YOURSELF |

1. Consider an economy described by the following set of equations:

$$C = 120 + 0.80DI$$
$$I = 320$$
$$G = 480$$
$$(X - IM) = -80$$
$$T = 200 + 0.25Y$$

Find the equilibrium level of GDP. Next, find the multipliers for government purchases and for fixed taxes. If full employment comes at $Y = 1,800$, what are some policies that would move GDP to that level?

2. This question is a variant of the previous problem that approaches things in the way that a fiscal policy planner might. In an economy whose consumption function and tax function are as given in Test Yourself Question 1, with investment fixed at 320 and net exports fixed at -80, find the value of G that would make GDP equal to 1,800.

3. You are given the following information about an economy:

$$C = 0.90DI$$
$$I = 100$$
$$G = 540$$
$$(X - IM) = -40$$
$$T = -\tfrac{1}{3}Y$$

a. Find equilibrium GDP and the budget deficit.

b. Suppose the government, unhappy with the budget deficit, decides to cut government spending by precisely the amount of the deficit you just found. What actually happens to GDP and the budget deficit, and why?

4. **(More difficult)** In the economy considered in Test Yourself Question 3, suppose the government, seeing that it has not wiped out the deficit, keeps cutting G until it succeeds in balancing the budget. What level of GDP will then prevail?

MONEY AND THE BANKING SYSTEM

[Money] is a machine for doing quickly and commodiously what would be done, though less quickly and commodiously, without it.

JOHN STUART MILL

The circular flow diagrams of earlier chapters showed a "financial system" in the upper-left corner. (Look back, for example, at Figure 1 of Chapter 9 on page 177.) Saving flowed into this system and investment flowed out. Something obviously goes on inside the financial system to channel the saving back into investment, and it is time we learned just what this something is.

There is another, equally important, reason for studying the financial system. The government exercises significant control over aggregate demand by manipulating monetary policy as well as fiscal policy. Indeed, most observers nowadays see monetary policy as the more important stabilization tool. To understand how monetary policy works (the subject of Chapters 13 and 14), we must first acquire some understanding of the banking and financial system. By the end of this chapter, you will have that understanding.

CONTENTS

ISSUE: WHY ARE BANKS SO HEAVILY REGULATED?

Banking has long been one of the most heavily regulated industries in America. But the pendulum of bank regulation has swung back and forth.

In the late 1970s and early 1980s, the United States eased several restrictions on interest rates and permissible bank activities. Then, after a number of banks and savings institutions went bankrupt in the 1980s, Congress and the bank regulatory agencies cracked down with stiffer regulation and much closer scrutiny. Later, the pendulum swung back in the deregulatory direction, with two landmark banking laws passed in the 1990s. Most restrictions on banking across state lines were lifted in 1994, and the once-strict separation of banking from insurance and investment banking was more or less ended in 1999. More recently, the mortgage meltdown that began in 2007 has raised new questions about what further regulations might be needed.

In brief, we have spent decades wrestling with the question: How much bank regulation is enough—or too much? But to answer this question intelligently, we must first address a more basic one: Why are banks so heavily regulated in the first place?

A first reason is something we will learn in the next chapter: that the major "output" of the banking industry—*the nation's money supply—is an important determinant of aggregate demand.* Bank managers are paid to do what is best for their stockholders. But as we will see, what is best for bank stockholders may not always be best for the economy as a whole. Consequently, the government does not allow bankers to determine the money supply and interest rates strictly on profit considerations.

A second reason for the extensive web of bank regulation is concern for the *safety of depositors.* In a free-enterprise system, new businesses are born and die every day; and no one other than the people immediately involved takes much notice. When a firm goes bankrupt, stockholders lose money and employees may lose their jobs. But, except for the case of very large firms, that is about all that happens.

But banking is different. If banks were treated like other firms, depositors would lose money whenever one went bankrupt. That outcome is bad enough by itself, but the real danger emerges in the case of a **run on a bank.** When depositors get nervous about the security of their money, they may all rush to cash in their accounts. For reasons we will learn in this chapter, most banks could not survive such a "run" and would be forced to shut their doors.

Worse yet, this disease is highly contagious. If one family hears that their neighbors just lost their life savings because their bank went broke, they are likely to rush to their own bank to withdraw their funds. In fact, fear of contagion is precisely what prompted British bank regulators to act in September 2007 when Northern Rock, a bank specializing in home mortgages, experienced a highly publicized run. (See the box "It's Not Such a Wonderful Life" on page 249.) They first guaranteed all deposits in Northern Rock and later extended the guarantee to all British banks.[1]

Without modern forms of bank regulation, therefore, one bank failure might lead to another. Indeed, bank failures were common throughout most of U.S. history. (See Figure 1(a).) But since the 1930s, bank failures have been less common. (See Figure 1(b), and notice the sharply different scale.) And they have rarely been precipitated by runs because the government has taken steps to ensure that such an infectious disease will not spread. It has done so in several ways that we will mention in this chapter.

> A **run on a bank** occurs when many depositors withdraw cash from their accounts all at once.

THE NATURE OF MONEY

Money is so much a part of our daily existence that we take it for granted and fail to appreciate all that it accomplishes. But money is in no sense "natural." Like the wheel, it had to be invented.

---

[1] The United Kingdom did not have a deposit insurance system comparable to the Federal Deposit Insurance Corporation (FDIC) in the United States.

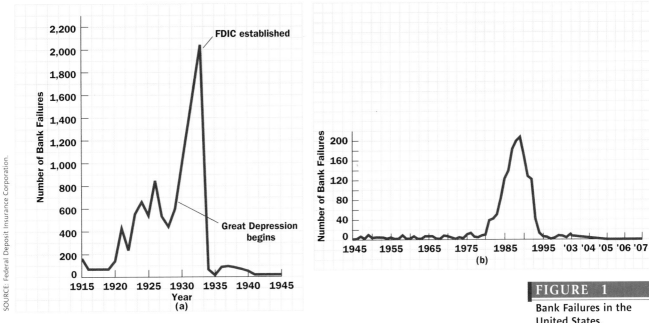

SOURCE: Federal Deposit Insurance Corporation.

FIGURE 1

Bank Failures in the United States, 1915–2007

Barter is a system of exchange in which people directly trade one good for another, without using money as an intermediate step.

The most obvious way to trade commodities is not by using money, but by **barter**—a system in which people exchange one good directly for another. And the best way to appreciate what monetary exchange accomplishes is to imagine a world without it.

Barter versus Monetary Exchange

Under a system of direct barter, if Farmer Jones grows corn and has a craving for peanuts, he has to find a peanut farmer, say, Farmer Smith, with a taste for corn. If he finds such a person (a situation called the *double coincidence of wants*), the two farmers make the trade. If that sounds easy, try to imagine how busy Farmer Jones would be if he had to repeat the sequence for everything he consumed in a week. For the most part, the desired double coincidences of wants are more likely to turn out to be double wants of coincidence. (See the accompanying cartoon.) Jones gets no peanuts and Smith gets no corn. Worse yet, with so much time spent looking for trading partners, Jones would have far less time to grow corn. In brief:

> **Money greases the wheels of exchange and thus makes the whole economy more productive.**

SOURCE: By permission of Johnny Hart and Creators Syndicate, Inc.

Dealing by Wheeling on Yap

Primitive forms of money still exist in some remote places, as this extract from an old newspaper article shows.

Yap, Micronesia—On this tiny South Pacific Island . . . the currency is as solid as a rock. In fact, it is rock. Limestone to be precise.

For nearly 2,000 years the Yapese have used large stone wheels to pay for major purchases, such as land, canoes and permission to marry. Yap is a U.S. trust territory, and the dollar is used in grocery stores and gas stations. But reliance on stone money . . . continues.

Buying property with stones is "much easier than buying it with U.S. dollars," says John Chodad, who recently purchased a building lot with a 30-inch stone wheel. "We don't know the value of the U.S. dollar."

Stone wheels don't make good pocket money, so for small transactions, Yapese use other forms of currency, such as beer. . . .

SOURCE: University of Pennsylvania Museum (58–21338)

Besides stone wheels and beer, the Yapese sometimes spend *gaw*, consisting of necklaces of stone beads strung together around a whale's tooth. They also can buy things with *yar*, a currency made from large seashells. But these are small change.

The people of Yap have been using stone money ever since a Yapese warrior named Anagumang first brought the huge stones over from limestone caverns on neighboring Palau, some 1,500 to 2,000 years ago. Inspired by the moon, he fashioned the stone into large circles. The rest is history. . . .

By custom, the stones are worthless when broken. You never hear people on Yap musing about wanting a piece of the rock.

SOURCE: Excerpted from Art Pine, "Hard Assets, or Why a Loan in Yap Is Hard to Roll Over," *The Wall Street Journal*, March 29, 1984, p. 1.

Under a monetary system, Farmer Jones gives up his corn for money. He does so not because he wants the money per se, but because of what that money can buy. Now he need simply locate a peanut farmer who wants money. And what peanut farmer does not? For these reasons, monetary exchange replaced barter at a very early stage of human civilization, and only extreme circumstances, such as massive wars and runaway inflations, have been able to bring barter (temporarily) back.

The Conceptual Definition of Money

Money is the standard object used in exchanging goods and services. In short, money is the **medium of exchange**.

The **medium of exchange** is the object or objects used to buy and sell other items such as goods and services.

The **unit of account** is the standard unit for quoting prices.

A **store of value** is an item used to store wealth from one point in time to another.

Under monetary exchange, people trade **money** for goods when they purchase something, and they trade goods for money when they sell something, but they do not trade goods directly for other goods. This practice defines money's principal role as the **medium of exchange.** But once it has become accepted as the medium of exchange, whatever serves as money is bound to serve other functions as well. For one, it will inevitably become the **unit of account**—that is, the standard unit for quoting prices. Thus, if inhabitants of an idyllic tropical island use coconuts as money, they would be foolish to quote prices in terms of seashells.

Money also may come to be used as a **store of value.** If Farmer Jones's corn sales bring him more cash than he wants to spend right away, he may find it convenient to store the difference temporarily in the form of money. He knows that money can be sold easily for goods and services at a later date, whereas land, gold, and other stores of value might not be. Of course, if inflation is substantial, he may decide to forgo the convenience of money and store his wealth in some other form rather than see its purchasing power eroded. So money's role as a store of value is far from inevitable.

Because money may not always serve as a store of value, and because other commodities may act as stores of value, we will not include the store-of-value function as part of our conceptual definition of money. Instead, we simply label as "money" whatever serves as the medium of exchange.

What Serves as Money?

Anthropologists and historians can testify that a bewildering variety of objects have served as money in different times and places. Cattle, stones, candy bars, cigarettes, woodpecker

Remaking America's Paper Money

Over the last few years, the U.S. Treasury has replaced much of America's paper money with new notes designed to be much more difficult to counterfeit. Several of the new anticounterfeiting features are visible to the naked eye. By inspecting one of the new $20 bills—the ones with the big picture of Andrew Jackson that looks like it's been through a washing machine—you can easily see several of them. (Others are harder to detect.)

Most obvious are the various shades of coloration, including the silver blue eagle to Jackson's left. Next, hold the bill up to a light, with Jackson facing you. Near the left edge, you will find some small type set vertically, rather than horizontally. If your eyesight is good, you will be able to read what it says. But, if you were a counterfeiter, you would find this line devilishly difficult to duplicate. Third, twist the bill and see how the gold numeral "20" in the lower-right corner glistens and changes color. An optical illusion? No, a clever way to make life hard on counterfeiters.

© AP Images

scalps, porpoise teeth, and giraffe tails provide a few of the more colorful examples. (For another example, see the box "Dealing by Wheeling on Yap" on the previous page.)

In primitive or less organized societies, the commodities that served as money generally held value in themselves. If not used as money, cattle could be slaughtered for food, cigarettes could be smoked, and so on. But such **commodity money** generally runs into several severe difficulties. To be useful as a medium of exchange, a commodity must be easily divisible—which makes cattle a poor choice. It must also be of uniform, or at least readily identifiable, quality so that inferior substitutes are easy to recognize. This shortcoming may be why woodpecker scalps never achieved great popularity. The medium of exchange must also be storable and durable, which presents a serious problem for candy-bar money. Finally, because people will carry and store commodity money, it is helpful if the item is compact—that is, if it has high value per unit of volume and weight.

All of these traits make it natural that gold and silver have circulated as money since the first coins were struck about 2,500 years ago. Because they have high value in nonmonetary uses, a lot of purchasing power can be carried without too much weight. Pieces of gold are also storable, divisible (with a little trouble), and of identifiable quality (with a little more trouble).

The same characteristics suggest that paper would make an even better money. The Chinese invented paper money in the eleventh century, and Marco Polo brought the idea to Europe. Because we can print any number on it that we please, we can make paper money as divisible as we like. People can also carry a large value of paper money in a lightweight and compact form. Paper is easy to store and, with a little cleverness, we can make counterfeiting challenging, though never impossible. (See the box "Remaking America's Paper Money" above.)

Paper cannot, however, serve as commodity money because its value per square inch in alternative uses is so low. A paper currency that is repudiated by its issuer can, perhaps, be used as wallpaper or to wrap fish, but these uses will surely represent only a small fraction of the paper's value as money.[2] Contrary to the popular expression, such a currency

Commodity money is an object in use as a medium of exchange, but that also has a substantial value in alternative (nonmonetary) uses.

---

[2] The first paper money issued by the U.S. federal government, the Continental dollar, was essentially repudiated. (Actually, the new government of the United States redeemed the Continentals for 1 cent on the dollar in the 1790s.) This event gave rise to the derisive expression, "It's not worth a Continental."

Fiat money is money that is decreed as such by the government. It is of little value as a commodity, but it maintains its value as a medium of exchange because people have faith that the issuer will stand behind the pieces of printed paper and limit their production.

literally *is* worth the paper it is printed on—which is to say that it is not worth much. Thus, paper money is always **fiat money.**

Money in the contemporary United States is almost entirely fiat money. Look at a dollar bill. Next to George Washington's picture it states: "This note is legal tender for all debts, public and private." Nowhere on the certificate is there a promise, stated or implied, that the U.S. government will exchange it for anything else. A dollar bill is convertible into, say, 4 quarters or 10 dimes—but not into gold, chocolate, or any other commodity.

Why do people hold these pieces of paper? Because they know that others are willing to accept them for things of intrinsic value—food, rent, shoes, and so on. If this confidence ever evaporated, dollar bills would cease serving as a medium of exchange and, given that they make ugly wallpaper, would become virtually worthless.

But don't panic. This series of events is hardly likely to occur. Our current monetary system has evolved over hundreds of years, during which *commodity money* was first replaced by *full-bodied paper money*—paper certificates that were backed by gold or silver of equal value held in the issuer's vaults. Then the full-bodied paper money was replaced by certificates that were only partially backed by gold and silver. Finally, we arrived at our present system, in which paper money has no "backing" whatsoever. Like hesitant swimmers who first dip their toes, then their legs, then their whole body into a cold swimming pool, we have "tested the water" at each step of the way—and found it to our liking. It is unlikely that we will ever take a step back in the other direction.

HOW THE QUANTITY OF MONEY IS MEASURED

Because the amount of money in circulation is important for the determination of national product and the price level, the government must know how much money there is. Thus we must devise some *measure* of the money supply.

Our conceptual definition of money as the medium of exchange raises difficult questions about just which items to include and which items to exclude when we count up the money supply. Such questions have long made the statistical definition of money a subject of dispute. In fact, the U.S. government has several official definitions of the money supply, two of which we will meet shortly.

Some components are obvious. All of our coins and paper money—the small change of our economic system—clearly should count as money. But we cannot stop there if we want to include the main vehicle for making payments in our society, for the lion's share of our nation's payments are made neither in metal nor in paper money, but by check.

Checking deposits are actually no more than bookkeeping entries in bank ledgers. Many people think of checks as a convenient way to pass coins or dollar bills to someone else. But that is not so. For example, when you pay the grocer $50 by check, dollar bills rarely change hands. Instead, that check normally travels back to your bank, where $50 is deducted from the bookkeeping entry that records your account and $50 is added to the bookkeeping entry for your grocer's account. (If you and the grocer hold accounts at different banks, more books get involved, but still no coins or bills will likely move.) The volume of money held in the form of checkable deposits far exceeds the volume of currency.

M1

So it seems imperative to include checkable deposits in any useful definition of the money supply. Unfortunately, this is not an easy task nowadays, because of the wide variety of ways to transfer money by check. Traditional checking accounts in commercial banks are the most familiar vehicle. But many people can also write checks on their savings accounts, on their deposits at credit unions, on their mutual funds, on their accounts with stockbrokers, and so on.

One popular definition of the money supply draws the line early and includes only coins, paper money, traveler's checks, conventional checking accounts, and certain other checkable deposits in banks and savings institutions. In the official U.S. statistics, this narrowly defined concept of money is called **M1.** The upper part of Figure 2 shows the composition of M1 as of December 2007.

M2

But other types of accounts allow withdrawals by check, so they are also candidates for inclusion in the money supply. Most notably, *money market deposit accounts* allow their owners to write only a few checks per month but pay market-determined interest rates. Consumers have found these accounts attractive, and balances in them now exceed all the checkable deposits included in M1.

In addition, many mutual fund organizations and brokerage houses offer *money market mutual funds.* These funds sell shares and use the proceeds to purchase a variety of short-term securities. But the important point for our purposes is that owners of shares in money market mutual funds can withdraw their funds by writing checks. Thus, depositors can use their holdings of fund shares just like checking accounts.

Finally, although you cannot write a check on a *savings account,* modern banking procedures have blurred the distinction between checking balances and savings balances. For example, most banks these days offer convenient electronic transfers of funds from one account to another, by telephone, Internet, or by pushing a button on an automatic teller machine (ATM). Consequently, savings balances can become checkable almost instantly. For this reason, savings accounts are included—along with money market deposit accounts and money market mutual fund shares—in the broader definition of the money supply known as **M2.**

The composition of M2 as of December 2007 is shown in the lower part of Figure 2. You can see that savings deposits predominate, dwarfing M1. Figure 2 illustrates that our money supply comes not only from banks but also from savings institutions, brokerage houses, and mutual fund organizations. Even so, banks still play a predominant role.

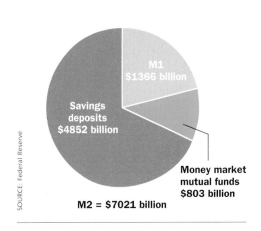

FIGURE 2

Two Definitions of the Money Supply, December 2007

SOURCE: Federal Reserve

Other Definitions of the Money Supply

Some economists do not want to stop counting at M2; they prefer still broader definitions of money (M3, and so on), which include more types of bank deposits and other closely related assets. The inescapable problem, however, is that there is no obvious place to stop, no clear line of demarcation between those assets that *are* money and those that are merely *close substitutes* for money—so-called **near moneys.**

If we define an asset's **liquidity** as the ease with which its holder can convert it into cash, there is a spectrum of assets of varying degrees of liquidity. Everything in M1 is completely liquid, the money market fund shares and passbook savings accounts included in M2 are a bit less so, and so on, until we encounter items such as short-term government bonds, which, while still quite liquid, would not be included in anyone's definition of the money supply. Any number of different Ms can be defined—and have been—by drawing the line in different places.

And yet more complexities arise. For example, credit cards clearly serve as a medium of exchange. Should they be included in the money supply? Of course, you say. But how much *money* does your credit card represent? Is it the amount you currently owe on the card, which may be zero? Or is it your entire line of credit, even though you may never use it all? Neither choice seems sensible. Furthermore, you will probably wind up writing a check (which is included in M1) to pay your credit card bill. These are two reasons why economists have so far ignored credit cards in their definitions of money.

The narrowly defined money supply, usually abbreviated **M1**, is the sum of all coins and paper money in circulation, plus certain checkable deposit balances at banks and savings institutions.[3]

The broadly defined money supply, usually abbreviated **M2**, is the sum of all coins and paper money in circulation, plus all types of checking account balances, plus most forms of savings account balances, plus shares in money market mutual funds.

Near moneys are liquid assets that are close substitutes for money.

An asset's **liquidity** refers to the ease with which it can be converted into cash.

---

[3] This amount includes travelers' checks and NOW (negotiable order of withdrawal) accounts.

We could mention further complexities, but an introductory course in economics is not the place to get bogged down in complex definitional issues. So we will simply adhere to the convention that:

"Money" consists only of coins, paper money, and checkable deposits.

THE BANKING SYSTEM

Now that we have defined money and seen how to measure it, we turn our attention to the principal creators of money—the banks. Banking is a complicated business—and getting more so. If you go further in your study of economics, you will probably learn more about the operations of banks. But for present purposes, a few simple principles will suffice. Let's start at the beginning.

How Banking Began

When Adam and Eve left the Garden of Eden, they did not encounter an ATM. Banking had to be invented. With a little imagination, we can see how the first banks must have begun.

When money was made of gold or other metals, it was inconvenient for consumers and merchants to carry it around and weigh and assay its purity every time they made a transaction. So the practice developed of leaving gold in a goldsmith's safe storage facilities and carrying in its place a receipt stating that John Doe did indeed own 5 ounces of gold. When people began trading goods and services for the goldsmiths' receipts, rather than for the gold itself, the receipts became an early form of paper money.

At this stage, paper money was fully backed by gold. Gradually, however, the goldsmiths began to notice that the amount of gold they were actually required to pay out in a day was but a small fraction of the total gold they had stored in their warehouses. Then one day some enterprising goldsmith hit upon a momentous idea that must have made him fabulously wealthy.

His thinking probably ran something like this: "I have 2,000 ounces of gold stored away in my vault, for which I collect storage fees from my customers. But I am never called upon to pay out more than 100 ounces on a single day. What harm could it do if I lent out, say, half the gold I now have? I'll still have more than enough to pay off any depositors who come in for withdrawals, so no one will ever know the difference. And I could earn 30 additional ounces of gold each year in interest on the loans I make (at 3 percent interest on 1,000 ounces). With this profit, I could lower my service charges to depositors and so attract still more deposits. I think I'll do it."

With this resolution, the modern system of **fractional reserve banking** was born. This system has three features that are crucially important to this chapter.

Bank Profitability By getting deposits at zero interest and lending some of them out at positive interest rates, goldsmiths made profits. The history of banking as a profit-making industry was begun and has continued to this date. *Banks, like other enterprises, are in business to earn profits.*

Bank Discretion over the Money Supply When goldsmiths decided to keep only fractions of their total deposits on reserve and lend out the balance, they acquired the ability to *create money.* As long as they kept 100 percent reserves, each gold certificate represented exactly 1 ounce of gold. So whether people decided to carry their gold or leave it with their goldsmiths did not affect the money supply, which was set by the volume of gold.

With the advent of fractional reserve banking, however, new paper certificates appeared whenever goldsmiths lent out some of the gold they held on deposit. The loans, in effect, created new money. In this way, the total amount of money came to depend on

> **Fractional reserve banking** is a system under which bankers keep as reserves only a fraction of the funds they hold on deposit.

the amount of gold that each goldsmith felt compelled to keep in his vault. For any given volume of gold on deposit, the lower the reserves the goldsmiths kept, the more loans they could make, and therefore the more money would circulate.

Although we no longer use gold to back our money, this principle remains true today. *Bankers' decisions on how much to hold in reserves influence the supply of money.* A substantial part of the rationale for modern monetary policy is, as we have mentioned, that profit-seeking bankers might not create the amount of money that is best for society.

Exposure to Runs   A goldsmith who kept 100 percent reserves never had to worry about a run on his vault. Even if all his depositors showed up at the door at once, he could always convert their paper receipts back into gold. But as soon as the first goldsmith decided to get by with only fractional reserves, the possibility of a run on the vault became a real concern. If that first goldsmith who lent out half his gold had found 51 percent of his customers at his door one unlucky day, he would have had a lot of explaining to do. Similar problems have worried bankers for centuries. *The danger of a run on the bank has induced bankers to keep prudent reserves and to lend out money carefully.*

Runs on banks are, for the most part, a relic of the past. You may have seen the famous bank-run scene in Frank Capra's 1946 movie classic *It's a Wonderful Life*, with Jimmy Stewart playing a young banker named George Bailey. But you've probably never seen an actual bank run. In September 2007, however, quite a few people in England did see one when depositors "ran" Northern Rock, a large mortgage bank. (See the box "It's Not Such a Wonderful Life" below.) As we observed earlier, avoiding bank runs is one of the main rationales for bank regulation.

It's Not Such a Wonderful Life

The subprime mortgage crisis of 2007 (described in greater detail later on page 251) quickly spread beyond the borders of the United States. One of its victims was a large British mortgage lender called Northern Rock. In mid-September, rumors that the bank was in trouble precipitated the first bank run in England since the nineteenth century. Here is the scene as described in the online version of The Times (of London) on September 14, 2007:

> Long queues formed outside branches of Northern Rock today as anxious customers waited to withdraw savings after the bank was forced to seek an emergency bailout from the Bank of England. Savers went in person to Northern Rock's branches to withdraw their money, after facing difficulties contacting the bank on the phone or via the internet.
>
> William Gough, 75, arriving at a Northern Rock branch in Central London this morning, said he did not believe the bank's assurances that his savings were safe and intended to withdraw his funds. ". . . At the time I put the money in I wouldn't have imagined something like this would happen," Mr Gough said while joining the back of a 40-strong queue.
>
> Customers queued for up to an hour and, as news of the Bank of England bailout spread, the throng inside the branch was so dense that some struggled to open the door.
>
> Gary Diamond beat the crowd by arriving early. "I came down here to withdraw my funds because I'm concerned that Northern Rock are not still going to be in existence," he said after closing his accounts. He added that there was a danger that if others followed suit it could worsen Northern Rock's posi-

tion. "But I don't want to be the mug left without my savings," he said.

> [Other] customers said they were not concerned about the stability of the bank but had been forced to act over fears of a bank run. Paul De Lamare, a 46-year-old consultant, said: ". . . I don't think the Bank of England would allow anything to happen. But I'm just trying to avoid getting caught short, so I've taken out cash."

SOURCE: © AP Images/Andrew Milligan/PA

SOURCE: Times Online, September 14, 2007.

Principles of Bank Management: Profits versus Safety

Bankers have a reputation for conservatism in politics, dress, and business affairs. From what has been said so far, the economic rationale for this conservatism should be clear. Checking deposits are pure fiat money. Years ago, these deposits were "backed" by nothing more than a particular bank's promise to convert them into currency on demand. If people lost trust in a bank, it was doomed.

Thus, bankers have always relied on a reputation for prudence, which they achieved in two principal ways. First, they maintained a sufficiently generous level of reserves to minimize their vulnerability to runs. Second, they were cautious in making loans and investments, because large losses on their loans could undermine their depositors' confidence.

It is important to realize that banking under a system of fractional reserves is an inherently risky business that is rendered safe only by cautious and prudent management. America's long history of bank failures (see Figure 1) bears sober testimony to the fact that many bankers were neither cautious nor prudent. Why not? Because caution is not the route to high profits. Bank profits are maximized by keeping reserves as low as possible and by making at least some loans to borrowers with questionable credit standing who will pay higher interest rates.

The art of bank management is to strike the appropriate balance between the lure of profits and the need for safety. If a banker errs by being too stodgy, his bank will earn inadequate profits. If he errs by taking unwarranted risks, his bank may not survive at all.

Bank Regulation

But governments in virtually every society have decided that profit-minded bankers will not necessarily strike the balance between profits and safety exactly where society wants it. So they have constructed a web of regulations designed to ensure depositors' safety and to control the money supply.

Deposit insurance is a system that guarantees that depositors will not lose money even if their bank goes bankrupt.

Deposit Insurance   The principal innovation that guarantees the safety of bank deposits is **deposit insurance.** Today, most U.S. bank deposits are insured against loss by the *Federal Deposit Insurance Corporation (FDIC)*—an agency of the federal government. If your bank belongs to the FDIC, as almost all do, your account is insured for up to $100,000 regardless of what happens to the bank. Thus, while bank failures may spell disaster for the bank's stockholders, they do not create concern for many depositors. Deposit insurance eliminates the motive for customers to rush to their bank just because they hear some bad news about the bank's finances. Many observers give this innovation much of the credit for the pronounced decline in bank failures after the FDIC was established in 1933—which is apparent in Figure 1.

Despite this achievement, some critics of FDIC insurance worry that depositors who are freed from any risk of loss from a failing bank will not bother to shop around for safer banks. This problem is an example of what is called the **moral hazard** problem: the general idea that, when people are well insured against a particular risk, they will put little effort into making sure that the risk does not occur. (Example: A business with good fire insurance may not install an expensive sprinkler system.) In this context, some of the FDIC's critics argue that high levels of deposit insurance actually make the banking system less safe.

Moral hazard is the idea that people insured against the consequences of risk will engage in riskier behaviors.

Bank Supervision   Partly for this reason, the government takes several steps to see that banks do not get into financial trouble. For one thing, various regulatory authorities conduct periodic *bank examinations* to keep tabs on the financial conditions and business practices of the banks under their purview. After a rash of bank failures in the late 1980s and early 1990s (visible in Figure 1(b)), U.S. bank supervision was tightened by legislation that permits the authorities to intervene early in the affairs of financially troubled banks. Other laws and regulations *limit the kinds and quantities of assets in which banks may invest.* For example, banks are permitted to own only limited amounts of common stock. Both of these forms of regulation, and others, are clearly aimed at keeping banks safe. That said, there is no such thing as perfect safety, as the subprime mortgage debacle of 2007 illustrated (see the box on the next page).

What Happened to the Subprime Mortgage Market?

One valuable, but also somewhat risky, innovation in American banking during the past decade was the rapid expansion of so-called subprime mortgages, meaning loans to prospective homeowners with less-than-stellar credit histories. Often, these borrowers were low-income and poorly educated people. Naturally, bankers expected higher default rates on subprime loans than on prime loans, and so they charged higher interest rates to compensate for expected future losses. That was all perfectly sound banking practice.

But a few things went wrong, especially in 2005 and 2006. For one thing, subprime loans started to be made with little or no evidence that the homeowners had enough regular income (for example, a large-enough paycheck) to meet their monthly payments. That is *not* sound banking practice. Second, many subprime loans carried "adjustable rates," which in practice meant that the monthly mortgage payment was almost certain to skyrocket after, say, two years. That created a ticking time bomb that should have raised serious questions about affordability of the mortgages—but apparently did not. Third, about half of these risky loans were not made by regulated banks at all, but rather by mortgage brokers—who were not regulated by the federal government and who sometimes followed unscrupulous sales practices. Finally, the general euphoria over housing (the housing "bubble") led many people to believe that all these dangers would be papered over by ever-rising home prices.

When house prices stopped rising so fast in 2005–2006, the game of musical chairs ended abruptly. Default rates on subprime mortgages soared. Then, in 2007, the subprime market virtually shut down, precipitating a near panic in financial markets in the United States and around the world. In the United States, the Federal Reserve stepped in to quell the panic by lending massively to banks and then cutting interest rates.

The medicine helped a bit, but losses from the housing downturn continued, banks remained jittery, and credit became harder to obtain. By early 2008, talk of an impending recession was rampant.

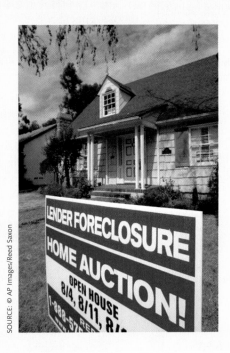

SOURCE: © AP Images/Reed Saxon

Reserve Requirements   A final type of regulation also has some bearing on safety but is motivated primarily by the government's desire to control the money supply. We have seen that the amount of money any bank will issue depends on the amount of reserves it elects to keep. For this reason, most banks are subject by law to minimum **required reserves.** Although banks may (and sometimes do) keep reserves in excess of these legal minimums, they may not keep less. This regulation places an upper limit on the money supply. The rest of this chapter is concerned with the details of this mechanism.

> **Required reserves** are the minimum amount of reserves (in cash or the equivalent) required by law. Normally, required reserves are proportional to the volume of deposits.

THE ORIGINS OF THE MONEY SUPPLY

Our objective is to understand how the money supply is determined. But before we can fully understand the process by which money is "created," we must acquire at least a nodding acquaintance with the mechanics of modern banking.

How Bankers Keep Books

The first thing to know is how to distinguish assets from liabilities. An **asset** of a bank is something of value that the bank *owns*. This "thing" may be a physical object, such as the bank building or a computer, or it may be a piece of paper, such as an IOU signed by a customer to whom the bank has made a loan. A **liability** of a bank is something of value that the bank *owes*. Most bank liabilities take the form of bookkeeping entries. For example, if you have an account in the Main Street Bank, your bank balance is a liability of the bank. (It is, of course, an asset to you.)

There is an easy test for whether some piece of paper or bookkeeping entry is a bank's *asset* or *liability*. Ask yourself a simple question: If this paper were converted into cash, would the bank receive the cash (if so, it is an asset) or pay it out (if so, it is a liability)?

> An **asset** of an individual or business firm is an item of value that the individual or firm owns.

> A **liability** of an individual or business firm is an item of value that the individual or firm owes. Many liabilities are known as *debts*.

This test makes it clear that loans to customers are assets of the bank (when a loan is repaid, the bank collects), whereas customers' deposits are bank liabilities (when a deposit is cashed in, the bank pays). Of course, things are just the opposite to the bank's customers: The loans are liabilities and the deposits are assets.

When accountants draw up a complete list of all the bank's assets and liabilities, the resulting document is called the bank's **balance sheet.** Typically, the value of all the bank's assets exceeds the value of all its liabilities. (On the rare occasions when this is not so, the bank is in serious trouble.) In what sense, then, do balance sheets "balance"?

A **balance sheet** is an accounting statement listing the values of all assets on the left side and the values of all liabilities and *net worth* on the right side.

They balance because accountants have invented the concept of **net worth** to balance the books. Specifically, they define the net worth of a bank to be the *difference* between the value of all its assets and the value of all its liabilities. Thus, by definition, when accountants add net worth to liabilities, the sum they get must be equal to the value of the bank's assets:

Net worth is the value of all assets minus the value of all liabilities.

$$\text{Assets} = \text{Liabilities} + \text{Net worth}$$

Table 1 illustrates this point with the balance sheet of a fictitious bank, Bank-a-mythica, whose finances are extremely simple. On December 31, 2007, it had only two kinds of assets (listed on the left side of the balance sheet)—$1 million in cash reserves and $4.5 million in outstanding loans to its customers, that is, in customers' IOUs. And it had only one type of liability (listed on the right side)—$5 million in checking deposits. The difference between total assets ($5.5 million) and total liabilities ($5.0 million) was the bank's net worth ($500,000), also shown on the right side of the balance sheet.

TABLE 1

Balance Sheet of Bank-a-mythica, December 31, 2007

Assets		Liabilities and Net Worth	
Assets		**Liabilities**	
Reserves	$1,000,000	Checking deposits	$5,000,000
Loans outstanding	$4,500,000		
Total	**$5,500,000**	**Net Worth**	
Addendum: Bank Reserves		Stockholders' equity	$500,000
Actual reserves	$1,000,000	Total	**$5,500,000**
Required reserves	1,000,000		
Excess reserves	0		

BANKS AND MONEY CREATION

Let us now turn to the process of deposit creation. Many bankers will deny that they have any ability to "create" money. The phrase itself has a suspiciously hocus-pocus sound to it. But the protesting bankers are not quite right. Although any individual bank's ability to create money is severely limited, the banking system as a whole can achieve much more than the sum of its parts. Through the modern alchemy of **deposit creation,** it can turn one dollar into many dollars. But to understand this important process, we had better proceed step-by-step, beginning with the case of a single bank, our hypothetical Bank-a-mythica.

Deposit creation refers to the process by which a fractional reserve banking system turns $1 of bank reserves into several dollars of bank deposits.

The Limits to Money Creation by a Single Bank

According to the balance sheet in Table 1, Bank-a-mythica holds cash reserves of $1 million, equal to 20 percent of its $5 million in deposits. Assume that this is the reserve ratio prescribed by law and that the bank strives to keep its reserves down to the legal minimum; that is, it strives to keep its **excess reserves** at zero.

Excess reserves are any reserves held in excess of the legal minimum.

Now let us suppose that on January 2, 2008, an eccentric widower comes into Bank-a-mythica and deposits $100,000 in cash in his checking account. The bank now has $100,000 more in cash reserves and $100,000 more in checking deposits. But because deposits are up by $100,000, *required* reserves rise by only $20,000, leaving $80,000 in *excess* reserves. Table 2 illustrates the effects of this transaction on Bank-a-mythica's balance sheet. Tables such as

TABLE 2

Changes in Bank-a-mythica's Balance Sheet, January 2, 2008

Assets		Liabilities	
Reserves	+$100,000	Checking deposits	+$100,000
Addendum: Changes in Reserves			
Actual reserves	+$100,000		
Required reserves	+$ 20,000		
Excess reserves	**+$ 80,000**		

this one, which show *changes* in balance sheets rather than the balance sheets themselves, will help us follow the money-creation process.[4]

Bank-a-mythica is unlikely to be happy with the situation illustrated in Table 2, for it is holding $80,000 in excess reserves on which it earns no interest. So as soon as possible, it will lend out the extra $80,000—let us say to Hard-Pressed Construction Company. This loan leads to the balance sheet changes shown in Table 3: Bank-a-mythica's loans rise by $80,000 while its holdings of cash reserves fall by $80,000.

TABLE 3

Changes in Bank-a-mythica's Balance Sheet, January 3–6, 2008

Assets		Liabilities
Loans outstanding	+$80,000	No change
Reserves	−$80,000	
Addendum: Changes in Reserves		
Actual reserves	−$80,000	
Required reserves	No change	
Excess reserves	**−$80,000**	

By combining Tables 2 and 3, we arrive at Table 4, which summarizes the bank's transactions for the week. Reserves are up $20,000, loans are up $80,000, and, now that the bank has had a chance to adjust to the inflow of deposits, it no longer holds excess reserves.

Looking at Table 4 and keeping in mind our specific definition of money, it appears at first that the chairman of Bank-a-mythica is right when he claims not to have engaged in the nefarious-sounding practice of "money creation." All that happened was that, in exchange for the $100,000 in cash it received, the bank issued the widower a checking balance of $100,000. This transaction does not change M1; it merely converts one form of money (currency) into another (checking deposits).

TABLE 4

Changes in Bank-a-mythica's Balance Sheet, January 2–6, 2008

Assets		Liabilities	
Reserves	+$20,000	Checking deposits	+$100,000
Loans outstanding	+$80,000		
Addendum: Changes in Reserves			
Actual reserves	+$20,000		
Required reserves	+$20,000		
Excess reserves	**No change**		

[4] In all such tables, which are called *T accounts,* the two sides of the ledger must balance. This balance is required because changes in assets and changes in liabilities must be equal if the balance sheet is to balance both before and after the transaction.

But wait. What happened to the $100,000 in cash that the eccentric man brought to the bank? The table shows that Bank-a-mythica retained $20,000 in its vault. Because this currency is no longer in circulation, it no longer counts in the official money supply, M1. (Notice that Figure 2 included only "currency outside banks.") But the other $80,000, which the bank lent out, is still in circulation. It is held by Hard-Pressed Construction Company, which probably will redeposit it in some other bank. But even before this new deposit is made, the original $100,000 in cash has supported an increase in the money supply. There is now $100,000 in checking deposits and $80,000 of cash in circulation, making a total of $180,000—whereas prior to the original deposit there was only the $100,000 in cash. The money-creation process has begun.

Multiple Money Creation by a Series of Banks

By tracing the $80,000 in cash, we can see how the process of money creation gathers momentum. Suppose that Hard-Pressed Construction Company, which banks across town at the First National Bank, deposits the $80,000 in its bank account. First National's reserves increase by $80,000. But because its deposits rise by $80,000, its *required* reserves increase by 20 percent of this amount, or $16,000. If First National Bank behaves like Bank-a-mythica, it will lend out the $64,000 of excess reserves.

Table 5 shows the effects of these events on First National Bank's balance sheet. (We do not show the preliminary steps corresponding to Tables 2 and 3 separately.) At this stage in the chain, the original $100,000 in cash has led to $180,000 in deposits—$100,000 at Bank-a-mythica and $80,000 at First National Bank—and $64,000 in cash, which is still in circulation (in the hands of the recipient of First National's loan—Al's Auto Shop). Thus, instead of the original $100,000, a total of $244,000 worth of money ($180,000 in checking deposits plus $64,000 in cash) has been created.

TABLE 5
Changes in First National Bank's Balance Sheet

Assets		Liabilities	
Reserves	+$16,000	Checking deposits +$80,000	
Loans outstanding	+$64,000		
Addendum: Changes in Reserves			
Actual reserves	+$16,000		
Required reserves	+$16,000		
Excess reserves	**No change**		

But, to coin a phrase, the bucks do not stop there. Al's Auto Shop will presumably deposit the proceeds from its loan into its own account at Second National Bank, leading to the balance sheet adjustments shown in Table 6 when Second National makes an additional loan of $51,200 rather than hold on to excess reserves. You can see how the money creation process continues.

TABLE 6
Changes in Second National Bank's Balance Sheet

Assets		Liabilities	
Reserves	+$12,800	Checking deposits +$64,000	
Loans outstanding	+$51,200		
Addendum: Changes in Reserves			
Actual reserves	+$12,800		
Required reserves	+$12,800		
Excess reserves	**No change**		

Figure 3 summarizes the balance sheet changes of the first five banks in the chain (from Bank-a-mythica through the Fourth National Bank) graphically, based on the assumptions that (1) each bank holds exactly the 20 percent required reserves, and (2) each loan recipient redeposits the proceeds in the next bank. But the chain does not end there. The Main Street Movie Theatre, which received the $32,768 loan from the Fourth National Bank, deposits these funds into the Fifth National Bank. Fifth National has to keep only 20 percent of this deposit, or $6,553.60, on reserve and will lend out the balance. And so the chain continues.

Where does it all end? The running sums on the right side of Figure 3 show what eventually happens to the entire banking system. The initial deposit of $100,000 in cash is ultimately absorbed in bank reserves (column 1), leading to a total of $500,000 in new deposits (column 2) and $400,000 in new loans (column 3). The money supply rises by $400,000 because the nonbank public eventually holds $100,000 *less* in currency and $500,000 *more* in checking deposits.

As we see, there really is some hocus-pocus. Somehow, an initial deposit of $100,000 leads to $500,000 in new bank deposits—a multiple expansion of $5 for every original dollar—and a net increase of $400,000 in the money supply. We need to understand *why* this is so. But first let us verify that the calculations in Figure 3 are correct.

If you look carefully at the numbers, you will see that each column forms a geometric progression; specifically, each entry is equal to exactly 80 percent of the entry before it. Recall that in our discussion of the multiplier in Chapter 9 we learned how to sum an infinite

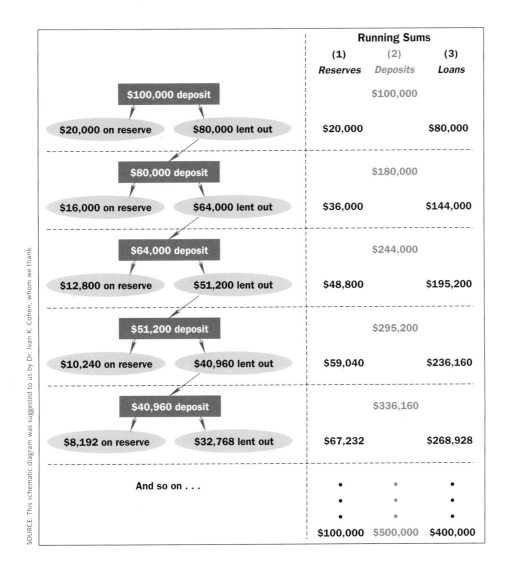

FIGURE 3

The Chain of Multiple Deposit Creation

SOURCE: This schematic diagram was suggested to us by Dr. Ivan K. Cohen, whom we thank.

geometric progression, which is just what each of these chains is. In particular, if the common ratio is R, the sum of an infinite geometric progression is:

$$1 + R + R^2 + R^3 + \ldots = \frac{1}{1 - R}$$

By applying this formula to the chain of checking deposits in Figure 3, we get:

$$\$100{,}000 + \$80{,}000 + \$64{,}000 + \$51{,}200 + \ldots$$
$$= \$100{,}000 \times (1 + 0.80 + 0.64 + 0.512 + \ldots)$$
$$= \$100{,}000 \times (1 + 0.80 + 0.80^2 + 0.80^3 + \ldots)$$
$$= \$100{,}000 \times \frac{1}{1 - 0.80} = \frac{\$100{,}000}{0.20} = \$500{,}000$$

Proceeding similarly, we can verify that the new loans sum to $400,000 and that the new required reserves sum to $100,000. (Check these figures as exercises.) Thus the numbers in Figure 3 are correct. Let us, therefore, think through the logic behind them.

The chain of deposit creation ends only when there are no more *excess* reserves to be loaned out—that is, when the entire $100,000 in cash is tied up in *required* reserves. That explains why the last entry in column (1) of Figure 3 must be $100,000. But, with a reserve ratio of 20 percent, excess reserves disappear only when checking deposits expand by $500,000—which is the last entry in column (2). Finally, because balance sheets must balance, the sum of all newly created assets (reserves plus loans) must equal the sum of all newly created liabilities ($500,000 in deposits). That leaves $400,000 for new loans—which is the last entry in column (3).

More generally, if the reserve ratio is some number m (rather than the one-fifth in our example), each dollar of deposits requires only a fraction m of a dollar in reserves. The common ratio in the preceding formula is, therefore, $R = 1 - m$, and deposits must expand by $1/m$ for each dollar of new reserves that are injected into the system. This suggests the general formula for multiple money creation when the required reserve ratio is some number m:

OVERSIMPLIFIED MONEY MULTIPLIER FORMULA

The **money multiplier** is the ratio of newly created bank deposits to new reserves.

If the required reserve ratio is some fraction, m, the banking system as a whole can convert each $1 of reserves into $1/m$ in new money. That is, the so-called money multiplier is given by:

Change in money supply = $(1/m)$ × Change in reserves

Although this formula correctly describes what happens in our example, it leaves out an important detail. The initial deposit of $100,000 in cash at Bank-a-mythica constitutes $100,000 in new reserves (see Table 2 on page 253). Applying a multiplier of $1/m = 1/0.20 = 5$ to this $100,000, we conclude that bank deposits will rise by $500,000—which is just what happens. But remember that the process started when the eccentric widower took $100,000 in cash and deposited it in his bank account. Thus the public's holdings of *money*—which includes both checking deposits and cash—increase by only $400,000 in this case: There is $500,000 more in deposits, but $100,000 less in cash.

The Process in Reverse: Multiple Contractions of the Money Supply

Let us now briefly consider how this deposit-creation mechanism operates in reverse—as a system of deposit *destruction*. In particular, suppose that our eccentric widower returned to Bank-a-mythica to withdraw $100,000 from his checking account and return it to his mattress, where it rightfully belongs. Bank-a-mythica's *required* reserves would fall by $20,000 as a result of this transaction (20 percent of $100,000), but its *actual* reserves would fall by $100,000. The bank would be $80,000 short, as indicated in Table 7(a).

TABLE 7

Changes in the Balance Sheet of Bank-a-mythica

(a)				(b)		
Assets		**Liabilities**		**Assets**		**Liabilities**
Reserves	−$100,000	Checking deposits	−$100,000	Reserves	+$80,000	No Change
				Loans outstanding	−$80,000	
Addendum: Changes in Reserves				**Addendum: Changes in Reserves**		
Actual reserves	−$100,000			Actual reserves	+$80,000	
Required reserves	−$20,000			Required reserves	No Change	
Excess reserves	**−$80,000**			Excess reserves	**+$80,000**	

How would the bank react to this discrepancy? As some of its outstanding loans are routinely paid off, it will cease granting new ones until it has accumulated the necessary $80,000 in required reserves. The data for Bank-a-mythica's contraction are shown in Table 7(b), assuming that borrowers pay off their loans in cash.[5]

But where did the borrowers get this money? Probably by making withdrawals from other banks. In this case, assume that the funds came from First National Bank, which loses $80,000 in deposits and $80,000 in reserves. It finds itself short some $64,000 in reserves, as shown in Table 8(a), and therefore must reduce its loan commitments by $64,000, as in Table 8(b). This reaction, of course, causes some other bank to suffer a loss of reserves and deposits of $64,000, and the whole process repeats just as it did in the case of deposit expansion.

TABLE 8

Changes in the Balance Sheet of First National Bank

(a)				(b)		
Assets		**Liabilities**		**Assets**		**Liabilities**
Reserves	−$80,000	Checking deposits	−$80,000	Reserves	+$64,000	No Change
				Loans outstanding	−$64,000	
Addendum: Changes in Reserves				**Addendum: Changes in Reserves**		
Actual reserves	−$80,000			Actual reserves	+$64,000	
Required reserves	−$16,000			Required reserves	No Change	
Excess reserves	**−$64,000**			Excess reserves	**+$64,000**	

After the entire banking system had become involved, the picture would be just as shown in Figure 3, except that all the numbers would have *minus signs* in front of them. Deposits would shrink by $500,000, loans would fall by $400,000, bank reserves would be reduced by $100,000, and the M1 money supply would fall by $400,000. As suggested by

---

[5] In reality, the borrowers would probably pay with checks drawn on other banks. Bank-a-mythica would then cash these checks to acquire the reserves.

our money multiplier formula with $m = 0.20$, the decline in the bank deposit component of the money supply is $1/0.20 = 5$ times as large as the decline in reserves.

One of the authors of this book was a student in Cambridge, Massachusetts, during the height of the radical student movement of the late 1960s. One day a pamphlet appeared urging citizens to withdraw all funds from their checking accounts on a prescribed date, hold them in cash for a week, and then redeposit them. This act, the circular argued, would wreak havoc upon the capitalist system. Obviously, some of these radicals were well schooled in modern money mechanics, for the argument was basically correct. The tremendous multiple contraction of the banking system and subsequent multiple expansion that a successful campaign of this sort could have caused might have seriously disrupted the local financial system. But history records that the appeal met with little success. Apparently, checking account withdrawals are not the stuff of which revolutions are made.

WHY THE MONEY-CREATION FORMULA IS OVERSIMPLIFIED

So far, our discussion of the process of money creation has seemed rather mechanical. If everything proceeds according to formula, each $1 in new reserves injected into the banking system leads to a $1/m$ increase in new deposits. But, in reality, things are not this simple. Just as in the case of the expenditure multiplier, the oversimplified money multiplier is accurate only under very particular circumstances. These circumstances require that

1. Every recipient of cash must redeposit the cash into another bank rather than hold it.
2. Every bank must hold reserves no larger than the legal minimum.

The "chain" diagram in Figure 3 on page 255 can teach us what happens if either of these assumptions is violated.

Suppose first that the business firms and individuals who receive bank loans decide to redeposit only a fraction of the proceeds into their bank accounts, holding the rest in cash. Then, for example, the first $80,000 loan would lead to a deposit of less than $80,000—and similarly down the chain. The whole chain of deposit creation would therefore be reduced. Thus:

If individuals and business firms decide to hold more cash, the multiple expansion of bank deposits will be curtailed because fewer dollars of cash will be available for use as reserves to support checking deposits. Consequently, the money supply will be smaller.

The basic idea here is simple. Each $1 of cash held *inside* a bank can support several dollars (specifically, $1/m$) of money. But each $1 of cash held *outside* the banking system is exactly $1 of money; it supports no deposits. Hence, any time cash moves from inside the banking system into the hands of a household or a business, the money supply will decline. And any time cash enters the banking system, the money supply will rise.

Next, suppose bank managers become more conservative or that the outlook for loan repayments worsens because of a recession. In such an environment, banks might decide to keep more reserves than the legal requirement and lend out less than the amounts assumed in Figure 3. If this happens, banks further down the chain receive smaller deposits and, once again, the chain of deposit creation is curtailed. Thus:

If banks wish to keep excess reserves, the multiple expansion of bank deposits will be limited. A given amount of cash will support a smaller supply of money than would be the case if banks held no excess reserves.

The latter problem afflicted Japan for many years in the 1990s and continuing into this decade. Because they had so many bad loans on their books, Japanese bankers became supercautious about lending money to any but their most creditworthy borrowers. So even though bank reserves soared, the money supply did not. Something similar happened in the U.S. in 2007 and 2008, when banks got jittery.

THE NEED FOR MONETARY POLICY

If we pursue these two points a bit farther, we will see why the government must regulate the money supply in an effort to maintain economic stability. We have just suggested that banks prefer to keep excess reserves when they do not foresee profitable and secure opportunities to make loans. This scenario is most likely to arise when business conditions are depressed. At such times, the propensity of banks to hold excess reserves can turn the deposit-creation process into one of deposit destruction, as happened recently in the U.S. and elsewhere. In addition, if depositors become nervous, they may decide to hold on to more cash. Thus:

> **During a recession, profit-oriented banks would be prone to reduce the money supply by increasing their excess reserves and declining to lend to less creditworthy applicants—if the government did not intervene. As we will learn in subsequent chapters, the money supply is an important influence on aggregate demand, so such a contraction of the money supply would aggravate the recession.**

This is precisely what happened—with a vengeance—during the Great Depression of the 1930s. Although total bank reserves grew, the money supply contracted violently because banks preferred to hold excess reserves rather than make loans that might not be repaid. And something similar has been happening in Japan for years: The supply of reserves has expanded much more rapidly than the money supply because nervous bankers have been holding on to their excess reserves.

By contrast, banks want to squeeze the maximum money supply possible out of any given amount of cash reserves by keeping their reserves at the bare minimum when the demand for bank loans is buoyant, profits are high, and secure investment opportunities abound. This reduced incentive to hold excess reserves in prosperous times means that

> **During an economic boom, profit-oriented banks will likely make the money supply expand, adding undesirable momentum to the booming economy and paving the way for inflation. The authorities must intervene to prevent this rapid money growth.**

Regulation of the money supply, then, is necessary because profit-oriented bankers might otherwise provide the economy with a money supply that dances to and amplifies the tune of the business cycle. Precisely how the authorities control the money supply is the subject of the next chapter.

| SUMMARY |

1. It is more efficient to exchange goods and services by using **money** as a medium of exchange than by **bartering** them directly.

2. In addition to being the **medium of exchange,** whatever serves as money is likely to become the standard **unit of account** and a popular **store of value.**

3. Throughout history, all sorts of items have served as money. **Commodity money** gave way to full-bodied paper money (certificates backed 100 percent by some commodity, such as gold), which in turn gave way to partially backed paper money. Nowadays, our paper money has no commodity backing whatsoever; it is pure **fiat money.**

4. One popular definition of the U.S. money supply is **M1,** which includes coins, paper money, and several types of checking deposits. Most economists prefer the **M2** definition, which adds to M1 other types of checkable accounts and most savings deposits. Much of M2 is held outside of banks by investment houses, credit unions, and other financial institutions.

5. Under our modern system of fractional reserve banking, banks keep cash reserves equal to only a fraction of their total deposit **liabilities.** This practice is the key to their profitability, because the remaining funds can be loaned out at interest. But it also leaves banks potentially vulnerable to **runs.**

6. Because of this vulnerability, bank managers are generally conservative in their investment strategies. They also keep a prudent level of reserves. Even so, the government keeps a watchful eye over banking practices.

7. Before 1933, bank failures were common in the United States. They declined sharply when **deposit insurance** was instituted.

8. Because it holds only fractional reserves, the banking system as a whole can create several dollars of deposits for each dollar of reserves it receives. Under

certain assumptions, the ratio of new bank deposits to new reserves will be $1/m$, where m is the **required reserve** ratio.

9. The same process works in reverse, as a system of money destruction, when cash is withdrawn from the banking system.

10. Because banks and individuals may want to hold more cash when the economy is shaky, the money supply would probably contract under such circumstances if the government did not intervene. Similarly, the money supply would probably expand rapidly in boom times if it were unregulated.

| KEY TERMS |

Run on a bank   242

Barter   243

Money   244

Medium of exchange   244

Unit of account   244

Store of value   244

Commodity money   245

Fiat money   246

M1   247

M2   247

Near moneys   247

Liquidity   247

Fractional reserve banking   248

Deposit insurance   250

Moral hazard   250

Federal Deposit Insurance Corporation (FDIC)   250

Required reserves   251

Asset   251

Liability   251

Balance sheet   252

Net worth   252

Deposit creation   252

Excess reserves   252

Money multiplier   256

| TEST YOURSELF |

1. Suppose banks keep no excess reserves and no individuals or firms hold on to cash. If someone suddenly discovers $12 million in buried treasure and deposits it in a bank, explain what will happen to the money supply if the required reserve ratio is 10 percent.

2. How would your answer to Test Yourself Question 1 differ if the reserve ratio were 25 percent? If the reserve ratio were 100 percent?

3. Use tables such as Tables 2 and 3 to illustrate what happens to bank balance sheets when each of the following transactions occurs:

   a. You withdraw $100 from your checking account to buy concert tickets.

   b. Sam finds a $100 bill on the sidewalk and deposits it into his checking account.

   c. Mary Q. Contrary withdraws $500 in cash from her account at Hometown Bank, carries it to the city, and deposits it into her account at Big City Bank.

4. For each of the transactions listed in Test Yourself Question 3, what will be the ultimate effect on the money supply if the required reserve ratio is one-eighth (12.5 percent)? Assume that the oversimplified money multiplier formula applies.

| DISCUSSION QUESTIONS |

1. If ours were a barter economy, how would you pay your tuition bill? What if your college did not want the goods or services you offered in payment?

2. How is "money" defined, both conceptually and in practice? Does the U.S. money supply consist of commodity money, full-bodied paper money, or fiat money?

3. What is fractional reserve banking, and why is it the key to bank profits? (*Hint:* What opportunities to make profits would banks lose if reserve requirements were 100 percent?) Why does fractional reserve banking give bankers discretion over how large the money supply will be? Why does it make banks potentially vulnerable to runs?

4. During the 1980s and early 1990s, a rash of bank failures occurred in the United States. Explain why these failures did not lead to runs on banks.

5. Each year during Christmas shopping season, consumers and stores increase their holdings of cash. Explain how this development could lead to a multiple contraction of the money supply. (As a matter of fact, the authorities prevent this contraction from occurring by methods explained in the next chapter.)

6. Excess reserves make a bank less vulnerable to runs. Why, then, don't bankers like to hold excess reserves? What circumstances might persuade them that it would be advisable to hold excess reserves?

7. If the government takes over a failed bank with liabilities (mostly deposits) of $2 billion, pays off the depositors, and sells the assets for $1.5 billion, where does the missing $500 million come from? Why?

MANAGING AGGREGATE DEMAND: MONETARY POLICY

Victorians heard with grave attention that the Bank Rate had been raised. They did not know what it meant. But they knew that it was an act of extreme wisdom.

JOHN KENNETH GALBRAITH

Armed with our understanding of the rudiments of banking, we are now ready to bring money and interest rates into our model of income determination and the price level. Up to now, we have taken investment (*I*) to be a fixed number. But this is a poor assumption. Not only is investment highly variable but it also depends on interest rates—which are, in turn, heavily influenced by **monetary policy**. The main task of this chapter is to explain how monetary policy affects interest rates, investment, and aggregate demand. By the end of the chapter, we will have constructed a complete macroeconomic model, which we will use in subsequent chapters to investigate a variety of important policy issues.

Monetary policy refers to actions that the Federal Reserve System takes to change interest rates and the money supply. It is aimed at affecting the economy.

CONTENTS

The financial crisis of 2007–2008 had been simmering below the surface for a while. But when it burst into the open in August 2007, every eye in the financial world, it seemed, turned to Ben Bernanke, who had been installed as chairman of the Federal Reserve Board just 18 months earlier. Why? Because many observers see the Federal Reserve chairman as the most powerful person in the economic world.

Bernanke is a brilliant but unassuming economist who taught for many years at Princeton University. But now when he speaks, people in financial markets around the world dote on his remarks with an intensity that was once reserved for utterances from behind the Kremlin walls. The reason for all the attention is that, in the view of many economists, the Federal Reserve's decisions on interest rates are the single most important influence on aggregate demand—and hence on economic growth, unemployment, and inflation. And the financial crisis made people worried about the health of the economy.

Bernanke heads America's central bank, the *Federal Reserve System*. The "Fed," as it is called, is a bank—but a very special kind of bank. Its customers are banks rather than individuals, and it performs some of the same services for them as your bank performs for you. Although it makes enormous profits, profit is not its goal. Instead, the Fed tries to manage interest rates according to what it perceives to be the national interest. This chapter will teach you how the Fed does its job and why its decisions affect our economy so profoundly. In brief, it will teach you why people listen so intently whenever Ben Bernanke speaks.

" SOMEONE STARTED A RUMOR THAT BEN BERNANKE HAS A COLD."

MONEY AND INCOME: THE IMPORTANT DIFFERENCE

But first we must get some terminology straight. The words money and income are used almost interchangeably in common parlance. Here, however, we must be more precise.

Money is a snapshot concept. It answers questions such as "How much money do you have right now?" or "How much money did you have at 3:32 P.M. on Friday, November 5?" To answer these questions, you would add up the cash you are (or were) carrying and whatever checkable balances you have (or had), and answer something like: "I have $126.33," or "On Friday, November 5, at 3:32 P.M., I had $31.43."

Income, by contrast, is more like a motion picture; it comes to you over a period of time. If you are asked, "What is your income?", you must respond by saying "$1,000 *per week*," or "$4,000 *per month*," or "$50,000 *per year*," or something like that. Notice that a unit of time is attached to each of these responses. If you just answer, "My income is $45,000," without indicating whether it is per week, per month, or per year, no one will understand what you mean.

That the two concepts are very different is easy to see. A typical American family has an *income* of about $45,000 per year, but its *money* holdings at any point in time (using the M1 definition) may be less than $2,000. Similarly, at the national level, nominal GDP at the end of 2007 was around $14 trillion, while the money stock (M1) was under $1.4 trillion.

Although money and income are different, they are certainly related. This chapter focuses on that relationship. Specifically, we will look at how interest rates and the stock of *money* in existence at any moment of time influences the rate at which people earn *income*—that is, how *monetary policy* affects GDP.

AMERICA'S CENTRAL BANK: THE FEDERAL RESERVE SYSTEM

When Congress established *the Federal Reserve System* in 1914, the United States joined the company of most other advanced industrial nations. Until then, the United States, distrustful of centralized economic power, was almost the only important nation without a **central bank.** The Bank of England, for example, dates back to 1694.

A **central bank** is a bank for banks. The United States' central bank is the *Federal Reserve System.*

Origins and Structure

It was painful experiences with economic reality, not the power of economic logic, that provided the impetus to establish a central bank for the United States. Four severe banking panics between 1873 and 1907, in which many banks failed, convinced legislators and bankers alike that a central bank that would regulate credit conditions was not a luxury but a necessity. The 1907 crisis led Congress to study the shortcomings of the banking system and, eventually, to establish the Federal Reserve System.

Although the basic ideas of central banking came from Europe, the United States made some changes when it imported the idea, making the Federal Reserve System a uniquely American institution.[1] Because of the vastness of our country, the extraordinarily large number of commercial banks, and our tradition of shared state-federal responsibilities, Congress decided that the United States should have not one central bank but twelve.

Technically, each Federal Reserve Bank is a corporation; its stockholders are its member banks. But your bank, if it is a member of the system, does not enjoy the privileges normally accorded to stockholders: It receives only a token share of the Federal Reserve's immense profits (the bulk is turned over to the U.S. Treasury), and it has virtually no say in corporate decisions. In fact, the private banks are more like customers of the Fed than owners.

Who, then, controls the Fed? Most of the power resides in the seven-member Board of Governors of the Federal Reserve System in Washington, and especially in its chairman. The governors are appointed by the President of the United States, with the advice and consent of the Senate, for fourteen-year terms. The president also designates one of the members to serve a four-year term as chairman of the board and thus to be the most powerful central banker in the world.

The Federal Reserve is independent of the rest of the government. As long as it stays within the authority granted to it by Congress, it alone has responsibility for determining the nation's monetary policy. The power of appointment, however, gives the president some long-run influence over Federal Reserve policy. For example, it was President George W. Bush in 2006 who selected Ben Bernanke, a former adviser, to be the Fed's next chairman.

Closely allied with the Board of Governors is the powerful Federal Open Market Committee (FOMC), which meets eight times a year in Washington. For reasons to be explained shortly, FOMC decisions largely determine short-term interest rates and the size of the U.S. money supply. This twelve-member committee consists of the seven governors of the Federal Reserve System, the president of the Federal Reserve Bank of New York, and, on a rotating basis, four of the other eleven district bank presidents.[2]

"I'm sorry, sir, but I don't believe you know us well enough to call us the Fed."

---

[1] Ironically, when the European Central Bank was established in 1999, its structure was patterned on that of the Federal Reserve.

[2] Alan Blinder was the vice chairman of the Federal Reserve Board, and thus a member of the Federal Open Market Committee, from 1994 to 1996.

A Meeting of the Federal Open Market Committee

Meetings of the Federal Open Market Committee are serious and formal affairs. All 19 members—7 governors and 12 reserve bank presidents—sit around a mammoth table in the Fed's cavernous but austere board room. A limited number of top Fed staffers join them at and around the table, for access to FOMC meetings is strictly controlled.

At precisely 9 A.M.—for punctuality is a high virtue at the Fed—the doors are closed and the chairman calls the meeting to order. No press is allowed and, unlike most important Washington meetings, nothing said there will leak. Secrecy is another high virtue at the Fed.

After hearing a few routine staff reports, the chairman calls on each of the members in turn to give their views of the current economic situation. District bank presidents offer insights into their local economies, and all members comment on the outlook for the national economy. Committee members also offer their views on what changes in monetary policy, if any, are appropriate. Disagreements are raised, but voices are not, for politeness is another virtue. Strikingly, in this most political of cities, politics is almost never mentioned.

Once he has heard from all the others, the chairman summarizes the discussion, offers his own views of the economic situation and of the policy options, and recommends a course of action. Most members normally agree with the chairman, though some note differences of opinion. Then the chairman asks the secretary to call the roll. Only the 12 voting members answer, saying yes or no. Negative votes are rare, for the FOMC tries to operate by consensus and a dissent is considered a loud objection.

The meeting adjourns, and at precisely 2:15 P.M. a Fed spokesman announces the decision to the public. Within minutes, financial markets around the world react.

SOURCE: Courtesy of the Federal Reserve Board

Central Bank Independence

Central bank independence refers to the central bank's ability to make decisions without political interference.

For decades a debate raged, both in the United States and in other countries, over the pros and cons of **central bank independence.**

Proponents of central bank independence argued that it enables the central bank to take the long view and to make monetary policy decisions on objective, technical criteria—thus keeping monetary policy out of the "political thicket." Without this independence, they argued, politicians with short time horizons might try to force the central bank to expand the money supply too rapidly, especially before elections, thereby contributing to chronic inflation and undermining faith in the country's financial system. They pointed to historical evidence showing that countries with more independent central banks have, on average, experienced lower inflation.

Opponents of this view countered that there is something profoundly undemocratic about letting a group of unelected bankers and economists make decisions that affect every citizen's well-being. Monetary policy, they argued, should be formulated by the elected representatives of the people, just as fiscal policy is.

The high inflation of the 1970s and early 1980s helped resolve this issue by convincing many governments around the world that an independent central bank was essential to controlling inflation. Thus, one country after another has made its central bank independent over the past 20 to 25 years. For example, the Maastricht Treaty (1992), which committed members of the European Union to both low inflation and a single currency (the euro), required each member state to make its central bank independent. All did so, even though several have still not joined the monetary union. Japan also decided to make its central bank independent in 1998. In Latin America, several formerly high-inflation countries like Brazil and Mexico found that giving their central banks more independence helped them control inflation. And some of the formerly socialist countries of Europe, finding themselves saddled with high inflation and "unsound" currencies, made their central banks more independent for similar reasons. Thus, for practical purposes, the debate over central bank independence is now all but over.

The new debate is over how to hold such independent and powerful institutions *accountable* to the political authorities and to the broad public. For example, most central banks have now abandoned their former traditions of secrecy and have become far more open to public scrutiny. Some, the "inflation targeters," even announce specific numerical targets for inflation, thereby making it easy for outside observers to judge the central bank's success or failure. The Federal Reserve does not do this explicitly, but it reveals enough information in its long-run forecast that people pretty much know its inflation target.

IMPLEMENTING MONETARY POLICY: OPEN-MARKET OPERATIONS

When it wants to change interest rates, the Fed normally relies on **open-market operations,** which is the tool it relied upon when it lowered interest rates in response to the financial crisis of 2007–2008. Open-market operations either give banks more reserves or take reserves away from them, thereby triggering the sort of multiple expansion or contraction of the money supply described in the previous chapter.

Open-market operations refer to the Fed's purchase or sale of government securities through transactions in the open market.

How does this process work? If the Federal Open Market Committee decides to lower interest rates, it can bring them down by providing banks with more reserves. Specifically, the Federal Reserve System would normally *purchase* a particular kind of short-term U.S. government security called a *Treasury bill* from any individual or bank that wished to sell them, paying with newly created bank reserves. To see how this open-market operation affects interest rates, we must understand how *the market for bank reserves,* which is depicted in Figure 1, works.

The Market for Bank Reserves

The main sources of supply and demand in the market on which bank reserves are traded are straightforward. On the supply side, the Fed decides how many dollars of reserves to provide. Thus the label on the supply curve in Figure 1 indicates that *the position of the supply curve depends on Federal Reserve policy.* The Fed's decision on the quantity of bank reserves is the essence of monetary policy, and we are about to consider how the Fed makes that decision.

On the demand side of the market, the main reason why banks hold reserves is something we learned in the previous chapter: Government regulations require them to do so. In Chapter 12, we used the symbol m to denote the required reserve ratio (which is 0.1 in the United States). So if the volume of transaction deposits is D, the demand for *required reserves* is simply $m \times D$. The demand for reserves thus reflects the demand for transactions deposits in banks.

FIGURE 1

The Market for Bank Reserves

Quantity of Bank Reserves

The demand for bank deposits depends on many factors, but the principal determinant is the dollar value of transactions. After all, people and businesses hold bank deposits in order to conduct transactions. Real GDP (Y) is typically used as a convenient indicator of the *number* of transactions, and the price level (P) is a natural measure of the *average price per transaction.* So the volume of bank deposits, D, *and therefore the demand for bank reserves,* *depends on both Y and P*—as indicated by the label on the demand curve in Figure 1.

The quick brown fox.

The **federal funds rate** is the interest rates that banks pay and receive when they borrow reserves from one another.

There is more to the story, however, for we have not yet explained why the the demand curve *DD* slopes down and the supply curve *SS* slopes up. The interest rate measured along the vertical axis of Figure 1 is called the **federal funds rate.** It is the rate that applies when banks borrow and lend reserves to one another. When you hear on the evening news that "the Federal Reserve today cut interest rates by ¼ of a point today," it is the federal funds rate that the reporter is talking about.

Now where does this borrowing and lending come from? As we mentioned in the previous chapter, banks sometimes find themselves with either insufficient or excess reserves. Neither situation leaves bankers happy. Keeping actual reserves below the required level is not allowed. Holding reserves in excess of requirements is perfectly legal, but since reserves pay no interest, a bank can put excess reserves to better use by lending them out rather than keeping them idle. So banks have developed an active market in which those with excess reserves lend them to those with reserve deficiencies. These bank-to-bank loans provide an additional source of *both* supply *and* demand—and one that (unlike required reserves) is interest sensitive.

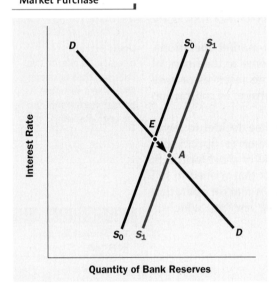

FIGURE 2

The Effects of an Open-Market Purchase

Any bank that wants to borrow reserves must pay the federal funds rate for the privilege. Naturally, as the funds rate rises, borrowing looks more expensive and so fewer reserves are demanded. In a word, the demand curve for reserves (*DD*) slopes downward. Similarly, the supply curve for reserves (*SS*) slopes upward because lending reserves becomes more attractive as the federal funds rate rises.

The equilibrium federal funds rate is established, as usual, at point *E* in Figure 1—where the demand and supply curves cross. Now suppose the Federal Reserve wants to push the federal funds rate *down*. It can provide additional reserves to the market by purchasing Treasury bills (often abbreviated as *T-bills*) from banks.[3] This *open-market purchase* would shift the supply curve of bank reserves outward, from S_0S_0 to S_1S_1, in Figure 2. Equilibrium would therefore shift from point *E* to point *A*, which, as the diagram shows, implies a lower interest rate and more bank reserves. That is precisely what the Fed does when it wants to reduce interest rates.[4]

The Mechanics of an Open-Market Operation

The bookkeeping behind such an open-market purchase is illustrated by Table 1, which imagines that the Fed purchases $100 million worth of T-bills from commercial banks. When the Fed buys the securities, the ownership of the T-bills shifts from the banks to the Fed—as indicated by the black arrows in Table 1. Next, *the Fed makes payment by giving the banks $100 million in new reserves,* that is, by adding $100 million to the bookkeeping entries that represent the banks' accounts at the Fed—called "bank reserves" in the table. These reserves, shown in blue in the table, are liabilities of the Fed and assets of the banks.

You may be wondering where the Fed gets the money to pay for the securities. It could pay in cash, but it normally does not. Instead, it manufactures the funds out of thin air or, more literally, by punching a keyboard. Specifically, the Fed pays the banks by adding the appropriate sums to the reserve accounts that the banks maintain at the Fed. Balances held in these accounts constitute bank reserves, just like cash in bank vaults. Although this process of adding to bookkeeping entries at the Federal Reserve is sometimes referred to as "printing money," the Fed does not literally run any printing presses. Instead, it simply

---

[3] It is not important that banks be the buyers. Test Yourself Question 3 at the end of the chapter shows that the effect on bank reserves and the money supply is the same if bank customers purchase the securities.

[4] There are many interest rates in the economy, but they all tend to move up and down together. So, in a first course in economics, we need not distinguish one interest rate from another.

TABLE 1

Effects of an Open-Market Purchase of Securities on the Balance Sheets of Banks and the Fed

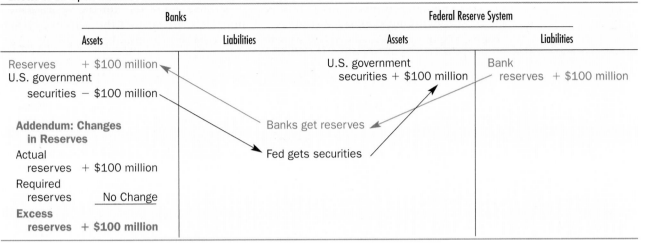

trades its IOUs for an existing asset (a T-bill). But unlike other IOUs, the Fed's IOUs constitute bank reserves and thus can support a multiple expansion of the money supply just as cash does. Let's see how this works.

It is clear from Table 1 that bank deposits have not increased at all—yet. So *required* reserves are unchanged by the open-market operation. But *actual* reserves are increased by $100 million. So, if the banks held only their required reserves initially, they now have $100 million in *excess reserves*. As banks rid themselves of these excess reserves by making more loans, a multiple expansion of the banking system is set in motion—as described in the previous chapter. It is not difficult for the Fed to estimate the ultimate increase in the money supply that will result from its actions. As we learned in the previous chapter, each dollar of newly created bank reserves can support up to $1/m$ dollars of checking deposits, if m is the required reserve ratio. In the example in the last chapter, $m = 0.20$; hence, $100 million in new reserves would support $100 million $\div$ 0.2 = $500 million in new money.

But *estimating* the ultimate monetary expansion is a far cry from *knowing it* with certainty. We know from the previous chapter that the oversimplified money multiplier formula is predicated on two assumptions: that people will want to hold no more cash, and that banks will want to hold no more excess reserves, as the monetary expansion proceeds. In practice, these assumptions are unlikely to be literally true. So to predict the eventual effect of its action on the money supply, the Fed must *estimate* both the amount that firms and individuals will add to their currency holdings and the amount that banks will add to their excess reserves. Neither of these can be estimated with utter precision. In summary:

> When the Federal Reserve wants lower interest rates, it purchases U.S. government securities in the open market. It pays for these securities by creating new bank reserves, which lead to a multiple expansion of the money supply. Because of fluctuations in people's desires to hold cash and banks' desires to hold excess reserves, the Fed cannot predict the consequences of these actions for the money supply with perfect accuracy. But the Fed can always put the federal funds rate where it wants by buying just the right volume of securities.[5]

For this reason, in this and subsequent chapters, we will simply proceed as if the Fed controls the federal funds rate directly.

---

[5] Why? Because the federal funds rate is observable in the market every minute and hence need not be estimated. If interest rates do not fall as much as the Fed wants, it can simply purchase more securities. If interest rates fall too much, the Fed can purchase less. And these adjustments can be made very quickly.

The procedures followed when the FOMC wants to *raise* interest rates are just the opposite of those we have just explained. In brief, it *sells* government securities in the open market. This takes reserves *away* from banks, because banks pay for the securities by drawing down their deposits at the Fed. A multiple *contraction* of the banking system ensues. The principles are exactly the same—and so are the uncertainties.

Open-Market Operations, Bond Prices, and Interest Rates

The *expansionary monetary policy* action we have been using as an example began when the Fed bought more Treasury bills. When it goes into the open market to purchase more of these bills, the Federal Reserve naturally drives up their prices. This process is illustrated by Figure 3, which shows an *inward shift* of the (vertical) supply curve of T-bills *available to private investors*—from S_0S_0 to S_1S_1—indicating that the Fed's action has taken some of the bills off the private market. With an unchanged (private) demand curve, *DD,* the price of T-bills rises from P_0 to P_1 as equilibrium in the market shifts from point *A* to point *B*.

Rising prices for Treasury bills—or for any other type of bond—translate directly into falling interest rates. Why? The reason is simple arithmetic. Bonds pay a fixed number of dollars of interest per year. For concreteness, consider a bond that pays $60 each year. If the bond sells for $1,000, bondholders earn a 6 percent return on their investment (the $60 interest payment is 6 percent of $1,000). We therefore say that *the interest rate on the bond is 6 percent.* Now suppose that the price of the bond rises to $1,200. The annual interest payment is still $60, so bondholders now earn just 5 percent on their money ($60 is 5 percent of $1,200*). The effective interest rate on the bond has fallen to 5 percent.* This relationship between bond prices and interest rates is completely general:

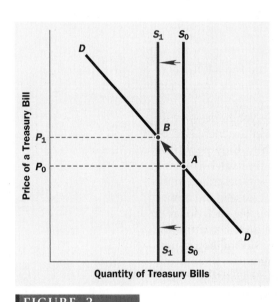

> When bond prices rise, interest rates fall because the purchaser of a bond spends more money than before to earn a given number of dollars of interest per year. Similarly, when bond prices fall, interest rates rise.

In fact, the relationship amounts to nothing more than two ways of saying the same thing. Higher interest rates *mean* lower bond prices; lower interest rates *mean* higher bond prices.[6] Thus Figure 3 is another way to look at the fact that Federal Reserve open-market operations influence interest rates. Specifically:

> An open-market purchase of Treasury bills by the Fed not only raises the money supply but also drives up T-bill prices and pushes interest rates down. Conversely, an open-market sale of bills, which reduces the money supply, lowers T-bill prices and raises interest rates.

FIGURE 3

Open-Market Purchases and Treasury Bill Prices

OTHER METHODS OF MONETARY CONTROL

When the Federal Reserve System was first established, its founders did not intend it to pursue an active monetary policy to stabilize the economy. Indeed, the basic ideas of stabilization policy were unknown at the time. Instead, the Fed's founders viewed it as a means of preventing the supplies of money and credit from drying up during banking panics, as had happened so often in the pre-1914 period.

[6] For further discussion and examples, see Test Yourself Question 4 at the end of the chapter.

You Now Belong to a Distinctive Minority Group

When the financial panic hit in 2007, more and more investors became attracted to U.S. government bonds as a safe place to park funds. But an amazing number of investors do not understand even the elementary facts about bond investing—including the relationship between bond prices and interest rates.

The Wall Street Journal reported back in November 2001 that "One of the bond basics about which many investors are clueless, for instance, is the fundamental seesaw relationship between interest rates and bond prices. Only 31% of 750 investors participating in the American Century [a mutual fund company] telephone survey knew that when interest rates rise, bond prices generally fall."* Imagine how many fewer, then, could explain *why* this is so.

* Karen Damato, "Investors Love Their Bond Funds—Too Much?," *The Wall Street Journal*, November 9, 2001, p. C1.

SOURCE: © Sidney Harris, www.sciencecartoonsplus.com

"When interest rates go up, bond prices go down. When interest rates go down, bond prices go up. But please don't ask me why."

Lending to Banks

One of the principal ways in which Congress intended the Fed to provide such insurance against financial panics was to act as a "lender of last resort." When risky business prospects made commercial banks hesitant to extend new loans, or when banks were in trouble, the Fed would step in by lending money to the banks, thus inducing them to lend more to their customers. If that sounds familiar, it should, since it is exactly what the Fed and other central banks did beginning in the summer and fall of 2007, when the financial crisis made banks wary of lending. Mammoth amounts of central bank lending to commercial banks help keep the financial system functioning and eased the panic for a while. Later, in 2008, the Fed actually began a new program of lending to *securities firms*—something it had not done since the 1930s.

The mechanics of Federal Reserve lending are illustrated in Table 2. When the Fed makes a loan to a bank in need of reserves, that bank receives a credit in its deposit account at the Fed—$5 million in the example. That $5 million represents newly created reserves. So it expands the supply of reserves just as was shown in Figure 2. Furthermore, because bank deposits, and hence required reserves, have not yet increased, this addition to the supply of bank reserves creates *excess reserves*, which should lead to an expansion of the money supply.

TABLE 2

Balance Sheet Changes for Borrowing from the Fed

Banks			Federal Reserve System	
Assets	Liabilities		Assets	Liabilities
Reserves　+ $5 million	Loan from Fed　+ $5 million		Loan to bank　+ $5 million	Bank reserves　+ $5 million
Addendum: Changes in Reserves		Bank borrows $5 million and		
Actual reserves　+ $5 million		the proceeds are credited to its reserve account		
Required reserves　No Change				
Excess reserves　**+ $5 million**				

The **discount rate** is the interest rate the Fed charges on loans that it makes to banks.

Federal Reserve officials can try to influence the amount banks borrow by manipulating the *rate of interest charged on these loans,* which is known as the **discount rate.** If the Fed wants banks to have more reserves, it can reduce the interest rate that it charges on loans, thereby tempting banks to borrow more—which is exactly what it did repeatedly in 2007 and 2008. Alternatively, it can soak up reserves by raising its rate and persuading the banks to reduce their borrowings.

But when it changes its discount rate, the Fed cannot know for sure how banks will react. Sometimes they may respond vigorously to a cut in the rate, borrowing a great deal from the Fed and lending a correspondingly large amount to their customers. At other times they may essentially ignore the change in the discount rate. In fact, when it first cut the discount rate in 2007, the Fed was disappointed in the banks' meager response because it wanted to add reserves to the system. This episode illustrates a general point: that the link between the discount rate and the volume of bank reserves may be a loose one.

Some foreign central banks use their versions of the discount rate *actively* as the centerpiece of monetary policy. But in the United States, the Fed normally lends infrequently and in very small amounts. It relies instead on open-market operations to conduct monetary policy. The Fed typically adjusts its discount rate *passively,* to keep it in line with market interest rates. But in a crisis, the Fed does use the discount window to supplement and support open-market operations. It did so massively in 2007 and 2008.

Changing Reserve Requirements

In principle, the Federal Reserve has a third way to conduct monetary policy: varying the minimum required reserve ratio. To see how this works, imagine that banks hold reserves that just match their required minimums. In other words, excess reserves are zero. If the Fed decides that lower interest rates are warranted, it can reduce the required reserve ratio, thereby transforming some previously *required* reserves into *excess* reserves. No new reserves are created directly by this action. But we know from the previous chapter that such a change will set in motion a multiple expansion of the banking system. Looked at in terms of the market for bank reserves (Figure 1 on page 265), a reduction in reserve requirements shifts the demand curve *inward* (because banks no longer need as many reserves), thereby lowering interest rates. Similarly, raising the required reserve ratio will raise interest rates and set off a multiple contraction of the banking system.

In point of fact, however, the Fed has not used the reserve ratio as a weapon of monetary control for years. Current law and regulations provide for required reserves equal to 10 percent of transaction deposits—a figure that has not changed since 1992.

HOW MONETARY POLICY WORKS

Remembering that monetary policy actions by the Fed are almost always open-market operations, the two panels of Figure 4 illustrate the effects of *expansionary monetary policy* (an open-market purchase) and *contractionary monetary policy* (an open-market sale). Panel (a) looks just like Figure 2 on page 266. So expansionary monetary policy actions lower interest rates and contractionary monetary policy actions raise interest rates. But then what happens?

To find out, let's go back to the analysis of earlier chapters, where we learned that aggregate demand is the sum of consumption spending (C), investment spending (I), government purchases of goods and services (G), and net exports ($X - IM$). We know that *fiscal policy* controls G directly and influences both C and I through the tax laws. We now want to understand how *monetary policy* affects total spending.

Most economists agree that, of the four components of aggregate demand, investment and net exports are the most sensitive to monetary policy. We will study the effects of monetary and fiscal policy on net exports in Chapter 19, after we have learned about international exchange rates. For now, we will assume that net exports are *fixed* and focus on monetary policy's influence on investment.

Investment and Interest Rates

Given recent events in the housing market, it is important to remember that the *I* in $C + I + G + (X - IM)$ includes both *business investment* in new factories and machinery and *investment in housing*. Because the interest cost of a home mortgage is the major component of the total cost of owning a house, fewer families will want to purchase new homes as interest rates rise. Thus, higher interest rates will reduce expenditures on housing. Business investment is also sensitive to interest rates, for reasons explained in earlier chapters.[7] Because the rate of interest that must be paid on borrowings is part of the cost of an investment, business executives will find investment prospects less attractive as interest rates rise. Therefore, they will spend less. We conclude that

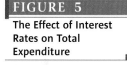

FIGURE 4

The Effects of Monetary Policy on Interest Rates

> **Higher interest rates lead to lower investment spending. But investment (*I*) is a component of total spending, $C + I + G + (X - IM)$. Therefore, when interest rates rise, total spending falls. In terms of the 45° line diagram of previous chapters, a higher interest rate leads to a lower expenditure schedule. Conversely, a lower interest rate leads to a higher expenditure schedule.**

Figure 5 depicts this situation graphically.

Monetary Policy and Total Expenditure

The effect of interest rates on spending provides the chief mechanism by which monetary policy affects the macroeconomy. We know from our analysis of the market for bank reserves (repeated in Figure 4) that monetary policy can move interest rates up or down. Let us, therefore, trace the impacts of monetary policy, starting there.

Suppose the Federal Reserve, worried that the economy might slip into a recession, increases the supply of bank reserves. It would normally do so by purchasing government securities in the open market, thereby shifting the supply schedule for reserves outward—as indicated by the shift from the black line S_0S_0 to the brick-colored line S_1S_1 in Figure 4(a). This is essentially what the Fed did in 2007 and 2008.

With the demand schedule for bank reserves, *DD*, temporarily fixed, such a shift in the supply curve has the effect that an increase in supply always has in a free market: It lowers the price, as Figure 4(a) shows. In this case, the relevant price is the rate of interest that must be paid for borrowing reserves, *r* (the federal funds rate). So *r* falls.

Next, for reasons we have just outlined, investment spending on housing and business equipment (*I*) rises in response to the lower interest rates. But,

FIGURE 5

The Effect of Interest Rates on Total Expenditure

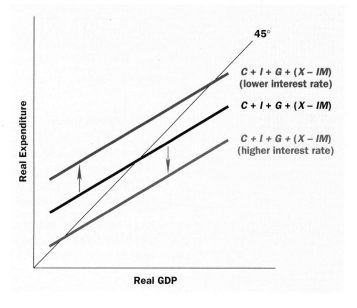

[7] See, for example, Chapter 7, pages 138–139.

as we learned in Chapter 9, such an autonomous rise in investment kicks off a multiplier chain of increases in output and employment.

This sequence of events summarizes the linkages from the supply of bank reserves to the level of aggregate demand. In brief, monetary policy works as follows:

> **Expansionary monetary policy leads to lower interest rates (r), and these lower interest rates encourage investment (I), which has multiplier effects on aggregate demand.**

This process operates equally well in reverse. By contracting bank reserves and the money supply, the central bank can push interest rates up, which is precisely what the Fed did between mid-2004 and August 2006. Higher rates will cause investment spending to fall and pull down aggregate demand via the multiplier mechanism.

This, in outline form, is how monetary policy influences the economy in the Keynesian model. Because the chain of causation is fairly long, the following schematic diagram may help clarify it:

In this causal chain, Link 1 indicates that the Federal Reserve's open-market operations affect both interest rates and the money supply. Link 2 stands for the effect of interest rates on investment. Link 3 simply notes that investment is one component of total spending. Link 4 is the multiplier, relating an autonomous change in investment to the ultimate change in aggregate demand. To see what economists must study if they are to estimate the effects of monetary policy, let us briefly review what we know about each of these four links.

Link 1 is the subject of this chapter. It was depicted in Figure 4(a), which shows how injections of bank reserves by the Federal Reserve push the interest rate down. Thus, the first thing an economist must know is how sensitive interest rates are to changes in the supply of bank reserves.

Link 2 translates the lower interest rate into higher investment spending. To estimate this effect in practice, economists must study the sensitivity of investment to interest rates—a topic we first took up in Chapter 7.

Link 3 instructs us to enter the rise in I as an autonomous upward shift of the $C + I + G + (X - IM)$ schedule in a 45° line diagram. Figure 6 carries out this next step. The expenditure schedule rises from $C + I_0 + G + (X - IM)$ to $C + I_1 + G + (X - IM)$.

Finally, Link 4 applies multiplier analysis to this vertical shift in the expenditure schedule to obtain the eventual increase in real GDP demanded. This change is shown in Figure 6 as a shift in equilibrium from E_0 to E_1, which raises real GDP by $500 billion in the example. Of course, the size of the multiplier itself must also be estimated. To summarize:

> **The effect of monetary policy on aggregate demand depends on the sensitivity of interest rates to open-market operations, on the responsiveness of investment spending to the rate of interest, and on the size of the basic expenditure multiplier.**

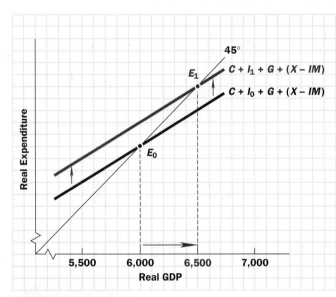

FIGURE 6

The Effect of Expansionary Monetary Policy on Total Expenditure

NOTE: Figures are in billions of dollars per year.

MONEY AND THE PRICE LEVEL IN THE KEYNESIAN MODEL

Our analysis up to now leaves one important question unanswered: What happens to the price level? To find the answer, we must recall that aggregate demand *and* aggregate supply *jointly* determine prices and output. Our analysis of monetary policy so far has shown us how expansionary monetary policy boosts total spending: It increases the *aggregate quantity demanded at any given price level.* But to learn what happens to the price level and to real output, we must consider *aggregate supply* as well.

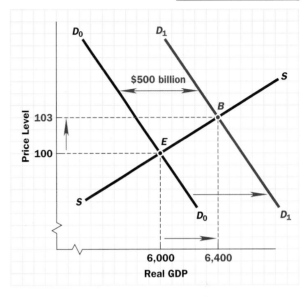

FIGURE 7

The Inflationary Effects of Expansionary Monetary Policy

Specifically, when considering shifts in aggregate demand caused by *fiscal policy* in Chapter 11, we noted that an upsurge in total spending normally induces firms to increase output somewhat *and* to raise prices somewhat. This is precisely what an upward-sloping aggregate supply curve shows. Whether the responses come more in the form of real output or more in the form of price depends on the slope of the aggregate supply curve (see Figure 7). Exactly the same analysis of output and price responses applies to monetary policy or, for that matter, to anything that raises the aggregate demand curve. So we conclude that

> **Expansionary monetary policy causes some inflation under normal circumstances. But exactly how much inflation it causes depends on the slope of the aggregate supply curve.**

The effect of expansionary monetary policy on the price level is shown graphically on an aggregate supply and demand diagram in Figure 7. In the example depicted in Figure 6, the Fed's actions lowered interest rates enough to increase aggregate demand (through the multiplier) by

NOTE: GDP figures are in billions of dollars per year.

$500 billion. We enter this increase as a $500 billion *horizontal* shift of the aggregate demand curve in Figure 7, from D_0D_0 to D_1D_1. The diagram shows that this expansionary monetary policy pushes the economy's equilibrium from point E to point B—the price level therefore rises from 100 to 103, or 3 percent. The diagram also shows that real GDP rises by only $400 billion, which is less than the $500 billion stimulus to aggregate demand. The reason, as we know from earlier chapters, is that rising prices stifle real aggregate demand.

By taking account of the effect of an increase in the money supply on the price level, we have completed our story about the role of monetary policy in the Keynesian model. We can thus expand our schematic diagram of monetary policy as follows:

The last link now recognizes that *both* output *and* prices normally are affected by changes in interest rates and the money supply.

Application: Why the Aggregate Demand Curve Slopes Downward[8]

This analysis of the effect of monetary policy on the price level puts us in a better position to understand why higher prices reduce aggregate quantity demanded—that is, why the aggregate demand curve slopes downward. In earlier chapters, we explained this phenomenon in two ways. First, we observed that rising prices reduce the purchasing power of certain assets held by consumers, especially money and government bonds, and that falling real wealth in turn retards consumption spending. Second, we noted that higher domestic prices depress exports and stimulate imports.

There is nothing wrong with this analysis; it is just incomplete. Higher prices have another important effect on aggregate demand, through a channel that we are now in a position to understand.

---

[8] This section contains somewhat more difficult material, which can be skipped in shorter courses.

FIGURE 8

The Effect of a Higher
Price Level on the
Market for Bank
Reserves

Bank deposits are demanded primarily to conduct transactions. As we noted earlier in this chapter, an increase in the *average money cost* of each transaction—that is, a rise in the price level—will increase the quantity of deposits demanded, and hence increase the demand for bank reserves. Thus, when spending rises for any reason, the price level will also rise, and more reserves will therefore be demanded at any given interest rate—that is, the demand curve for bank reserves will shift outward to the right, as shown in Figure 8.

If the Fed does not increase the *supply* of reserves, this outward shift of the demand curve will force the cost of borrowing reserves—the federal funds rate—to rise, as Figure 8 makes clear. As we know, increases in interest rates reduce investment and, hence, reduce aggregate demand. This is the main reason why the economy's aggregate demand curve has a negative slope, meaning that aggregate quantity demanded is lower when prices are higher. In sum:

At higher price levels, the quantity of bank reserves demanded is greater. If the Fed holds the supply schedule fixed, a higher price level must therefore lead to higher interest rates. Because higher interest rates discourage investment, aggregate quantity demanded is lower when the price level is higher—that is, the aggregate demand curve has a negative slope.

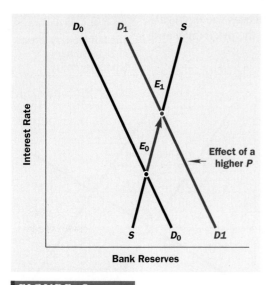

SOURCE: © Harley Schwadron / CartoonStock.com

FROM MODELS TO POLICY DEBATES

You will no doubt be relieved to hear that we have now provided just about all the technical apparatus we need to analyze stabilization policy. To be sure, you will encounter many graphs in the next few chapters. Most of them, however, repeat diagrams with which you are already familiar. Our attention now turns from *building* a theory to *using* that theory to address several important policy issues.

The next three chapters take up a trio of controversial policy debates that surface regularly in the media: the debate over the conduct of stabilization policy (Chapter 14), the continuing debate over budget deficits and the effects of fiscal and monetary policy on growth (Chapter 15), and the controversy over the trade-off between inflation and unemployment (Chapter 16).

| SUMMARY |

1. A **central bank** is bank for banks.

2. The **Federal Reserve System** is America's central bank. There are 12 Federal Reserve banks, but most of the power is held by the Board of Governors in Washington and by the Federal Open Market Committee.

3. The Federal Reserve acts independently of the rest of the government. Over the past 20 to 25 years, many countries have decided that **central bank independence** is a good idea and have moved in this direction.

4. The Fed has three major monetary policy weapons: **open-market operations,** reserve requirements, and its

lending policy to banks. But only open-market operations are used frequently.

5. The Fed increases the supply of bank reserves by purchasing government securities in the open market. When it pays banks for such purchases by creating new reserves, the Fed lowers interest rates and induces a multiple expansion of the money supply. Conversely, open-market sales of securities take reserves from banks, raise interest rates, and lead to a contraction of the money supply.

6. When the Fed buys bonds, bond prices rise and interest rates fall. When the Fed sells bonds, bond prices fall and interest rates rise.

7. The Fed can also pursue a more expansionary monetary policy by allowing banks to borrow more reserves, perhaps by reducing the interest rate it charges on such loans **(the discount rate)** or by reducing **reserve requirements.**

8. None of these weapons, however, gives the Fed perfect control over the money supply in the short run, because it cannot predict perfectly how far the process of deposit creation or destruction will go. The Fed can, however, control the interest rate paid to borrow bank reserves, which is called the **federal funds rate,** much more tightly.

9. Investment spending (*I*), including business investment and investment in new homes, is sensitive to interest rates (*r*). Specifically, *I* is lower when *r* is higher.

10. **Monetary policy** works in the following way in the Keynesian model: Raising the supply of bank reserves leads to lower interest rates; the lower interest rates stimulate investment spending; and this investment stimulus, via the multiplier, then raises aggregate demand.

11. Prices are likely to rise as output rises. The amount of inflation caused by expansionary monetary policy depends on the slope of the aggregate supply curve. Much inflation will occur if the supply curve is steep, but little inflation if it is flat.

12. The main reason why the aggregate demand curve slopes downward is that higher prices increase the demand for bank deposits, and hence for bank reserves. Given a fixed supply of reserves, this higher demand pushes interest rates up, which, in turn, discourages investment.

| KEY TERMS |

Monetary policy   261

Central bank   263

Federal Reserve System   263

Federal Open Market Committee (FOMC)   264

Central bank independence   264

Open-market operations   265

Equilibrium in the market for bank reserves   265

Federal funds rate   266

Bond prices and interest rates   268

Federal Reserve lending to banks   269

Discount rate   270

Reserve requirements   270

Why the aggregate demand curve slopes downward   273

| TEST YOURSELF |

1. Suppose there is $120 billion of cash and that half of this cash is held in bank vaults as *required* reserves (that is, banks hold no *excess* reserves). How large will the money supply be if the required reserve ratio is 10 percent? 12 ½ percent? 16 ⅔ percent?

2. Show the balance sheet changes that would take place if the Federal Reserve Bank of New York purchased an office building from Citigroup for a price of $100 million. Compare this effect to the effect of an open-market purchase of securities shown in Table 1. What do you conclude?

3. Suppose the Fed purchases $5 billion worth of government bonds from Bill Gates, who banks at the Bank of America in San Francisco. Show the effects on the balance sheets of the Fed, the Bank of America, and Gates. (*Hint:* Where will the Fed get the $5 billion to pay Gates?) Does it make any difference if the Fed buys bonds from a bank or an individual?

4. Treasury bills have a fixed face value (say, $1,000) and pay interest by selling at a discount. For example, if a one-year bill with a $1,000 face value sells today for $950, it will pay $1,000 − $950 = $50 in interest over its life. The interest rate on the bill is therefore $50/$950 = 0.0526, or 5.26 percent.

   a. Suppose the price of the Treasury bill falls to $925. What happens to the interest rate?

   b. Suppose, instead, that the price rises to $975. What is the interest rate now?

   c. **(More difficult)** Now generalize this example. Let *P* be the price of the bill and *r* be the interest rate. Develop an algebraic formula expressing *r* in terms of *P*. (*Hint:* The interest earned is $1,000 − *P*. What is the *percentage* interest rate?) Show that this formula illustrates the point made in the text: Higher bond prices mean lower interest rates.

5. Explain what a $5 billion increase in bank reserves will do to real GDP under the following assumptions:

   a. Each $1 billion increase in bank reserves reduces the rate of interest by 0.5 percentage point.

   b. Each 1 percentage point decline in interest rates stimulates $30 billion worth of new investment.

   c. The expenditure multiplier is 2.

   d. The aggregate supply curve is so flat that prices do not rise noticeably when demand increases.

6. Explain how your answers to Test Yourself Question 5 would differ if each of the assumptions changed. Specifically, what sorts of changes in the assumptions would weaken the effects of monetary policy?

7. **(More difficult)** Consider an economy in which government purchases, taxes, and net exports are all zero, the consumption function is

$$C = 300 + 0.75Y$$

and investment spending (I) depends on the rate of interest (r) in the following way:

$$I = 1,000 - 100r$$

Find the equilibrium GDP if the Fed makes the rate of interest (a) 2 percent ($r = 0.02$), (b) 5 percent, and (c) 10 percent.

| DISCUSSION QUESTIONS |

1. Why does a modern industrial economy need a central bank?

2. What are some reasons behind the worldwide trend toward greater central bank independence? Are there arguments on the other side?

3. Explain why the quantity of bank reserves supplied normally is higher and the quantity of bank reserves demanded normally is lower at higher interest rates.

4. From September 2007 through April 2008, the Fed believed that interest rates needed to fall and took steps to reduce them, eventually cutting the federal funds rate from 5.25 percent to 2.0 percent. How did the Fed reduce the federal funds rate? Illustrate your answer on a diagram.

5. Explain why both business investments and purchases of new homes rise when interest rates decline.

6. In the early years of this decade, the federal government's budget deficit rose sharply because of tax cuts and increased spending. If the Federal Reserve wanted to maintain the same level of aggregate demand in the face of large increases in the budget deficit, what should it have done? What would you expect to happen to interest rates?

14

THE DEBATE OVER MONETARY AND FISCAL POLICY

The love of money is the root of all evil.

THE NEW TESTAMENT

Lack of money is the root of all evil.

GEORGE BERNARD SHAW

U p to now, our discussion of stabilization policy has been almost entirely objective and technical. In seeking to understand how the national economy works and how government policies affect it, we have mostly ignored the intense economic and political controversies that surround the actual conduct of monetary and fiscal policy. Chapters 14 through 16 are precisely about these issues.

We begin this chapter by introducing an alternative theory of how monetary policy affects the economy, known as *monetarism.* Although the monetarist and Keynesian *theories* seem to contradict one another, we will see that the conflict is more apparent than real. However, important differences *do* arise among economists over the appropriate design and execution of monetary *policy.* These differences are the central concern of the chapter. We will learn about the continuing debates over the nature of aggregate supply, over the relative virtues of monetary versus fiscal policy, and over whether the Federal Reserve should try to control the money stock or interest rates. As we will see, the resolution of these issues is crucial to the proper conduct of stabilization policy and, indeed, to the decision of whether the government should try to stabilize the economy at all.

CONTENTS

ISSUE: **SHOULD WE FORSAKE STABILIZATION POLICY?**

We have suggested several times in this book that well-timed changes in fiscal or monetary policy can mitigate fluctuations in inflation and unemployment. For example, when the U.S. economy sagged after the terrorist attacks in September 2001, both fiscal policy and monetary policy turned more expansionary. Congress cut taxes and the Federal Reserve cut interest rates. These actions might be called "textbook responses" to the threat of recession. Similarly, when the financial crisis of 2007–2008 threatened to throw the economy into recession, the Fed cut interest rates again and the government enacted a large "stimulus package." These policy decisions were all consistent with the lessons you have learned in Chapters 11 and 13.

But some economists argue that these lessons are best forgotten. In practice, they claim, attempts at macroeconomic stabilization are likely to do more harm than good. Policy makers are therefore best advised to follow fixed *rules* rather than use their best judgment on a case-by-case basis.

Nothing we have said so far leads to this conclusion. But we have not yet told the whole story. By the end of the chapter you will have encountered several arguments in favor of rules, and so you will be in a better position to make up your own mind.

VELOCITY AND THE QUANTITY THEORY OF MONEY

Velocity indicates the number of times per year that an "average dollar" is spent on goods and services. It is the ratio of nominal gross domestic product (GDP) to the number of dollars in the money stock. That is:

$$Velocity = \frac{Nominal\ GDP}{Money\ stock}$$

In the previous chapter, we studied the *Keynesian* view of how monetary policy influences real output and the price level. But another, older model provides a different way to look at these matters. This model, known as the *quantity theory of money*, will be easy to understand once we introduce one new concept: **velocity.**

In Chapter 12, we learned that because barter is so cumbersome, virtually all economic transactions in advanced economies use money. Thus, if there are $10 trillion worth of transactions in an economy during a particular year, and there is an average money stock of $2 trillion during that year, then each dollar of money must have been used an average of five times during the year.

The number 5 in this example is called the *velocity of circulation,* or *velocity* for short, because it indicates the *speed* at which money circulates. For example, a particular dollar bill might be used to buy a haircut in January; the barber might use it to purchase a sweater in March; the storekeeper might then use it to pay for gasoline in May; the gas station owner could pay it out to a house painter in October; and the painter might spend it on a Christmas present in December. In this way, the same dollar is used five times during the year. If it were used only four times during the year, its velocity would be 4, and so on.

No one has data on every transaction in the economy. To make velocity an operational concept, economists need a workable measure of the dollar volume of all transactions. As mentioned in the previous chapter, the most popular choice is nominal gross domestic product (GDP), even though it ignores many transactions that use money, such as the huge volume of activity in financial markets. If we accept nominal GDP as our measure of the money value of transactions, we are led to a concrete definition of velocity as the ratio of nominal GDP to the number of dollars in the money stock. Because nominal GDP is the product of real GDP (Y) times the price level (P), we can write this definition in symbols as follows:

$$Velocity = \frac{Value\ of\ transactions}{Money\ stock} = \frac{Nominal\ GDP}{M} = \frac{P \times Y}{M}$$

The **equation of exchange** states that the money value of GDP transactions must be equal to the product of the average stock of money times velocity. That is:

$$M \times V = P \times Y$$

By multiplying both sides of the equation by M, we arrive at an identity called the **equation of exchange,** which relates the money supply and nominal GDP:

Money supply × Velocity = Nominal GDP

Alternatively, stated in symbols, we have

$$M \times V = P \times Y$$

The equation of exchange provides an obvious link between the stock of money, *M*, and the nominal value of the nation's output, *P* × *Y*. This connection is merely a matter of arithmetic, however—not of economics. For example, it does not imply that the Fed can raise nominal GDP by increasing *M*. Why not? Because *V* might simultaneously fall enough to prevent the product *M* × *V* from rising. In other words, if more dollar bills circulated than before, but each bill changed hands more slowly, total spending might not rise. Thus, we need an auxiliary assumption to change the arithmetic identity into an economic theory.

The **quantity theory of money** transforms the equation of exchange from an arithmetic identity into an economic model by assuming that changes in velocity are so minor that velocity can be taken to be virtually constant.

You can see that if *V* never changed, the equation of exchange would be a marvelously simple model of the determination of nominal GDP—far simpler than the Keynesian model that took us several chapters to develop. To see this, it is convenient to rewrite the equation of exchange in terms of growth rates:

$$\%\Delta M + \%\Delta V = \%\Delta P + \%\Delta Y$$

If *V* was constant, making its percentage change zero, this equation would say, for example, that if the Federal Reserve wanted to make nominal GDP grow by 4.7 percent per year, it need merely raise the money supply by 4.7 percent per year. In such a simple world, economists could use the equation of exchange to *predict* nominal GDP growth by predicting the growth rate of money. And policy makers could *control* nominal GDP growth by controlling growth of the money supply.

In the real world, things are not so simple because velocity is not a fixed number. But variable velocity does not necessarily destroy the usefulness of the quantity theory. As we explained in Chapter 1, all economic models make assumptions that are at least mildly unrealistic. Without such assumptions, they would not be models at all, just tedious descriptions of reality. The question is really whether the assumption of constant velocity is a useful abstraction from annoying detail or a gross distortion of the facts.

Figure 1 sheds some light on this question by showing the behavior of velocity since 1929. Note that the figure includes two different measures of velocity, labeled V_1 and V_2. Why? Recall from Chapter 12 that we can measure money in several ways, the most popular of which are M1 and M2. Because velocity (*V*) is simply nominal GDP divided by the money stock (*M*), we get a *different* measure of *V* for *each* measure of *M*. Figure 1 shows the velocities of both M1 and M2.

The **quantity theory of money** assumes that velocity is (approximately) constant. In that case, nominal GDP is proportional to the money stock.

FIGURE 1

Velocity of Circulation, 1929–2007

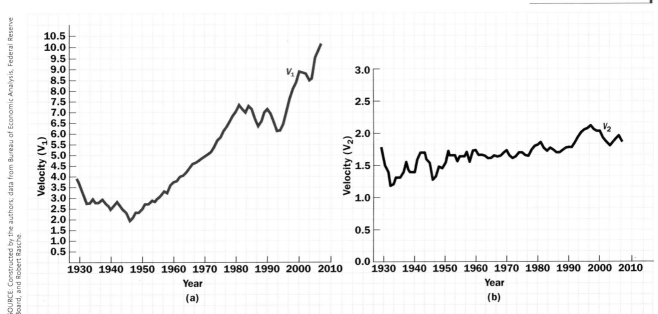

SOURCE: Constructed by the authors; data from Bureau of Economic Analysis, Federal Reserve Board, and Robert Rasche.

You will undoubtedly notice the stark difference in the behavior of V_1 versus V_2. V_1 is nowhere near constant; it displays a clear downward trend from 1929 until 1946, a pronounced upward trend until about 1981, and quite erratic behavior since then. V_2 is much closer to constant, but it has risen noticeably since the 1980s. Furthermore, closer examination of monthly or quarterly data reveals rather substantial fluctuations in velocity, by either measure. Because velocity is not constant in the short run, predictions of nominal GDP growth based on assuming constant velocity have not fared well, regardless of how M is measured. In a word, the strict quantity theory of money is not an adequate model of aggregate demand.

Some Determinants of Velocity

Because it is abundantly clear that velocity is a variable, not a constant, the equation of exchange is useful as a model of GDP determination only if we can explain movements in velocity. What factors decide whether a dollar will be used to buy goods and services four or five or six times per year? While numerous factors are relevant, two are important enough to merit discussion here.

Efficiency of the Payments System

Money is convenient for conducting transactions, which is why people hold it. But money has one important *dis*advantage: Cash pays no interest, and ordinary checking accounts pay very little. Thus, if it were possible to convert interest-bearing assets into money on short notice and at low cost, rational individuals might prefer to use, say, credit cards for most purchases, making periodic transfers to their checking accounts as necessary. That way, the same volume of transactions could be accomplished with lower money balances. By definition, velocity would rise.

The incentive to limit cash holdings thus depends on the ease and speed with which it is possible to exchange money for other assets—which is what we mean by the "efficiency of the payments system." As computerization has speeded up banks' bookkeeping procedures, as financial innovations have made it possible to transfer funds rapidly between checking accounts and other assets, and as credit cards have come to be used instead of cash, the need to hold money balances has declined and velocity has risen.

In practice, improvements in the payments system pose severe practical problems for analysts interested in predicting velocity. A host of financial innovations, beginning in the 1970s and continuing right up to the present day (some of which were mentioned in Chapter 12's discussion of the definitions of money), have transformed forecasting velocity into a hazardous occupation. In fact, many economists believe the task is impossible and should not even be attempted.

Interest Rates

A second key determinant of velocity is the rate of interest. The reason is implicit in what we have already said: The higher the rate of interest, the greater the *opportunity cost* of holding money. Therefore, as interest rates rise, people want to hold smaller cash balances—which means that the existing stock of money circulates faster, and velocity rises.

> It is this factor that most directly undercuts the usefulness of the quantity theory of money as a guide for monetary policy. In the previous chapter, we learned that expansionary monetary policy, which increases bank reserves and the money supply, also decreases the interest rate. But if interest rates fall, other things being equal, velocity (V) also falls. Thus, *when the Fed raises the money supply (M), the product $M \times V$ should increase by a smaller percentage than does M itself.*

Thus, we conclude that

> Velocity is not a strict constant but depends on such things as the efficiency of the financial system and the rate of interest. Only by studying these determinants of velocity

can we hope to predict the growth rate of nominal GDP from knowledge of the growth rate of the money supply.

Monetarism: The Quantity Theory Modernized

Adherents to a school of thought called **monetarism** try to do precisely that. Monetarists realize that velocity changes, but they claim that such changes are fairly *predictable*—certainly in the long run and perhaps even in the short run. As a result, they conclude that the best way to study economic activity is to start with the equation of exchange in growth-rate form:

$$\%\Delta M + \%\Delta V = \%\Delta P + \%\Delta Y$$

From here, careful study of the determinants of money growth (which we provided in the previous two chapters) and of changes in velocity (which we just sketched) can be used to *predict* the growth rate of nominal GDP. Similarly, given an understanding of movements in V, controlling M can give the Fed excellent control over nominal GDP. These ideas are the central tenets of monetarism.

The monetarist and Keynesian approaches can be thought of as two competing theories of aggregate demand. Keynesians divide economic knowledge into four neat compartments marked C, I, G, and $(X - IM)$ and then add them all up to obtain aggregate demand. In Keynesian analysis, as we have learned, money affects the economy by first affecting interest rates. Monetarists, by contrast, organize their knowledge into two alternative boxes labeled M and V and then multiply the two to obtain aggregate demand. In the monetarist model, the role of money is not necessarily limited to working through interest rates.

The bit of arithmetic that multiplies M and V to get $P \times Y$ is neither more nor less profound than the one that adds up C, I, G and $(X \times IM)$ to get Y, and certainly both are correct. The real question is which framework is more *useful* in practice. That is, which approach works better as a model of aggregate demand?

Although there is no generally correct answer for all economies in all periods of time, a glance back at Figure 1 (page 279) will show you why most economists had abandoned monetarism by the early 1990s. During the 1960s and 1970s, velocity (at least V_2) was fairly stable, which helped monetarism win many converts—in the United States and around the world. Since then, however, velocity has behaved so erratically here and in many other countries that there are few monetarists left.

Nonetheless, as we will see later in this chapter, some faint echoes of the debate between Keynesians and monetarists can still be heard. Furthermore, few economists doubt that there is a strong *long-run* relationship between M and P. They just question whether this relationship is useful in the short run. (See the box "Does Money Growth Always Cause Inflation?" on the next page.)

*Sidebar:* Monetarism is a mode of analysis that uses the equation of exchange to organize and analyze macroeconomic data.

FISCAL POLICY, INTEREST RATES, AND VELOCITY

As we learned in the previous chapter, Keynesian economics provides a powerful and important role for *monetary* policy: An increase in bank reserves and the money supply reduces interest rates, which, in turn, stimulates the demand for investment. But *fiscal* policy also exerts a powerful influence on interest rates.

To see how, think about what happens to real output and the price level following, say, a rise in government spending. We have learned that both real GDP (Y) and the price level (P) rise, so nominal GDP certainly rises. But the previous chapter's analysis of the market for bank reserves taught us that rising prices and/or rising output—by increasing the money volume of transactions—push the demand curve for bank reserves outward to the right. If there is no change in the supply of reserves, the rate of interest must rise. So *expansionary fiscal policy raises interest rates.*

POLICY DEBATE

DOES MONEY GROWTH ALWAYS CAUSE INFLATION?

Monetarists have long claimed that, in the famous words of the late Milton Friedman, "inflation is always and everywhere a monetary phenomenon." By this statement, Friedman meant that changes in the growth rate of the money supply (%ΔM) are far and away the principal cause of changes in the inflation rate (%ΔP)—in all places and at all times.

Few economists question the dominant role of rapid money growth in accounting for extremely high rates of inflation. During the German hyperinflation of the 1920s, for example, money was being printed so fast that the printing presses had a difficult time keeping up the pace! But most economists question the words "always and everywhere" in Friedman's dictum. Aren't many cases of moderate inflation driven by factors other than the growth rate of the money supply?

The answer appears to be "yes." The accompanying charts use recent U.S. history as an illustration. In the scatter diagram on the left, each point records both the growth rate of the M2 money supply and the inflation rate (as measured by the Consumer Price Index) for a particular year between 1979 and 2007. Because of the years 1979–1981, there seems to be a weak positive relationship between the two variables. But no relationship at all appears for the years 1982–2007.

Monetarists often argue that this comparison is unfair because the effect of money supply growth on inflation operates with a lag of perhaps two years. So the right-hand scatter diagram compares inflation with money supply growth *two years earlier*. It tells essentially the same story. More sophisticated versions of scatter plots like these have led most economists to reject the monetarist claim that inflation and money supply growth are tightly linked.

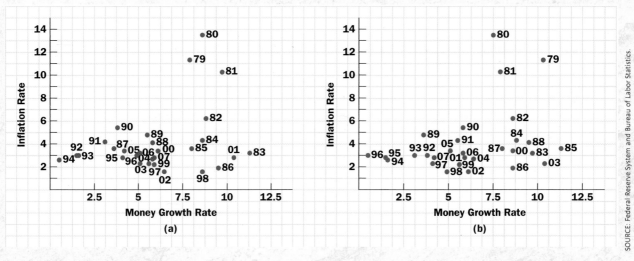

NOTE: All figures are in percent.

SOURCE: Federal Reserve System and Bureau of Labor Statistics.

If the government uses its spending and taxing weapons in the opposite direction, the same process works in reverse. Falling output and (possibly) falling prices shift the demand curve for reserves inward to the left. With a fixed supply curve, equilibrium in the market for bank reserves leads to a lower interest rate. Thus:

Monetary policy is not the only type of policy that affects interest rates. Fiscal policy does, too. Specifically, increases in government spending or tax cuts normally push interest rates up, whereas restrictive fiscal policies normally pull interest rates down.

The apparently banal fact that changes in fiscal policy move interest rates up and down has several important consequences. Here are two.

Application: The Multiplier Formula Revisited

We have just noted that expansionary fiscal policy raises interest rates. We also know that higher interest rates deter private investment spending. So when the government raises the G component of C + I + G + (X − IM), one side effect will probably be a reduction in the I component. Consequently, total spending will rise by *less* than simple multiplier analysis might suggest. The fact that a surge in government demand (G) discourages some private demand (*I*) provides another reason why the oversimplified multiplier formula of earlier chapters, $1/(1 - \text{MPC})$, exaggerates the size of the multiplier:

> Because a rise in *G* (or, for that matter, an autonomous rise in any component of total expenditure) pushes interest rates higher, and hence deters some investment spending, the increase in the sum $C + I + G + (X - IM)$ is smaller than what the oversimplified multiplier formula predicts.

Combining this observation with our previous analysis of the multiplier, we now have the following complete list of

REASONS WHY THE OVERSIMPLIFIED FORMULA OVERSTATES THE MULTIPLIER

1. It ignores variable imports, which reduce the size of the multiplier.
2. It ignores price-level changes, which reduce the size of the multiplier.
3. It ignores the income tax, which reduces the size of the multiplier.
4. It ignores the rising interest rates that accompany any autonomous increase in spending, which also reduce the size of the multiplier.

With so many reasons, it is no wonder that the actual multiplier, which is estimated to be less than 2 for the U.S. economy, is so much less than the oversimplified formula suggests.

Application: The Government Budget and Investment

One major argument for reducing the government's budget deficit is that lower deficits should lead to higher levels of private investment spending. We can now understand why. To reduce its budget deficit, the government must engage in *contractionary* fiscal policies: lower spending or higher taxes. But as we have now just learned, any such measure should *reduce* real interest rates. These lower real interest rates should spur investment spending. This simple insight—that lower budget deficits should lead to more private investment—will play a major role in the next chapter.

DEBATE: SHOULD WE RELY ON FISCAL OR MONETARY POLICY?

The Keynesian and monetarist approaches are like two different languages. But it is well known that language influences attitudes in subtle ways. For example, the Keynesian language biases things toward thinking first about fiscal policy simply because *G* is a part of $C + I + G + (X - IM)$. By contrast, the monetarist approach, working through the equation of exchange, $M \times V = P \times Y$, puts the spotlight on *M*. In fact, years ago economists engaged in a spirited debate in which extreme monetarists claimed that fiscal policy was futile, whereas extreme Keynesians argued that monetary policy was useless. Today, such arguments are rarely heard.

Instead of arguing over which type of policy is more *powerful*, economists nowadays debate which type of medicine—fiscal or monetary—works *faster*. Until now, we have ignored questions of timing and pretended that the authorities noticed the need for stabilization policy instantly, decided on a course of action right away, and administered the appropriate medicine at once. In reality, each of these steps takes time.

First, delays in data collection mean that the most recent data describe the state of the economy a few months ago. Second, one of the prices of democracy is that the government often takes a distressingly long time to decide what should be done, to muster the necessary political support, and to put its decisions into effect. Finally, our $14 trillion economy is a bit like a sleeping elephant that reacts rather sluggishly to moderate fiscal and monetary prods. As it turns out, these *lags in stabilization policy*, as they are called, play a pivotal role in the choice between fiscal and monetary policy. Here's why.

The main policy tool for manipulating consumer spending (*C*) is the personal income tax, and Chapter 8 documented why the fiscal policy planner can feel fairly confident that each $1 of tax reduction will lead to about 90 to 95 cents of additional spending *eventually*. But not all of this extra spending happens at once.

First, consumers must learn about the tax change. Then they may need to be convinced that the change is permanent. Finally, there is simple force of habit: Households need time to adjust their spending habits when circumstances change. For all these reasons, consumers may increase their spending by only 30 to 50 cents for each $1 of additional income within the first few months after a tax cut. Only gradually will they raise their spending up to about 90 to 95 cents for each additional dollar of income.

Lags are much longer for investment (I), which provides the main vehicle by which monetary policy affects aggregate demand. Planning for capacity expansion in a large corporation is a long, drawn-out process. Ideas must be submitted and approved, plans must be drawn up, funding acquired, orders for machinery or contracts for new construction placed. And most of this activity occurs *before* any appreciable amount of money is spent. Economists have found that much of the response of investment to changes in either interest rates or tax provisions takes several *years* to develop.

The fact that C responds more quickly than I has important implications for the choice among alternative stabilization policies. The reason is that the most common varieties of fiscal policy either affect aggregate demand directly—because G is a component of $C + I + G + (X - IM)$—or work through consumption with a relatively short lag, whereas monetary policy primarily affects investment. Therefore:

> **Conventional types of fiscal policy actions, such as changes in G or in personal taxes, probably affect aggregate demand much more promptly than do monetary policy actions.**

So is fiscal policy therefore a superior stabilization tool? Not necessarily. The lags we have just described, which are beyond policy makers' control, are not the only ones affecting the timing of stabilization policy. Additional lags stem from the behavior of the policy makers themselves. We refer here to the delays that occur while policy makers study the state of the economy, contemplate which steps they should take, and put their decisions into effect.

Here monetary policy has a huge advantage. The Federal Open Market Committee (FOMC) meets eight times each year, and more often if necessary. So monetary policy decisions are made frequently. And once the Fed decides on a course of action, it executes its plan immediately by buying or selling Treasury bills in the open market.

In contrast, federal budgeting procedures operate on an annual budget cycle. Except in unusual cases, major fiscal policy initiatives can occur only at the time of the annual budget. In principle, tax laws can be changed at any time. But the wheels of Congress normally grind slowly and are often gummed up by partisan politics. For these reasons, it may take many months for Congress to change fiscal policy. That said, Congress has proven twice in this decade that it can act very quickly in a perceived emergency. First in 2001, and then again in 2008, both houses rapidly passed, and the president signed, fiscal stimulus bills that put checks into the hands of consumers when the economy was threatened by recession—even though, in the second case, the White House and Congress were controlled by different parties. This recent experience now has many observers rethinking the old conventional wisdom, which held that:

> **Policy lags are normally much shorter for monetary policy than for fiscal policy.**

Could it be that this is no longer true?

So where does the combined effect of expenditure lags and policy lags leave us? With nothing very conclusive, we are afraid. In practice, however, most students of stabilization policy have come to believe that the unwieldy and often partisan nature of our political system make active use of fiscal policy for stabilization purposes quite difficult. Monetary policy, they claim, is the only realistic game in town and therefore must bear most of the burden of stabilization policy.

DEBATE: SHOULD THE FED CONTROL THE MONEY SUPPLY OR INTEREST RATES?

Another major controversy that raged for decades focused on how the Federal Reserve should conduct monetary policy. Most economists argued that the Fed should use its open-market operations to control the rate of interest (r), which is how we have portrayed monetary policy up to now. But others, especially monetarists, insisted that the Fed should concentrate on controlling bank reserves or some measure of the money supply (*M*) instead. This debate echoes even today in Europe, where the European Central Bank (ECB), unlike the Fed, *claims* to pay considerable attention to the growth of the money supply. (Many skeptics doubt that it actually does so, however.)

To understand the nature of this debate, we must first understand why the Fed cannot control both *M* and *r* at the same time. Figure 2 will help us see why. It looks just like Figure 8 of the previous chapter (on page 274), except that the horizontal axis now measures the *money supply* instead of *bank reserves*. The switch from reserves to money is justified by something we learned in earlier chapters: that the money supply is "built up" from the Fed's supply of bank reserves via the process of multiple expansion.[1] As you will recall, this process leads to an approximately proportional relationship between the two—meaning that if bank reserves go up by *X* percent, then the money supply rises by approximately *X* percent, too.[2] Because *M* is basically proportional to bank *reserves*, anything we can analyze in the market for reserves can be analyzed in just the same way in the market for *money*—which is the market depicted in Figure 2.

FIGURE 2

The Federal Reserve's Policy Dilemma

The diagram shows an initial equilibrium in the money market at point *E*, where money demand curve $M_0 D_0$ crosses money supply curve *MS*. Here the interest rate is *r* = 5 percent and the money stock is *M* = $830 billion. We assume that these are the Fed's targets: It wants to keep the money supply and interest rates just where they are.

If the demand curve for money holds still, everything works out fine. But suppose the demand for money is not so obliging. Suppose, instead, that the demand curve shifts outward to the position indicated by the brick-colored line $M_1 D_1$ in Figure 2. We learned in the previous chapter that such a shift might occur because output increases or because prices rise, thereby increasing the volume of transactions. Or it might happen simply because people decide to hold more bank deposits. But whatever the reason, once the shift occurs, the Fed can no longer achieve *both* previous targets.

If the Fed does nothing, the outward shift of the demand curve will push up both the quantity of money (*M*) and the rate of interest (*r*). Figure 2 depicts these changes as the move from point *E* to point *A*. In the example, if the demand curve for money shifts outward from $M_0 D_0$ to $M_1 D_1$, and monetary policy does not change (leaving the supply curve unchanged), the money stock rises to $840 billion and the interest rate rises to 7 percent.

Now suppose the Fed is targeting the money supply and is unwilling to let *M* rise. In that case, it must use *contractionary* open-market operations to prevent *M* from rising. But in so doing, it will push *r* up even higher, as point *W* in Figure 2 shows. After the demand curve for money shifts outward, point *E* is no longer attainable. The Fed must instead choose from among the points on the brick-colored line $M_1 D_1$, and point *W* is the point on this line that keeps the money supply at $830 billion. To hold *M* at $830 billion, the Fed must reduce bank reserves just enough to pull the money supply curve *inward* so that it passes through point *W*. (Pencil this shift in for yourself on the diagram.) But the interest rate will then skyrocket to 9 percent.

Alternatively, if the Federal Reserve is pursuing an interest rate target, it might decide that the rise in *r* must be avoided. In this case, the Fed would be forced to engage in *expansionary* open-market operations to prevent the outward shift of the demand curve for money

---

[1] If you need to review this process, turn back to Chapter 12, especially pages 252–258.

[2] For further details on this proportionality relationship, including some numerical examples, see Test Yourself Question 5 at the end of this chapter.

from pushing r up. In terms of Figure 2, the interest rate can be held at 5 percent by adding just enough bank reserves to shift the money supply curve *outward* so that it passes through point Z. But doing this will push the money supply up to $850 billion. (Again, try penciling in the required shift of the money supply curve.) To summarize this discussion:

> **When the demand curve for money shifts outward, the Fed must tolerate a rise in interest rates, a rise in the money stock, or both. It cannot control *both* the supply of money *and* the interest rate. If it tries to keep *M* steady, then *r* will rise even more. Conversely, if it tries to stabilize *r*, then *M* will rise even more.**

Two Imperfect Alternatives

For years, economists debated how a central bank should deal with its inability to control both the money supply and the rate of interest. Should it adhere rigidly to a target growth path for bank reserves and the money supply, regardless of the consequences for interest rates—which is the monetarist policy? Should it hold interest rates steady, even if that requires sharp gyrations in reserves and the money stock—which is roughly what the Fed does now? Or is some middle ground more appropriate? Let us first explore the issues and then consider what has actually been done.

The main problem with imposing rigid targets on the *supply* of money is that the *demand* for money does not cooperate by growing smoothly and predictably from month to month; instead it dances around quite a bit in the short run. This variability presents the recommendation to control the money supply with two problems:

1. It is almost impossible to achieve. Because the volume of money in existence depends on *both* the demand *and* the supply curves, keeping *M* on target in the face of significant fluctuations in the demand for money requires exceptional dexterity.
2. For reasons just explained, rigid adherence to money-stock targets might lead to wide fluctuations in interest rates, which could create an unsettled atmosphere for business decisions.

But powerful objections can also be raised against exclusive concentration on interest rate movements. Because increases in output and prices shift the demand schedule for money outward (as shown in Figure 2), a central bank determined to keep interest rates from rising would have to expand the money supply in response. Conversely, when GDP sagged, it would have to contract the money supply to keep rates from falling. Thus, interest rate pegging would make the money supply expand in boom times and contract in recessions, with potentially grave consequences for the stability of the economy. Ironically, this is precisely the sort of monetary behavior the Federal Reserve System was designed to prevent. Hence, if the Fed is to control interest rates, it had better formulate flexible targets, not fixed ones.

What Has the Fed Actually Done?

For most of post–World War II history, the predominant view held that the interest rate was much the more important of the two targets. The rationale was that gyrating interest rates could cause abrupt and unsettling changes in investment spending, which in turn would make the entire economy fluctuate. Stabilizing interest rates was therefore believed to be the best way to stabilize GDP. If doing so required fluctuations in the money supply, so be it. Consequently, the Fed focused on interest rates and paid little attention to the money supply—which is more or less the Fed's view today as well.

During the 1960s, however, this prevailing view came under withering attack from Milton Friedman and other monetarists. These economists argued that the Fed's obsession with stabilizing interest rates actually *destabilized* the economy by making the money supply fluctuate too much. For this reason, they urged the Fed to stop worrying so much about fluctuations in interest rates and, instead, make the money supply grow at a constant rate from month to month and year to year.

Monetarism made important inroads at the Fed during the inflationary 1970s, especially in October 1979 when then-Chairman Paul Volcker announced a major change in the conduct of monetary policy. Henceforth, he asserted, the Fed would stick more closely to its target for money-stock growth regardless of the implications for interest rates. Interest rates would go wherever supply and demand took them.

According to our analysis, this change in policy should have led to wider fluctuations in interest rates—and it did. Unfortunately, the Fed also ran into some bad luck. The ensuing three years were marked by un-usually severe gyrations in the demand for money, so the ups and downs of interest rates were even more ex-treme than anyone had expected. Figure 3 shows just how volatile interest rates were between late 1979 and late 1982. As you might imagine, this erratic perform-ance provoked some heavy criticism of the Fed.

Then, in October 1982, Chairman Volcker announced that the Fed was temporarily abandoning its attempts to stick to a target growth path for the money supply. Although he did not say so, his announcement presumably meant that the Fed went back to paying more attention to interest rates. As you can see in Figure 3, interest rates did become much more stable after the change in policy. Most observers think this greater stability was no coincidence.

FIGURE 3

The Behavior of Interest Rates, 1979–1985

After 1982, the Fed gradually distanced itself from the proposition that the money sup-ply should grow at a constant rate. Finally, in 1993, then-Chairman Alan Greenspan offi-cially confirmed what many people already knew: that the Fed was no longer using the various *M*s to guide policy. He strongly hinted that the Fed was targeting interest rates, especially *real* interest rates, instead—a hint that has been repeated many times since then. In truth, the Fed had little choice. The demand curve for money behaved so erratically and so unpredictably in the 1980s and 1990s that stabilizing the money stock was probably im-possible and certainly undesirable. And at least so far, the Fed has shown little interest in returning to the *M*s.

DEBATE: THE SHAPE OF THE AGGREGATE SUPPLY CURVE

Another lively debate over stabilization policy revolves around the shape of the econ-omy's aggregate supply curve. Many economists think of the aggregate supply curve as quite flat, as in Figure 4(a) on the next page, so that large increases in output can be achieved with little inflation. But other economists envision the supply curve as steep, as shown in Figure 4(b), so that prices respond strongly to changes in output. The differences for public policy are substantial.

If the aggregate supply curve is flat, expansionary fiscal or monetary policy that raises the aggregate demand curve can buy large gains in real GDP at low cost in terms of infla-tion. In Figure 5(a) on the next page, stimulation of demand pushes the aggregate demand curve outward from D_0D_0 to D_1D_1, thereby moving the economy's equilibrium from point *E* to point *A*. The substantial rise in output ($400 billion in the diagram) is accompanied by only a pinch of inflation (1 percent). So the antirecession policy is quite successful.

Conversely, when the supply curve is flat, a restrictive stabilization policy is not a very effective way to bring inflation down. Instead, it serves mainly to reduce real output, as Figure 5(b) shows. Here a leftward shift of the aggregate demand curve from D_0D_0 to D_2D_2 moves equilibrium from point *E* to point *B*, lowering real GDP by $400 billion but cutting the price level by merely 1 percent. Fighting inflation by contracting aggregate demand is obviously quite costly in this example.

FIGURE 4

Alternative Views of
the Aggregate Supply
Curve

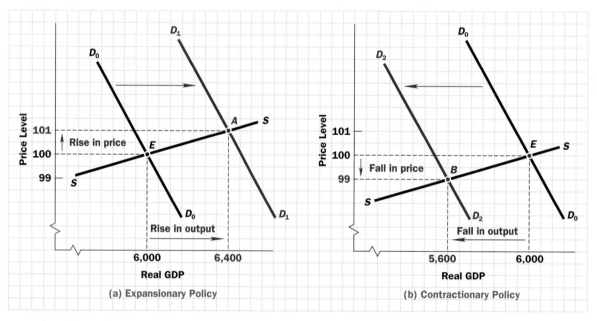

NOTE: Real GDP in billions of dollars per year.

FIGURE 5

Stabilization Policy
with a Flat Aggregate
Supply Curve

Things are just the reverse if the aggregate supply curve is steep. In that case, expansionary fiscal or monetary policies will cause a good deal of inflation without boosting real GDP much. This situation is depicted in Figure 6(a) on the next page, in which expansionary policies shift the aggregate demand curve outward from D_0D_0 to D_1D_1, thereby moving the economy's equilibrium from E to A. Output rises by only $100 billion but prices shoot up 10 percent.

Similarly, contractionary policy is an effective way to bring down the price level without much sacrifice of output, as shown by the shift from E to B in Figure 6(b). Here it takes only a $100 billion loss of output (from $6,000 billion to $5,900 billion) to "buy" 10 percent less inflation.

Thus, as we can see, deciding whether the aggregate supply curve is steep or flat is clearly of fundamental importance to the proper conduct of stabilization policy. If the supply curve is flat, stabilization policy is much more effective at combating recession than inflation. If the supply curve is steep, precisely the reverse is true.

But why does the argument persist? Why can't economists just measure the slope of the aggregate supply curve and stop arguing? The answer is that supply conditions in the real

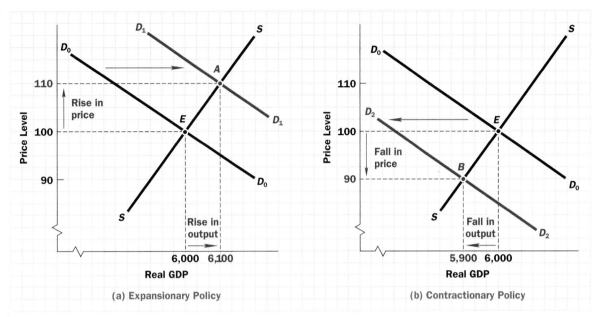

(a) Expansionary Policy   (b) Contractionary Policy

NOTE: Real GDP in billions of dollars per year.

FIGURE 6

Stabilization Policy
with a Steep Aggregate
Supply Curve

world are far more complicated than our simple diagrams suggest. Some industries may have flat supply curves, whereas others have steep ones. For reasons explained in Chapter 10, supply curves shift over time. And, unlike laboratory scientists, economists cannot perform controlled experiments that would reveal the shape of the aggregate supply curve directly. Instead, they must use statistical inference to make educated guesses.

Although empirical research continues, our understanding of aggregate supply remains less settled than our understanding of aggregate demand. Nevertheless, many economists believe that the outline of a consensus view has emerged. This view holds that *the steepness of the aggregate supply schedule depends on the time period under consideration.*

In the very short run, the aggregate supply curve is quite flat, making Figure 5 the more relevant picture of reality. Over short time periods, therefore, fluctuations in aggregate demand have large effects on output but only minor effects on prices. In the long run, however, the aggregate supply curve becomes quite steep, perhaps even vertical. In that case, Figure 6 is a better representation of reality, so that changes in demand affect mainly prices, not output.[3] The implication is that

> Any change in aggregate demand will have most of its effect on *output* in the short run but on *prices* in the long run.

DEBATE: SHOULD THE GOVERNMENT INTERVENE?

We have yet to consider what may be the most fundamental and controversial debate of all—the issue posed at the beginning of the chapter. Is it likely that government policy can successfully stabilize the economy? Or are even well-intentioned efforts likely to do more harm than good?

This controversy has raged for several decades, with no end in sight. In part, the debate is political or philosophical. Liberal economists tend to be more intervention-minded and hence more favorably disposed toward an activist stabilization policy. Conservative economists are more inclined to

*"Daddy's not mad at you, dear—
Daddy's mad at the Fed."*

SOURCE: From *The Wall Street Journal*—Permission, Cartoon Features Syndicate

---

[3] The reasoning behind the view that the aggregate supply curve is flat in the short run but steep in the long run will be developed in Chapter 16.

The Fed Fights Recession

From June 2004 until June 2006, the Federal Reserve raised the Federal funds rate—at first to bring it up to more "normal" levels and then because it was worried about inflation. The Fed then left the funds rate constant (at 5.25%) for more than a year as it pondered what to do next. (See chart.) Then the financial panic which erupted in August 2007 changed everything.

Worried that the financial shock might disrupt not only the financial markets but also the economy, the Fed cut interest rates by ½ percentage point (a large move by Fed standards) on September 18. But that was just the beginning. It soon followed with several more cuts, including two particularly sharp rate reductions just eight days apart in January 2008. Yet the financial crisis persisted and, by some measures, got worse. By the end of April 2008, the federal funds rate was down to 2%, as the Fed worked hard to avert a recession. At the time this book went to press, Fed watchers were guessing that the Fed would stop cutting rates at 2%, but no one was quite sure.

Federal Funds Rate, 2004–2008

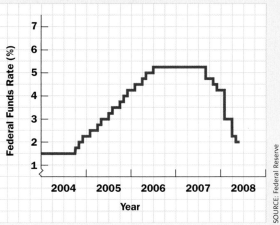

SOURCE: Federal Reserve

keep the government's hands off the economy and hence advise adhering to fixed rules. Such political differences are not surprising. But more than ideology propels the debate. We need to understand the economics.

Critics of stabilization policy point to the lags and uncertainties that surround the operation of both fiscal and monetary policies—lags and uncertainties that we have stressed repeatedly in this and earlier chapters. Will the Fed's actions have the desired effects on the money supply? What will these actions do to interest rates and spending? Can fiscal policy actions be taken promptly? How large is the expenditure multiplier? The list could go on and on.

These skeptics look at this formidable catalog of difficulties, add a dash of skepticism about our ability to forecast the future state of the economy, and worry that stabilization policy may fail. They therefore advise both the fiscal and monetary authorities to pursue a passive policy rather than an active one—adhering to fixed rules that, although incapable of ironing out every bump and wiggle in the economy's growth path, will at least keep it roughly on track in the long run.

Advocates of active stabilization policies admit that perfection is unattainable. But they are much more optimistic about the prospects for success, and they are much *less* optimistic about how smoothly the economy would grow in the absence of demand management. They therefore advocate discretionary increases in government spending (or decreases in taxes) and lower interest rates when the economy has a recessionary gap—and the reverse when the economy has an inflationary gap. Such policies, they believe, will help keep the economy closer to its full-employment growth path.

Each side can point to evidence that buttresses its own view. Activists look back with pride at the tax cut of 1964 and the sustained period of economic growth that it ushered in. They also point to the tax cut of 1975 (which was quickly enacted at just about the trough of a severe recession) and the even speedier fiscal stimulus packages enacted after 9/11 and then again in February 2008. Advocates of using discretionary monetary policy extol the Federal Reserve's switch to "easy money" in 1982, its expert steering of the economy between 1992 and 2000, and its quick responses to the threats to the economy after 9/11 and again after the financial panic in August 2007. Advocates of rules remind us of the government's refusal to curb what was obviously a situation of runaway demand during the 1966–1968 Vietnam buildup, its overexpansion of the economy in 1972, the monetary overkill that helped bring on the sharp recession of 1981–1982, and the inadequate antirecession policies of the early 1990s. Some also argue that the Fed helped fuel the housing "bubble" by holding interest rates too low in 2003–2005.

The historical record of fiscal and monetary policy is far from glorious. Although the authorities have sometimes taken appropriate and timely actions to stabilize the economy, at other times they clearly either took inappropriate steps or did nothing at all. The question of whether the government should adopt passive rules or attempt an activist stabilization policy therefore merits a closer look. As we shall see, the *lags* in the effects of policy discussed earlier in this chapter play a pivotal role in the debate.

Lags and the Rules-versus-Discretion Debate

Lags lead to a fundamental difficulty for stabilization policy—a difficulty so formidable that it has prompted some economists to conclude that attempts to stabilize economic activity are likely to do more harm than good. To see why, refer to Figure 7, which charts the behavior of both actual and potential GDP over the course of a business cycle in a hypothetical economy with no stabilization policy. At point *A*, the economy begins to slip into a recession and does not recover to full employment until point *D*. Then, between points *D* and *E*, it overshoots potential GDP and enters an inflationary boom.

The argument in favor of stabilization policy runs something like this: Policy makers recognize that the recession is a serious problem at point *B*, and they take appropriate actions very soon. These actions have their major effects around point *C* and therefore limit both the depth and the length of the recession.

But suppose the lags are really longer and less predictable than those just described. Suppose, for example, that actions do not come until point *C* and that stimulative policies do not have their major effects until after point *D*. Then policy will be of little help during the recession and will actually do harm by overstimulating the economy during the ensuing boom. Thus:

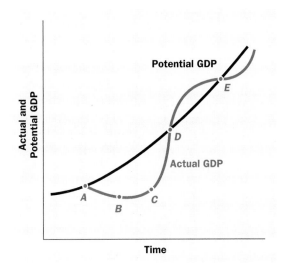

FIGURE 7

A Typical Business Cycle

> **In the presence of long lags, attempts at stabilizing the economy may actually succeed in destabilizing it.**

For this reason, some economists argue that we are better off leaving the economy alone and relying on its natural self-corrective forces to cure recessions and inflations. Instead of embarking on periodic programs of monetary and fiscal stimulus or restraint, they advise policy makers to stick to fixed rules that ignore current economic events.

For monetary policy, we have already mentioned the monetarist policy rule: The Fed should keep the money supply growing at a constant rate. For fiscal policy, proponents of rules often recommend that the government resist the temptation to manage aggregate demand actively and rely instead on the economy's automatic stabilizers, which we discussed in Chapter 11 (see page 225).

DIMENSIONS OF THE RULES-VERSUS-DISCRETION DEBATE

Are the critics right? Should we forget about discretionary policy and put the economy on autopilot—relying on automatic stabilizers and the economy's natural, self-correcting mechanisms? As usual, the answer depends on many factors.

How Fast Does the Economy's Self-Correcting Mechanism Work?

In Chapter 10, we emphasized that the economy has a self-correcting mechanism. If that self-correcting mechanism is fast and efficient, so that recessions and inflations will disappear quickly by themselves, the case for policy intervention is weak. Indeed, if such problems typically last only a short time, then lags in discretionary stabilization policy might mean that the medicine has its major effects only after the disease has run its course. In terms of Figure 7, this is a case in which point *D* comes very close to point *A*. In fact, a distinct minority of economists used precisely this reasoning to argue against a fiscal stimulus after the September 11, 2001, terrorist attacks and again after the financial panic of 2007–2008.

Although extreme advocates of rules argue that this is indeed what happens, most economists agree that the economy's self-correcting mechanism is slow and not terribly reliable, even when supplemented by the automatic stabilizers. On this count, then, a point is scored for discretionary policy.

How Long Are the Lags in Stabilization Policy?

We just explained why long and unpredictable lags in monetary and fiscal policy make it hard for stabilization policy to do much good. Short, reliable lags point in just the opposite direction. Thus advocates of fixed rules emphasize the length of lags while proponents of discretion tend to discount them.

Who is right depends on the circumstances. Sometimes policy makers take action promptly, and the economy receives at least some stimulus from expansionary policy within a year after slipping into a recession. The tax reductions and sharp cuts in interest rates that followed both the 9/11 tragedy and the financial crisis of 2007–2008 are the most recent examples. Although far from perfect, the effects of such timely actions were certainly felt soon enough to do some good. But, as we have seen, very slow policy responses may actually prove destabilizing. Because history offers examples of each type, we can draw no general conclusion.

How Accurate Are Economic Forecasts?

One way to compress the policy-making lag dramatically is to forecast economic events accurately. If we could see a recession coming a full year ahead of time (which we certainly *cannot* do), even a rather sluggish policy response would still be timely. In terms of Figure 7, this would be a case in which the recession is predicted well before point *A*.

Over the years, economists in universities, government agencies, and private businesses have developed a number of techniques to assist them in predicting what the economy will do. Unfortunately, none of these methods is terribly accurate. To give a rough idea of magnitudes, forecasts of either the inflation rate or the real GDP growth rate for the year ahead typically err by $\pm \frac{3}{4}$ to 1 percentage point. But, in a bad year for forecasters, errors of 2 or 3 percentage points occur.

Is this forecasting record good enough? That depends on how the forecasts are used. It is certainly not good enough to support so-called *fine-tuning*—that is, attempts to keep the economy always within a hair's breadth of full employment. But it probably is good enough for policy makers interested in using discretionary stabilization policy to close persistent and sizable gaps between actual and potential GDP.

The Size of Government

One bogus argument that is sometimes heard is that active fiscal policy must inevitably lead to a growing public sector. Because proponents of fixed rules tend also to be opponents of big government, they view this growth as undesirable. Of course, others think that a larger public sector is just what society needs.

This argument, however, is completely beside the point because, as we pointed out in Chapter 11: *One's opinion about the proper size of government should have nothing to do with one's view on stabilization policy.* For example, President George W. Bush is as conservative as they come and, at least rhetorically, he is devoted to shrinking the size of the public sector.[4] But his tax-cutting initiatives in 2001–2003 constituted an extremely

---

[4] In fact, the size of the federal government has expanded rapidly during his presidency, in part because of national security concerns, but also because of domestic spending.

activist fiscal policy to spur economic growth. Furthermore, most stabilization policy these days consists of monetary policy, which neither increases nor decreases the size of government.

Uncertainties Caused by Government Policy

Advocates of rules are on stronger ground when they argue that frequent changes in tax laws, government spending programs, or monetary conditions make it difficult for firms and consumers to formulate and carry out rational plans. They argue that the authorities can provide a more stable environment for the private sector by adhering to fixed rules so that businesses and consumers know exactly what to expect.

No one disputes that a more stable environment is better for private planning. But supporters of discretionary policy emphasize that *stability in the economy* is more important than *stability in the government budget* (or in Federal Reserve operations). The whole idea of stabilization policy is to *prevent* gyrations in the pace of economic activity by *causing* timely gyrations in the government budget (or in monetary policy). Which atmosphere is better for business, they ask: one in which fiscal and monetary rules keep things peaceful on Capitol Hill and at the Federal Reserve while recessions and inflations wrack the economy, or one in which government changes its policy abruptly on occasion but the economy grows more smoothly? They think the answer is self-evident. The question, of course, is whether stabilization policy can succeed in practice.

A Political Business Cycle?

A final argument put forth by advocates of rules is political rather than economic. Fiscal policy decisions are made by elected politicians: the president and members of Congress. When elections are on the horizon (and for members of the House of Representatives, they *always*

Between Rules and Discretion

In recent years, a number of economists and policy makers have sought a middle ground between saddling monetary policy makers with rigid rules and giving them complete discretion, as the Federal Reserve has in the United States.

One such approach is called "inflation targeting." As practiced in the United States, for example, inflation targeting starts when an elected official (the Chancellor of the Exchequer, who is roughly equivalent to the U.S. Secretary of the Treasury) chooses a numerical target for the inflation rate—currently, this target is 2 percent for consumer prices. The United Kingdom's central bank, the Bank of England, is then bound by law to try to reach this target. In that sense, the system functions somewhat like a *rule*. However, monetary policy makers are given complete *discretion* as to how they go about trying to achieve this goal. Neither the Chancellor nor Parliament interferes with day-to-day monetary policy decisions. The Federal Reserve's current chairman, Ben Bernanke, was a big advocate of inflation targeting when he was a professor at Princeton University. But the Fed has not adopted it officially.

Another approach is called the "Taylor rule," after Professor John Taylor of Stanford University. More than a decade ago, Taylor noticed that the Fed's interest rate decisions during the chairmanship of Alan Greenspan could be described by a simple algebraic equation. This equation, now called the Taylor rule, starts with a 2 percent *real* interest rate, and then instructs the Fed to *lower* the rate of interest in proportion to any recessionary gap and to *raise* the

interest rate in proportion to any excess of inflation above 2 percent (which is the Fed's presumed inflation goal). No central bank uses the Taylor rule as a mechanical rule; nor did Taylor intend it that way. But many central banks around the world, including the Fed, find the Taylor rule useful as a benchmark to guide their decision making—thus blending, once again, features of both rules and discretion.

The Bank of England's Monetary Policy Committee

SOURCE: © David Devins/newscast

are), these politicians may be as concerned with keeping their jobs as with doing what is right for the economy. This situation leaves fiscal policy subject to "political manipulation"— lawmakers may take inappropriate actions to attain short-run political goals. A system of purely automatic stabilization, its proponents argue, would eliminate this peril.

It is certainly *possible* that politicians could deliberately *cause* economic instability to help their own reelection. Indeed, some observers of these "political business cycles" have claimed that several American presidents have taken full advantage of the opportunity. Furthermore, even without any insidious intent, politicians may take the wrong actions for perfectly honorable reasons. Decisions in the political arena are never clear-cut, and it certainly is easy to find examples of grievous errors in the history of U.S. fiscal policy.

Taken as a whole, then, the political argument against discretionary fiscal policy seems to have a great deal of merit. But what are we to do about it? It is unrealistic to believe that fiscal decisions could or should be made by a group of objective and nonpartisan technicians. Tax and budget policies require inherently *political* decisions that, in a democracy, should be made by elected officials.

This fact may seem worrisome in view of the possibilities for political chicanery. But it should not bother us any more (or any less) than similar maneuvering in other areas of policy making. After all, the same problem besets international relations, national defense, formulation and enforcement of the law, and so on. Politicians make all these decisions for us, subject only to sporadic accountability at elections. Is there really any reason why fiscal decisions should be different?

But monetary policy *is* different. Because Congress was concerned that elected officials focused on the short run would pursue inflationary monetary policies, it long ago gave day-to-day decision-making authority over monetary policy to the unelected technocrats at the Federal Reserve. Politics influences monetary policy only indirectly: The Fed must report to Congress, and the president has the power to appoint Federal Reserve governors whose views are to his liking. For the most part, however, the Fed is apolitical.

A Nobel Prize for the Rules-versus-Discretion Debate

In 2004, the economists Finn Kydland of Carnegie-Mellon University and Edward Prescott of Arizona State University were awarded the Nobel Prize for a fascinating contribution to the rules-versus-discretion debate. They called attention to a general problem that they labeled "time inconsistency," and their analysis of this problem led them to conclude that the Fed should follow a rule.

A close-to-home example will illustrate the basic time inconsistency problem. Suppose your instructor announces in September that a final exam will be given in December. The main purpose of the exam is to ensure that students study and learn the course materials, and the exam itself creates both work for the faculty and stress for the students. So, when December rolls around, it may seem "optimal" to call off the exam at the last moment. Of course, if that happened

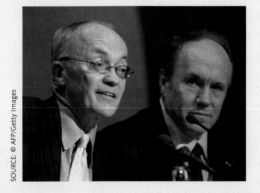

SOURCE: © AFP/Getty Images

regularly, students would soon stop studying for exams. So actually giving the exam is the better long-run policy. One way to solve this time inconsistency problem is to adopt a simple *rule* stating that announced exams will always be given, rather than allowing individual faculty members to cancel exams at their *discretion*.

Kydland and Prescott argued that monetary policy makers face a similar time inconsistency problem. They first announce a stern anti-inflation policy (analogous to giving an exam). But then, when the moment of truth (December) arrives, they may relent because they don't want to cause unemployment (all that work and stress). Their suggested solution: The Fed and other central banks should adopt *rules* that remove period-by-period *discretion*.

So where do we come out on the question posed at the start of this chapter? On balance, is it better to pursue the best discretionary policy we can, knowing full well that we will never achieve perfection? Or is it wiser to rely on fixed rules and the automatic stabilizers?

In weighing the pros and cons, your basic view of the economy is crucial. Some economists believe that the economy, if left unmanaged, would generate a series of ups and downs that would be difficult to predict, but that it would correct each of them by itself in a relatively short time. They conclude that, because of long lags and poor forecasts, our ability to anticipate whether the economy will need stimulus or restraint by the time policy actions have their effects is quite limited. Consequently, they advocate fixed rules.

Other economists liken the economy to a giant glacier with a great deal of inertia. Under this view, if we observe an inflationary or recessionary gap today, it will likely still be there a year or two from now because the self-correcting mechanism works slowly. In such a world, accurate forecasting is not imperative, even if policy lags are long. If we base policy on a forecast of a 4 percent gap between actual and potential GDP a year from now, and the gap turns out to be only 2 percent, we still will have done the right thing despite the inaccurate forecast. So holders of this view of the economy tend to support discretionary policy.

There is certainly no consensus on this issue, either among economists or politicians. After all, the question touches on political ideology as well as economics, and liberals often look to government to solve social problems, whereas conservatives consistently point out that many efforts of government fail despite the best intentions. A prudent view of the matter might be that

The case for active discretionary policy is strong when the economy has a serious deficiency or excess of aggregate demand. However, advocates of fixed rules are right that it is unwise to try to iron out every little wiggle in the growth path of GDP.

But one thing seems certain: The rules-versus-discretion debate is likely to go on for quite some time.

| SUMMARY |

1. **Velocity** (V) is the ratio of nominal GDP to the stock of money (M). It indicates how quickly money circulates.

2. One important determinant of velocity is the rate of interest (r). At higher interest rates, people find it less attractive to hold money because money pays zero or little interest. Thus, when r rises, money circulates faster, and V rises.

3. **Monetarism** is a type of analysis that focuses attention on velocity and the money supply (M). Although monetarists realize that V is not constant, they believe that it is predictable enough to make it a useful tool for policy analysis and forecasting.

4. Because it increases the volume of transactions, and hence increases the demands for bank deposits and therefore bank reserves, expansionary fiscal policy pushes interest rates higher. Higher interest rates reduce the multiplier by deterring some types of spending, especially investment.

5. Because fiscal policy actions affect aggregate demand either directly through G or indirectly through C, the expenditure lags between fiscal actions and their effects on aggregate demand are probably fairly short. By con-

trast, monetary policy operates mainly on investment, I, which responds slowly to changes in interest rates.

6. However, the policy-making lag normally is much longer for fiscal policy than for monetary policy. Hence, when the two lags are combined, it is not clear which type of policy acts more quickly.

7. Because it cannot control the demand curve for money, the Federal Reserve cannot control both M and r. If the demand for money changes, the Fed must decide whether it wants to hold M steady, hold r steady, or adopt some compromise position.

8. Monetarists emphasize the importance of stabilizing the growth path of the money supply, whereas the predominant Keynesian view puts more emphasis on keeping interest rates on target.

9. In practice, the Fed has changed its views on this issue several times. For decades, it attached primary importance to interest rates. Between 1979 and 1982, it stressed its commitment to stable growth of the money supply. But, since then, the focus has clearly returned to interest rates.

10. When the aggregate supply curve is very flat, changes in aggregate demand will have large effects on the nation's real output but small effects on the price level. Under those circumstances, stabilization policy works well as an antirecession device, but it has little power to combat inflation.

11. When the aggregate supply curve is steep, changes in aggregate demand have small effects on real output but large effects on the price level. In such a case, stabilization policy can do much to fight inflation but is not a very effective way to cure unemployment.

12. The aggregate supply curve is likely to be relatively flat in the short run but relatively steep in the long run. Hence, stabilization policy affects mainly output in the short run but mainly prices in the long run.

13. When the lags in the operation of fiscal and monetary policy are long and unpredictable, attempts to stabilize economic activity may actually destabilize it.

14. Some economists believe that our imperfect knowledge of the channels through which stabilization policy works, the long lags involved, and the inaccuracy of forecasts make it unlikely that discretionary stabilization policy can succeed.

15. Other economists recognize these difficulties but do not believe they are quite as serious. They also place much less faith in the economy's ability to cure recessions and inflations on its own. They therefore think that discretionary policy is not only advisable, but essential.

16. Stabilizing the economy by fiscal policy need not imply a tendency toward "big government."

| KEY TERMS |

Velocity   278

Equation of exchange   278

Quantity theory of money   279

Effect of interest rate on velocity   280

Monetarism   281

Effect of fiscal policy on interest rates   281

Lags in stabilization policy   283

Controlling *M* versus controlling *r*   284

Rules versus discretionary policy   291

| TEST YOURSELF |

1. How much money by the M1 definition (cash plus checking account balances) do you typically have at any particular moment? Divide this amount into your total income over the past 12 months to obtain your own personal velocity. Are you typical of the nation as a whole?

2. The following table provides data on nominal gross domestic product and the money supply (M1 definition) in recent selected years. Compute velocity in each year. Can you see any trend? How does it compare with the trend that prevailed from 1975 to 1995?

Year	End-of-Year Money Supply (M1)	Nominal GDP
2004	$1,376	$11,686
2005	1,375	12,434
2006	1,367	13,195
2007	1,364	13,841

NOTE: Amounts are in billions.

3. Use a supply-and-demand diagram similar to Figure 2 to show the choices open to the Fed following an unexpected *decline* in the demand for money. If the Fed is following a monetarist policy, what will happen to the rate of interest?

4. Which of the following events would strengthen the argument for the use of discretionary policy, and which would strengthen the argument for rules?

   a. Structural changes make the economy's self-correcting mechanism work more quickly and reliably than before.

   b. New statistical methods are found that improve the accuracy of economic forecasts.

   c. A Republican president is elected when there is an overwhelmingly Democratic Congress. Congress and the president differ sharply on what should be done about the national economy.

5. **(More difficult)** The money supply (*M*) is the sum of bank deposits (*D*) plus currency in the hands of the public (call that *C*). Suppose the required reserve ratio is 20 percent and the Fed provides $50 billion in bank reserves (*R* = $50 billion).

   a. First assume that people hold no currency (*C* = 0). How large will the money supply (*M*) be? If the Fed increases bank reserves to *R* = $60 billion, how large will *M* be then?

   b. Next, assume that people hold 20 cents worth of currency for each dollar of bank deposits, that is, *C* = 0.2*D*. Define the *monetary base* (*B*) as the sum of reserves (*R*) plus currency (*C*): *B* = *R* + *C*. If the Fed now creates $50 billion worth of monetary base, how large will *M* be? (Hint: You will need a little bit of algebra to figure this out. Remember that the $50 billion monetary base is divided between two purposes: bank reserves and currency.) Now, if the Fed increases the monetary base to *B* = $60 billion, how large will *M* be?

   c. What do you notice about the relationship between *M* and *B*?

| DISCUSSION QUESTIONS |

1. Use the concept of opportunity cost to explain why velocity is higher at higher interest rates.

2. How does monetarism differ from the quantity theory of money?

3. Given the behavior of velocity shown in Figure 1, would it make more sense for the Federal Reserve to formulate targets for M1 or M2?

4. Distinguish between the expenditure lag and the policy lag in stabilization policy. Does monetary or fiscal policy have the shorter expenditure lag? What about the policy lag?

5. Explain why their contrasting views on the shape of the aggregate supply curve lead some economists to argue much more strongly for stabilization policies to fight unemployment and other economists to argue much more strongly for stabilization policies to fight inflation.

6. Explain why lags make it possible that policy actions intended to stabilize the economy will actually destabilize it.

7. Many observers think that the Federal Reserve succeeded in using deft applications of monetary policy to "fine-tune" the U.S. economy into the full-employment zone in the 1990s without worsening inflation. Use the data on money supply, interest rates, real GDP, unemployment, and the price level given on the inside back cover of this book to evaluate this claim.

8. During the year 2007, U.S. economic performance deteriorated sharply. Can this decline be blamed on inferior monetary or fiscal policy? (You may want to ask your instructor about this question.)

BUDGET DEFICITS IN THE SHORT AND LONG RUN

Blessed are the young, for they shall inherit the national debt.

HERBERT HOOVER

Monetary policy and fiscal policy are typically thought of as tools for short-run economic *stabilization*—that is, as ways to combat either inflation or unemployment. Debates over the Federal Reserve's next interest-rate decision, or over this year's federal budget, are normally dominated by short-run considerations such as: Does the economy need to be stimulated or restrained *right now?*

But the monetary and fiscal choices the government makes today also have profound effects on our economy's ability to produce goods and services *in the future*. We began Part 2 by emphasizing long-run growth, and especially the role of capital formation (see Chapters 6 and 7). But for most of Part 3, we have been preoccupied with the shorter-run issues of inflation, unemployment, and recession. This chapter integrates the two perspectives by considering both the long-run and short-run implications of fiscal and monetary policy decisions. What differences does it make if we stimulate (or restrain) the economy with fiscal or monetary policy? Should we strive to balance the budget? What are the economic virtues and vices of large budget deficits, both now and in the future?

CONTENTS

IS THE FEDERAL GOVERNMENT BUDGET DEFICIT TOO LARGE?

Several of these questions were brought into sharp relief by the partisan debate over the budget deficit during the 2008 presidential campaign.

During the primary season, virtually all the Democratic candidates railed against the large budget deficits of the Bush years. Most—including both Hillary Clinton and Barack Obama—proposed to repeal parts of the tax cuts enacted in 2001 and 2003, especially those that benefited upper-income groups, in order to shrink the budget deficit—which, they said, was a danger to the nation's economic health.

By contrast, virtually all the Republican candidates, including John McCain, vowed to maintain the Bush tax cuts, arguing that repealing them would harm the economy. While these candidates also objected to large budget deficits, they stoutly defended most of the Bush administration's spending initiatives as well. Since you cannot reduce the budget deficit without either raising taxes or cutting spending, they were implicitly saying that reducing the budget deficit was not a high priority.

Which side was right? Is it important to shrink the budget deficit? Or is it more advisable to maintain both the tax cuts and the spending? Politics aside, by the end of the chapter, you will be in an excellent position to make an informed judgment on this important policy issue for yourself.

SHOULD THE BUDGET ALWAYS BE BALANCED? THE SHORT RUN

Americans have long been attracted by the idea of balancing the government budget year after year—so much so that a constitutional amendment to require a balanced budget has been proposed and debated many times. Let us begin our examination of the virtues and vices of a balanced budget by reviewing the basic principles of fiscal policy that we have learned so far (especially in Chapter 11).

These principles certainly do *not* imply that we should always maintain a balanced budget, much as that notion may appeal to our intuitive sense of prudent financial management. Rather, they instruct fiscal policy makers to focus on *balancing aggregate supply and aggregate demand*. They therefore point to the desirability of budget *deficits* when private demand, $C + I + (X - IM)$, is weak and of budget *surpluses* when private demand is strong. The budget should be balanced, according to these principles, only when $C + I + G + (X - IM)$ under a balanced-budget policy approximately equals potential GDP. This situation may sometimes prevail, but it will not necessarily be the norm.

The reason why a balanced budget is not always advisable should be clear from our earlier discussion of stabilization policy. Consider the fiscal policy that the federal government would follow if its goal were to maintain a balanced budget every year, as most of the 50 states do. Suppose the budget was initially balanced and private spending sagged for some reason, as it did in 2007–2008. The multiplier would pull GDP down. Because personal and corporate tax receipts fall sharply when GDP declines, the budget would automatically swing into the red. To restore budget balance, the government would then have to *cut spending* or *raise taxes*—exactly the opposite of the appropriate fiscal policy response to a recessionary gap, and exactly the opposite of what the federal government actually did. Thus:

Attempts to balance the budget during recessions—as was done, say, during the Great Depression—will prolong and deepen slumps.

This is precisely what many observers feel happened to Japan when it raised taxes in a weak economy in 1997. In fact, Ryutaro Hashimoto, Japan's prime minister from 1996 to 1998, was disparagingly called the "Herbert Hoover of Japan" because he sought to reduce the budget deficit despite Japan's sinking economy. State and local governments in the United States also often raise taxes or cut spending during recessions because they have balanced-budget requirements.

This problem arises in both directions. Budget balancing also can lead to inappropriate fiscal policy under boom conditions. If rising tax receipts induce a budget-balancing government to spend more or to cut taxes, then fiscal policy will "boom the boom"—with unfortunate inflationary consequences.

The Importance of the Policy Mix

Actually, the issue is even more complicated than we have indicated so far. As we know, fiscal policy is not the only way for the government to affect aggregate demand. It also can influence aggregate demand through its *monetary policy*. For this reason,

> The appropriate fiscal policy depends, among other things, on the current stance of monetary policy. Although a balanced budget may be appropriate under one monetary policy, a deficit or a surplus may be appropriate under another monetary policy.

An example will illustrate the point. Suppose Congress and the president believe that the aggregate supply and demand curves will intersect approximately at full employment if the budget is balanced. Then a balanced budget would seem to be the appropriate fiscal policy.

Now suppose monetary policy turns contractionary, pulling the aggregate demand curve inward to the left, as shown by the brick-colored arrow in Figure 1, and thereby creating a recessionary gap. If the fiscal authorities wish to restore GDP to its original level, they must shift the aggregate demand curve back to its original position, D_0D_0, as indicated by the blue arrow. To do so, they must either raise spending or cut taxes, thereby opening up a budget deficit. Thus, the tightening of *monetary* policy changes the appropriate *fiscal* policy from a balanced budget to a deficit, because both monetary and fiscal policies affect aggregate demand.

By the same token, a given target for aggregate demand implies that any change in *fiscal* policy will alter the appropriate *monetary* policy. For example, we can reinterpret Figure 1 as indicating the effects of increasing the budget deficit by raising government spending or cutting taxes (the blue arrow). Then, if the Fed wants real GDP to remain at Y_1, it must raise interest rates enough to restore the aggregate demand curve to D_1D_1.

It is precisely the preferred *mix* of policy—a smaller budget deficit balanced by easier money—that the U.S. government managed to engineer with great success in the 1990s. Congress raised taxes and cut spending, which reduced aggregate demand. But the Federal Reserve pursued a sufficiently expansionary policy to return this "lost" aggregate demand to the economy by keeping interest rates low.

So we should not expect a balanced budget to be the norm. How, then, can we tell whether any particular deficit is too large or too small? From the discussion so far, it would appear that the answer depends on the strength of private-sector aggregate demand and the stance of monetary policy. But those are not the only considerations.

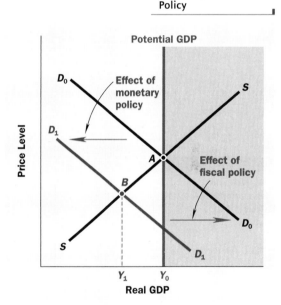

FIGURE 1

The Interaction of Monetary and Fiscal Policy

SURPLUSES AND DEFICITS: THE LONG RUN

One implication of what we have just said is that various *combinations* of fiscal and monetary policy can lead to the *same* level of aggregate demand, and hence to the same real GDP and price level, in the short run. For example, the government could reduce aggregate demand by raising taxes, but the Fed could make up for it by cutting interest rates. Or the reverse could happen: The government could cut taxes while the Fed raises interest rates, leaving aggregate demand unchanged. The long-run consequences of these alternative mixes of monetary and fiscal policy may be quite different, however.

In previous chapters, we learned that more expansionary fiscal policy (tax cuts or higher government spending) and tighter money should produce *higher* real interest rates and therefore *lower* investment. Thus, such a policy mix should shift the composition of total expenditure, $C + I + G + (X - IM)$, toward more G, more C (from tax cuts), and less I.[1] The expected result is less capital formation, and therefore slower growth of potential GDP. As we shall see shortly, it was precisely that policy mix—large tax cuts and very tight money—that the U.S. government inadvertently chose in the early 1980s and, to a lesser extent, in the years 2004–2006.

But the opposite policy mix—tighter budgets and looser monetary policy—should produce the opposite outcomes: lower real interest rates, more investment, and hence faster growth of potential GDP. That was the direction U.S. macroeconomic policy took in the 1990s—with excellent results. Lowering the budget deficit and then turning it into a surplus, economists believe, was an effective way to increase the investment share of GDP, which soared from 12 percent in 1992 to 17 percent in 2000. The general point is

> The composition of aggregate demand is a major determinant of the rate of economic growth. If a larger fraction of GDP is devoted to investment, the nation's capital stock will grow faster and the aggregate supply schedule will shift more quickly to the right, accelerating growth.

International data likewise show a positive relationship between growth and the share of GDP invested. Figure 2 displays, for a set of 24 countries on four continents, both investment as a share of GDP and growth in per-capita output over two decades (the 1970s and 1980s). Countries with higher investment rates clearly experienced higher growth, on average.

FIGURE 2

Growth and Investment in 24 Countries

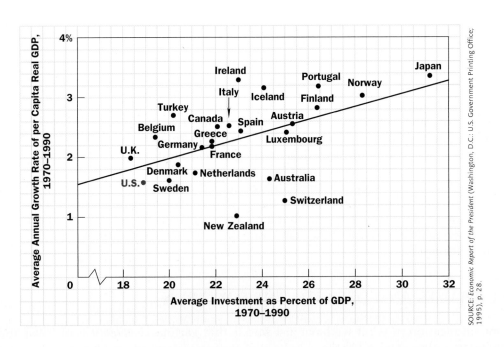

SOURCE: *Economic Report of the President* (Washington, D.C.: U.S. Government Printing Office, 1995), p. 28.

---

[1] Assume for the moment that net exports, $X - IM$, *are fixed*. We will deal with the consequences of fiscal and monetary policy on exports and imports in Chapter 19.

So it appears that when we ask whether the budget should be in balance, in deficit, or in surplus, we have posed a good but complicated question. Before attempting to answer it, we need to get some facts straight.

DEFICITS AND DEBT: TERMINOLOGY AND FACTS

First, some critical terminology. People frequently confuse two terms that have different meanings: *budget deficits* and the *national debt*. We must learn to distinguish between the two.

The **budget deficit** is the amount by which the government's expenditures exceed its receipts during some specified period of time, usually a year. If, instead, receipts exceed expenditures, we have a **budget surplus.** For example, during fiscal year 2007, the federal government raised $2.568 trillion in revenue and spent $2.730 trillion, resulting in a deficit of $162 billion.[2]

The **national debt,** also called the *public debt,* is the total value of the government's indebtedness at a moment in time. Thus, for example, the U.S. national debt at the end of fiscal year 2007 was almost $9 *trillion.*

These two concepts—deficit and debt—are closely related because the government accumulates *debt* by running *deficits* or reduces its debt by running *surpluses.* The relationship between the debt and the deficit or surplus can be explained by a simple analogy. As you run water into a bathtub ("run a deficit"), the accumulated volume of water in the tub ("the debt") rises. Alternatively, if you let water out of the tub ("run a surplus"), the level of the water ("the debt") falls. Analogously, budget deficits raise the national debt, whereas budget surpluses lower it. But, of course, getting rid of the deficit (shutting off the flow of water) does not eliminate the accumulated debt (drain the tub).

Some Facts about the National Debt

Now that we have made this distinction, let us look at the size and nature of the accumulated public debt and then at the annual budget deficit. How large a public debt do we have? How did we get it? Who owes it? Is it growing or shrinking?

To begin with the simplest question, the public debt is enormous. At the end of 2007, it amounted to nearly $30,000 for every man, woman, and child in America. But just under half of this outstanding debt was held by agencies of the U.S. government—in other words, one branch of the government owed it to another. If we deduct this portion, the net national debt was about $5 trillion, or approximately $16,500 per person.

Furthermore, when we compare the debt with the gross domestic product—the volume of goods and services our economy produces in a year—it does not seem so large after all. With a GDP approaching $14 trillion in late 2007, the net debt was only about 35 percent of the nation's yearly income. By contrast, many families who own homes owe *several years'* worth of income to the banks that granted them mortgages. Many U.S. corporations also owe their bondholders much more than 35 percent of a year's sales.

But before these analogies make you feel too comfortable, we should point out that simple analogies between public and private debt are almost always misleading. For one thing, individuals do not live forever. But the federal government does—or at least we hope so—which increases its capacity to carry debt.

On the other hand, a family with a large mortgage debt also owns a home whose value presumably exceeds the mortgage. And a solvent business firm has assets (factories, machinery, inventories, and so forth) that far exceed its outstanding debt in value. Is the same

The **budget deficit** is the amount by which the government's expenditures exceed its receipts during a specified period of time, usually a year. If receipts exceed expenditures, it is called a **budget surplus** instead.

The **national debt** is the federal government's total indebtedness at a moment in time. It is the result of previous budget deficits.

---

[2] *Reminder:* The fiscal year of the U.S. government ends on September 30. Thus, fiscal year 2007 ran from October 1, 2006, to September 30, 2007.

thing true of the U.S. government? No one knows for sure. How much is the White House worth? Or the national parks? And what about military bases, both here and abroad? Because these government assets are not sold on markets, no one really knows their true value. But some people think the value of the government's assets may be almost as large as the value of its debt.

Figure 3 charts the path of the *net* national debt from 1915 to 2007, expressing each year's net debt as a fraction of that year's nominal GDP. Looking at the debt *relative to GDP* is important for two reasons. First, we must remember that everything grows in a growing economy. Given that private debt has expanded greatly since 1915, it would be surprising indeed if the public debt had not grown as well. In fact, federal debt grew more slowly than did either private debt or GDP for most of the period since World War II. The years from 1980 to about 1994 stand out as an aberration in Figure 3, with the debt-to-GDP ratio climbing sharply.

Second, the debt is measured in dollars and, as long as there is any inflation, the amount of purchasing power that each dollar represents declines each year. Dividing the debt by nominal GDP, as is done in Figure 3, adjusts for both real growth and inflation, and so puts the debt numbers in better perspective.

Figure 3 shows us how and when the U.S. government acquired all this debt. Notice the sharp increases in the ratio of debt to GDP during World War I, the Great Depression, and especially World War II. Thereafter, you see an unmistakable downward trend until the recession of 1974–1975. In 1945, the national debt was the equivalent of about a year's worth of GDP. By 1974, this figure had been whittled down to just two months' worth.

Thus, until the 1980s, the U.S. government had acquired most of its debt either to finance wars or during recessions. As we will see later, the *cause* of the debt is quite germane to the question of whether the debt is a burden. So it is important to remember that

Until about 1983, almost all of the U.S. national debt stemmed from financing wars and from the losses of tax revenues that accompany recessions.

But then things changed. From the early 1980s until 1993, the national debt grew faster than nominal GDP, reversing the pattern that had prevailed since 1945. This growth spurt happened with no wars and only one recession. By 1993, the debt exceeded five months' GDP—nearly triple its value in 1974. This development alarmed many economists and public figures.

FIGURE 3

The U.S. National Debt Relative to GDP, 1915–2007

SOURCE: Constructed by the authors from data in *Historical Statistics of the United States* and *Economic Report of the President.*

At that point, the government took decisive actions to reduce the budget deficit. The ratio of debt to GDP then fell for years. But President Bush's large tax cuts reversed the trend for a few years after 2001. Lately, the ratio of debt to GDP has been falling modestly again.

INTERPRETING THE BUDGET DEFICIT OR SURPLUS

We have observed that the federal government ran extremely large budget deficits from the early 1980s until the mid 1990s, and then again for a few years in this decade. As Figure 4 shows, the budget deficit ballooned from $79 billion in fiscal year 1981 to $208 billion by fiscal year 1983—setting a record that was subsequently eclipsed several times. As late as fiscal year 1995, the deficit was still $164 billion. These are enormous, even mind-boggling, numbers. But what do they mean? How should we interpret them?

The Structural Deficit or Surplus

First, it is important to understand that the same fiscal program can lead to a deficit or a surplus, depending on the state of the economy. Failure to appreciate this point has led many people to assume that a larger deficit always signifies a more expansionary fiscal policy—which is not the case.

Think, for example, about what happens to the budget during a recession. As GDP falls, the government's major sources of tax revenue—income taxes, corporate taxes, and payroll taxes—all shrink because firms and people pay lower taxes when they earn less. Similarly, some types of government spending, notably transfer payments such as unemployment benefits, rise when GDP falls because more people are out of work. Recall that the deficit is the difference between government expenditures, which are either purchases or transfer payments, and tax receipts:

$$\text{Deficit} = G + \text{Transfers} - \text{Taxes} = G - (\text{Taxes} - \text{Transfers}) = G - T$$

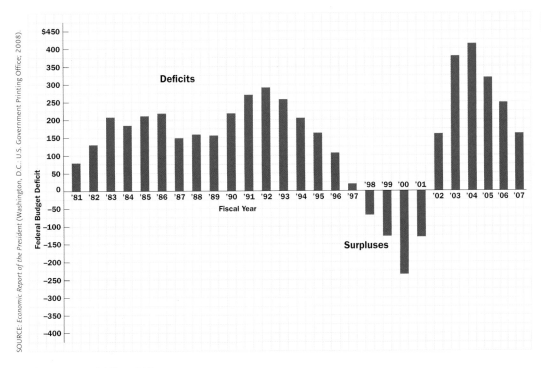

FIGURE 4

Official Fiscal-Year Budget Deficits, 1981–2007

SOURCE: *Economic Report of the President* (Washington, D.C.: U.S. Government Printing Office, 2008).

NOTE: Amounts are in billions of dollars.

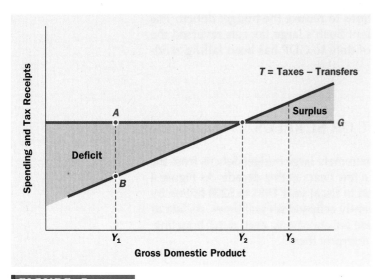

Because a falling GDP leads to higher transfer payments and lower tax receipts,

> **The deficit rises in a recession and falls in a boom, even with no change in fiscal policy.**

Figure 5 depicts this relationship between GDP and the budget deficit. The government's fiscal program is summarized by the blue and brick-colored lines. The horizontal blue line labeled G indicates that federal purchases of goods and services are approximately unaffected by GDP. The rising brick-colored line labeled T (for taxes minus transfers) indicates that taxes rise and transfer payments fall as GDP rises. Notice that the same fiscal policy (that is, the same two lines) leads to a large deficit if GDP is Y_1, a balanced budget if GDP

FIGURE 5

The Effect of the Economy on the Budget

The **structural budget deficit or surplus** is the hypothetical deficit or surplus we *would have* under current fiscal policies if the economy were operating near full employment.

is Y_2, or a surplus if GDP is as high as Y_3. Clearly, the deficit itself is not a good measure of the government's fiscal policy.

To seek a better measure, economists pay more attention to what is called the **structural budget deficit or surplus.** This hypothetical measure replaces both the spending and taxes in the *actual* budget by estimates of how much the government *would be* spending and receiving, given current tax rates and expenditure rules, if the economy were operating at some fixed, high-employment level. For example, if the high-employment benchmark in Figure 5 was Y_2, although actual GDP was only Y_1, the structural deficit would be zero even though the actual deficit would be AB.

Because it is based on the spending and taxing the government *would be* doing at some fixed level of GDP, rather than on *actual* expenditures and receipts, the structural deficit does not depend on the state of the economy. It changes *only* when policy changes, *not* when GDP changes. For that reason, most economists view it as a better measure of the thrust of fiscal policy than the actual deficit.

This new concept helps us understand the changing nature of the large budget deficits of the 1980s, the stunning turn to surpluses in the late 1990s, and the rapid swing back to large deficits since 2001. The first two columns of data in Table 1 show both the actual surplus and the structural surplus every other year since 1981. (Most of the numbers are negative, indicating *deficits*.) Because of recessions in 1983 and 1991, the actual deficit was far larger than the structural deficit in those years. But the difference between the two was negligible in 1987 and small in 1995, when the economy was near full employment, and then changed sign (the structural deficit was larger than the actual deficit) in 1997–2001. By 2007, the two measures were quite close again.

Four interesting facts stand out when we compare the numbers in the first and second columns. First, even though the *official* deficit was smaller in fiscal 1995 than in fiscal 1983, the *structural* deficit was larger in 1995—despite years of budget "stringency." Second, the structural deficit rose between 1989 and 1993. It was this trend toward larger structural deficits that alarmed keen students of the federal budget. Third, the stunning $381 billion swing in the budget deficit from 1993 to 1999 (from a deficit of $255 billion to a surplus of $126 billion) far exceeds the change in the structural deficit, which fell by "only" $192 billion. This last number, which is still impressive, is a better indicator of how much fiscal policy changed during the period. Fourth, the swing from a moderate-sized structural surplus in 2001 to a large structural deficit in 2003 was both rapid and huge—$381 billion in just two years. Fortunately, both the actual and the structural deficit have come down dramatically since then.

TABLE 1

Alternative Budget Concepts, 1981–2007

Fiscal Year	Total Surplus (1)	Structural Surplus (2)	On-Budget Surplus (3)	Off-Budget Surplus (4)
1981	−79	−17	−74	−5
1983	−208	−112	−208	0
1985	−212	−179	−222	+10
1987	−150	−156	−168	+18
1989	−153	−117	−205	+52
1991	−269	−150	−321	+52
1993	−255	−193	−300	+45
1995	−164	−146	−226	+62
1997	−22	−80	−103	+81
1999	+126	−1	+2	+124
2001	+128	+105	−32	+160
2003	−378	−276	−538	+160
2005	−318	−237	−494	+176
2007	−162	−166	−344	+182

NOTE: Amounts in billions of dollars.

SOURCE: Congressional Budget Office

On-Budget versus Off-Budget Surpluses

When you read about the budget in the newspapers, you may see references to the "off-budget" surplus or deficit and the "on-budget" surplus or deficit. What do those terms mean?

Because Social Security benefits are financed by an earmarked revenue source—the payroll tax—Social Security and a few minor items have traditionally been segregated in the federal fiscal accounts. Specifically, both Social Security expenditures and the payroll tax receipts that finance them are treated as off-budget items, whereas most other expenditures and receipts are classified as on-budget. Thus:

Overall budget deficit = Off-budget deficit + On-budget deficit

Because the Social Security System has been running sizable surpluses in recent years, the difference between the overall and on-budget deficits has been substantial. For example, in fiscal year 2007, the overall budget showed a $162 billion deficit (column 1). But this was composed of a whopping $344 billion on-budget *deficit* (column 3) less a $182 billion Social Security *surplus* (column 4). Some people claim that such a large discrepancy must mean that the Social Security surplus is "hiding" the "true" deficit. That's a matter of semantics. Nothing is really hidden; the facts are as given in Table 1. But you need to interpret the facts correctly. If you are interested in knowing how much the federal government must borrow each year, the total deficit (column 1) gives the number you want.

Conclusion: What Happened after 1981?

Table 1 helps us understand the remarkable ups and downs of the federal budget deficit since the early 1980s. Column 1 shows the overall surplus (if positive) or deficit (if negative) every other year from 1981 to 2007, and column 2 shows the corresponding *structural* surplus. Finally, columns 3 and 4 break the overall surplus into its *on-budget* and *off-budget* components. The table tells the following story about the evolution of the budget deficit.

The large Reagan tax cuts in the early 1980s ballooned the budget deficit from $79 billion to $212 billion, and more than 100 percent of this deterioration was structural (see column 2). Late in the 1980s, the deficit started rising again—even though Social Security began to run sizable surpluses (see column 4). The overall deficit reached $269 billion in 1991, but then began to shrink. One reason was the burgeoning Social Security surplus, which increased by $115 between 1993 and 2001. The strong economy helped, too. Notice that the actual surplus rose more than the structural surplus. But most of the deficit-reducing "work" was on-budget and structural, as tax increases and expenditure restraint during the Clinton years finally got the budget under control—briefly, as it turned out.

By 2003, a combination of large tax cuts, a burst of spending on antiterrorism and the war in Iraq, and weaker economic growth had pushed the deficit up to a record $378 billion—a record that was topped in fiscal year 2004. But both the actual budget deficit (column 1) and the structural budget deficit (column 2) have fallen since then.

WHY IS THE NATIONAL DEBT CONSIDERED A BURDEN?

Now that we have gained some perspective on the facts, let us consider the charge that budget deficits place intolerable burdens on future generations. Perhaps the most frequently heard reason is that *future Americans will be burdened by heavy interest payments*, which will necessitate higher taxes. But think about who will receive those interest payments: mostly the future Americans who own the bonds. Thus, one group of future Americans will be making interest payments to another group of future Americans—which cannot be a burden on the nation as a whole.[3]

---

[3] However, the future taxes that will have to be raised to pay the interest may reduce the efficiency of the economy.

But there *is* a future burden to the extent that the debt is held by foreigners. The share of the net U.S. national debt owned by foreign individuals, businesses, and governments has been rising rapidly and is now over 52 percent. Paying interest on this portion of the debt will indeed burden future Americans in a very concrete way: For years to come, a portion of America's GDP will be sent abroad to pay interest on the debts we incurred in the 1980s, 1990s, and 2000s. For this reason, many thoughtful observers are becoming concerned that the United States is borrowing too much from abroad.[4] Thus, we conclude that

> **If the national debt is owned by domestic citizens, future interest payments just transfer funds from one group of Americans to another. But the portion of the national debt owned by foreigners does constitute a burden on the nation as a whole.**

Many people also worry that every nation has a limited capacity to borrow, just like every family and every business. If it exceeds this limit, it is in danger of being unable to pay its creditors and may go bankrupt—with calamitous consequences for everyone. For some countries, this concern is indeed valid and serious. Debt crises have done major damage to many countries in Latin America, Asia, and Africa over the years.

But the U.S. government need not worry about defaulting on its debt for one simple reason. *The American national debt is an obligation to pay U.S. dollars:* Each debt certificate obligates the Treasury to pay the holder so many U.S. dollars on a prescribed date. But think about where those dollars come from. The U.S. government prints them up! So, in the worst case, if the U.S. government had no better way to pay off its creditors, it could always print whatever money it needed to do so. In a word, *no nation need default on debts that call for repayment in its own currency.*[5] However, printing up the necessary money is not an option for countries whose debts call for payment, say, in U.S. dollars, as a number of Southeast Asian countries learned in 1997 and as Argentina learned in 2001.

It does not, of course, follow that acquiring more debt through budget deficits is necessarily a good idea for the United States. Sometimes, it is clearly a bad idea. Nonetheless:

> **There is a fundamental difference between nations that borrow in their own currency (such as the United States) and nations that borrow in some other currency (which is, normally, the U.S. dollar). The former need never default on their debts; the latter might have to.**

BUDGET DEFICITS AND INFLATION

We now turn to the effects of deficits on macroeconomic outcomes. It often is said that deficit spending is a cause of inflation. Let us consider that argument with the aid of Figure 6, which is a standard aggregate supply-and-demand diagram.

Initially, equilibrium is at point *A*, where demand curve D_0D_0 and supply curve *SS* intersect. Output is $7,000 billion, and the price index is 100. In the diagram, the aggregate demand and supply curves intersect precisely at potential GDP, indicating that the economy is operating at full employment. Let us also assume that the budget is initially balanced.

Suppose the government now raises spending or cuts taxes enough to shift the aggregate demand schedule outward from D_0D_0 to D_1D_1. Equilibrium shifts from point *A* to point *B*, and the graph shows the price level rising from 100 to 106, or 6 percent. But that is not the end of the story, because point *B* represents an inflationary gap. We know from previous chapters that inflation will continue until the aggregate supply curve shifts far enough inward that it passes through point *C*, at which point the inflationary gap is gone. In this example, deficit spending will eventually raise the price level 12 percent.

Thus, the cries that budget deficits are inflationary have the ring of truth. How much truth they hold depends on several factors. One is the slope of the aggregate supply curve.

---

[4] We will discuss the linkages between the federal budget deficit and foreign borrowing in greater detail in Chapter 19.

[5] However, Russia astounded the financial world in 1998 by defaulting on its ruble-denominated debt.

Figure 6 clearly shows that a steep supply curve would lead to more inflation than a flat one. A second factor is the degree of resource utilization. Deficit spending is more inflationary in a fully employed economy (such as that depicted in Figure 6) than in an economy with lots of slack.

Finally, we must remember that the Federal Reserve's monetary policy can always cancel out the potential inflationary effects of deficit spending by pulling the aggregate demand curve back to its original position. Once again, the *policy mix* is crucial.

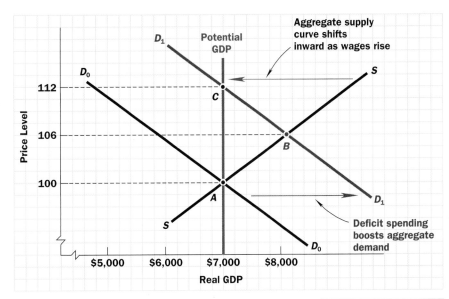

NOTE: Real GDP amounts are in billions of dollars.

FIGURE 6

The Inflationary Effects of Deficit Spending

The Monetization Issue

But will the Federal Reserve always neutralize the expansionary effect of a higher budget deficit? This question brings up another reason why some people worry about the inflationary consequences of deficits. They fear that the Federal Reserve may feel compelled to "monetize" part of the deficit by purchasing some of the newly issued government debt. Let us explain, first, why the Fed might make such purchases and, second, why these purchases are called **monetizing the deficit**.

The central bank is said to **monetize the deficit** when it purchases bonds issued by the government.

Deficit spending, we have just noted, normally drives up both real GDP and the price level. As we emphasized in Chapter 13, such an economic expansion shifts the demand curve for bank reserves outward to the right—as depicted by the movement from D_0D_0 to D_1D_1 in Figure 7. The diagram shows that, if the Federal Reserve takes no action to shift the supply curve, interest rates will rise as equilibrium moves from point A to point B.

Suppose now that the Fed does not want interest rates to rise. What can it do? To prevent the incipient rise in r, it would have to engage in *expansionary monetary policy* that creates new bank reserves, thereby shifting the supply curve for reserves outward to the right—as indicated in Figure 8 on the next page. With the blue supply curve S_1S_1, equilibrium would be at point C rather than at point B, leaving interest rates unchanged. Because the Federal Reserve usually pursues expansionary monetary policy by purchasing Treasury bills in the open market, deficit spending might therefore induce the Fed to buy more government debt.

But why is this process called *monetizing* the deficit? The reason is simple. As we learned in Chapter 12, creating more bank reserves generally leads, via the multiple expansion process, to an increase in the money supply. By this indirect route, then, larger budget deficits may lead to a larger money supply. To summarize:

If the Federal Reserve takes no countervailing actions, an expansionary fiscal policy that increases the budget deficit will raise real GDP and prices, thereby raising the demand for bank reserves and

FIGURE 7

Fiscal Expansion and Interest Rates

Quantity of Bank Reserves

FIGURE 8

Monetization and Interest Rates

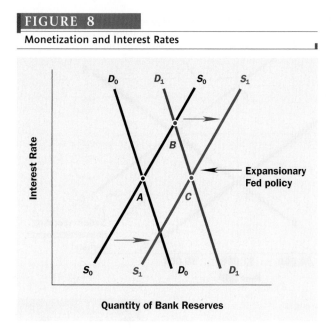

Quantity of Bank Reserves

driving up interest rates (Figure 7). If the Fed does not want interest rates to rise, it can engage in expansionary open-market operations; that is, it can purchase more government debt. If the Fed does so, both bank reserves and the money supply will increase (Figure 8). In this case, we say that part of the deficit is *monetized*.

Monetized deficits are more inflationary than nonmonetized deficits for the simple reason that expansionary monetary and fiscal policies *together* are more inflationary than expansionary fiscal policy *alone*. But is this a real worry? Does the Fed actually monetize any substantial portion of the deficit? Normally, it does not. The clearest evidence is the fact that the Fed managed to *reduce* inflation in the 1980s, and again in the early years of this decade, even as the government ran huge budget deficits. But over the years, monetization of deficits *has* been a serious cause of inflation in many other countries, ranging from Latin America to Russia, Israel, and elsewhere.

DEBT, INTEREST RATES, AND CROWDING OUT

So far, we have looked for possible problems that the national debt might cause on the *demand* side of the economy. But the real worry comes on the *supply* side. In brief, large budget deficits discourage investment and thereby retard the growth of the nation's capital stock.

The mechanism is easy to understand by presuming (as is generally the case) that the Fed does not engage in any substantial monetization. In that case, we have just seen, budget deficits tend to *raise* interest rates. But we know from earlier chapters that the rate of interest (r) is a major determinant of investment spending (I). In particular, higher r leads to less I. Lower investment today, in turn, means that the nation will have less capital tomorrow—and the size of *potential* GDP will be smaller. This, according to most economists, is the true sense in which a larger national debt may burden future generations—and, conversely, a smaller national debt may help them:

> A larger national debt may lead a nation to bequeath less physical capital to future generations. If they inherit less plant and equipment, these generations will be burdened by a smaller productive capacity—a lower potential GDP. By that mechanism, large deficits may retard economic growth. By the same logic, budget surpluses can stimulate capital formation and economic growth.

Crowding out occurs when deficit spending by the government forces private investment spending to contract.

Phrasing this point another way explains why this result is often called the **crowding-out** effect. Consider what happens in financial markets when the government engages in deficit spending. When it spends more than it takes in, the government must borrow the rest. It does so by selling bonds, which compete with corporate bonds and other financial instruments for the available supply of funds. As some savers decide to buy government bonds, the funds remaining to invest in private bonds must shrink. Thus, some private borrowers get "crowded out" of the financial markets as the government claims an increasing share of the economy's total saving.

Some critics of deficit spending have taken this lesson to its illogical extreme by arguing that each $1 of government spending crowds out exactly $1 of private spending, leaving "expansionary" fiscal policy with no net effect on total demand. In their view, when G rises, I falls by an equal amount, leaving the total of $C + I + G + (X - IM)$ unchanged. Under normal circumstances, we would not expect this to occur. Why? First, moderate budget deficits push up interest rates only slightly. Second, private spending is only moderately sensitive to interest rates. Even at the higher interest rates that government deficits cause, most corporations will continue to borrow to finance their capital investments.

Furthermore, in times of economic slack, a counterforce arises that we might call the **crowding-in** effect. Deficit spending presumably quickens the pace of economic activity. That, at least, is its purpose. As the economy expands, businesses find it more profitable to add to their capacity in order to meet the greater consumer demands. Because of this *induced investment*, as we called it in earlier chapters, any increase in G may *increase* investment, rather than *decrease* it as the crowding-out hypothesis predicts.

The strength of the crowding-in effect depends on how much additional real GDP is stimulated by government spending (that is, on the size of the multiplier) and on how sensitive investment spending is to the improved business opportunities that accompany rapid growth. It is even conceivable that the crowding-in effect could dominate the crowding-out effect in the short run, so that I rises, on balance, when G rises.

But how can this be true in view of the crowding-out argument? Certainly, if the government borrows more *and the total volume of private saving is fixed,* then private industry must borrow less. That's just arithmetic. The fallacy in the strict crowding-out argument lies in supposing that the economy's flow of saving is really fixed. If government deficits succeed in raising output, we will have more income and therefore more saving. In that way, *both* government *and* industry can borrow more.

Which effect dominates—crowding out or crowding in? Crowding *out* stems from the increases in interest rates caused by deficits, whereas crowding *in* derives from the faster real economic growth that deficits sometimes produce. In the short run, the crowding-in effect—which results from the outward shift of the aggregate demand curve—is often the more powerful, especially when the economy is at less than full employment.

In the long run, however, the supply side dominates because, as we have learned, the economy's self-correcting mechanism pushes actual GDP toward potential GDP. When the economy is approximately at potential, the crowding-out effect takes over: Higher interest rates lead to less investment, causing the capital stock and potential GDP to grow more slowly. Turned on its head, this is the basic long-run argument for reducing the budget deficit: Smaller budget deficits should raise investment and speed up economic growth.

Crowding in occurs when government spending, by raising real GDP, induces increases in private investment spending.

"Would you mind explaining again how high interest rates and the national deficit affect my allowance?"

The Bottom Line

Let us summarize what we have learned so far about the crowding-out controversy.

- The basic argument of the crowding-out hypothesis is sound: *Unless the economy produces enough additional saving*, more government borrowing will force out some private borrowers, who are discouraged by the higher interest rates. This process will reduce investment spending and cancel out some of the expansionary effects of higher government spending.
- But crowding out is rarely strong enough to cancel out the *entire* expansionary thrust of government spending. Some net stimulus to the economy remains.
- If deficit spending induces substantial GDP growth, then the crowding-in effect will lead to more income *and* more saving—perhaps so much more that private industry can borrow *more* than it did previously, despite the increase in government borrowing.
- The crowding-out effect is likely to dominate in the long run or when the economy is operating near full employment. The crowding-in effect is likely to dominate in the short run, especially when the economy has a great deal of slack.

THE MAIN BURDEN OF THE NATIONAL DEBT: SLOWER GROWTH

This analysis of crowding out versus crowding in helps us understand whether or not the national debt imposes a burden on future generations:

When government budget deficits take place in a high-employment economy, the crowding-out effect probably dominates. So deficits exact a toll by leaving a smaller

capital stock, and hence lower potential GDP to future generations. However, deficits in an economy with high unemployment may well lead to more investment rather than less. In this case, in which the crowding-in effect dominates, deficit spending increases growth and the new debt is a blessing rather than a burden.

Which case applies to the U.S. national debt? To answer this question, let us go back to the historical facts and recall how we accumulated all that debt prior to the 1980s. The first cause was the financing of wars, especially World War II. Because this debt was contracted in a fully employed economy, it undoubtedly constituted a burden in the formal sense of the term. After all, the bombs, ships, and planes that it financed were used up in the war, not bequeathed as capital to future generations.

Yet today's Americans may not feel terribly burdened by the decisions of those in power in the 1940s, for consider the alternatives. We could have financed the entire war by taxation and thus placed the burden on consumption rather than on investment. But that choice would truly have been ruinous, and probably impossible, given the colossal wartime expenditures. Alternatively, we could have printed money, which would have unleashed an inflation that nobody wanted. Finally, the government could have spent much less money and perhaps not have won the war. Compared to those alternatives, Americans of subsequent generations probably have not felt burdened by the massive deficit spending undertaken in the 1940s.

A second major contributor to the national debt prior to 1983 was a series of recessions. But these are precisely the circumstances under which budget deficits might prove to be a blessing rather than a burden. So it was only in the 1980s that we began to have the type of deficits that are truly burdensome—deficits acquired in a fully employed, peacetime economy.

This sharp departure from historical norms is what made those budget deficits worrisome. The tax cuts of 1981–1984 blew a large hole in the government budget, and the recession of 1981–1982 ballooned the deficit even further. By the late 1980s, the U.S. economy had recovered to full employment, but a structural deficit of $100–$150 billion per year remained. This persistent deficit was something that had never happened before. Such large structural deficits posed a real threat of crowding out and constituted a serious potential burden on future generations. After a brief interlude of budget surpluses in the late 1990s, large structural deficits reemerged in the early years of this decade, caused by a combination of large tax cuts and rapid spending growth. Current projections also foresee very large deficits in the future, which worries economists and budget analysts.

Let us now summarize our evaluation of the actual burden of the U.S. national debt:

- **The national debt will not lead the nation into bankruptcy. But it does impose a burden on future generations to the extent that it is sold to foreigners or contracted in a fully employed, peacetime economy. In the latter case, it will reduce the nation's capital stock.**

- **Under some circumstances, budget deficits are appropriate for stabilization-policy purposes.**

- **Until the 1980s, the actual public debt of the U.S. government was mostly contracted as a result of wars and recessions—precisely the circumstances under which new debt does not constitute a burden. However, the large deficits of the 1980s and 2000s were not mainly attributable to recessions, and are therefore worrisome.**

- **The shift from budget surpluses back to deficits in this decade may retard capital formation and future economic growth.**

ISSUE REVISITED: IS THE BUDGET DEFICIT TOO LARGE?

We are now in a position to address the issue posed at the beginning of this chapter: Is the federal budget deficit too large? To tackle this question, we need to understand how and why fiscal policy changed, and we need to distinguish between the short-run (demand side) and long-run (supply side) effects of budget deficits.

The federal budget was in surplus by $236 billion in fiscal year 2000 (which ended September 30, 2000). By fiscal 2003, there was a deficit of $378 billion—a swing of $614 billion in just three years. How did this happen? Three main factors contributed.

One was the tax cuts of 2001 and 2003, which were even larger than George W. Bush had proposed as a candidate in the 2000 campaign. As we have noted in this chapter, whether such large tax cuts were wise or foolish policy is still hotly debated. But this much is clear: Given the 2001 recession and the weak economy that followed it, the stimulus to aggregate demand from the tax cuts was welcome. The debate is over whether the government should have reduced the fiscal stimulus when the economy strengthened in 2004–2006.

The second major factor was the recession of 2001 and its aftermath—a period of time during which GDP was consistently below potential. As we have emphasized in this chapter (see especially Figure 5 on page 306), it is perfectly natural for the budget to deteriorate when the economy does—and then to improve when the economy does.

The third major factor was a surge in federal spending during President Bush's first term. From fiscal year 2001 to fiscal year 2005, total federal spending increased by 33 percent while nominal GDP rose by just 22 percent. Some of this additional spending was on the war in Iraq, another policy whose wisdom is hotly debated. But other types of spending rose, too.

Those were the fiscal policies. What were their effects?

In the short run, aggregate demand factors dominate economic performance, and the stimulus from both higher spending and tax cuts provided an expansionary force just when the economy needed one. Moving from surpluses to deficits probably cushioned the recession and sped up the recovery by boosting aggregate demand, as shown in Figure 9.

But in the long run, however, output gravitates toward potential GDP, no matter what happens to aggregate demand. So aggregate supply rules the roost. And that is where the long-run costs of fiscal stimulus emerge. Large budget deficits lead to higher real interest rates and hence to lower levels of private investment. That makes the nation's capital stock grow more slowly, thereby retarding the growth rate of potential GDP. This slower growth is depicted in Figure 10, which shows budget deficits leading to a potential GDP of Y_1 instead of Y_0 in the future. With the same aggregate demand curve, DD, the result is lower real GDP.

So, on balance, were the deficits appropriate? The answer is not clear. In the short run, the economy clearly did need stimulus in 2001–2003, as it did once again in 2008. But because large deficits deter some investment spending, they slow down the economy's potential growth rate in the long run. That is why thoughtful proponents of fiscal stimulus in 2001 urged the government to make any increases in spending or reductions in taxes temporary. We should reduce the budget surplus in the short run, they argued, but maintain it in the long run. That advice was not heeded in 2001. But it was heeded when the government enacted a large stimulus package in 2008, which was explicitly temporary.

FIGURE 9

The Short-Run Effect of Larger Deficits or Smaller Surpluses

FIGURE 10

The Long-Run Effect of Larger Deficits or Smaller Surpluses

THE ECONOMICS AND POLITICS OF THE U.S. BUDGET DEFICIT

Given what we have learned in this chapter about the theory and facts of budget deficits, we can now address some of the major issues that have been debated in the political arena for years.

SOURCE: From *The Wall Street Journal*—Permission, Cartoon Features Syndicate

"The 'Twilight Zone' will not be seen tonight, so that we may bring you the followng special on the federal budget."

1. *Have the deficits of the 1980s, 1990s, and 2000s been a problem?* In 1981–1982, 1990–1991, and again in 2001, the U.S. economy suffered through recessions. And in late 2007-2008, the economy was very weak again. Under such circumstances, crowding out is not a serious concern, and actions to close the deficit during or right after these recessions would have threatened the subsequent recoveries. According to the basic principles of fiscal policy, growing deficits were appropriate in each case.

   But in each case, crowding out became a more serious issue as the economy recovered toward full employment. Budget deficits should decline under such circumstances—as they did in the 1990s and again from 2004 to 2007. But the deficit did not fall in the 1980s nor in the period from 2002 to 2004. Instead, the structural deficit rose. Worries about the burden of the national debt, once mostly myths, became all too realistic.

2. *How did we get rid of the deficit in the 1990s?* In part, we did it the old-fashioned way: by raising taxes and reducing spending in three not-so-easy steps. There was a contentious but bipartisan budget agreement in 1990, a highly partisan deficit-reduction package in 1993 (which passed without a single Republican vote), and a smaller bipartisan budget deal in 1997.

   Taxing more and spending less produces a contractionary fiscal policy that reduces aggregate demand. This effect did not hurt the U.S. economy in the 1990s because fiscal and monetary policies were well coordinated. If fiscal policy turns contractionary to reduce the deficit, monetary policy can turn expansionary to counteract the effects on aggregate demand. In this way, we can hope to shrink the deficit without shrinking the economy. Such a change in the policy mix should also bring down interest rates, because both tighter budgets and easier money tend to have that effect. Indeed, that is just what happened in the 1990s. Interest rates fell, and the Fed made sure that aggregate demand was sufficient to keep the economy growing.

   In addition, surprisingly rapid economic growth in the late 1990s generated much more tax revenue than anyone thought likely only a few years earlier. And the so-called off-budget surplus also increased. Both of these developments helped the federal budget turn rapidly from deficit into surplus.

3. *How did the surplus give way to such large deficits so rapidly?* As we have just noted, the answer comes in three parts: recession, tax cuts, and higher levels of spending, especially on national defense and homeland security. It is hardly a mystery that sharply rising expenditures and rapidly falling revenue push the budget from the black into the red.

4. *What are the future prospects for the federal budget deficit?* In a word, not very good. Beginning in 2011, baby boomers born in the years after 1946 will start reaching the magic age of 65—making them eligible for Medicare and, soon thereafter, for full Social Security benefits. So it is all but certain that federal spending will start to rise sharply. But as of now, Congress has not enacted the future tax increases that will be needed to fund these expanding retirement and health-care programs. Nor has it cut the promised benefits. So, if nothing changes, the budget deficit will start to grow again. Economists are not terribly concerned about the triple-digit budget deficits of 2007 and 2008. But they are worried about how the U.S. government will pay its bills in 2020, 2030, and 2040.

| SUMMARY |

1. Rigid adherence to budget balancing would make the economy less stable, by reducing aggregate demand (via tax increases and reductions in government spending) when private spending is low and by raising aggregate demand when private spending is high.

2. Because both monetary and fiscal policy influence aggregate demand, the appropriate **budget deficit or surplus** depends on monetary policy. Similarly, the appropriate monetary policy depends on budget policy.

3. The same level of aggregate demand can be generated by more than one **mix of fiscal and monetary policy**. But the composition of GDP will be different in each case. Larger budget deficits and tighter money tend to produce higher interest rates, a smaller share of investment in GDP, and slower growth. Smaller budget deficits and looser monetary policy lead to a larger investment share and faster growth.

4. One major reason for the large budget deficits of the early 1980s and early 1990s was the fact that the economy operated well below full employment. In those years, the **structural deficit,** which uses estimates of what the government's receipts and outlays would be at full employment to correct for business-cycle fluctuations, was much smaller than the official deficit.

5. The need to make future interest payments on the public debt is a burden only to the extent that the national debt is owned by foreigners.

6. The argument that a large **national debt** can bankrupt a country like the United States ignores the fact that our national debt consists entirely of obligations to pay U.S. dollars—a currency that the government can raise by increasing taxes or create by printing money.

7. Budget deficits can be inflationary because they expand aggregate demand. They are even more inflationary if they are **monetized**—that is, if the central bank buys some of the newly issued government debt in the open market.

8. Unless the deficit is substantially monetized, deficit spending forces interest rates higher and discourages private investment spending. This process is called the **crowding-out effect.** If a great deal of crowding out occurs, then deficits impose a serious burden on future generations by leaving them a smaller capital stock with which to work.

9. But higher government spending (G) may also produce a **crowding-in effect.** If expansionary fiscal policy succeeds in raising real output (Y), more investment will be induced by the higher Y.

10. Whether crowding out or crowding in dominates largely depends on the time horizon. In the short run, and especially when unemployment is high, crowding in is probably the stronger force, so higher G does not cause lower investment. But, in the long run, the economy will be near full employment, and the proponents of the crowding-out hypothesis will be right: High government spending will mainly displace private investment.

11. Larger deficits may spur growth (via aggregate demand) in the short run but deter growth (via aggregate supply and potential GDP) in the long run.

12. Whether or not deficits create a burden depends on how and why the government incurred the deficits in the first place. If the government runs deficits to fight recessions, more investment may be crowded in by rising output than is crowded out by rising interest rates. Deficits contracted to carry on wars certainly impair the future capital stock, although they may not be considered a burden for noneconomic reasons. Because these two cases account for most of the debt the U.S. government contracted until the mid-1980s, that debt cannot reasonably be considered a serious burden. However, some of the deficits since 1984 are more worrisome on this score.

| KEY TERMS |

Mix of monetary and
fiscal policy   301

Budget deficit   303

Budget surplus   303

National debt   303

Structural budget deficit or
surplus   306

Monetizing the deficit   309

Crowding out   310

Crowding in   311

Burden of the national debt   311

| TEST YOURSELF |

1. Explain the difference between the budget deficit and the national debt. If the deficit gets turned into a surplus, what happens to the debt?

2. Explain in words why the *structural* budget might show a surplus while the *actual* budget is in deficit. Illustrate your answer with a diagram like Figure 5 (page 306).

3. If the Federal Reserve lowers interest rates, what will happen to the government budget deficit? (*Hint:* What will happen to tax receipts and interest expenses?) If the government wants to offset the effects of the Fed's actions on aggregate demand, what might it do? How will this action affect the deficit?

| DISCUSSION QUESTIONS |

1. Explain how the U.S. government managed to accumulate a debt of over $9 trillion. To whom does it owe this debt? Is the debt a burden on future generations?

2. Comment on the following: "Deficit spending paves the road to ruin. If we keep it up, the whole nation will go bankrupt. Even if things do not go this far, what right have we to burden our children and grandchildren with these debts while we live high on the hog?"

3. Newspaper reports frequently suggest that the administration (regardless of who is president) is pressuring the Fed to lower interest rates. In view of your answer to Test Yourself Question 3, why do you think that might be?

4. Explain the difference between crowding out and crowding in. Given the current state of the economy, which effect would you expect to dominate today?

5. Given the current state of the economy, what sort of fiscal-monetary policy mix seems most appropriate to you now? (*Note:* There is no one correct answer to this question. It is a good question to discuss in class.)

THE TRADE-OFF BETWEEN INFLATION AND UNEMPLOYMENT

We must seek to reduce inflation at a lower cost in lost output and unemployment.

JIMMY CARTER

Imagine that you were Ben Bernanke, Chairman of the Federal Reserve Board, cutting interest rates in 2007 and 2008 in order to boost aggregate demand. Two things you would have liked to know is how much your actions were likely to speed up real GDP growth, and hence reduce unemployment, and how much they were likely to increase inflation—because monetary policy normally moves unemployment and inflation in opposite directions in the short run.

This is an idea we first encountered in our list of *Ideas for Beyond the Final Exam* in Chapter 1. Back then, we noted that there is a bothersome *trade-off between inflation and unemployment*: High-growth policies that reduce unemployment tend to raise inflation, and slow-growth policies that reduce inflation tend to raise unemployment. We subsequently observed, in Chapter 14, that the trade-off looks rather different in the short run than in the long run because the aggregate supply curve is fairly flat in the short run but quite steep (or vertical) in the long run. A statistical relationship called the *Phillips curve* seeks to summarize the quantitative dimensions of the trade-off between inflation and unemployment in both the short and long runs. This chapter is about the Phillips curve; that is, it is about one of the things that Chairman Bernanke was wondering in 2007 and 2008.

CONTENTS

ISSUE: Is the Trade-Off Between Inflation and Unemployment a Relic of the Past?

In the late 1990s, unemployment in the United States fell to extremely low levels—the lowest in 30 years. Yet, in stark contrast to prior experience, inflation did not rise. In fact, it fell slightly. This pleasant conjunction of events, which was nearly unprecedented in U.S. history, set many people talking about a glorious "New Economy" in which there was no longer any trade-off between inflation and unemployment. The soaring stock market, especially for technology stocks, added to the euphoria.

Is the long-feared trade-off really just a memory now? Can the modern economy speed along without fear of rising inflation? Or does faster growth eventually have inflationary consequences? These are questions the Federal Reserve wrestled with in 2007 and 2008, and they are the central questions for this chapter. Our answers, in brief, are: no, no, and yes. And we will devote most of this chapter to explaining why.

DEMAND-SIDE INFLATION VERSUS SUPPLY-SIDE INFLATION: A REVIEW

We begin by reviewing some of what we learned about inflation in earlier chapters. One major cause of inflation, although certainly not the only one, is *rapid growth of aggregate demand*. We know that any autonomous increase in spending—whether initiated by consumers, investors, the government, or foreigners—has multiplier effects on aggregate demand. So each additional $1 of C or I or G or $(X - IM)$ leads to more than $1 of additional demand. We also know that firms normally find it profitable to supply additional output only at higher prices; that is, the aggregate supply curve slopes upward. Hence, a stimulus to aggregate demand normally pulls up both real output and prices.

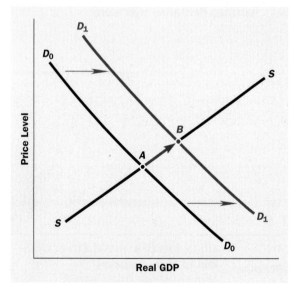

FIGURE 1

Inflation from the Demand Side

Figure 1, which is familiar from earlier chapters, reviews this conclusion. Initially, the economy is at point A, where aggregate demand curve D_0D_0 intersects aggregate supply curve SS. Then something happens to increase spending, and the aggregate demand curve shifts horizontally to D_1D_1. The new equilibrium is at point B, where both prices and output are higher than they were at A. Thus, the economy experiences both inflation and increased output. The slope of the aggregate supply curve measures the amount of inflation that accompanies any specified rise in output and therefore calibrates the trade-off between inflation and economic growth.

But we also have learned in this book (especially in Chapter 10) that inflation does not always originate from the demand side. Anything that retards the growth of aggregate supply—for example, an increase in the price of foreign oil—can shift the economy's aggregate supply curve inward. This sort of inflation is illustrated in Figure 2, where the aggregate supply curve shifts inward from S_0S_0 to S_1S_1, and the economy's equilibrium consequently moves from point A to point B. Prices rise as output falls. We have *stagflation*.

Thus, although inflation can emanate from either the demand side or the supply side of the economy, a crucial difference arises between the two sources. **Demand-side inflation** is normally accompanied by rapid growth of real GDP (as in Figure 1), whereas **supply-side inflation** is normally accompanied by stagnant or even falling GDP (as in Figure 2). This distinction has major practical importance, as we will see in this chapter.

Demand-side inflation is a rise in the price level caused by rapid growth of aggregate demand.

Supply-side inflation is a rise in the price level caused by slow growth (or decline) of aggregate supply.

ORIGINS OF THE PHILLIPS CURVE

Let us begin by supposing that most economic fluctuations are driven by gyrations in *aggregate demand*. In that case, we have just seen that GDP growth and inflation should rise and fall together. Is this what the data show?

We will see shortly, but first let us translate the prediction into a corresponding statement about the relationship between inflation and *unemployment*. Faster growth of real output naturally means faster growth in the number of jobs and, hence, lower unemployment. Conversely, slower growth of real output means slower growth in the number of jobs and, hence, higher unemployment. So we conclude that if business fluctuations emanate from the demand side, unemployment and inflation should move in opposite directions. Unemployment should fall when inflation rises high and rise when inflation falls.

Figure 3 illustrates the idea. The unemployment rate in the United States in 2007 averaged 4.6 percent (which we approximate by 5 percent in the figure), and the Consumer Price Index was 2.8 percent higher than in 2006 (which we approximate by 2 percent). Point *B* in Figure 3 records these two numbers. Had aggregate demand grown faster, inflation would have been higher and unemployment would have been lower. To create a concrete example, let us suppose that unemployment would have been 4 percent and inflation would have been 3 percent—as shown by point *A* in Figure 3. By contrast, had aggregate demand grown more slowly than it actually did, unemployment would have been higher and inflation lower. In Figure 3, we suppose that unemployment would have been 6 percent and inflation would have been just 1 percent (point *C*). This figure displays the principal empirical implication of our theoretical model:

> If fluctuations in economic activity are caused primarily by variations in the rate at which the aggregate demand curve shifts outward from year to year, then the data should show an inverse relationship between unemployment and inflation.

Now we are ready to look at real data. Do we actually observe such an inverse relationship between inflation and unemployment? About 50 years ago, the economist A. W. Phillips plotted data on unemployment and the rate of change of money *wages* (not prices) for several extended periods of British history on a series of scatter diagrams, one of which is reproduced on the next page as Figure 4. He then sketched a curve that seemed to fit the data well. This type of curve, which we now call a **Phillips curve,** shows that wage inflation normally is high when unemployment is low and is low when unemployment is high. So far, so good. These data illustrate the short-run trade-off between inflation and unemployment, one of our *Ideas for Beyond the Final Exam.*

Phillips curves are more commonly constructed for price inflation; Figure 5 on the next page shows a Phillips-type diagram for the post–World War II United States. This curve also appears to fit the data well. As viewed through the eyes of our theory, these facts suggest that economic fluctuations in Great Britain between 1861 and 1913 and in the United States between 1954 and 1969 probably arose primarily from changes in the growth rate of

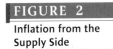

FIGURE 2

Inflation from the Supply Side

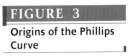

FIGURE 3

Origins of the Phillips Curve

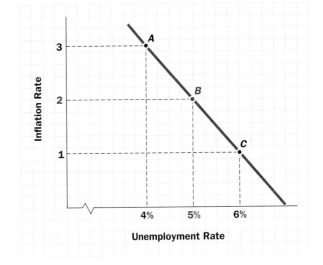

A **Phillips curve** is a graph depicting the rate of unemployment on the horizontal axis and either the rate of inflation or the rate of change of money wages on the vertical axis. Phillips curves are normally downward-sloping, indicating that higher inflation rates are associated with lower unemployment rates.

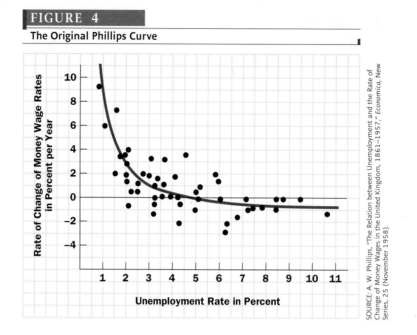

FIGURE 4

The Original Phillips Curve

Rate of Change of Money Wage Rates in Percent per Year

Unemployment Rate in Percent

SOURCE: A. W. Phillips, "The Relation between Unemployment and the Rate of Change of Money Wages in the United Kingdom, 1861–1957," *Economica*, New Series, 25 (November 1958).

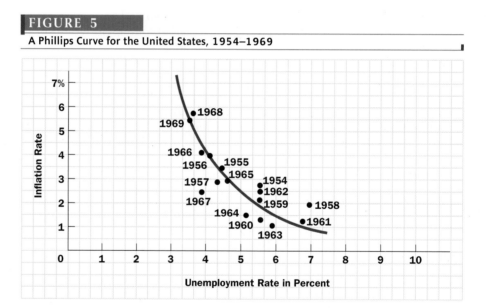

FIGURE 5

A Phillips Curve for the United States, 1954–1969

Inflation Rate

Unemployment Rate in Percent

aggregate demand. The simple model of demand-side inflation really does seem to describe what happened.

During the 1960s and early 1970s, many economists thought of the Phillips curve as a "menu" of choices available to policy makers. In this view, policy makers could opt for low unemployment and high inflation—as in 1969—or for high unemployment and low inflation—as in 1961. The Phillips curve was thought to measure the quantitative trade-off between inflation and unemployment. And for a number of years it seemed to work.

Then something happened. The economy in the 1970s and early 1980s behaved far worse than the historical Phillips curve had led economists to expect. In particular, given the unemployment rates in each of those years, inflation was astonishingly high by past standards. This fact is shown clearly by Figure 6, which simply adds to Figure 5 the data points for 1970 to 1984. So something went badly wrong with the old view of the Phillips curve as a menu for policy choices. But what? There are two major answers to this question, and a full explanation contains elements of each.

SUPPLY-SIDE INFLATION AND THE COLLAPSE OF THE PHILLIPS CURVE

We begin with the simpler answer, which is that much of the inflation in the years from 1972 to 1982 did not emanate from the demand side at all. Instead, the 1970s and early 1980s were full of adverse "supply shocks"—events such as crop failures in 1972–1973 and oil price increases in 1973–1974 and again in 1979–1980. These events pushed the economy's aggregate supply curve inward to the left, as was shown in Figure 2 (page 319). What kind of "Phillips curve" will be generated when economic fluctuations come from the supply side?

Figure 2 reminds us that output will decline (or at least grow more slowly) and prices will rise when the economy is hit by an adverse supply shock. Now, in a growing population with more people looking for jobs each year, a stagnant economy that does not generate enough new jobs will suffer a rise in unemployment. Thus inflation and unemployment will rise together:

If fluctuations in economic activity emanate from the supply side, higher rates of inflation will be associated with higher rates of unemployment, and lower rates of inflation will be associated with lower rates of unemployment.

FIGURE 6

A Phillips Curve for the United States?

The major supply shocks of the 1970s stand out clearly in Figure 6. (Remember—these are real data, not textbook examples.) Food prices soared from 1972 to 1974, and again in 1978. Energy prices skyrocketed in 1973–1974, and again in 1979–1980. Clearly, the inflation and unemployment data generated by the U.S. economy in 1972–1974 and in 1978–1980 are consistent with our model of supply-side inflation. Most economists believe that supply shocks, not demand shocks, dominated the decade from 1972 to 1982.

Explaining the Fabulous 1990s

Now let's stand this analysis of supply shocks on its head. Suppose the economy experiences a *favorable* supply shock, rather than an adverse one, so that the aggregate supply curve shifts *outward* at an unusually rapid rate. Any number of factors—such as a drop in oil prices, bountiful harvests, or exceptionally rapid technological advance—can have this effect.

Whatever the cause, Figure 7 (which duplicates Figure 14 of Chapter 10) depicts the consequences. The aggregate demand curve shifts outward as usual, but the aggregate supply curve shifts out more than it would in a "normal" year. So the economy's equilibrium winds up at point B rather than at point C, meaning that economic growth is *faster* (B is to the right of C) and inflation is *lower* (B is below C). Thus, inflation falls while rapid growth reduces unemployment.

Figure 7 more or less characterizes the experience of the U.S. economy from 1996 to 1998. Oil prices plummeted, lowering costs to American businesses and households. Stunning advances in technology made computer prices drop even more rapidly than usual. And the rising value of

FIGURE 7

The Effects of a Favorable Supply Shock

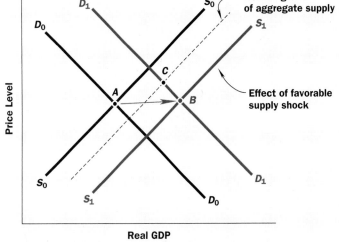

the U.S. dollar made imported goods cheaper to Americans.[1] Thus, we benefited from a series of favorable supply shocks, and the effects were as depicted in Figure 7. The U.S. economy grew rapidly, and inflation and unemployment fell together.

ISSUE RESOLVED: WHY INFLATION AND UNEMPLOYMENT BOTH DECLINED

We now have the answer to the question posed at the start of this chapter. We do not need to add anything new or mysterious to explain the marvelous economic performance of the second half of the 1990s. According to the basic macroeconomic theory taught in this book, favorable supply shocks should produce rapid economic growth with falling inflation—which is just what happened. The U.S. economy did so well, in part, because we were so fortunate.

WHAT THE PHILLIPS CURVE IS NOT

So one view of what went wrong with the Phillips curve is that adverse supply shocks dominated the 1970s and early 1980s. But there is another view, one that holds that policy makers misinterpreted the Phillips curve and tried to pick combinations of inflation and unemployment that were simply unsustainable.

Specifically, we have learned that the Phillips curve is a *statistical relationship* between inflation and unemployment that we expect to emerge *if business cycle fluctuations arise mainly from changes in the growth of aggregate demand.* But in the 1970s and 1980s, the curve was widely misinterpreted as depicting a number of *alternative equilibrium points* from which policy makers could choose.

To understand the flaw in this reasoning, let us quickly review an earlier lesson. We know from Chapter 10 that the economy has a *self-correcting mechanism* that will cure both inflations and recessions *eventually,* even if the government does nothing. This idea is important in this context because it tells us that many combinations of output and prices cannot be maintained indefinitely. Some will self-destruct. Specifically, if the economy finds itself far from the normal full-employment level of unemployment, forces will be set in motion that tend to erode the inflationary or recessionary gap.

Figure 8 depicts the case of a recessionary gap where aggregate supply curve S_0S_0 intersects aggregate demand curve DD at point A. With equilibrium output well below potential GDP, the economy has unused industrial capacity and unsold output, so inflation will be tame. At the same time, the availability of unemployed workers eager for jobs limits the rate at which labor can push up wage rates. But since wages are the main component of business costs, when they decline (relative to what they would have been without a recession) so do costs. These lower costs, in turn, stimulate greater production. Figure 8 illustrates this process by an outward shift of the aggregate supply curve—from S_0S_0 to the brick-colored curve S_1S_1.

As the figure shows, the outward shift of the aggregate supply curve brought on by the recession pushes equilibrium output up as the economy moves from point A to point B. Thus, the size of the recessionary gap begins to shrink. This process continues until the aggregate supply curve reaches the position indicated by the blue curve S_2S_2

FIGURE 8

The Elimination of a Recessionary Gap

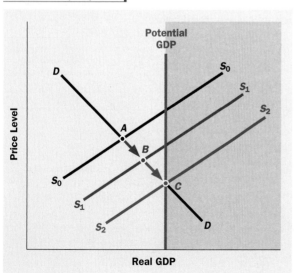

---

[1] The dollar and imports will be discussed in detail in Chapter 19.

in Figure 8. Here wages have fallen enough to eliminate the recessionary gap, and the economy has reached a full-employment equilibrium at point C.[2]

We can relate this sequence of events to our discussion of the origins of the Phillips curve with the help of Figure 9, which is a hypothetical Phillips curve. Point a in Figure 9 corresponds to point A in Figure 8: It shows the initial recessionary gap with unemployment (assumed to be 6.5 percent) above full employment, which we assume to occur at 5 percent.

But we have just seen that point A in Figure 8—and therefore also point a in Figure 9—is not sustainable. The economy tends to rid itself of the recessionary gap through the disinflation process just described. The adjustment path from A to C depicted in Figure 8 would appear on our Phillips curve diagram as a movement toward less inflation and less unemployment—something like the blue arrow from point a to point c in Figure 9.

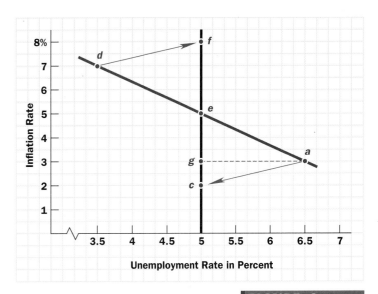

FIGURE 9

The Vertical Long-Run Phillips Curve

Similarly, points representing inflationary gaps—such as point d in Figure 9—are also not sustainable. They, too, are gradually eliminated by the self-correcting mechanism that we studied in Chapter 10. Wages are forced up by the abnormally low unemployment, which in turn pushes prices higher. Higher prices deter investment spending by forcing up interest rates, and they deter consumer spending by lowering the purchasing power of consumer wealth. The inflationary process continues until the amount people want to buy is brought into line with the amount firms want to sell at normal full employment. During such an adjustment period, unemployment and inflation both rise—as indicated by the blue arrow from point d to point f in Figure 9. Putting these two conclusions together, we see that

> On a Phillips curve diagram such as Figure 9, neither points corresponding to an inflationary gap (like point d) nor points corresponding to a recessionary gap (like point a) can be maintained indefinitely. Inflationary gaps lead to rising unemployment and rising inflation. Recessionary gaps lead to falling inflation and falling unemployment.

All the points that are sustainable in the long run (such as c, e, and f), therefore, correspond to the *same* rate of unemployment, which is therefore called the **natural rate of unemployment.** The natural rate corresponds to what we have so far been calling the "full-employment" unemployment rate.

Thus, the Phillips curve connecting points d, e, and a is not a menu of policy choices at all. Although we can move from a point such as e to a point such as d by stimulating aggregate demand sufficiently, the economy will not be able to remain at d. We cannot keep unemployment at such a low level indefinitely. Instead, policy makers must choose from among points such as c, e, and f, all of which correspond to the same "natural" rate of unemployment. For obvious reasons, the line connecting these points has been dubbed the **vertical long-run Phillips curve.** It is this vertical Phillips curve, connecting points such as e and f, that represents the true long-run menu of policy choices. We thus conclude:

THE TRADE-OFF BETWEEN INFLATION AND UNEMPLOYMENT In the short run, it is possible to "ride up the Phillips curve" toward lower levels of unemployment by stimulating aggregate demand. (See, for example, point d in Figure 9.) Conversely, by restricting the growth of demand, it is possible to "ride down the Phillips curve" toward lower rates of

The economy's self-correcting mechanism always tends to push the unemployment rate back toward a specific rate of unemployment that we call the **natural rate of unemployment.**

The **vertical (long-run) Phillips curve** shows the menu of inflation/ unemployment choices available to society in the long run. It is a vertical straight line at the natural rate of unemployment.

IDEAS FOR BEYOND THE FINAL EXAM

---

[2] This simple analysis assumes that the aggregate demand curve does not move during the adjustment period. If it is shifting to the right, the recessionary gap will disappear even faster, but inflation will not slow down as much. (*Exercise:* Construct the diagram for this case by adding a shift of the aggregate demand curve to Figure 8.)

inflation (such as point *a* in Figure 9). Thus, there is a *short run trade-off between unemployment and inflation*. Stimulating demand will improve the unemployment picture but worsen inflation; restricting demand will lower inflation but aggravate the unemployment problem.

However, there is no such trade-off in the long run. The economy's self-correcting mechanism ensures that unemployment will eventually return to the natural rate no matter what happens to aggregate demand. In the long run, faster growth of demand leads only to higher inflation, not to lower unemployment; and slower growth of demand leads only to lower inflation, not to higher unemployment.

FIGHTING UNEMPLOYMENT WITH FISCAL AND MONETARY POLICY

Now let us apply this analysis to a concrete policy problem—one that has often troubled policy makers in the United States and in many other countries. Should the government use its ability to manage aggregate demand through fiscal and monetary policy to combat unemployment? And if so, how? To focus the discussion, we will deal with a recent, real-world example.

The unemployment rate in the United States bottomed out at 3.8 percent in April 2000, a rate that most economists thought was well below the natural rate of unemployment (something like point *d* in Figure 9). It then began to creep up gradually, and by August 2001 stood at 4.9 percent—which may be close to the natural rate (see point *e* in the figure). Then the terrorist attacks of September 11, 2001 occurred, and within a few months unemployment had risen to 5.7 percent. By December, the economy was in a position resembling point *a* in Figure 9, with a recessionary gap.

Even if fiscal and monetary policy makers did nothing, the economy's self-correcting mechanism would have gradually eroded the recessionary gap. Both unemployment and inflation would have declined gradually as the economy moved along the blue arrow from point *a* to point *c* in Figure 9. Eventually, as the diagram shows, the economy would have returned to its natural rate of unemployment (assumed here to be 5 percent) and inflation would have fallen—in the example, from 3 percent to 2 percent.

This eventual outcome is quite satisfactory: Both unemployment and inflation are lower at the end of the adjustment period (point *c*) than at the beginning (point *a*). But it may take an agonizingly long time to get there. And American policy makers in 2001 did not view patience as a virtue. Rather than keep hands off, the Federal Reserve started cutting interest rates almost immediately after the terrorist attacks. Fiscal policy reacted as well. Spending on defense and security was increased immediately after the attacks, the first phase of the 2001 tax cut kicked in, and Congress passed a small fiscal stimulus package.

According to the theory we have learned, such a large dose of expansionary fiscal and monetary policy should push the economy up the short-run Phillips curve from a point like *a* toward a point like *e* in Figure 9. Compared to simply relying on the self-correcting mechanism, then, the strong policy response presumably led to a faster recovery from the 2001 recession—which was certainly the intent of the president, Congress, and the Fed. But Figure 9 points out that it also probably left us with a higher inflation rate (5 percent in the figure, about 2 percent in reality).

This example illustrates the range of choices open to policy makers. They can wait patiently while the economy's self-correcting mechanism pulls unemployment down to the natural rate—leading to a long-run equilibrium like point *c* in Figure 9. Or they can rush the process along with expansionary monetary and fiscal policy—and wind up with the same unemployment rate but higher inflation (point *e*). In what sense, then, do policy makers face a *trade-off* between inflation and unemployment? The answer, illustrated by this diagram, is

The cost of reducing unemployment more rapidly by expansionary fiscal and monetary policies is a permanently higher inflation rate.

WHAT SHOULD BE DONE?

Should the government pay the inflationary costs of fighting unemployment? When the transitory benefit (lower unemployment for a while) is balanced against the permanent cost (higher inflation), have we made a good bargain?

We have noted that the U.S. government opted for a strong policy response in 2001. Thus two forces were at work simultaneously: The self-correcting mechanism was pulling the economy toward point *c* in Figure 9, and expansionary monetary and fiscal policies were pushing it toward point *e*. The net result was an intermediate path—something like the dotted line leading to point *g* in Figure 9. As the economy returned to full employment over the years from 2003 to 2006, growth was reasonably strong and inflation rose only a little.

How do policy makers make decisions like this? Our analysis highlights three critical issues on which the answer depends.

The Costs of Inflation and Unemployment

In Chapter 6, we examined the social costs of inflation and unemployment. Many of the benefits of lower unemployment are readily measured in dollars and cents. Basically, we need only estimate how much higher real GDP is each year. However, the costs of the permanently higher inflation rate are more difficult to measure. So there is considerable controversy over the costs and benefits of using demand management to fight unemployment.

Economists and political leaders who believe that inflation is extremely costly may deem it unwise to accept the inflationary consequences of reducing unemployment faster. And indeed, a few dissenters in both 2001 and 2007 (when the Fed once again cut interest rates to stave off recession) were worried about future inflation. Most U.S. policy makers apparently disagreed with that view, however. They decided that reducing unemployment was the higher priority. But things do not always work out that way. In recent decades, European authorities have often avoided expansionary stabilization policies, and allowed unemployment to remain high, rather than accept even slightly higher inflation.

The Slope of the Short-Run Phillips Curve

The shape of the short-run Phillips curve is also critical. Look back at Figure 9, and imagine that the Phillips curve connecting points *a, e,* and *d* was much steeper. In that case, the inflationary costs of using expansionary policy to reduce unemployment would be more substantial. By contrast, if the short-run Phillips curve was much flatter than the one shown in Figure 9, unemployment could be reduced with less inflationary cost.

The Efficiency of the Economy's Self-Correcting Mechanism

We have emphasized that once a recessionary gap opens, the economy's natural self-correcting mechanism will eventually close it—even in the absence of any policy response. The obvious question is: How long must we wait? If the self-correcting mechanism—which works through reductions in wage inflation—is fast and reliable, high unemployment will not last very long. So the costs of waiting will be small. But if wage inflation responds only slowly to unemployment, the costs of waiting may be enormous. That has evidently been true in much of Europe, where unemployment has remained persistently high for years.

The efficacy of the self-correcting mechanism is also surrounded by controversy. Most economists believe that the weight of the evidence points to extremely sluggish wage behavior: Wage inflation appears to respond slowly to economic slack. In terms of Figure 9, this lag means that the economy will traverse the path from *a* to *c* at an agonizingly slow pace, so that a long period of weak economic activity will be necessary to bring down inflation.

But a significant minority opinion finds this assessment far too pessimistic. Economists in this group argue that the costs of reducing inflation are not nearly so severe and that

Inflation Targeting and the Phillips Curve

In Chapter 14, we mentioned *inflation targeting* as a new approach to monetary policy that is gaining adherents in many countries. In practice, inflation targeting requires monetary policy makers to rely heavily on the Phillips curve. Why? Because a central bank with, say, a 2 percent inflation target is obligated to pursue a monetary policy that it believes will drive the inflation rate to 2 percent after, say, a year or two. But how does the central bank know which policy will accomplish this goal?

Knowing the proper policy with certainty is, of course, out of the question. But a central bank can use a model similar to the aggregate supply/demand model taught in this book to *estimate* how its policy choices will affect the unemployment rate, say, this year and next. Then it can use a Phillips curve to *estimate* how that unemployment path will affect inflation. In fact, that is more or less what inflation-targeting central banks from New Zealand to Norway now do.

the key to a successful anti-inflation policy is how it affects people's *expectations* of inflation. To understand this argument, we must first understand why expectations are relevant to the Phillips curve.

INFLATIONARY EXPECTATIONS AND THE PHILLIPS CURVE

Recall from Chapter 10 that the main reason the economy's aggregate supply curve slopes upward—that is, why output increases as the price level rises—is that businesses typically purchase labor and other inputs under long-term contracts that fix input costs in money terms. (The money wage rate is the clearest example.) As long as such contracts are in force, *real* wages fall as the prices of goods rise. Labor therefore becomes cheaper in real terms, which persuades businesses to expand employment and output. Buying low and selling high is, after all, the route to higher profits.

Table 1 illustrates this general idea in a concrete example. We suppose that workers and firms agree today that the money wage to be paid a year from now will be $10 per hour. The table then shows the real wage corresponding to each alternative inflation rate. For example, if inflation is 4 percent, the real wage a year from now will be $10.00/1.04 = $9.62. Clearly, the higher the inflation rate, the higher the price level at the end of the year and the lower the real wage.

Lower real wages provide an incentive for firms to increase output, as we have just noted. But lower real wages also impose losses of purchasing power on workers. Thus, workers are, in some sense, "cheated" by inflation if they sign a contract specifying a fixed money wage in an inflationary environment.

Many economists doubt that workers will sign such contracts *if they can see inflation coming*. Wouldn't it be wiser, these economists ask, to insist on being compensated for the coming inflation? After all, firms should be willing to offer higher money wages if they expect inflation, because they realize that higher money wages need not imply higher *real* wages.

Table 2 illustrates the mechanics of such a deal. For example, if people expect 4 percent inflation, the contract could stipulate that the wage rate be increased to $10.40 (which is 4 percent more than $10) at the end of the year. That would keep the real wage at $10 (because $10.40/1.04 = $10.00), the same as it would be under zero inflation. The other money wage figures in Table 2 are derived similarly.

TABLE 1

Money and Real Wages under Unexpected Inflation

Inflation Rate	Price Level 1 Year from Now	Wage per Hour 1 Year from Now	Real Wage per Hour 1 Year from Now
0%	100	$10.00	$10.00
2	102	10.00	9.80
4	104	10.00	9.62
6	106	10.00	9.43

NOTE: Each real wage figure is obtained by dividing the $10 nominal wage by the corresponding price level a year later and multiplying by 100. Thus, for example, when the inflation rate is 4 percent, the real wage at the end of the year is ($10.00/104) × 100 = $9.62.

TABLE 2

Money and Real Wages under Expected Inflation

Expected Inflation Rate	Expected Price Level 1 Year from Now	Wage per Hour 1 Year from Now	Expected Real Wage per Hour 1 Year from Now
0%	100	$10.00	$10.00
2	102	10.20	10.00
4	104	10.40	10.00
6	106	10.60	10.00

If workers and firms behave this way, and if they forecast inflation accurately, then the real wage will remain unchanged as the price level rises. (Notice that, in Table 2, the expected future real wage is $10 per hour regardless of the expected inflation rate.) Prices and wages will go up together. So workers will not lose from inflation, and firms will not gain. But then there is no reason for firms to raise production when the price level rises. In a word, the aggregate supply curve becomes vertical. In general:

> If workers can see inflation coming, and if they receive compensation for it, inflation does not erode *real* wages. But if real wages do not fall, firms have no incentives to increase production. In such a case, the economy's aggregate supply curve will not slope upward, but, rather, will be a vertical line at the level of output corresponding to potential GDP.

Such a curve is shown in Panel (a) of Figure 10. Because a vertical aggregate supply curve leads to a vertical Phillips curve, it follows that even the *short-run* Phillips curve would be vertical under these circumstances, as in Panel (b) of Figure 10.[3]

If this analysis is correct, it has profound implications for the costs and benefits of fighting inflation. To see this, refer once again to Figure 9 (page 323), but now use the graph to depict the strategy of fighting inflation by causing a recession. Suppose we start at point *e*, with 5 percent inflation. To move to point *c* (representing 2 percent inflation), the economy must take a long and unpleasant detour through point *a*. Specifically, contractionary policies must push the economy down the Phillips curve toward point *a* before the self-correcting mechanism takes over and moves the economy from *a* to *c*. In words, we must suffer through a recession to reduce inflation.

But what if even the *short-run* Phillips curve were *vertical* rather than downward-sloping? In this case, the unpleasant recessionary detour would not be necessary. Instead, inflation could fall without unemployment rising. The economy could move vertically downward from point *e* to point *c*.

Does this optimistic analysis describe the real world? Can we really slay the inflationary dragon so painlessly? Not necessarily, for our discussion of expectations so far has made at least one unrealistic assumption: that businesses and workers can predict inflation accurately. Under this assumption, as Table 2 shows, real wages are unaffected by inflation—leaving the aggregate supply curve vertical, even in the short run.

But forecasts of inflation are often inaccurate. Suppose workers underestimate inflation. For example, suppose they expect 4 percent inflation but actually get 6 percent. Then

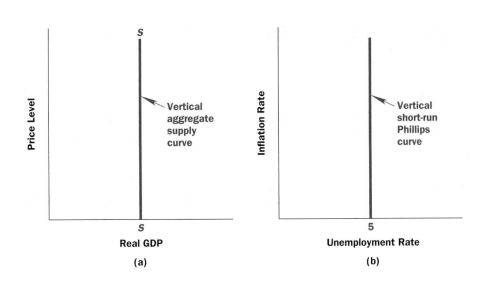

FIGURE 10

A Vertical Aggregate Supply Curve and the Corresponding Vertical Phillips Curve

---

[3] Test Yourself Question 1 at the end of the chapter asks you to demonstrate that a vertical aggregate supply curve leads to a vertical Phillips curve.

real wages will decline by 2 percent. More generally, real wages will fall if workers underestimate inflation at all. The effects of inflation on real wages will be somewhere in between those shown in Tables 1 and 2.[4] So firms will retain some incentive to raise production as the price level rises, which means that the aggregate supply curve will retain some upward slope. We thus conclude that

> The short-run aggregate supply curve is *vertical* when inflation is predicted accurately but *upward-sloping* when inflation is underestimated. Thus, only *unexpectedly* high inflation will raise output, because only unexpected inflation reduces real wages.[5] Similarly, only an *unexpected* decline in inflation will lead to a recession.

Because people often fail to anticipate changes in inflation correctly, this analysis seems to leave our earlier discussion of the Phillips curve almost intact for practical purposes. Indeed, most economists nowadays believe that the Phillips curve slopes downward in the short run but is vertical in the long run.

THE THEORY OF RATIONAL EXPECTATIONS

Rational expectations are forecasts that, while not necessarily correct, are the best that can be made given the available data. Rational expectations, therefore, cannot err systematically. If expectations are rational, forecasting errors are pure random numbers.

However, an influential minority of economists disagrees. This group, believers in the hypothesis of **rational expectations,** insists that the Phillips curve is vertical even in the short run. To understand their point of view, we must first explain what rational expectations are. Then we will see why rational expectations have such radical implications for the trade-off between inflation and unemployment.

What Are Rational Expectations?

In many economic contexts, people must formulate expectations about what the future will bring. For example, those who invest in the stock market need to forecast the future prices of the stocks they buy and sell. Likewise, as we have just discussed, workers and businesses may want to forecast future prices before agreeing on a money wage. Rational expectations is a controversial hypothesis about how such forecasts are made.

As used by economists, a forecast (an "expectation") of a future variable is considered rational if the forecaster makes *optimal* use of all relevant information that is *available* at the time of the forecast. Let us elaborate on the two italicized words in this definition, using as an example a hypothetical stock market investor who has rational expectations.

First, proponents of rational expectations recognize that *information is limited*. An investor interested in Google stock would like to know how much profit the company will make in the coming years. Armed with such information, she could predict the future price of Google stock more accurately. But that information is simply unavailable. The investor's forecast of the future price of Google shares is not "irrational" just because she cannot foresee the future. On the other hand, if Google stock normally goes down on Fridays and up on Mondays, she should be aware of this fact.

Next, we have the word *optimal*. As used by economists, it means using proper statistical inference to process all the relevant information that is available before making a forecast. In brief, to have rational expectations, your forecasts do not have to be correct, but they cannot have systematic errors that you could avoid by applying better statistical methods. This requirement, although exacting, is not quite as outlandish as it may seem. A good billiards player makes expert use of the laws of physics even without understanding the theory. Similarly, an experienced stock market investor may make good use of information even without formal training in statistics.

[4] To make sure you understand why, construct a version of Table 2 based on the assumption that workers expect 4 percent inflation (and hence set next year's wage at $10.40 per hour), regardless of what the actual rate of inflation is. If you create this table correctly, it will show that higher inflation leads to lower real wages, as in Table 1.

[5] To see this point, compare Tables 1 and 2.

But if interest rates on loans were indexed, none of this would occur. Borrowers and lenders would agree on a fixed *real* rate of interest, and the borrower would compensate the lender for whatever actual inflation occurred. No one would have to guess what the inflation rate would be.[6]

A second social cost mentioned in Chapter 6 stems from the fact that our tax system levies taxes on nominal interest and nominal capital gains. As we learned, this flaw in the tax system leads to extremely high effective tax rates in an inflationary environment. But indexing can cure this problem. We need only rewrite the tax code so that only *real* interest payments and *real* capital gains are taxed.

In the face of all these benefits, why does our economy not employ more indexing? One obvious reason is that inflation has been low for years. Indexing received much more attention years ago, when inflation was much higher. A second reason is that some economists fear that indexing will erode society's resistance to inflation. With the costs of inflation so markedly reduced, they ask, what will stop governments from inflating more and more? They fear that the answer is: Nothing. Voters who stand to lose nothing from inflation are unlikely to pressure their legislators into stopping it. Opponents of indexing worry that a mild inflationary disease could turn into a ravaging epidemic in a highly indexed economy.

| SUMMARY |

1. Inflation can be caused either by rapid growth of aggregate demand or by sluggish growth of aggregate supply.

2. When fluctuations in economic activity emanate from the **demand side,** prices will rise rapidly when real output grows rapidly. Because rapid growth means more jobs, unemployment and inflation will be inversely related.

3. This inverse relationship between unemployment and inflation is called the **Phillips curve.** In the United States, data for the 1950s and 1960s display a clear Phillips-curve relation, but data for the 1970s and 1980s do not.

4. The Phillips curve is not a menu of long-run policy choices for the economy, because the self-correcting mechanism guarantees that neither an inflationary gap nor a recessionary gap can last indefinitely.

5. Because of the self-correcting mechanism, the economy's true long-run choices lie along a **vertical long-run Phillips curve,** which shows that the so-called **natural rate of unemployment** is the only unemployment rate that can persist indefinitely.

6. In the short run, the economy can move up or down along its short-run Phillips curve. Temporary reductions in unemployment can be achieved at the cost of higher inflation, and temporary increases in unemployment can be used to fight inflation. This **short-run trade-off between inflation and unemployment** is one of our *Ideas for Beyond the Final Exam.*

7. Whether it is advisable to use unemployment to fight inflation depends on four principal factors: the relative social costs of inflation versus unemployment, the efficiency of the economy's self-correcting mechanism, the shape of the short-run Phillips curve, and the speed at which inflationary expectations are adjusted.

8. If workers expect inflation to occur, and if they demand (and receive) compensation for inflation, output will be independent of the price level. Both the aggregate supply curve and the short-run Phillips curve are vertical in this case.

9. Errors in predicting inflation will change real wages and therefore the quantity of output that firms wish to supply. Thus, unpredicted movements in the price level will lead to a normal, upward-sloping aggregate supply curve.

10. According to the **rational expectations** hypothesis, errors in predicting inflation are purely random. As a consequence, except for some random gyrations, the aggregate supply curve is vertical even in the short run.

11. Many economists reject the rational expectations view. Some deny that expectations are "rational" and believe instead that people tend, for example, to underpredict inflation when it is rising. Others point out that contracts signed years ago may not embody expectations that are "rational" in terms of what we know today.

12. When fluctuations in economic activity are caused by shifts of the aggregate supply curve, output will grow slowly (causing unemployment to rise) when inflation rises. Hence, the rates of unemployment and inflation will be positively correlated. Many observers feel that this sort of stagflation is why the Phillips curve collapsed in the 1970s. Similarly, a series of favorable supply shocks help explain the 1990s combination of low inflation and strong economic growth.

---

[6] For example, an indexed loan with a 2 percent real interest rate would require a 5 percent nominal interest payment if inflation were 3 percent, a 7 percent nominal interest payment if inflation were 5 percent, and so on.

13. Even if inflation is initiated by supply-side problems, so that inflation and unemployment rise together, the monetary and fiscal authorities still face this trade-off: Anything they do to improve unemployment is likely to worsen inflation, and anything they do to reduce inflation is likely to aggravate unemployment. (This is part of one of our *Ideas for Beyond the Final Exam*.) The reason is that monetary and fiscal policy mainly influence the aggregate demand curve, not the aggregate supply curve.

14. Policies that improve the functioning of the labor market—including retraining programs and employment services—can, in principle, lower the natural rate of unemployment. To date, however, the U.S. government has enjoyed only modest success with these measures.

15. **Indexing** is another way to approach the trade-off problem. Instead of trying to improve the trade-off, it concentrates on reducing the social costs of inflation. Opponents of indexing worry, however, that the economy's resistance to inflation may be lowered by indexing.

| KEY TERMS |

Demand-side inflation   318

Supply-side inflation   318

Phillips curve   319

Stagflation caused by supply shocks   321

Self-correcting mechanism   322

Natural rate of unemployment   323

Vertical (long-run) Phillips curve   323

Trade-off between unemployment and inflation in the short run and in the long run   323

Rational expectations   328

Indexing   332

Real versus nominal interest rates   333

| TEST YOURSELF |

1. Show that if the economy's aggregate supply curve is vertical, fluctuations in the growth of aggregate demand produce only fluctuations in inflation with no effect on output.

2. Long-term government bonds now pay approximately 5 percent nominal interest. Would you prefer to trade yours in for an indexed bond that paid a 3 percent real rate of interest? What if the real interest rate offered were 2 percent? What if it were 1 percent? What do your answers to these questions reveal about your personal attitudes toward inflation?

| DISCUSSION QUESTIONS |

1. When inflation and unemployment fell together in the 1990s, some observers claimed that policy makers no longer faced a trade-off between inflation and unemployment. Were they correct?

2. "There is no sense in trying to shorten recessions through fiscal and monetary policy because the effects of these policies on the unemployment rate are sure to be temporary." Comment on both the truth of this statement and its relevance for policy formulation.

3. Why is it said that decisions on fiscal and monetary policy are, at least in part, political decisions that cannot be made on "objective" economic criteria?

4. What is a Phillips curve? Why did it seem to work so much better in the period from 1954 to 1969 than it did in the 1970s?

5. Explain why expectations of inflation affect the wages that result from labor-management bargaining.

6. What is meant by "rational" expectations? Why does the hypothesis of rational expectations have such stunning implications for economic policy? Would believers in rational expectations want to shorten a recession by expanding aggregate demand? Would they want to fight inflation by reducing aggregate demand? Relate this analysis to your answer to Test Yourself Question 1.

7. It is often said that the Federal Reserve Board typically cares more about inflation and less about unemployment than the administration. If this is true, why might presidents often worry about what the Fed might do to interest rates?

8. The year 2007 closed with the unemployment rate around 5 percent, real GDP barely growing, inflation above 2 percent and apparently rising a bit, and the federal budget showing a large deficit.

   a. Give one or more arguments for engaging in expansionary monetary or fiscal policies under these circumstances.

   b. Give one or more arguments for engaging in contractionary monetary or fiscal policies under these circumstances.

   c. Which arguments do you find more persuasive?

The United States in the World Economy

"Globalization" became a buzzword in the 1990s—and it remains one today. Some people extol its virtues and view it as something to be encouraged. Others deplore its (real or imagined) costs and seek to stop globalization in its tracks. For example, globalization is often viewed as a threat to the livelihoods of American workers.

We will examine several aspects of the globalization debate in Part 4. But love it or hate it, one thing is clear: The United States is thoroughly integrated into a broader world economy. What happens in the United States influences other countries, and events abroad reverberate back here. Trillions of dollars' worth of goods and services—American software, Chinese toys, Japanese cars—are traded across international borders each year. A vastly larger dollar volume of financial transactions—trade in stocks, bonds, and bank deposits, for example—takes place in the global economy at lightning speed.

We have mentioned these subjects before, but Part 4 brings international factors from the wings to center stage. Chapter 17 studies the factors that underlie *international trade*, and Chapter 18 takes up the determination of *exchange rates*—the prices at which the world's currencies are bought and sold. Then Chapter 19 integrates these international influences into our model of the macroeconomy.

If you want to understand why so many Americans are worried about international trade, why many thoughtful observers think we need to overhaul the international monetary system, or why there was so much economic turmoil in Southeast Asia, Russia, and Latin America during the last 15 years or so, read these three chapters with care.

CHAPTERS

INTERNATIONAL TRADE AND COMPARATIVE ADVANTAGE

No nation was ever ruined by trade.

BENJAMIN FRANKLIN

Economists emphasize international trade as the source of many of the benefits of "globalization"—a loosely defined term that indicates a closer knitting together of the world's national economies. Of course, countries have always been linked in various ways. The Vikings, after all, landed in North America—not to mention Christopher Columbus. In recent decades, however, dramatic improvements in transportation, telecommunications, and international relations have drawn the nations of the world ever closer together economically. This process of globalization is often portrayed as something new. But in fact, it is not, as the box "Is Globalization Something New?" on the next page points out. Still, it is changing the way the peoples of the world live.

Economic events in other countries affect the United States for both macroeconomic and microeconomic reasons. For example, we learned in Parts 2 and 3 that the level of net exports is an important determinant of a nation's output and employment. But we did not delve very deeply into the factors that determine a nation's exports and imports. Chapters 18 and 19 will take up these *macroeconomic* linkages in greater detail. First, however, this chapter studies some of the *microeconomic* linkages among nations: How are patterns and prices of world trade determined? How and why do governments often interfere with foreign trade? The central idea of this chapter is one we have encountered before (in Chapters 1 and 3): the *principle of comparative advantage*.

CONTENTS

Is Globalization Something New?

Few people realize that the industrialized world was, in fact, highly globalized prior to World War I, before the ravages of two world wars and the Great Depression severed many international linkages. Furthermore, as the British magazine *The Economist* pointed out more than a decade ago, globalization has not gone nearly as far as many people imagine.

> Despite much loose talk about the "new" global economy, today's international economic integration is not unprecedented. The 50 years before the first world war saw large cross-border flows of goods, capital and people. That period of globalisation, like the present one, was driven by reductions in trade barriers and by sharp falls in transport costs, thanks to the development of railways and steamships. The present surge of globalisation is in a way a resumption of that previous trend. . . .
>
> Two forces have been driving [globalization]. The first is technology. With the costs of communication and computing falling rapidly, the natural barriers of time and space that separate national markets have been falling too. The cost of a three-minute telephone call between New York and London has fallen from $300 (in 1996 dollars) in 1930 to $1 today . . .
>
> The second driving force has been liberalisation. . . . Almost all countries have lowered barriers to trade. . . . [T]he ratio of trade to output . . . has increased sharply in most countries since 1950. But by this measure Britain and France are only slightly more open to trade today than they were in 1913. . . .
>
> Product markets are still nowhere near as integrated across borders as they are within nations. Consider the example of trade between the United States and Canada, one of the least restricted trading borders in the world. On average, trade between a Canadian province and an American state is 20 times smaller than domestic trade between two Canadian provinces, after adjusting for distance and income levels.
>
> The financial markets are not yet truly integrated either. Despite the newfound popularity of international investing, capital markets were by some measures more integrated at the start of this century than they are now. . . . [And] labour is less mobile than it was in the second half of the 19th century, when some 60m people left Europe for the New World.

SOURCE: © AP Images

SOURCE: "Schools Brief: One World?" from *The Economist*, October 18, 1997. Copyright © 1997 The Economist Newspaper Ltd. All rights reserved. Reprinted with permission. Further reproduction prohibited. http://www.economist.com.

ISSUE: ## HOW CAN AMERICANS COMPETE WITH "CHEAP FOREIGN LABOR"?

Americans (and the citizens of many other nations) often want their government to limit or prevent import competition. Why? One major reason is the common belief that imports take bread out of American workers' mouths. According to this view, "cheap foreign labor" steals jobs from Americans and pressures U.S. businesses to lower wages. For many years, attention focused on the phenomenon of manufacturing jobs moving abroad. Lately, there has been a great deal of concern over the "offshoring" of a wide variety of service jobs—ranging from call center operators to lawyers. Such worries were prominently voiced in the 2008 presidential campaign. For example, during the Democratic primaries, Senators Hillary Clinton and Barack Obama competed over who could be more disparaging toward the North American Free Trade Agreement (NAFTA), arguing that competition from cheap Mexican labor had destroyed many good American jobs.

Oddly enough, the facts appear to be grossly inconsistent with the theory that trade kills jobs. For one thing, wages in most countries that export to the United States have risen dramatically in recent decades—much faster than wages here. Table 1 shows hourly compensation rates in eight countries on three continents, each expressed as a percentage of hourly compensation in the United States, in 1975 and 2005. Only workers in Mexico lost ground to American workers over this 30-year period. Labor in

Europe gained substantially on their U.S. counterparts—rising in Britain, for example, from just above half the U.S. standard to above-U.S. levels. And the wage gains in Asia were nothing short of spectacular. Labor compensation in South Korea, for example, soared from just 5 percent of U.S. levels to more than half.[1] Yet, while all this was going on, American imports of automobiles from Japan, electronics from Taiwan, and textiles from Korea expanded rapidly.

Ironically, then, the United States' dominant position in the international marketplace *deteriorated* just as wage levels in Europe and Asia were rising closer to our own. Clearly, something other than exploiting cheap foreign labor must be driving international trade—in contrast to what the "common sense" view of the matter suggests. In this chapter, we will see precisely what is wrong with this commonsense view.

TABLE 1		
Labor Costs in Industrialized Countries as a Percentage of U.S. Labor Costs		
	1975	2005
France	73%	104%
United Kingdom	54	109
Spain	41	75
Japan	48	92
South Korea	5	57
Taiwan	6	27
Mexico	24	11
Canada	99	101

SOURCE: U.S. Bureau of Labor Statistics.

NOTE: Data are compensation estimates per hour, converted at exchange rates, and relate to production workers in the manufacturing sector.

WHY TRADE?

The earth's resources are distributed unequally across the planet. Although the United States produces its own coal and wheat, it depends almost *entirely* on the rest of the world for such basic items as rubber and coffee. Similarly, the Persian Gulf states have little land that is suitable for farming but sit atop huge pools of oil—something we are constantly reminded of by geopolitical events. Because of the seemingly whimsical distribution of the earth's resources, every nation must trade with others to acquire what it lacks.

Even if countries had all the resources they needed, other differences in natural endowments such as climate, terrain, and so on would lead them to engage in trade. Americans *could* grow their own bananas and coffee in hothouses, albeit with great difficulty. But these crops are grown much more efficiently in Honduras and Brazil, where the climates are appropriate.

The skills of a nation's labor force also play a role. If New Zealand has a large group of efficient farmers and few workers with industrial experience, while the opposite is true in Japan, it makes sense for New Zealand to specialize in agriculture and let Japan concentrate on manufacturing.

Finally, a small country that tried to produce every product its citizens want to consume would end up with many industries that are simply too small to utilize modern mass-production techniques or to take advantage of other economies of large-scale operations. For example, some countries operate their own international airlines for reasons that can only be described as political, not economic.

To summarize, the main reason why nations trade with one another is to exploit the many advantages of **specialization**, some of which were discussed in Chapter 3. International trade greatly enhances living standards for all parties involved because:

Specialization means that a country devotes its energies and resources to only a small proportion of the world's productive activities.

1. **Every country lacks some vital resources that it can get only by trading with others.**

2. **Each country's climate, labor force, and other endowments make it a relatively efficient producer of some goods and a relatively inefficient producer of others.**

3. **Specialization permits larger outputs via the advantages of large-scale production.**

Mutual Gains from Trade

Many people have long believed that one nation gains from trade only at the expense of another. After all, nothing new is produced by the mere act of trading. So if one country gains from a swap, it has been argued for centuries, the other country must necessarily lose. One consequence of this mistaken belief was and continues to be attitudes that call for each country to try to take advantage of its trading partners on the (fallacious) grounds that one nation's gain must be another's loss.

---

[1] China would be an even more extreme example, but we lack Chinese data dating back to 1975.

Yet, as Adam Smith emphasized, and as we learned in Chapter 3, both parties must expect to gain something from any *voluntary exchange*. Otherwise, why would they agree to trade?

But how can mere exchange of goods leave both parties better off? The answer is that although trade does not increase the total output of goods, it does allow each party to acquire items better suited to its tastes. Suppose Levi has four cookies and nothing to drink, while Malcolm has two glasses of milk and nothing to eat. A trade of two of Levi's cookies for one of Malcolm's glasses of milk will not increase the total supply of either milk or cookies, but it almost certainly will make both boys better off.

By exactly the same logic, both the United States and Mexico must reap gains when Mexicans voluntarily ship their tomatoes to the United States in return for American chemicals. In general, as we emphasized in Chapter 3:

IDEAS FOR BEYOND THE FINAL EXAM

TRADE IS A WIN-WIN SITUATION Both parties must expect to gain from any *voluntary exchange*. Trade brings about mutual gains by redistributing products so that both parties end up holding more preferred combinations of goods than they held before. This principle, which is one of our *Ideas for Beyond the Final Exam*, applies to nations just as it does to individuals.

INTERNATIONAL VERSUS INTRANATIONAL TRADE

The 50 states of the United States may be the most eloquent testimonial to the large gains that can be realized from specialization and free trade. Florida specializes in growing oranges, Michigan builds cars, California makes software and computers, and New York specializes in finance. All of these states trade freely with one another and, as a result, enjoy great prosperity. Try to imagine how much lower your standard of living would be if you consumed only items produced in your own state.

The essential logic behind international trade is no different from that underlying trade among different states; the basic reasons for trade are equally applicable within a country or among countries. Why, then, do we study international trade as a special subject? There are at least three reasons.

Political Factors in International Trade

First, domestic trade takes place under a single national government, whereas foreign trade always involves at least two governments. But a nation's government is normally much less concerned about the welfare of other countries' citizens than it is about its own. So, for example, the U.S. Constitution prohibits tariffs on trade among states, but it does not prohibit the United States from imposing tariffs on imports from abroad. One major issue in the economic analysis of international trade is the use and misuse of political impediments to international trade.

The Many Currencies Involved in International Trade

Second, all trade within the borders of the United States is carried out in U.S. dollars, whereas trade across national borders almost always involves at least two currencies. Rates of exchange between different currencies can and do change. In 1985, it took about 250 Japanese yen to buy a dollar; now it takes fewer than half that many. Variability in exchange rates brings with it a host of complications and policy problems.

Impediments to Mobility of Labor and Capital

Third, it is much easier for labor and capital to move about within a country than to move from one nation to another. If jobs are plentiful in California but scarce in Ohio, workers can move freely to follow the job opportunities. Of course, personal costs such as the financial burden of moving and the psychological burden of leaving friends and familiar surroundings may discourage mobility. But such relocations are not inhibited by immigration quotas, by laws restricting the employment of foreigners, or by the need to learn a new language.

There are also greater impediments to the transfer of capital across national boundaries than to its movement within a country. For example, many countries have rules limiting foreign ownership. Even the United States limits foreign ownership of broadcast outlets and airlines and, recently, political furors arose when a Chinese company sought to purchase a U.S. oil company and when a Middle Eastern company offered to take over the management of several U.S. ports. Foreign investment is also subject to special political risks, such as the danger of outright expropriation or nationalization after a change in government.

But even if nothing as extreme as expropriation occurs, capital invested abroad faces significant risks from exchange rate variations. An investment valued at 250 million yen is worth $2.5 million to American investors when the dollar is worth 100 yen, but it is worth only $1 million when it takes 250 yen to buy a dollar.

THE LAW OF COMPARATIVE ADVANTAGE

The gains from international specialization and trade are clear and intuitive when one country is better at producing one item and its trading partner is better at producing another. For example, no one finds it surprising that Brazil sells coffee to the United States and the United States exports software to Brazil. We know that coffee can be produced using less labor and other inputs in Brazil than in the United States. Likewise, the United States can produce software at a lower resource cost than can Brazil.

In such a situation, we say that Brazil has an **absolute advantage** in coffee production, and the United States has an absolute advantage in software production. In such cases, it is obvious that both countries can gain by producing the item in which they have an absolute advantage and then trading with one another.

What is much less obvious, but equally true, is that these gains from international trade still exist *even if one country is more efficient than the other in producing everything*. This lesson, the principle of **comparative advantage,** is one we first encountered in Chapter 3.[2] It is, in fact, one of the most important of our *Ideas for Beyond the Final Exam*, so we repeat it here for convenience.

> **THE SURPRISING PRINCIPLE OF COMPARATIVE ADVANTAGE** Even if one country is at an absolute *dis*advantage relative to another country in the production of every good, it still has a *comparative advantage* in making the good at which it is *least inefficient* (compared with the other country).
>
> The great classical economist David Ricardo (1772–1823) discovered about 200 years ago that two countries can still gain from trade even if one is more efficient than the other in *every* industry—that is, even if one has an absolute advantage in producing every commodity.
>
> In determining the most efficient patterns of production, it is *comparative* advantage, not *absolute* advantage, that matters. Thus a country can gain by importing a good even if that good can be produced more efficiently at home. Such imports make sense if they enable the country to specialize in producing goods at which it is *even more* efficient.

The Arithmetic of Comparative Advantage

Let's see precisely how comparative advantage works using a hypothetical example first suggested in Chapter 3. Table 2 gives a rather exaggerated impression of the trading positions of the United States and Japan a few years ago. We imagine that labor is the only

One country is said to have an **absolute advantage** over another in the production of a particular good if it can produce that good using smaller quantities of resources than can the other country.

One country is said to have a **comparative advantage** over another in the production of a particular good relative to other goods if it produces that good less inefficiently as compared with the other country.

IDEAS FOR BEYOND THE FINAL EXAM

---

[2] To review, see page 49.

TABLE 2

Alternative Outputs from One
Year of Labor Input

	In the U.S.	In Japan
Computers	50	10
Televisions	50	40

input used to produce computers and television sets in the two countries and that the United States has an absolute advantage in manufacturing both goods. In this example, one year's worth of labor can produce either 50 computers or 50 TV sets in the United States but only 10 computers or 40 televisions in Japan. So the United States is the more efficient producer of both goods. Nonetheless, as we will now show, it pays for the United States to specialize in producing computers and trade with Japan to get the TV sets it wants.

To demonstrate this point, we begin by noting that the United States has a comparative advantage in *computers,* whereas Japan has a comparative advantage in producing *televisions.* Specifically, the numbers in Table 2 show that the United States can produce 50 televisions with one year's labor, whereas Japan can produce only 40, giving the United States a 25 percent efficient edge over Japan. However, the United States is five times as efficient as Japan in producing computers: It can produce 50 per year of labor rather than 10. Because America's competitive edge is far greater in computers than in televisions, we say that the United States has a *comparative advantage* in computers.

From the Japanese perspective, these same numbers indicate that Japan is only *slightly less* efficient than the United States in TV production but *drastically less* efficient in computer production. So Japan's comparative advantage is in producing televisions. According to Ricardo's law of comparative advantage, then, the two countries can gain if the United States specializes in producing computers, Japan specializes in producing TVs, and the two countries trade.

TABLE 3

Example of the Gains from Trade

	U.S.	Japan	Total
Computers	+25,000	−10,000	**+15,000**
Televisions	−25,000	+40,000	**+15,000**

Let's verify that this conclusion is true. Suppose Japan transfers 1,000 years of labor out of the computer industry and into TV manufacturing. According to the figures in Table 2, its computer output will fall by 10,000 units, while its TV output will rise by 40,000 units. This information is recorded in the middle column of Table 3. Suppose, at the same time, the United States transfers 500 years of labor out of television manufacturing (thereby losing 25,000 TVs) and into computer making (thereby gaining 25,000 computers). Table 3 shows us that these transfers of resources between the two countries increase the *world's* production of *both* outputs. Together, the two countries now have 15,000 additional TVs and 15,000 additional computers—a nice outcome.

Was there some sleight of hand here? How did *both* the United States *and* Japan gain *both* computers *and* TVs? The explanation is that the process we have just described involves more than just a swap of a fixed bundle of commodities, as in our earlier cookies-and-milk example. It also involves *a change in the production arrangements.* Some of Japan's inefficient computer production is taken over by more efficient American makers. And some of America's TV production is taken over by Japanese television companies, which are *less inefficient* at making TVs than Japanese computer manufacturers are at making computers. In this way, *world productivity is increased.* The underlying principle is both simple and fundamental:

> **When every country does what it can do best, all countries can benefit because more of every commodity can be produced without increasing the amounts of labor and other resources used.**

Where does the United States hold and lack comparative advantage? Among our big export powerhouses are the aerospace industry, agriculture, chemicals, high-tech services, financial services, entertainment, and higher education. We are, of course, huge importers of petroleum, television sets, automobiles, computers, clothing, toys, and much else.

The Graphics of Comparative Advantage

The gains from trade also can be illustrated graphically, and doing so helps us understand whether such gains are large or small.

The lines *US* and *JN* in Figure 1 are closely related to the production possibilities frontiers of the two countries, differing only in that they pretend that each country has the same amount of labor available.[3] In this case, we assume that each has 1 million person-years of labor. For example, Table 2 tells us that for each 1 million years of labor, the United States can produce 50 million TVs and no computers (point *U* in Figure 1), 50 million computers and no TVs (point *S*), or any combination between (the line *US*). Similar reasoning leads to line *JN* for Japan.

America's *actual* production possibilities frontier would be even higher, relative to Japan's, than shown in Figure 1 because the U.S. population is larger. But Figure 1 is more useful because it highlights the differences in *efficiency* (rather than in mere size), and this is what determines both absolute and comparative advantage. Let's see how.

The fact that line *US* lies *above* line *JN* means that the United States can manufacture more televisions and more computers than Japan *with the same amount of labor.* This difference reflects our assumption that the United States has an *absolute* advantage in both commodities.

America's *comparative* advantage in computer production and Japan's comparative advantage in TV production are shown in a different way: by the relative *slopes* of the two lines. Look back to Table 2, which shows that the United States can acquire a computer on its own by giving up one TV. Thus, the *opportunity cost* of a computer in the United States is one television set. This opportunity cost is depicted graphically by the slope of the U.S. production possibilities frontier in Figure 1, which is $OU/OS = 50/50 = 1$.

Table 2 also tells us that the opportunity cost of a computer in Japan is four TVs. This relationship is depicted in Figure 1 by the slope of Japan's production possibilities frontier, which is $OJ/ON = 40/10 = 4$.

> A country's *absolute* advantage in production over another country is shown by its having a higher per-capita production possibilities frontier. The difference in the *comparative* advantages between the two countries is shown by the difference in the slopes of their frontiers.

Because opportunity costs differ in the two countries, gains are possible if the two countries specialize and trade with one another. Specifically, it is cheaper, in terms of real resources forgone, for *either* country to acquire its computers in the United States. By a similar line of reasoning, the opportunity cost of TVs is higher in the United States than in Japan, so it makes sense for both countries to acquire their televisions in Japan.[4]

Notice that if the slopes of the two production possibilities frontiers, *JN* and *US*, were equal, then opportunity costs would be the same in each country. In that case, no potential gains would arise from trade. Gains from trade arise from *differences* across countries, not from similarities. This is an important point about which people are often confused. It is often argued that two very different countries, such as the United States and Mexico, cannot gain much by trading with one another. The fact is just the opposite:

> Two very similar countries may gain little from trade. Large gains from trade are most likely when countries are very different.

The pattern is apparent in U.S. trade statistics—with one big exception. Canada, a country very similar to the United States, is our biggest trading partner. But that is mainly because the two nations share a huge and very porous border. However, our next three biggest

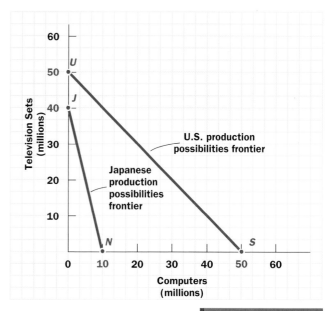

FIGURE 1

Production Possibilities Frontiers for Two Countries (per million years of labor)

---

[3] To review the concept of the production possibilities frontier, see Chapter 3.

[4] As an exercise, provide this line of reasoning.

trading partners, in order, are China, Mexico, and Japan—three countries very different from the United States.

How nations divide the gains from trade depends on the prices that emerge from world trade—a complicated topic taken up in the appendix to this chapter. But we already know enough to see that world trade must, in our example, leave a computer costing more than one TV and less than four. Why? Because if a computer bought less than one TV (its opportunity cost in the United States) on the world market, the United States would produce its own TVs rather than buying them from Japan. And if a computer cost more than four TVs (its opportunity cost in Japan), Japan would prefer to produce its own computers rather than buy them from the United States. So we conclude that, if both countries are to trade, the rate of exchange between TVs and computers must end up somewhere between 4:1 and 1:1. Generalizing:

> **If two countries voluntarily trade two goods with one another, the rate of exchange between the goods must fall in between the price ratios that would prevail in the two countries in the absence of trade.**

To illustrate the gains from trade in our concrete example, suppose the world price ratio settles at 2:1—meaning that one computer costs as much as two televisions. How much, precisely, do the United States and Japan gain from world trade in this case?

Figure 2 helps us visualize the answers. The blue production possibilities frontiers, *US* in Panel (b) and *JN* in Panel (a), are the same as in Figure 1. But the United States can do better than line *US*. Specifically, with a world price ratio of 2:1, the United States can buy two TVs for each computer it gives up, rather than just one (which is the opportunity cost of a computer in the United States). Hence, if the United States produces only computers—point *S* in Figure 2(b)—and buys its TVs from Japan, America's *consumption possibilities* will be as indicated by the brick-colored line that begins at point *S* and has a slope of 2—that is, each computer sold brings the United States two television sets. (It ends at point *A* because 40 million TV sets is the most that Japan can produce.) Because trade allows the United States to choose a point on *AS* rather than on *US*, trade opens up consumption possibilities that were simply not available before (shaded gray in the diagram).

FIGURE 2

The Gains from Trade

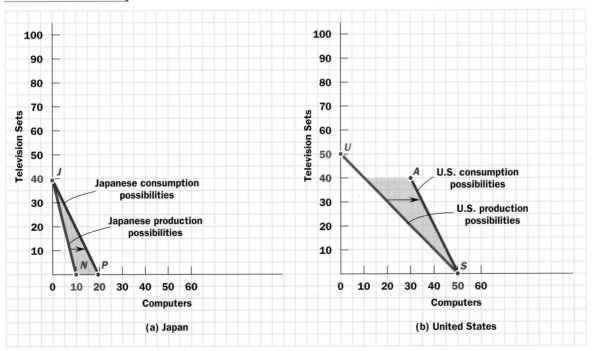

(a) Japan

(b) United States

NOTE: Quantities are in millions.

A similar story applies to Japan. If the Japanese produce only television sets—point *J* in Figure 2(a)—they can acquire a computer from the United States for every two TVs they give up as they move along the brick-colored line *JP* (whose slope is 2). This result is better than they can achieve on their own, because a sacrifice of two TVs in Japan yields only one-half of a computer. Hence, world trade enlarges Japan's consumption possibilities from *JN* to *JP*.

Figure 2 shows graphically that gains from trade arise to the extent that world prices (2:1 in our example) differ from domestic opportunity costs (4:1 and 1:1 in our example). How the two countries share the gains from trade depends on the exact prices that emerge from world trade. As explained in the appendix, that in turn depends on relative supplies and demands in the two countries.

Must Specialization be Complete?

In our simple numerical and graphical examples, international specialization is always *complete*—for example, the United States makes all the computers and Japan makes all the TV sets. But if you look at the real world, you will find mostly *incomplete* specialization. For example, the United States is the world's biggest importer of both petroleum and automobiles. But we also manufacture lots of cars and drill for lots of oil at home. In fact, we even export some cars. This stark discrepancy between theory and fact might worry you. Is something wrong with the theory of comparative advantage?

Actually, there are many reasons why specialization is typically incomplete, despite the validity of the principle of comparative advantage. Two of them are simple enough to merit mentioning right here.

First, some countries are just too small to provide the world's entire output, even when they have a strong comparative advantage in the good in question. In our numerical example, Japan just might not have enough labor and other resources to produce the entire world output of televisions. If so, some TV sets would have to be produced in the United States.

Second, you may have noticed that in this chapter we have drawn all the production possibilities frontiers (PPFs) as *straight lines*, whereas they were always *curved* in previous chapters. The reason is purely pedagogical: We wanted to create simple examples that lend themselves to numerical solutions. It is undoubtedly more realistic to assume that PPFs are curved. But that sort of technology leads to incomplete specialization, which is a complication best left to more advanced courses.

ISSUE RESOLVED: COMPARATIVE ADVANTAGE EXPOSES THE

"CHEAP FOREIGN LABOR" FALLACY

The principle of comparative advantage takes us a long way toward understanding the fallacy in the "cheap foreign labor" argument described at the beginning of this chapter. Given the assumed productive efficiency of American labor, and the inefficiency of Japanese labor, we would expect wages to be much higher in the United States.

In these circumstances, one might expect American workers to be apprehensive about an agreement to permit open trade between the two countries: "How can we hope to meet the unfair competition of those underpaid Japanese workers?" Japanese laborers might also be concerned: "How can we hope to meet the competition of those Americans, who are so efficient in producing everything?"

The principle of comparative advantage shows us that both fears are unjustified. As we have just seen, when trade opens up between Japan and the United States, *workers in both countries will be able to earn higher real wages than before* because of the increased productivity that comes through specialization.

As Figure 2 shows, once trade opens up, Japanese workers should be able to acquire more TVs and more computers than they did before. As a consequence, their living standards should rise, even though they have been left vulnerable to competition from the super-efficient Americans. Workers in the United States should also end up with more TVs and more computers. So their living standards should also rise, even though they have been exposed to competition from cheap Japanese labor.

These higher standards of living, of course, reflect the higher real wages earned because workers become more productive in both countries. The lesson to be learned here is elementary:

Nothing helps raise living standards more than a greater abundance of goods.

TARIFFS, QUOTAS, AND OTHER INTERFERENCES WITH TRADE

Despite the large mutual gains from international trade, nations often interfere with the free movement of goods and services across national borders. In fact, until the rise of the free-trade movement about 200 years ago (with Adam Smith and David Ricardo as its vanguard), it was taken for granted that one of the essential tasks of government was to impede trade, presumably in the national interest.

Then, as now, many people argued that the proper aim of government policy was to promote exports and discourage imports, for doing so would increase the amount of money foreigners owed the nation. According to this so-called **mercantilist** view, a nation's wealth consists of the amount of gold or other monies at its command.

> **Mercantilism** is a doctrine that holds that exports are good for a country, whereas imports are harmful.

Obviously, governments can pursue such a policy only within certain limits. A country *must* import vital foodstuffs and critical raw materials that it cannot provide for itself. Moreover, mercantilists ignore a simple piece of arithmetic: It is mathematically impossible for *every* country to sell more than it buys, because one country's exports must be some other country's imports. If everyone competes in this game by cutting imports to the bone, then exports must shrivel up, too. The result is that everyone will be deprived of the mutual gains from trade. Indeed, that is precisely what happens in a trade war.

After the protectionist 1930s, the United States moved away from mercantilist policies designed to impede imports and gradually assumed a leading role in promoting free trade. Over the past 60 years, tariffs and other trade barriers have come down dramatically.

In 1995, the United States led the world to complete the Uruguay Round of tariff reductions and, just before that, the country joined Canada and Mexico in the North American Free Trade Agreement (NAFTA). The latter caused a political firestorm in the United States in 1993 and 1994, with critic (and 1992 presidential candidate) Ross Perot predicting a "giant sucking sound" as American workers lost their jobs to competition from "cheap Mexican labor." (Does that argument sound familiar?) Most of the world's trading nations are now engaged in a new multiyear round of trade talks, under guidelines adopted at an important meeting in Doha, Qatar, in 2001. (See "Liberalizing World Trade: The Doha Round.")

Modern governments use three main devices when seeking to control trade: tariffs, quotas, and export subsidies.

> A **tariff** is a tax on imports.

A **tariff** is simply a tax on imports. An importer of cars, for example, may be charged $2,000 for each auto brought into the country. Such a tax will, of course, make automobiles more expensive and favor domestic models over imports. It will also raise revenue for the government. In fact, tariffs were a major source of tax revenue for the U.S. government during the eighteenth and nineteenth centuries—and also a major source of political controversy. But the United States is a low-tariff country nowadays, with only a few notable exceptions. However, many other countries rely on heavy tariffs to protect their industries. Indeed, tariff rates of 100 percent or more are not unknown in some countries.

> A **quota** specifies the maximum amount of a good that is permitted into the country from abroad per unit of time.

A **quota** is a legal limit on the amount of a good that may be imported. For example, the government might allow no more than 5 million foreign cars to be imported in a year. In some cases, governments ban the importation of certain goods outright—a quota of zero. The United States now imposes quotas on a smattering of goods, including textiles, meat, and sugar. Most imports, however, are not subject to quotas. By reducing supply, quotas naturally raise the prices of the goods subject to quotas. For example, sugar is vastly more expensive in the United States than it is elsewhere in the world.

An **export subsidy** is a government payment to an exporter. By reducing the exporter's costs, such subsidies permit exporters to lower their selling prices and compete more effectively in world trade. Overt export subsidies are minor in the United States. But some foreign governments use them extensively to assist their domestic industries—a practice that provokes bitter complaints from American manufacturers about "unfair competition." For example, years of heavy government subsidies helped the European Airbus consortium take a sizable share of the world commercial aircraft market away from U.S. manufacturers like Boeing and McDonnell-Douglas—a trend that has lately reversed.

> An **export subsidy** is a payment by the government to exporters to permit them to reduce the selling prices of their goods so they can compete more effectively in foreign markets.

Tariffs versus Quotas

Although both tariffs and quotas reduce international trade and increase the prices of domestically produced goods, there are some important differences between these two ways to protect domestic industries.

First, under a quota, profits from the higher price in the importing country usually go into the pockets of the foreign and domestic sellers of the products. Limitations on supply (from abroad) mean (a) that customers in the importing country must pay more for the product and (b) that suppliers, whether foreign or domestic, receive more for every unit they sell. For example, the right to sell sugar in the United States under the tight sugar quota has been extremely valuable for decades. Privileged foreign and domestic firms can make a lot of money from quota rights.

By contrast, when trade is restricted by a tariff instead, some of the "profits" go as tax revenues to the government of the importing country. (Domestic producers still benefit, because they are exempt from the tariff.) In this respect, a tariff is certainly a better proposition than a quota for the country that enacts it.

Another important distinction between the two measures arises from their different implications for productive efficiency. Because a tariff handicaps all foreign suppliers

Liberalizing World Trade: The Doha Round

The time and place were not auspicious: an international gathering in the Persian Gulf just two months after the September 11, 2001 terrorists attacks. Nerves were frayed, security was extremely tight, and memories of a failed trade meeting in Seattle in 1999 lingered on. Yet representatives of more than 140 nations, meeting in Doha, Qatar, in November 2001, managed to agree on the outlines of a new round of comprehensive trade negotiations—one that now appears unlikely to be completed.

The so-called Doha Round focuses on bringing down tariffs, subsidies, and other restrictions on world trade in agriculture, services, and a variety of manufactured goods. It also seeks greater protection for intellectual property rights, while making sure that poor countries have access to modern pharmaceuticals at prices they can afford. Reform of the World Trade Organization's own rules and procedures is also on the agenda. Perhaps most surprisingly, the United States has even promised to consider changes in its antidumping laws, which are used to keep many foreign goods out of U.S. markets. (Dumping is explained at the end of this chapter.)

Large-scale trade negotiations such as this one, involving more than 100 countries and many different issues, take years to complete. (The last one, the Uruguay Round, took seven years.) And the Doha Round almost collapsed in 2003 and again in 2006 when negotiating sessions got nowhere. In early 2008, there was not much optimism that the contentious agricultural issues could be resolved, leaving many observers doubting that the Doha Round would ever be completed. But no one knows what the future may bring.

SOURCE: © Patrick Baz/AFP/Getty Images

equally, it awards sales to those firms and nations that can supply the goods most cheaply—presumably because they are more efficient. A quota, by contrast, necessarily awards its import licenses more or less capriciously—perhaps in proportion to past sales or even based on political favoritism. There is no reason to expect the most efficient suppliers will get the import permits. For example, the U.S. sugar quota was for years suspected of being a major source of corruption in the Caribbean.

If a country must inhibit imports, two important reasons support a preference for tariffs over quotas:

1. **Some of the revenues resulting from tariffs go to the government of the importing country rather than to foreign and domestic producers.**

2. **Unlike quotas, tariffs offer special benefits to more efficient exporters.**

WHY INHIBIT TRADE?

To state that tariffs provide a better way to inhibit international trade than quotas leaves open a far more basic question: Why limit trade in the first place? It has been estimated that trade restrictions cost American consumers more than $70 billion per year in the form of higher prices. Why should they be asked to pay these higher prices? A number of answers have been given. Let's examine each in turn.

Gaining a Price Advantage for Domestic Firms

A tariff forces foreign exporters to sell more cheaply by restricting their market access. If the foreign firms do not cut their prices, they will be unable to sell their goods. So, in effect, a tariff amounts to government intervention to rig prices in favor of domestic producers.[5]

Not bad, you say. However, this technique works only as long as foreigners accept the tariff exploitation passively—which they rarely do. More often, they retaliate by imposing tariffs or quotas of their own on imports from the country that began the tariff game. Such tit-for-tat behavior can easily lead to a trade war in which everyone loses through the resulting reductions in trade. Something like this, in fact, happened to the world economy in the 1930s, and it helped prolong the worldwide depression. Preventing such trade wars is one main reason why nations that belong to the World Trade Organization (WTO) pledge not to raise tariffs.

Tariffs or quotas can benefit particular domestic industries in a country that is able to impose them without fear of retaliation. But when every country uses them, every country is likely to lose in the long run.

Protecting Particular Industries

The second, and probably more frequent, reason why countries restrict trade is to protect particular favored industries from foreign competition. If foreigners can produce steel or shoes more cheaply, domestic businesses and unions in these industries are quick to demand protection. And their governments may be quite willing to grant it.

The "cheap foreign labor" argument is most likely to be invoked in this context. Protective tariffs and quotas are explicitly designed to rescue firms that are too inefficient to compete with foreign exporters in an open world market. But it is precisely this harsh competition that gives consumers the chief benefits of international specialization: better products at lower prices. So protection comes at a cost.

---

[5] For more details on this, see the appendix to this chapter.

Thinking back to our numerical example of comparative advantage, we can well imagine the indignant complaints from Japanese computer makers as the opening of trade with the United States leads to increased imports of American-made computers. At the same time, American TV manufacturers would probably express outrage over the flood of imported TVs from Japan. Yet it is Japanese specialization in televisions and U.S. specialization in computers that enables citizens of both countries to enjoy higher standards of living. If governments interfere with this process, consumers in both countries will lose out.

Industries threatened by foreign competition often argue that some form of protection against imports is needed to prevent job losses. For example, the U.S. steel industry has made exactly this argument time and time again since the 1960s—most recently in 2001, when world steel prices plummeted and imports surged. And the U.S. government has usually delivered some protection in response. But basic macroeconomics teaches us that there are better ways to stimulate employment, such as raising aggregate demand.

A program that limits foreign competition will be more effective at preserving employment *in the particular protected industry*. But such job gains typically come at a high cost to consumers and to the economy. Table 4 estimates some of the costs to American consumers of using tariffs and quotas to save jobs in selected industries. In every case, the costs far exceed the annual wages of the workers in the protected industries—ranging as high as $600,000 per job for the sugar quota.

Nevertheless, complaints over proposals to reduce tariffs or quotas may be justified unless something is done to ease the cost to individual workers of switching to the product lines that trade makes profitable.

TABLE 4	
Estimated Costs of Protectionism to Consumers	
Industry	Cost per Job Saved
Apparel	$139,000
Costume jewelry	97,000
Shipping	415,000
Sugar	600,000
Textiles	202,000
Women's footwear	102,000

SOURCE: Gary C. Hufbauer and Kimberly Ann Elliott, *Measuring the Costs of Protectionism in the United States* (Washington, D.C.: Institute for International Economics; January 1994), Table 1.3, pp. 12–13.

The argument for free trade between countries cannot be considered airtight if governments do not assist the citizens in each country who are harmed whenever patterns of production change drastically—as would happen, for example, if governments suddenly reduced tariff and quota barriers.

Owners of television factories in the United States and of computer factories in Japan may see large investments suddenly rendered unprofitable. Workers in those industries may see their special skills and training devalued in the marketplace. Displaced workers also pay heavy intangible costs—they may need to move to new locations and/or new industries, uprooting their families, losing old friends and neighbors, and so on. Although the *majority* of citizens undoubtedly gain from free trade, that is no consolation to those who are its victims.

To mitigate these problems, the U.S. government follows two basic approaches. First, our trade laws offer temporary protection from sudden surges of imports, on the grounds that unexpected changes in trade patterns do not give businesses and workers enough time to adjust.

Second, the government has set up **trade adjustment assistance** programs to help workers and businesses that lose their jobs or their markets to imports. Firms may be eligible for technical assistance, government loans or loan guarantees, and permission to delay tax payments. Workers may qualify for retraining programs, longer periods of unemployment compensation, and funds to defray moving costs. Each form of assistance is designed to ease the burden on the victims of free trade so that the rest of us can enjoy its considerable benefits.

Trade adjustment assistance provides special unemployment benefits, loans, retraining programs, and other aid to workers and firms that are harmed by foreign competition.

National Defense and Other Noneconomic Considerations

A third rationale for trade protection is the need to maintain national defense. For example, even if the United States were not the most efficient producer of aircraft, it might still be rational to produce our own military aircraft so that no foreign government could ever cut off supplies of this strategic product.

How Popular Is Protectionism?

Since World War II, the world has mainly been moving toward freer trade and away from protection. But the people of the world are not convinced that this trend is desirable. In what was probably the most comprehensive polling ever conducted on the subject, a Canadian firm asked almost 13,000 people in 22 countries the following question in 1998: "Which of the following two broad approaches do you think would be the best way to improve the economic and employment situation in this country—protecting our local industries by restricting imports, or removing import restrictions to increase our international trade?" The protectionist response narrowly outnumbered the free-trade response by a 47 percent to 42 percent margin. (The rest were undecided.) Protectionist sentiment was much stronger in the United States, however, where the margin was 56 percent to 37 percent. (See the accompanying graph.)

That was in 1998. In the United States (and elsewhere), there is clear evidence that protectionist sentiment is actually gaining in popularity. For example, a *Wall Street Journal*/NBC News poll in 1999 found that 39 percent of Americans believed that trade agreements have helped the United States, while 30 percent believed they had hurt. When that same question was asked in 2007, only 28 percent thought trade agreements had helped, while 46 percent thought they had hurt.

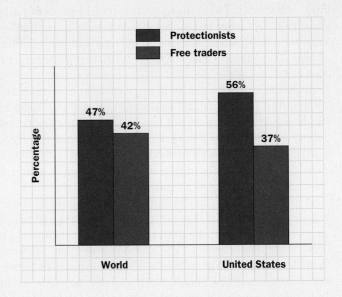

SOURCES: "How Popular Is Protectionism?" *The Economist*, January 2, 1999; and Grant Aldonas, Robert Lawrence, and Matthew Slaughter, *Succeeding in the Global Economy*, Financial Services Forum Policy Research, June 2007, p. 10.

The national defense argument is fine as far as it goes, but it poses a clear danger: Even industries with the most peripheral relationship to defense are likely to invoke this argument on their behalf. For instance, for years the U.S. watchmaking industry argued for protection on the grounds that its skilled craftsmen would be invaluable in wartime!

Similarly, the United States has occasionally banned either exports to or imports from nations such as Cuba, Iran, and Iraq on political grounds. Such actions may have important economic effects, creating either bonanzas or disasters for particular American industries. But they are justified by politics, not by economics. Noneconomic reasons also explain quotas on importation of whaling products and on the furs of other endangered species.

The Infant-Industry Argument

The **infant-industry argument** for trade protection holds that new industries need to be protected from foreign competition until they develop and flourish.

Yet a fourth common rationale for protectionism is the so-called **infant-industry argument**, which has been prominent in the United States at least since Alexander Hamilton wrote his *Report on Manufactures*. Promising new industries often need breathing room to flourish and grow. If we expose these infants to the rigors of international competition too soon, the argument goes, they may never develop to the point where they can survive on their own in the international marketplace.

This argument, although valid in certain instances, is less defensible than it seems at first. Protecting an infant industry is justifiable only if the prospective future gains are sufficient to repay the up-front costs of protectionism. But if the industry is likely to be so profitable in the future, why doesn't private capital rush in to take advantage of the prospective net profits? After all, the annals of business are full of cases in which a new product or a new firm lost money at first but profited handsomely later on. In recent times, Apple, Yahoo, Google, and eBay all lost money in their early days.

The infant-industry argument for protection stands up to scrutiny only if private funds are unavailable for some reason, despite an industry's glowing profit prospects. Even then it may make more sense to provide a government loan rather than to provide trade protection.

In an advanced economy such as ours, with well-developed capital markets to fund new businesses, it is difficult to think of legitimate examples where the infant-industry argument applies. Even if such a case were found, we would have to be careful that the industry not remain in diapers forever. In too many cases, industries are awarded protection when young and, somehow, never mature to the point where protection can be withdrawn. We must be wary of infants that never grow up.

Strategic Trade Policy

A stronger argument for (temporary) protection has substantially influenced trade policy in the United States and elsewhere. Proponents of this line of thinking agree that free trade for all is the best system. But they point out that we live in an imperfect world in which many nations refuse to play by the rules of the free-trade game. And they fear that a nation that pursues free trade in a protectionist world is likely to lose out. It therefore makes sense, they argue, to threaten to protect your markets unless other nations agree to open theirs.

The United States has followed this strategy in trade negotiations with several countries in recent years. In one prominent case, the U.S. government threatened to impose high tariffs on several European luxury goods unless Europe opened its markets to imported bananas from the Americas. A few years later, the European Union turned the tables, threatening to increase tariffs on a variety of U.S. goods unless we changed a tax provision that amounted to an export subsidy. In each case, a dangerous trade war was narrowly averted when an agreement was struck at the eleventh hour.

The **strategic argument for protection** is a difficult one for economists to counter. Although it recognizes the superiority of free trade, it argues that *threatening* protectionism is the best way to achieve that end. (See the box "Can Protectionism Save Free Trade?") Such a strategy might work, but it clearly involves great risks. If threats that the United States will turn protectionist induce other countries to scrap their existing protectionist policies, then the gamble will have succeeded. But if the gamble fails, protectionism increases.

> The **strategic argument for protection** holds that a nation may sometimes have to threaten protectionism to induce other countries to drop their own protectionist measures.

CAN CHEAP IMPORTS HURT A COUNTRY?

One of the most curious—and illogical—features of the protectionist position is the fear of low import prices. Countries that subsidize their exports are often accused of **dumping**—of getting rid of their goods at unjustifiably low prices. Economists find this argument strange. As a nation of consumers, we should be indignant when foreigners charge us *high* prices, not *low* ones. That common-sense rule guides every consumer's daily life. Only from the topsy-turvy viewpoint of an industry seeking protection are low prices seen as counter to the public interest.

> **Dumping** means selling goods in a foreign market at lower prices than those charged in the home market.

Ultimately, the best interests of any country are served when its imports are as cheap as possible. It would be ideal for the United States if the rest of the world were willing to provide us with goods at no charge. We could then live in luxury at the expense of other countries.

But, of course, benefits to the United States as a whole do not necessarily accrue to every single American. If quotas on, say, sugar imports were dropped, American consumers and industries that purchase sugar would gain from lower prices. At the same time, however, owners of sugar fields and their employees would suffer serious losses in the form of lower profits, lower wages, and lost jobs—losses they would fight fiercely to prevent. For this reason, politics often leads to the adoption of protectionist measures that would likely be rejected on strictly economic criteria.

ISSUE: LAST LOOK AT THE "CHEAP FOREIGN LABOR" ARGUMENT

The preceding discussion reveals the fundamental fallacy in the argument that the United States as a whole should fear cheap foreign labor. The average American worker's living standard must rise, not fall, if other countries willingly supply their products to us more cheaply. As long as the government's monetary and fiscal policies succeed in maintaining high levels of employment, we cannot possibly lose by getting world products at bargain prices. Indeed, this is precisely what happened to the U.S. economy in the late 1990s. Even though imports poured in at low prices, unemployment in the United States fell to its lowest rate in a generation. Even in 2007, with a financial crisis and a massive trade deficit equal to 5.1 percent of GDP, the U.S. unemployment rate averaged only 4.6 percent.

We must add a few important qualifications, however. First, our macroeconomic policy may not always be effective. If workers displaced by foreign competition cannot find new jobs, they will indeed suffer from international trade. But high unemploy-

Can Protectionism Save Free Trade?

In this classic column, William Safire shook off his long-standing attachment to free trade and argued eloquently for retaliation against protectionist nations.

Free trade is economic motherhood. Protectionism is economic evil incarnate. . . . Never should government interfere in the efficiency of international competition.

Since childhood, these have been the tenets of my faith. If it meant that certain businesses in this country went belly-up, so be it. . . . If it meant that Americans would be thrown out of work by overseas companies paying coolie wages, that was tough. . . .

The thing to keep in mind, I was taught, was the Big Picture and the Long Run. America, the great exporter, had far more to gain than to lose from free trade; attempts to protect inefficient industries here would ultimately cost more American jobs.

While playing with my David Ricardo doll and learning nursery rhymes about comparative advantage, I was listening to another laissez-fairy tale: Government's role in the world of business should be limited to keeping business honest and competitive. In God we antitrusted. Let businesses operate in the free marketplace.

Now American businesses are no longer competing with foreign companies. They are competing with foreign governments who help their local businesses. That means the world arena no longer offers a free marketplace; instead, most other governments are pushing a policy that can be called helpfulism.

Helpfulism works like this: A government like Japan decides to get behind its baseball-bat industry. It pumps in capital, knocks off marginal operators, finds subtle ways to discourage imports of Louisville Sluggers, and selects target areas for export blitzes. Pretty soon, the favored Japanese companies are driving foreign competitors batty.

How do we compete with helpfulism? One way is to complain that it is unfair; that draws a horselaugh. Another way is to demand a "Reagan Round" of trade negotiations under GATT, the Gentlemen's Agreement To Talk, which is equally laughable.

Yet another way is to join the helpfuls by subsidizing our exports and permitting our companies to try monopolistic tricks abroad not permitted at home. But all that makes us feel guilty, with good reason.

The other way to deal with helpfulism is through—here comes the dreadful word—protection. Or, if you prefer a euphemism, retaliation. Or if that is still too severe, reciprocity. Whatever its name, it is a way of saying to the cutthroat cartelists we sweetly call our trading partners: "You have bent the rules out of shape. Change your practices to conform to the agreed-upon rules, or we will export a taste of your own medicine."

A little balance, then, from the free trade theorists. The demand for what the Pentagon used to call "protective reaction" is not demagoguery, not shortsighted, not self-defeating. On the contrary, the overseas pirates of protectionism and exemplars of helpfulism need to be taught the basic lesson in trade, which is: tit for tat.

SOURCE: William Safire, "Smoot-Hawley Lives," *The New York Times*, March 17, 1983. Copyright © 1983 by The New York Times Company. Reprinted by permission.

SOURCE: © David Burnett/Contact Press Images

ment reflects a shortcoming of the government's monetary and fiscal policies, not of its international trade policies.

Second, we have noted that an abrupt stiffening of foreign competition can hurt U.S. workers by not allowing them adequate time to adapt to the new conditions. If change occurs fairly gradually, workers can be retrained and move into the industries that now require their services. Indeed, if the change is slow enough, normal attrition may suffice. But competition that inflicts its damage overnight is certain to impose real costs on the affected workers—costs that are no less painful for being temporary. That is why our trade laws make provisions for people and industries damaged by import surges.

In fact, the economic world is constantly changing. The recent emergence of China, India, and other third-world countries, for example, has created stiff new competition for workers in America and other rich nations—competition they never imagined when they signed up for jobs that may now be imperiled by international trade. The same is true of many workers in service jobs (ranging from call center operators to lawyers) who never dreamed that their jobs might be done electronically from thousands of miles away. It is not irrational, and it is certainly not protectionist, for countries like the United States to use trade adjustment assistance and other tools to cushion the blow for these workers.

But these are, after all, only qualifications to an overwhelming argument. They call for intelligent monetary and fiscal policies and for transitional assistance to unemployed workers, not for abandonment of free trade. In general, the nation as a whole need not fear competition from cheap foreign labor.

In the long run, labor will be "cheap" only where it is not very productive. Wages will be high in countries with high labor productivity, and this high productivity will enable those countries to compete effectively in international trade despite their high wages. It is thus misleading to say that the United States held its own in the international marketplace until recently *despite* high wages. Rather, it is much more accurate to note that the higher wages of American workers were a result of higher

Unfair Foreign Competition

Satire and ridicule are often more persuasive than logic and statistics. Exasperated by the spread of protectionism under the prevailing mercantilist philosophy, the French economist Frédéric Bastiat decided to take the protectionist argument to its illogical conclusion. The fictitious petition of the French candlemakers to the Chamber of Deputies, written in 1845 and excerpted below, has become a classic in the battle for free trade.

> We are subject to the intolerable competition of a foreign rival, who enjoys, it would seem, such superior facilities for the production of light, that he is enabled to inundate our national market at so exceedingly reduced a price, that, the moment he makes his appearance, he draws off all custom for us; and thus an important branch of French industry, with all its innumerable ramifications, is suddenly reduced to a state of complete stagnation. This rival is no other than the sun.
>
> Our petition is, that it would please your honorable body to pass a law whereby shall be directed the shutting up of all windows, dormers, skylights, shutters, curtains, in a word, all openings, holes, chinks, and fissures through which the light of the sun is used to penetrate our dwellings, to the prejudice of the profitable manufactures which we flatter ourselves we have been enabled to bestow upon the country. . . .
>
> We foresee your objections, gentlemen; but there is not one that you can oppose to us . . . which is not equally opposed to your own practice and the principle which guides your policy. . . . Labor and nature concur in different proportions, according to country and climate, in every article of production. . . . If a Lisbon orange can be sold at half the price of a Parisian one, it is because a natural and gratuitous heat does for the one what the other only obtains from an artificial and consequently expensive one. . . .
>
> Does it not argue the greatest inconsistency to check as you do the importation of coal, iron, cheese, and goods of foreign manufacture, merely because and even in proportion as their price approaches zero, while at the same time you freely admit, and without limitation, the light of the sun, whose price is during the whole day at zero?

SOURCE: © Culver Pictures

SOURCE: F. Bastiat, *Economic Sophisms* (New York: G. P. Putnam's Sons, 1922).

worker productivity, which gave the United States a major competitive edge—an edge we still have, by the way.

Remember, where standards of living are concerned, it is *absolute* advantage, not *comparative* advantage, that counts. The country that is most efficient in producing every output can pay its workers more in every industry.

| SUMMARY |

1. Countries trade for many reasons. Two of the most important are that differences in their natural resources and other inputs create discrepancies in the efficiency with which they can produce different goods, and that specialization offers greater economies of large-scale production.

2. Voluntary trade will generally be advantageous to both parties in an exchange. This concept is one of our *Ideas for Beyond the Final Exam.*

3. International trade is more complicated than trade within a nation because of political factors, differing national currencies, and impediments to the movement of labor and capital across national borders.

4. Two countries will gain from trade with each other if each nation exports goods in which it has a **comparative advantage.** Even a country that is inefficient across the board will benefit by exporting the goods in whose production it is *least inefficient.* This concept is another of the *Ideas for Beyond the Final Exam.*

5. When countries specialize and trade, each can enjoy consumption possibilities that exceed its production possibilities.

6. The "cheap foreign labor" argument ignores the principle of comparative advantage, which shows that real wages (which determine living standards) can rise in both importing and exporting countries as a result of **specialization.**

7. **Tariffs** and **quotas** aim to protect a country's industries from foreign competition. Such protection may sometimes be advantageous to that country, but not if foreign countries adopt tariffs and quotas of their own in retaliation.

8. From the point of view of the country that imposes them, tariffs offer at least two advantages over quotas: Some of the gains go to the government rather than to foreign producers, and they provide greater incentive for efficient production.

9. When a nation eliminates protection in favor of free trade, some industries and their workers will lose out. Equity then demands that these people and firms be compensated in some way. The U.S. government offers protection from import surges and various forms of **trade adjustment assistance** to help those workers and industries adapt to the new conditions.

10. Several arguments for protectionism can, under the right circumstances, have validity. They include the national defense argument, the infant-industry argument, and the use of trade restrictions for strategic purposes. But each of these arguments is frequently abused.

11. **Dumping** will hurt certain domestic producers, but it benefits domestic consumers.

| KEY TERMS |

"Cheap foreign labor" argument   340

Imports   340

Exports   340

Specialization   341

Mutual gains from trade   341

Absolute advantage   343

Comparative advantage   343

Mercantilism   348

Tariff   348

Quota   348

Export subsidy   349

Trade adjustment assistance   351

Infant-industry argument   352

Strategic argument for protection   353

Dumping   353

| TEST YOURSELF |

1. The following table describes the number of yards of cloth and barrels of wine that can be produced with a week's worth of labor in England and Portugal. Assume that no other inputs are needed.

	In England	In Portugal
Cloth	8 yards	12 yards
Wine	2 barrels	6 barrels

   a. If there is no trade, what is the price of wine in terms of cloth in England?

   b. If there is no trade, what is the price of wine in terms of cloth in Portugal?

   c. Suppose each country has 1 million weeks of labor available per year. Draw the production possibilities frontier for each country.

   d. Which country has an absolute advantage in the production of which good(s)? Which country has a comparative advantage in the production of which good(s)?

   e. If the countries start trading with each other, which country will specialize and export which good?

   f. What can be said about the price at which trade will take place?

2. Suppose that the United States and Mexico are the only two countries in the world and that labor is the only productive input. In the United States, a worker can produce 12 bushels of wheat *or* 2 barrels of oil in a day. In Mexico, a worker can produce 2 bushels of wheat *or* 4 barrels of oil per day.

   a. What will be the price ratio between the two commodities (that is, the price of oil in terms of wheat) in each country if there is no trade?

   b. If free trade is allowed and there are no transportation costs, which commodity would the United States import? What about Mexico?

   c. In what range would the price ratio have to fall under free trade? Why?

   d. Picking one possible post-trade price ratio, show clearly how it is possible for both countries to benefit from free trade.

| DISCUSSION QUESTIONS |

1. You have a dozen shirts and your roommate has six pairs of shoes worth roughly the same amount of money. You decide to swap six shirts for three pairs of shoes. In financial terms, neither of you gains anything. Explain why you are nevertheless both likely to be better off.

2. In the eighteenth century, some writers argued that one person in a trade could be made better off only by gaining at the expense of the other. Explain the fallacy in this argument.

3. Country A has a cold climate with a short growing season, but a highly skilled labor force (think of Finland). What sorts of products do you think it is likely to produce? What are the characteristics of the countries with which you would expect it to trade?

4. After the removal of a quota on sugar, many U.S. sugar farms go bankrupt. Discuss the pros and cons of removing the quota in the short and long runs.

5. Country A has a mercantilist government that believes it is always best to export more than it imports. As a consequence, it exports more to Country B every year than it imports from Country B. After 100 years of this arrangement, both countries are destroyed in an earthquake. What were the advantages or disadvantages of the surplus to Country A? To Country B?

6. Under current trade law, the president of the United States must report periodically to Congress on countries engaging in unfair trade practices that inhibit U.S. exports. How would you define an "unfair" trade practice? Suppose Country X exports much more to the United States than it imports, year after year. Does that constitute evidence that Country X's trade practices are unfair? What would constitute such evidence?

7. Suppose the United States finds Country X guilty of unfair trade practices and penalizes it with import quotas. So U.S. imports from Country X fall. Suppose, further, that Country X does not alter its trade practices in any way. Is the United States better or worse off? What about Country X?

| APPENDIX | *Supply, Demand, and Pricing in World Trade*

As noted in the text, price determination in a world market with free trade depends on supply and demand conditions in each of the countries participating in the market. This appendix works out some of the details in a two-country example.

When applied to international trade, the usual supply-demand model must deal with (at least) *two demand curves:* that of the exporting country and that of the importing country. In addition, it may also involve *two supply curves,* because the importing country may produce part of its own consumption. (For example, the United States, which is the world's biggest importer of oil, nonetheless produces quite a bit of domestic oil.) Furthermore, equilibrium does *not* take place at the intersection point of *either* pair of supply-demand curves. Why? Because if the two countries trade at all, the exporting nation must supply more than it demands while the importing nation must demand more than it supplies.

All three of these complications are illustrated in Figure 3, which shows the supply and demand curves of a country that *exports* wheat in Panel (a) and of a country that *imports* wheat in Panel (b). For simplicity, we assume that these countries do not deal with anyone else. Where will the two-country wheat market reach equilibrium?

Under free trade, the equilibrium price must satisfy two requirements:

1. **The quantity of wheat *exported* by one country must equal the quantity of wheat *imported* by the other country, for that is how *world* supply and demand balance.**

2. **The price of wheat must be the same in both countries.[6]**

In Figure 3, these two conditions are met at a price of $2.50 per bushel. At that price, the distance *AB* between what the exporting country produces and what it consumes equals the distance *CD* between what the importing country consumes and what it produces. This means that the amount the exporting country wants to sell at $2.50 per bushel exactly equals the amount the importing country wants to buy at that price.

At any higher price, producers in both countries would want to sell more and consumers in both countries would want to buy less. For example, if the price rose to $3.25 per bushel, the exporter's quantity supplied would rise from *B* to *F* and its quantity demanded would fall from *A* to *E*, as shown in Panel (a). As a result, more wheat would be available for export—*EF* rather than *AB*. For exactly the same reason, the price increase would cause higher production and lower sales in the importing country, leading to a reduction in imports from *CD* to *GH* in Panel (b).

But this means that the higher price, $3.25 per bushel, cannot be sustained in a free and competitive international market. With export supply *EF* far greater than import demand *GH*, there would be pressure on price to fall back toward the $2.50 equilibrium price.

FIGURE 3

Supply-Demand Equilibrium in the International Wheat Trade

(a) Exporting Country   **(b) Importing Country**

---

[6] To keep things simple, we ignore such details as the costs of shipping wheat from one country to the other.

Similar reasoning shows that no price below $2.50 can be sustained. Thus:

> In international trade, the equilibrium price is the one that makes the exporting country want to export exactly the amount that the importing country wants to import. Equilibrium will thus occur at a price at which the horizontal distance *AB* in Figure 3(a) (the excess of the exporter's quantity supplied over its quantity demanded) is equal to the horizontal distance *CD* in Figure 3(b) (the excess of the importer's quantity demanded over its quantity supplied). At this price, the *world's* quantity demanded equals the *world's* quantity supplied.

HOW TARIFFS AND QUOTAS WORK

However, as noted in the text, nations do not always let markets operate freely. Sometimes they intervene with quotas that limit imports or with tariffs that make imports more expensive. Although both tariffs and quotas restrict supplies coming from abroad and drive up prices, they operate slightly differently. A tariff works by raising prices, which in turn reduces the quantity of imports demanded. The sequence associated with a quota is just the reverse—a restriction in supply forces prices to rise.

The supply and demand curves in Figure 4 illustrate how tariffs and quotas work. Just as in Figure 3, the equilibrium price of wheat under free trade is $2.50 per bushel (in both countries). At this price, the exporting country produces 125 million bushels—point *B* in Panel (a)—and consumes 80 million

(point *A*). So its exports are 45 million bushels—the distance *AB*. Similarly, the importing country consumes 95 million bushels—point *D* in Panel (b)—and produces only 50 million (point *C*), so its imports are also 45 million bushels—the distance *CD*.

Now suppose the government of the importing nation imposes a *quota* limiting imports to 30 million bushels. The free-trade equilibrium with imports of 45 million bushels is now illegal. Instead, the market must equilibrate at a point where both exports and imports are only 30 million bushels. As Figure 4 indicates, this requirement implies that there must be different prices in the two countries.

Imports in Panel (b) will be 30 million bushels—the distance *QT*—only when the price of wheat in the importing nation is $3.25 per bushel, because only at this price will quantity demanded exceed domestic quantity supplied by 30 million bushels. Similarly, exports in Panel (a) will be 30 million bushels—the distance *RS*—only when the price in the exporting country is $2.00 per bushel. At this price, quantity supplied exceeds quantity demanded in the exporting country by 30 million bushels. Thus, the quota *raises* the price in the importing country to $3.25 and *lowers* the price in the exporting country to $2.00. In general:

> An import quota on a product normally reduces the volume of that product traded, raises the price in the importing country, and reduces the price in the exporting country.

A tariff can accomplish exactly the same restriction of trade. In our example, a quota of 30 million bushels

---

FIGURE 4

Quotas and Tariffs in International Trade

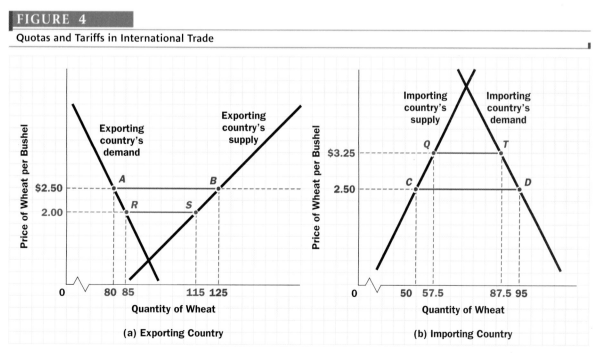

NOTE: Quantities are in millions of bushels.

leads to a price that is $1.25 higher in the importing country than in the exporting country ($3.25 versus $2.00). Suppose that, instead of a quota, the importing nation were to impose a $1.25 per bushel *tariff.* International trade equilibrium would then have to satisfy the following two requirements:

1. The quantity of wheat *exported* by one country must equal the quantity of wheat *imported* by the other, just as before.

2. The price that consumers in the importing country pay for wheat must *exceed* the price that suppliers in the exporting country receive by the amount of the *tariff* (which is $1.25 in the example).

By consulting the graphs in Figure 4, you can see exactly where these two requirements are met. If the exporter produces at *S* and consumes at *R*, while the importer produces at *Q* and consumes at *T*, then exports and imports are equal (at 30 million bushels), and the two domestic prices differ by exactly $1.25. (They are $3.25 and $2.00.) But this is exactly the same equilibrium we found under the quota. What we have just discovered is a general result of international trade theory:

Any restriction of imports that is accomplished by a quota normally can also be accomplished by a tariff.

In this case, the tariff corresponding to an import quota of 30 million bushels is $1.25 per bushel.

We mentioned in the text that a tariff (or a quota) forces foreign producers to sell more cheaply. Figure 4 shows how this works. Suppose, as in Panel (b), that a $1.25 tariff on wheat raises the price in the importing country from $2.50 to $3.25 per bushel. This higher price drives down imports from an amount represented by the length of the brick-colored line *CD* to the smaller amount represented by the blue line *QT.* In the exporting country, this change means an equal reduction in exports, as illustrated by the change from *AB* to *RS* in Panel (a).

As a result, the price at which the exporting country can sell its wheat is driven down—from $2.50 to $2.00 in the example. Meanwhile, producers in the importing country, which are exempt from the tariff, can charge $3.25 per bushel. Thus, as noted in the text, a tariff (or a quota) can be thought of as a way to "rig" the domestic market in favor of domestic firms.

| SUMMARY |

1. The prices of goods traded between countries are determined by supply and demand, but one must consider explicitly the demand curve and the supply curve of *each* country involved. Thus the equilibrium price must make the excess of quantity supplied over quantity demanded in the exporting country equal to the excess of quantity demanded over quantity supplied in the importing country.

2. When trade is restricted, the combinations of prices and quantities in the various countries that are achieved by a quota can also be achieved by a tariff.

3. Tariffs or quotas favor domestic producers over foreign producers.

| TEST YOURSELF |

1. The following table presents the demand and supply curves for microcomputers in Japan and the United States.

Price per Computer	Quantity Demanded in U.S.	Quantity Supplied in U.S.	Quantity Demanded in Japan	Quantity Supplied in Japan
1	90	30	50	50
2	80	35	40	55
3	70	40	30	60
4	60	45	20	65
5	50	50	10	70
6	40	55	0	75

NOTE: Price and quantity are in thousands.

a. Draw the demand and supply curves for the United States on one diagram and those for Japan on another one.

b. If the United States and Japan do not trade, what are the equilibrium price and quantity in the computer market in the United States? In Japan?

c. Now suppose trade is opened up between the two countries. What will be the equilibrium price in the world market for computers? What has happened to the price of computers in the United States? In Japan?

d. Which country will export computers? How many?

e. When trade opens, what happens to the quantity of computers produced, and therefore employment, in the computer industry in the United States? In Japan? Who benefits and who loses *initially* from free trade?

THE INTERNATIONAL MONETARY SYSTEM: ORDER OR DISORDER?

Cecily, you will read your Political Economy in my absence. The chapter on the Fall of the Rupee you may omit. It is somewhat too sensational.

MISS PRISM IN OSCAR WILDE'S *THE IMPORTANCE OF BEING EARNEST*

Miss Prism, the Victorian tutor, may have had a better point than she knew. In the summer of 1997, the Indonesian rupiah (not the Indian rupee) fell and economic disaster quickly followed. The International Monetary Fund rushed to the rescue with billions of dollars and pages of advice. But its plan failed, and some say it may even have helped precipitate the bloody riots that led to the fall of the Indonesian government.

Like the demure Miss Prism, this chapter does not concentrate on sensational political upheavals. Rather, it focuses on a seemingly mundane topic: how the market determines rates of exchange among different national currencies. Nevertheless, events in Southeast Asia in 1997–1998, in Brazil and Russia in 1998–1999, and in Turkey and Argentina in 2001–2002 have amply demonstrated that dramatic exchange rate movements can have severe human as well as financial consequences. Even in the United States, some people are now worried about the consequences of the declining value of the dollar. This chapter and the next will help you understand why.

CONTENTS

PUZZLE: WHY HAS THE DOLLAR SAGGED?

Many observers speak of "American exceptionalism." One way in which America differs from other countries is that its media and citizens almost never pay much attention to the international value of its currency. But 2007 proved to be an exception to the exceptionalism. The dollar fell so low against the euro, the British pound, and, especially, the Canadian dollar that—at least for a few days—it grabbed the headlines. The euro flirted with $1.50 (which it later surpassed), the pound topped $2, and the Canadian dollar became more valuable than the U.S. dollar.

These events in foreign currency markets had a lot of people scratching their heads. What caused the dollar to fall so far? Will it fall further? Does the decline signal some deep-seated problem with the U.S. economy? We will learn some of the answers to these and related questions in this chapter. But to do that, we first need to understand what determines exchange rates.

WHAT ARE EXCHANGE RATES?

> The **exchange rate** states the price, in terms of one currency, at which another currency can be bought.

We noted in the previous chapter that international trade is more complicated than domestic trade. There are no national borders to be crossed when, say, California lettuce is shipped to Massachusetts. The consumer in Boston pays with *dollars*, just the currency that the farmer in Modesto wants. If that same farmer ships her lettuce to Japan, however, consumers there will have only Japanese yen with which to pay, rather than the dollars the farmer in California wants. Thus, for international trade to take place, there must be some way to convert one currency into another. The rates at which such conversions are made are called **exchange rates.**

There is an exchange rate between every pair of currencies. For example, one British pound is currently the equivalent of about $2. The exchange rate between the pound and the dollar, then, may be expressed as roughly "$2 to the pound" (meaning that it costs $2 to buy a pound) or about "50 pence to the dollar" (meaning that it costs half a British pound to buy a dollar).

Exchange rates vis-à-vis the United States dollar have changed dramatically over time. In a nutshell, the dollar soared in the period from mid-1980 to early 1985, fell relative to most major currencies from early 1985 until early 1988, and then fluctuated with no clear trend until the spring of 1995. From then until early 2002, the dollar was mostly on the rise. Then, from February 2002 through December 2004, the dollar reversed course and fell steadily. From then until 2007, the dollar was relatively stable, on balance until early 2007 when, as noted above, it started dropping once again. This chapter seeks to explain such currency movements.

> A nation's currency is said to **appreciate** when exchange rates change so that a unit of its currency can buy more units of foreign currency.

Under our present system, currency rates change frequently. When other currencies become more expensive in terms of dollars, we say that they have **appreciated** relative to the dollar. Alternatively, we can look at this same event as the dollar buying less foreign currency, meaning that the dollar has **depreciated** relative to another currency.

What is a depreciation to one country must be an appreciation to the other.

> A nation's currency is said to **depreciate** when exchange rates change so that a unit of its currency can buy fewer units of foreign currency.

For example, if the cost of a pound *rises* from $1.50 to $2, the cost of a U.S. dollar in terms of pounds simultaneously *falls* from 67 pence to 50 pence. The United Kingdom has experienced a currency *appreciation* while the United States has experienced a currency *depreciation*. In fact, the two mean more or less the same thing. As you may have noticed, these two ways of viewing the exchange rate are reciprocals of one another, that is, 1/1.5 = 0.67 and 1/2 = 0.50. And of course, when a number goes up, its reciprocal goes down.

When many currencies are changing in value at the same time, the dollar may be appreciating with respect to one currency but depreciating with respect to another. Table 1 offers a selection of exchange rates prevailing in July 1980, February 1985, June 1995, April

SOURCE: International Financial Statistics and *The Wall Street Journal.*

TABLE 1
Exchange Rates with the U.S. Dollar

Country	Currency	Symbol	Cost in Dollars					
			July 1980	Feb. 1985	June 1995	April 2002	April 2005	April 2008
Australia	dollar	$	$1.16	$0.74	$0.72	$0.53	$0.77	$0.93
Canada	dollar	$	0.87	0.74	0.73	0.63	$0.82	$0.99
France	franc	FF	0.25	0.10	0.20	*	*	*
Germany	mark	DM	0.57	0.30	0.71	*	*	*
Italy	lira	L	0.0012	0.00049	0.0061	*	*	*
Japan	yen	¥	0.0045	0.0038	0.0118	0.0076	0.0092	0.0096
Mexico	new peso	$	44.0†	5.0†	0.16	0.11	0.09	0.09
Sweden	krona	Kr	0.24	0.11	0.14	0.10	0.14	0.17
Switzerland	franc	S.Fr.	0.62	0.36	0.86	0.60	0.83	0.98
United Kingdom	pound	£	2.37	1.10	1.59	1.44	1.88	1.99
—	euro	€	—	—	—	0.88	1.29	1.58

NOTE: Exchange rates are in U.S. dollars per unit of foreign currency.

*These exchange rates were locked together at the start of the euro in January 1999.

†On January 1, 1993, the peso was redefined so that 1,000 old pesos were equal to 1 new peso. Hence, the numbers 44 and 5 listed for July 1980 and February 1985 were actually 0.044 and 0.005 on the old basis.

2002, April 2005, and April 2008, showing how many dollars or cents it cost at each of those times to buy each unit of foreign currency. Between February 1985 and April 2002, the dollar *depreciated* sharply relative to the Japanese yen and most European currencies. For example, the British pound rose from $1.10 to $1.44. During that same period, however, the dollar *appreciated* dramatically relative to the Mexican peso; it bought about 0.2 pesos in 1985 but more than 9 in 2002.[1] Since April 2002, the dollar has depreciated against most currencies, and sharply against the euro.

Although the terms "appreciation" and "depreciation" are used to describe movements of exchange rates in free markets, a different set of terms is employed to describe decreases and increases in currency values that are set by government decree. When an officially set exchange rate is altered so that a unit of a nation's currency can buy fewer units of foreign currency, we say that a **devaluation** of that currency has occurred. When the exchange rate is altered so that the currency can buy more units of foreign currency, we say that a **revaluation** has taken place. We will say more about devaluation and revaluation shortly, but first let's look at how the free market determines exchange rates.

A **devaluation** is a reduction in the official value of a currency.

A **revaluation** is an increase in the official value of a currency.

EXCHANGE RATE DETERMINATION IN A FREE MARKET

In 1999, eleven European countries adopted a new common currency, the euro. But why does a euro now cost about $1.50 and not $1.25 or $1.75? In a world of **floating exchange rates,** with no government interferences, the answer would be straightforward. Exchange rates would be determined by the forces of supply and demand, just like the prices of apples, computers, and haircuts.

In a leap of abstraction, imagine that the dollar and the euro are the only currencies on earth, so the market need determine only one exchange rate. Figure 1 on the next page depicts the determination of this exchange rate at the point (denoted *E* in the figure) where demand curve *DD* crosses supply curve *SS*. At this price ($1.50 per euro), the number of euros demanded is equal to the number of euros supplied.

Floating exchange rates are rates determined in free markets by the law of supply and demand.

> In a free market, exchange rates are determined by supply and demand. At a rate below the equilibrium level, the number of euros demanded would exceed the number supplied, and the price of a euro would be bid up. At a rate above the equilibrium level, quantity supplied would exceed quantity demanded, and the price of a euro would fall. Only at the equilibrium exchange rate is there no tendency for the rate to change.

[1] In fact, the dollar bought about 200 pesos in February 1985, but that is because the old peso was replaced by a new peso in January 1993, which moved the decimal point three places.

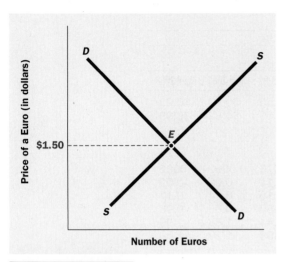

FIGURE 1

Determination of
Exchange Rates in a
Free Market

As usual, supply and demand determine price. But in this case, we must ask: Where do the supply and demand come from? Why does anyone demand a euro? The answer comes in three parts:

1. *International trade in goods and services.* This factor was the subject of the previous chapter. If, for example, Jane Doe, an American, wants to buy a new BMW, she will first have to buy euros with which to pay the car dealer in Munich.[2] Thus, Jane's demand for a European car leads to a demand for European currency. In general, *demand for a country's exports leads to demand for its currency.*[3]

2. *Purchases of physical assets such as factories and machinery overseas.* If IBM wants to buy a small French computer manufacturer, the owners will no doubt want to receive euros. So IBM will first have to acquire European currency. In general, *direct foreign investment leads to demand for a country's currency.*

3. *International trade in financial instruments such as stocks and bonds.* If American investors want to purchase Italian stocks, they will first have to acquire the euros that the sellers will insist on for payment. In this way, demand for European financial assets leads to demand for European currency. Thus, *demand for a country's financial assets leads to demand for its currency.* In fact, nowadays the volume of international trade in financial assets among the major countries of the world is so large that it swamps the other two sources of demand.

Now, where does the supply come from? To answer this question, just turn all of these transactions around. Europeans who want to buy U.S. goods and services, make direct investments in the United States, or purchase U.S. financial assets will have to offer their euros for sale in the foreign-exchange market (which is mainly run through banks) to acquire the needed dollars. To summarize:

The *demand* for a country's currency is derived from the demands of foreigners for its export goods and services and for its assets—including financial assets, such as stocks and bonds, and real assets, such as factories and machinery. The *supply* of a country's currency arises from its imports, and from foreign investment by its own citizens.

To illustrate the usefulness of even this simple supply-and-demand analysis, think about how the exchange rate between the dollar and the euro should change if Europeans become worried about the safety of U.S. assets, as happened during the financial crisis of 2007–2008. As European investors reduce their desires to buy U.S. assets, they will supply fewer euros for sale (in order to buy the necessary dollars). In terms of the supply-and-demand diagram in Figure 2, that decreased sale of euros will shift the supply curve inward from the black line S_1S_1 to the brick-colored line S_2S_2. Equilibrium would shift from point E to point A, and the exchange rate would rise from $1.30 per euro to $1.50 per euro. Thus, the decreased supply of euros by European citizens would cause the euro to *appreciate* relative to the dollar—which is just what happened.

Exercise Test your understanding of the supply-and-demand analysis of exchange rates by showing why each of the following events would lead to an appreciation of the euro (a depreciation of the dollar) in a free market:

1. American investors are attracted by prospects for profit on the German stock market.
2. A recession in Italy cuts Italian purchases of American goods.

----

[2] Actually, she will not do so because banks generally handle foreign-exchange transactions for consumers. An American bank probably will buy the euros for her. Even so, the effect is exactly the same as if Jane had done it herself.

[3] See Discussion Question 2 at the end of this chapter.

3. Interest rates on government bonds rise in France but are stable in the United States. (*Hint:* Which country's citizens will be attracted to invest by high interest rates in the other country?)

To say that supply and demand determine exchange rates in a free market is at once to say everything and to say nothing. If we are to understand the reasons why some currencies appreciate whereas others depreciate, we must look into the factors that move the supply and demand curves. Economists believe that the principal determinants of exchange rate movements differ significantly in the short, medium, and long runs. So in the next three sections, we turn to the analysis of exchange rate movements over these three "runs," beginning with the short run.

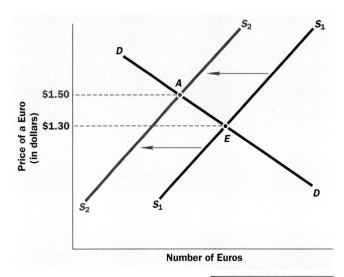

FIGURE 2

The Effect of Declining Demand for U.S. Assets on the Exchange Rate

Interest Rates and Exchange Rates: The Short Run

Most experts in international finance agree that interest rates and financial flows are the major determinants of exchange rates—certainly in the short run, and probably in the medium run as well. Specifically, one variable that often seems to call the tune in the short run is *interest rate differentials*. A multitrillion-dollar pool of so-called *hot money*—owned by banks, investment funds, multinational corporations, and wealthy individuals of all nations—travels rapidly around the globe in search of the highest interest rates.

As an example, suppose British government bonds pay a 5 percent rate of interest when yields on equally safe American government securities rise to 7 percent. British investors will be attracted by the higher interest rates in the United States and will offer pounds for sale in order to buy dollars, planning to use those dollars to buy American securities. At the same time, American investors will find it more attractive to keep their money at home, so fewer pounds will be demanded by Americans.

When the demand schedule for pounds shifts inward and the supply curve shifts outward, the effect on price is predictable: The pound will depreciate, as Figure 3 shows. In the figure, the supply curve of pounds shifts outward from S_1S_1 to S_2S_2 when British investors seek to sell pounds in order to purchase more U.S. securities. At the same time, American investors wish to buy fewer pounds because they no longer desire to invest as much in British securities. Thus, the demand curve shifts inward from D_1D_1 to D_2D_2. The result, in our example, is a depreciation of the pound from $2.10 to $1.80. In general:

> Other things equal, countries that offer investors higher rates of return attract more capital than countries that offer lower rates. Thus, a rise in interest rates often will lead to an appreciation of the currency, and a drop in interest rates often will lead to a depreciation.

It is useful to think of interest rate differentials as standing in for the relative returns on all sorts of financial assets in the two countries. In the late 1990s and the early part of this decade, prospective returns on American assets rose well above comparable returns in most other countries—especially those in Europe and Japan. In consequence, foreign capital was attracted here, American capital stayed at home, and the dollar soared—to levels that proved

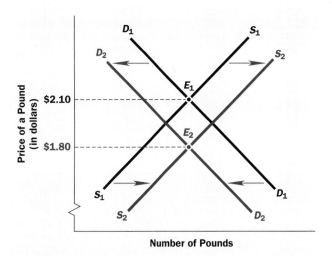

unsustainable. Similarly, if a nation suffers from capital flight, as Argentina did in 2001, it must offer extremely high interest rates to attract foreign capital.

Economic Activity and Exchange Rates: The Medium Run

The medium run is where the theory of exchange rate determination is most unsettled. Economists once reasoned as follows: Because consumer spending increases when income rises and decreases when income falls, the same thing is likely to happen to spending on imported goods. So *a country's imports will rise quickly when its economy booms and rise only slowly when its economy stagnates.*

For the reasons illustrated in Figure 4, then, a boom in the United States should shift the *demand* curve for euros *outward* as Americans seek to acquire more euros to buy more European goods. And that, in turn, should lead to an appreciation of the euro (depreciation of the dollar). In the figure, the euro rises in value from $1.50 to $1.60.

However, if Europe was booming at the same time, Europeans would be buying more American exports, which would shift the *supply* curve of euros outward. (Europeans must offer more euros for sale to get the dollars they want.) On balance, the value of the dollar might rise or fall. It appears that what matters is whether exports are growing faster than imports.

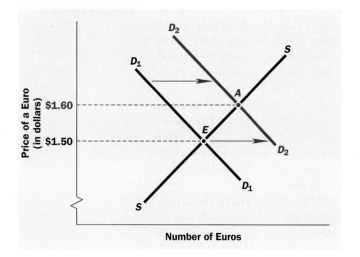

FIGURE 4

The Effect of an Economic Boom Abroad on the Exchange Rate

A country that grows faster than the rest of the world normally finds its imports growing faster than its exports. Thus, its demand curve for foreign currency shifts outward more rapidly than its supply curve. *Other things equal*, that will make its currency depreciate.

This reasoning is sound—so far as it goes. And it leads to the conclusion that a "strong economy" might produce a "weak currency." But the three most important words in the preceding paragraph are "other things equal." Usually, they are not. Specifically, a booming economy will normally offer more attractive prospects to investors than a stagnating one—higher interest rates, rising stock market values, and so on. This difference in prospective investment returns, as we noted earlier, should attract capital and boost its currency value.

So there appears to be a kind of tug of war. Thinking only about trade in goods and services leads to the conclusion that faster growth should *weaken* the currency. But thinking instead about trade in financial assets (such as stocks and bonds) leads to precisely the opposite conclusion: Faster growth should *strengthen* the currency. Which side wins this tug of war?

As we have suggested, it is usually no contest—at least among the major currencies of the world. In the modern world, the evidence seems to say that trade in financial assets is the dominant factor. For example, rapid growth and soaring imports in the United States in the second half of the 1990s were accompanied by a sharply *appreciating* dollar as investors from all over the world brought funds to America. We conclude that

> Stronger economic performance often leads to currency *appreciation* because it improves prospects for investing in the country.

The Purchasing-Power Parity Theory: The Long Run

We come at last to the long run, where an apparently simple principle ought to govern exchange rates. As long as goods can move freely across national borders, exchange rates should eventually adjust so that the same product costs the same amount of money, whether measured in dollars in the United States, euros in Germany, or yen in Japan—except for differences in transportation costs and the like. This simple statement forms the basis of the major theory of exchange rate determination in the long run:

> The *purchasing-power parity theory of exchange rate determination* holds that the exchange rate between any two national currencies adjusts to reflect differences in the price levels in the two countries.

An example will illustrate the basic truth in this theory and also suggest some of its limitations. Suppose German and American steel are identical and that these two nations are the only producers of steel for the world market. Suppose further that steel is the only tradable good that either country produces.

Question: If American steel costs $300 per ton and German steel costs 200 euros per ton, what must be the exchange rate between the dollar and the euro?

Answer: Because 200 euros and $300 each buy a ton of steel, the two sums of money must be of equal value. Hence, each euro must be worth $1.50. Why? Any higher price for a euro, such as $1.60, would mean that steel would cost $320 per ton (200 euros at $1.60 each) in Germany but only $300 per ton in the United States. In that case, all foreign customers would shop for their steel in the United States—which would increase the demand for dollars and decrease the demand for euros. Similarly, any exchange rate below $1.50 per euro would send all the steel business to Germany, driving the value of the euro up toward its purchasing-power parity level.

Exercise   Show why an exchange rate of $1.25 per euro is too low to lead to an equilibrium in the international steel market.

The purchasing-power parity theory is used to make long-run predictions about the effects of inflation on exchange rates. To continue our example, suppose that steel (and other) prices in the United States rise while prices in Europe remain constant. The purchasing-power parity theory predicts that the euro will appreciate relative to the dollar. It also predicts the amount of the appreciation. After the U.S. inflation, suppose that the price of American steel is $330 per ton, while German steel still costs 200 euros per ton. For these two prices to be equivalent, 200 euros must be worth $330, or one euro must be worth $1.65. The euro, therefore, must rise from $1.50 to $1.65.

> According to the purchasing-power parity theory, differences in domestic inflation rates are a major cause of exchange rate movements. If one country has higher inflation than another, its exchange rate should be depreciating.

For many years, this theory seemed to work tolerably well. Although precise numerical predictions based on purchasing-power parity calculations were never very accurate (see "Purchasing Power Parity and the Big Mac" on the following page), nations with higher inflation did at least experience depreciating currencies. But in the 1980s and 1990s, even this rule broke down. For example, although the U.S. inflation rate was consistently higher than both Germany's and Japan's, the dollar nonetheless rose sharply relative to both the German mark and the Japanese yen from 1980 to 1985. The same thing happened again between 1995 and 2002. Clearly, the theory is missing something. What?

Many things. But perhaps the principal failing of the purchasing-power parity theory is, once again, that it focuses too much on trade in goods and services. Financial assets such as stocks and bonds are also traded actively across national borders—and in vastly greater dollar volumes than goods and services. In fact, the astounding *daily* volume of foreign-exchange transactions exceeds $3 trillion, which is far more than an entire *month's* worth of world trade in goods and services. The vast majority of these transactions are financial. If investors decide that, say, U.S. assets are a better bet than Japanese assets, the dollar will rise, even if our inflation rate is well above Japan's. For this and other reasons,

> Most economists believe that other factors are much more important than relative price levels for exchange rate determination in the short run. But in the long run, purchasing-power parity plays an important role.

Purchasing-Power Parity and the Big Mac

Since 1986, *The Economist* magazine has been using a well-known international commodity—the Big Mac—to assess the purchasing-power parity theory of exchange rates, or as the magazine once put it, "to make exchange-rate theory more digestible."

Here's how it works. In theory, the local price of a Big Mac, when translated into U.S. dollars by the exchange rate, should be the same everywhere in the world. The following numbers show that the theory does not work terribly well.

For example, although a Big Mac cost an average of $3.22 in the United States in January 2007, it sold for about 11 yuan in China. Using the official exchange rate of 7.77 yuan to the dollar, that amounted to just $1.41. Thus, according to the hamburger parity theory, the yuan was grossly undervalued.

By how much? The price in China was just 44 percent of the price in the United States ($1.41/$3.22 = 0.438). So the yuan was 56 percent below its Big Mac parity—and therefore should appreciate. The other numbers in the table have similar interpretations.

True Big Mac aficionados may find these data helpful when planning international travel. But can deviations from Big Mac parity predict exchange rate movements? Surprisingly, they can.

When economist Robert Cumby studied Big Mac prices and exchange rates in 14 countries over a 10-year period, he found that deviations from hamburger parity were transitory. Their "half-life" was just a year, meaning that 50 percent of the deviation tended to disappear within a year. Thus, the undervalued currencies in the accompanying table would be predicted to appreciate during 2007, whereas the overvalued currencies would be expected to depreciate.

Deviations from Big Mac Purchasing Power Parity, January 2007		
Country	Big Mac Prices (converted to dollars)	Percent Over (+) or Under (−) Valuation Against Dollar
United States	$3.22	—
Norway	6.63	+106%
Great Britain	3.90	+21
Euro area	3.82	+19
Canada	3.08	−4
Mexico	2.66	−17
Japan	2.31	−28
Russia	1.85	−43
China	1.41	−56

Market Determination of Exchange Rates: Summary

You have probably noticed a theme here: International trade in financial assets certainly dominates short-run exchange rate changes, may dominate medium-run changes, and also influences long-run changes. We can summarize this discussion of exchange rate determination in free markets as follows:

1. We expect to find *appreciating* currencies in countries that offer investors *higher rates of return* because these countries will attract capital from all over the world.

2. To some extent, these are the countries that are *growing faster* than average because strong growth tends to produce attractive investment prospects. However, such fast-growing countries will also be importing relatively more than other countries, which tends to pull their currencies *down*.

3. Currency values generally will appreciate in countries with *lower inflation rates* than the rest of the world's, because buyers in foreign countries will demand their goods and thus drive up their currencies.

Reversing each of these arguments, we expect to find *depreciating* currencies in countries with relatively high inflation rates, low interest rates, and poor growth prospects.

WHEN GOVERNMENTS FIX EXCHANGE RATES: THE BALANCE OF PAYMENTS

Many exchange rates today are truly floating, determined by the forces of supply and demand without government interference. Others are not. Furthermore, some people claim that exchange rate fluctuations are so troublesome that the world would be better off with fixed exchange rates. For these reasons, we turn next to a system of **fixed exchange rates,** or rates that are set by governments.

Fixed exchange rates are rates set by government decisions and maintained by government actions.

Naturally, under such a system the exchange rate, being fixed, is not closely watched. Instead, international financial specialists focus on a country's *balance of payments*—a term we must now define—to gauge movements in the supply of and demand for a currency.

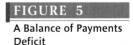

FIGURE 5

A Balance of Payments Deficit

To understand what the balance of payments is, look at Figure 5, which depicts a situation that might represent, say, Argentina in the winter of 2001–2002—an overvalued currency. Although the supply and demand curves for pesos indicate an equilibrium exchange rate of $0.50 to the peso (point *E*), the Argentine government is holding the rate at $1.00. Notice that, at $1 per peso, more people supply pesos than demand them. In the example, suppliers offer to sell 8 billion pesos per year, but purchasers want to buy only 4 billion. This gap between the 8 billion pesos that some people wish to sell and the 4 billion pesos that others wish to buy is what we mean by Argentina's **balance of payments deficit**—4 billion pesos (or $4 billion) per year in this hypothetical case. It appears as the horizontal distance between points *A* and *B* in Figure 5.

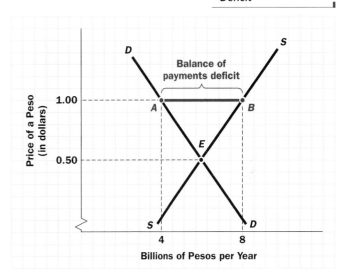

How can governments flout market forces in this way? Because sales and purchases on any market must be equal, the excess of quantity supplied over quantity demanded—or 4 billion pesos per year in this example—must be bought by the Argentine government. To purchase these pesos, it must give up some of the foreign currency that it holds as reserves. Thus, the Central Bank of Argentina would be losing about $4 billion in reserves per year as the cost of keeping the peso at $1.

The **balance of payments deficit** is the amount by which the quantity supplied of a country's currency (per year) exceeds the quantity demanded. Balance of payments deficits arise whenever the exchange rate is pegged at an artificially high level.

Naturally, this situation cannot persist forever, as the reserves eventually will run out. This is the fatal flaw of a fixed exchange rate system. Once speculators become convinced that the exchange rate can be held for only a short while longer, they will sell the currency in massive amounts rather than hold on to money whose value they expect to fall. That is precisely what began to happen to Argentina in 2001. Lacking sufficient reserves, the Argentine government succumbed to market forces and let the peso float in early 2002. It promptly depreciated.

For an example of the reverse case, a severely undervalued currency, we can look at contemporary China. Figure 6 on the next page depicts demand and supply curves for Chinese yuan that intersect at an equilibrium price of 15 cents per yuan (point *E* in the diagram). Yet, in the example, we suppose that the Chinese authorities are holding the rate at 12 cents. At this rate, the quantity of yuan demanded (1,000 billion) greatly exceeds the quantity supplied (600 billion). The difference is China's **balance of payments surplus,** shown by the horizontal distance *AB*.

The **balance of payments surplus** is the amount by which the quantity demanded of a country's currency (per year) exceeds the quantity supplied. Balance of payments surpluses arise whenever the exchange rate is pegged at an artificially low level.

China can keep the rate at 12 cents only by selling all the additional yuan that foreigners want to buy—400 billion yuan per year in this example. In return, the country must buy the equivalent amount of U.S. dollars ($48 billion). All of this activity serves to increase China's reserves of U.S. dollars. But notice one important difference between this case and the overvalued peso:

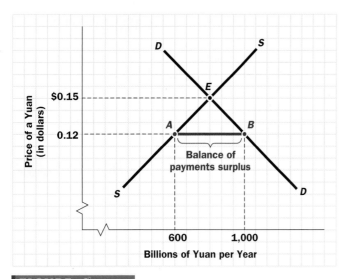

FIGURE 6

A Balance of Payments Surplus

The **current account** balance includes international purchases and sales of goods and services, cross-border interest and dividend payments, and cross-border gifts to and from both private individuals and governments. It is approximately the same as net exports.

The **capital account** balance includes purchases and sales of financial assets to and from citizens and companies of other countries.

The accumulation of reserves rarely will force a central bank to revalue in the way that losses of reserves can force a devaluation.

Thus China has been keeping its currency undervalued and accumulating huge dollar reserves for years, although it has shown some recent signs of backing away from this policy recently.

This asymmetry is a clear weakness in a fixed exchange rate system. In principle, an exchange rate disequilibrium can be cured either by a *devaluation* by the country with a balance of payments deficit or by an upward *revaluation* by the country with a balance of payments surplus. In practice, though, only deficit countries are forced to act.

Why do surplus countries refuse to revalue? One reason is often a stubborn refusal to recognize some basic economic realities. They tend to view the disequilibrium as a problem only for the deficit countries and, therefore, believe that the deficit countries should take the corrective steps. This view, of course, is nonsense in a worldwide system of fixed exchange rates. Some currencies are overvalued *because* some other currencies are undervalued. In fact, the two statements mean exactly the same thing.

The other reason why surplus countries resist upward revaluations is that such actions would make their products more expensive to foreigners and thus cut into their export sales. This, in fact, is the main reason why China maintains an undervalued currency despite the protestations of many other nations. China's leaders believe that vibrant export industries are the key to growth and development.

The balance of payments comes in two main parts. The **current account** totes up exports and imports of goods and services, cross-border payments of interest and dividends, and cross-border gifts. It is close, both conceptually and numerically, to what we have called *net exports* ($X - IM$) in previous chapters. The United States has been running extremely large current account deficits for years.

But the current account represents only one part of our balance of payments, for it leaves out all purchases and sales of assets. Purchases of U.S. assets by foreigners bring foreign currency to the United States, and purchases of foreign assets cost us foreign currency. Netting the capital flows in each direction gives us our surplus or deficit on **capital account.** In recent years, this part of our balance of payments has registered persistently large *surpluses* as foreigners have acquired massive amounts of U.S. assets.

In what sense, then, does the overall balance of payments balance? There are two possibilities. If the exchange rate is *floating,* all *private* transactions—current account plus capital account—must add up to zero because dollars purchased = dollars sold. But if, instead, the exchange rate is *fixed,* as shown in Figures 5 and 6, the two accounts need not balance one another. Government purchases or sales of foreign currency make up the surplus or deficit in the overall balance of payments.

A BIT OF HISTORY: THE GOLD STANDARD AND THE BRETTON WOODS SYSTEM

It is difficult to find examples of strictly fixed exchange rates in the historical record. About the only time exchange rates were truly fixed was under the old gold standard, at least when it was practiced in its ideal form.[4]

---

[4] As a matter of fact, although the gold standard lasted (on and off) for hundreds of years, it was rarely practiced in its ideal form. Except for a brief period of fixed exchange rates in the late nineteenth and early twentieth centuries, governments periodically adjusted exchange rates even under the gold standard.

The Classical Gold Standard

Under the **gold standard,** governments maintained fixed exchange rates by an automatic equilibrating mechanism that went something like this: All currencies were defined in terms of gold; indeed, some were actually made of gold. When a nation ran a balance of payments *deficit*, it had to *sell gold* to finance the deficit. Because the domestic money supply was based on gold, losing gold to foreigners meant that the money supply fell *automatically,* thus raising interest rates. Those higher interest rates attracted foreign capital. At the same time, this restrictive "monetary policy" pulled down output and prices, which discouraged imports and encouraged exports. The balance of payments problem quickly rectified itself.

This automatic adjustment process meant, however, that under the gold standard no nation had control of its domestic monetary policy. An analogous problem arises in any system of fixed exchange rates, regardless of whether it makes use of gold:

> Under fixed exchange rates, monetary policy must be dedicated to pegging the exchange rate. It cannot, therefore, be used to manage aggregate demand.

The gold standard posed one other serious difficulty: The world's commerce was at the mercy of gold discoveries. Major gold finds would mean higher prices and booming economic conditions, through the standard monetary-policy mechanisms that we studied in earlier chapters. But when the supply of gold failed to keep pace with growth of the world economy, prices had to fall in the long run and employment had to fall in the short run.

The **gold standard** is a way to fix exchange rates by defining each participating currency in terms of gold and allowing holders of each participating currency to convert that currency into gold.

The Bretton Woods System

The gold standard collapsed for good amid the financial chaos of the Great Depression of the 1930s and World War II. Without it, the world struggled through a serious breakdown in international trade.

As the war drew to a close, representatives of the industrial nations, including John Maynard Keynes of Great Britain, met at a hotel in Bretton Woods, New Hampshire, to devise a stable monetary environment that would enable world trade to resume. Because the United States held the lion's share of the world's reserves at the time, these officials naturally turned to the dollar as the basis for the new international economic order.

The Bretton Woods agreements reestablished fixed exchange rates based on the free convertibility of the U.S. dollar into gold. The United States agreed to buy or sell gold to maintain the $35 per ounce price that President Franklin Roosevelt had established in 1933. The other signatory nations, which had almost no gold in any case, agreed to buy and sell *dollars* to maintain their exchange rates at agreed-upon levels.

The Bretton Woods system succeeded in refixing exchange rates and restoring world trade—two notable achievements. But it also displayed the flaws of any fixed exchange rate system. Changes in exchange rates were permitted only as a last resort—which, in practice, came to mean that the country had a chronic *deficit* in the balance of payments of sizable proportions. Such nations were allowed to *devalue* their currencies relative to the dollar. So the system was not really one of fixed exchange rates but, rather, one in which rates were "fixed until further notice." Because devaluations came only after a long run of balance of payments deficits had depleted the country's reserves, these devaluations often could be clearly foreseen and normally had to be large. Speculators therefore saw glowing opportunities for profit and would "attack" weak currencies with waves of selling.

A second problem arose from the asymmetry mentioned earlier: Deficit nations could be forced to devalue while surplus nations could resist upward revaluations. Because the value of the U.S. dollar was fixed in terms of gold, the United States was the one nation in the world that had no way to devalue its currency. The only way the dollar could fall was if the surplus nations would revalue their currencies upward. But they did not adjust frequently enough, so the United States developed an overvalued currency and chronic balance of payments deficits.

The overvalued dollar finally destroyed the Bretton Woods system in 1971, when President Richard Nixon unilaterally ended the game by announcing that the United States would no longer buy or sell gold at $35 per ounce.

ADJUSTMENT MECHANISMS UNDER FIXED EXCHANGE RATES

Under the Bretton Woods system, devaluation was viewed as a last resort, to be used only after other methods of adjusting to payments imbalances had failed. What were these other methods?

We encountered most of them in our earlier discussion of exchange rate determination in free markets. Any factor that *increases the demand* for, say, Argentine pesos or that *reduces the supply* will push the value of the peso upward—if it is free to adjust. But if the exchange rate is pegged, the balance of payments deficit will shrink instead. (Try this for yourself using Figure 5 on page 369.)

Recalling our earlier discussion of the factors that underlie the demand and supply curves, we see that one way a nation can shrink its balance of payments deficit is to *reduce its aggregate demand,* thereby discouraging imports and cutting down its demand for foreign currency. Another is to *lower its rate of inflation,* thereby encouraging exports and discouraging imports. Finally, it can *raise its interest rates* to attract more foreign capital.

In other words, deficit nations are expected to follow restrictive monetary and fiscal policies *voluntarily,* just as they would have done *automatically* under the classical gold standard. However, just as under the gold standard, this medicine is often unpalatable.

A surplus nation could, of course, take the opposite measures: pursuing *expansionary* monetary and fiscal policies to increase economic growth and *lower* interest rates. By increasing the supply of the country's currency and reducing the demand for it, such actions would reduce that nation's balance of payments surplus. But surplus countries often do not relish the inflation that accompanies expansionary policies, and so, once again, they leave the burden of adjustment to the deficit nations. The general point about fixed exchange rates is that

> **Under a system of fixed exchange rates, a country's government loses some control over its domestic economy. Sometimes balance of payments considerations may force it to contract its economy in order to cut down its demand for foreign currency, even though domestic needs call for expansion. At other times, the domestic economy may need to be reined in, but balance of payments considerations suggest expansion.**

That was certainly the case in Argentina in 2002, when interest rates soared to attract foreign capital and the government pursued contractionary fiscal policies to curb the country's appetite for imports. Both contributed to a long and deep recession. Argentina took the bitter medicine needed to defend its fixed exchange rate for quite a while. But high unemployment eventually led to riots in the streets, toppled the government, and persuaded the Argentine authorities to abandon the fixed exchange rate.

WHY TRY TO FIX EXCHANGE RATES?

"Then it's agreed. Until the dollar firms up, we let the clamshell float."

In view of these and other problems with fixed exchange rates, why did the international financial community work so hard to maintain them for so many years? And why do some nations today still fix their exchange rates? The answer is that floating exchange rates also pose problems.

Chief among these worries is the possibility that freely floating rates might prove to be highly variable rates, thereby adding an unwanted element of risk to foreign trade. For example, if the exchange rate is $1.50 to the euro, then a Parisian dress priced at 400 euros will cost $600. But should the euro appreciate to $1.75, that same dress would cost $700. An American department store thinking of buying the dress may need to place its order far in advance and will want to know the cost *in dollars.* It may be worried about the possibility that the value of the euro will rise, making the dress cost more than $600. And such worries might inhibit trade.

There are two responses to this concern. First, freely floating rates might prove to be fairly stable in practice. Prices of most ordinary goods and services, for example, are determined by supply and demand in free markets and do not fluctuate unduly. Unfortunately, experience since 1973 has dashed this hope. Exchange rates have proved to be extremely volatile, which is why some observers now favor greater fixity in exchange rates.

A second possibility is that speculators might relieve business firms of exchange rate risks—for a fee, of course. Consider the department store example. If each euro costs $1.50 today, the department store manager can assure herself of paying exactly $600 for the dress several months from now by arranging for a speculator to deliver 400 euros to her at $1.50 per euro on the day she needs them. If the euro appreciates in the interim, the speculator, not the department store, will take the financial beating. Of course, if the euro depreciates, the speculator will pocket the profits. Thus, speculators play an important role in a system of floating exchange rates.

The widespread fears that speculative activity in free markets will lead to wild gyrations in prices, although occasionally valid, are often unfounded. The reason is simple.

> To make profits, international currency speculators must *buy* a currency when its value is low (thus helping to support the currency by pushing up its demand curve) and *sell* it when its value is high (thus holding down the price by adding to the supply curve). This means that successful speculators must come into the market as *buyers* when demand is weak (or when supply is strong) and come in as *sellers* when demand is strong (or supply is scant). In doing so, they help limit price fluctuations. Looked at the other way around, speculators can *destabilize* prices only if they are systematically willing to lose money.[5]

Notice the stark—and ironic—contrast to the system of fixed exchange rates in which speculation often leads to wild "runs" on currencies that are on the verge of devaluation—as happened in Mexico in 1995, several Southeast Asian countries in 1997–1998, Brazil in 1999, and Argentina in 2001. Speculative activity, which may well be *destabilizing* under fixed rates, is more likely to be *stabilizing* under floating rates.[6]

We do not mean to imply that speculation makes floating rates trouble-free. At the very least, speculators will demand a fee for their services—a fee that adds to the costs of trading across national borders. In addition, speculators will not assume *all* exchange rate risks. For example, few contracts on foreign currencies last more than, say, a year or two. Thus, a business cannot easily protect itself from exchange rate changes over periods of many years. Finally, speculative markets can and do get carried away from time to time, moving currency rates in ways that are difficult to understand, that frustrate the intentions of governments, and that devastate some people—as happened in Mexico in 1995 and in Southeast Asia in 1997.

Despite all of these problems, international trade has flourished under floating exchange rates. So perhaps exchange rate risk is not as burdensome as some people think.

THE CURRENT "NONSYSTEM"

The international financial system today is an eclectic blend of fixed and floating exchange rates, with no grand organizing principle. Indeed, it is so diverse that it is often called a "nonsystem."

Some currencies are still pegged in the old Bretton Woods manner. The most prominent example is probably China, which for years maintained a fixed value for its currency (the yuan) by standing ready to buy or sell U.S. dollars as necessary. Over the years, the pegging policy required the Chinese to buy dollars steadily and in large volume. So China has acquired over $1 *trillion* in foreign currency reserves. Lately, the Chinese authorities seem to be backing away from their currency peg, albeit in small steps, and the yuan has appreciated relative to the dollar.

---

[5] See Test Yourself Question 4 at the end of the chapter.

[6] After their respective currency crises in 1995 and 1999, both Mexico and Brazil floated their currencies. Each weathered the subsequent international financial storms rather nicely. But Argentina, with its fixed exchange rate, struggled.

A few small countries, such as Panama and Ecuador, have taken the more extreme step of actually adopting the U.S. dollar as their domestic currencies. Other nations tie their currencies to a hypothetical "basket" of several foreign currencies, rather than to just one.

More nations, however, let their exchange rates float, although not always freely. Such floating rates change slightly on a day-to-day basis, and market forces determine the basic trends, up or down. But governments do not hesitate to intervene to moderate exchange movements whenever they feel such actions are appropriate. Typically, interventions are aimed at ironing out what are deemed to be transitory fluctuations. But sometimes central banks oppose basic exchange rate trends. For example, the Federal Reserve and other central banks sold dollars aggressively in 1985 to push the dollar *down* and then bought dollars in 1994 and 1995 to push the dollar *up*. As we will discuss in the next chapter, the Japanese acquired hundreds of billions of dollars earlier in this decade trying to prevent the yen from floating up too much. The terms *dirty float* or *managed float* have been coined to describe this mongrel system.

The Role of the IMF

The International Monetary Fund (IMF), which was established at Bretton Woods in 1944, examines the economies of all its member nations on a regular basis. When a country runs into serious financial difficulties, it may turn to the Fund for financial assistance. The IMF typically provides loans, but with many strings attached. For example, if the country has a large current account deficit—as is normally the case when countries come to the IMF—the Fund will typically insist on contractionary fiscal and monetary policies to curb the country's appetite for imports. Often, this mandate spells recession.

During the 1990s, the IMF found itself at the epicenter of a series of very visible economic crises: in Mexico in 1995, in Southeast Asia in 1997, in Russia in 1998, and in Brazil in 1999. In 2001, Turkey and Argentina ran into trouble and appealed to the IMF for help. Although each case was different, they shared some common elements.

Most of these crises were precipitated by the collapse of a fixed exchange rate pegged to the U.S. dollar. In each case, the currency plummeted, with ruinous consequences. Questions were raised about the country's ability to pay its bills. In each case, the IMF arrived on the scene with lots of money and lots of advice, determined to stave off default. In the end, each country suffered through a severe recession—or worse.

The IMF's increased visibility naturally brought it increased criticism. Some critics complained that the Fund set excessively strict conditions on its client states, requiring them, for example, to cut their government budgets and raise interest rates during recessions—which made bad economic situations even worse.

Other critics worried that the Fund was serving as a bill collector for banks and other financial institutions from the United States and other rich countries. Because the banks loaned money irresponsibly, these critics argued, they deserved to lose some of it. By bailing them out of their losses, the IMF simply encouraged more reckless behavior in the future.

Numerous suggestions for reform were offered, and some minor changes in the IMF's policies and procedures were made. While the debate over IMF reform rages on to this day, it is mostly behind the scenes. The reason is simple. As the world economy improved, and the nations that formerly needed IMF help no longer required it, the Fund's list of client states diminished and so did the prominence of the IMF. Whether this placid situation will continue is anyone's guess.

The Volatile Dollar

As mentioned earlier, floating exchange rates have proven to be volatile exchange rates. No currency illustrates this point better than the U.S. dollar (see Figure 7). As Table 1 showed, in July 1980 a U.S. dollar bought less than 2 German marks, about 4 French francs, and about 830 Italian lire. Then it started rising like a rocket (see Figure 7). By the time it peaked in February 1985, the mighty dollar could buy more than 3 German marks,

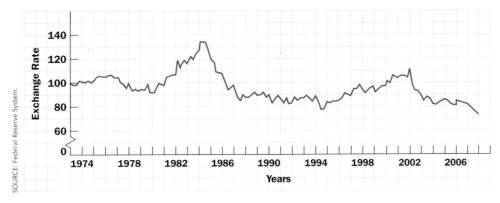

SOURCE: Federal Reserve System.

FIGURE 7

The Ups and Downs of the Dollar

NOTE: Exchange rate relative to major currencies, March 1973 = 100.

about 10 French francs, and more than 2,000 Italian lire. Such major currency changes affect world trade dramatically.

The rising dollar was a blessing to Americans who traveled abroad or who bought foreign goods—because foreign prices, when translated to dollars by the exchange rate, looked cheap to Americans.[7] But the arithmetic worked just the other way around for U.S. firms seeking to sell their goods abroad; foreign buyers found everything American very expensive.[8] It was no surprise, therefore, that as the dollar climbed our exports fell, our imports rose, and many of our leading manufacturing industries were decimated by foreign competition. An expensive currency, Americans came to learn, is a mixed blessing.

From early 1985 until early 1988, the value of the dollar fell even faster than it had risen. The cheaper dollar curbed American appetites for imports and alleviated the plight of our export industries, many of which boomed. However, rising prices for imported goods and foreign vacations were a source of consternation to many American consumers.

Over the following seven years, the overall value of the dollar did not change very much—although there was a small downward drift. Then, in the spring of 1995, the dollar began another sizable ascent which lasted until early 2002. After that, as we noted earlier in this chapter, the dollar fell for about two years and then was pretty stable until 2007–2008, when it tumbled again. All in all, the behavior of the dollar has been anything but boring. Fortunes have been made and lost speculating on what it will do next.

The Birth and Adolescence of the Euro

As noted earlier, floating exchange rates are no panacea. One particular problem confronted the members of the European Union (EU). As part of their long-range goal to create a unified market like that of the United States, they perceived a need to establish a single currency for all member countries—a monetary union.

The process of convergence to a single currency took place in steps, more or less as prescribed by the Treaty of Maastricht (1992), over a period of years. Member nations encountered a number of obstacles along the way. But to the surprise of many skeptics, all such obstacles were overcome, and the euro became a reality on schedule. Electronic and checking transactions in 11 EU nations were denominated in euros rather than in national currencies in 1999, euro coins and paper money were introduced successfully in 2002, and

---

[7] *Exercise:* How much does a 100-euro hotel room in Paris cost in dollars when the euro is worth $1.25? $1? 80 cents?

[8] *Exercise*: How much does a $55 American camera cost a German consumer when the euro is worth $1.20? $1? 80 cents?

the number of participating countries has since risen in stages to 15. All of these transformations went remarkably smoothly.

That said, the euro did not spring into life as a fully grown adult. In its earlier years, there were still plenty of doubters. And perhaps for that reason, the new European currency, which made its debut at $1.18 in January 1999, fell to a low point of $0.83 in October 2000—a stunning 30 percent decline in less than two years. Since then, however, the euro has mostly been climbing in value relative to the dollar, reaching about $1.57 in April 2008.

The establishment of the euro was a great economic experiment that marked a giant step beyond merely fixing exchange rates. A government can end a fixed exchange rate regime at any time. And, as we have seen, speculators sometimes break fixed exchange rates even when governments want to maintain them. But the single European currency was created by an international treaty and is more or less invulnerable to speculative attack because it *abolished* exchange rates among the participating nations. Just as there has long been no exchange rate between New York and New Jersey, now there is no exchange rate between Germany and France. Monetary unions may create other problems, but exchange rate instability should not be one of them.

PUZZLE RESOLVED: WHY THE DOLLAR ROSE AND THEN FELL

What we have learned in this chapter helps us understand what brought the dollar down between 2002 and 2004, and then again in 2007 and 2008. The story actually begins well before that.

During the Great Boom of the late 1990s, the United States was *the* place to invest. Funds poured in from all over the world to purchase American stocks, American bonds, and even American companies—especially in the information technology field. Yahoo! was indeed a fitting name for the age. As we have learned in this chapter, the rising demand for U.S. assets should have bid up the price of U.S. currency—and it did (see Figure 7 again).

"His mood is pegged to the dollar"

But the soaring dollar sowed the seeds of its own destruction. Two of its major effects were (a) to make U.S. goods and services look much more expensive to potential buyers abroad and (b) to make foreign goods look much cheaper to Americans. So our imports grew much faster than our exports. In brief, we developed a huge *current account deficit* (which is roughly exports *minus* imports) to match our large *capital account surplus*.

The Internet bubble, of course, started to burst in 2000, pulling the stock market down with it. Then the September 11, 2001, terrorist attacks raised doubts about the strength of the U.S. economy. For these and other reasons, foreign investors apparently began to question the wisdom of holding so many American assets. With the U.S. current account still deeply in the red, and the foreign demand for U.S. capital sagging, there was only one way for the (freely floating) dollar to go: down. And so it did.

The real mystery was why the depreciation of the dollar stopped at the end of 2004; most economists felt that further depreciation was necessary, given the huge (and growing) current account deficit. But before that question was answered, the dollar fell again in 2007 and into the early part of 2008 and the current account deficit finally began to shrink.

| SUMMARY |

1. **Exchange rates** state the value of one currency in terms of other currencies and thus translate one country's prices into the currencies of other nations. Exchange rates therefore influence patterns of world trade.

2. If governments do not interfere by buying or selling their currencies, exchange rates will be determined in free markets by the usual laws of supply and demand. Such a system is said to be based on **floating exchange rates.**

3. Demand for a nation's currency is derived from foreigners' desires to purchase that country's goods and services or to invest in its assets. Under floating rates, anything that increases the demand for a nation's currency will cause its exchange rate to **appreciate.**

4. Supply of a nation's currency is derived from the desire of that country's citizens to purchase foreign goods and services or to invest in foreign assets. Under floating rates, anything that increases the supply of a nation's currency will cause its exchange rate to **depreciate.**

5. Purchasing-power parity plays a major role in very-long-run exchange rate movements. The **purchasing-power parity theory** states that relative price levels in any two countries determine the exchange rate between their currencies. Therefore, countries with relatively low inflation rates normally will have appreciating currencies.

6. Over shorter periods, however, purchasing-power parity has little influence over exchange rate movements. The pace of economic activity and, especially, the level of interest rates exert greater influences.

7. Capital movements are typically the dominant factor in determining exchange rates in the short and medium runs. A nation that offers international investors higher interest rates, or better prospective returns on investments, will typically see its currency appreciate.

8. An exchange rate can be fixed at a nonequilibrium level if the government is willing and able to mop up any excess of quantity supplied over quantity demanded or provide any excess of quantity demanded over quantity

supplied. In the first case, the country is suffering from a **balance of payments deficit** because of its overvalued currency. In the second case, an undervalued currency has given it a **balance of payments surplus.**

9. The **gold standard** was a system of **fixed exchange rates** in which the value of every nation's currency was fixed in terms of gold. This system created problems because nations could not control their own money supplies and because the world could not control the total supply of gold.

10. After World War II, the gold standard was replaced by the **Bretton Woods system,** in which exchange rates were fixed in terms of U.S. dollars and the dollar was in turn tied to gold. This system broke up in 1971, when the dollar became chronically overvalued.

11. Since 1971, the world has moved toward a system of relatively free exchange rates, but with plenty of exceptions. We now have a thoroughly mixed system of "dirty" or "managed" floating, which continues to evolve and adapt.

12. Floating rates are not without their problems. For example, importers and exporters justifiably worry about fluctuations in exchange rates.

13. Under floating exchange rates, investors who speculate on international currency values provide a valuable service by assuming the risks of those who do not wish to speculate. Normally, speculators stabilize rather than destabilize exchange rates, because that is how they make profits.

14. The value of the U.S. dollar has been volatile. It rose dramatically from 1980 to 1985, making our imports cheaper and our exports more expensive. From 1985 to 1988, the dollar tumbled, which had precisely the reverse effects. Then the dollar climbed again between 1995 and 2002, leading once again to a large trade imbalance. From 2002 to 2004, and then again in 2007–2008, the dollar fell further.

15. The European Union has established a single currency, the euro, for most of its member nations.

| KEY TERMS |

| TEST YOURSELF |

1. Use supply and demand diagrams to analyze the effect of the following actions on the exchange rate between the dollar and the yen:

   a. Japan opens its domestic markets to more foreign competition.

   b. Investors come to believe that values on the Tokyo stock market will fall.

   c. The Federal Reserve cuts interest rates in the United States.

   d. The U.S. government, to help settle the problems of the Middle East, gives huge amounts of foreign aid to Israel and her Arab neighbors.

   e. The United States has a recession while Japan booms.

   f. Inflation in the United States exceeds that in Japan.

2. For each of the following transactions, indicate how it would affect the U.S. balance of payments if exchange rates were fixed:

   a. You spent the summer traveling in Europe.

   b. Your uncle in Canada sent you $20 as a birthday present.

   c. You bought a new Honda, made in Japan.

   d. You bought a new Honda, made in Ohio.

   e. You sold some stock you own on the Tokyo Stock Exchange.

3. Suppose each of the transactions listed in Test Yourself Question 2 was done by many Americans. Indicate how each would affect the international value of the dollar if exchange rates were floating.

4. We learned in this chapter that successful speculators buy a currency when demand is weak and sell it when demand is strong. Use supply and demand diagrams for two different periods (one with weak demand, the other with strong demand) to show why this activity will limit price fluctuations.

| DISCUSSION QUESTIONS |

1. What items do you own or routinely consume that are produced abroad? From what countries do these items come? Suppose Americans decided to buy fewer of these things. How would that affect the exchange rates between the dollar and these currencies?

2. If the dollar appreciates relative to the euro, will the German camera you have wanted become more or less expensive? What effect do you imagine this change will have on American demand for German cameras? Does the American demand curve for euros, therefore, slope upward or downward? Explain.

3. During the first half of the 1980s, inflation in (West) Germany was consistently lower than that in the United States. What, then, does the purchasing-power parity theory predict should have happened to the exchange rate between the mark and the dollar between 1980 and 1985? (Look at Table 1 on page 363 to see what actually happened.)

4. How are the problems of a country faced with a balance of payments deficit similar to those posed by a government regulation that holds the price of milk above the equilibrium level? (*Hint:* Think of each in terms of a supply-demand diagram.)

5. Under the old gold standard, what do you think happened to world prices when a huge gold strike occurred in California in 1849? What do you think happened when the world went without any important new gold strikes for 20 years or so?

6. Explain why the members of the Bretton Woods conference in 1944 wanted to establish a system of fixed exchange rates. What flaw led to the ultimate breakdown of the system in 1971?

7. Suppose you want to reserve a hotel room in London for the coming summer but are worried that the value of the pound may rise between now and then, making the room too expensive for your budget. Explain how a speculator could relieve you of this worry. (Don't actually try it—speculators deal only in very large sums!)

8. In 2003 and 2004, market forces raised the international value of the Japanese yen. Why do you think the government of Japan was unhappy about this currency appreciation? (*Hint:* Japan was trying to emerge from a recession at the time.) If they wanted to stop the yen's appreciation, what actions could the Bank of Japan (Japan's central bank) and the Federal Reserve have taken? Why might the central banks have failed in this attempt?

EXCHANGE RATES AND THE MACROECONOMY

No man is an island, entire of itself.

JOHN DONNE

One prominent aspect of globalization is that economic events that originate in one country reverberate quickly around the globe, sometimes at the speed of electricity. A stunning example arose in 2007, after the housing boom ended in the United States. A number of so-called subprime mortgages (meaning mortgages granted to people with questionable credit) started to go bad. As the trickle of defaults turned into a flood, it triggered a worldwide financial crisis when several financial businesses in—of all places—France and Germany ran into serious trouble. Why there? It turned out that these institutions, thousands of miles away, had invested heavily in *U.S.* subprime mortgages. It is indeed a small world.

This was just one example of a general phenomenon. Fluctuations in foreign growth, inflation, and interest rates profoundly affect the U.S. economy. And economic events that originate in our country reverberate around the globe. Anyone who ignores these international linkages cannot hope to understand how the modern world economy works.

The macroeconomic model we developed in earlier chapters does a bit of that, but not enough because it ignores such crucial influences as exchange rates and international financial movements. The previous chapter showed how major macroeconomic variables such as gross domestic product (GDP), prices, and interest rates affect exchange rates. In this chapter, we complete the circle by studying how changes in the exchange rate affect the domestic economy. Then we bring international capital flows into the picture and learn how monetary and fiscal policy work in an **open economy.** In particular, we build a model suitable for a *large open* economy with *substantial capital flows* and a *floating exchange rate*—in short, a model meant to resemble the contemporary United States, which is indeed not "an island, entire of itself."

An **open economy** is one that trades with other nations in goods and services, and perhaps also trades in financial assets.

CONTENTS

ISSUE: SHOULD THE U.S. GOVERNMENT TRY TO STOP THE DOLLAR FROM FALLING?

For years before it actually started happening, economists predicted that America's huge trade deficits would eventually drive the international value of the U.S. dollar down. In early 2002, this prophecy finally started to come true. However, the dollar declined only for about two years, before stabilizing at the end of 2004. Then, after a two-year hiatus, dollar depreciation resumed in 2007 and into 2008, when the greenback tumbled sharply. This time the dollar's weakness even grabbed the headlines—a rare event in our country. People looked on in amazement as the British pound topped $2, the euro soared above $1.50, and the Canadian dollar became worth more than the U.S. dollar for the first time since the 1970s.

Some observers were alarmed by the falling dollar. They urged the United States government to fight the dollar's decline. Both European and Japanese businesspeople complained that they were losing export markets to the Americans, which was damaging European and Japanese growth. But there was also a bright side: The massive U.S. trade deficit at last started to shrink. Weighing the pros and cons, the U.S. government decided that currency values should remain "flexible," that is, determined in world markets by the forces of supply and demand that we studied in the previous chapter. It refused to intervene to try to stop the dollar from falling.

Who was right? We will examine this question as the chapter progresses.

INTERNATIONAL TRADE, EXCHANGE RATES, AND AGGREGATE DEMAND

We know from earlier chapters that a country's net exports, $(X - IM)$, are one component of its aggregate demand, $C + I + G + (X - IM)$. It follows that an autonomous increase in exports or decrease in imports has a multiplier effect on the economy, just like an increase in consumption, investment, or government purchases.[1] Figure 1 depicts this conclusion on an aggregate demand-and-supply diagram. A rise in net exports shifts the aggregate demand curve outward to the right, pushing equilibrium from point *A* to point *B*. Both GDP and the price level therefore rise.

FIGURE 1

The Effects of Higher Net Exports

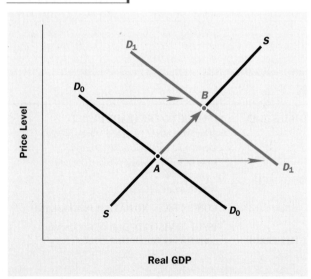

Real GDP

But what forces might make net exports increase? One factor mentioned in Chapter 8 was a rise in *foreign incomes*. If foreign economies boom, their citizens are likely to spend more on a wide variety of products, some of which will be American exports. Thus, Figure 1 illustrates the effect on the U.S. economy of more rapid growth in foreign countries. By like reasoning, a recession abroad would reduce U.S. exports and shift the U.S. aggregate demand curve inward. Thus, as we learned in Chapter 9:

Booms or recessions in one country tend to be transmitted to other countries through international trade in goods and services.

A second important determinant of net exports was mentioned in Chapter 8, but not discussed in depth there: the relative prices of foreign and domestic goods. The idea is a simple application of the law of demand. Namely, if the prices of the goods of Country X rise, people everywhere will tend to buy fewer of them—and

---

[1] An appendix to Chapter 9 showed that international trade lowers the numerical value of the multiplier. Autonomous changes in C, I, G, and $(X - IM)$ all have the same multiplier.

more of the goods of Country Y. As we will see next, this simple idea holds the key to understanding how *exchange rates* affect international trade.

Relative Prices, Exports, and Imports

First assume—just for this short section—that exchange rates are *fixed*. Think about what happens if the prices of American goods fall while, say, Japanese prices are constant. With U.S. products now less expensive *relative to Japanese products,* both Japanese and American consumers will buy more American goods and fewer Japanese goods. That means America's exports will rise and its imports will fall, thus adding to aggregate demand in the United States. Conversely, a rise in American prices (relative to Japanese prices) will *decrease* U.S. net exports and aggregate demand. Thus:

> A *fall* in the relative prices of a country's exports tends to *increase* that country's net exports and, thereby, to raise its real GDP. Analogously, a *rise* in the relative prices of a country's exports will *decrease* that country's net exports and GDP.

Precisely the same logic applies to changes in Japanese prices. If Japanese prices rise, Americans will export more to and import less from Japan. So $X - IM$ in the U.S. will rise, boosting GDP here. Figure 1 applies to this case without change. By similar reasoning, falling Japanese prices decrease U.S. net exports and depress our economy. Thus:

> Price increases for foreign products raise a country's net exports and hence its GDP. Price decreases for foreign products have the opposite effects.

The Effects of Changes in Exchange Rates

From here, it is a simple matter to figure out how changes in exchange rates affect a country's net exports, because *currency appreciations or depreciations change international relative prices.*

Recall that the basic role of an exchange rate is to convert one country's prices into another country's currency. Table 1 uses two examples of U.S.–Japanese trade to remind us of this role. Suppose the dollar depreciates from 120 yen to 100 yen. Then, from the American consumer's viewpoint, a television set that costs ¥30,000 in Japan goes up in price from $250 (that is, 30,000/120) to $300 (that is, 30,000/100). To Americans, it is just as if Japanese manufacturers had raised TV prices by 20 percent. Naturally, Americans will react by purchasing fewer Japanese products, so American imports will decline.

TABLE 1				
Exchange Rates and Home Currency Prices				
	¥30,000 Japanese TV Set		$1,000 U.S. Home Computer	
Exchange Rate	Price in Japan	Price in the U.S.	Price in the U.S.	Price in Japan
$1 = 120 yen	¥30,000	$250	$1,000	¥120,000
$1 = 100 yen	¥30,000	$300	$1,000	¥100,000

Now consider the implications for Japanese consumers interested in buying American personal computers that cost $1,000. When the dollar falls from 120 yen to 100 yen, they see the price of these computers falling from ¥120,000 to ¥100,000. To them, it is just as if American producers had offered a 16.7 percent markdown. Under such circumstances, we expect U.S. sales to the Japanese to rise, so U.S. exports should increase. Putting these two findings together, we conclude that

> A currency *depreciation* should *raise* net exports and therefore *increase* aggregate demand. Conversely, a currency *appreciation* should *reduce* net exports and therefore *decrease* aggregate demand.

The aggregate supply-and-demand diagram in Figure 2 on the next page illustrates this conclusion. If the currency depreciates, net exports rise and the aggregate demand curve shifts outward from D_0D_0 to D_1D_1. Both prices and output rise as the economy's equilibrium moves from E_0 to E_1. If the currency appreciates instead, everything operates in reverse: Net exports fall, the aggregate demand curve shifts inward to D_2D_2, and both prices and output decline.

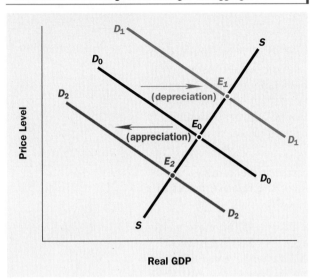

FIGURE 2

The Effects of Exchange Rate Changes on Aggregate Demand

This simple analysis helps us understand why the U.S. trade deficit grew so enormously in the late 1990s and early 2000s and has fallen a bit recently. We learned in the previous chapter that the international value of the dollar began to climb in 1995. According to the reasoning we have just completed, within a few years such an appreciation of the dollar should have boosted U.S. imports and damaged U.S. exports. That is precisely what happened. In constant dollars, American imports soared by over 40 percent between 1997 and 2002, while American exports rose by only 7 percent. The result was that a $105 billion real net export deficit in 1997 turned into a monumental $471 billion deficit by 2002. More recently, the dollar's decline has helped push the trade deficit down from a record $625 billion in 2006 to "only" $556 billion in 2007.

AGGREGATE SUPPLY IN AN OPEN ECONOMY

So far we have concluded that a currency depreciation increases aggregate demand and that a currency appreciation decreases it. To complete our model of macroeconomics in an open economy, we must turn to the implications of international trade for *aggregate supply*.

Part of the story is already familiar. We know from previous chapters that the United States, like all economies, purchases some of its productive inputs from abroad. Oil is by far the most prominent example. But we also rely on foreign suppliers for metals such as titanium, raw agricultural products such as coffee beans, and thousands of other items used by American industry. When the dollar depreciates, all of these imported inputs cost more in U.S. dollars—just as if foreign prices had risen.

The consequence is clear: With imported inputs more expensive, American firms will be forced to charge higher prices at any given level of output. Graphically, this means that *the aggregate supply curve will shift upward* (or inward to the left).

FIGURE 3

The Effects of Exchange Rate Changes on Aggregate Supply

When the dollar *depreciates*, the prices of imported inputs rise. The U.S. aggregate supply curve therefore shifts *inward*, pushing up the prices of American-made goods and services. By exactly analogous reasoning, an *appreciation* of the dollar makes imported inputs cheaper and shifts the U.S. aggregate supply curve *outward*, thus pushing American prices down. (See Figure 3.)

Beyond this, a depreciating dollar has additional inflationary effects that do not even show up on an aggregate demand-and-supply diagram, because the price level depicted on the vertical axis is *the price of gross domestic product*. Most obviously, prices of imported goods are included in U.S. price indexes like the Consumer Price Index (CPI). So when the dollar prices of Japanese cars, French wine, and Swiss watches increase, the CPI goes up *even if no American prices rise*. For this and other reasons, the inflationary impact of a dollar depreciation on *consumer* prices is greater than that indicated by Figure 3.

THE MACROECONOMIC EFFECTS OF EXCHANGE RATES

Let us now put aggregate demand and aggregate supply together and think through the macroeconomic effects of changes in exchange rates.

First, suppose the international value of the dollar falls. Referring back to the blue lines in Figures 2 and 3, we see that this depreciation will shift the aggregate demand curve *outward* and the aggregate supply curve *inward*. The result, as Figure 4 shows, is that the U.S. price level certainly rises. But whether real GDP rises or falls depends on whether the supply or demand shift is the dominant influence. The evidence strongly suggests that aggregate *demand* shifts are usually larger, so we expect GDP to rise. Hence:

A currency depreciation is inflationary and probably also expansionary.

The intuitive explanation for this result is clear. When the dollar falls, foreign goods become more expensive to Americans. That effect is directly inflationary. At the same time, aggregate demand in the United States is stimulated by rising net exports. As long as the expansion of demand outweighs the adverse shift of the aggregate supply curve brought on by currency depreciation, real GDP should rise.

But wait. By this reasoning, the massive depreciations of several Southeast Asian currencies in 1997 and 1998 should have given these economies tremendous boosts. But instead, the so-called Asian Tigers suffered horrific slumps—as did Mexico when the peso tumbled in 1995. Why? The answer is that our simple analysis of aggregate supply and demand omits a detail that, while unimportant for the United States, is critical in many developing nations.

Countries that borrow in foreign currency will see their debts increase whenever their currency values decline. For example, an Indonesian business that borrowed $1,000 in July 1997, when $1 was worth 2,500 rupiah, thought it owed 2.5 million rupiah. But when the dollar suddenly became worth 10,000 rupiah, the company's debt skyrocketed to 10 million rupiah. Many businesses found themselves unable to cope with their crushing debt burdens and simply went bankrupt. So although currency depreciation is expansionary in the United States, it was sharply contractionary in Indonesia.

Returning to rich countries such as the United States, let's now reverse direction and look at what happens when the currency *appreciates*. In this case, net exports *fall*, so the aggregate demand curve shifts *inward*. At the same time, imported inputs become cheaper, so the aggregate supply curve shifts *outward*. Both of these shifts are shown in Figure 5. Once again, as the diagram shows, we can be sure of the movement of the price level: It falls. Output also falls if the demand shift is larger than the supply shift, as is likely. Thus:

A currency appreciation is disinflationary and probably also contractionary.

This analysis explains why many economists and financial experts cringed a bit when the yen and the euro appreciated relative to the dollar in 2002–2004 and then again in 2007. Japan, in particular, was just emerging from deflation, and growth there was mediocre. The last thing it needed, they argued, was a decrease in aggregate demand.

FIGURE 4

The Effects of a Currency Depreciation

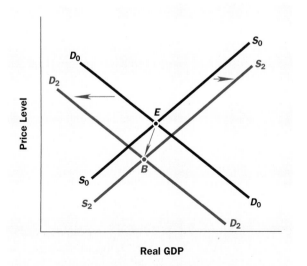

FIGURE 5

The Effects of a Currency Appreciation

Interest Rates and International Capital Flows

One important piece of our international economic puzzle is still missing. We have analyzed international trade in goods and services in some detail, but we have ignored international movements of *capital* up to now.

For some nations, this omission is inconsequential because they rarely receive or lend international capital. But things are quite different for the United States because the vast majority of international financial flows involve either buying or selling assets whose values are stated in U.S. dollars. In addition, we cannot hope to understand the origins of the various international financial crises of the 1990s and 2000s without incorporating capital flows into our analysis. Fortunately, given what we have just learned about the effects of exchange rates, this omission is easily rectified.

Recall from the previous chapter that interest rate differentials and capital flows are typically the most important determinants of exchange rate movements. Specifically, suppose interest rates in the United States rise while foreign interest rates are unchanged. We learned in the previous chapter that this change in relative interest rates will attract capital to the United States and cause the dollar to appreciate. This chapter has just taught us that an appreciating dollar will, in turn, reduce net exports, prices, and output in the United States—as indicated in Figure 5. Thus:

> **A rise in interest rates tends to contract the economy by appreciating the currency and reducing net exports.**

Notice that this conclusion has a familiar ring. When we studied monetary policy in Chapter 13, we observed that higher interest rates deter investment spending and hence reduce the I component of $C + I + G + (X - IM)$. Now, in studying an open economy with **international capital flows**, we see that higher interest rates also reduce the $X - IM$ component. Thus, *international capital flows strengthen the negative effects of interest rates on aggregate demand.*

If interest rates fall in the United States, or rise abroad, everything we have just said is turned in the opposite direction. The conclusion is

> **A decline in interest rates tends to expand the economy by depreciating the currency and raising net exports.**

Exercise   Provide the reasoning behind this conclusion.

International capital flows are purchases and sales of financial assets across national borders.

FISCAL AND MONETARY POLICIES IN AN OPEN ECONOMY

We are now ready to use our model to analyze how fiscal and monetary policies work when capital is internationally mobile and the exchange rate floats. Doing so will teach us how international economic relations modify the effects of stabilization policies that we learned about in earlier chapters. Fortunately, no new theoretical apparatus is necessary; we need merely remember what we have learned in the chapter up to this point. Specifically:

- A rise in the domestic interest rate leads to capital *inflows*, which make the exchange rate *appreciate*. A currency appreciation *reduces* aggregate demand and *raises* aggregate supply (see Figure 5).
- A fall in the domestic interest rate leads to capital *outflows*, which make the exchange rate *depreciate*. A currency depreciation *raises* aggregate demand and *reduces* aggregate supply (see Figure 4).

Fiscal Policy Revisited

With these points in mind, suppose the government cuts taxes or raises spending. Aggregate demand increases, which pushes up both real GDP and the price level in the usual manner. This effect is shown as the shift from D_0D_0 to the blue line D_1D_1 in Figure 6. In a

closed economy, that is the end of the story. But in an *open economy* with international capital flows, we must add in the macroeconomic effects that work through the exchange rate. We do this by answering two questions.

First, what will happen to the exchange rate? We know from earlier chapters that a fiscal expansion pushes up interest rates. At higher interest rates, American securities become more attractive to foreign investors, who go to the foreign-exchange markets to buy dollars with which to purchase them. This buying pressure drives up the value of the dollar. Thus, at least for a rich country that can easily sell its bonds on the world market,

A **closed economy** is one that does not trade with other nations in either goods or assets.

A fiscal expansion normally makes the exchange rate appreciate.

Second, what are the effects of a higher dollar? We know that when the dollar rises in value, American goods become more expensive abroad and foreign goods become cheaper here. So exports fall and imports rise, driving down the $X - IM$ component of aggregate demand. The fiscal expansion thus winds up increasing both America's *capital account surplus* (by attracting foreign capital) and its *current account deficit* (by reducing net exports). In fact, the two must rise by equal amounts because, under floating exchange rates, it is always true that[2]

Current account surplus + Capital account surplus = 0

Because a fiscal expansion leads in this way to a trade deficit, many economists believe that the large U.S. trade deficits of the 1980s were a side effect of the large tax cuts made early in the decade—and that the tax cuts of 2001–2003 once again pushed the trade deficit up. We will return to that issue shortly.

FIGURE 6

A Fiscal Expansion in an Open Economy

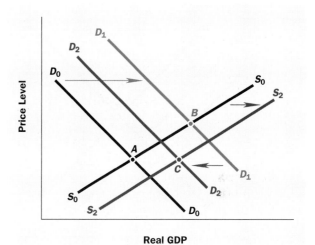

Real GDP

For now, note that the induced rise in the dollar will shift the aggregate supply curve *outward* and the aggregate demand curve *inward,* as we saw in Figure 5. Figure 6 adds these two shifts (in brick-colored lines) to the effect of the original fiscal expansion (in blue). The final equilibrium in an open economy is point *C*, whereas in a closed economy it would be point *B*. By comparing points *B* and *C*, we can see how international linkages change the picture of fiscal policy that we painted earlier in the book.

Two main differences arise. First, a higher exchange rate makes imports cheaper and thereby offsets part of the inflationary effect of a fiscal expansion. Second, a higher exchange rate reduces the expansionary effect on real GDP by reducing $X - IM$. Here we have a new kind of "crowding out," different from the one we studied in Chapter 15. There we learned that an increase in G will crowd out some *private investment* spending by raising interest rates. Here an increase in G, by raising both interest rates and the exchange rate, crowds out *net exports*. But the effect is the same: The fiscal multiplier is reduced. Thus, we conclude that

International capital flows reduce the power of fiscal policy.

Table 2, which shows actual U.S. data, suggests that this new international variety of crowding out was much more important than the traditional type of crowding out during the huge fiscal expansion of the 1980s. Between 1981 and 1986, the share of investment in GDP barely changed despite the rise in the shares of both consumer spending and government purchases. Only the share of net exports, $X - IM$, fell—from +0.2 percent to -2.8 percent.

American economists thus learned an important lesson. In 1981, many economists worried that large government budget deficits

TABLE 2

Percentage Shares of Real GDP in the United States, 1981 and 1986

Year	C	I	G	X − IM
1981	64.5%	14.3%	20.5%	0.2%
1986	67.3	14.5	21.2	−2.8
Change	+2.8	+0.2	+0.7	−3.0

NOTE: Totals do not add up because of rounding and deflation.

would crowd out private investment. By the end of the decade, most were more concerned that deficits were crowding out net exports and producing a massive trade deficit.

Monetary Policy Revisited

FIGURE 7

A Monetary
Contraction in an
Open Economy

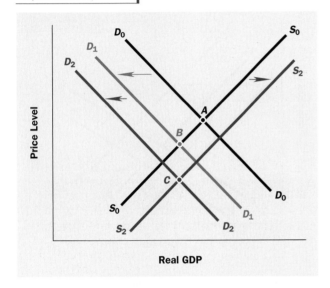

Now let us consider how *monetary policy* works in an open economy with floating exchange rates and international capital mobility. To remain consistent with the history of the 1980s, we consider a *tightening,* rather than a *loosening,* of monetary policy.

As we know from earlier chapters, contractionary monetary policy *reduces* aggregate demand, which lowers both real GDP and prices. This situation is shown in Figure 7 by the shift from D_0D_0 to the blue line D_1D_1, and it looks like the exact opposite of a fiscal expansion. Without international capital flows, that would be the end of the story.

But in the presence of internationally mobile capital, we must also think through the consequences for interest rates and exchange rates. As we know from previous chapters, a monetary contraction *raises* interest rates—just like a fiscal expansion. Hence, tighter money attracts foreign capital into the United States in search of higher rates of return. The exchange rate therefore *rises.* The appreciating dollar encourages imports and discourages exports; so $X - IM$ falls. America therefore winds up with an inflow of capital and an increase in its trade deficit. In Figure 7, the two effects of the exchange rate appreciation appear in the brick-colored lines S_2S_2 and D_2D_2: aggregate supply shifts *outward* and aggregate demand shifts *inward.* This time, as you can see in the figure,

International capital flows increase the power of monetary policy.

In a closed economy, higher interest rates *reduce investment* spending, I. In an open economy, these same higher interest rates also appreciate the currency and reduce *net exports,* $X - IM$. Thus, the effect of monetary policy is enhanced.

It may seem puzzling that capital flows *strengthen* monetary policy but *weaken* fiscal policy. The explanation of these contrasting results lies in their effects on interest rates. The main international repercussion of either a fiscal *expansion* or a monetary *contraction* is to raise interest rates and the exchange rate, thereby crowding out net exports. But that means that the initial effects of a fiscal expansion on aggregate demand are *weakened,* whereas the initial effects of a monetary contraction are *strengthened.*

INTERNATIONAL ASPECTS OF DEFICIT REDUCTION

We have now completed our theoretical analysis of the macroeconomics of open economies. Let us put the theory to work by applying it to the events of the 1990s, when fiscal policy was tightened and monetary policy was eased. Should reducing the budget deficit (or raising the surplus) strengthen or weaken the dollar?

As discussed in Chapter 15, the U.S. government transformed its mammoth budget deficit into a notable surplus during the 1990s by raising taxes and cutting expenditures. Column (1) of Table 3 reviews the predicted effects of a fiscal contraction: It should lower real interest rates, make the dollar depreciate, reduce real GDP, and be less disinflationary than normal because of the falling dollar. This information is recorded by entering + signs for increases and − signs for decreases.

Eliminating the budget deficit reduced aggregate demand. But the Federal Reserve restored the missing demand by lowering interest rates so that the economy would not suffer a slump. According to the analysis in this chapter, such a monetary expansion should lower real interest rates, make the dollar depreciate, raise real GDP, and be a bit more inflationary than usual because of the falling dollar. These effects are recorded in column (2) of Table 3.

Column (3) puts the two pieces together. We conclude that a policy mix of fiscal *contraction* and monetary *expansion* should reduce interest rates strongly, push down the value of the dollar, and strongly stimulate our foreign trade. The net effects on output and inflation are uncertain, however: The balance depends on whether the fiscal contraction overwhelms the monetary expansion, or vice versa.

TABLE 3			
Expected Effects of Policy			
	(1)	(2)	(3)
Variable	Fiscal Contraction	Monetary Expansion	Combination
Real interest rate	−	−	−
Exchange rate	−	−	−
Net exports	+	+	+
Real GDP	−	+	?
Inflation	−	+	?

What actually happened? First, interest rates did fall, just as predicted. The rate on 10-year U.S. government bonds dropped from almost 7 percent in late 1992 to just over 4.5 percent in December 1998, and by 1998 American households were enjoying the lowest home mortgage rates since the 1960s. Second, the U.S. economy expanded rapidly between 1992 and 1998; apparently, the monetary stimulus overwhelmed the fiscal contraction. Third, inflation fell despite such rapid growth. As we explained in Chapter 10, one major reason was a series of favorable supply shocks that pushed inflation down.

But what about the exchange rate and international trade? Here the theory did less well. The dollar generally declined from 1993 to 1995, just as the theory predicts. But then it turned around and rose sharply from 1995 to 1998, just when the budget deficit was turning into a surplus. America's trade performance was even more puzzling. According to the theory, a lower budget deficit should have led to a lower exchange rate, and therefore to a smaller **trade deficit.** But, in fact, America's real net exports sagged from just −$16 billion in 1992 to −$204 billion in 1998. What went wrong?

A country's **trade deficit** is the excess of its imports over its exports. If, instead, exports exceed imports, the country has a **trade surplus**.

The Loose Link between the Budget Deficit and the Trade Deficit

To answer this question, let's explore the connection between the budget deficit and the trade deficit in more detail. To do so, we need one simple piece of arithmetic.

Begin with the familiar equilibrium condition for GDP in an open economy:

$$Y = C + I + G + (X - IM)$$

Because GDP can either be spent, saved, or taxed away,[3]

$$Y = C + S + T$$

Equating these two expressions for Y gives

$$C + I + G + (X - IM) = C + S + T$$

Finally, subtracting C from both sides and bringing the I and G terms over to the right-hand side leads to an accounting relationship between the trade deficit and the budget deficit:

$$X - IM = (S - I) - (G - T)$$

Notice that this equation is a matter of *accounting*, not economics. It must hold in *all* countries at *all* times, and it has nothing to do with any particular economic theory. In words, it says that a trade deficit—a *negative* value of $(X - IM)$—can arise from one of two sources: a government budget deficit (G larger than T) or an excess of investment over saving (I larger than S).

Now let's apply this accounting relationship to actual U.S. events in the 1990s. As we know, the government deficit, $G - T$, fell precipitously. Other things equal, that should

---

[3] If you do not see why, recall that GDP equals disposable income (DI) plus taxes (T), $Y = DI + T$, and that disposable income can either be consumed or saved, $DI = C + S$. These two definitions together imply that $Y = C + S + T$.

have *reduced* the trade deficit. But other things were not equal. The equation reminds us that the balance between saving and investment matters, too. As shares of GDP, business investment boomed while household saving declined from 1992 to 1998. So $S - I$ moved sharply in the negative direction. And that change, as our equation shows, should *raise* the trade deficit (reduce net exports).

In brief, taken by itself, deficit reduction would have increased net exports. But in reality, sharp changes in private economic behavior—specifically, less saving and more investment—overwhelmed the government's actions and made net exports fall instead. The link from the budget deficit to the trade deficit can be a loose one.

SHOULD WE WORRY ABOUT THE TRADE DEFICIT?

The preceding explanation suggests that the large U.S. trade deficits over the past decade are a symptom of a deeper trouble: The nation as a whole—including both the government and the private sector—has been consuming more than it has been producing for years. The United States has therefore been forced to borrow the difference from foreigners. The trade deficit is just the mirror image of the required capital inflows.

Those who worry about trade deficits point out that these capital inflows create debts on which interest and principal payments must be made in the future. In this view, we Americans have been mortgaging our futures to finance higher consumer spending.

But another, quite different, interpretation of the trade deficit is possible. Suppose foreign investors come to see the United States as an especially attractive place to invest their funds. Then capital will flow here, not because Americans need to *borrow* it, but because foreigners are eager to *lend* it. The desire of foreigners to acquire American assets should push the value of the dollar up, which should in turn push America's net exports down. In that case, the trade deficit would still be the mirror image of the capital inflows. But it would signify America's economic *strength*, not its weakness.

Each view has elements of truth, but the second raises a critical question: How long can it go on? As long as the United States continues to run large trade deficits, foreigners will have to continue to accumulate large amounts of U.S. assets—one way or another. As we noted in the previous chapter, starting in 2002 private investors abroad began concluding that they had acquired about all the American assets they wanted. That would have marked the day of reckoning for the United States but for one important fact: The governments of Japan and China decided to buy hundreds of billions of dollars (selling equivalent amounts of their own currencies) rather than let the yen and the yuan appreciate. These large *government* capital inflows allowed the U.S. to continue to run mammoth trade deficits for a few more years. Then in 2007, with the U.S. economy looking weaker than in the past, foreigners decided to buy fewer U.S. assets, and the dollar declined again.

ON CURING THE TRADE DEFICIT

How can we ameliorate our foreign trade problem and reduce our addiction to foreign borrowing? There are four basic ways.

Change the Mix of Fiscal and Monetary Policy

The fundamental equation

$$X - IM = (S - I) - (G - T)$$

suggests that a *decrease in the budget deficit* (that is, shrinking $G - T$) would be one good way to reduce the trade deficit. According to the analysis in this chapter, a reduction in G or an increase in T would lead to lower real interest rates in the United States, a depreciating dollar, and, eventually, a smaller trade deficit.

When the government curtails its spending or raises taxes, aggregate demand falls. If we do not want the shrinking budget deficit to slow economic growth, we must therefore compensate for it by providing monetary stimulus. Like contractionary fiscal policy, expansionary monetary policy lowers interest rates, depreciates the dollar, and should therefore help reduce the trade deficit. So the policy recommendation actually amounts to tightening *fiscal* policy and loosening *monetary* policy.

As we have just noted, the U.S. government—after years of vacillation—changed the policy mix decisively in this direction in the 1990s. But our trade deficit rose anyway because private investment spending soared while private saving stagnated. Then, starting in 2001, the federal budget turned rapidly from a substantial surplus to a record-high deficit, which pushed the trade deficit up further. What else might work?

More Rapid Economic Growth Abroad

One factor behind the growing U.S. trade deficit is that the economies of many foreign nations—the customers for our exports—grew more slowly than the U.S. economy for years. If foreign economies would grow faster, the U.S. government frequently argued, they would buy more American goods, thereby raising U.S. exports and reducing our trade deficit. So we have regularly urged our major trading partners to stimulate their economies and to open their markets more to American goods—but with only modest success. When the U.S. economy slowed down in 2000–2001, our trade deficit did recede a bit—albeit temporarily. And the same thing happened again in 2007–2008. But no one thought slower U.S. growth was a very good remedy.

Raise Domestic Saving or Reduce Domestic Investment

Our fundamental equation calls attention to two other routes to a smaller trade deficit: more saving or less investment.

The U.S. personal saving rate (saving as a share of disposable income) has hit postwar lows in recent years. The approximately ½ percent saving rates recorded in both 2005 and 2006 were the lowest since the Great Depression of the 1930s! If Americans would simply save more, we would need to borrow less from abroad. This solution, too, would lead to a cheaper dollar and a smaller trade deficit.

The trouble is that no one has yet found a reliable way to induce Americans to save more. The government has implemented a variety of tax incentives for saving, and more are suggested every year. But little evidence suggests that any of them has worked. Instead, large increases in stock market wealth in the second half of the 1990s, and then in housing wealth in the early 2000s, convinced Americans that it was prudent to save *even less* than they used to.

If the other cures for our trade deficit fail to work, the deficit may cure itself in a particularly unpleasant way: by reducing U.S. domestic investment. The 2001 recession accomplished this to some extent, reducing the share of investment in real GDP from 17.7 percent in 2000 to 15.1 percent in 2003. (It also curbed our appetite for imports.) And with fear of recession rampant in 2008, those effects were expected again. But these side-effects of recession are only temporary, and the longer-run problem mentioned above remains: If our trade deficit persists, we will have to borrow more and more from foreigners who, at some point, will start demanding higher interest rates. At best, higher interest rates will lead to lower investment in the United States. At worst, interest rates will skyrocket, and we will experience a severe recession.

Protectionism

We have saved the worst remedy for last. One seemingly obvious way to cure our trade deficit is to limit imports by imposing stiff tariffs, quotas, and other protectionist devices. We discussed protectionism, and the reasons why almost all economists oppose it, in Chapter 17. Despite the economic arguments against it, protectionism has an undeniable political allure. It seems, superficially, to "save American jobs," and it conveniently shifts the blame for our trade problems onto foreigners.

"But we're not just talking about buying a car—we're talking about confronting this country's trade deficit with Japan."

In addition to depriving us and other countries of the benefits of comparative advantage, protectionism might not even succeed in reducing our trade deficit, however. One reason is that other nations may retaliate. If we erect trade barriers to reduce our imports, *IM* will fall. But if foreign countries erect corresponding barriers to our exports, *X* will fall, too. On balance, our *net* exports, *X − IM*, may or may not improve. But world trade will surely suffer. This game may have no winners, only losers.

Even if other nations do not retaliate, tariffs and quotas may not improve the U.S. trade deficit much. Why? If they succeed in reducing American spending on imports, tariffs and quotas will thereby reduce the supply of dollars on the world market—which will push the value of the dollar up. A rising dollar, of course, would hurt U.S. exports and encourage more imports. The fundamental equation

$$X - IM = (S - I) - (G - T)$$

reminds us that protectionism can raise *X − IM* only if it raises the budget surplus, raises saving, or reduces investment.[4]

CONCLUSION: NO NATION IS AN ISLAND

When the poet John Donne wrote that "no man is an island," he was not referring to economic globalization. But in the modern world, no nation is isolated from economic developments elsewhere on the globe. Instead, we live in a world economy in which the fates of nations are intertwined. The major trading countries are linked by exports and imports, by capital flows, and by exchange rates. What happens to national income, prices, and interest rates in one country affects other nations. No events make this point clearer than the international financial crises that erupt from time to time.

As we noted in Chapter 18, one root cause of almost all of the crises of the 1990s was countries' decisions to fix their exchange rates to the U.S. dollar. Unfortunately for nations such as Thailand, Indonesia, and South Korea, the dollar rose spectacularly from 1995 to 1997. With their exchange rates tied to the dollar, the Thai baht, the Indonesian rupiah, and the Korean won automatically appreciated relative to most other currencies—making their exports more costly. Soon these one-time export powerhouses found themselves in an unaccustomed position: running large trade deficits.

Then the crisis hit, and all four of these countries watched their currencies tumble in value. The sharp depreciations restored their international competitiveness, but they also impoverished many of their citizens. Naturally, the shrinking Asian economies curbed their appetites for American goods, so our exports to the region fell—which contributed to further deterioration in the U.S. trade deficit.

Thus, a primarily American development (the rise of the dollar) harmed the Asian economies, and then a primarily Asian development (deep recessions in the Asian Tigers) hurt the U.S. economy. Similarly, the subprime mortgage crisis of 2007–2008, an *American* phenomenon, threatened economic growth around the world. The nations of the world are indeed linked economically.

---

[4] Here tariffs, which raise revenue for the government, have a clear advantage over quotas, which do not.

ISSUE REVISITED: SHOULD THE UNITED STATES LET THE DOLLAR FALL?

 Recall the question with which we began this chapter: Should the United States let the dollar fall or try to stop it? Remember that a falling dollar boosts exports and growth in the United States but reduces exports and growth in, say, Europe and Japan. With economic growth in both Japan and Europe already slow, it was easy to understand why foreign leaders wanted the U.S. government to stop, or at least slow down, the dollar's rapid descent in 2007 and 2008.

But it was also easy to understand why the United States was not eager to do so, especially with elections on the horizon, because a falling dollar could reasonably be expected to help the United States grow faster—even if that meant that Europe and Japan would grow slower. And indeed, foreign demand for U.S. goods helped support the weakening U.S. economy in 2007 and 2008.

Unfortunately, there is no way to avoid this conflict of interests. A cheaper dollar means a dearer euro and a dearer yen. For better or for worse, we all live in one world.

| SUMMARY |

1. The nations of the world are linked together economically because national income, prices, and interest rates in one country affect those in other countries. They are thus **open economies.**

2. Because one country's imports are another country's exports, rapid (or sluggish) economic growth in one country contributes to rapid (or sluggish) growth in other countries.

3. A country's net exports depend on whether its prices are high or low relative to those of other countries. Because exchange rates translate one country's prices into the currencies of other countries, the exchange rate is a key determinant of net exports.

4. If the currency depreciates, net exports rise and aggregate demand increases, thereby raising both real GDP and the price level. A depreciating currency also reduces aggregate supply by making imported inputs more costly.

5. If the currency appreciates, net exports fall and aggregate demand, real GDP, and the price level all decrease. An appreciating currency also increases aggregate supply by making imported inputs cheaper.

6. **International capital flows** respond strongly to rates of return on investments in different countries. For example, higher domestic interest rates lead to currency appreciations, and lower interest rates lead to depreciations.

7. Contractionary monetary policies raise interest rates and therefore make the currency appreciate. Both the higher interest rates and the stronger currency reduce aggregate demand. Hence, international capital flows make monetary policy more powerful than it would be in a closed economy.

8. Expansionary fiscal policies also raise interest rates and make the currency appreciate. But in this case, the international repercussions cancel out part of the demand-expanding effects of the policies. Hence, international capital flows make fiscal policy less powerful than it would be in a closed economy.

9. Because eliminating the budget deficit in the 1990s combined tighter fiscal policy with looser monetary policy, it lowered interest rates. That should have pushed the dollar down and led to a smaller **trade deficit** in the United States. However, changes in private economic behavior—specifically, lower saving and higher investment—offset the presumed international effects of deficit reduction, and the trade deficit kept growing.

10. Budget deficits and trade deficits are linked by the fundamental equation $X - IM = (S - I) - (G - T)$.

11. It follows from this equation that the U.S. trade deficit must be cured by some combination of lower budget deficits, higher savings, and lower investment.

12. Protectionist policies might not cure the U.S. trade deficit because (a) they will make the dollar appreciate and (b) they may provoke foreign retaliation.

| KEY TERMS |

Open economy   379

Net exports   380

Exchange rate   381

Appreciation   381

Depreciation   381

International capital flows   384

Closed economy   385

Trade deficit   387

Budget deficits and trade
deficits   387

$X - IM = (S - I) - (G - T)$ 387

| TEST YOURSELF |

1. Use an aggregate supply-demand diagram to analyze the effects of a currency appreciation.

2. Explain why $X - IM = (S - I) - (G - T)$. Now multiply both sides of this equation by –1 to get

$$IM - X = (I - S) + (G - T)$$

and remember that the trade deficit, $IM - X$, is the amount we have to borrow from foreigners to get

Borrowing from foreigners $= (I - S) + (G - T)$

Explain the common sense behind this version of the fundamental equation.

3. **(More difficult)** Suppose consumption and investment are described by the following:

$$C = 150 + 0.75DI$$
$$I = 300 + 0.2Y - 50r$$

Here DI is disposable income, Y is GDP, and r, the interest rate, is measured in percentage points. (For example,

a 5 percent interest rate is $r = 5$.) Exports and imports are as follows:

$$X = 300$$
$$IM = 250 + 0.2Y$$

Government purchases are $G = 800$, and taxes are 20 percent of income. The price level is fixed and the central bank uses its monetary policy to peg the interest rate at $r = 8$.

a. Find equilibrium GDP, the budget deficit or surplus, and the trade deficit or surplus.

b. Suppose the currency appreciates and, as a result, exports and imports change to

$$X = 250$$
$$IM = 0.2Y$$

Now find equilibrium GDP, the budget deficit or surplus, and the trade deficit or surplus.

| DISCUSSION QUESTIONS |

1. For years, the U.S. government has been trying to get Japan and the European Union to expand their economies faster. Explain how more rapid growth in Japan would affect the U.S. economy.

2. If inflation is lower in Germany than in Spain (as it is), and the exchange rate between the two countries is fixed (as it is, because of the monetary union), what is likely to happen to the balance of trade between the two countries?

3. Explain why a currency depreciation leads to an improvement in a country's trade balance.

4. Explain why American fiscal policy is less powerful and American monetary policy is more powerful than

indicated in the closed-economy model described earlier in this book.

5. Given what you now know, do you think it was a good idea for the United States to adopt a policy mix of tight money and large government budget deficits in the early 1980s? Why or why not? What were the benefits and costs of reversing that policy mix in the 1990s?

6. In 2001, 2002, and 2003, Congress passed the series of tax cuts that President Bush had requested. What effect did this policy likely have on the U.S. trade deficit? Why?

7. In 2007 and 2008, the international value of the dollar fell. This development was viewed with alarm in Japan. Why?

Answers to odd-numbered Discussion Questions are available on the text support site at academic.cengage.com/economics/baumol.

CHAPTER 1:
What Is Economics?

Answers to Appendix Questions

1.

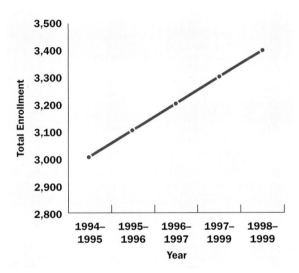

Slope is 100 interpreted as 100 new students each academic year.

Slope is 25 interpreted as 25 new economics students each academic year.

3.

A marginal increase in the number of job offers is relatively larger with the first good grade compared to additional good grades.

5. $A =>$ 30 hr labor and 40 yd cloth = 20 units of output.

$B =>$ 40 hr labor and 28 yd cloth = 20 units of output.

Common: 20 units of output; Difference: Amount of labor and cloth charge—more labor, less cloth.

CHAPTER 3:
The Fundamental Economic Problem: Scarcity and Choice

1. This question asks the students to apply opportunity cost to a straightforward decision: to rent or buy. After buying the house, the person would no longer have to pay $24,000 annual rent. On the other hand, she would lose the $8,000 she currently earns in interest from her bank account. She would be ahead by $16,000, and the purchase is therefore a good deal. In order to get a service (housing) for which she had been willing to pay $24,000, she only has to give up (that is, the opportunity cost is) goods and services worth $8,000. It is worth pointing out to students that if she did continue to rent the house, it must be because the services she receives from the landlord are worth more than $16,000. Also, it is important to realize that this question is very simplified—it ignores home equity, property taxes, etc.

3. In case (b), the production possibilities frontier will be further from the origin in 2007, since Stromboli will have more pizza ovens with which it can produce more pizzas.

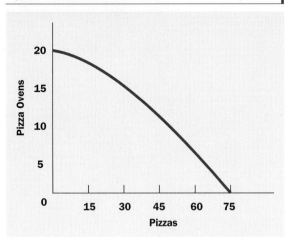

FIGURE 1

(Pizza numbers in Millions; ovens in thousands)

y-axis: Pizza Ovens — 0, 5, 10, 15, 20
x-axis: Pizzas — 15, 30, 45, 60, 75

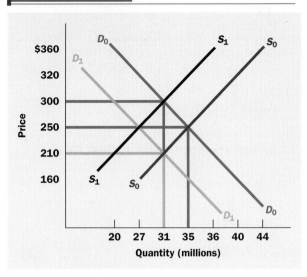

FIGURE 2

y-axis: Price — $360, 320, 300, 250, 210, 160
x-axis: Quantity (millions) — 20, 27, 31, 35, 36, 40, 44
Curves: D_0, D_1, S_1, S_0

CHAPTER 4:
Supply and Demand: An Initial Look

1. (a) The demand curve for a medicine that means life or death for a patient will be vertical, provided the patient has access to any money at all. One would not expect a decline in quantity demanded as the price rises, if that decline meant that the patient would die.

   (b) The demand curve for french fries in a food court with many other stands will be fairly flat, perhaps even horizontal. If the firm raises its price at all, many if not most of its customers will just move to a different stand. Thus a small change in price results in a large change in the amount of fries bought.

3. The answers to all three parts are shown in Figure 2.

   (a) Initially, the equilibrium price is $250, and the equilibrium quantity is 35 million bicycles, as shown by the intersection of D_0 and S_0.

   (b) If demand falls by 8 million bikes per year, the new demand curve is D_1. The price falls to $210, and the quantity falls to 31 million, as shown by the intersection of D_1 and S_0. Although demand falls by 8 million at each price, the quantity exchanged falls by only 4 million because the price fall has induced a movement out along the new demand curve, as well as a movement back along the old supply curve.

   (c) If supply falls by 8 million bikes per year, the new supply curve is S_1. The price rises to $300, and the quantity falls to 31 million, as shown by the intersection of D_0 and S_1. Although supply falls by 8 million at each price, the quantity exchanged falls by only 4 million because the price increase has induced a movement out along the new supply curve, as well as a movement back along the old demand curve.

   (d) If demand and supply each fall by 8 million bikes per year, the equilibrium price is $250, and the equilibrium quantity is 27 million bicycles, as shown by the intersection of D_1 and S_1.

5. The same diagram, Figure 4, can be used for all three cases, because they all entail a decline in demand, from D_0 to D_1. Price falls from P_0 to P_1, and quantity falls from Q_0 to Q_1.

(a) In a drought, people have less need for umbrellas, so demand falls.

(b) Popcorn is a complement for movie tickets, so when popcorn prices rise, the demand for tickets falls.

(c) Coca-Cola is a substitute for coffee, so when the price of the soda falls, the demand for coffee falls.

FIGURE 4

y-axis: Price — P_0, P_1
x-axis: Quantity — Q_1, Q_0
Curves: D_0, D_1, S

CHAPTER 5:
An Introduction to Macroeconomics

1. Microeconomist: (a) and (d); Macroeconomist: (b) and (c)

3. (a) Raises GDP by $50,000.

   (b) Raises GDP by $10,000.

   (c) GDP does not rise, because there is no market transaction.

(d) GDP rises by $500,000, the value of the newly constructed house.

(e) GDP does not rise, because nothing new was produced.

(f) Raises GDP by $25,000.

(g) GDP actually falls by $100. The casino is selling "gambling services" to you, which are measured by how much you lose. Winning $100 therefore reduces sales of gambling services.

(h) GDP does not rise. Because nothing new is produced, capital gains and losses do not count in GDP.

(i) GDP does not change because you did not produce a good or service.

(j) Raises GDP by $100.

CHAPTER 6:
The Goals of Macroeconomic Policy

1. After 25 years Country A's economy has grown by 109% because $(1.03)^{25} = 2.09$. After 25 years Country B's economy has grown by 167% because $(1.04)^{25} = 2.67$. If we index both countries' GDP to be 100 at the start of the 25-year period, by the end of the period, Country A's GDP would be 209 and Country B's would be 267. Therefore, Country B's economy would be roughly 28% larger than that of Country A because $(267 - 209)/(209) = .28$.

   The gap between the GDPs of the two countries is *larger than* 25% due to the *compounding* of a 1% higher growth rate for 25 years.

3. If actual GDP grew slower than potential GDP from 2000 to 2003, unemployment should have increased, which it did. Similarly, from 2003 to 2006, unemployment should have decreased because actual GDP was growing faster than potential. Unemployment did, in fact, fall between 2003 and 2006.

5. (a) 18 percent (b) 14 percent (c) 10 percent (d) 3 percent (e) −2 percent

Answers to Appendix Questions

1.

	1970	1980	1990	2000
Dow Jones Industrial Average (DJIA)	753	891	2,679	10,735
CPI	38.8	82.4	130.7	172.2
Deflated DJIA	1,941	1,081	2,050	6,234

The deflated DJIA is found by dividing the DJIA by the CPI of the same year, then multiplying by the base year CPI, which is 100. Stock prices do not rise every decade. They declined notably during the decade between 1970 and 1980 but then rose between 1980 and 2000. Stocks were most valuable in 2000. (Incidentally, both nominal and real stock prices fell between 2000 and 2003, before recovering.)

3.

	2005	2006	2007
Nominal GDP	12,434	13,195	**13,843**
Real GDP	11,003	11,319	**11,567**
GDP Deflator	113.0	116.6	**119.7**

5.

	1970	1980	1990	2000
Money wages	$3.23	$6.66	$10.01	$13.75
CPI	38.8	82.4	130.7	172.2
Real wages	$8.32	$8.08	$7.66	$7.98

	1970–80	1980–90	1990–00
Growth, money wages	106.2%	50.3%	37.4%
Growth, real wages	−2.9%	−5.2%	4.2%

Money wages grew fastest in the decade 1970–1980, but real wages grew fastest in 1990–2000. In fact, real wages declined in the preceding two decades.

CHAPTER 7:
Economic Growth: Theory and Policy

1. The productivity growth for each country is shown in the fourth column below.

	1997 Output per Hour	2007 Output per Hour	Productivity Growth 1997–2007
Country A	$40.00	$48.00	20%
Country B	25.00	35.00	40%
Country C	2.00	3.00	50%
Country D	0.50	0.60	20%

Productivity growth was highest for Country C, which had a very low initial level of productivity. But note that the productivity growth for Country D lagged far behind countries B and C despite Country D's lower starting point. As mentioned in the text, not all countries (such as Country D here) are able to participate in the convergence process. However, Countries B and C did close some of the gap on Country A.

3. The prices of items b, d, and e would be expected to rise rapidly over time, as each of these are personally provided services for which productivity improvements are difficult or impossible. By contrast, items a and c are not personally provided. In fact, productivity in these two electronically delivered services has increased dramatically over time, pushing down their prices.

5. Draw a graph similar to Figure 1 in the text. Higher levels of capital increase labor productivity, resulting in higher levels of output produced with the same quantity of labor. For example, in Figure 1 increasing the amount of capital from K_1 to K_2 increases the output from Y_a to Y_b. Labor

productivity increases when the capital stock is larger because workers can use the additional capital to produce more goods and services. For example, imagine loading and unloading a semitrailer truck by hand vs. using a forklift. One forklift operator can load and unload the truck in far less time then can be done by hand.

FIGURE 1

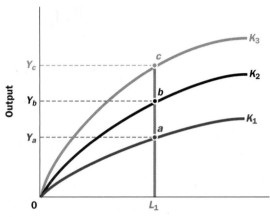

Hours of Labor Input

CHAPTER 8:
Aggregate Demand and the Powerful Consumer

1. Consumption (largest), government spending, investment, net exports (smallest—actually negative in the U.S.)

3. Line C_0 is the consumption function for Simpleland. The marginal propensity to consume can be calculated from the data for any pair of years. For example, for the period 2006–2007:

$$MPC = [C(2007) - C(2006)]/[Y(2007) - Y(2006)]$$
$$= (2,160 - 1,920)/(2,700 - 2,400)$$
$$= 240/300$$
$$= 0.8$$

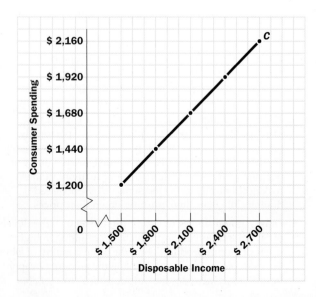

Disposable Income

Answers to Appendix Questions

1. (a) Included: GDP rises by $25,000.

   (b) Not included, because it was produced in another country. Actually, it is *included* as part of C, but then *deducted* as part of IM, which enters *negatively* in $C + I + G + (X - IM)$.

   (c) Not included, since it was not produced this year.

   (d) Included: GDP rises by $500 million (in investment, I).

   (e) Not included; it's a government transfer payment.

   (f) Included, as investment in inventory: GDP rises by $15 million.

   (g) Included, as consumption (legal services): GDP rises by $10,000.

   (h) Not included: previously produced.

3.

GDP as the Sum of Final Demands (all figures in millions)

| | Source | | | | |
	Specific Motors	Super Duper	Government	Rest of World	Total
C		4.8	14.0	1.0	19.8
I		0.8			0.8
G		0.3		0.8	1.1
X		0.9			0.9
−IM				−1.0	−1.0
Y					21.6

GDP as the Sum of Incomes (all figures in millions)

| | Source | | | | |
	Specific Motors	Super Duper	Farmers	Government	Total
Wages	3.8	4.5		0.8	9.1
+ Interest	0.1	0.2	0.7		1.0
+ Rent	0.2	1.0	2.0		3.2
+ Profits	1.6	0.9	4.3		6.8
= Nat. Income					20.1
+ Ind. Bus.Tax	0.5	0.2			0.7
= NNP					20.8
+ Depreciation	0.6	0.2			0.8
= GDP					21.6

Personal income = National income + Transfer payments
$$= 20.1 + 1.2 = 21.3$$

Disposable income = Personal income − Taxes
$$= 21.3 - 1.33 = 19.97$$

(since taxes are 10% of wages + interest + rent, which total 13.3)

Note: Profits were computed as follows:

	Specific Motors	Super Duper	Farmers
Revenues	6.8	14.0	7.0
– Wages	–3.8	–4.5	
– Interest	–0.1	–0.2	–0.7
– Rent	–0.2	–1.0	–2.0
– Intermediate Goods		–7.0	
– Depreciation		–0.6	–0.2
– Ind. taxes	–0.5	–0.2	
= Profits	–1.6	0.9	4.3

CHAPTER 9:
Demand-Side Equilibrium: Unemployment or Inflation?

1.

FIGURE 1

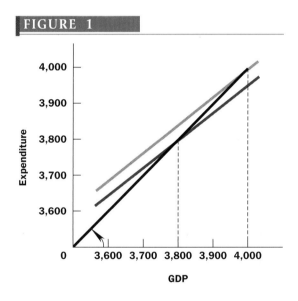

The original equilibrium GDP is at $Y = 3,800$, where spending equals output. This is shown by the intersection of the lower of the two expenditure lines in the graph above with the 45° line. The MPC calculated from the data is 0.90, so the multiplier is 10. If investment spending rises by $20 (to $260) the equilibrium GDP will increase by $20 \times 10 = 200, which is represented by a vertical shift (by $20) to the upper expenditure function in the diagram.

3.

FIGURE 2

At lower prices, the real value of money and other assets that are denominated in money terms is higher. Since wealth influences consumption, at lower prices consumption is higher.

5. $Y = C + I + G + (X − IM)$
$C = 300 + 0.75DI$
$C = 300 + 0.75(Y − 1,200)$
$C = 300 + 0.75Y − 900$
$C = −600 + 0.75Y$
$Y = −600 + 0.75Y + 1,100 + 1,300 − 100$
$Y = 0.75Y + 1,700$
$0.25Y = 1,700$
$Y = 4 \times 1,700 = 6,800$

This algebraic model yields the same equilibrium GDP as Table 3 and Figure 10 in the chapter.

Compared to the answer to Test Yourself Question 4, we find $800 more in GDP from a $200 increase in I. Thus this question demonstrates that the multiplier of 4 applies to changes in I as well as to changes in C.

7.

FIGURE 3

| Income | Before Shift | | After Shift | |
	Consumption	Expenditure	Consumption	Expenditure
1,080	880	1,160	920	1,200
1,140	920	1,200	960	1,240
1,200	960	1,240	1,000	1,280
1,260	1,000	1,280	1,040	1,320
1,320	1,040	1,320	1,080	1,360
1,380	1,080	1,360	1,120	1,400
1,440	1,120	1,400	1,160	1,440
1,500	1,160	1,440	1,200	1,480
1,560	1,200	1,480	1,240	1,520

The graph above indicates that equilibrium GDP rises from 1,320 to 1,440, or by 120. The oversimplified multiplier formula can be used in this case. The marginal propensity to consume can be calculated between any two income levels. The numbers in the table above show that each $60 of additional income leads to $40 more in consumer spending, so the MPC is 40/60 = 2/3, and the multiplier is $1/[1 - (2/3)] = 3$. So a shift in consumption of 40 should raise equilibrium GDP by 120, which it does.

Answers to Appendix A Questions

1. $Y = C + I + G + (X - IM)$

   $C = 150 + 0.75(Y - 400)$

   $C = 150 + 0.75Y - 300$

   $C = -150 + 0.75Y$

   $Y = -150 + 0.75Y + 300 + 400 - 50$

   $Y = 0.75Y + 500$

   $0.25Y = 500$

   $Y = 4 \times 500 = 2,000$

3. Saving is equal to disposable income minus consumption. In Question 1: $S = (Y - T) - C$

   $S = (2,000 - 400) - [-150 + 0.75(2000)]$

   $S = 1,600 - (-150 + 1,500)$

   $S = 1,600 - 1,350$

   $S = 250$

   S is *not* equal to I. (In Question 2, S is equal to I. The difference is that X and IM are equal in Question 2 but unequal in Question 1.

5. (a) $Y = C + I + G + (X - IM)$

   $C = 100 + 0.8(Y - 500)$

   $C = 100 + 0.8Y - 400$

   $C = -300 + 0.8Y$

   $Y = -300 + 0.8Y + 700 + 500 + 0$

   $Y = 0.8Y + 900$

   $0.2Y = 900$

   $Y = 5 \times 900 = 4,500$

(b) $S = (Y - T) - C$

   $S = (4,500 - 500) - [-300 + 0.8(4,500)]$

   $S = 4,300 - 3,600 = 700$, which is equal to investment, so $S = I$.

(c) Now $X - IM = 100$, so the last four lines of 5(a) above are replaced by

   $Y = -300 + 0.8Y + 700 + 500 + 100$

   $Y = 0.8Y + 1,000$

   $0.2Y = 1,000$

   $Y = 5 \times 1,000 = 5,000$

   $S = (Y - T) - C$

   $S = (5,000 - 500) - [-300 + 0.8(5,000)]$

   $S = 4,800 - 4,000 = 800$

   Now, S is not equal to I.

Answers to Appendix B Questions

1.

GDP	Exports	Imports	Net Exports
2,500	400	250	150
3,000	400	300	100
3,500	400	350	50
4,000	400	400	0
4,500	400	450	–50
5,000	400	500	–100

FIGURE 4

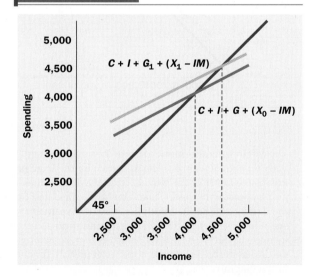

3. In Figure 4, the intersection of the upper expenditure line with the 45° line shows an equilibrium GDP of 4,500. (The lower expenditure line shows the solution to Test Yourself Question 2, with a GDP of 4,000.) Exports have risen by 250, and GDP has risen by 500, so the multiplier is 2.

CHAPTER 10:
Supply-Side Equilibrium: Unemployment *and* Inflation?

1.

Equilibrium real output is $3,000, while the price level is 100. Since full employment is at $2,800 billion, there is an inflationary gap of 200.

3.

FIGURE 2

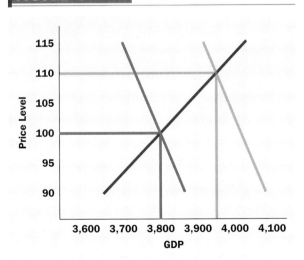

(a) In Chapter 9, Test Yourself Question 2, the marginal propensity to consume was 0.9, and the (oversimplified) multiplier was therefore 10. The table in this question confirms that when investment rises by 20, from 240 to 260, aggregate demand rises by 200 at any given price level. For example, at a price level of 105, aggregate demand rises from 3,770 to 3,970.

(b) Initial equilibrium: $P = 100$, $Y = 3,800$. Eventual equilibrium: $P = 110$, $Y = 3,940$. The multiplier, taking account of price increases, is $140/20 = 7$, which is less than 10.

CHAPTER 11:
Managing Aggregate Demand: Fiscal Policy

1.

GDP	Taxes	Disposable Income	Consumption	Total Expenditure
1,360	400	960	720	1,450
1,480	400	1,080	810	1,540
1,600	400	1,200	900	1,630
1,720	400	1,320	990	1,720
1,840	400	1,440	1,080	1,810

FIGURE 1

Equilibrium GDP is 1,720 (see diagram). The marginal propensity to consume is 0.75 and the multiplier is 4. If government purchases fall by 60, and the price level is unchanged, GDP would fall by $4 \times 60 = 240$, that is, to 1,480.

3. At each level of GDP, G is now higher by 120, while C is lower by ¾ of 120, or 90. Therefore, there is a net *increase* in total expenditure of 30 at each level of GDP, as shown in the following table:

GDP	Taxes	Disposable Income	Consumption	Total Expenditure
1,360	520	840	630	1,480
1,480	520	960	720	1,570
1,600	520	1,080	810	1,660
1,720	520	1,200	900	1,750
1,840	520	1,320	990	1,840

Equilibrium GDP is now 1,840, which is 120 more than in Test Yourself Question 1.

5. The answer to Test Yourself Question 2 is 1,720. So you want to increase GDP by 120 (raising it to 1,840). Because the marginal propensity to consume is 0.75, and the marginal tax rate is ⅓, the multiplier is 2. Therefore, you must take some action that will have the initial effect of raising expenditure by 60. You may raise government spending on GDP by 60, or you may lower taxes or raise transfer payments by 80 (since ¾ of 80 is 60).

Answers to Appendix A Questions

1. (a) variable tax (as GDP rises, people drive more); (b) variable tax; (c) fixed tax; (d) variable tax

3. The higher fixed tax reduces consumer spending, but the lower income-tax rate increases consumer spending. The question is: which effect is larger? The answer is found by seeing which tax change is larger, since C depends on $DI = Y - T$. At a GDP of $Y = 10,000$ billion, a two percentage point cut in the income-tax rate reduces tax receipts by \$200 billion, which is larger than the \$100 billion fixed-tax increase. So C, and hence equilibrium GDP on the demand side, rises.

Answers to Appendix B Questions

1. $Y = C + I + G + (X - IM)$
   $C = 120 + 0.8DI$
   $DI = Y - T$
   $DI = Y - (200 + 0.25Y)$
   $DI = 0.75Y - 200$
   $C = 120 + 0.8(0.75Y - 200)$
   $C = 120 + 0.6Y - 160$
   $C = 0.6Y - 40$
   $Y = 0.6Y - 40 + 320 + 480 - 80$
   $Y = 0.6Y + 680$
   $0.4Y = 680$
   $Y = (1/0.4) \times 680$
   $Y = 2.5 \times 680 = 1,700$

   Equilibrium GDP is 1,700.

   There are three different ways to find the multipliers, any one of which is correct.

   for government purchases:

   1. Note from the preceding equations that equilibrium GDP is 2.5 times all autonomous spending. Since G is autonomous spending, the multiplier for G is 2.5.

   2. Raise G from 480 to 481. Working through the algebra above, this comes to $0.4Y = 681$, which implies that $Y = 1,702.5$. So the increase in G of 1 has raised Y by 2.5, and the multiplier is 2.5.

   3. From the formula in the appendix, the multiplier is
      $1/1 - b(1 - t) = 1/[1 - 0.8(1 - 0.25)] = 1/[1 - 0.8(0.75)]$
      $= 1/(1 - 0.6) = 1/0.4 = 2.5$

   for fixed taxes:

   Note that a rise in fixed taxes decreases GDP (so the sign of the multiplier is negative) and that it increases

spending in the first round by the marginal propensity to consume times the tax reduction. So the tax multiplier is the multiplier found above, multiplied by (minus) the MPC, or $2.5 \times (-0.8) = -2$.

2. Raise fixed taxes in the model from 200 to 201. Working through the algebra, this comes to $0.4Y = 679.2$, or $Y = 1,698$. So an increase in taxes of 1 has reduced GDP by 2, and the multiplier is -2.

3. From the formula in the appendix, the tax multiplier is
   $-b/1 - b(1 - t) = -0.8/[1 - 0.8(1 - 0.25)] = -0.8/[1 - 0.8(0.75)] = -0.8/(1 - 0.6) = -0.8/0.4 = -2$

To raise GDP by 100, the government can (a) raise G by 40, and the multiplier of 2.5 will do the rest, or (b) lower taxes or raise transfer payments by 50, and the multiplier of –2 will do the rest.

3. (a) $Y = C + I + G + (X - IM)$
   $C = 0.9(Y - T)$
   $C = 0.9[Y - (\frac{1}{3})Y]$
   $C = 0.9[(\frac{2}{3})Y]$
   $C = 0.6Y$
   $Y = 0.6Y + 100 + 540 - 40$
   $Y = 0.6Y + 600$
   $0.4Y = 600$
   $Y = (1/0.4) \times 600$
   $Y = 2.5 \times 600 = 1,500$
   Budget deficit $= G - T$
   $= 540 - [(\frac{1}{3}) \times 1500]$
   $= 540 - 500$
   $= 40$

   (b) Since the budget deficit in part a is 40, the government would reduce its purchases by 40, to 500. Repeating the steps above, but now with $G = 500$:
   $Y = 0.6Y + 100 + 500 - 40$
   $Y = 0.6Y + 560$
   $0.4Y = 560$
   $Y = (1/0.4) \times 560$
   $Y = 2.5 \times 560 = 1,400$
   Budget deficit $= G - T$
   $= 500 - [(\frac{1}{3}) \times 1,400]$
   $= 500 - 466\frac{2}{3}$
   $= 33\frac{1}{3}$

   GDP falls by 100, to 1,400. That drop reduces tax receipts, which are one-third of GDP, by 33⅓ (to 466⅔). So in the new equilibrium, the deficit has fallen by only 6⅔ (to 33⅓), not by the full 40 in lower spending. Although G fell by the amount of the deficit, this in turn caused Y to fall, which in turn lowered taxes, and the deficit persisted.

CHAPTER 12:
Money and the Banking System

1. Under those conditions, the money multiplier is 1/.10, or 10, so an infusion of \$12 million into reserves will support an increase in money of \$120 million.

3.

(a)		(b)		(c)	
Assets	Liabilities	Assets	Liabilities	Assets	Liabilities
Reserves −100	Deposits −100	Reserves +100	Deposits +100	**HomeTown Bank**	
				Reserves −500	Deposits −500
				Big City Bank	
				Reserves +500	Deposits +500
				All Banks	
				Reserves no change	Deposits no change

CHAPTER 13:
Managing Aggregate Demand: Monetary Policy

1. In each case, there is $60 billion in the form of cash in circulation, and the rest of the money supply is held in bank deposits, backed by $60 billion in reserves. The total money supply is calculated as follows:

Reserve Ratio	Money Multiplier	Total Deposits	Money Supply
10%	10	600	660
12.5%	8	480	540
16 2/3%	6	360	420

The M1 money supply always exceeds total deposits by the $60 billion in cash outside banks.

3. Note: all figures are in billions of dollars.

Bill Gates		Bank of America		Federal Reserve	
Assets	Liabilities	Assets	Liabilities	Assets	Liabilities
Deposit at B of A +5	no change	Reserves +5	Deposits +5 Bonds −5	Bonds +5	Bank reserves +5

The Fed simply creates the $5 billion (in the form of bank reserves) to buy the bonds. In the long run, it makes no difference whether the Fed buys the bonds from a bank or from an individual. In this case, Bank of America's $5 billion in new reserves are offset by $5 billion in new deposits, so that not all of the new reserves are *excess* reserves, whereas if the Fed had bought the bonds from Bank of America directly there would have been no change in deposits, and all the new reserves would have been excess. In the long run, however, the new reserves of $5 billion will support the same increase in deposits. Why? Because in this case, the original transaction between the Fed and Bill Gates already creates $5 billion in new deposits.

5. (a) A $5 billion increase in the bank reserves lowers interest rates by 2.5 percentage points.

(b) A reduction in interest rates of 2.5 percentage points stimulates $75 billion of new investment spending.

(c) Aggregate demand rises by $150 billion.

(d) The aggregate supply curve is horizontal, and GDP rises by $150 billion.

7. There are several ways to solve this problem. Investment (I) can be found at the three different interest rates, and then equilibrium GDP can be calculated three times using the three different values for I. Alternatively, a more general solution just works with the symbol r for the interest rate:

$$Y = C + I$$
$$C = 300 + 0.75Y$$
$$I = 1{,}000 - 100r$$
$$Y = 300 + 0.75Y + 1{,}000 - 100r$$
$$Y = 1{,}300 + 0.75Y - 100r$$
$$0.25Y = 1{,}300 - 100r$$
$$Y = 4(1{,}300 - 100r)$$
$$Y = 5{,}200 - 400r$$

Therefore:

(a) If $r = 0.02$, $Y = 5{,}192$.

(b) If $r = 0.05$, $Y = 5{,}180$.

(c) If $r = 0.1$, $Y = 5{,}160$.

CHAPTER 14:
The Debate over Monetary and Fiscal Policy

1. Based on recent data, the velocity of money in the United States, for M1, is about 9.5–10. Students will probably calculate a much higher velocity for themselves.

3. In Figure 1, M_0S_0 is the initial money supply. The demand for money falls from M_0D_0 to M_1D_1; as a consequence, the quantity of money in the economy falls from M_0 to M_1, and the interest rate falls from r_0 to r_1. The Fed has three choices.

(a) It can accept the new money supply and interest rate.

(b) It can restore the previous interest rate, r_0, by lowering the money supply curve to M_1S_1. This will further reduce the quantity of money to M_2.

(c) If it follows a monetarist policy, it can restore the original quantity of money, M_0, by increasing the supply curve to M_2S_2. This will have the effect of reducing the interest rate still further, to r_2.

FIGURE 1

5. (a) Since people hold no currency, $M = D$. Both M and D will therefore be $(1/0.2) \times \$50$ billion $= 5 \times \$50$ billion $= \$250$ billion. If the Fed increases reserves to $\$60$ billion, M and D will rise to $\$300$ billion instead. The money multiplier is therefore $\$50/\$10 = 5$.

(b) Now, since people hold currency, $M = C + D = 1.2D$, because $C = 0.2D$. The $\$50$ billion monetary base ($B = 50$) must now serve *two* purposes: bank reserves plus currency, $B = R + C$. Since $R = 0.2D$ (reserve requirements) and $C = 0.2D$ (currency holdings), this means $B = 0.4D$. With $B = 50$, $D = 125$ now. But now people also hold $0.2 \times \$125 = \$25$ billion in currency, so the money supply is $M = D + C = \$150$. Notice that the money supply is much less than in part (a). The reason is that half of the monetary base is now used as currency rather than as bank reserves. (Notice that required reserves are $0.2 \times \$125 = \$25$ billion and cash holdings are also $\$25$ billion.)

When the Fed increases the monetary base to $\$60$ billion, the equation $B = R + C$ now becomes $60 = .4D$, so deposits rise to $D = \$150$ billion ($\$60/0.4$). With an additional $C = \$30$ billion in cash in circulation ($0.2 \times \$150$), the money supply will rise to $M = D + C = \$150 + \$30 = \$180$. So the money multiplier is just $\$30/\$10 = 3$ now.

(c) As the monetary base increases, the money supply M increases as well. However, the size of the increase in the money supply depends *both* on the required reserve ratio (0.2) in the example and how much the

public holds in currency (zero in part (a), 0.2D in part (b)). In part (a), the monetary base ($B = R + C$) and bank reserves are identical because $C = 0$. So all $\$10$ billion in new monetary base goes into bank reserves, where it supports $\$50$ billion in new deposits. But in part (b), half of the new $\$10$ billion in monetary base gets absorbed by currency holdings, leaving an increase of only $\$5$ billion in bank reserves—which supports only $\$25$ billion in new deposits.

CHAPTER 15:
Budget Deficits in the Short and Long Run

1. The budget deficit is an annual-flow concept. It is the excess of government expenditures over government revenues in a given year. The national debt is an accumulated stock of debt. It is increased each year by the deficit or reduced by the surplus. If the deficit becomes a surplus, the debt will fall (although the accumulated debt may still be very large).

3. Expansionary monetary policy will raise GDP, and this will raise tax receipts. The lower interest rates will also decrease the government's interest payments. Both changes will reduce the government's budget deficit. If the government tries to counteract the Fed's positive effect on aggregate demand, it will institute a more contractionary fiscal policy by decreasing government spending or raising taxes, or both. The deficit will shrink still more.

CHAPTER 16:
The Trade-Off between Inflation and Unemployment

1. Figure 1 shows that when the aggregate supply curve is vertical, shifting aggregate demand curves change only the price level, not output.

FIGURE 1

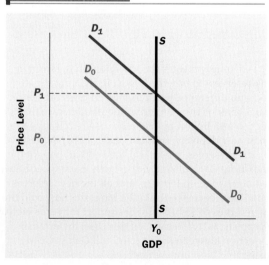

CHAPTER 17:
International Trade and Comparative Advantage

1. (a) In the absence of trade, 1 barrel of wine costs 4 yards of cloth in England.

   (b) In the absence of trade, 1 barrel of wine costs 2 yards of cloth in Portugal.

   (c)

FIGURE 1

(a) England   (b) Portugal

Wine (million barrels)

   (d) Portugal has the absolute advantage in the production of both goods, and the comparative advantage in wine. England has the comparative advantage in cloth.

   (e) When trade opens, England will specialize in cloth and export it to Portugal, which in turn will specialize in wine and export it to England.

   (f) In the international market, the price of a barrel of wine will wind up somewhere between 4 yards and 2 yards of cloth, perhaps 3. Stated another way, the price of 1 yard of cloth will be between ½ gallon of wine and ¼ gallon of wine.

Answers to Appendix Questions

1. (a)

FIGURE 3

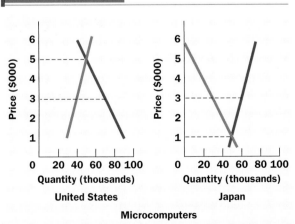

United States   Japan

Microcomputers

(b) If there is no trade, in the United States the equilibrium price is $5,000 and the equilibrium quantity is 50,000 units. In Japan, the price is $1,000 and the quantity is 50,000.

(c) The new world price will be $3,000 because, at that price, *world* quantity demanded is 100,000 units (70,000 plus 30,000) and *world* quantity supplied is also 100,000 units (40,000 plus 60,000). The price of computers has fallen in the United States and risen in Japan. (*Note:* To arrive at the answer graphically, construct *world* demand and supply curves. The equilibrium will be found at a world price of $3,000.)

(d) Japan will export 30,000 computers.

(e) In the United States, computer production falls from 50,000 to 40,000, and therefore employment in the computer industry falls. In Japan, computer production rises from 50,000 to 60,000, with a consequent increase in employment. Initially, American consumers and Japanese computer producers (both employers and employees) are helped by free trade, while American computer producers and Japanese consumers are hurt.

CHAPTER 18:
The International Monetary System: Order or Disorder?

1. One can use supply and demand curves for either the yen or the dollar. If one chooses the market for dollars, then the exchange rate measured on the vertical axis is the price of a dollar in yen:

(a) Japanese imports increase and U.S. exports increase. So the demand for dollars rises, and the dollar therefore appreciates.

(b) Because Japanese stocks are less attractive, there is less capital outflow from the United States to Japan to buy stocks. The supply of dollars decreases, and the dollar therefore appreciates.

(c) With lower interest rates, American financial assets become less attractive. So capital flows out of the United States (or less flows in). This increases the supply of dollars, leading to a depreciation of the dollar.

(d) The increase in foreign aid increases the supply of dollars and leads to a depreciation of the dollar.

(e) Because the Japanese economy booms and the U.S. economy is in a recession, Japanese imports increase while U.S. imports fall. Japanese demand for dollars therefore increases, while US supply of dollars decreases. So the dollar appreciates.

(f) At any given exchange rate, higher U.S. inflation causes an increase in imports and a decrease in exports. This leads to consequent increases in the supply of dollars and decreases in the demand for dollars. Therefore, the dollar depreciates.

3. Items (a) and (c) would lead to a depreciation of the dollar. Items (b) and (e) would lead to an appreciation. Item (d) would have no effect on the value of the dollar because it is purely a domestic transaction.

CHAPTER 19:
Exchange Rates and the Macroeconomy

1. In Figure 1, the economy begins at A, with price P_0 and output Y_0, resulting from aggregate demand D_0 and aggregate supply S_0. The currency appreciation leads to a decrease in exports and therefore a decrease in aggregate demand to D_1. Because imported inputs become less expensive, it also leads to an increase in aggregate supply to S_1. The price level will definitely fall, to P_1 in the diagram. Whether output falls or rises depends on the relative strength of the aggregate demand and aggregate supply effects, but since the aggregate demand shift is probably greater, output is likely to decrease, as shown in the diagram, to Y_1.

FIGURE 1

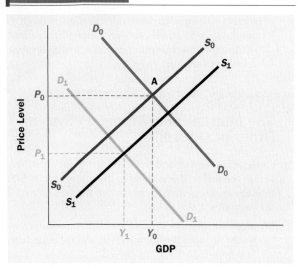

3. (a)

$$Y = C + I + G + (X - IM)$$
$$C = 150 + .75DI$$
$$C = 150 + .75(.8)Y$$
$$C = 150 + .6Y$$
$$I = 300 + .2Y - 50(r)$$
$$I = 300 + .2Y - 50(8)$$

$$I = .2Y - 100$$
$$(X - IM) = 300 - (250 + .2Y)$$
$$(X - IM) = 50 - .2Y$$
$$Y = 150 + .6Y + .2Y - 100 + 800 + 50 - .2Y$$
$$Y = 900 + .6Y$$
$$.4Y = 900$$
$$Y = 2.5(900)$$
$$Y = 2,250$$
$$G - T = 800 - .2(2,250)$$
$$G - T = 800 - 450$$
$$G - T = 350$$
$$X - IM = 50 - .2(2,250)$$
$$X - IM = 50 - 450$$
$$X - IM = -400$$

(b)

$$Y = C + I + G + (X - IM)$$
$$C = 150 + .75DI$$
$$C = 150 + .75(.8)Y$$
$$C = 150 + .6Y$$
$$I = 300 + .2Y - 50(r)$$
$$I = 300 + .2Y - 50(8)$$
$$I = .2Y - 100$$
$$(X - IM) = 250 - (.2Y)$$
$$(X - IM) = 250 - .2Y$$
$$Y = 150 + .6Y + .2Y - 100 + 800 + 250 - .2Y$$
$$Y = 1,100 + .6Y$$
$$.4Y = 1,100$$
$$Y = 2.5(1,100)$$
$$Y = 2,750$$
$$G - T = 800 - .2(2,750)$$
$$G - T = 800 - 55$$
$$G - T = 250$$
$$X - IM = 250 - .2(2,750)$$
$$X - IM = 250 - 550$$
$$X - IM = -300$$

GLOSSARY

Absolute advantage One country is said to have an absolute advantage over another in the production of a particular good if it can produce that good using smaller quantities of resources than can the other country. (p. 343)

Abstraction Abstraction means ignoring many details so as to focus on the most important elements of a problem. (p. 8)

Aggregate demand Aggregate demand is the total amount that all consumers, business firms, and government agencies spend on final goods and services. (p. 154)

Aggregate demand curve The aggregate demand curve shows the quantity of domestic product that is demanded at each possible value of the price level. (pp. 86, 180)

Aggregate supply curve The aggregate supply curve shows, for each possible price level, the quantity of goods and services that all the nation's businesses are willing to produce during a specified period of time, holding all other determinants of aggregate quantity supplied constant. (pp. 86, 200)

Aggregation Aggregation means combining many individual markets into one overall market. (p. 84)

Allocation of resources Allocation of resources refers to the society's decisions on how to divide up its scarce input resources among the different outputs produced in the economy and among the different firms or other organizations that produce those outputs. (p. 47)

Appreciate A nation's currency is said to appreciate when exchange rates change so that a unit of its currency can buy more units of foreign currency. (pp. 362, 381)

Asset An asset of an individual or business firm is an item of value that the individual or firm owns. (p. 251)

Automatic stabilizer An automatic stabilizer is a feature of the economy that reduces its sensitivity to shocks, such as sharp increases or decreases in spending. (p. 225)

Autonomous increase in consumption An autonomous increase in consumption is an increase in consumer spending without any increase in consumer incomes. It is represented on a graph as a shift of the entire consumption function. (p. 189)

Balance of payments deficit The balance of payments deficit is the amount by which the quantity supplied of a country's currency (per year) exceeds the quantity demanded. Balance of payments deficits arise whenever the exchange rate is pegged at an artificially high level. (p. 369)

Balance of payments surplus The balance of payments surplus is the amount by which the quantity demanded of a country's currency (per year) exceeds the quantity supplied. Balance of payments surpluses arise whenever the exchange rate is pegged at an artificially low level. (p. 369)

Balance sheet A balance sheet is an accounting statement listing the values of all assets on the left side and the values of all liabilities and net worth on the right side. (p. 252)

Barter Barter is a system of exchange in which people directly trade one good for another, without using money as an intermediate step. (p. 243)

Budget deficit The budget deficit is the amount by which the government's expenditures exceed its receipts during a specified period of time, usually a year. If receipts exceed expenditures, it is called a budget surplus instead. (pp. 303, 387)

Budget surplus The budget surplus is the amount by which the government's receipts exceed its expenditures during a specified period of time, usually a year. If expenditures exceed receipts, it is called a budget deficit instead. (p. 303)

Capital A nation's capital is its available supply of plant, equipment, and software. It is the result of past decisions to make *investments* in these items. (pp. 138)

Capital account The capital account balance includes purchases and sales of financial assets to and from citizens and companies of other countries. (p. 370)

Capital formation Capital formation is synonymous with investment. It refers to the process of building up the capital stock. (p. 138)

Capital gain A capital gain is the difference between the price at which an asset is sold and the price at which it was bought. (p. 122)

Central bank A central bank is a bank for banks. The United States' central bank is the *Federal Reserve System*. (p. 263)

Central bank independence Central bank independence refers to the central bank's ability to make decisions without political interference. (p. 264)

Closed economy A closed economy is one that does not trade with other nations in either goods or assets. (pp. 24, 385)

Commodity money Commodity money is an object in use as a medium of exchange, but that also has a substantial value in alternative (nonmonetary) uses. (p. 245)

Comparative advantage One country is said to have a comparative advantage over another in the production of a particular good *relative to other goods* if it produces that good less inefficiently as compared with the other country. (pp. 49, 343)

Consumer expenditure Consumer expenditure (*C*) is the total amount spent by consumers on newly produced goods and services (excluding purchases of new homes, which are considered investment goods). (p. 154)

Consumer Price Index (CPI) The Consumer Price Index (CPI) is measured by pricing the items on a list representative of a typical urban household budget. (p. 128)

Consumption function The consumption function shows the relationship between total consumer expenditures and total disposable income in the economy, holding all other determinants of consumer spending constant. (p. 160)

Convergence hypothesis The convergence hypothesis holds that nations with low levels of productivity tend to have high productivity growth rates, so that international productivity differences shrink over time. (p. 137)

Coordination failure A coordination failure occurs when party A would like to change his behavior if party B would change hers, and vice versa, and yet the two changes do not take place because the decisions of A and B are not coordinated. (p. 184)

Correlated Two variables are said to be correlated if they tend to go up or down together. Correlation need not imply causation. (p. 10)

Cost disease of the personal services The cost disease of the personal services is the tendency of the costs and prices of these services to rise persistently faster than those of the average output in the economy. (p. 146)

Crowding in Crowding in occurs when government spending, by raising real GDP, induces increases in private investment spending. (p. 311)

Crowding out Crowding out occurs when deficit spending by the government forces private investment spending to contract. (p. 310)

Current account The current account balance includes international purchases and sales of goods and services, crossborder interest and dividend payments, and cross-border gifts to and from both private individuals and governments. It is approximately the same as net exports. (p. 370)

Cyclical unemployment Cyclical unemployment is the portion of unemployment that is attributable to a decline in the economy's total production. Cyclical unemploymentrises during recessions and falls as prosperity is restored. (p. 114)

Deflating Deflating is the process of finding the real value of some monetary magnitude by dividing by some appropriate price index. (p. 129)

Deflation Deflation refers to a sustained decrease in the general price level. (p. 93)

Demand curve A demand curve is a graphical depiction of a demand schedule. It shows how the quantity demanded of some product will change as the price of that product changes during a specified period of time, holding all other determinants of quantity demanded constant. (p. 58)

Demand schedule A demand schedule is a table showing how the quantity demanded of some product during a specified period of time changes as the price of ̇at product changes, holding all other ͬminants of quantity demanded con- ͺ(p. 58)

Demand-side inflation Demand-side inflation is a rise in the price level caused by rapid growth of aggregate demand. (p. 318)

Deposit creation Deposit creation refers to the process by which a fractional reserve banking system turns $1 of bank reserves into several dollars of bank deposits. (p. 252)

Deposit insurance Deposit insurance is a system that guarantees that depositors will not lose money even if their bank goes bankrupt. (p. 250)

Depreciate A nation's currency is said to depreciate when exchange rates change so that a unit of its currency can buy fewer units of foreign currency. (p. 362)

Depreciation Depreciation is the value of the portion of the nation's capital equipment that is used up within the year. It tells us how much output is needed just to maintain the economy's capital stock. (pp. 171, 381)

Devaluation A devaluation is a reduction in the official value of a currency. (p. 363)

Development assistance Development assistance ("foreign aid") refers to outright grants and low-interest loans to poor countries from both rich countries and multinational institutions like the World Bank. The purpose is to spur economic development. (p. 147)

Discount rate The discount rate is the interest rate the Fed charges on loans that it makes to banks. (p. 270)

Discouraged worker A discouraged worker is an unemployed person who gives up looking for work and is therefore no longer counted as part of the labor force. (p. 114)

Disposable income Disposable income (*DI*) is the sum of the incomes of all individuals in the economy after all taxes have been deducted and all transfer payments have been added. (p. 155)

Division of labor Division of labor means breaking up a task into a number of smaller, more *specialized* tasks so that each worker can become more adept at a particular job. (p. 48)

Dumping Dumping means selling goods in a foreign market at lower prices than those charged in the home market. (p. 353)

Economic model An economic model is a simplified, small-scale version of some

aspect of the economy. Economic models are often expressed in equations, by graphs, or in words. (p. 10)

Efficiency A set of outputs is said to be produced efficiently if, given current technological knowledge, there is no way one can produce larger amounts of any output without using larger input amounts or giving up some quantity of another output. (p. 47)

Equation of exchange The equation of exchange states that the money value of GDP transactions must be equal to the product of the average stock of money times velocity. That is: $M \times V = P \times Y$ (p. 278)

Equilibrium An equilibrium is a situation in which there are no inherent forces that produce change. Changes away from an equilibrium position will occur only as a result of "outside events" that disturb the status quo. (pp. 65, 176)

Excess reserves Excess reserves are any reserves held in excess of the legal minimum. (p. 252)

Exchange rate The exchange rate states the price, in terms of one currency, at which another currency can be bought. (pp. 362, 381)

Expenditure schedule An expenditure schedule shows the relationship between national income (GDP) and total spending. (p. 179)

Export subsidy An export subsidy is a payment by the government to exporters to permit them to reduce the selling prices of their goods so they can compete more effectively in foreign markets. (p. 349)

Factors of production Inputs or factors of production are the labor, machinery, buildings, and natural resources used to make outputs. (p. 22)

Federal funds rate The federal funds rate is the interest rates that banks pay and receive when they borrow reserves from one another. (p. 266)

Fiat money Fiat money is money that is decreed as such by the government. It is of little value as a commodity, but it maintains its value as a medium of exchange because people have faith that the issuer will stand behind the pieces of printed paper and limit their production. (p. 246)

Final goods and services Final goods and services are those that are purchased by their ultimate users. (p. 89)

Fiscal policy The government's fiscal policy is its plan for spending and taxation. It can be used to steer aggregate demand in the desired direction. (pp. 95, 221, 301)

Fixed exchange rates Fixed exchange rates are rates set by government decisions and maintained by government actions. (p. 369)

Fixed taxes Fixed taxes are taxes that do not vary with the level of GDP. (p. 235)

Floating exchange rates Floating exchange rates are rates determined in free markets by the law of supply and demand. (p. 363)

Foreign direct investment Foreign direct investment is the purchase or construction of real business assets—such as factories, offices, and machinery—in a foreign country. (p. 147)

45° line Rays through the origin with a slope of 1 are called 45° lines because they form an angle of 45° with the horizontal axis. A 45° line marks off points where the variables measured on each axis have equal values. (p. 17)

45° line diagram An income-expenditure diagram, or 45° line diagram, plots total real expenditure (on the vertical axis) against real income (on the horizontal axis). The 45° line marks off points where income and expenditure are equal. (p. 180)

Fractional reserve banking Fractional reserve banking is a system under which bankers keep as reserves only a fraction of the funds they hold on deposit. (p. 248)

Frictional unemployment Frictional unemployment is unemployment that is due to normal turnover in the labor market. It includes people who are temporarily between jobs because they are moving or changing occupations, or are unemployed for similar reasons. (p. 114)

Full employment Full employment is a situation in which everyone who is willing and able to work can find a job. At full employment, the measured unemployment rate is still positive. (p. 115)

GDP deflator The price index used to deflate nominal GDP is called the GDP deflator. It is a broad measure of economywide inflation; it includes the prices of all goods and services in the economy. (p. 129)

Gold standard The gold standard is a way to fix exchange rates by defining each participating currency in terms of gold and allowing holders of each participating currency to convert that currency into gold. (p. 371)

Government purchases Government purchases (G) refer to the goods (such as airplanes and paper clips) and services (such as school teaching and police protection) purchased by all levels of government. (p. 155)

Gross domestic product (GDP) Gross domestic product (GDP) is the sum of the money values of all final goods and services produced in the domestic economy and sold on organized markets during a specified period of time, usually a year. (pp. 23, 88, 168)

Gross national product (GNP) Gross national product (GNP) is a measure of all final production, making no adjustment for the fact that some capital is used up each year and thus needs to be replaced. (p. 171)

Gross private domestic investment (I) Gross private domestic investment includes business investment in plant, equipment, and software; residential construction; and inventory investment. (p. 169)

Growth policy Growth policy refers to government policies intended to make the economy grow faster in the long run. (p. 106)

Human capital Human capital is the amount of skill embodied in the workforce. It is most commonly measured by the amount of education and training. (p. 136)

Income-expenditure diagram An income-expenditure diagram, or 45° line diagram, plots total real expenditure (on the vertical axis) against real income (on the horizontal axis). The 45° line marks off points where income and expenditure are equal. (p. 180)

Indexing Indexing refers to provisions in a law or a contract whereby monetary payments are automatically adjusted whenever a specified price index changes. Wage rates, pensions, interest payments on bonds, income taxes, and many other things can be indexed in this way, and have been. Sometimes such contractual provisions are called *escalator clauses*. (p. 332)

Index number An index number expresses the cost of a market basket of goods relative to its cost in some "base" period, which is simply the year used as a basis of comparison. (p. 127)

Index number problem When relative prices are changing, there is no such thing as a "perfect price index" that is correct for every consumer. Any statistical index will understate the increase in the cost of living for some families and overstate it for others. At best, the index can represent the situation of an "average" family. (p. 127)

Induced increase in consumption An induced increase in consumption is an increase in consumer spending that stems from an increase in consumer incomes. It is represented on a graph as a movement along a fixed consumption function. (p. 189)

Induced investment Induced investment is the part of investment spending that rises when GDP rises and falls when GDP falls. (p. 179)

Infant-industry argument The infant-industry argument for trade protection holds that new industries need to be protected from foreign competition until they develop and flourish. (p. 352)

Inflation Inflation refers to a sustained increase in the general price level. Inflation occurs when prices in an economy rise rapidly. The rate of inflation is calculated by averaging the percentage growth rate of the prices of a selected sample of commodities. (p. 87)

Inflationary gap The inflationary gap is the amount by which equilibrium real GDP exceeds the full-employment level of GDP. (pp. 183, 205)

Innovation Innovation is the process that begins with invention and includes improvement to prepare the invention for practical use and marketing of the invention or its products. (p. 142)

Inputs Inputs or factors of production are the labor, machinery, buildings, and natural resources used to make outputs. (pp. 22, 42, 105)

Intermediate good An intermediate good is a good purchased for resale or for use in producing another good. (p. 89)

International capital flows International capital flows are purchases and sales of financial assets across national borders. (p. 384)

Invention Invention is the act of discovering new products or new ways of making products. (p. 142)

Investment Investment is the *flow* of resources into the production of new capital. It is the labor, steel, and other inputs devoted to the *construction* of factories, warehouses, railroads, and other pieces of capital during some period of time. (p. 138)

Investment spending Investment spending (*I*) is the sum of the expenditures of business firms on new plant and equipment and households on new homes. Financial "investments" are not included, nor are resales of existing physical assets. (p. 155)

Invisible hand The invisible hand is a phrase used by Adam Smith to describe how, by pursuing their own self-interests, people in a market system are "led by an invisible hand" to promote the well-being of the community. (p. 56)

Labor force The labor force is the number of people holding or seeking jobs. (p. 108)

Labor productivity Labor productivity is the amount of output a worker turns out in an hour (or a week, or a year) of labor. If output is measured by GDP, it is GDP per hour of work. (p. 107)

Law of supply and demand The law of supply and demand states that in a free market the forces of supply and demand generally push the price toward the level at which quantity supplied and quantity demanded are equal. (p. 66)

Liability A liability of an individual or business firm is an item of value that the individual or firm owes. Many liabilities are known as *debts*. (p. 251)

Liquidity An asset's liquidity refers to the ease with which it can be converted into cash. (p. 247)

M1 The narrowly defined money supply, usually abbreviated M1, is the sum of all coins and paper money in circulation, plus certain checkable deposit balances at banks and savings institutions. (p. 247)

M2 The broadly defined money supply, usually abbreviated M2, is the sum of all coins and paper money in circulation, plus all types of checking account balances, plus most forms of savings account balances, plus shares in money market mutual funds. (p. 247)

Marginal propensity to consume (MPC) The marginal propensity to consume (MPC) is the ratio of changes in consumption relative to changes in disposable income that produce the change in consumption. On a graph, it appears as the slope of the consumption function. (p. 160)

Market system A market system is a form of economic organization in which resource allocation decisions are left to individual producers and consumers acting in their own best interests without central direction. (p. 50)

Medium of exchange The medium of exchange is the object or objects used to buy and sell other items such as goods and services. (p. 244)

Mercantilism Mercantilism is a doctrine that holds that exports are good for a country, whereas imports are harmful. (p. 348)

Mixed economy A mixed economy is one with some public influence over the workings of free markets. There may also be some public ownership mixed in with private property. (p. 36)

Monetarism Monetarism is a mode of analysis that uses the equation of exchange to organize and analyze macroeconomic data. (p. 281)

Monetary policy Monetary policy refers to actions taken by the Federal Reserve to influence aggregate demand by changing interest rates. (pp. 97, 261, 301)

Monetize the deficit The central bank is said to monetize the deficit when it purchases bonds issued by the government. (p. 309)

Money Money is the standard object used in exchanging goods and services. In short, money is the medium of exchange. (p. 244)

Money-fixed asset A money-fixed asset is an asset whose value is a fixed number of dollars. (p. 162)

Money multiplier The money multiplier is the ratio of newly created bank deposits to new reserves. (p. 256)

Moral hazard Moral hazard refers to the tendency of insurance to discourage policyholders from protecting themselves from risk. (p. 250)

Multinational corporations Multinational corporations are corporations, generally large ones, which do business in many countries. Most, but not all, of these corporations have their headquarters in developed countries. (p. 147)

Multiplier The multiplier is the ratio of the change in equilibrium GDP (Y) divided by the original change in spending that causes the change in GDP. (p. 185)

National debt The national debt is the federal government's total indebtedness at a moment in time. It is the result of previous budget deficits. (p. 303)

National income National income is the sum of the incomes that all individuals in the country earn in the forms of wages, interest, rents, and profits. It includes indirect business taxes, but excludes transfer payments and makes no deduction for income taxes. (p. 155, 170)

National income accounting The system of measurement devised for collecting and expressing macroeconomic data is called national income accounting. (p. 168)

Natural rate of unemployment The economy's self-correcting mechanism always tends to push the unemployment rate back toward a specific rate of unemployment that we call the natural rate of unemployment. (p. 323)

Near moneys Near moneys are liquid assets that are close substitutes for money. (p. 247)

Net exports Net exports, or $X - IM$, is the difference between exports (X) and imports (IM). It indicates the difference between what we sell to foreigners and what we buy from them. (pp. 155, 380)

Net national product (NNP) Net national product (NNP) is a measure of production. NNP is conceptually identical to national income. However, in practice, national income accountants estimate income and production independently; and so the two measures are never precisely equal. (p. 170)

Net worth Net worth is the value of all assets minus the value of all liabilities. (p. 252)

Nominal GDP Nominal GDP is calculated by valuing all outputs at current prices. (p. 88)

Nominal rate of interest The nominal rate of interest is the percentage by which the money the borrower pays back exceeds the money that was borrowed, making no adjustment for any decline in the purchasing power of this money that results from inflation. (p. 121)

On-the-job training On-the-job training refers to skills that workers acquire while at work, rather than in school or in formal vocational training programs. (p. 141)

Open economy An open economy is one that trades with other nations in goods and services, and perhaps also trades in financial assets. (pp. 24, 379)

Open-market operations Open-market operations refer to the Fed's purchase or sale of government securities through transactions in the open market. (p. 265)

Opportunity cost The opportunity cost of some decision is the value of the next best alternative that must be given up because of that decision (for example, working instead of going to school). (pp. 4, 41)

Optimal decision An optimal decision is one that best serves the objectives of the decision maker, whatever those objectives may be. It is selected by explicit or implicit comparison with the possible alternative choices. The term *optimal* connotes neither approval nor disapproval of the objective itself. (p. 42)

Origin (of a graph) The "0" point in the lower-left corner of a graph where the axes meet is called the origin. Both variables are equal to zero at the origin. (p. 13)

Outputs The outputs of a firm or an economy are the goods and services it produces. (pp. 22, 42, 105)

Phillips curve A Phillips curve is a graph depicting the rate of unemployment on the horizontal axis and either the rate of inflation or the rate of change of money wages on the vertical axis. Phillips curves are normally downward sloping, indicating that higher inflation rates are associated with lower unemployment rates. (p. 319)

Potential GDP Potential GDP is the real GDP that the economy would produce if its labor and other resources were fully employed. (p. 108)

Price ceiling A price ceiling is a maximum that the price charged for a commodity cannot legally exceed. (p. 70)

Price floor A price floor is a legal minimum below which the price charged for a commodity is not permitted to fall. (p. 73)

Principle of increasing costs The principle of increasing costs states that as the production of a good expands, the opportunity cost of producing another unit generally increases. (p. 44)

Production function The economy's production function shows the volume of output that can be produced from given inputs (such as labor and capital), given the available technology. (p. 108)

Production indifference map A production indifference map is a graph whose axes show the quantities of two inputs that are used to produce some output. A curve in the graph corresponds to some given quantity of that output, and the different points on that curve show the different quantities of the two inputs that are just enough to produce the given output. (p. 18)

Production possibilities frontier The production possibilities frontier is a curve that shows the maximum quantities of outputs it is possible to produce with the available resource quantities and the current state of technological knowledge. (p. 43)

Productivity Productivity is the amount of output produced by a unit of input. (p. 202)

Progressive tax A progressive tax is one in which the average tax rate paid by an individual rises as income rises. (p. 35)

Property rights Property rights are laws and/or conventions that assign owners the rights to use their property as they see fit (within the law)—for example, to sell the property and to reap the benefits (such as rents or dividends) while they own it. (p. 140)

Purchasing power The purchasing power of a given sum of money is the volume of goods and services that it will buy. (p. 117)

Quantity demanded The quantity demanded is the number of units of a good that consumers are willing and can afford to buy over a specified period of time. (p. 57)

Quantity supplied The quantity supplied is the number of units that sellers want to sell over a specified period of time. (p. 61)

Quantity theory of money The quantity theory of money assumes that velocity is (approximately) constant. In that case, nominal GDP is proportional to the money stock. (p. 279)

Quota A quota specifies the maximum amount of a good that is permitted into the country from abroad per unit of time. (p. 348)

Rational expectations Rational expectations are forecasts that, while not necessarily correct, are the best that can be made given the available data. Rational expectations, therefore, cannot err systematically. If expectations are rational, forecasting errors are pure random numbers. (p. 328)

Ray through the origin (or Ray) Lines whose Y-intercept is zero have so many special uses in economics and other disciplines that they have been given a special name: a ray through the origin, or a ray. (p. 16)

Real GDP Real GDP is calculated by valuing outputs of different years at common prices. Therefore, real GDP is a far better measure than nominal GDP of changes in total production. (p. 88)

Real GDP per capita Real GDP per capita is the ratio of real GDP divided by population. (p. 92)

Real rate of interest The real rate of interest is the percentage increase in purchasing power that the borrower pays to the lender for the privilege of borrowing. It indicates the increased ability to purchase goods and services that the lender earns. (p. 121)

Real wage rate The real wage rate is the wage rate adjusted for inflation. Specifically, it is the nominal wage divided by the price index. The real wage thus indicates the volume of goods and services that the nominal wages will buy. (p. 117)

Recession A recession is a period of time during which the total output of the economy declines. (pp. 24, 87)

Recessionary gap The recessionary gap is the amount by which the equilibrium level of real GDP falls short of potential GDP. (pp. 183, 205)

Relative price An item's relative price is its price in terms of some other item rather than in terms of dollars. (p. 119)

Required reserves Required reserves are the minimum amount of reserves (in cash or the equivalent) required by law. Normally, required reserves are proportional to the volume of deposits. (p. 251)

Research and development (R&D) Research and development (R&D) is the activity of firms, universities, and government agencies that seeks to invent new products and processes and to improve those inventions so that they are ready for the market or other users. (p. 142)

Resources Resources are the instruments provided by nature or by people that are used to create goods and services. Natural resources include minerals, soil, water, and air. Labor is a scarce resource, partly because of time limitations (the day has only 24 hours) and partly because the number of skilled workers is limited. Factories and machines are resources made by people. These three types of resources are often referred to as *land, labor,* and *capital*. They are also called *inputs* or *factors of production*. (p. 40)

Revaluation A revaluation is an increase in the official value of a currency. (p. 363)

Run on a bank A run on a bank occurs when many depositors withdraw cash from their accounts all at once. (p. 242)

Scatter diagram A scatter diagram is a graph showing the relationship between two variables (such as consumer spending and disposable income). Each year is represented by a point in the diagram, and the coordinates of each year's point show the values of the two variables in that year. (p. 158)

Self-correcting mechanism The economy's self-correcting mechanism refers to the way money wages react to either a recessionary gap or an inflationary gap. Wage changes shift the aggregate supply curve and therefore change equilibrium GDP and the equilibrium price level. (pp. 209, 322)

Shift in a demand curve A shift in a demand curve occurs when any relevant variable other than price changes. If consumers want to buy *more* at any and all given prices than they wanted previously, the demand curve shifts to the right (or outward). If they desire *less* at any given price, the demand curve shifts to the left (or inward). (p. 59)

Shortage A shortage is an excess of quantity demanded over quantity supplied. When there is a shortage, buyers cannot purchase the quantities they desire at the current price. (p. 65)

Slope of a curved line The slope of a curved line at a particular point is defined as the slope of the straight line that is tangent to the curve at that point. (p. 15)

Slope of a straight line The slope of a straight line is the ratio of the vertical change to the corresponding horizontal change as we move to the right along the line or, as it is often said, the ratio of the "rise" over the "run." (p. 14)

Specialization Specialization means that a country devotes its energies and resources to only a small proportion of the world's productive activities. (p. 341)

Stabilization policy Stabilization policy is the name given to government programs designed to prevent or shorten recessions and to counteract inflation (that is, to *stabilize* prices). (p. 99)

Stagflation Stagflation is inflation that occurs while the economy is growing slowly ("stagnating") or in a recession. (pp. 96, 210, 318)

Store of value A store of value is an item used to store wealth from one point in time to another. (p. 244)

Strategic argument for protection The strategic argument for protection holds that a nation may sometimes have to threaten protectionism to induce other countries to drop their own protectionist measures. (p. 353)

Structural budget deficit or surplus The structural budget deficit or surplus is the hypothetical deficit or surplus we *would have* under current fiscal policies if the economy were operating near full employment. (p. 306)

Structural unemployment Structural unemployment refers to workers who have lost their jobs because they have been displaced by automation, because their skills are no longer in demand, or because of similar reasons. (p. 114)

Supply curve A supply curve is a graphical depiction of a supply schedule. It shows how the quantity supplied of some product will change as the price of that product changes during a specified period of time, holding all other determinants of quantity supplied constant. (p. 62)

Supply-demand diagram A supply-demand diagram graphs the supply and demand curves together. It also determines the equilibrium price and quantity. (p. 64)

Supply schedule A supply schedule is a table showing how the quantity supplied of some product changes as the price of that product changes during a specified period of time, holding all other determinants of quantity supplied constant. (p. 61)

Supply-side inflation Supply-side inflation is a rise in the price level caused by slow growth (or decline) of aggregate supply. (p. 318)

Surplus A surplus is an excess of quantity supplied over quantity demanded. When there is a surplus, sellers cannot sell the quantities they desire to supply at the current price. (p. 65)

Tangent A tangent to the curve is *straight* line that *touches*, but does not *cut*, the curve at a particular point. (p. 15)

Tariff A tariff is a tax on imports. (p. 348)

Theory A theory is a deliberate simplification of relationships used to explain how those relationships work. (p. 9)

Trade adjustment assistance Trade adjustment assistance provides special unemployment benefits, loans, retraining programs, and other aid to workers and firms that are harmed by foreign competition. (p. 351)

Trade deficit A country's trade deficit is the excess of its imports over its exports. If, instead, exports exceed imports, the country has a trade surplus. (p. 387)

Trade surplus A country's trade surplus is the excess of its exports over its imports. If, instead, imports exceed exports, the country has a trade deficit. (p. 387)

Transfer payments Transfer payments are sums of money that the government gives certain individuals as outright grants rather than as payments for services rendered to employers. Some common examples are Social Security and unemployment benefits. (pp. 35, 157)

Unemployment insurance Unemployment insurance is a government program that replaces some of the wages lost by eligible workers who lose their jobs. (p. 116)

Unemployment rate The unemployment rate is the number of unemployed people, expressed as a percentage of the labor force. (p. 111)

Unit of account The unit of account is the standard unit for quoting prices. (p. 244)

Value added The value added by a firm is its revenue from selling a product minus the amount paid for goods and services purchased from other firms. (p. 171)

Variable A variable is something measured by a number; it is used to analyze what happens to other things when the size of that number changes (varies). (p. 13)

Variable taxes Variable taxes are taxes that vary with the level of GDP. (p. 235)

Velocity Velocity indicates the number of times per year that an "average dollar" is spent on goods and services. It is the ratio of nominal gross domestic product (GDP) to the number of dollars in the money stock. That is:

$$\text{Velocity} = \frac{\text{Nominal GDP}}{\text{Money stock}} \text{ (p. 278)}$$

Vertical (long-run) Phillips curve The vertical (long-run) Phillips curve shows the menu of inflation/unemployment choices available to society in the long run. It is a vertical straight line at the natural rate of unemployment. (p. 323)

Y-intercept The Y-intercept of a line or a curve is the point at which it touches the vertical axis (the Y-axis). The X-intercept is defined similarly. (p. 16)

INDEX